Guide to
Operating Systems,
Second Edition

Michael Palmer
Michael Walters
Tom Badgett
Niels Jonker

**COURSE
TECHNOLOGY**
™
THOMSON LEARNING

Australia • Canada • Mexico • Singapore • Spain • United Kingdom • United States

Guide to Operating Systems, Second Edition

By Michael Palmer, Michael Walters, Tom Badgett, and Niels Jonker

Acquisitions Editor:
Will Pitkin

Product Manager:
Laura Hildebrand

Production Editor:
Anne Valsangiacomo

Technical Editor:
Kelly Caudle

Reviewers:
Will Holt, Pamela Silvers

Development Editor:
Dave George

Quality Assurance Manager:
John Bosco

MQA Technical Lead:
Nicole Ashton

Associate Product Manager:
Tim Gleeson

Editorial Assistant:
Nick Lombardi

Marketing Manager:
Toby Shelton

Text Designer:
GEX Publishing Services

Compositor:
GEX Publishing Services

Cover Design:
Julie Malone

BRIEF
Contents

TABLE OF
Contents

CHAPTER FIVE
Upgrading to a Newer Operating System Version   **221**

Introduction

This book is very basic. It also covers complex material. A paradox? In a way, yes. Any broad-based discussion of operating systems must be somewhat complex, but the operating system also is the most basic component of any computer system. So, basic and complex does, indeed, describe the contents of this book.

But you needn't be concerned. This basic-complex discussion begins at the beginning with a description of general operating system concepts, including how system-level software works with your computer hardware. From there, you'll read detailed descriptions of individual operating systems—Windows and its various configurations, MAC OS, and UNIX. You'll learn how each of these systems works with specific hardware components such as printers and modems, and you'll review basic procedures such as OS initial installations, OS upgrades, hardware driver installation, and more. Chapters eight and nine deal with networking and connectivity issues, and so the discussion of operating systems extends to Novell NetWare and Windows NT/2000/.NET Server, the most widely used network operating systems.

In addition, you can review your progress in learning these topics with extensive Hands-on projects, case projects, key terms, team projects, and review questions at the end of each chapter.

FEATURES

To aid you in fully understanding Operating Systems concepts, there are many features in this book designed to improve its pedagogical value.

- **Chapter Objectives.** Each chapter in this book begins with a detailed list of the concepts to be mastered within that chapter. This list provides you with a quick reference to the contents of that chapter, as well as a useful study aid.

- **Illustrations and Tables.** Numerous illustrations of operating system screens and components aid you in the visualization of common setup steps, theories, and concepts. In addition, many tables provide details and comparisons of both practical and theoretical information.

- **Chapter Summaries.** Each chapter's text is followed by a summary of the concepts it has introduced. These summaries provide a helpful way to recap and revisit the ideas covered in each chapter.

- **Key Terms.** A listing of the terms, along with definitions, which were introduced throughout the chapter.

- **Review Questions.** End-of-chapter assessment begins with a set of review questions that reinforce the ideas introduced in each chapter.

- **Hands-on Projects.** The goal of this book is to provide you with the practical knowledge and skills to troubleshoot desktop operating systems in use in business today. To this end, along with theoretical explanations, each chapter provides numerous Hands-on Projects aimed at providing you with real-world implementation experience.

- **Case Projects.** Located at the end of each chapter are a case project and two optional team projects. These extensive case examples allow you to implement the skills and knowledge gained in the chapter through real-world operating system support and administration scenarios.

HARDWARE AND SOFTWARE REQUIREMENTS

You can study the operating system concepts in this book without any hardware. Screen shots and other illustrations help support the discussions presented here. However, to get the most of this material you should step through the Hands-on Projects. For this, you'll need access to at least one computer and operating system. To pursue a complete, broad-based study of operating systems as presented in this book, you will need several computers and operating systems or a large hard drive that you can partition and load with multiple operating systems.

Here are suggestions for each of the operating systems covered here:

Windows 95

Windows 95 represents a major upgrade from Windows 3.x. The user interface is improved and the system is improved operationally as well. A truly functional Windows 95 installation includes a Pentium 100 CPU, 16 Mbytes of RAM (at least!), 2 GB hard drive, floppy disk, and CD-ROM drive. You'll be amazed at how much improved Windows 95 operation will be with at least 32 Mbytes of RAM.

Windows 98

Windows 98 is a significant step up from Windows 95, and it needs a similar increase in hardware capability for successful operation. You can use the same configuration for Windows 98 as was suggested for Windows 95, but if you use all of Windows 98's capabilities active desktop, direct World Wide Web interface, Internet communications, and so on—then you'll crave more hardware. A Pentium II running at 233 MHz, 64 Mbytes of RAM, 4 GB hard drive, floppy disk, and CD-ROM will run Windows 98 nicely.

Windows Me

Windows Me is very similar to Windows 98. Therefore the hardware used for a Windows 98 setup will also work for Windows Me. We do recommend a little more CPU power—a Pentium II running at 300 MHz, 64 Mbytes of RAM, 4 GB hard drive, floppy disk, and CD-ROM. The more memory you have the better Windows Me will perform.

Windows XP

Windows XP is a substantial upgrade to the Windows 98/Me operating systems. The Home version is for recreational users while the Professional version is intended for office and networked environments. We recommend a Pentium 500 MHz, with 256 Mbytes of RAM, 10 GB hard drive, floppy disk and DVD drive for the Home version. For the Professional version, we suggest a Pentium 900 Mhz, with 512 Mbytes of RAM.

Windows NT

Windows NT was developed by Microsoft as their high-end operating system. Windows NT 4.0 will run on a low-end Pentium 100 MHz, with 64 Mbytes of RAM, 4 GB hard drive, floppy disk, and CD-ROM. Depending on the number of clients using the server or the functions being performed on the workstation, you may choose to increase the CPU speed, amount of memory, and the size of the hard drive.

Windows 2000

Windows 2000 is a significant upgrade to Windows NT and as such, you will want to run it on a more powerful computer. We recommend a Pentium III 667 MHz, with 256 Mbytes of RAM, 4 GB hard drive, floppy disk, and CD-ROM. Depending on the use of this Windows 2000 computer, you may want to replace the CD-ROM with a DVD drive.

Mac OS

As with Windows, Mac OS has many versions. Earlier versions can get by with basic hardware, but the latest Mac OS needs a machine comparable to one for Windows 98. You can get along with a basic IMAC (G3 processor) and 32 Mbytes of RAM for Mac OS 9.x. However, as with Windows 98, more RAM—64 or 128 Mbytes—will give you a more pleasant Mac OS experience. For Mac OS X we recommend a G4 processor with at least 64 Mbytes of RAM.

UNIX

Virtually any medium to high-end Intel box produced in the last three years can make a reasonable UNIX platform, say a high-end Pentium or above computer that operates at 200 MHz or faster and that has 64 Mbytes of RAM and at least 1.8 GB of disk space (to install X Window interfaces). This is particularly true if you're experimenting with versions of Linux such as Red Hat Linux. However, if you are putting UNIX through commercial paces, doing real work with it, you should consider a RISC-based workstation, say a Sun or HP machine with as much RAM as you can afford. A machine with 250 to 500 Mbytes of RAM in a commercial environment isn't all that uncommon.

TEXT AND GRAPHIC CONVENTIONS

Wherever appropriate, additional information and exercises have been added to this book to help you better understand what is being discussed in the chapter. Icons throughout the text alert you to additional materials. The icons used in this textbook are described below.

 The Note icon is used to present additional helpful material related to the subject being described.

 Each hands-on activity in this book is preceded by the Hands-on icon and a description of the exercise that follows.

 Tips are included from the authors' experiences that provide extra information about how to attack a problem or what to do to in certain real-world situations.

 The Cautions are included to help you anticipate potential mistakes or problems so you can prevent them from happening.

 Case Project icons mark each case project. These are more involved, scenario-based assignments. In these extensive case examples, you are asked to implement independently what you have learned.

 Optional Team Case Project icons mark the team case projects. These are projects designed for a group of students to work on as a team. There are normally two team case projects in each chapter.

INSTRUCTOR'S MATERIALS

The following supplemental materials are available when this book is used in a classroom setting. All of the supplements available with this book are provided to the instructor on a single CD-ROM.

Electronic Instructor's Manual. The Instructor's Manual that accompanies this textbook includes:

- Additional instructional material to assist in class preparation, including suggestions for lecture topics, suggested lab activities, tips on setting up a lab for the hands-on assignments, and alternative lab setup ideas in situations where lab resources are limited.

- Solutions to all end-of-chapter materials, including the Review Questions, Hands-on Projects, Case and Optional Team Case assignments.

ExamView Pro 3.0. This textbook is accompanied by ExamView®, a powerful testing software package that allows instructors to create and administer printed, computer (LAN-based), and Internet exams. ExamView includes hundreds of questions that correspond to the topics covered in this text, enabling students to generate detailed study guides that include page references for further review. The computer-based and Internet testing components allow students to take exams at their computers, and also save the instructor time by grading each exam automatically. .

PowerPoint presentations. This book comes with Microsoft PowerPoint slides for each chapter. These are included as a teaching aid for classroom presentation, to make available to students on the network for chapter review, or to be printed for classroom distribution. Instructors, please feel at liberty to add your own slides for additional topics you introduce to the class.

ACKNOWLEDGMENTS

Writing a book is really a story about people working together to bring ideas to life on the printed page. There are many people who have played a significant role in creating the second edition of this book. First, we thank managing editor Stephen Solomon and acquisitions editor Will Pitkin for their support of this project. We offer particular thanks to Laura Hildebrand our product manager who has guided the making of this book from start to finish; and to Dave George the development editor for his work and advice on every page. Dave George's experienced eye has truly made a difference in creating a more thorough and readable book.

The production editor, Anne Valsangiacomo has provided able production and copyedit services. Further, our technical editor Kelly Caudle has offered sound advice in every chapter to help us provide more comprehensive and solid coverage of each operating system, as have our reviewers Will Holt and Pamela Silvers. Also, the quality assurance and validation team of Nick Atlas, Nicole Ashton, John Freitas, Serg Palladino, and Chris Scriver, have been invaluable in helping to assure the accuracy of the text, review questions, and projects. And we thank you, the reader for purchasing this book and for your interest in the operating systems we have described.

DEDICATIONS

Michael Palmer — I dedicate this book to two incredible professionals, Kent Nelson and Timothy Wirt.

Michael Walters — I dedicate this book to my wife, Donna. Your support and encouragement were invaluable. I would also like to dedicate this to Michael Palmer, a true friend, teacher, and mentor.

1

OPERATING SYSTEM THEORY

After reading this chapter and completing the exercises you will be able to:

♦ Understand what an operating system does

♦ Describe the types of operating systems

♦ Understand the history of operating system development

♦ Discuss single tasking versus multitasking

♦ Differentiate between single-user and multi-user operating systems

♦ List and briefly describe current operating systems

An operating system is the software that makes it possible for you to start the basic functions of a computer, view text on a computer's display, access the Internet, and run applications. Without the operating system, a computer is just a helpless box of electronic parts. There are many kinds of operating systems, but only a few have really captured a wide audience. Most of these are operating systems that you use on the computers that fit on your desktop. This book is a study guide and reference for the popular operating systems used on most modern computers. In the following chapters, you will take an in-depth look at the desktop operating systems: Windows 95/98, Windows Me, Windows NT, Windows 2000, and Windows XP; UNIX (focusing on the Linux variation); and Macintosh OS 9.x/X. Also, later in the book, you will examine popular server operating systems that include Windows NT, Windows 2000, Windows .NET Server, Mac OS X server and NetWare. This chapter introduces some of the theoretical concepts common to all operating systems. It is one of the few chapters in the book that is primarily theoretical, and is placed at the beginning of the book to give you an understanding of some general operating system theory. With this theory under your belt, you will have a solid frame of reference to understand operating system specifics as they are discussed later.

UNDERSTANDING OPERATING SYSTEMS

An **operating system (OS)** is a set of basic programming instructions to the lowest levels of computer **hardware**, forming a basic layer of programming **code** on which most other functions of the computer are built. The two types of operating systems that are the focus of this book are desktop and server operating systems. A **desktop operating system** typically is one installed on a PC type of computer that is used by one person at a time, and that may or may not be connected to a network. A **server operating system** is usually on a more powerful computer that is connected to a network, and can act in many roles to enable multiple users to access information, such as electronic mail, files, and software.

In its lowest form, the operating system takes care of what are known as basic **input/output (I/O)** functions, which let other programs easily talk to the computer hardware. It is essentially the task of the I/O functions to take requests from the software the user runs (the application software) and translate them into low-level requests that the hardware can understand and carry out. In general, an operating system serves as an interface between application software and hardware, as shown in Figure 1-1. Operating systems perform the following tasks:

- Handle input from the keyboard and mouse
- Handle output to the screen and printer
- Handle communications using a modem
- Handle network communications, such as for the Internet
- Control input/output with all bus devices, such as a network interface card
- Control information storage and retrieval using various types of disk and CD-ROM drives
- Enable multimedia use for voice and video reproduction, such as playing music through speakers

The operating system communicates directly with all of these devices. Some operating system programs exchange information with specific hardware (chips) inside the computer. This code is typically referred to as a **device driver**. A device driver translates computer code to display text on a screen, or translates movements of a mouse into action, for example. A separate device driver is usually present for each individual device inside the computer, as shown in Figure 1-2. In general, operating systems have a standardized way to communicate with a certain type of device driver. The device driver then contains the actual code (instructions) to communicate with the chips on the device. This way, if another piece of hardware is introduced into the computer, the operating system code does not have to change. All that needs to be done to make the computer capable of communicating with the new device is to load a new driver onto the operating system.

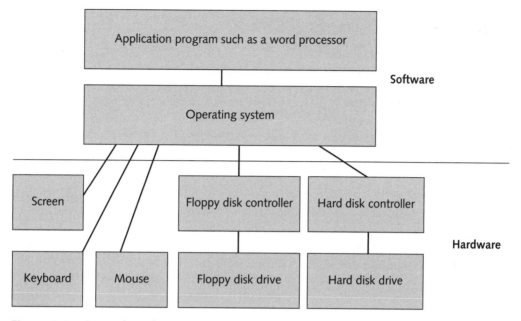

Figure 1-1 General configuration for all operating systems

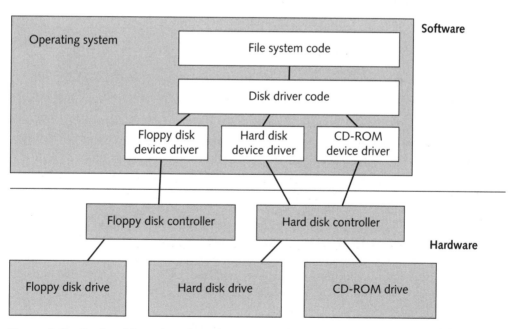

Figure 1-2 Device drivers interface the operating system with various hardware devices

If a particular device is not working, one way to troubleshoot the problem is to obtain a new device driver from that device's manufacturer, which can usually be downloaded from the manufacturer's Web site.

A good example of a device is a **compact disc read only Memory (CD-ROM)** drive. CD-ROM drives for computers were introduced a long time after many operating systems were written. However, since they are similar to other types of disk drives, most operating systems can be expanded to use CD-ROM drives by loading a few simple drivers for the operating system. You may encounter device drivers that interface with your operating system for other devices, including:

- Floppy and hard disk drives
- Computer monitors
- Keyboards
- Mouse and trackball devices
- Modems
- Scanners
- Printers
- Tape drives, Zip drives, and other removable media
- Specialty devices such as digital cameras
- Audio transfer hardware
- DVD players
- CD–ROM

In addition to communicating with computer hardware, the operating system communicates with the application software running on the computer, as in Figure 1-3. **Application software** is a fairly vague term; it can mean a word processor, spreadsheet, database, computer game, or many types of other applications. Basically, it means any program a user may choose to run on the computer. If an application program accesses a piece of hardware, it sends a request to the operating system to execute the job. For example, the application program may have to access the keyboard to see if a user has pressed a key, or the screen to show the user a message. This makes the application programmer's job easier because she does not have to know exactly how to manipulate the chips in the computer to communicate with the keyboard, screen, or printer. She only has to know how to communicate with the operating system.

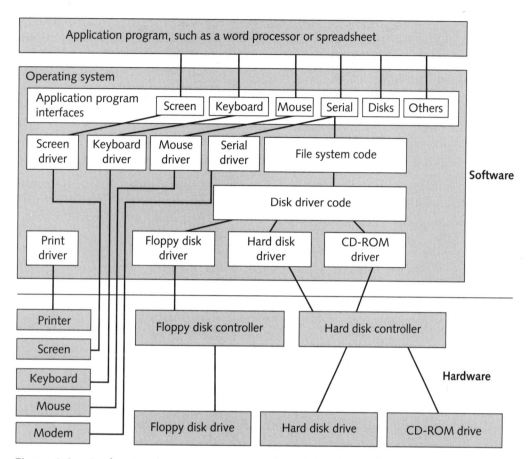

Figure 1-3 Application programs communicate with hardware through the operating system

You can therefore say that in its most basic form, an operating system provides a level of management among the application programs, the user, and the computer. This level of management allows application programmers to concentrate on applications that will run on any hardware, as long as the operating system can control them. In other words, an application program can submit a general request to the operating system, such as "write this information to disk," and the operating system handles the details. The application programmer doesn't have to worry about how to queue data, update the disk directory, or physically copy the data from memory to the disk drive.

Of course there are some applications—particularly those that are designed for DOS or UNIX (both early operating systems)—that directly access hardware devices. At one time, many programmers designed code to do this to improve overall application performance, but this frequently occurred at the expense of software compatibility. Although software performance may be improved by writing directly to I/O ports or other hardware devices, it isn't necessarily good programming practice (even though it is still done for some specific needs).

Some operating systems, such as Windows 2000 and Windows XP, do not allow the programmer to directly access hardware. Instead, the programmer must call on an intermediary process that decides how to handle the request. This design means that it is harder for an application program to "crash" a computer, such as when two application programs access the same memory location at the same time.

The general operating system we describe provides only the most basic input and output functions, so it is called a **Basic Input/Output System**, or **BIOS**. Every PC has a BIOS, which is stored in **Read Only Memory**, or **ROM**. Figure 1-4 shows a sample BIOS setup screen on a computer. ROM is a special kind of memory that does not lose its contents when the power is removed from the computer. Whenever you turn on your PC, the machine wakes up and jumps to a startup program inside the BIOS. This program initializes the screen and keyboard, tests some central computer hardware, such as the **central processing unit (CPU)** and memory, initializes the floppy drive and other disk drives, and then loads other parts of the operating system that can provide more advanced functionality for application programs. Figure 1-5 shows a general conceptual drawing of various operating system components.

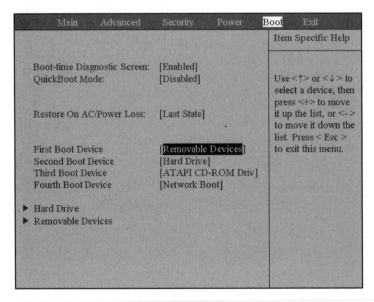

Figure 1-4   Sample BIOS setup screen

1

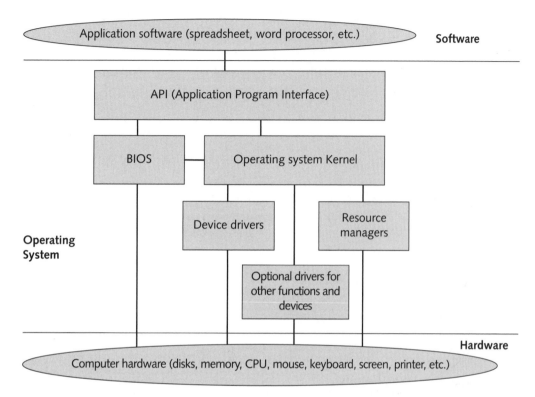

Figure 1-5   General operating system design

If a computer is turned on, but cannot access a device, such as the main disk drive or display monitor, check the BIOS settings to make sure that the BIOS knows about that disk drive or monitor.

The elements in Figure 1-5 include the following, from the application down:

- *Application software*, such as a spreadsheet or word processor

- ***API (Application Program Interface)***, software designed to communicate with the application software and the user. The API translates requests from the application into code that the operating system **kernel** can understand and pass on to the hardware device drivers, and translates data from the kernel and device drivers so the application can use it. It also provides an interface to the BIOS. This is the part of the operating system most visible to users.

- *BIOS*, which provides the basic input/output functions to communicate with system devices, such as disks, monitor, and keyboard. BIOS resides in ROM, so it is always present in the computer. It usually loads other operating system components on startup.

- *Operating system kernel*, the core of the operating system that coordinates operating system functions, such as control of memory and storage. The kernel communicates with the BIOS, device drivers, and the API to perform these functions. It also interfaces with the **resource managers**.

- *Device drivers*, programs that take requests from the API via the kernel and translate them into commands to manipulate specific hardware devices, such as disks, tape drives, keyboards, monitors, modems, and printers.

- *Resource managers*, programs that manage computer memory and central processor use.

- *Optional drivers*, for other functions and devices, such as sound.

- *Computer hardware*, disks, storage, CPU, mouse, keyboard, monitor, printer, and so on.

Although all operating systems incorporate the basic I/O functions, the operating systems you are accustomed to, such as Mac OS, Microsoft Windows, or UNIX, include many additional functions. Examples include the logic to handle files, time and date functions, memory management, and other more advanced features to deal with the various devices connected to the system. Some features that most operating systems have in common are:

- Provide an interface between the computer hardware and application programs

- Act as an intermediary between the user and applications

- Provide a user interface into computer hardware and application programs

- Manage memory and central processor use

- Manage peripheral devices, such as printers, monitors, keyboards, and modems

TYPES OF OPERATING SYSTEMS

There are many types of computer operating systems, which work in very different ways, intended for very different purposes. The functions a computer requires, to a large extent, dictate what the operating system will do and how it will do it. As an example, the computer in a microwave oven needs device drivers for the **LED (Light Emitting Diode)** display, numeric keypad, and door close switches, whereas the computer in a television needs drivers to monitor the remote control and tell the tuner to change the channel. The same goes for various types of small and large computers; a computer designed to handle a high volume of numerical operations for many users needs different functions from the PC used to run a word processor.

In general, operating systems are organized by the size, type, and purpose of the computer on which they run. This book discusses personal computer (PC) operating systems. PC-class computers are designed for individual users to perform tasks, such as word processing, database and spreadsheet management, and networking with other computers. Over the years, PCs have become faster, more complex, and more powerful, offering the user more features. As a result, many PCs now can handle complex operations that go beyond simply running a user's application software. This has resulted in advanced, elaborate operating systems that are designed to deal with more hardware, and provide advanced functions. The lines of division by size, type, and purpose are therefore getting a little more vague every day. Hardware is becoming more compact, and the operating systems are getting more complex. As operating systems get more complex, functionality is also enhanced. (Interestingly enough, prices on these smaller, more powerful machines are declining at the same time.)

One example of how PC operating systems have become more complex is the comparison of lines of code in Windows 95 to Windows XP. The number of lines of code in Windows 95 is only a couple of million. The number of lines of code in Windows XP is over 50 million.

For instance, in the seventies, corporate computing was confined to mainframe- and mini-computer-class devices. These were refrigerator-sized or larger computers that required a full staff to manage them, and large, expensive air-conditioned rooms to hold them. The operating systems for these machines were quite complex and often included such intrinsic functions as text editing (not quite "word processing" by today's standards), database management, networking, and communications. There were few PC-class devices at the time. Those that were available were capable of minimal functionality, and used what could only be described as rudimentary operating systems. Many of those early devices didn't support any storage hardware (disk drives), or if they did, it was frequently serial, low-density tape. In this comparison, it should be easy to see that operating systems for large machines were very different from operating systems used for small ones.

At the same time, applications for these machines were written with efficient code so they could maximize all of the resources on the computer. As a result, appearance, programming, and management were very terse and basic.

To a lesser extent, this is still true today. There are still "big" machines and "small" machines, except that none of today's computer equipment is physically large. The days of room-sized, or even refrigerator-sized, computers are about gone. A "big" machine today simply has more processing power, more memory, more storage (disk drive capacity), and better network connectivity. To operate these more powerful computers, more powerful and more capable operating systems are employed. For example, a company that sells computer time to thousands of other users—an Internet service provider (ISP), for instance—requires computers capable of performing multiple tasks for many users at the same time.

Fifteen years ago, an IBM mainframe and its disk drives of several million bytes consisted of two "boxes," each the size of three or four very large refrigerators. A couple of drives for the mainframe were another refrigerator-sized box. Today, a more powerful IBM mainframe and its disk drives containing many gigabytes of storage, plus a couple of tape drives, is about the size of three or four PCs.

Although the computers used for such installations don't look much different from the PC or Macintosh designed for a single user, they are quite different inside. They use a network operating system (such as a version of UNIX, Windows 2000 or .NET Server) or another multitasking, multi-user operating system. Also, they may include multiple CPUs and have more powerful I/O capabilities. The differences are significant, but also subtle. For example, Linux is a popular desktop operating system (used by a single person) based on UNIX, and it is also applied in the Internet business as a network operating system to power Web servers, mail servers, and other multi-user applications. Again, the hardware used for an individual Linux box is likely much different from the design of these Internet service computers, even though the operating system is the same. On the other hand, even with the enhanced hardware, an Internet service provider wouldn't likely replace Linux or any other multi-user operating system on these machines with Windows 95, Windows 98, or Windows Me, and certainly not with MS-DOS/PC-DOS.

So-called "high-end" workstations are used by engineers for graphical design, or by editors for film design and animation. Again, these machines may look much like a school or home PC, but inside they include extremely fast hard disk controllers, high-speed networking interfaces, 3D graphics interfaces, lots of memory, and, often, support for multiple CPUs. The needs of these workstations are very different from the multitasking, multi-user needs of an Internet server, but they too have specialty requirements that can't be met by some operating systems. Although some graphics applications use Linux or UNIX, the Windows 2000, Windows XP, and Mac OS operating systems are more popular foundations for these applications. Windows 2000, Windows XP, and Mac OS are now powerful enough for business, graphics, engineering, and even movie editing applications.

So there must be other factors that differentiate high-end from low-end computers. The main factor is the application software used with the computers. Again, the differentiation among computers is getting more vague. You have seen some of these factors, but the confusing concept is that even high-end applications often can run on what are considered low-end machines, and they might even share an operating system. When this is the case, the main differentiating factor is the hardware: speed of the disk controller, size and speed of the hard disk, amount of memory, or type of display adapter.

One way to look at computer and operating system differences is to consider that there are really two main groups of computers: older, large computers with traditional operating systems, and newer, small hardware with similar but specialized operating systems. In general, mainframe-class computers are used to conduct massive calculations or manipulate huge amounts of data. These computers are common at scientific institutions, banks, and insurance companies. They are built to quickly perform tasks, such as keeping track of thousands of checking account balances. Most of their work is done in batches—clearing two million checks and updating their associated bank accounts—instead of single, sequential repetitive tasks. When the batch job is finished—all checks have been posted, for example—the statements can be printed. These large operating systems are designed to perform these batch processes. In addition, there often are many clerks and ATM machines that use this computer to do daily transactions. They all share the resources, or processor time, of the large machine. These systems are referred to as **time-sharing systems**.

Notice that these time-sharing systems, and other large computers, frequently conduct what are termed **batch processes**. Today's smaller, interactive systems are more prone to use **sequential processing**, where each process request is completed and the data returned before the next process is started.

 Big batch processing jobs, or multiple batch jobs that must occur in a specific order on large computers, are often scheduled to run after work hours because they require so many machine resources. This makes batch processing less convenient than the instant response you get with a sequential process.

Medium-sized computers, which are replacing these large systems at an incredible rate, can perform many of the same tasks with less hardware because new hardware is faster and more efficient. Many of these machines run a real-time operating system instead of the batch-oriented systems used on mainframes. **Real-time systems** are what most of us are familiar with today. PC-based operating systems, such as Windows 98 or Windows XP, interact directly with the user—even multiple users (on shared drives)—and respond in real time with the required information. In this environment, multiple users can do many different things on the machine at the same time. Still, all users are using one machine or a group of machines to do all their work. This is known as a **multi-user environment**.

One of the newest types of large computing and operating system environments is known as the **client/server systems**. Again, hardware is physically smaller, faster, and more efficient than the older machines, and where the actual work is done also is very different. In the two systems above, all work is done on the big machine. In the client/server model, only a small part of the work is done on the central computer or computers. It may hold all the data and files, and it may even perform some of the database functions or calculations required, but much of work is performed on the client side, the computer at the user's desk. If you have used PC-class computers in a networked environment, chances are you have used the client/server model, at least to some degree. A Macintosh computer running Mac OS, or a minimally configured Windows 2000 computer connected to a network that includes a Windows NT, 2000, or .NET server, for example, is well suited for client/server operations. Notice, again, the importance of the combination of operating system and application. Operating system differences are beginning to narrow, but the applications that run on them help differentiate how the computer is used. Client/server computing was not possible until the PC was introduced. After all, it requires a computer at the user's desk, a facility that was not available until the introduction of the PC.

Taking client/server systems a step further is Microsoft's .NET architecture. .NET incorporates the Internet and focuses on integrating data and user functions so that they can be accomplished at any location on many kinds of devices, including handheld devices and cell phones. It also integrates different programming languages so that they can be used to build one large-scale application, taking advantage of old, tested program code, and coupling it with new code that can be used by a Web server, a single user's PC, or a pen computing device. With .NET, the distinctions between desktop and server computers grow much less distinct because desktop computers can potentially play some roles in data and resource sharing that are now associated with server operating systems.

A SHORT HISTORY OF OPERATING SYSTEMS

The history of operating systems is a very elaborate subject. As a matter of fact, there are many books on this subject. This short history is not meant to be comprehensive; it merely presents enough background information to show how some of the features in modern PCs and PC operating systems work.

Initially, computers were used as large automated calculators to solve all sorts of mathematical and statistical problems. Computers were extremely large, often taking up entire rooms. Although you can legitimately trace the history of today's digital computers back 100 years or more, there were no practical designs used by significant numbers of people until the late fifties and early sixties. Scientists programmed these computers to perform precise tasks, the exact tasks for which they were built. The operating systems were rudimentary, often not able to do more than read punch cards or tape, and write output to Teletype machines. A tape or deck of cards was loaded, a button was pushed on the machine to indicate the input was ready, and the machine started to read the tape and perform the operations requested. If all went well, the work was done and the output was generated. This output would be sent to the Teletype, and that was that.

Yes, there was computer history before this point, but it did not involve any sort of operating system. Any program that the computer ran had to include all logic to control the computer. Since this logic was rather complex, and not all scientists were computer scientists, the operating system was a tool that allowed non-computer scientists to use computers for their purposes. That reduced programming work and increased efficiency. Obviously, there was not all that much to "operate" on, mainly the punch card and punch tape readers for input, and the Teletype printer for output. There also was not that much to operate with; memory capacity was very limited and the processing speed of the computer was slow by our standards (but fast for that time). The art in operating systems design, therefore, largely was to keep them very small and efficient.

It did not take long (in terms of world history, at least) before computer applications evolved to actually do something useful for a broader audience. Although computers of the late sixties and early seventies were crude by today's standards, they were quite capable and handled extremely complex tasks. These computers contributed to the development of space travel, submarine-based ballistic missiles, and a growing global financial community (all on much less than 1 MB of memory). This period also saw the beginning of a global, computer-based communications system called the Internet. Applications became logically more complex, requiring larger programs and large amounts of data. With more useful applications being developed, the wait to "run" programs became longer.

As always, necessity was the mother of invention. Input and output devices were created, and computer memory capacity and speed increased. With more devices to manage, operating systems became more complex and extensive, but the rule of thumb, small and fast, was still extremely important. This round of evolution, which really began to take off in the mid seventies, included the display terminal, a Teletype machine with a keyboard that did not print on paper, but projected letters on a screen. The initial "glass Teletype" was later followed by a terminal that could also show simple graphics. The magnetic tape drive, used to store and retrieve data and programs on tape, could store more, and was less operator-intensive than paper tape. It was quickly followed by numerous incarnations of magnetic disks.

The next evolution was the ability to share computer resources among various programs. After all, if a computer was very fast and could quickly switch among various programs, you could do several tasks seemingly all at once, and serve many people simultaneously. Some of the operating systems that evolved in this era are long lost to all but those who worked directly with them. But there are some notable players that were responsible for setting the stage for the full-featured functionality we take for granted today. Digital Equipment Corporation's PDP series computers, for example, ran the DEC operating system, simply known as OS, in one version or another. A popular one was OS/8, which came in various versions, such as Release 3Q, and was released in 1968. PDP series could also run Multics, which was the basis for the development of the first version of UNIX, a multi-user, multitasking operating system. (Multics is widely considered to be the first multi-user, multitasking operating system.)

The original UNIX was developed at AT&T Bell Labs in 1969 by Kenneth Thompson and Dennis Ritchie as an improvement on Multics. Later Digital VAXs used VMS, a powerful, multitasking, multi-user system that was strong on networking. IBM mainframes made a series of operating systems popular, including GM-NAA I/O in the early sixties, an operating system that effectively enabled the machine to perform batch processing jobs. The letters "GM" indicate the company for which this OS was originally developed. Many others would follow, including CICS, which is still in use today. However, this company's minicomputers used OS/VM and TS, systems aimed at batch processing and time-sharing applications.

Programming computers at this time was still a very complicated process best left to scientists. In the mid sixties, right after the first interactive computer game was invented at MIT, a simple programming language was developed, aimed at the non-programmer. It was dubbed **BASIC**, or **Beginner's All-purpose Symbolic Instruction Code**. A few years later, in 1975, Bill Gates discovered BASIC, and became interested enough to write a compiler (software that turns computer code written by people into code that is understood by computers) for it, which he sold to a company called MITS (Micro Instrumentation Telemetry Systems). MITS was the first company to produce a desktop computer that was widely accepted, and could conduct useful work at the hands of any knowledgeable programmer. That same year, Gates dropped out of Harvard to dedicate his time to writing software. Other programming languages introduced at about this time included Pascal, C, and other versions of BASIC supplied by various computer manufacturers. In addition, Microsoft and others, only a couple of years later released FORTRAN, COBOL, and other mainframe and minicomputer languages for desktop computers. There were also highly proprietary languages that gained some popularity—languages primarily designed for database programming, for example—but they neither lasted, nor are they significant to our discussion in this book.

The introduction of the microcomputer in the mid seventies was probably the most exciting thing to happen to operating systems. These machines typically had many of the old restrictions, including slow speed and little memory. Many microcomputers came with a small operating system and ROM that did no more than provide an elementary screen, keyboard, printer, and disk input and output. Bill Gates saw an opportunity and put together a team at Microsoft, consisting of Paul Allen, Bob O'Rear, and himself, to adapt a fledging version of a new microcomputer operating system called 86-DOS to run on a prototype of a new microcomputer being developed by IBM, called the personal computer (PC). 86-DOS, which was originally written by Tim Patterson (from Seattle Computer Products) for the new 8086 microprocessor, evolved in 1980, through a cooperative effort between Patterson and Microsoft, into the **Microsoft Disk Operating System**, or **MS-DOS**. MS-DOS became a runaway success for the five-year-old Microsoft company. And it was the first widely distributed operating system for microcomputers that had to be loaded from disk or tape. There were earlier systems, including CP/M (Control Program/Microcomputer) that used some of the features and concepts of the existing UNIX operating system designs, but when IBM adopted MS-DOS for its machine, the die was cast.

When IBM introduced the first PC in 1981, it caused a revolution—not necessarily because the machine itself was revolutionary (many argue that it was not), but because it was designed around an "open standard." Anyone who wanted to was welcome to make PCs that worked like IBM's PC, or hardware that would work with it. And when IBM needed an operating system for its PC, the company bought a license for Microsoft DOS (MS-DOS *with* a hyphen). IBM dubbed the new operating system PC DOS (*without* a hyphen), and Bill Gates once again showed his entrepreneurial spirit. He approached all the people then making PC hardware and sold them licenses to MS-DOS. The vendors needed MS-DOS to be truly compatible with the IBM PC, and Microsoft was the only game in town. It is reported that Microsoft had more than 100 companies licensing the MS-DOS system in less than two years.

What did this MS-DOS do? It provided the basic operating system functions described earlier in this chapter, and it was amazingly similar to what was used before on larger computers. It supported very basic functions, such as keyboard, disk and printer I/O, and communications with the outside world. As time went on, more and more support functions were added, including such things as hard disks. Then graphical user interfaces became the thing of the day. Initially, Microsoft chose to wait on development of a graphical user interface, but after Microsoft saw the successful reception of the interface on Apple Macintosh computers, it developed one of its own.

The Macintosh was introduced in 1984, and it seemed to be light years ahead of the IBM PC. Its operating system came with a standard **graphical user interface (GUI)**, at a time when MS-DOS was still text-based. Also, the Macintosh OS managed the computer memory closely for the software, something MS-DOS did not do. And because Mac OS managed all computer memory for the application programs, you could start several programs sequentially and switch among them. It was also years ahead in such things as printer management. In MS-DOS, a program was on its own when it came to controlling the printer; all MS-DOS did was provide the most rudimentary interface. On Mac OS, many I/O functions were part of the operating system.

Microsoft, however, did not fall far behind. In 1990, Microsoft introduced an extension to its DOS operating system, called Microsoft Windows which provided a GUI and many of the same functions as the Mac OS. The first Windows was really an operating environment running on top of an operating system, made to look like a single operating system. Today's Windows is more unified than the early versions.

Although Apple was six years ahead of Microsoft in offering a friendly GUI-based OS, Apple ultimately fell well behind Microsoft in sales because it chose not to license the Mac OS to outside hardware vendors.

The incarnations of operating systems since those days have been numerous, maybe 10 versions of Windows and 10 of Mac OS. Today, they are both very similar in what they can do and how they can do it; they have a wealth of features and drivers that make the original DOS look elementary. Their principal functions are unchanged, however: to provide an interface between the application programs and hardware, and provide a user interface for basic functions, such as file and disk management.

Let's review the important pieces of operating system development history. Although pre-1980s computing history is interesting, it doesn't hold much relevance to what we do with computers today. Table 1-1 shows the major milestones in operating system development. Note that we mention 16-, 32-, and 64-bit operating systems in the table. In general, a 64-bit operating system is more powerful and faster than a 32-bit system, which is more powerful and faster than a 16-bit system. You will learn more information on the differences in Chapter 2.

Table 1-1   Operating System Releases

Operating System	Approximate Date	Bits	Comments
UNIX (Bell/AT&T)	1968	8	First widely used multi-user, multitasking operating system for minicomputers
CP/M	1975	8	First operating system that allowed serious business work on small personal computers. VisiCalc, released in 1978, was the first business calculation program for CP/M, and to a large extent made CP/M a success.
MS-DOS	1980	16	First operating system for the very successful IBM PC family of computers. Lotus 1-2-3 was to MS-DOS in 1981 what VisiCalc was to CP/M. Also in 1981, Microsoft introduced the first version of Word for the PC.
PC DOS	1981	16	IBM version of Microsoft MS-DOS
Mac OS	1984	16	The first widely distributed operating system that was totally graphical in its user interface. Also, the Mac OS introduced the use of a mouse to PC-based systems.
Windows 3.0	1990	16	First usable version of a graphical operating system for the PC. Earlier releases, such as Windows 286, are not significant to this discussion.
Windows for Workgroups (Windows 3.11)	1993	16	First version of Microsoft Windows with peer-to-peer networking support for the PC
Windows NT (New Technology or Network)	1993	32	Microsoft's first attempt to bring a true 32-bit, preemptive, multitasking operating system with integrated network functionality to the world of personal computing. Windows NT was later offered in a Workstation version and a Server version.

Table 1-1   Operating System Releases (continued)

Operating System	Approximate Date	Bits	Comments
Windows 95	1995	16/32	An upgrade to Windows 3.x, with a much-improved user interface, and increased support for hardware and mostly 32-bit code. Native support to run 32-bit applications, and many networking features. Windows 95 represented a different direction than Windows NT because it was intended to provide backward compatiblity for 16-bit applications, and it continued to allow direct access of applications to hardware functions.
Windows 98	1998	32	Implemented many bug fixes to Windows 95, more extended hardware support, and fully 32-bit
Windows 2000	2000	32	A major revision of the Windows NT operating system, with the notable characteristics that it is much faster and more reliable than Windows NT. The Windows 2000 kernel contains over 45 million lines of code, compared to 15 million for Windows NT. Windows 2000 comes in several versions, including Professional, Server, Advanced Server, and Datacenter.
Windows Millennium Edition (Me)	2000	32	Microsoft's operating system upgrade of Windows 98, designed specifically for the home user
Windows XP (Experience) Home/Professional	2001	32/64	The successor to Windows Me and Windows NT Professional. It is available in Home and Professional editions. The Home Edition is a 32-bit system that focuses on home use for photos, music, and other multimedia files. The Professional Edition, available in 32-bit and 64-bit versions, is intended for office and professional users who need more computing power and extensive networking capabilities.

Table 1-1   Operating System Releases (continued)

Operating System	Approximate Date	Bits	Comments
Windows Advanced Server, Limited Edition	2001	64	A 64-bit server edition (actually a temporary release of Windows .NET Advanced Server Beta 2) offered as an interim operating system for the new Intel 64-bit titanium processors, preceding the formal release of Windows .NET Server
Windows .NET Server	2002	32/64	Available at this writing in Standard Server, Enterprise Server, and Datacenter versions, this operating system is designed as a server platform for Microsoft's .NET initiative, which is integrating all types of devices—PCs, handheld computers, cell phones, and home appliances—for communications over the Internet.

And what have all these PC operating systems done to the dynasty of the big machines? They have changed their roles. Many big machines are now obsolete; others are used for calculation and data storage, as back-end functions for the PC. Even in this arena, they are threatened today, as PC operating systems and hardware extend further and further.

Many older operating systems are no longer around because of hardware changes. In the next chapter, we will look more closely at hardware architecture and what it means for the operating system. A good example of hardware that is no longer a feasible option to run an OS is the Z80 CPU produced by Zilog. When the cheaper and more flexible Intel 8088 and 8086 microprocessors were introduced in the IBM PC, the MS-DOS platform was a more attractive choice for most users. The Z80 and CP/M slowly died out. The same happened to some operating systems that used the IBM PC hardware for other reasons. A prime example is IBM's own OS/2 operating system. The OS/2 system required extensive hardware, and it could not run older MS-DOS applications. Many people wished to continue to run MS-DOS applications, so OS/2 was not a big hit. Because new software for OS/2 was slow to come, and offered no substantial new features, users were hesitant to use OS/2. Today, you will find OS/2 mainly in environments where it is used to interface to large IBM mainframes with custom-developed applications. For an operating system to be successful, many things must work together: availability of hardware and application programs, the right mix of features, and a little luck. Try Hands-on Project 1-1 to learn more about the history of operating systems.

SINGLE-TASKING VERSUS MULTITASKING

There are a few aspects of operating systems that deserve a closer look. As pointed out, today's PC operating systems go way beyond basic I/O. In practice, almost every resource in the computer, such as the memory and the **microprocessor** (central processing unit or CPU), is managed by the operating system. This is both good and bad; it results in a lot more consistency and a lot of added functionality. However, application programs can no longer directly access hardware in creative ways, as they could before, particularly under MS-DOS. A good example of this is the chip used to make sound. This chip includes an electronic timer that can be accessed by external programs. Many older MS-DOS programs use this chip as a timer to halt program execution for a specified period of time. This is done by manipulating the internal workings of the chip directly from the application program, without the intervention of MS-DOS. Some versions of Windows, such as Windows 3.x, Windows 95, Windows 98, and Windows Me still enable programs to directly access hardware, whereas Windows NT, Windows 2000, and Windows XP do not.

 A common complaint about Windows 95 and Windows 98, in particular, is that these systems sometimes hang or crash. This is because in order to achieve backward compatibility with older 16-bit Windows and MS-DOS programs, these operating systems allow programs to directly access hardware resources—and are therefore more susceptible to experiencing conflicts in hardware management between two or more programs running at the same time.

One of the major reasons for giving the operating system so much control over resources is to facilitate **multitasking**, a technique that allows a computer to run two or more programs at the same time. Since most personal computers have only one CPU chip, which can in general only do one thing at a time, multitasking is generally achieved by splitting processor time between applications, switching so rapidly that the user is not aware of any discontinuity.

There are two general types of multitasking. The first method is known as **cooperative multitasking**. In this method, the operating system hands over control to a program, sits back, and waits for the program to hand control back to the operating system. The assumption here is that the program will do some work, and then give control back to the operating system. If, for some reason, the program does not hand control back to the operating system, this one program will hog the CPU until its operations are complete, while all other programs on the computer are on hold. If the program does not release control, for example, because it is stuck in an endless loop, the operating system may never regain control. As a result, no other programs can run until the computer is reset—an undesirable scenario. This could also be a problem if some of the programs on the computer are time sensitive. If a program must collect data every second, or regularly update a clock, a cooperative multitasking environment may cause trouble. You will find this behavior in systems such as Windows 3.1. If you format a floppy disk and try to play

Solitaire at the same time, you will find that you cannot play a card until the floppy disk is completely formatted. Figure 1-6 shows the basic concept of cooperative multitasking.

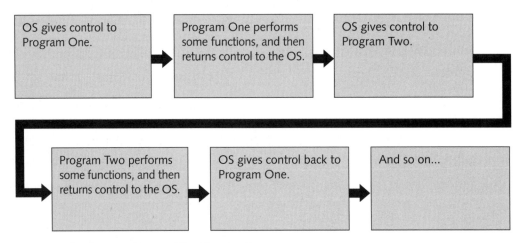

Figure 1-6   Cooperative multitasking basics

A better method is the second alternative, **preemptive multitasking**, illustrated in Figure 1-7. In this scenario, the operating system is in control of the computer at all times. It lets programs execute a little bit of code at a time, but immediately after the code executes, it forces the program to relinquish control of the CPU back to the operating system. It then takes the next program and repeats the same process. Because the operating system is in charge, it has a lot of control over how much of the computer's resources are allocated to each program. As a result, the computer must use more of its processor power and memory to support the operating system, but the behavior of programs and the computer as a whole are a little more predictable. Playing Solitaire while formatting a floppy disk in any of Windows NT, 2000, or XP operating systems is not a problem; preemptive multitasking results in both processes getting some CPU time to do their jobs. Windows 95, 98, and Me all use an enhanced version of cooperative multitasking, so you can format a floppy disk and play Solitaire with less delay than in earlier versions of Windows. One reason is that the program code used to format the floppy disk was rewritten to be more cooperative. If you compare the speed and response of Solitaire in Windows 95, 98, or Me against the speed and response of Solitaire in Windows NT, 2000, or XP, while both are formatting a floppy disk, you will see a slight to significant difference in favor of Windows NT, 2000, and XP (particularly because applications run up to 30 percent faster in Windows 2000 and XP).

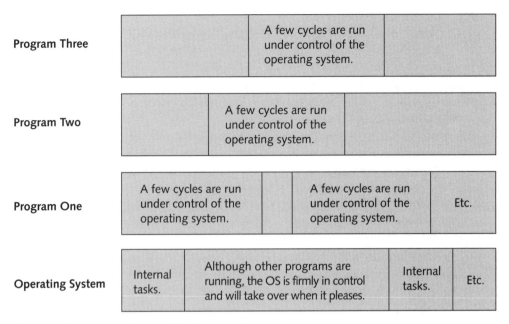

Figure 1-7   Preemptive multitasking basics

There are still some single-tasking operating systems used on PCs. A **single-tasking** operating system executes one program at a time (see Figure 1-8). To do something else, one program must be stopped, and a new program must be loaded and executed. Since there is normally never a situation in which there are multiple programs trying to use the same resources, single-tasking operating systems are a lot simpler. This is, however, considered older technology, and as new operating systems are released, they are seldom single-tasking. An example of a single-tasking operating system is MS-DOS. New single-tasking operating systems are found only in computers with very limited processor capacity, such as **Personal Digital Assistants (PDAs)**. An exception is Windows CE, which is designed for PDAs, but also can be multitasking. In addition, the Apple Newton PDA, now an older product, can handle basic multitasking, but Apple discontinued support for the Newton beginning in 1999.

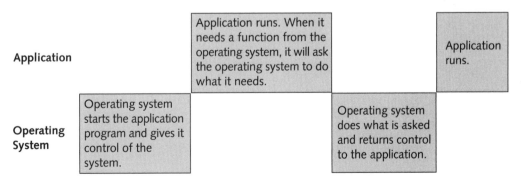

Figure 1-8   Single-tasking operating system

A special note must be made of a hybrid system called a **task-switching** operating system. This system offers many of the device management functions of the multitasking operating system, and it can load multiple application programs at once. It will, though, actively execute only one of these programs. If the user wants to use another application, he can ask the operating system to switch to that task. When the switch is made, the operating system gives control to the newly selected task. Obviously, many of the programs associated with switching among various applications and their use of various devices do not have to be addressed, making this a less complicated type of operating system. This is also considered an older technology that isn't used in any of the new PC operating systems. Many versions of Mac OS are task switching, as are some of the operating systems found on much older PCs made by companies such as Atari (the ST series) and Commodore (the Amiga series), which focus more on the home computer market. You can see the concept of task switching in Figure 1-9.

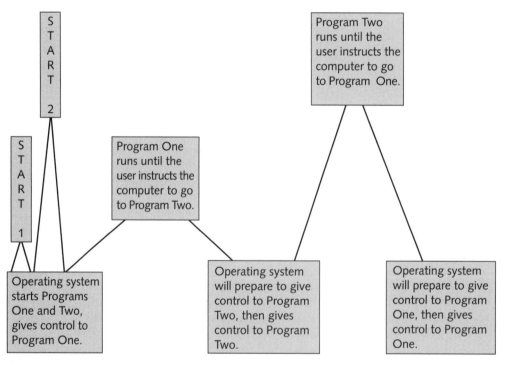

Figure 1-9   Task switching

SINGLE-USER VERSUS MULTI-USER OPERATING SYSTEMS

Some operating systems, in addition to being able to run multiple programs at the same time with multitasking technology, allow multiple users to use an application simultaneously. These are known as **multi-user** operating systems. A system that is a multi-user system is almost, by definition, also a multitasking system. Most multi-user systems use preemptive, multitasking technology. The desktop operating systems covered in this book initially were designed as **single-user** systems (only one user at a time), with the exception of UNIX, which is a multi-user operating system by design. UNIX is included here since its role in business seems to be increasing over recent years, even though UNIX is over 25 years old. Windows NT, Windows 2000, and Windows .NET Server also are designed as multi-user systems, particularly the Server versions.

You might think that the operating systems used to run client/server or .NET networks would be considered multi-user operating systems; however, this is not always the case. An OS can be multitasking without being multi-user. For example, although one computer on the network may act as a network server, making files or printers available to many other computers, and thereby to many other users, the operating system that performs those tasks is not always a multi-user operating system. In general, to qualify as multi-user, the operating system must allow multiple users to run individual applications simultaneously. For this reason, many client/server and .NET operating systems are not strictly multi-user. Some experts predict that client/server, and particularly .NET computing, will eventually make multi-user systems obsolete, but the trend to client/server, and particularly to .NET technologies, really enables all types of operating systems to work together seamlessly. A good example of an operating system that is multitasking but not multi-user is Windows 98.

CURRENT OPERATING SYSTEMS

The operating systems surveyed in this book are the most common in today's computing environments, and they fall into several families:

- Windows 95, Windows 98, and Windows Me

- Windows NT, Windows 2000, Windows XP, and Windows .NET Server

- The different flavors of UNIX operating systems

- Apple Macintosh Mac OS systems

In Chapter 2, you will be introduced to each of these families in more detail. This section gives a brief summary.

As this book is written, there are two popular desktop operating systems used in corporate America—Windows 98 and Windows 2000 Professional. In a short time, Windows XP Professional is likely to gain over both Windows 98 and Windows 2000 Professional. Windows 2000 Professional and Windows XP Professional offer a stable work environment that is appealing for office use. Some organizations still use Windows 95 and Windows NT Workstation, but these operating systems are likely to be replaced by Windows XP Professional because Windows XP offers more device drivers for more modern computing hardware, and is considerably faster. It is also possible to find some users hanging on to Windows 95 because they have older and more resource-limited machines, machines that cannot run later versions of Windows, such as Windows NT, 2000, or XP. The exact requirements for the various hardware platforms are discussed later in this book.

The dynamic multi-user UNIX operating system has been popular among industrial-strength users for many years. It is especially appealing to members of the scientific and research communities for its power to perform complex tasks and maintain large databases. There are many flavors of UNIX. You will look at a group of UNIX operating systems called the POSIX Compliant, System V, Release 4 systems (pronounced "System 5, Release 4" or "SVR4" for short). POSIX is an interface standard supported by both schools of UNIX, as well as non-UNIX operating systems like Windows NT, 2000, and XP. It was designed so applications can be resource compliant across multiple operating systems.

Still popular in the education and graphics industries is the Mac OS operating system for Apple Macintosh computers. In certain sectors, this OS is strongly represented, but typically you will not find it much in corporate America. You *will* find the Mac OS in education—colleges and some secondary schools—and in the graphics industry, particularly in video editing.

In Chapter 2, you will take a closer look at the individual operating systems mentioned here. You will read more about the hardware required to run each operating system, and which versions you will see in what environment and for what reason. Try Hands-on Projects 1-2 through 1-8 to learn more about the Windows-based, UNIX, and Mac OS operating systems, including how to use tools for obtaining system information, how to view device drivers, and how to see multitasking in operation.

CHAPTER SUMMARY

- ❐ You should now have a good idea how an operating system works in general terms. You should understand the input and output functions provided by the BIOS, and the other parts of the operating system. You were introduced to the concept of device drivers, and the functions the operating system provides to application programs. The types of operating systems in use were briefly discussed, as well as the differentiation that can be made based on the computer environment in which the operating system is used.

- ❐ A short operating system history touched on some of the highlights in computer development from the standpoint of operating systems. Also introduced were single-tasking operating systems, which run only one application at a time, and multitasking operating systems, which can run multiple applications at once. The single-user operating system can only service one user at a time, while the multi-user operating system services multiple users at once.

- ❐ Finally, some modern PC operating systems you will find in use today were described. This theoretical beginning will provide a good background for the following chapter, which provides a comparison of the basic features of some of today's popular operating systems.

KEY TERMS

Application Program Interface (API) — Functions or programming features in an operating system that programmers can use for network links, links to messaging services, or interfaces to other systems.

application software — A word processor, spreadsheet, database, computer game, or other type of application that a user runs on a computer. Application software consists of computer code that is formatted so that the computer or its operating system can translate that code into a specific task, such as writing a document.

Beginner's All-purpose Symbolic Instruction Code (BASIC) — An English-like computer programming language originally designed as a teaching tool, but which evolved into a useful and relatively powerful development language.

batch processing — A computing style frequently employed by large systems. A request for a series of processes is submitted to the computer; information is displayed or printed when the batch is complete. Batches might include processing all of the checks submitted to a bank for a day, or all of the purchases in a wholesale inventory system, for example. Compare to *sequential processing*.

Basic Input/Output System (BIOS) — Low-level computer program code that conducts basic hardware and software communications inside the computer. A computer's BIOS basically resides between computer hardware and the higher level operating system, such as UNIX or Windows.

Compact Disc Read Only Memory (CD-ROM) — A hardware device used to play, and in some cases record, computer data, music, and other multimedia information often in write-once, read-many format.

client/server systems — A computer hardware and software design in which different portions of an application execute on different computers, or on different components of a single computer. Typically, client software supports user I/O, and server software conducts database searches, manages printer output, and the like.

code — Instructions written in a computer programming language.

cooperative multitasking — A computer hardware and software design in which the operating system temporarily hands off control to an application and waits for the application to return control to the operating system. Compare to *preemptive multitasking*.

central processing unit (CPU) — In today's computer, typically a single chip (the microprocessor) with support devices that conducts the majority of the computer's calculations.

desktop operating system — A computer operating system that typically is installed on a PC type of computer, used by one person at a time, and may or may not be connected to a network.

device driver — Computer software designed to provide the operating system and application software access to specific computer hardware.

Disk Operating System (DOS) — The generic computer code used to control many low-level computer hardware and software functions. Also the specific name for the operating system popular with IBM-compatible PC computers, also called MS-DOS and PC DOS.

graphical user interface (GUI) — An interface between the user and an operating system, which presents information in an intuitive graphical format that employs multiple colors, figures, icons, windows, toolbars, and other features. A GUI is usually deployed with a pointing device, such as a mouse, to make the user more productive.

hardware — The physical devices in a computer that you can touch (if you have the cover off), such as the CPU, circuit boards (cards), disk drives, monitor, and modem.

input/output (I/O) — Input is information taken in by a computer device to handle or process, such as characters typed at a keyboard. Output is information sent out by a computer device after that information is handled or processed, such as displaying the characters typed at the keyboard on the monitor.

kernel — An essential set of programs and computer code built into a computer operating system to control processor, disk, memory, and other functions central to the basic operation of a computer. The kernel communicates with the BIOS, device drivers, and the API to perform these functions. It also interfaces with the resource managers.

Light Emitting Diode (LED) — An electronic device frequently used to display information in electronic devices, such as watches, clocks, and stereos.

microprocessor — A solid-state electronic device that controls the major computer functions and operations. See also *CPU*.

multitasking — A technique that allows a computer to run two or more programs at the same time.

multi-user — A computer hardware and software system designed to service multiple users who access the computer's hardware and software applications simultaneously.

multi-user environment — A computer environment that supports multi-user access to a computer's hardware and software facilities.

operating system (OS) — Computer software code that interfaces with user application software and the computer's BIOS to allow the applications to interact with the computer hardware.

Personal Digital Assistant (PDA) — A small hand-held computer used as a personal organizer.

preemptive multitasking — A computer hardware and software design for multitasking of applications in which the operating system retains control of the computer at all times. See *cooperative multitasking* for comparison.

real-time systems — An operating system that interacts directly with the user, and responds in real time with required information.

Read Only Memory (ROM) — Special memory that contains information that is not erased when the power is removed from the memory hardware. ROM is used to store computer instructions that must be available at all times, such as the BIOS code.

resource managers — Programs that manage computer memory and CPU use.

sequential processing — A computer processing style in which each operation is submitted, acted upon, and the results displayed before the next process is started. Compare to *batch processing*.

server operating system — A computer operating system usually found on more powerful PC-based computers than those used for desktop operating systems, which is connected to a network, and that can act in many roles to enable multiple users to access information, such as electronic mail, files, and software.

single-tasking — A computer hardware and software design that can manage only a single task at a time.

single-user — A computer hardware and software system that enables only one user to access its resources at a particular time.

task switching — A single-tasking computer hardware and software design that permits the user or application software to switch among multiple single-tasking operations.

time-sharing system — A central computer system, such as a mainframe, that is used by multiple users and applications simultaneously.

REVIEW QUESTIONS

1. An operating system acts as an interface between _____ and _____.

2. Which operating system was developed first?
   a. MS-DOS
   b. Windows 95
   c. UNIX
   d. Mac OS
   e. CP/M

3. One company created a revolution of sorts when it introduced an open standard and desktop computing hardware. Which company was this?

4. Which of the following statements is true of a computer's BIOS?
   a. It conducts high-level software and hardware operations.
   b. It communicates with the computer hardware at the lowest, most basic levels.
   c. It is required in some form of all computer systems.
   d. It serves as an intermediary between the operating system and the computer hardware.
   e. all of the above
   f. only a and b
   g. only b, c, and d

5. The _____ operating system was the first system used by IBM for its PC computer.

6. Who is responsible for the MS-DOS operating system, and in what year was it developed?

7. You connected a new printer to your computer, but it is not printing. Which of the following is most likely the problem?

   a. The printer is not Web compatible.

   b. Most new printers must be configured so that everyone on a local network can use them.

   c. You forgot to install the device driver for that printer.

   d. The printer must be set up to print in screen mode.

8. What is the main difference between a cooperative multitasking system and a pre-emptive multitasking system?

9. Apple Computer Corporation's operating system is called _____.

10. Which of the following is (are) at this writing the most prevalent operating system(s) currently used on desktop computers in the corporate world?

    a. Windows 3.11

    b. Windows 98

    c. Windows 2000

    d. Mac OS

    e. all of the above

    f. only a and c

    g. only b and c

    h. only a, c, and d

11. _____ is a technique that allows a user or a computer application to switch among multiple applications, running one program at a time.

12. Why did IBM's OS/2 operating system fail to catch on?

13. Why is it a problem for an operating system to enable a software application to directly access hardware, such as memory or a disk drive?

    a. because the software application can phyically damage the hardware interrupts

    b. because most hardware has memory that should only be managed by that hardware

    c. because the software application can cause the entire operating system to hang or crash

    d. because users should directly manage hardware, rather than programs or operating systems

14. One of the earliest widely used programming languages was called BASIC, which stands for _____.

15. Linux is an operating system that closely resembles Windows 98 because it was developed by Microsoft. True or false?

16. Which of the following is used to manage computer memory?

    a. Application Program Interface (API)

    b. resource manager

    c. batch process

    d. diplomatic intermediary

17. Very large early business computers were called _____.

18. The medium-sized computers that preceded PCs and were used for serious business and engineering applications were called _____.

19. Microsoft Windows was the first graphics-oriented user interface for small desktop computers. True or false?

20. The more powerful the computer, the larger it has to be. True or false?

HANDS-ON PROJECTS

Project 1-1

Today's Internet is a rich resource for finding current and historical computer information. This project enables you to use the Internet to learn how to find more information about the history of computers.

To view World Wide Web sites that house additional history about the information covered in this chapter:

1. Point your browser to the online address:

    http://www.computerhistory.org/timeline/index.page

2. Answer the following questions based on your investigation of this Web site:

    a. The IBM PC, introduced in 1981, used what type of central processing unit (CPU)? What was the speed of this processor in MHz?

    b. What was the first personal computer, and how much memory did it have?

    c. What was the first computer "bug"? Who coined this term?

    d. In what year did Kenneth Thompson and Dennis Ritchie develop UNIX, and for what organization did they work?

    e. What promotional technique did Apple use to introduce the first Macintosh in 1984? What short-lived IBM computer was introduced that same year? What successful computer did IBM introduce in 1984, and what CPU did it use?

f. What CPUs were both introduced in 1989?

g. What major operating system was first shipped in 1990?

3. Point your browser to the online address:

   http://www.digitalcentury.com/encyclo/update/mits.html

4. Answer the following questions based on your investigation of this Web site:

   a. Who were the co-developers of the MITS Altair computer, mentioned earlier in this chapter?

   b. What two Boston-based programmers responded to the first Altair ads with excitement because they had a computer program that might run on it?

Project 1-2

All operating systems have tools that enable you to find out information about them. In this project, you'll learn how to obtain information about Windows-based, UNIX, and Mac OS systems.

To enter commands and discover information from the MS-DOS or command prompt in a Windows-based operating system:

1. In Windows 95/98, click **Start**, point to **Programs**, and click **MS-DOS Prompt**. In Windows NT, click **Start**, point to **Programs**, and click **Command Prompt**. In Windows Me, click **Start**, point to **Programs**, point to **Accessories**, and click **MS-DOS Prompt**. In Windows 2000, click **Start**, point to **Programs**, point to **Accessories**, and click **Command Prompt**. And in Windows XP, click **Start**, point to **All Programs**, point to **Accessories**, and click **Command Prompt**.

2. At the MS-DOS or command prompt, type the command **chkdsk** and press **Enter**. What information appears?

3. Type **mem/ꟓc** and press **Enter**. What information does this command provide about how your computer's memory is used?

4. Type **Exit** and press **Enter** to leave the MS-DOS or Command Prompt window.

If possible, try these steps on different operating systems, such as Windows 98, Windows NT, and Windows 2000 or XP, and note the similarities and differences in the results.

To discover some version and memory information about your Windows 95/98, Windows Me, Windows NT, or Windows 2000/XP operating system:

1. Double-click **My Computer** on the desktop, click the **Help** menu, and choose **About Windows** from the pull-down options. What information does the dialog box provide? How might this information be useful if you have to contact technical support for your operating system?

1

2. Close each window (About Windows and My Computer) individually by clicking the **X** in the upper-right corner.

To discover some information about your Mac OS 9.x operating system:

1. In Mac OS 9.x, click **Help** at the right side of the main menu bar.

2. Choose **Help Center**.

3. Choose **Mac Help**.

4. Notice the topics for which you can find help, such as "What's New," "Basics," and "Disks."

5. How would you find help about opening files and running programs?

6. Where would you get help for solving problems?

7. Close the Mac Help window by clicking the **close** box in the upper-left corner of the window.

To discover some information about your Mac OS X operating system:

1. In Mac OS X, click **Help** at the right side of the main menu bar. Next, click **MacHelp** on the drop down menu.

2. Locate the search field at the top of the dialog box, enter **Printer**, and click the **Ask** button.

3. What type of dialog box appears next, and how might it help you answer a question about a printer?

4. Close the dialog box when you are finished.

To enter commands and discover some information about your UNIX operating system:

1. At a UNIX system prompt, type the command **man ls** (for Red Hat Linux) or **help ls** (for other UNIX versions), and press **Enter** to view help information about the *ls* command that is used to list files. (You must use *man ls* in Red Hat Linux, because it does not support the help command.)

2. Type the command **ls –la**, and press **Enter**. What information about files and directories do you see?

3. If you are using a Red Hat Linux terminal window, type **exit**, and press **Enter** to exit the UNIX command line session (check with your instructor if you need to use a different exit command).

Some UNIX systems, particularly Red Hat Linux, have an X Windows interface. If your system uses an X Windows interface, find out from your instructor how to open a terminal or "konsole" window to execute commands. For example, in the GNOME interface typically installed with Red Hat Linux, a terminal window is opened by clicking the terminal emulation icon on the taskbar at the bottom of the screen.

Project 1-3

In this project, you'll learn how to use the UNIX *cat* command to directly control the display of input and output (I/O) to the screen, and view the contents of a file.

To display information to the screen:

1. Type **cat** at the command prompt, and type enter. What happens after you type cat? Your results are an example of how you can directly influence the input and output of an operating system.

2. Type **UNIX is an operating system**, and press **Enter**.

3. What is displayed back on the screen after you press Enter?

4. If the cat input/output mode is not stopped when you press Enter, press **Ctrl+C** (see Figure 1-10, which illustrates using a GNOME terminial window in Red Hat Linux).

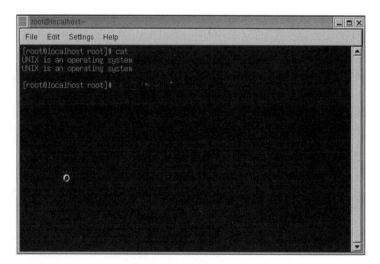

Figure 1-10   Using the cat command

To display the contents of a file:

1. First ask your instructor for the name and location of two files, such as the greeting file that automatically displays information when you log onto a UNIX system, and the motd (message of the day) file that displays additional information with the greeting.

2. Type **cat**, and then type the file path. For example, to view the contents of the greeting file, type **cat /etc/greeting**. What are the contents of the file that you displayed?

3. Next display the contents of two files at the same time by typing both file paths after the cat command, such as **cat /etc/greeting /etc/motd**.

Project 1-4

Windows 2000 and Windows XP offer extensive information about these operating systems through use of the system information features. This project shows you how to access the system information in both systems.

To access system information in Windows 2000:

1. Click **Start**, point to **Programs**, point to **Accessories**, point to **System Tools**, and click **System Information**. (Another way to access the system information is to right-click the My Computer icon on the desktop, and click Manage. Next, double-click System Information in the tree.)

2. What categories of information can be viewed in the left pane?

3. Select **System Summary** in the tree, if it is not already selected.

4. What system information is displayed in the right pane?

5. Double-click **Hardware Resources** in the tree, and click **Memory**. What information appears?

6. Double-click **Software Environment** in the tree, and click **Running Tasks**. Notice the executable programs that are currently running.

7. Close the System Information dialog box.

To access system information in Windows XP:

1. Click **Start**, point to **All Programs**, point to **Accessories**, point to **System Tools**, and click **System Information** (see Figure 1-11).

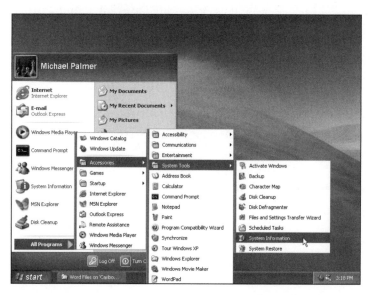

Figure 1-11   Viewing system information in Windows XP

2. What categories of information can be viewed in the left pane?

3. What system information appears in the right pane?

4. Double-click **Hardware Resources**, and then click **Conflicts/Sharing**. How might this information help you resolve a hardware conflict between two cards in the computer, for example?

5. Double-click **Software Environment**. What information can you access about the software environment?

6. Click **System Drivers** in the left pane and notice the information in the right pane that shows what drivers are loaded.

7. Close the System Information dialog box.

 Although the system information available in Windows 2000 and in Windows XP appears in similar fashion, there are several differences. If both systems are available to you, see if you can determine some of these differences.

Project 1-5

You can find information about the system and device drivers in Windows 95/98/Me by using the Device Manager in these systems.

To use the Device Manager:

1. Click **Start**, point to **Settings**, and click **Control Panel**.

2. Double-click the **System** icon (also called the System applet). In Windows Me, if the System icon does not appear, click **View all Control Panel Options**.

3. Click the **Device Manager** tab (see Figure 1-12).

4. Double-click one of the devices, such as **Mouse**.

5. Double-click the specific device on which you want to find driver information, such as **PS/2 Compatible Mouse Port**.

6. Click the **Driver** tab. What information appears on the tab?

7. In Windows 98 and Me, click the **Driver File Details** button. What driver files are associated with the device?

8. Close all the windows that you opened that are associated with the System icon, including the System Properties dialog box.

9. Close Control Panel.

1

Figure 1-12 Device Manager tab in Windows 98

Project 1-6

In this project, you'll list the contents of a particular UNIX driver file. UNIX systems have two types of driver files: block special files and character special files. A *block special file* enables communication between a device and a device driver using blocks of characters, compared to a *character special file* in which only one character is sent at a time during communications. In this example, the *sda1* (sda and the number one) file contains driver information pertaining to media, such as hard drives.

To view the contents of a device file:

1. Type **ls –l /dev/sda1** at the command prompt (note that this file has different names in non–Linux versions of UNIX, such as "ad0sla" in BSD UNIX, "vg00" in HP-UNIX, and "hd4" in IBM's AIX).

2. What information appears on the screen?

Project 1-7

Microsoft Windows 95, 98, Me, NT, 2000, and XP are good examples of widely distributed multitasking operating systems. In this project, you'll learn how to start multiple application windows in these operating systems.

To start several applications and view some information about their operation:

1. Click **Start** on the taskbar, and point to **Programs** (or **All Programs** in Windows XP).

2. In Windows 95, 98, or NT, click **Windows Explorer** (or **Windows NT Explorer** for Windows NT). In Windows Me, 2000, or Windows XP, click **Accessories**, and then click **Windows Explorer**. What information can you access using the Windows Explorer application?

3. Click **Start**, point to **Programs** (or **All Programs** in Windows XP), and point to **Accessories**. What applications can you start from the shortcut menu that appears? (In Windows Me, 2000, and XP, you may need to click the down arrows to display all of the programs).

4. Click **Notepad** on the shortcut menu.

5. Click **Start**, point to **Programs** (or **All Programs**), point to **Accessories**, and click **Calculator**.

6. Click **Start**, point to **Programs** (or **All Programs**), point to **Accessories**, and click **Address Book**. How many applications (and windows) are now running at the same time?

7. In Windows NT, 2000, and XP, press **Ctrl+Alt+Del** and complete Step 8. This control key combination displays the windows Security dialog box. Click the **Task Manager** button and make sure that the Applications tab appears. What information is available from the Applications tab? Also, notice that a CPU Usage Meter now appears on the right side of the taskbar near the time.

8. While you still have the Task Manager open, click the **Performance** tab. This tab displays information about the system resources that are in use, such as the CPU and memory usage. Close one or two applications and observe the effect on the use of resources (observe both the Performance tab and the CPU Usage Meter). Close **Task Manager**. What happens to the CPU Usage Meter when you close Task Manager?

9. In Windows 95/98/Me, press **Ctrl+Alt+Del**. What information about applications appears? Close the dialog box.

1

10. Also in Windows 95/98/Me, click **Start**, point to **Programs**, point to **Accessories**, point to **System Tools**, and click **Resource Meter**. (In Windows 98 and Me, the Resource Meter is not installed by default. If it is not installed, ask your instructor about how to install it.) Click **OK** if you see a dialog box warning that the Resource Meter may cause your system to run more slowly. Observe that the Resource Meter appears on the right side of the taskbar near the time. Double-click the **Resource Meter** icon in the taskbar to display it on the desktop as shown in Figure 1-13. Close one or two applications and notice how this affects the Resource Meter.

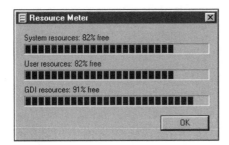

Figure 1-13   Windows 98 Resource Meter

11. Right-click the **Resource Meter** icon and click **Exit**.

12. Close all of the open programs.

Project 1-8

The Mac OS is another example of a multitasking system. In this project, you open two programs at the same time in the Mac OS.

To multitask in the Mac OS 9.x:

1. Open the Apple menu by clicking the **Apple** icon.

2. What options appear on this menu?

3. Click **Calculator** on the menu.

4. Open the Apple menu again.

5. Click **Clock**, **Address book**, or another application on the menu.

6. How would you compare using multitasking in Mac OS to using multitasking in a Windows-based operating system, as in Hands-on Project 1-7?

7. Close the two applications.

To multitask in Mac OS X:

1. Open **Macintosh HD**.

2. Choose **Applications**.

3. What applications appear on this menu?

4. Select **Calculator**.

5. From the Applications window, select **Address Book**, or another icon in the window.

6. Close the applications you've opened.

7. Close the Applications window.

CASE PROJECT

The National Water Research Association is currently working to upgrade several aging computer systems. For example, they have 20 computers running Mac OS 8.0 and earlier, and 15 computers running Windows 95. All of these computers are relatively slow for the kinds of applications that are used, resulting in valuable employee time lost while waiting on these computers. Further, the association wishes to add high-speed Internet service and faster servers that are accessed by users.

1. The National Water Research Association has traditional business and office software that includes accounting, word processing, spreadsheets, and Internet browsers. What operating system should be recommended for the new computers on the basis of the discussion of operating system capabilities in this chapter? Is there an operating system that you would not recommend?

2. Most of the association's computer users use multiple applications simultaneously, such as using accounting software and spreadsheets. What capability and type of operating system are necessary to enable them to run several applications at once?

3. One employee in the association has a 10-year-old, single-tasking UNIX computer (running Digital Equipment's ultrix) that he primarily uses to create documentation and newsletters for the company. The work has expanded over the years, requiring more and more graphics, tables, photos, and other complex information to be inserted into text. Do you recommend upgrading this computer, and if so, what operating system and type of computer would you upgrade to?

4. The executive director's administrative assistant has a computer on which the monitor does not seem to be communicating with the CPU. On the basis of what you learned in this chapter, what might be the problem?

5. As you discuss your recommendations with the executive director, she asks for your opinion about the most important historical developments in computers, such as CPUs, memory, peripheral devices, and operating systems, that have had an impact on the way the association uses computers. What is your answer?

OPTIONAL CASE PROJECTS FOR TEAMS

Many organizations use project or task teams to plan a new computer installation, install new software, or solve a problem. The Optional Case Projects for Teams are presented at the end of each chapter to enable you to practice working in a team environment, similar to the environment you might encounter in an employment situation.

Team Case One

Form a small team. Use the Internet or another resource to determine the average salaries of four or five types of jobs that involve computer use. Next, compare the advantages of single-tasking operating systems to multitasking systems. On the basis of your salary research, roughly project in dollars how a multitasking operating system can help make an employee more productive than a single-tasking operating system. For example, an accountant might, on average, earn $40,000 per year (about $20 an hour). That accountant may often need to use a word processor, spreadsheet, database, and accounting program to make a budget projection. At $20 per hour, how productive is that accountant in a single-tasking system compared to a multitasking system?

Team Case Two

Have your team study the operating system releases shown in Table 1-1 of this chapter. Work to achieve a team consensus about which operating system has most affected today's use of computers. Explain the reasons for the team's conclusion.

2

CURRENT HARDWARE AND PC OPERATING SYSTEMS

After reading this chapter and completing the exercises you will be able to:

♦ Explain operating system hardware, such as design type, speed, cache, address bus, data bus, and control bus

♦ Describe the basic features and system architecture of popular PC processors

♦ Identify the basic features and characteristics of popular PC operating systems

♦ Understand the development history of popular PC operating systems

♦ Understand how hardware components interact with operating systems

Operating systems and hardware work in a unified relationship to make computers useful for business, personal, and network computing applications. The features of an operating system used for a particular application depend on the capabilities of the hardware. In many cases, older hardware does not support modern operating systems. When you upgrade an operating system, you may need to upgrade the hardware to match the new operating system's capabilities.

This chapter gives you a foundation in hardware basics, including the design of CPUs, clock speeds, and types of computer buses. Also, you will learn about modern CPUs and how they are used by particular operating systems. After you learn about the hardware, you will examine the features of the most popular operating systems, enabling you to become acquainted with the general characteristics of each operating system, its strengths and weaknesses, and its hardware requirements. With this overview, you will understand how to choose the operating system that is best suited for a particular work or home environment, and for specific hardware. You'll know which operating system to use when new computers are installed, or when existing computers are upgraded. You'll also be able to identify situations in which the wrong operating system is used.

UNDERSTANDING CPUs

As you learned in the previous chapter, one of the main functions of the operating system is to provide the interface between the various application programs running on a computer and the hardware inside. Central to understanding the hardware is the system architecture of the computer, which is built around the central processing unit (CPU), or processor. The **system architecture** includes the number and type of CPUs in the hardware, and the communication routes, called **buses**, between the CPUs and other hardware components, such as memory and disk storage.

The CPU is the chip that performs the actual computational and logic work. Most modern PCs have one such chip, and are referred to as **single-processor computers**. In reality, for complete functionality, the CPU requires several support chips, such as chips that help manage communications with devices and device drivers. There are also computers that have multiple CPUs; many have two, some have as many as 64 or more. These computers are generally referred to as **multiprocessor computers**. You will take a closer look at single-processor and multiprocessor computers later in this chapter.

CPUs can be classified by several hardware elements, the most important of which are:

- Design type
- Speed
- Cache
- Address bus
- Data bus
- Control bus

Each of these elements is considered in the following sections.

Design Type

Two general CPU designs are used in today's computers: **CISC (Complex Instruction Set Computer)** and **RISC (Reduced Instruction Set Computer)**. The main difference between the two is the number of different instructions the chip can process. When a program executes on a computer, the CPU reads instruction after instruction from the program to perform the tasks the program wants completed. When the CPU has read such an instruction, it carries out the operations associated with it. In the current generation of PCs, the CPU can process as many as 20 million complex operations per second on the low end, and several billion on the high end. Clock speed and CPU design are the factors that determine how fast operations are executed. Obviously, it is convenient for the programmer to have many instructions available to do many different operations.

Let's say, for example, that the programmer wants to multiply two numbers. It would be convenient to give the CPU the two numbers, then tell it to multiply them, and display the result. Since different kinds of numbers (such as integers and real numbers) must be treated differently, it would be nice if there were functions to perform this multiplication on all number types. You can see that as we require the CPU to perform more and more functions, the number of instructions can rapidly increase. At the same time, the **instruction set**, or the list of commands the CPU can understand and carry out, can get quite complex. As programs perform more functions, the instruction set gets more complicated. A processor that works like this is called a Complex Instruction Set Computer (CISC) CPU. When a CISC CPU gets a command, it assigns specific instructions to different parts of the chip. When a command is finished and the CPU gets the next command, it typically uses the same parts of the chip it used before to carry out this command. Current versions of CISC-based chips typically recognize over 200 different instructions.

The CISC CPU offers advantages and disadvantages. A big advantage is that you need only general-purpose hardware to carry out commands. If you later want to add new commands to a new revision of your chip, that likely can be done with the same general-purpose hardware. Another big advantage is that the chip is driven mainly by software, which is cheaper to produce than hardware. Major disadvantages to the CISC design include the complexity of hardware needed to perform many functions, and the complexity of on-chip software needed to make the hardware do the right thing. An even bigger disadvantage is, ironically, the need to continually reprogram the on-chip hardware. If you use the same part of the chip to add a number as you use to multiply a number—two functions that are obviously related but slightly different—you must reconfigure the hardware in between the multiplication and addition operations. This reconfiguration takes a little time, which is one reason a CISC chip can be a little slower than other designs.

Also, when you use general-purpose hardware to perform specific functions, the functions won't always be executed in the most efficient way, which can slow the CPU's execution of program code. One solution to this problem is to customize hardware for specific functions. You can add a module that is optimized to do all computational functions (a **math coprocessor**), for example. Such a trick increases CPU performance, but it also increases the price. Fast hardware is expensive.

 Early system architectures have a processor and an optional slot for a math coprocessor. The math coprocessor is used to perform complex math calculations, such as those required for computations in a spreadsheet. Modern system architectures have a CPU with a built-in math coprocessor.

Considering the disadvantages of the design of the CISC CPU, it is easy to understand the idea behind the other major CPU design, the Reduced Instruction Set Computer (RISC) CPU. The complex operations that a CISC CPU carries out slow it down because all sorts of hardware on the chip must be set up to perform specific functions.

The RISC CPU design, on the other hand, requires very little setup for specific tasks because it has hardware on the chip that is specially designed and optimized to perform particular functions. As mentioned before, the disadvantage of this approach is that you need a lot of hardware to carry out instructions, which will make the chip more expensive because it is more complex. This is the main reason a RISC CPU has so few instructions; most of the instructions it performs are conducted by hardware on the chip that is dedicated to perform just that function. Since most of the hardware on the RISC CPU is not shared among many instructions, RISC CPUs typically use a technique called **pipelining**, which allows the processor to operate on one instruction at the same time it is fetching one or more subsequent instructions from the operating system or application. The difference between the RISC approach and the CISC approach is best explained by the example in Figure 2-1, which shows how each design carries out five multiplications. Motorola manufactures a RISC chip for the Apple Power Mac computers (PowerPC), for example.

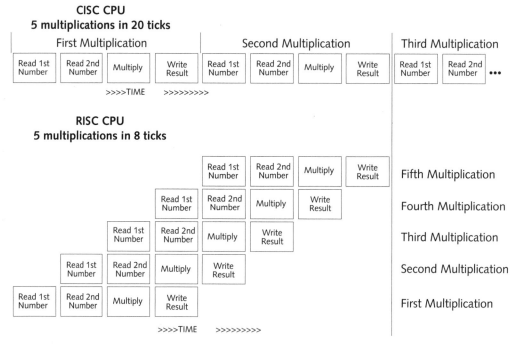

Figure 2-1   CISC versus RISC processing

The general steps required to perform the multiplications are as follows:

1. Read the first number out of memory.

2. Read the second number out of memory.

3. Multiply the two numbers.

4. Write the result back to memory.

5. Repeat Steps 1-4 for each of the four remaining multiplications.

On a simple CISC CPU, the CPU is first configured to get (read) the numbers. It then reads the numbers. Next, the CPU is configured to multiply the numbers. Then the numbers are multiplied. Next, the CPU is configured to write the result to memory. Then the numbers are written to memory. If you wish to multiply five sets of numbers in this way, the whole process must be repeated five times.

On a simple RISC CPU, the process looks slightly different. A piece of hardware on the CPU is dedicated to reading the first number. When this operation is complete, another piece of hardware reads the second number. When that operation is complete, yet another piece of hardware performs the multiplication, and when that is complete, yet another piece of hardware writes the result to memory. If this operation must happen five times in a row, the piece of RISC hardware dedicated to obtaining the first number from memory obtains the first number for the second operation while the second number for the first operation is obtained. And while the first two numbers are being multiplied, the second number for the second operation is retrieved from memory, while the first number for the third operation is obtained. As the first result is written back to memory, the second multiplication is performed, while the second number for the third operation is read from memory, while the first number for the fourth operation is read from memory, and so on. As you can see, when many operations must be performed, the RISC CPU's pipelining performs a lot more efficiently than a CISC CPU. Intel, Motorola, and AMD are three of the most popular manufacturers of this CPU.

The RISC processor design has evolved into a relatively new concept called **Explicitly Parallel Instruction Computing (EPIC)**, created as a joint project by Intel and Hewlett Packard. EPIC enables the processor to handle massive numbers of operations simultaneously by implementing large storage registers and executing parallel instruction sets. The EPIC technology enables a single processor to execute as many as 20 operations at a time.

EPIC employs a built-in compiler as part of the software that drives the CPU. The built-in compiler enables the chip to predict and speculate about which operations are likely in the future. For example, if many mathematical operations have already been requested to obtain and multiply certain data, EPIC makes predictions that additional similar operations will occur in the future. Through prediction and speculation, the chip actually performs some operations before they are requested. For other operations, it sets up rotating registers, or work areas, so that the tools needed for similar operations are already present, and those operations are handled one after the other. EPIC can support up to 256 64-bit registers, far more registers than CISC and traditional RISC processors. By using more registers, EPIC reduces or eliminates contention at the processor, which enables the processor to work faster without bottlenecks.

Another advantage of a RISC-based EPIC processor is that it can build three instructions into one "word." A word is like a single communication with the processor, and

CISC and traditional RISC processors use one instruction per word. By using three instructions per word, EPIC enables the processor to work much faster. Also, EPIC instructions can be combined into instruction groups, consisting of multiple words, and it attempts to execute all of the instructions in one group at the same time, if possible. The number of instructions in one instruction group is theoretically unlimited.

By performing parallel operations, the EPIC processor can do several things simultaneously. For example, in Figure 2-1, the CISC processor takes 20 ticks to perform five multiplications and the RISC processor takes eight ticks. The RISC-based EPIC processor can do five multiplications in one tick, and at the same time it predicts additional tasks or completes other tasks for a different software application.

Speed

The speed of a CPU defines how fast it can perform operations. There are many ways to indicate speed, but the most obvious indicator is the **internal clock speed** of the CPU. As you may know, a CPU runs on a very rigid schedule along with the rest of the computer. The clock provides this schedule to make sure that all the chips know what to expect at what time. The internal clock speed tells you how many clock pulses, or ticks, are available per second. Typically, the CPU performs some action on every tick. The more ticks per second, the faster the CPU executes commands, and the harder the electronics on the CPU must work. The clock speed for a CPU can be lower than 1 million ticks per second (1 megahertz or MHz), and higher than 2 billion ticks per second (2 gigahertz or GHz). The faster the clock, the faster the CPU, the more expensive the hardware. Also, as more components are needed to make a CPU, the chip uses more energy to do its work. Part of this energy is converted to heat, causing faster CPUs to run warmer.

Note

RISC CPU hardware is less complicated than CISC CPU hardware, so a RISC CPU can theoretically operate at higher clock speeds. RISC CPUs operating at clock speeds of 700 MHz have been around for years. Some designs are now available that run at speeds over 2 GHz.

In addition to performing fast operations inside the CPU, the chips also must be able to communicate with the other chips in the computer. This is where the **external clock speed** of the CPU comes in. While a CPU may run internally at a speed of 1.5 GHz, it typically uses a lower clock speed to communicate with the rest of the computer. The reason for this is again, to a large extent, cost. It would be extremely expensive to make every component in the computer run as fast as the CPU. It is therefore common practice to run the other components in the computer at a reduced clock rate. Usually, the external clock speed is one-half, one-third, one-fourth, or one-eighth the speed of the internal CPU clock. This is the speed at which the processor can communicate with the memory and the other devices in the computer.

2

Cache

If a CPU wants to get a few numbers out of memory, and its internal clock speed is four times faster than its external clock speed, it obviously must wait on the external clock, which could be very inefficient. To avoid this problem, most modern CPUs have **cache memory** built into the chip. This memory is extremely fast—it typically runs at the same speed as the processor—and therefore expensive. If the processor needs a number stored in the cache memory on the CPU, it probably won't have to wait to obtain that number. This memory is referred to as **Level 1 (L1) cache**. Some CPUs have one or two more levels of cache memory, which are typically on a separate chip. This is called **Level 2 (L2) cache**, and it normally runs at the same speed as the external CPU clock. For example, L2 cache is generally accessed faster than other memory in the computer, except for L1 cache.

When both L1 and L2 cache are built into the processor chip, the cache on a separate chip is called **Level 3 (L3) cache**. This cache structure is used on some modern chips, particularly those that employ EPIC architectures. The combination of L1, L2, and L3 caching can significantly reduce bottlenecks at the processor.

The amount of L1 and L2/L3 cache, especially for larger CPUs, determines the speed of the CPU. In many cases, up to 90% of the data a CPU needs to transfer to and from memory is present in the L1, L2, or L3 cache when the CPU needs it. This is because there is a specialized piece of hardware called the **cache controller** that predicts what data will be needed, and makes that data available in cache before it is needed. Most modern CPUs also can use the cache to write data to memory to ensure that the CPU will not have to wait when it wishes to write results to memory. You can see that intelligent, fast cache controllers and large amounts of L1, L2, and L3 cache are important components for increasing the speed of a CPU.

 One way to improve the performance of a Web server that is often slow is to upgrade to a processor that has a large amount of fast L2 cache, or a combination of L1, L2, and L3 cache.

Address Bus

The **address bus** is an internal communications pathway that specifies the source and target addresses for memory reads and writes. It is instrumental in the transfer of data to and from computer memory. The address bus typically runs at the external clock speed of the CPU. The address, like all data in the computer, is in digital form and is conveyed in the form of a series of bits. The width of the address bus is the number of bits that can be used to address memory. A wider bus means the computer can address more memory, and therefore store more data or larger, more complex programs. For example, a 16-bit wide address bus can address 64 kilobytes (KB) (64,000 bytes) of memory. This bus size is no longer found in PCs sold today. Most PCs today use a 32-bit address bus, which allows them to address roughly four billion (4,000,000,000) memory addresses, or four gigabytes (GB). However, many systems, although they have a 32-bit address bus, cannot actually address that much memory. Newer processors have even wider address buses, some as wide as 64 bits, allowing them to address 16 terabytes of memory.

Data Bus

The **data bus** allows computer components, such as the CPU, display adapter, and main memory, to share information. The number of bits in the data bus indicates how many bits of data can be transferred from memory to the CPU, or vice versa, in one clock tick. A CPU with an external clock speed of 1 GHz will have 1 billion ticks per second to the external bus. If this CPU has a 16-bit data bus, it could theoretically transfer two GB (2,000,000,000 bytes) of data to and from memory every second. (One byte consists of eight bits, so 1 billion x 16 bits ÷ 8 bits per second = 2 GB per second.) A CPU with an external clock speed of 1 GHz and a 32-bit data bus could transfer as much as 4 GB per second (1 billion x 32 bits ÷ 8 bits per byte). That is twice as much data in the same time period, so in theory, the CPU will work twice as fast.

There are a couple of catches here. First, the software must be able to instruct the CPU to use all of the data bus, and the rest of the computer must be fast enough to keep up with the CPU. Most CPUs work internally with the same number of bits as on the data bus. In other words, a CPU with a 32-bit data bus typically can perform operations on 32 bits of data at a time. Almost all CPUs can also be instructed to work with chunks of data narrower than the data bus width, but in this case the CPU is not as efficient since the same number of clock cycles is required to perform an operation, whether or not all bits are used.

Control Bus

The CPU is kept informed of the status of resources and devices connected to the computer, such as the memory and disk drives, by information that is transported on the **control bus**. The most basic information that is transported across the control bus is whether or not a particular resource is active and can be accessed. If a disk drive becomes active, for example, the disk controller provides this information to the CPU over the control bus. Other information that may be transported over the control bus includes whether a particular function is for input or output. Memory read and write status is transported on this bus, as well as **Interrupt Requests (IRQs)**. An interrupt request is a request to the processor for a currently operating process, such as a read from a disk drive, to be interrupted by another process, such as a write into memory.

POPULAR PC PROCESSORS

The following sections give an overview of the CPUs most often found in personal computers. These CPUs are:

- Intel
- Intel Itanium

- AMD

- Motorola

- SPARC

- Alpha

Intel

The most popular CPUs in use in PCs today are designed by Intel, and typically found in what are often called IBM-based PCs, a PC line started by IBM. The first player in this line of processors was the 8088, the CPU found in the original IBM PC. It originally had an internal and external CPU clock speed of roughly 4.7 MHz, and there was no L1 or L2 cache. Cache memory wasn't needed because the memory ran at the same speed as the external and internal CPU clock. The address bus on the CPU was 20 bits wide, a number chosen to enable the computer to address 1,048,576 bytes of memory, or 1 MB. This was 16 times the customary 65,536 bytes (commonly referred to as 64K) of memory common on CPUs in those days, a capacity many engineers thought would be more than a personal computer would ever need. The address bus of this CPU was eight bits wide, but internal operations could be performed either with 8- or 16-bit logic. The 8-bit data bus made it cheap and easy to build computers around the chip.

The 8088 was followed by the 8086, which was the first Intel CPU to have a 16-bit data path. Apart from that, it was identical to the 8088. Later on, clock speeds on these CPUs increased to as much as 20 MHz. Intel has built on this CPU ever since, following it up with other processors that became popular in PC computers. The 80286 was the beginning of the 80x86 line, featuring more advanced chip functionality to provide more commands to the end user, and higher clock speeds of 8, 16, and even 20 MHz. This chip also ran at identical internal and external clock speeds, and had no L1 and L2 cache.

The 80386 introduced a 32-bit address and data bus, and still higher clock speeds of 16, 20, and 40 MHz. This chip was the first in the Intel 80x86 chip family that could perform operations using 32 bits of data at a time. Because the chips were so fast, running at speeds over 16 MHz, they were the first Intel chips in this line to support external, or L2, cache. The internal and external clocks on the chip were still the same, but new instructions were introduced. Like the 8088 and 8086 combination, this chip also came in two data port variations. The 80386 was officially called the 80386DX and had a 32-bit data path. For reasons of economy, there was also an 80386SX, which had a 16-bit external data path and 24-bit address bus width.

The next chips released were the 80486 family, the first line of chips in which Intel used different internal and external clocks. This chip is the first one to have L1 cache on the chip, which runs at the internal CPU speed, as well as features for external L2 cache, which runs at the speed of the external clock. Unique in the 80486 was the inclusion of hardware dedicated to performing mathematical operations. Some 486 models, the initial ones known as DX chips, ran at the same internal and external clock speed. Newer models, identified as DX2 or DX4 chips, ran internally at two or four times the external clock. This is the last series of chips Intel made that had a "little brother" with a reduced data path, referred to as the 80486SX.

After the 80486 chip family, Intel left the 80x86 numbering scheme and started naming chips. The first model with a name was the Pentium. Penta is the Greek word for five, so this is really the 80586 (if Intel had followed previous conventions and hadn't run into copyright problems regarding the "586" name). More instructions were added and L1 cache was made more efficient. Otherwise, not much differed from the 80486. Next came the Pentium Pro, which is optimized for running 32-bit instructions faster than a Pentium chip. Then Intel released something called the **Multimedia Extension (MMX)**. These chips are nearly identical to a regular Pentium, but they have a few new instructions to deal with multimedia—for example graphics and video—and the chip design is optimized for handling large amounts of data. The data bus is 32 bits wide with a 36-bit address bus; the chip runs at external clock speeds of up to 66 MHz, and at internal clock speeds as fast as 233 MHz for desktop computers and 300 MHz for mobile computers.

Following the basic Pentium chip is the Pentium II family. Added features on these chips include an internal clock raised to as high as 550 MHz. External clock speed for these chips is 66 or 100 MHz. Unique in the Pentium II design is the inclusion of L1 cache, running at internal clock speed, as well as L2 cache, running at external or twice external clock speed, built right onto the CPU module. Table 2-1 summarizes the development of Intel CPUs.

The internal clock speed is raised yet again with the Pentium III and Pentium 4 chips. At this writing, the Pentium III processor has internal bus speeds of 1.2 GHz and higher, and usually comes with 512 KB L2 cache. The external bus speed of the Pentium III goes up to 133 MHz. At this writing, the Pentium 4 processor is offered with an internal clock speed of up to 2 GHz. The external system bus speed is an impressive 400 MHz. Another innovation with the Pentium 4 is the presence of two math coprocessing units, called **arithmetic logic units (ALUs)**, for handling math-related calculations. Other Pentium chips have only one ALU. Each Pentium 4 ALU operates at twice the internal clock speed.

The Xeon is another Pentium-based processor made by Intel. Initially, the Xeon processor was offered as a version of the Pentium II and Pentium III processors. Xeon processors are sold with 512 KB of L2 cache that can be expanded to 1 MB. One original advantage of the Xeon processor is that it uses a daughter-board L2 caching technique that is twice as fast as non-Xeon processors. At this writing, the newest version of the Xeon processor has a similar architecture to the Pentium 4, with the addition of "execution-based cache," which is even faster than the original Xeon cache. Newer Xeon chips also have a new instruction set that is meant to improve video, encryption, and authentication performance—all features that are particularly important for busy Web servers.

Table 2-1   Intel CPUs

CPU	Introduced	Data Bus/Address Bus Bits	Int Clock MHz	Ext Clock MHZ	Cache
8088	1978	8/20	4–8	4–8	No
8086	1978	16/20	4–16	4–16	No
80286	1982	16/24	8–40	8–40	No
80386SX	1985	16/24	16–40	16–40	No
80386DX	1985	32/24	16–40	16–40	No
80486SX	1989	16/24	16–80	16–40	Yes
80486DX	1989	32/24	16–120	16–40	Yes
Pentium	1993	32/28	16–233	16–66	Yes
Pentium (for mobile computers)	1993	32/28	16-300	16-66	Yes
Pentium Pro	1995	64/28	33–200	33–50	Yes
Pentium II	1997	64/36	66–550	66–100	Yes
Xeon	1998	64/36	500–2000	400	Yes
Pentium III	1999	64/36	600–1260	100–133	Yes
Pentium 4	2001	64/36	1300–2000	400	Yes

A very important feature of the whole line of Intel CPUs discussed here is backward compatibility, which means that a significant number of features from an older chip can function on a newer chip. Code written to run on an 8088 processor runs on a newer CPU without change. Since the 8088 code is only 16-bit code, it does not use many of the advanced features of the newer CPUs, therefore it runs slower than code written especially for the CPU. But the code does run without being rewritten, one of the major reasons for the success of the Intel line of CPUs.

Intel Itanium

The Intel Itanium processor is a significant departure from previous Intel processors in two respects: it is built on the RISC–based EPIC architecture and it is a 64–bit chip. These differences alone are enough to make this a very fast processor. Beyond these differences, Intel built in other factors that make the chip even faster. The internal clock speed is currently offered in 733 MHz and 800 MHz versions (with higher clock speeds on the way), and the 64-bit system bus has multiprocessor capability of up to 2.1 gigabits per second. Both the L1 and L2 cache are built into the processor chip for faster response. L3 cache can be either 2 MB or 4 MB, operating at full internal clock speed. The Itanium chip features the complete EPIC design allotment of 256 64-bit registers that can operate as rotating registers.

The Intel Itanium processor is intended for very large-scale operations that match powerful mainframes. For this reason, the chip architecture and bus design include the capability to run over 1,000 processors as a group. Of course, currently there are no server operating systems that can run this many processors in one computer, but the Itanium processor design is setting the stage for this future possibility.

Try Hands-on Projects 2-1 and 2-2 to practice monitoring Intel-type processor usage in a Windows-based operating system. Also, try Hands-on Project 2-3 to test the processor.

AMD

Advanced Micro Devices, Inc. (AMD) is a manufacturer of Microsoft Windows-compatible processor chips and non-volatile (flash) memory, which compete with Intel products in the processor market. AMD CPU chips include the AMD Duron and the AMD Athlon. The AMD Duron is available for desktop and notebook computers. The latest chips are in the 750 MHz to 1 GHz range. The AMD Athlon is available for desktops, notebooks, and servers. These chips range from 1 GHz to 1.6 GHz. Older CPU products included the AMD-K6-2, the AMD-K6, the AMD-K5, the Am5x86, and the Enhanced Am486.

Motorola

Motorola is the next most popular CPU maker, and its chips are typically found in Macintosh computers. Its line of CISC CPUs is used in many older Macintosh computers, as well as in many UNIX computers. The popular models include the 68000, 68020, 68030, and 68040. The development of the features in the chips is roughly similar to the development in the Intel line; the 68020 shows many similarities to the 80286, the 68030 is similar to the 80386, and the 86040 is similar to the 80486. Although there are major differences between the Intel and Motorola chip lines, and they are in no way interchangeable, their development was similar.

The 680x0 processors' instruction sets are divided into supervisory instructions, which are intended for use by an operating system, and user instructions, which are intended for use by a program. This, and the memory layout of these CPUs, made them very popular for task switching, multitasking, and multi-user operating systems. A later entry in this line of CPUs is the 68060, but this chip is aimed at the market for embedded devices; Motorola will not market this chip to computer vendors so as not to compete with its new high-end chip, the PowerPC chip.

PowerPC

Although Motorola continues to develop chips in the 68xxx line, modern Macintosh computers do not use this line of chips. A new non-compatible line of chips—chips that use different instruction sets and a different general architecture than the 68xxx line—was developed jointly by IBM, Motorola, and Apple Computer. These are RISC chips known as the PowerPC line. The initial PowerPC chips, known as models 601, 602, 603, and 603e, were similar in design and functionality. As the model number increased, so did the internal clock speeds, L1 cache size, and the efficiency of the chip designs.

The newest chip in the PowerPC line is the G4 (for 4th generation), which is the family of 64-bit RISC-based MPC74xx chips. At this writing, the internal clock speed of the MPC7450 chip is 733 MHz, with an external clock speed of up to 100 MHz. The MPC74xx chips offer a 64-bit data bus, and have both L1 and L2 cache built into the processor. L3 cache is fast and operates via a 64-bit bus between the processor and the separate cache board. The system bus operates at up to 500 MHz, which is five times faster than the previous generation (G3) of the chip. The MPC74xx chips also feature a technology that enables them to use less power than previous chips, and to save additional power by using the doze, nap, and sleep modes—all designed to shut down various parts of the computer while it is idle.

SPARC

It is useful to briefly mention a few other RISC processors, one of which is the SPARC processor designed by Sun Microsystems. SPARC CPUs have gone through many incarnations, and the RISC processor is the most popular on the market today. The UltraSPARC III is the current version of the SPARC processor at this writing. It is a 64-bit chip with both 64-bit address and data buses. The internal clock on this chip is currently available at speeds up to 900 MHz, with designs in the works for chips that operate at 1.5 GHz and beyond. The external clock speed is 150 MHz. L1 cache is similar to other chips at 64 KB. The external L2 cache, however, can be relatively large, at up to 8 MB.

Primarily you'll see various implementations of the UNIX operating system running on these CPUs, performing high-end engineering and networking duties. The most popular operating system using the chip is Sun Microsystem's SunOS UNIX and Solaris (Solaris is the SunOS with a desktop window system). Versions of Linux and BSD UNIX are also available for SPARC architectures.

Alpha

Another CPU of interest is the Alpha CPU, originally designed by Digital Equipment Corporation (DEC), which was purchased by Compaq. Today, the Alpha CPU is found in high-end Compaq servers. This CPU also has a 64-bit data bus and a 64-bit address bus. The internal clock speed can be as high as 1 GHz. The Alpha uses a traditional 64 KB L1 cache and an external L2 cache that can go up to 8 MB. Similar to the SPARC, Alpha chips are widely used in the UNIX environment. And, like the SPARC, Alpha chips are found in computers conducting heavy networking, engineering, and graphics duties. There are now many proprietary devices, such as file servers, **firewall** products, and routers, that run custom operating systems based on an Alpha architecture.

> **Note** Compaq announced that it plans to gradually move away from implementing Alpha chips in its high-end server computers, replacing the Alpha with the Intel Itanium chip.

Of course, there are many other CPUs, and there are many details about these chips that are beyond the focus of this book. The CPUs discussed here are those that are most popular in PCs today.

POPULAR PC OPERATING SYSTEMS

There are many popular operating systems available for today's computers. In the following sections, we present the most popular operating systems for personal computers. We begin by giving you a little history of operating systems, such as MS-DOS, PC DOS, and Windows 3.x. For the Microsoft operating systems, we discuss them generally in their order of development for desktop operating systems and for more powerful operating systems like Windows XP. In the following sections, we also present UNIX and Mac operating systems because they are popular personal computer operating systems.

The Kernel and APIs

The term **kernel** is mentioned throughout this chapter and in Chapter 1. It is a set of core operating system programs that handle several functions, including talking to the CPU and peripheral devices. These programs reside in the system directory. Needed portions of the kernel are loaded into memory or virtual memory, which is space used on a disk to extend memory. An Application Program Interface (API) is like a key that unlocks a little door into the kernel that handles a specific function. For example, when you use Microsoft Outlook or Microsoft Word to send e-mail, they use an API to unlock that part of the kernel.

MS-DOS and PC DOS

Microsoft wrote the original operating system for the IBM PC hardware platform, called MS-DOS or more simply DOS (Disk Operating System). DOS runs on any of the Intel 8088, 80x86, or Pentium-class CPUs implemented in a PC hardware platform. The version of MS-DOS that runs on early IBM computers is called PC DOS because it was customized and marketed by IBM.

DOS is a 16-bit, single-tasking, single-user operating system. Most programs operating under DOS use a simple text-based command-line user interface. Figure 2-2 illustrates a typical DOS screen. Although DOS was widely used in early PCs, its limitations in terms of lack of support for current software applications and graphical user interfaces have all but relegated it to the annals of computer history.

```
C>dir

  Volume in drive C is 123
  Volume Serial Number is 2C1D-19D4
  Directory of C:\

CONFIG    SYS           713   08-06-98   6:27p
COMMAND   COM        93,812   08-24-96  11:11a
AUTOEXEC  BAT         4,320   08-06-98   6:27p
WRPLOG    TXT           489   08-06-98   6:11p
BORLAND         <DIR>         08-06-98   6:11p
PROGRAMS        <DIR>         08-06-98   6:11p
DOCUMENT        <DIR>         08-06-98   6:26p
CICOMNDD  LOG           450   09-12-98  11:08p
          5 file(s)        99,774 bytes
          3 dir(s)     41,831,680 bytes free

C>mkdir test

C>cd test

C>cd
C:\TEST\

C>
```

Figure 2-2   Typical DOS screen

Table 2-2 provides a list of the advantages and disadvantages of DOS.

Table 2-2   DOS Advantages and Disadvantages

Advantage	Disadvantage
Runs on minimal hardware	Doesn't support some newer hardware features, and lacks support for modern 32-bit applications
Small size. Early versions could fit on a single floppy disk.	Includes minimal utilities and user support features
Requires minimal memory. Some applications run faster under DOS.	Early versions can't support large memory of new computers.
Command-line interface gives operator direct control	Command-line interface requires considerable knowledge and training

Windows 3.x

Implementing a GUI interface to compete with the Apple Macintosh, Microsoft released the first version of Windows, which was targeted for 80286 computers, in 1985. This early version of Windows was quite slow and Microsoft Windows was not well accepted until five years later when Windows 3.0 was released. Windows 3.0 was targeted for larger computers, such as the 80386, because only a computer with a faster processor and more memory could make Windows run fast enough to enable user productivity.

When Windows 3.1 came on the scene, with its popular GUI, Microsoft Windows was well on the way to becoming the dominant PC operating system for desktop computers.

Windows 3.0 and 3.1 were a significant step up from MS-DOS, but their memory, software applications, and networking abilities were limited. With Windows 3.11, Microsoft added significant networking capabilities to Windows, such as the options to have workgroups, and set up shared drives. In fact, Windows 3.11 is also referred to as Windows for Workgroups (WFW), and represents Windows' true initiation into networking. WFW is a **peer-to-peer network operating system**, which means each computer on a network can communicate with other computers on the same network. Peer-to-peer communications open the way for sharing resources such as files and directories. For example, the File Manager application in Windows was upgraded in WFW to include icons that distinguish directories shared with others from locally available resources.

One significant limitation of Windows 3.11 is the lack of security options to protect shared files. This is because when Windows 3.11 was first introduced, security was not recognized as the critical issue it is today.

The Windows 3.x (Windows 3.0, 3.1, and 3.11 versions) operating systems run on top of the MS-DOS or PC DOS operating system on the IBM PC system architecture. Although it is possible to run Windows 3.x on the oldest generation of this architecture, it will only run a very limited set of applications because it is running in **real mode** (16-bit mode). The limitations are mainly dictated by the way software can use memory. There are extensions to Windows 3.x that allow it to run 32-bit software (386 enhanced mode), and there are also some upgrades that replace parts of the Windows system itself with 32-bit code, but at the heart of Windows 3.x is a 16-bit operating system, running on top of MS-DOS.

Windows 95

As the PC platform became more powerful and the Pentium architecture more common, Microsoft recognized that it was time to build a more powerful operating system to match the capabilities of Pentium computers. Microsoft decided to create a true 32-bit operating system that would use the functionality of the new 32-bit computer architectures. The task turned out to be extremely complex because, as with all versions of DOS and Windows up to this point, backward compatibility had to be maintained. Windows 95 is the first in the Windows series of operating systems that does not rely on MS-DOS to provide underlying functionality. Although there is a core operating system that lies underneath the graphical shell of Windows 95, and it looks and feels a lot like the old MS-DOS, including the shell and the commands, it is actually a totally new, 32-bit operating system. It eliminates the 640 KB memory limit and the 16-bit code. For this reason, Windows 95 does not run on the oldest 16-bit CPUs (8088 and 8086) of the IBM PC architecture.

2

 Windows 95 will run on 80386 (just barely) and 80486 computers, but it is much faster when running on a Pentium computer. The general minimum system requirements are an 80386DX processor, 4 MB of RAM, 45 MB of hard disk, a VGA monitor, and a mouse or pointing device. To use Internet Explorer, 8MB of RAM and an extra 3 MB or more of disk space are required. Remember that these are minimum requirements, and Windows 95 runs much better if the recommended requirements are used. These recommended requirements are discussed in Chapter 4.

The new functionality of Windows 95 requires a lot more of the hardware on which it runs, particularly in terms of CPU speed and memory. As compared to Windows 3.x, this version of Windows requires about twice the memory, twice the hard disk space, and twice the processor speed to provide similar performance. Because it requires more computer resources, Windows 95 also enables more advanced functions than previous versions of Windows. These include:

- A new GUI
- Plug and Play
- ActiveX and the Component Object Model (COM) capability
- The Registry
- Multitasking
- Enhanced network capabilities

User Interface

Windows 95 introduces the GUI, now called the desktop, which has become the basic foundation for the GUI used in all later versions of Windows, as shown in Figure 2-3. The Windows 95 GUI introduces the Start button that provides direct access to system utilities and application programs. Another GUI feature is the taskbar at the bottom of the screen, which contains icons that represent currently running programs and other information about the operation of the system.

With the new GUI, the user is provided a workspace, like a desktop workspace, in which to run programs, manipulate files, access a network or the Internet, and generally accomplish work or play—all in one seamless environment. For backward compatibility, it is still possible to run old MS-DOS and Windows 3.x programs.

In Windows 95, programs are started in several ways, such as clicking the Start button and pointing to Programs, using the Run option from the Start button, or double-clicking an icon on the desktop. The directories used in MS-DOS and Windows 3.x are now called folders in Windows 95. Folders and files are now managed by using Windows Explorer —a feature that can also be used to run programs, access control panels, and perform just about anything else on the Windows 95 computer or network to which it is connected.

Figure 2-3   Windows 95 desktop

Plug and Play

Plug and Play is possibly the most exciting hardware feature introduced in Windows 95 and continued in later versions of Windows (except Windows NT). **Plug and Play (PnP)** enables the operating system to automatically detect newly installed hardware. It is an extension of the system architecture that lets the operating system and the hardware communicate. When PnP detects new hardware, it determines vital information, such as what device drivers to use for that hardware, and what computer resources (IRQ and memory) to link with the hardware. Reciprocally, the hardware has some built-in functions that let the operating system dictate how to configure the hardware. PnP is a great time saver for computer users because it reduces many of the tedious tasks of configuring hardware and software, previously done manually.

Manually configuring hardware in MS-DOS and Windows 3.x often required hours of work and frustrating trial-and-error experimentation.

Not all hardware was PnP compatible when Windows 95 was introduced, but most hardware is PnP compatible today. If you upgrade an older computer with Windows 95, consider discarding any older non-PnP hardware, such as a scanner card or disk controller. The time you spend trying to make the hardware work on a new system is likely to cost more than purchasing a new card or equipment.

ActiveX and the Component Object Model (COM)

Much of the easy manipulation of the user interface in Windows 95 is made possible by a new technology called ActiveX. **ActiveX**, along with its parent, the **Component**

2

Object Model (COM), is a standardized way for objects, such as programs, files, computers, printers, control panels, windows, and icons, to communicate with each other. It is a simple but revolutionary concept. Objects (such as folders, icons, menus, and almost any other object you see on the desktop) consist of a series of properties. To show you a folder full of files, the operating system makes a folder, then places the file objects in the folder. The COM and ActiveX technologies enable an object to "sense" when it is interacting with other objects, such as the mouse pointer, the desktop, the trash can, or the Start menu. The COM and ActiveX technologies allow you to simply drag files from one place to another. The icons you drag, through the use of COM, make it possible for the object onto which they are dragged to know what to do with them. By building this concept into the operating system, Microsoft has provided a new level of user interface consistency and program interoperability in Windows 95. You can click from a window that manages your local files, into a window that manages the files on the network, into the printer manager, or even onto the Internet, without ever being aware that you are starting and stopping programs and accessing numerous resources. If you have the Active Desktop installed on your machine, the new ActiveX technology, which is part of the COM model, is available to you as well. You will see some new features, such as the ability to drag objects in and out of the Start menu, and more advanced features, such as folder listings. With ActiveX objects, you can have customized looks for every file folder, for example.

ActiveX and COM also allow shortcuts (see the arrow in Figure 2-4), small ActiveX objects, on the desktop. In addition, easy access to programs and the operating system is provided through the Start menu, which on the Active Desktop is nothing more than another ActiveX object. The use of COM and ActiveX made Windows 95 easier to use than its predecessors, and once again broadened the functionality provided by the operating system.

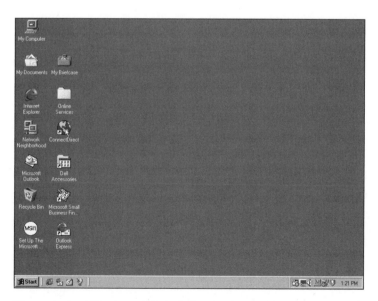

Figure 2-4   Windows 95 desktop shortcuts, Start button, and taskbar

The Registry

The Windows 95 design also introduced a new concept for changing the way information is stored and managed, and how software and hardware are configured. Up to this point, such information was kept in files in various locations on the hard disk. The new design is called the **Registry**, a database that stores information about hardware and software configuration, and all sorts of other data needed to make the operating system and applications run. Although the Registry was present in a primitive form in Windows 3.1, it was not used much. In Windows 95, the Registry is the only correct way to store configuration information, as well as much of the general information that is shared by multiple parts of the operating system or application programs to make COM and ActiveX work. The Windows 95 Registry is similar to the one used in Windows NT 3.51 and Windows NT 4.0. In later versions of Windows, the Registry is improved for even more functionality so that it is easier to install and remove programs, for example.

The Registry is a hierarchical database that provides the following information:

- Operating system configuration
- Service and device driver information and configuration
- Static tuning parameters
- Software and application parameters
- Hardware configuration
- Performance information
- Desktop configuration

Whenever any software needs to read from or write to the Registry, it uses operating system functions. The Registry central database repository may actually extend beyond the computer on which Windows 95 is running. It is possible to share Registry data over a network, a function that can be extremely useful in situations with many users and many computers.

 When you back up Windows 95 or later, make sure that you also back up the Registry because sometimes information in the Registry is corrupted from power failures, or because an application software installation may go bad and change important information in the Registry. With a backup, it is easy to restore the operating system without reinstalling it.

Multitasking

Multitasking in Windows 95 is still performed on a cooperative basis for 16-bit applications, but now uses preemptive multitasking for 32-bit applications. By the time Windows 95 was developed, Microsoft had greatly improved the multitasking mechanisms. Apart from communications functions, which still at times can bring multitasking to a halt in Windows 95, 16-bit cooperative multitasking yields mostly acceptable results. Windows 95 has a **task supervisor** that detects tasks that appear stuck, and that presents the option to close hung tasks without having to restarting the operating system. The methods used for cooperative multitasking in Windows 95 are also more advanced than the methods used in earlier versions of Windows, largely because of the COM technology. In Windows 95 preemptive multitasking, the operating system has complete control of the multitasking environment. This makes it very difficult for a program to gain absolute control of the CPU.

Network Capabilities and Communications

The networking functionality in Windows 95 is substantially extended from earlier versions of Windows, and completely rewritten. Unlike earlier versions of Windows, in Windows 95, the network drivers are part of the Windows operating system, instead of built into DOS. In all but the early versions of Windows 95, all the networking code is written as a 32-bit application. This results in a significant boost in network performance. The networking functions, as in Windows for Workgroups 3.11, consist of two parts, the client and the server. Windows 95 significantly increases the capabilities of both. Unlike Windows 3.11, Windows 95 can communicate over a network with many other operating systems, such as Novell NetWare, a popular server operating system.

Another important feature of Windows 95 is its integration with the Internet, the global network that can connect standalone workstations and networks for the exchange of information, advertising, e-mail, and many other purposes. When Windows 95 was originally released, Microsoft did not support Internet connectivity, but by 1997, Microsoft decided to embrace the Internet and integrate it into all of its operating systems. Initially, Internet connectivity was an add-on option in the form of Internet Explorer for Windows 95. Later, Internet connectivity was incorporated as an integral part of the operating system when Windows 98 was released. This resulted in extensive Internet support in Windows 95, in the form of **Web browsers**, **Web server** software, and the ability to share computer resources over the Internet.

 The United States Justice Department and Microsoft have been involved in litigation over several points, including the integration of the Internet into the OS.

In terms of communications, Windows 95 is a giant leap forward. In Windows 3.1, there was support for communications over serial ports, but tasks such as dialing the phone or making a connection were performed by the application software. In Windows 95, the operating system takes an active role. It manages the modem and provides relatively sophisticated communications features (for the mid nineties) to the user. With the popularity of the Internet, and the need to obtain remote access to corporate networks over telephone lines, Microsoft decided to include network drivers that support the use of modems to obtain remote access to a network and the Internet. **Dial-Up Networking (DUN)** can be used not only to make connections to remote networks or computers, but also to set up a Windows 95 computer as a **DUN server**, with the addition of the Plus!™ add-on set of utilities. A computer with a modem can be set up to answer a telephone line whenever it rings, authenticate the caller, and then give him access to all the shared resources available to the computer. Many people use DUN to gain access to their desktop computers in the office from their computers at home, or from laptops while they are on the road.

Another new communications feature of Windows 95 is built-in fax support. Out of the box, Windows 95 can send and receive fax transmissions. The only thing required is a modem capable of sending and receiving fax traffic. This modem does not even have to be connected to the computer that wants to send or receive a fax. Through Windows 95 networking, it is relatively easy to use any such modem connected to any computer in a Windows 95 workgroup.

Windows 98

Windows 98 is similar to Windows 95 in many ways. It runs on similar computers, and it provides roughly the same capabilities. Manly of the problems experienced with Windows 95 are solved in Windows 98, particularly Registry problems. If the Registry in Windows 95 got corrupted for any reason, the operating system was, in most cases, not able to restore it. Windows 98 includes Registry checks and automatic Registry repair when the computer is booted. The backup mechanisms are also greatly enhanced, and new networking capabilities were added, such as for high-speed networks. The look of the Windows 98 user interface is changed, especially if you choose the Web interface settings intrinsic to Windows 98. You can see some of the differences between Windows 95 and Windows 98 by comparing Figure 2-3 (shown earlier) with Figure 2-5.

Figure 2-5   Windows 98 desktop

A sampling of the changes from Windows 95 to Windows 98 includes:

- Expanded PnP support

- Advanced power management features

- Support for new hardware standards such as Universal Serial Bus (USB)

- Improved cooperative multitasking for 16-bit applications

- Greater integration of Internet and networking features

- Extended multimedia support

- Expanded network support for high-speed networking

- Ability to perform upgrades over the Internet

Windows 98 is written as a 32-bit application, much like Windows 95. PnP support is greatly expanded, and advanced **power management** features are now included in the operating system. These features make it possible to power down parts of the hardware that are not being used to conserve energy. This is especially important for users of battery-operated laptop computers. Windows 98 is also updated to support many new hardware standards, such as **Universal Serial Bus (USB)**, a relatively high-speed input/output port, and updated standards for multimedia, data storage, and networking.

 USB is a bus standard that enables you to attach all types of devices—keyboards, cameras, pointing devices, telephones, and tape drives, for example—to one bus port on a computer. Up to 127 devices can be attached to one port, and it is not necessary to power off the computer when you attach a device. USB was developed to replace the traditional serial and parallel bus technologies on computers.

Windows 98 uses improved cooperative multitasking for 16-bit applications and preemptive multitasking for 32-bit applications. The ActiveX technology was deployed as a standard feature in Windows 98, together with Internet integration and network functionality. In this version of Windows, the interface is now Internet-enabled. It is possible to put shortcuts to Internet objects right on the desktop through the use of ActiveX technology, and these objects can even be made to update automatically. Windows 98 also includes an Internet browser, as well as programs to provide Internet e-mail and other forms of multimedia Internet communication.

Windows 98 can be updated over the Internet. The system can automatically check whether updates are available online, and if they are, it can download and install them, either with or without user intervention. The networking functions were updated as well. Setting up dial-up connections and configuring the computer to use the Internet are simpler, plus there is support for high-speed networking, such as Asynchronous Transfer Mode (ATM). Windows 98 also includes new support for multimedia applications, ranging all the way from video conferencing to high-end video production.

Windows 98 is still found on many home PCs, portable computers, and general-purpose office desktop computers. Some small companies still use Windows 98 to run their entire operations, including all of the networking functions needed via a peer-to-peer workgroup.

 The minimum system requirements for Windows 98 are a bit higher than for Windows 95: 80486DX computer with a 66 MHz or faster processor, 16 MB of memory, 120 MB or higher of disk space, a VGA monitor, and a mouse or pointing device. It is important to remember that these are minimum requirements and Windows 98 runs much better if the recommended requirements are used, as discussed in Chapter 4.

Windows Millennium Edition

Windows Millennium Edition (Me) is the last in the 95/98 track of Windows operating systems that uses cooperative multitasking for 16-bit applications, preemptive multitasking for 32-bit applications, and retains substantial capability to run older 16-bit MS-DOS and Windows software. It is also the last in the line of Windows operating systems that gives software applications direct access to hardware, without going through the operating system kernel.

Windows Me was developed for home computer users, not office or professional users, because it implements better capabilities than Windows 95 or 98 for applications that appeal to home users. These applications include playing music, storing family photos, playing games, and accessing the Internet. Windows Me also makes it easier to connect all kinds of new devices to a computer, such as Internet cameras, digital cameras, scanners, read/write CD-ROM drives, TV converters, and specialized printers for color photo reproduction.

 Many users, including office and professional users, choose to use Windows 98 or Windows Me because they have older 16-bit MS-DOS and Windows applications for which there is no 32-bit equivalent. The limitation in using Windows Me on a corporate network is that there can be problems in getting it to communicate with a Windows NT or Windows 2000 domain—so such computers may have to be used as standalone computers that cannot fully communicate with others.

Windows Me enhances support for infrared devices, such as **Infrared Data Association (IrDA)** support, and implements the enhanced PnP standard, called **Universal Plug and Play (UPnP)**. UPnP provides better discovery of new devices, such as TVs and cameras, that can be connected to a computer. When a device is discovered through UPnP, a set of properties for that device is provided to the operating system. Also, with UPnP, modern devices can be shown through the My Network Places icon on the Windows Me desktop, so that the devices can be managed using a Web page type of interface.

Windows Me also comes with better networking capabilities for home use. Internet connections are easier to set up because the dial-up networking capabilities are improved over Windows 95 and 98. Included in these capabilities is the Connection Manager, which is used to manage and create network and dial-up connections, similar to the Connection Manager used in Windows 2000 (discussed later in this chapter).

The minimum system requirements for Windows Me are a Pentium 150 or faster processor, 32 MB of RAM, 480-645 MB of disk space, a mouse or pointing device, and a VGA monitor or better. Typically, Windows Me users also have a sound card, speakers, and a modem for connecting to the Internet. It is important to remember that these are minimum requirements and Windows Me runs much better if the recommended requirements (see Chapter 4) are used.

Windows NT

While Microsoft was developing the Windows line of operating systems to run on the lower end of IBM PC hardware, it was also developing a high-end operating system referred to as Windows New Technology, or Windows NT. Windows NT differs in many ways from other versions of Windows, the most significant being the system architecture for which it was developed. Over the course of its development, Windows NT has supported the IBM PC architecture, the DEC Alpha architecture, and for a while, the PowerPC architecture as each of these hardware platforms gained its time in the industry spotlight. As the Alpha and PowerPC moved out of the limelight, NT focus concentrated on Intel platforms. The idea was to make an operating system that could be used on some very powerful computers, with a choice of RISC or CISC processor architecture. The support for various system architectures has shifted over the years, but support for the high-end IBM PC architecture and the DEC Alpha architecture has been a constant for Windows NT.

Development of Windows NT began as early as 1988. Windows NT 3.1 was released in 1993 and version 3.5 was released in 1994. Windows NT was initially an extension to IBM's high-end operating system, OS/2, and was intended to support the emerging client/server networking environment. As client/server applications gained popularity, Windows NT development and the successive operating systems in the NT line, Windows 2000, Windows XP, and Windows .NET Server have experienced wide reception.

Windows NT, as is true of most operating systems, has gone through many iterations. You will find that there are very few installations of Windows NT prior to version 3.51 still in use because these versions were not stable or reliable. Windows NT 4.0 was successful, and today most installations have evolved or are evolving to Windows 2000, Windows XP, or Windows .NET. Windows NT 3.51 looks and feels much like Windows for Workgroups 3.11; the graphical interface is nearly identical, including the Program Manager, File Manager, and Control Panel.

Windows NT 4.0 looks and feels a lot like Windows 95 or Windows 98. Many of the GUI elements are the same, such as the desktop, Windows Explorer, and the taskbar with the Start menu, as shown in Figure 2-6. One very significant difference between Windows 95/98 and Windows NT is that the operating system kernel in Windows NT runs in privileged mode, which protects it from problems created by a malfunctioning program or process. The privileged mode gives the operating system an extra level of security from intruders, and prevents system crashes due to out-of-control applications. Privileged mode is a protected area in Windows NT from which the operating system kernel or program code runs. Direct access to the computer's memory or hardware is allowed from this mode. Application program threads that need to access memory and hardware issue a request to an operating system service, rather than to a direct memory or hardware instruction.

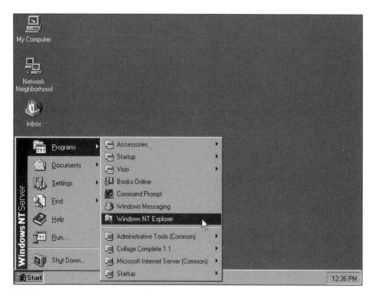

Figure 2-6   Windows NT desktop

Preemptive Multitasking

A significant improvement in Windows NT is the way it handles multitasking. Windows NT uses preemptive multitasking rather than cooperative multitasking. The advantage of preemptive multitasking is that the operating system is tightly in control of what the system will do at what time, which results in a much more predictable performance. Because Windows NT was built as a 32-bit operating system from the ground up, and the requirement to run all legacy 16-bit applications was set aside, Windows NT can significantly outperform Windows 95 and 98 running 32-bit applications. Besides preemptive multitasking, Windows NT 4.0 employs **multithreading**, which is the ability to run two or more program code blocks, known as threads, at the same time.

The performance comes at a price. Windows NT requires a faster CPU and more memory and disk space to run successfully, but it makes much better use of the resources available. Windows NT 4.0 can also function well in a hardware architecture that includes more than one CPU. Because the operating system is in tight control of how the resources in the computer are allocated to various processes, Windows NT Workstation can use up to two CPUs and Windows NT Server can use up to four. The system architecture that is used to perform this form of multiprocessing under Windows NT 4.0 consists of a set of CPUs that has access to the main memory of the computer. All the CPUs can carry out actions at the same time. This is known as **symmetric multiprocessing (SMP)**. Windows NT 3.51 and Windows NT 4.0 support SMP hardware architecture.

The system requirements for Windows NT are based on whether it is to be installed on a CISC or RISC computer. On a CISC computer, the requirements are: 80486 processor with a 33 MHz or higher clock speed, 16 MB RAM, 125 MB of disk space, a VGA monitor, and a mouse or pointing device. On a RISC processor, the requirements are: MIPS R4x00 or higher processor, Alpha AXP processor or a PowerPC processor, 16 MB of RAM, 160 MB of disk space, a VGA monitor, CD-ROM drive, and a mouse or other pointing device. Remember that these are minimum requirements and Windows NT runs much better if the recommended requirements (see Chapter 4) are used.

NT Server and NT Workstation

Windows NT is offered in two versions: Windows NT Workstation and Windows NT Server. Windows NT Workstation is the operating system for a person who needs a high-end, stable, and secure graphical operating system. Windows NT Server is designed as a multi-user, server operating system for access over a network. The core of the operating system, which oversees such things as multitasking and management of memory and shared resources, is the kernel.

In Windows NT Workstation, the kernel is optimized for maximum performance when used to run interactive applications, such as screen updates and fast retrieval and storage of data in memory and on disk. In the NT Server edition, the kernel is optimized to provide maximum network and disk performance. Everything the server kernel does is aimed at serving clients' requests rapidly. This is done at the expense of speed in the user interface and other interactive functions. The kernel of the Windows NT Server version provides a few extra functions that are not available in the NT Workstation kernel. All features of the NT Workstation kernel are included in the NT Server kernel. As a result, you can run any software that runs on Windows NT Workstation on Windows NT Server, but not all software that runs on NT Server can run on NT Workstation.

One important difference between Windows NT Server and Windows NT Workstation is the number of users who can simultaneously connect to these multi-user systems. With enough processor and system power, up to 15,000 users (theoretically) can connect to Windows NT Server at the same time. Only up to 10 simultaneous users can feasibly connect to Windows NT Workstation.

The Registry, mentioned earlier in the Windows 95 and Windows 98 sections, plays an equally important role in Windows NT. It is used as the central repository for configuration, hardware, software, and user information.

Networking Support

The networking features in Windows NT are more powerful than in Windows 95 or 98 because Windows NT is designed as a multi-user system. Windows NT supports network connectivity protocols that are compatible with IBM mainframes, UNIX computers, Macintosh computers, all Windows-based computers, Novell NetWare servers, and others. It also supports high-speed networking connectivity and remote access over telephone lines or the Internet.

Security

Security is a significant feature of Windows NT. The operating system requires the user to log on and be authenticated by submitting a username and password to gain access to the computer. This authentication process is stronger than that of Windows 3.x, 95, or 98. In fact, Windows NT 4.0 Server has a C2 top-secret security rating from the United States government. The C2 rating means that the Windows NT Server network operating system provides security at many levels, as follows:

- File and folder protection
- User accounts and passwords
- File, folder, and account auditing
- File server access protection on a network
- File server management controls

If an operating system running Windows 95 or 98, for example, is part of a Windows NT network that uses the domain system, these computers are able to use a similar kind of security to protect their resources. The **domain** is an integral part of the Windows NT security model. In every domain there is one primary domain controller (PDC). The PDC computer is responsible for keeping all usernames and passwords for all users who may want to contact the domain. Any other server that is part of the domain can request password and permission information from this PDC. This is convenient when there are many servers and users that must be tracked. In addition to user and password information, the PDC can also contain system policies, which provide general information on what certain users are and are not allowed to do on certain computers on the network, down to what function and features of the user interface should be enabled. The array of network services a computer running Windows NT can provide, using optional software, extends to central database management and Internet services.

Another networking feature of Windows NT is the **Remote Access Service (RAS)**. Although computers running Windows 95 and 98 can be used as dial-up hosts (computers that can be accessed via dial-up phone lines), security is limited because the client has access to any resources to which that computer has access. Through Windows NT RAS, the user information in a PDC can be used to grant or deny various levels of network access. This is a very powerful tool for allowing limited remote access to the resources available on the network. Remote access is a feature that enables workers to telecommute to work so that they can work from home during flexible hours.

Windows 2000

Built on the Windows NT technology, Microsoft Windows 2000 is a more robust operating system than Windows 95, 98, or NT. Originally, Windows 2000 was to be called Windows NT 5.0, but because the operating system represented a significant rewrite of the Windows NT kernel, and it was released in the year 2000, Microsoft chose to name it Windows 2000. One advantage of rewriting the kernel is that Windows 2000 runs about 30% faster than Windows NT. Like Windows 95, 98, and NT, you can use desktop features such as My Computer, and you can run programs from the Start button. Figure 2-7 illustrates the Windows 2000 desktop. Also, similar to its Windows NT predecessor, Windows 2000 uses preemptive multitasking, multithreading, and the kernel runs in the privileged mode.

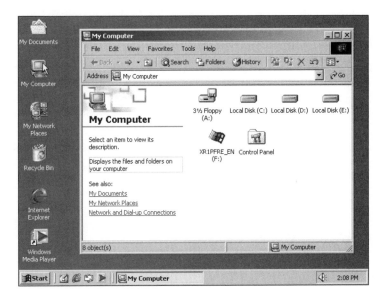

Figure 2-7   Windows 2000 desktop

Windows 2000 has more advanced networking support than Windows NT because it supports new networking technologies, such as **Virtual Private Networks (VPNs)**. A VPN is a private network that is like a tunnel through a larger network—such as the Internet, an enterprise network, or both—that is restricted only to designated member clients.

People who have experience troubleshooting problems with mismatched drivers, or who have overwritten portions of the operating system in previous versions of Windows, will like the built-in protection of the core operating system files and driver-signing features of Windows 2000. Windows 2000 keeps a copy of operating system files in a safe place, so if a critical file is overwritten or deleted, the operating system automatically replaces it. Driver signing means that you can set up all drivers so that they cannot be inadvertently overwritten by earlier driver versions, and only certified versions of drivers can be installed.

New Features Introduced in Windows 2000

Windows 2000 incorporates a wide range of new features, including:

- *Active Directory* – Active Directory is a database that is used to store information about resources such as user accounts, computers, and printers; and it groups resources at different levels (hierarchies) for local and universal management. These groupings are called containers because they are like storage bins that can hold network resources and other bins at lower levels. The Active Directory also provides a centralized means to quickly find a specific resource through indexing. Active Directory is managed by a Windows 2000 server, but its resources are used by both Windows 2000 Server and Professional.

- *Distributed network architecture (DNA)* – Windows 2000 offers new ways to distribute network and management resources to match the needs of all types of networks. In Windows 2000 Server, multiple servers can be designated as domain controllers, each containing a copy of Active Directory and able to verify a user who wants to log on to the network. This is an important change from Windows NT Server 4.0, in which one server, the primary domain controller (PDC), maintains the master copy of account and security information; and one or more servers, called backup domain controllers (BDC), keep copies of this information as a backup.

- *Kerberos security* – **Kerberos** is a security system that enables two parties on an open network to communicate without interception by an intruder. Kerberos works through a special communications protocol that enables a client to initiate contact with a server and request secure communication. The server responds by providing an encryption key that is unique to that communication session, and it does so by using a protected communication called a ticket. Kerberos is supported by Windows 2000 Server and Professional versions.

- *IntelliMirror* – IntelliMirror is a concept built into the combined use of Windows 2000 Server and Windows 2000 Professional. It is intended to enable Windows 2000 Professional clients to access the same desktop settings, applications, and data from wherever they access the network, or even if they are not on the network. IntelliMirror also uses information in Active Directory to ensure that consistent security and group policies apply to the client, and that the client's software is upgraded or removed on the basis of a central management scheme.

- *Power Management* – Power in Windows 2000 is handled through OnNow, which is similar to power management in Windows 98, enabling portions of a system, such as hard disks and the monitor, to "sleep" when they are not in use for a specific period of time.

- *International Language Compatibility* – Windows 2000 supports more languages and language capabilities than previous versions of Windows, including Hindi, Chinese, and multiple versions of English. This is an important feature because servers are used all over the world.

Windows 2000 Server and Windows 2000 Professional

Microsoft offers versions of Windows 2000 designed for server and workstation implementations. The basic server version is called Windows 2000 Server, and Windows 2000 Professional is designed for workstations. When it introduced Windows 2000, Microsoft's overall goal was to combine Windows 2000 Server and Windows 2000 Professional on a server-based network to achieve a lower **total cost of ownership (TCO)**. The TCO is the total cost of owning a network, including hardware, software, training, maintenance, and user support costs. Windows 2000 Professional is intended as a reliable, easy-to-configure, workstation operating system to be used in a business or professional environment. Recognizing that professionals are highly mobile, Windows 2000 Professional is designed to work equally well on a desktop computer or a laptop. Windows 2000 Server is intended to play a key management role on the network by administering **Active Directory**—a database of computers, users, groups, shared printers, folders, and other network resources—and a multitude of network services. Active Directory is also used to manage domains in Windows 2000. By combining Windows 2000 Professional workstations and Windows 2000 Server on the same network, along with Active Directory, it is possible to centralize software updates and workstation configuration via a server.

Windows 2000 Server supports up to four processors, while Windows 2000 Professional supports up to two. Windows 2000 Server also offers more services and user connectivity options that are appropriate for a server instead of a workstation. These services include the following:

- The capability to handle virtually unlimited numbers of users simultaneously (depending on the hardware platform; Windows 2000 Professional is designed optimally for only 10 simultaneous users)

- Active Directory management

- Network management

- Web-based management services

- Network-wide security management

- Network storage management

- Remote network access, network-wide communications services, and high-speed network connectivity

- Application services management

- Network printer management through Active Directory

 The minimum system hardware requirements for Windows 2000 Professional are a Pentium 133 MHz or faster processor, 32 MB of RAM (64 recommended), 650 MB of disk space (1 GB recommended), a VGA monitor, and a mouse or other pointing device. For Windows 2000 Server, the requirements are a Pentium 133 MHz processor, 128 MB of RAM (256 recommended), 1 GB of disk space (2 GB recommended), a VGA monitor, and a mouse or other pointing device. Unlike Windows NT, Windows 2000 has not been adapted to run on an Alpha or PowerPC processor. It is important to remember that these are minimum requirements and Windows 2000 runs much better if the recommended requirements (see Chapter 4) are used.

Windows 2000 Server, Advanced Server, and Datacenter Server

Windows 2000 Server is divided into three different products to match the network application: Windows 2000 Server, Windows 2000 Advanced Server, and Windows 2000 Datacenter Server. Windows 2000 Server provides a comprehensive set of server and Web services for up to four processor systems, and supports up to 4 GB of RAM. Windows 2000 Advanced Server is intended for high-end enterprise networks that require up to eight processor servers, clustered servers, or both. **Clustering** is a technique in which two or more servers are linked to equally share the server processor load, server storage, and other server resources (see Figure 2-8). Windows 2000 Advanced Server also has the ability to handle up to 8 GB of RAM. Windows 2000 Datacenter is targeted for large database and data manipulation services. The Datacenter version supports 64 GB of RAM, clustering, and individual servers with up to 32 processors.

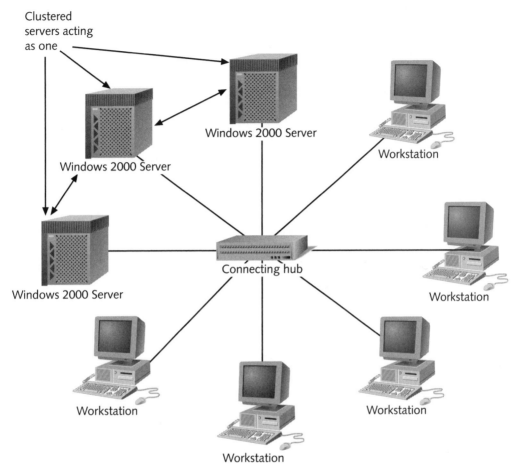

Figure 2-8   Server clustering

Windows XP and .NET Server

Windows 2000 has evolved into two products, both containing the core elements of the Windows 2000 kernel: Windows XP and Windows .NET Server. Windows XP is the desktop version of the new operating system, while Windows .NET Server is the server version. Both of these operating systems are a relatively minor upgrade of Windows 2000, but offer a new desktop GUI, as shown in Figure 2-9. Besides having a new GUI, the Windows XP and .NET Server desktop stresses removing the clutter of icons by incorporating more functions into the Start menu. Try Hands-on Project 2-4 to compare the Windows XP desktop to that of Windows 95/98 to see how much the desktop has evolved.

Figure 2-9   Windows XP desktop

Even though there is a new interface, users who are familiar with Windows 2000, and prefer its interface, can simulate it in Windows XP and Windows .NET Server by selecting the option to use the classic interface.

Besides the new GUI, Windows XP and Windows .NET Server offer more capabilities than Windows 2000 for keeping photo albums, playing music, running video and audio files, playing games, and using other multimedia applications. Windows XP and Windows .NET Server also offer better Internet security through a built-in firewall and the ability to remotely control the computer over an Internet connection via a tool called Remote Desktop. Remote Desktop is designed to be secure so that the computer being controlled must first grant access. Another new feature of both operating systems is that you must activate them after installation by contacting Microsoft for an activation code. The activation code is linked to a particular computer on which the operating system resides. If the operating system is moved to another computer, it is necessary to contact Microsoft to obtain a new activation code for that computer. The activation code is another mechanism, besides the key code, that is entered during installation to help ensure that software is not pirated.

Windows XP

Windows XP, which stands for "Windows Experience," comes in two versions: Windows XP Professional and Windows XP Home Edition. Windows XP Professional is the upgrade to Windows 2000 Professional, and is intended for office and professional use. This version of Windows XP has the ability to create accounts for different users who might use the operating system. Also, Windows XP Professional, like Windows 2000 Professional, can be used as a small server for up to 10 users. Windows XP Home Edition is meant as the next upgrade step from Windows Me, and is a scaled-down version of Windows Professional. For example, user accounts cannot be created in Windows XP Home Edition, nor is it designed to support 10 simultaneous users. Another difference is that Windows XP Professional can run on computers using up to two processors and on 64-bit Itanium computers, whereas Windows XP Home Edition only runs on 32-bit single-processor computers.

One change that is exclusive to both versions of Windows XP is a new "experiential" look and feel for the Control Panel. The Control Panel is used to customize all types of settings in Windows, such as display settings, mouse settings, system settings, power management, and many others. In previous versions of Windows, the Control Panel consists of icons or applets (see Figure 2-10). In Windows XP, the Control Panel is designed to reflect the user's experience of a particular setting, such as the "appearance and themes" of the desktop, which includes settings such as font, background, screensaver, and so on (see Figure 2-11). A theme for the desktop includes the presentation of the background, title bars, and windows to match a particular theme. Windows XP is one theme, which stresses the new Windows XP GUI look with a green Start button and light blue backgrounds. Windows Classic is another theme that uses the Windows 2000 GUI look. The new experiential categories that can be selected are:

- Appearance and Themes
- Network and Internet Connections
- Add or Remove Programs
- Sounds, Speech, and Audio Devices
- Performance and Maintenance
- Printers and Other Hardware
- User Accounts (in Windows XP Professional)
- Date, Time, Language, and Regional Options
- Accessibility Options

Figure 2-10   Windows 2000 Control Panel

Figure 2-11   Windows XP Professional Control Panel

A much improved feature of Windows XP is the help and support documentation. This documentation includes articles to help you become familiar with the new Windows XP desktop, and there are many "Troubleshooter" articles that can help users solve problems. There are options to help you reach others for assistance, and there is a "Do you know?"

2

section that contains new articles automatically updated daily via the Internet, which provides information about new releases and service packs. Try Hands-on Project 2-5 to practice using the help and support documentation.

Programs written for Windows 95 and earlier operating systems may not run in Windows XP without using the new Program Compatibility Wizard. The Program Compatibility Wizard is used by first selecting the program that you want to run, and then selecting the operating system, such as Windows 95, that the program is designed to run under. The operating system options that are available in the Program Compatibility Wizard are shown in Figure 2-12. Hands-on Project 2-6 enables you to practice using the Program Compatibility Wizard.

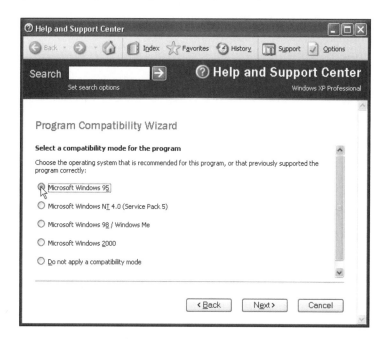

Figure 2-12   Windows XP Program Compatibility Wizard

At this writing, the minimum system requirements for Windows XP Professional and Windows Home Edition are the same: 233 MHz processor (300 MHz recommended), 64 MB RAM (128 MB recommended), a Super VGA display, 1.5 GB of disk space, CD-ROM or DVD drive, and a mouse or pointing device. Remember that these are minimum requirements and Windows XP runs much better if the recommended requirements are used, as discussed in Chapter 4.

Windows .NET Server

Windows .NET Server comes in four versions at this writing, which are similar to the versions that are available for Windows 2000 Server: Standard Server (formerly Server),

Enterprise Server (formerly Advanced Server), Datacenter Server, and Web Server (a new server version). A minor upgrade from Windows 2000, Windows .NET Server contains new features that include:

- The same new GUI interface used with Windows XP
- Improvements for faster network logon authentication through Active Directory
- Several hundred new group policies that can be set to manage user workstations via Active Directory
- New tools for managing server resources
- Ability to run on 64-bit Itanium computers
- Remote server management through the Remote Desktop tool
- Enhanced ability for users to run programs on the server, through Microsoft Terminal Services (Terminal Services were introduced as a service pack enhancement to Windows NT and perfected in Windows 2000.)
- Runtime code for the new Windows .NET development environment to run applications through the Internet on all types of devices

At this writing, Windows .NET Server is still under development and the system requirements are not available.

UNIX System V Release 4

The UNIX operating system comes in many different formats. Of all the operating systems covered in this book, it is the oldest, most diverse, and most complicated. The reason for this is that one manufacturer does not have the exclusive license for UNIX. After UNIX was developed at AT&T, the company never formally licensed the kernel to prevent others from using it and implementing their own specialized utilities. AT&T used the operating system within the company and made the source code available to people outside the company. The end result is that there are many UNIX versions with many diverse utilities.

All versions of UNIX that ship today adhere to one of the two main design standards, the **Berkeley Software Distribution (BSD)** standard or the System V Release 4 (SVR4) standard. Examples of BSD-style UNIX include the freely available NetBSD and FreeBSD operating systems, as well as the commercially available BSDi UNIX. SVR4 versions include the freely available Linux, and commercial versions such as Sun Microsystems Solaris and SCO UNIX. All UNIX systems include security features. Table 2-3 lists several versions of UNIX along with the manufacturer and origin.

Table 2-3   UNIX Versions

Version	Manufacturer	Origin
AIX	IBM	A combination of SVR4 and BSD
Digital Equipment UNIX (previously called Ultrix)	Compaq/Digital	BSD
HP UNIX (HP/UX)	Hewlett Packard	SVR4
Irix	Silicon Graphics	SVR4
Linux	There are several sources, but Red Hat is one popular commercial source.	SVR4
OSF1	Compaq/Digital	SVR4
OpenServer (new versions now integrated into UnixWare and not sold as OpenServer)	Santa Cruz Operation, Inc.	SVR4
SINUX	Siemens Nixdorf	BSD
Solaris	Sun Microsystems	BSD
SunOS	Sun Microsystems	BSD
UnixWare	Santa Cruz Operation, Inc.	SVR4

This book uses Linux for its UNIX examples; Linux is a version of UNIX that is available free of charge, but some enhanced versions of Linux must be purchased. Linux is considered to be "UNIX-like" because the kernel is new code based on the POSIX standards that were developed after UNIX originally came out. Linux runs on Intel-based and PowerPC computers.

Because UNIX comes in such a wide variety of implementations, it runs on almost any hardware platform; there are UNIX versions available for all platforms mentioned up to this point. For this reason, it is hard to define exactly what specifications a platform should meet to run UNIX.

UNIX is a true multitasking, multi-user operating system. This means, as we explained before, that it has the ability to fully serve all the computing needs of multiple users running multiple applications at the same time. Depending on the hardware, a single UNIX computer can support from one to over 1,000 users.

After startup, UNIX typically presents you with a request for a login, or username, followed by a request for a password. The username and password you provide determine what privileges you will be granted on the system. When your identity has been verified, you are presented with a **shell**. This is another point where UNIX is substantially different from most other operating systems: by default, most UNIX versions come with several different shells, and it is up to the user to pick the shell they wish to use. Different shells provide you with different levels of functionality, but all of the shells function much like the shell in MS-DOS, with a series of built-in commands and the ability to call **external commands** and programs by simply typing them in at the command line.

The most popular UNIX shells are the Bourne shell (sh) and its cousin the Bourne Again shell (bash), and a version of the Bourne shell in which some of the commands are formatted to be similar to the C programming language, called the C shell (csh). Overall, these shells function in the same way: you get a prompt, you type a command, and they do what you ask. Main commands are the same across the shells. To see the **path** of the directory you are in, you use the Print Working Directory or *pwd* command. To list the contents of the current directory, you use *ls*. Changing to another directory is done with the *cd* command, much like in MS-DOS. When you are done with the shell, you can exit from it by using the *exit* command. Typically, this returns you to the login prompt. Try Hands-on Project 2-7 to determine the UNIX shell you are using.

Many versions of UNIX can also provide you with a graphical user interface. The most popular interface is the X11 Window System, known commonly as X Window. **X Window** is similar to other windowed systems, and makes it easier to use a multitask-ing, multi-user operating system such as UNIX. A unique feature of X Window is that it is network enabled. Using an X terminal, it is possible to run X Window and all the application programs on a remote UNIX computer, and remotely interact with your applications. One UNIX system can support many X terminals and users. X Window is, however, an optional part of many UNIX versions. Just as there are many different UNIX versions, there are also many different versions of X Window. Linux will gener-ally use something called Xfree, a version that can be obtained for free. Other UNIX versions use X Window versions with added capabilities. X Window, by default, does not include programs like Windows Explorer for managing files, or the Windows-based Start menu for starting programs, but many utilities are available to provide file and applica-tion management.

Red Hat Linux, for example, offers an X Window type GUI interface called GNOME, which can be installed or omitted (see the example in Figure 2-13). Even when GNOME is installed, you can still execute regular Linux commands by starting the terminal emu-lation program window shown in Figure 2-14. To start the terminal emulation program in Red Hat Linux 7.x, for instance, click the icon on the taskbar at the bottom of the GNOME interface that resembles a computer monitor. Hands-on Project 2-8 enables you to learn more about the Red Hat Linux 7.2 GNOME interface.

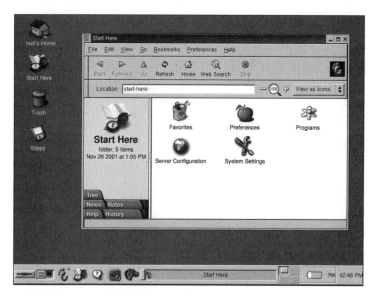

Figure 2-13   Linux GUI desktop

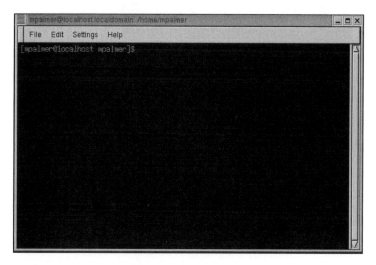

Figure 2-14   Linux terminal emulation window

All networking functions in UNIX are based on the BSD networking model, which provides support for the **TCP/IP (Transmission Control Protocol/Internet Protocol)**. This is the standard protocol in use on the Internet, and as such, UNIX computers are uniquely qualified to provide numerous Internet services (network protocols are discussed later in this book). The standard UNIX operating system does not provide many network functions. Most of these functions are provided by add-ons. The standard functions include login services, allowing a user to connect to the UNIX computer from another remote computer on the network; file transfers through the **File Transfer Protocol (FTP)**; and some form of e-mail service, usually the **Simple Mail Transfer Protocol (SMTP)**. Other services can be standard as well. In Linux, additional standard services include the **Network File System (NFS)**, and support for other network systems such as those used by Microsoft, Apple, and Novell. It is also possible to add modules to UNIX to provide other services, such as World Wide Web (WWW) service.

The security model in the UNIX operating system makes it a system of choice for providing many Internet functions, such as Internet server and firewall. It is possible to turn services on and off at the user's desire, and it is also possible to run services in ways that do not result in security issues for other services on the computer.

In addition to their roles as Internet server and firewall, UNIX computers are often used as database or application servers that many users can access at the same time. You will also find UNIX computers in use for technical design and industrial control applications.

Most versions of UNIX come with either a line editor, a text editor, or both. A line editor is an editor that is used to create text a line at a time. Line editors are often used to create scripts in which each line of the script executes a specific command. A text editor enables you to edit text in a full-screen mode. One of the most common UNIX text editors is Emacs.

One reason that UNIX is so popular is that it is compatible with an extensive range of programming tools, particularly program compilers and interpreters, which means that you can create nearly any kind of software application. For example, you can use the following programming languages with most versions of UNIX:

- FORTRAN
- Ada
- C
- C++
- Pascal
- LISP
- BASIC

UNIX is also compatible with many popular databases, such as Oracle and Informix. With the combined power of programming languages and databases, UNIX systems are frequently used for administrative computing, such as accounting systems, and for all kinds of scientific applications.

Mac OS

Apple Computer has always had a unique approach to operating systems. Its Macintosh line of personal computers revolutionized the world of operating systems. The Mac OS was truly the first operating system to have an all-graphical user interface and an all-graphical shell. Although there are subtle differences in the way Mac OS functions, you will see many similarities between it and Microsoft Windows, which many would say was designed to mimic the look and feel of the Mac OS. An example of Mac OS X is shown in Figure 2-15.

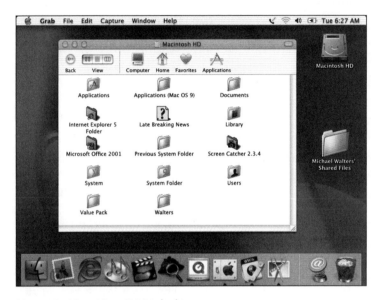

Figure 2-15   Mac OS X desktop

The hardware architecture of the Mac OS is substantially different from the architecture used on most other platforms, especially because many of the graphical functions are included in the BIOS functions, located in the ROM (Read Only Memory) of the hardware. (Apple calls this "firmware.") Beginning with System 7.1, Apple began using system enabler files that allowed the previous version of the operating system to support new hardware. When the next version of the operating system was released, support for the most recent Macs was included so the enabler file was no longer needed for that model. The hardware architecture needed to run Mac OS is very dependent on the version of the operating system. If you run Version 7.0, you could be using any Macintosh hardware architecture, except for the PowerPC platform, which is supported as of Version 7.5. If you are running the newest generation of hardware (G4), you must run Mac OS Versions 9.x or newer. Apple has always made the hardware and software closely interconnected, which results in strict requirements when it comes to operating system solutions.

One significant difference between the Mac OS and other operating systems covered in this chapter is that only one company makes hardware capable of running Mac OS, and that is Apple. A few years back, Apple licensed Power Computing, Motorola, and other companies to make Mac OS-compatible hardware, but that is no longer the case. In short, using Apple software means using Apple hardware.

After the Mac is started, you are presented with the all-graphical shell. This shell allows you to perform many operations with the mouse: starting programs, looking at the contents of directories, removing files, creating and removing folders (a folder is the Mac equivalent of a **directory**, a usage later adopted by most other graphical operating systems), and so on. The interface is extremely intuitive, and in many ways it is unchanged from the way it looked at its inception. The Mac makes no distinction between file management and the program start and stop functions.

Versions of Mac OS prior to 8.0 were not multitasking; they were essentially task switching with the aid of MultiFinder. Moreover, in Mac OS 8 and later, the multitasking functions are somewhat limited. While OS 8 Finder allows fairly significant multitasking operations, such as emptying the trash, opening programs, and performing multiple file copy tasks simultaneously, these multitasking services are not available to other programs. It is possible to start several programs and switch between them in Mac OS 7.x, but whenever you switch from one application to another, the application you switch from will stop running. It will stay in memory until you reactivate it, at which point it will pick up where it left off. The only exceptions to this are a few pieces of the operating system, such as the print spooler, which runs while other software is in control of the computer. In Mac OS Version 8.0 and newer, multitasking is a standard feature of the operating system that is available to all applications. When more than one application is active, the CPU resources are shared among them.

The network functions in Mac OS are fairly evolved. Peer-to-peer networking has been a standard feature of the Mac OS since its inception. The protocol used is called AppleTalk, which originated in the Macintosh world. However, you can run AppleTalk under Windows and Linux (using the *netatalk* command). The nice thing about AppleTalk is that it has remained compatible as new Mac OS versions arrived, and any Mac can be networked to any other Mac by simply plugging in a few cables and configuring some software. Apple implemented LocalTalk hardware with every Macintosh printer port, which uses an RS-422 interface to provide a combination networking and RS-232 serial solution in one inexpensive interface. This is, to our knowledge, the only hardware architecture and operating system combination that has consistently had these features. Through the use of optional clients, or through servers that can provide AppleTalk-compatible services, many Macintoshes can also be networked easily to other networks.

Not all Macintosh hardware is equipped with standard network hardware. Many older computers only have LocalTalk, a proprietary Apple hardware standard. For these computers to be able to network with other systems, additional hardware is needed.

Mac OS was always meant to be a desktop operating system, and there are no extended security features to keep users from getting access to files on the local computers. For networking, Mac OS allows the user to generate user profiles. A user can be given a username and a password. Based on this combination, a user may access some of the resources made available on the network. The Mac OS can use its networking features to share printer and disk resources. In Version 8.x and later, there are extensions that will let the Macintosh share resources using protocols other than AppleTalk, including TCP/IP, the standard Internet protocol, enabling greater flexibility in how Macs can be networked.

Throughout its history, the Mac OS has been known for its support of graphics, video, and sound capabilities. There has not been a version of Mac OS that does not support some kind of hardware that can produce sound. In this respect, Mac OS has been ahead of the industry. The same goes for sound capture, video capture and reproduction, and many other audiovisual functions. Because Apple has had tight control over both the Macintosh hardware architecture and operating system, and it chose to actively enhance the audiovisual functions of both hardware and software, you will find that the Mac and the Mac OS are favored by people in the graphics, sound, and video fields.

Macintosh computers are used in many different environments, especially those that deal with the creative process. The Mac font management and ColorSync color matching technologies have endeared it in the graphic arts and pre-press fields, while QuickTime has made the Mac popular for multimedia sound and video production. You will also find many Macs in the educational environment. The home computer market has a small but substantial share of computers running Mac OS. The Apple PowerBook laptops continue to be popular, even in organizations that have mostly settled on the Windows-Intel platform.

Mac OS 9.x introduces features for better hardware and Internet access. For example, Version 9.1 introduces a Printer Sharing panel to manage and share a USB printer on a network (try Hands-on Project 2-9). There is a capability to connect to another computer over the Internet by using the Point-to-Point Protocol, a network communications protocol designed for remote communications (you will learn more about protocols later in this book). Mac OS also has Personal Web Sharing for creating a Web page that others can access over the Internet, or through a private network. Also, Mac OS 9.x includes a runtime execution tool for running Java applets from the Finder tool. For users who are connected to a network, there is the Network Assist Client tool that is used by network administrators to control the computer.

Mac OS X

Mac OS X, where X means Version 10, is a significant update of the Mac OS because it sports a new interface called the "Aqua" interface (try Hands-on Project 2-10). One of the main changes for previous users of Mac OS 9.x and earlier is that some programs and utilities were replaced. This is first evident from the new Apple menu, which has these options:

- About This Mac
- Get Mac OS X Software
- System Preferences
- Dock
- Location
- Recent Items
- Force Quit
- Sleep
- Restart
- Shut Down
- Log Out

The Apple menu can no longer be customized as in the past. New menu features include System Preferences, which is similar to the Control Panel on Windows systems. System Preferences enables you to set functions such as the time and date, display settings, startup functions, energy saving functions, and network functions. The Dock function can now be customized through the System Preferences tool for the applications you wish to include. Through Dock, you can start multiple applications, and switch between them in a multitasking environment.

Out of the box, Mac OS X is already configured so that different users can access the operating system in their own workspaces, without affecting other users. If one user wants to logout, so that another user can access Mac OS X, the first user can now select the new Log Out option from the Apple menu, instead of turning off the computer and then rebooting.

Many windows in Mac OS X now can be customized so that their contents appear in columns, similar to Windows-based systems. Also, the title bar in a window displays buttons to close, minimize, or maximize (zone) that window. Throughout each window, the icons have a new modern look. Further, some windows have drawers that offer information that slides out of the windows like drawers out of file cabinets.

Internet connectivity is enhanced in Mac OS X through the new tool, Internet Connect, which performs functions that users of previous Mac OS versions associated

2

with the Remote Access tool. Internet Connect enables you to set up an Internet connection, configure a modem, and monitor the status of a connection. Internet applications include the Mail application, from Apple, used for e-mail; and the Internet Explorer application, is a Web browser from Microsoft.

CHAPTER SUMMARY

❐ Hardware and operating systems are interrelated because in many ways they grew up together. We've seen a steady march of hardware from the early 8088 chip to the modern 64-bit Itanium processor. Processors are much faster and more efficient, and operating systems paralleled this change to take advantage of the capabilities of new processors at each stage of development.

❐ The early computer operating systems, such as MS-DOS, are well suited to the early processors, which included the 8088, 8086, and 80286. As processors became faster and more advanced, so did operating systems such as the early Windows and Macintosh operating systems. UNIX operating systems, too, have grown to take advantage of improvements in 32-bit and 64-bit processors.

❐ Today, 32-bit processors, such as the Pentium 4, provide a foundation for operating systems like Windows XP to take advantage of high-speed networking and multimedia capabilities. Also, new 64-bit processors have emerged, such as the PowerPC G4 generation of processors, and new operating systems, such as Mac OS X, are there to take advantage of the new features of these processors.

❐ In your work with computers, one of the most basic steps is to ensure that the hardware resources are properly matched to the operating system. Trying to run Windows XP on an 80486 computer makes no sense because that level of computer cannot support Windows XP. An even subtler problem for troubleshooters is the situation in which the hardware meets the minimum required configuration for the operating system, but really does not have enough power to do justice to that system—resulting in slow service and frustration for the user. For example, Windows XP can run on a 233 MHz processor with 64 MB of RAM, but once several applications are started, the combination is likely to be slow. Consequently, some of the best preparation that you can have for diagnosing computer problems is to know the hardware and if it matches the requirements of the operating system loaded onto it.

KEY TERMS

Active Directory — A Windows 2000 database of computers, users, shared printers, shared folders, and other network resources and resource groupings that is used to manage a network and enable users to quickly find a particular resource.

ActiveX — An internal programming standard that allows various software that runs under the Windows operating system to communicate with the operating system and other programs.

address bus — An internal communications pathway inside a computer that specifies the source and target address for memory reads and writes. The address bus is measured by the number of bits of information it can carry. The wider the address bus (the more bits it moves at a time), the more memory available to the computer that uses it.

arithmetic logic unit (ALU) — A part of the CPU that handles all arithmetic computations.

Berkeley Software Distribution (BSD) — A variant of the UNIX operating system upon which a large proportion of today's UNIX software is based.

bus — A path or channel between a computer's CPU and the devices it manages, such as memory and disk storage.

cache controller — Internal computer hardware that manages the data going into and loaded from the computer's cache memory.

cache memory — Special computer memory that temporarily stores data used by the CPU. Cache memory is physically close to the CPU, and is faster than standard system memory, enabling faster retrieval and processing time.

client — In a networking environment, a computer that handles certain user-side software operations. For example, a network client may run software that captures user data input and presents output to the user from a network server.

clustering — The ability to share the computing load and resources by linking two or more discrete computer systems to function as though they are one.

Complex Instruction Set Computer (CISC) — A computer CPU architecture in which processor components are reconfigured to conduct different operations as required. Such computer designs require many instructions and more complex instructions than other designs.

Component Object Model (COM) — Standards that enable a software object, such as a graphic, to be linked from one software component into another one. COM is the foundation that makes Object Linking and Embedding (OLE) possible.

control bus — An internal communications pathway that keeps the CPU informed of the status of particular computer resources and devices, such as memory and disk drives.

data bus — An internal communications pathway that allows computer components, such as the CPU, display adapter, and main memory, to share information. Early personal computers used an 8-bit data bus. More modern computers use 32- or 64-bit data buses.

Dial-Up Networking (DUN) — A utility built into Windows 95, Windows 98, and Windows NT to permit operation of a hardware modem to dial a telephone number for the purpose of logging into a remote computer system via standard telephone lines.

directory — A special disk storage location that keeps track of filenames, file types, and storage locations on a computer storage device. Also a list of these files and file information produced by a program utility that reads and reports on the disk's directory structure.

Disk Operating System (DOS) — Computer software that manages the interface between the user and computer components, and among various components inside the computer. A Disk Operating System manages the low-level computer instructions for operation of and communication with such devices as storage hardware, a keyboard, a display adapter, and so on.

domain — A logical grouping of computers and computer resources that helps manage these resources and user access to them.

DUN server — In Windows 95, Windows 98, and Windows NT, a software utility that permits a desktop computer to answer incoming calls, log on a user, and, with other software, permits the user access to the computer's resources.

Explicitly Parallel Instruction Computing (EPIC) — A computer CPU architecture that grew out of the RISC-based architecture, and enables the processor to work faster by performing several operations at once, predicting and speculating about operations that will come next (so that they are even completed before requested). EPIC uses larger and more work area registers than CISC or traditional RISC-based CPU architectures.

external clock speed — The speed at which the processor communicates with the memory and other devices in the computer; usually one-fourth to one-half the internal clock speed.

external commands — Operating system commands that are stored in separate program files on disk. When these commands are required, they must be loaded from disk storage into memory before they are executed.

File Transfer Protocol (FTP) — In some networking environments, a software utility that facilitates the copying of computer files across the network connection from one computer to another.

firewall — In a networked environment, a computer that is configured with special software to control access from networked workstations to an external network, and vice versa.

Infrared Data Association (IrDA) — A group of peripheral manufacturers that developed a set of standards for transmitting data using infrared light. Printers were one of the first devices to support the IrDA specifications.

instruction set — In a computer CPU, the group of commands (instructions) the processor recognizes. These instructions are used to conduct the operations required of the CPU by the operating system and application software.

internal clock speed — The speed at which the CPU executes internal commands, measured in megahertz (millions of clock ticks per second) or gigahertz (billions of clock ticks per second). Internal clock speeds can be as low as 1 MHz and as high as over 2 GHz.

internal commands — Operating system commands that load with the main operating system kernel or command module.

Interrupt Request (IRQ) — A request to the processor so that a currently operating process, such as a read from a disk drive, can be interrupted by another process, such as a write into memory.

Kerberos — A security system developed by the Massachusetts Institute of Technology to enable two parties on an open network to communicate without interception by an intruder, creating a unique encryption key per each communication session.

kernel — In a computer operating system, the lowest level and most basic instructions.

Level 1 (L1) cache — Cache memory that is part of the CPU hardware. *See* cache memory.

Level 2 (L2) cache — Cache memory that, in most computer CPU designs, is located on hardware separate from, but close to, the CPU.

Level 3 (L3) cache — Cache memory that is located on a chip or daughter board, which is separate from, but close to the CPU, when L1 and L2 cache are both already built into the CPU.

math coprocessor — A module optimized to perform complex math calculations. Early system architectures have a processor and an optional slot for a math coprocessor. Modern system architectures have a CPU with a built-in math coprocessor.

Multimedia Extension (MMX) — A CPU design that permits the processor to manage certain multimedia operations—graphics, for example—faster and more directly. MMX technology improves computer performance when running software that requires multimedia operations.

multiprocessor computers — A computer that uses more than one CPU.

multithreading — Running several program processes or parts (threads) at the same time.

Network File System (NFS) — In UNIX and other operating systems, a system-level facility that supports loading and saving files to remote disk drives across the network.

path — In a computer directory structure, both a command and a path designation that specifies the complete location of a specific file or directory. Computer files are stored in files, which in turn reside in directories (folders). Directories can be stored within other directories. To access a specific file, you must also specify the series of directories, the path that must be traversed to reach the desired file.

peer-to-peer network operating system — A network operating system through which any computer can communicate with other networked computers on an equal or peer-like basis without going through an intermediary, such as a server or network host computer.

pipelining — A CPU design that permits the processor to operate on one instruction at the same time it is fetching one or more subsequent instructions from the operating system or application.

2

Plug and Play (PnP) — Software utilities that operate with compatible hardware to facilitate automatic hardware configuration. Windows versions starting with 95 recognize PnP hardware when it is installed, and, in many cases, can configure the hardware and install required software without significant user intervention.

√ **power management** — A hardware facility in modern computers that permits certain hardware to shut down automatically after a specified period of inactivity. Proper use of power management facilities reduces hardware wear and tear, as well as energy usage.

real mode — A limited, 16-bit operating mode in PCs running early versions of Windows.

Reduced Instruction Set Computer (RISC) — A computer CPU design that dedicates processor hardware components to certain functions. This design reduces the number and complexity of required instructions and, in many cases, results in faster performance than CISC CPUs.

√ **Registry** — A Windows database that stores information about a computer's hardware and software configuration.

Remote Access Service (RAS) — A computer operating system subsystem that manages user access to a computer from a remote location, including security access.

√ **shell** — The operating system user interface. In MS-DOS, UNIX, and some other systems, the shell interface is text based and command oriented.

Simple Mail Transfer Protocol (SMTP) — In a networked computer environment, a software utility that manages the transfer of electronic messages among various users.

single-processor computers — Computers capable of supporting only a single CPU.

√ **symmetric multiprocessing (SMP)** — A computer design that supports multiple, internal CPUs that can be configured to work simultaneously on the same set of instructions.

system architecture — The computer hardware design that includes the processor (CPU), and communication routes between the CPU and the hardware it manages, such as memory and disk storage.

√ **task supervisor** — A process in the operating system that keeps track of the applications that are running on the computer and the resources they use.

√ **total cost of ownership (TCO)** — The cost of installing and maintaining computers and equipment on a network, which includes hardware, software, maintenance, and support costs.

Transmission Control Protocol/Internet Protocol (TCP/IP) — A networking communications protocol. Used on the Internet and other UNIX networking environments.

Universal Plug and Play (UPnP) — An initiative of over 80 companies to develop products that can be quickly added to a computer or network. These include intelligent appliances for the home. More information can be found at the Web site, www.upnp.org.

√**Universal Serial Bus (USB)** — A relatively new serial bus designed to support up to 127 discrete devices with data transfer speeds up to 12 Mbps (megabits per second).

√**Virtual Private Network (VPN)** — A private network that is like a tunnel through a larger network—such as the Internet, an enterprise network, or both – and restricted to designated member clients.

√**Web browser** — Software to facilitate individual computer access to graphical data presented over the Internet on the World Wide Web, or over a local area network in a compatible format.

√**Web server** — In a networked environment, a computer that runs special software to host graphical data in a World Wide Web format. Data on a Web server is accessed with a computer running a Web browser.

√**X Window** — A windowed user interface for UNIX and other operating systems.

REVIEW QUESTIONS

1. A single processor computer is one that:

   a. can conduct only a single process at a time.

   b. contains only a single central processing unit (CPU).

   c. can connect on a network to only one other computer.

   d. none of the above

2. Two general CPU designs are used in modern computers. They are Complex _____ _____ _____ and Reduced _____ _____ _____.

3. The Mac OS that has a significantly new interface is called _____.

4. A CISC CPU design uses:

   a. hardware that is software configured to perform multiple operations.

   b. hardware that is dedicated to perform multiple operations.

   c. hardware that requires fewer instructions than other designs.

   d. hardware that requires more instructions than other designs.

5. Instruction pipelining is a processing technique used by _____ CPUs to improve performance.

6. One benchmark of the speed of a CPU is the number of instructions it can perform with each clock cycle. How many clock cycles will a 1.7 GHz computer have?

7. G4 is the _____ generation of the _____ processor.

8. Special memory that may reside on the CPU hardware and that can speed up computer operation is called _____ memory.

9. The Intel Pentium 4 processor operates at what internal clock speeds?

10. Describe L3 cache, and explain the main function of a cache controller.

11. A computer address bus is used to enable the computer to _____.

12. How many memory locations can a 32-bit address bus access? A 64-bit address bus?

13. The _____ bus is used to transport device status information to the _____.

14. The first widely used personal computer CPU was manufactured by Intel, their model:

   a. 68040.

   b. 60000.

   c. 8086.

   d. 8088.

15. The first popular graphical user interface (GUI) for the PC was:

   a. Windows 98.

   b. MS-DOS.

   c. Windows 3.1.

   d. UNIX.

16. The Intel Itanium processor is built on what architecture?

17. The most recent, graphical Windows desktop operating system designed for business applications by Microsoft is _____.

18. Mac OS is designed by the _____ company for its line of _____ computers.

19. What relatively high-speed input/output port was first supported in Windows 98?

20. What Windows-based operating system is the first to implement Kerberos security?

HANDS-ON PROJECTS

Project 2-1

In this project, you use the System Monitor tool in Windows 95/98 to monitor the processor response to system and network demands. The System Monitor can help you determine if the processor is meeting the usage demands, or if it needs to be upgraded. For example, a processor that is frequently at 80 to 100% usage may need to be upgraded.

To use the System Monitor:

1. Click **Start**, point to **Programs**, point to **Accessories**, point to **System Tools**, and click **System Monitor**.

2. What information is displayed and in what format?

3. Watch the monitor for several minutes and determine how the information changes.

4. Close the System Monitor.

Project 2-2

In Windows NT, 2000, and XP, you can monitor the processor usage through the Task Manager (you got a first glimpse of the Task Manager in Hands-on Project 1-7 in Chapter 1).

To monitor processor usage:

1. Right-click the **Task Bar** and click **Task Manager** on the shortcut menu.

2. Click the **Performance** tab.

3. Watch the CPU Usage and the CPU Usage History graphs. How do the graphs change as you are watching? Does the CPU ever go over 80% usage and stay at this level for a long time?

4. What other information can you monitor on the Performance tab? How can you determine the amount of RAM or physical memory in the computer? How much memory is used by the kernel?

5. Close the Task Manager.

It is not advised to leave the Task Manager running in the background while you are not using it because the Task Manager uses CPU and memory resources and could slow down the computer.

Project 2-3

Most Windows-based systems have the ability to show you if the processor (or any other hardware device) is working properly. This project shows you how to test the processor.

To test the processor in Windows 95/98:

1. Click **Start**, point to **Settings**, and click **Control Panel**.

2. Double-click the **System** icon.

3. Click the **Device Manager** tab.

4. Double-click **System devices** if the entities under it are not displayed.

5. What is displayed under System devices?

6. Find the processor in the list and double-click it (or click the processor's connection to a controller or bridge, such as the PCI bridge). Look for the device status box in the resulting dialog box. What is the device status? Close the dialog box for the processor.

7. Look at the list of devices under System devices. Is there an option to check the numeric or math coprocessor? Is there an option to check the Plug and Play BIOS?

8. Close the System Properties dialog box, and then close the Control Panel.

To test the processor in Windows Me/2000/XP:

1. In Windows 2000, right-click the **My Computer** icon on the desktop, and click **Manage**. Or, in Windows XP, click **Start**, right-click **My Computer**, and click **Manage**.

2. Double-click **System Tools** in the left pane, if necessary, to display the objects under it.

3. Click **Device Manager**.

4. For Windows XP, double-click **Processors** in the right pane. How many processors are displayed? Double-click a processor in the list (if there are more than one). In Windows 2000, double-click **System Devices** and notice the devices that are displayed. Double-click a processor in the list (or click the processor's connection to a controller or bridge, such as the PCI bridge).

5. Make sure that the General tab is shown, and if not, click it.

6. What is the status of the processor? Also, notice that there is a Troubleshoot button to help you diagnose a problem with the processor.

7. Close the Processor Properties dialog box, and then close the Computer Management Window.

Project 2-4

In this project, you compare the desktop of Windows 95/98 to Windows XP Home Edition or Professional.

To compare the desktops:

1. Log onto Windows 95 or Windows 98.

2. What icons are displayed on the desktop?

3. Click the **Start** button. What options do you see?

4. Log off Windows 95 or 98, and then log onto Windows XP.

5. What icons are displayed on the desktop? Compare the similarities and differences of the Windows 95/98 desktop to that of Windows XP.

6. Click the **Start** button. How is the Windows XP Start button menu different from that of Windows 95/98?

7. Log off Windows XP when you are finished examining the similarities and differences of the desktop to Windows 95/98.

Project 2-5

Windows XP has some of the most extensive help and support information available for an operating system. In this project, you have an opportunity to view the Windows XP Help and Support Center.

To view the Windows XP help and support information:

1. Click **Start**, and then click **Help and Support**.

2. What information categories are available?

3. Click **Windows basics**. How might this information help you learn more about Windows XP?

4. Click the **Back** arrow on the menu bar.

5. Click **Fixing a problem**.

6. Which option provides help with hardware problems? Which option offers help for software problems?

7. Click **Troubleshooting problems**.

8. Scroll the right pane and click **List of troubleshooters** under the Overviews, Articles, and Tutorials section. What are some of the Troubleshooters that you can access? Select one of the Troubleshooters to see how it can provide help for a problem.

9. Close the Help and Support Center tool.

Project 2-6

Windows XP has a Program Compatibility Wizard from which to run programs adapted to earlier operating systems, such as Windows 95. This project gives you the opportunity to use the Program Compatibility Wizard. You'll need to obtain from your instructor a program originally designed for Windows 95, such as Word 95.

To use the Program Compatibility Wizard:

1. Click **Start**, point to **All Programs**, point to **Accessories**, and click **Program Compatibility Wizard**.

2. Click **Next** after the wizard starts.

3. What options do you see for selecting programs?

4. Select the option **I want to locate the program manually**, and then click **Next**.

5. Enter the path to the program that you want to start, or click the **Browse** button to find and select the program.

6. Click **Next**.

7. What compatibility modes are available?

8. Select **Microsoft Windows 95**, and then click **Next**.

9. Select the appropriate display settings, such as 640 X 480 screen resolution (ask your instructor if you are unsure about what to select). Click **Next**.

10. Review the program, path, and compatibility settings. Click **Next**.

11. What happens after you click Next?

12. Test the program and then close it.

13. If the program ran successfully, click the option **Yes, set this program to always use these compatibility settings**, and click **Next**. If it did not run successfully, click **No, try different compatibility settings**, and repeat Steps 8 through 12, trying different settings.

14. Click **Yes** to send program compatibility information to Microsoft so that Microsoft can use this information for its own research. Click **Next**.

15. Click **Finish**.

Project 2-7

In this project, you learn how to determine what shell you are using while in the Linux operating system.

To determine the shell that you are using:

1. Access the command prompt, such as by opening a terminal window in the Red Hat Linux GNOME GUI interface. To open a terminal window, click the icon that resembles a monitor at the bottom of the screen, or click the **foot** (Main Menu), point to **System**, and click **GNOME terminal**.

2. Start by looking at the command prompt. The $ prompt means that you are in either the Bourne, Bourne Again, or Korn shell.

3. Enter **echo $SHELL**, making sure that the word "SHELL" is all capital letters. What response do you see? If /bin/sh appears, you are in the Bourne shell. A response of /bin/bash means you are using the Bourne Again shell. And /bin/ksh signifies the Korn shell.

4. If you get an error message in Step 2, enter **echo $shell** (making sure that the word "shell" is all lowercase letters). Now you should see the response /bin/csh, which means that you are in the C shell.

5. Type **exit** and press **Enter**, or click the **x** in the upper right corner of the window to close the terminal window.

Project 2-8

In Windows-based systems, you can start a program by beginning from the Start button and Programs option, for example. In Red Hat Linux 7.2, the X Window GNOME interface has a similar structure. For instance, you can click the Main Menu and select the Programs option to access many programs and utilities. In this project you have an opportunity to briefly become acquainted with the GNOME interface.

To become more acquainted with the GNOME interface:

1. Log on to Red Hat Linux 7.2, either using the root account or another account provided by your instructor.

2. What icons do you see already on the desktop?

3. The bottom of the screen contains the Panel, which is similar to the taskbar in Windows-based systems. Notice the icons on the Panel. The foot icon is the Main Menu. The icon that looks like a monitor opens the GNOME Terminal emulation program that enables you to enter command line commands. Other icons may include one to view documentation (a question mark), a starter's clock that opens the Start Here window, and other icons that can be installed by applications or that a user has placed on the Panel. There's also a clock on the right side of the Panel.

4. Click the **foot** icon to open the Main Menu. What options do you see?

5. Point to **Programs**. What options are on the Programs menu?

6. Point to **Applications**. What applications are available from this menu?

7. Move your pointer away from the menus and click in open space so that you close the menus.

Project 2-9

In this project, you view the new Mac OS 9.x option for USB printer sharing and determine if printer sharing is turned on.

To view the setup for USB printer sharing:

1. Open the Apple menu, point to **Control Panels**, and click **USB Printer Sharing**.

2. Click the **Start/Stop** tab, if it does not already appear.

3. What is the status of the USB printer; is it shared or not shared?

4. How can you start printer sharing if it is not enabled, or how can you turn it off if it is enabled?

5. If you enable sharing, next click the **My Printers** tab and make sure that the Share check box next to the printer that you want to share is selected with a checkmark.

6. Close the USB Printer Sharing dialog box.

Project 2-10

In this project, you examine the Mac OS X desktop.

To view the new desktop:

1. Start up Mac OS X and observe the desktop.

2. What features are on the desktop?

3. Click each of the menus at the top. What are some examples of options that you see?

4. What are some examples of applications in the Applications window?

5. How would you run an application?

CASE PROJECT

2

Oven Fresh Pastries makes doughnuts and pastries that are packaged and distributed to convenience stores. This company has a network of 278 computers consisting of:

❑ Eight Windows NT 4.0 servers

❑ Two Linux servers

❑ 20 computers running Mac OS 8.1

❑ 32 computers running Windows 95

❑ 216 computers running Windows 98

Oven Fresh Pastries has experienced record profits and now wants to upgrade all its computers.

1. The Accounting Department has all of the Windows 95 computers that are running on 90 MHz Pentium hardware. The accounting director wants to upgrade to Windows XP. What are the advantages of upgrading for this department in terms of the enhanced operating system functions that are available in Windows XP?

2. If the Accounting Department does upgrade to Windows XP, will it have to upgrade the processors, and if so, to what? Also, will the department be able to run a legacy 16-bit billing program that was designed for Windows 95?

3. The Marketing Department uses the Mac OS 8.1 computers, which are G3 computers. Since they plan to purchase new computers, what is the newest Mac operating system to which they can upgrade, and what new processor can they upgrade to? What would be the advantage of this upgrade for their department?

4. The president of Oven Fresh Pastries is convinced that the processor on his Windows 98 system is overloaded. How can you help him determine if there is a problem with the processor?

5. The new chief financial officer (CFO) believes that all of the Windows 98 computers should be upgraded to Windows Me because Windows XP Professional is too new. What are the advantages and disadvantages of upgrading to Windows Me compared to Windows XP Professional or Windows 2000 Professional?

6. What would be the advantage of upgrading the Windows NT servers, and if you recommend upgrading them, what operating system do you recommend? Why?

OPTIONAL CASE PROJECTS FOR TEAMS

Team Case One

Form a small team. Search for two or three computer vendors on the Internet and find the most current combinations of desktop computers that they offer, including CPUs, clock speeds, bus speeds, memory, and peripherals. Next, list the operating systems that could run on the computers with these configurations (list more than the operating systems that are already loaded on the computers).

Team Case Two

Have your team consider the following general types of applications:

❑ Using desktop publishing for large newsletters

❑ Using games, music, and Internet access at home

❑ Writing large-scale computer programs

❑ Offering a Web server

❑ Using word processing, spreadsheets, databases, and scientific programs

Describe the processors and operating systems that your team recommends, in general, for each of these applications.

3

FILE SYSTEMS

After reading this chapter and completing the exercises you will be able to:

♦ Understand the basic functions common to all file systems

♦ Explain the design of the Windows 95 (FAT16) and Windows 95, Windows 98, and Windows Me (FAT32) file systems

♦ Describe the Windows NT, Windows 2000, and Windows XP file system (NTFS)

♦ Describe the design of the UNIX file system

♦ Describe the basics of the Macintosh file system

Storing information in files is one of the primary functions of personal computers. Some files contain text, such as letters or book chapters. Other files contain program code that you can execute—word processing code, for example, that enables you to create the text for a letter or book chapter. A **file system** is a design for storing and managing files on storage media. Just as a good paper filing system enables you to store important papers and find them later, a computer file system enables you to easily find and use program, text, and other files. The file system is a vital function of every operating system because even operating system files in the kernel must be organized and managed to start the computer. The file system builds a logical system on top of the physical disk organization. It organizes how information is stored on disk, and affects how users interact with the operating system to work with files.

In this chapter, you'll learn the general characteristics and functions of file systems, including their organization and specific features. Next, you'll explore the design of the file systems used by Microsoft, UNIX, and Macintosh operating systems. You'll also examine typical file system problems and the tools that you can use to solve those problems.

UNDERSTANDING FILE SYSTEM FUNCTIONS

The file systems used by personal computer operating systems perform the following general functions:

- Enable files to be organized through directories and folders
- Partition and format disks to store and retrieve information
- Establish file-naming conventions
- Provide utilities for functions such as file compression and disk defragmentation
- Provide for file and data integrity
- Provide storage media management functions
- Enable error recovery or prevention

The overall purpose of a file system is to create a structure for filing data. The image that is typically used for a file system is that of file cabinets, file drawers, and file folders. For example, the computer could be considered the file cabinet, and the disk drives the drawers. Within each drawer (drive), information is organized into hanging folders (directories), manila folders (subdirectories), and individual documents (files), as shown in Figure 3-1.

A file is a set of data that is grouped in some logical manner, assigned a name, and stored on the disk. As the file is stored, the file system records where the file is located on the disk so that it has a way to later retrieve that file. Whenever the file is needed, the operating system is given the filename, and it retrieves the data in the file from the disk.

The data contained in files can be text, images, music and sounds, video, or Web pages for the Internet. But no matter what kind of data is stored in the file system, it must be converted into digital format—a series of 1s and 0s, or electrical signal "ons" and "offs"— that the computer understands. The operating system, along with the applications you use for word processing, graphics, and so on, performs this function of converting data into digital format for the computer, and back into the end user format as text or pictures, for example.

Moreover, there must be a way to write digital information onto disk, track it, update it when necessary, and call it back when the user, or a program under the user's control, wants it. To achieve all this, the operating system typically groups disk sectors in some logical way, creates a record of this structure, and builds a **directory** to track the type of data stored in each file. The directory connects names to the files that are stored on the disk, which makes it easy for users and programs to obtain the right data at the right time.

The term *directory* can have two meanings: the internal database maintained by the operating system to track file locations, sizes, and attributes; and the actual list of this information displayed and accessed by the user through the UNIX *ls* command or Windows Explorer, for example.

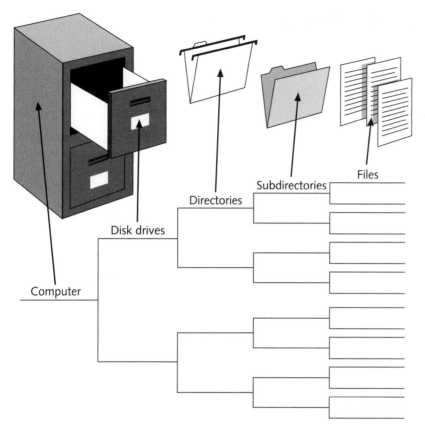

Figure 3-1   A file system

In addition to the names of files and where to find them on the disk, directories (and individual files) also store the following information:

- Date and time the directory or file was created (a timestamp for that directory or file)

- Date and time the directory or file was last modified (another form of timestamp)

- Directory or file size

- Directory or file attributes, such as security information, or if the directory or file was backed up

Figure 3-2 illustrates some of the information that is stored for a file in Windows XP, which can be displayed using Windows Explorer or My Computer (try Hands-on Project 3-1 to see how to select which file details to view in Windows XP). As you will learn later in this chapter, the way in which this information is stored depends on the design of the file system.

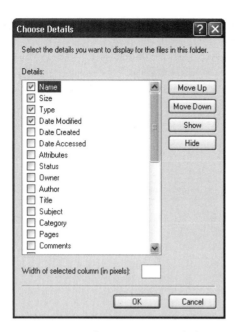

Figure 3-2   Information stored about Windows XP files

Designing a Directory Structure

For users, one of the most important features of a file system is the ability to store information according to a pattern of organization that is enabled by the use of directories. In the early Windows systems and UNIX systems, files are organized by directories, while in later Windows versions and the Mac OS, these are called **folders**. For example, in Windows NT, 2000, and XP, the default folder in which the system files are organized is called \Winnt. In UNIX, many system files are located in the /etc directory, while in the Mac OS, the System Folder contains the critical system files.

Directories and folders can be organized in a hierarchy that is similar to a tree structure. For example, in Windows XP, the \Winnt folder contains subfolders such as \Winnt\AddIns, \Winnt\Config, \Winnt\Help, \Winnt\Media, \Winnt\System, and \Winnt\System32. Many of these subfolders contain subfolders under them, such as the Restore and Spool subfolders under the System32 subfolder—giving the folder system a tree-like structure. In Red Hat Linux, the /etc directory has many subdirectories—/etc/gnome, /etc/mail, /etc/security, and /etc/sysconfig, to name a few. Building a hierarchy of folders and subfolders enables you to fine tune the organization of files and folders in a methodical way so that information is easy to find and use.

Without a well-designed directory or folder structure, it is common for a hard disk to become cluttered and disorganized with different versions of files and application software. Some personal computer users keep most of their files in the computer's primary level or **root directory**, or they load all application software into a single directory. As a partial solution, some application software programs use an automated setup that suggests folders for new programs, such as creating new subfolders under the Program Files folder in many Windows systems—but some users still have difficulty organizing files. A chaotic file structure makes it difficult to run or remove programs, or determine the most current versions. It also makes users spend unproductive time looking for specific files.

To avoid confusion, carefully design the file and folder structure from the start, particularly on servers that are accessed by many users. When you design a directory structure consider directories for the following:

- Operating system files
- Software applications
- Work files, such as word processing, graphics, spreadsheet, and database files
- Public files that you share over the network
- Utilities files
- Temporary files

In deciding how to allocate folders for specific types of files, consider following some general practices. For instance, the root folder should not be cluttered with files, or too many directories or folders. Each software application should have its own folder or subfolder, so updates and software removal are easy to administer. For easy access control, similar information should be grouped, such as accounting systems or office productivity software. Operating system files should be kept separate and protected so important files are not accidentally deleted by a user. Directories and folders should have names that clearly reflect their purposes. For example, consider a law office administrator who uses legal time accounting software, legal forms software, Microsoft Office, confidential and shared spreadsheets, and Word documents—all on a computer running Windows XP Professional. The same office administrator also maintains specialized Web pages for the law firm's Web site. The folder structure from the root might be as follows:

- *Winnt* for the system files
- *Program Files* for general software and utilities
- *Documents and Settings* for work files such as spreadsheets and Word documents
- *Shared* for spreadsheets that are shared over the network
- *Forms* for specific types of forms used by the legal forms software
- *Inetpub* for Web pages

Each major folder has subfolders to keep grouped files or application software separate. For example, the Program Files folder contains subfolders for each different software package, such as /Program Files/MSOffice for the Microsoft Office software, and /Program Files/Time Accounting for the legal time accounting software folder. The

Documents and Settings folder would have subfolders for confidential spreadsheets and Word documents, while shared spreadsheets would be in the Shared folder. Figure 3-3 illustrates this folder structure.

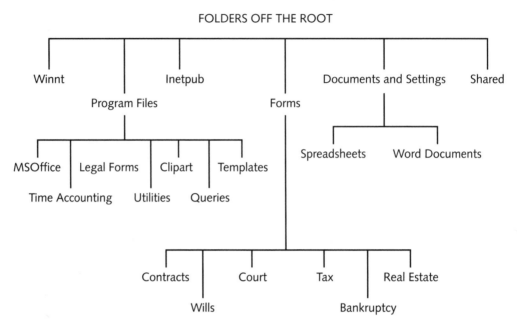

Figure 3-3   Sample folder structure for a Windows-based system

For UNIX systems, such as Red Hat Linux, a typical directory (or folder) structure is as follows:

- *bin* for user programs and utilities (binary files)
- *lib* for libraries
- *usr* for user files and programs
- *var* for files in which content often varies or that are used only temporarily
- *tmp* for files used only temporarily
- *dev* for devices
- *mnt* for floppy drives, CD–ROM drives, and other removable media that can be mounted
- *etc* for system and configuration files
- *sbin* for user programs and utilities (system binary files)
- *home* for users' home directories (or folders)
- *proc* for system resource tracking

Red Hat Linux now uses the term "folders" instead of "directories," as it had in earlier versions.

In the Mac OS, the default folder structure from the root includes:

- *Applications* for software applications
- *System Folder* for system files
- *Library* for library files (such as fonts)
- *Users* for user accounts
- *Documents* for documents

Try Hands-on Project 3-2 to practice making directories and folders in different operating systems.

Disk Storage Basics

When a hard disk is delivered from the manufacturer, it is low-level formatted. A **low-level format** is a software process that marks the location of disk tracks and sectors. Every disk is divided into **tracks**, which are like several circles around a disk. To visualize tracks, it helps to think of an old phonograph record filled with grooves. The number of tracks on a hard disk depends on the disk size and manufacturer, just as an old 45 rpm record (one song per side) is smaller and has fewer grooves than a 33.3 rpm record (six or seven songs per side). Each track is divided into sections of equal size called **sectors**. Figure 3-4 illustrates a hard disk divided into tracks and sectors.

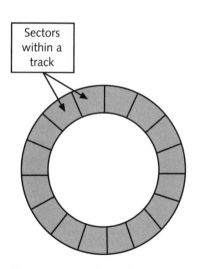
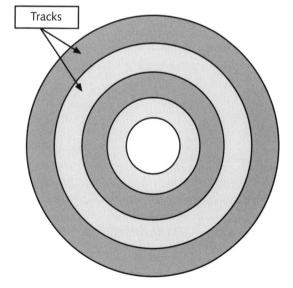

Figure 3-4 Disk tracks and sectors

Block Allocation

The operating systems discussed in this book use a method called **block allocation** to keep track of where specific files are stored on the disk. Rather than storing absolute track, sector, and head information for every sector on a disk, with block allocation the disk is divided into logical blocks (in MS-DOS and Windows these are called **clusters**), which are in turn mapped to sectors, heads, and tracks on the disk. Each hard disk platter has two sides, with a read-write head on each side. Tracks that line up on each platter from top to bottom are called cylinders, and are all read at the same time.

When the operating system needs to allocate some disk space, it does so based on a block address. Lower-level drivers translate block numbers into real disk addresses. The reference to a file in the directory and in the file allocation data is based on block numbers.

The data regarding block allocation is stored on the disk itself, using two techniques. One technique uses a fixed portion of the disk to store this data, such as the **FAT (file allocation table)** file system used by MS-DOS and supported by all versions of Windows (although some Windows versions, such as Windows NT/2000/XP, also support other file systems). The other technique uses various locations on the disk to store a special type of file that is used for directory and file allocation information, such as the **New Technology File System (NTFS)** and the UNIX file systems. As you can imagine, the areas of the disk in which allocation information and directory information are stored are very important; without this data, it would not be possible to access any of the files on the system.

If a system uses a specific area or set of areas on the disk to store this data, obviously this disk area is accessed frequently. This is why many problems with disks arise as problems in disk allocation tables and directory information (you'll learn about disk allocation tables later in this chapter). Since this data also is stored in a location separate from the actual file, you can see how when there is a problem with the disk, some of the directory or allocation data may not match the data actually stored on the disk. These occurrences are not uncommon, so it is very important to exercise proper care of disks to minimize such problems.

All operating systems have special tools that let you check, and sometimes repair, common file system and disk problems. Some operating systems can perform checks on the file system on an ongoing basis. These tools are discussed in more detail later in this chapter.

Partitions

Before a file system can be placed on a hard disk, the disk must be partitioned and formatted. **Partitioning** is the process of blocking a group of tracks and sectors to be used by a particular file system, such as FAT or NTFS. After a disk is partitioned, it must be **high-level formatted** (usually referred to as just formatted) so that the partition contains the disk divisions and patterns needed by a particular operating system to store files. With today's technology creating disks with more capacity, and as disks are used in more diverse applications, sometimes it is desirable to have more than one file system on a single disk, which is accomplished by having a partition for each file system. You might need multiple file systems to allow the installation of Windows 98 alongside Windows 2000 or XP, or to install Red Hat Linux and Windows 2000 on the same computer, for example. Multiple operating systems may be required on a single system to accommodate various applications.

When you want to have multiple file systems on one disk, you can partition the disk so that different file systems can be installed on different disk partitions. You can also create partitions in one operating system to segment a drive into multiple logical volumes to which you can assign distinct drive letters. This technique is useful to segment data—in Windows 2000 Server, for example—and necessary when you use older operating systems, such as MS-DOS and Windows 3.1, which don't recognize very large hard drives. Figure 3-5 illustrates a Windows 2000 system that has multiple partitions (FAT, NTFS, and **compact disc file system (CDFS)**) used for segmenting data on two hard disks and a CD-ROM drive.

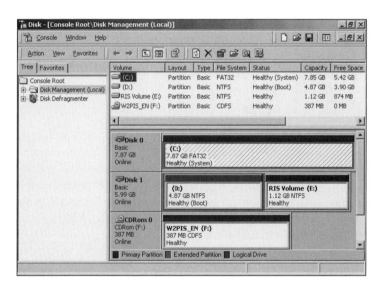

Figure 3-5   Multiple partitions used in one Windows 2000 system

  Partitioning can typically be done only on hard disks or large removable disks. Floppy disks and other low-capacity media do not support partitioning because there simply isn't enough room on these low-capacity disks to make partitioning practical.

The logical programming that creates disk partitions resides at an even lower level than the actual file system, and it lets you divide the disk into "slices." The slices are done at the low-level format portion of the disk, and stored in special sections of the hard drive itself, separate from the operating system. Obviously, the partitioning scheme must be communicated to the operating system and file system. On most disks, there is a separate area that stores the partition information. This area has room to hold information about a set number of partitions. Whenever you create a partition, information about that partition is stored in this special area of the disk. On systems in the IBM/Intel PC hardware architecture, for example, typically there is room to store information for up to four partitions on each disk. This area is known as the **partition table** in MS-DOS, Mac OS, and Windows, and the **disk label** in UNIX. In addition to the disk label and partition table, there is another piece of disk reserved, known as the **boot block** in UNIX, or the **Master Boot Record (MBR)** in MS-DOS and Windows. This area holds a tiny program used to begin booting an operating system from a disk. Try Hands-on Project 3-3 to see how to repair a Master Boot Record or a damaged boot sector in Windows NT or Windows 2000.

Not all operating systems support partitions in the same way, which you will discover in the following sections on file systems for individual operating systems. Each operating system also uses specific utilities to create partitions. When a disk partition is created, the file system is stored inside the partition. The directory structures are then built inside the file system. When files are stored on the disks, they are given some space inside the partition, and data about the files is written in the directory area.

THE BASIC MS-DOS FILE SYSTEM

The first Microsoft file system, called the file allocation table (FAT) file system started with MS-DOS in the early eighties, and later versions of FAT are in many ways similar to the earliest version. Even though the primary focus of this book is not on MS-DOS or Windows 3.x, it is valuable to understand the early MS-DOS and Windows 3.x FAT file system because it provides the basis on which the Windows 95 and Windows 98 FAT file systems are built. Also, several of the early FAT troubleshooting tools, such as Checkdisk (chkdsk) and ScanDisk, are still in use.

FAT uses a file allocation table to store directory information about files, such as filenames, file attributes, and file location. This table structure must be searched in sequential fashion, one entry at a time, whenever users access directories or files. FAT disks contain a series of clusters (called allocation units in later Windows versions) that form a partition. A cluster or allocation unit can consist of two, four, or eight sectors on a disk.

MS-DOS versions prior to 4.0 use the FAT12 file system in which the maximum size of a file system is 32 MB. Beginning with MS-DOS 4.0, the FAT16 file system is used, in which the maximum size of a volume is 4 GB, and the maximum size of a file is 2 GB. The FAT16 file system has been around for a long time, and many computers, even those that do not run MS-DOS, can read disks written in FAT format. Because the file system is simple, there is relatively little that can go wrong, which makes this a stable file system.

3

 It is possible to use the FAT16 file system with Windows 95, Windows 98, Windows NT, Windows 2000, and Windows XP. Many other operating systems support FAT12 and FAT16 as secondary file systems, which means these operating systems are able to read files from and write files to file systems of those types, something very useful when it comes to information exchange. However, using FAT with other operating systems limits the functionality offered by the native file systems of those operating systems.

Another important characteristic of FAT is its use of "8.3" filenames, which can be up to eight characters long, followed by a period and an **extension** of three characters, such as Filename.ext. This convention led to the proliferation of many common three-letter file extensions such as .txt for text files, .doc for word processing files, .xls for Excel spreadsheets, and so on. The limitations of this naming convention contributed to the development of an upgrade of FAT in Windows 95, which supports long filenames (see the section on Windows 95).

Partitioning

The FAT file system supports two partitions per hard drive, a primary partition and a secondary partition. The secondary partition may then be divided further into a maximum of three logical drives (see Figure 3-6). Each of these four possible logical drives can hold an individual MS-DOS file system. Under control of MS-DOS, up to 26 logical drives (pointers to separate file systems), each with its own file system, can be active at one time. A logical drive, remember, is a software definition that divides a physical hard drive into multiple drives for file storage. A floppy disk does not support multiple file systems, since each floppy drive is allocated as one removable file system. Under MS-DOS and Windows, a CD-ROM is always treated as one file system.

 Although 26 drive definitions are technically possible, MS-DOS reserves drives A: and B: for floppy drives, practically limiting the number of hard drives (including logical drives) to 24.

Primary Partition
It is normally active, so the system will boot from this partition.
In most cases, this file system is referred to as drive C:.

Secondary Partition, with logical drives

	First Logical Drive Typically, drive D:
	Second Logical Drive Typically, drive E:
	Third Logical Drive Typically, drive F:

Figure 3-6   Sample MS-DOS partition table structure

Each MS-DOS file system is assigned a letter followed by a colon: A:, B:, C:, and so on through Z:. This design lets you easily address the individual file systems by specifying a drive letter. Letters A: and B: are reserved for two removable file systems on floppy disk drives. Typically, C: is reserved for the first hard disk or removable disk file system (and is normally the system that contains the boot partition). All other file systems located on fixed disks that are controlled by the hard disk drivers in the operating system follow in sequential order. So, an MS-DOS machine with two hard disks with two partitions each will have the drive letters C: for the first partition on the first disk, D: for the second partition on the first disk, E: for the first partition on the second disk, and F: for the second partition on the second disk. Disks that require special drivers, such as CD-ROM drives or removable disks, can be assigned any unused drive letter. By default, they will be assigned the next letter after the drive letter used by the last hard disk. In the example above, a CD-ROM would be drive G:.

In MS-DOS (and in many versions of Windows), a program called *fdisk* is used to modify partition information. The name *fdisk* stands for fixed disk, an alternative name for hard disk. The *fdisk* utility is used to configure the information contained in the partition record.

 Extreme care should be taken when using the *fdisk* utility. If partition information is changed or removed using *fdisk*, all data in the related file system is permanently lost. You may want to consider utilities, like Norton Disk Editor, which allow you to do low-level disk editing and Master Boot Record modification.

If you start a computer in MS-DOS, you can use the *fdisk* utility to look at the contents of the partition record. When the *fdisk* command is issued, a menu appears, as shown in Figure 3-7. For systems that have more than one physical hard disk, there is an additional choice that lets you select a disk other than the default first hard disk.

```
                          FDISK Options

     Current fixed disk drive: 1

     Choose one of the following:

     1. Create DOS partition or Logical DOS Drive
     2. Set active partition
     3. Delete partition or Logical DOS Drive
     4. Display partition information


     Enter choice: [1]




     Press Esc to exit FDISK
```

Figure 3-7   *MS-DOS fdisk utility*

You can choose option 4 from the menu in Figure 3-7 to see what partitions are on the disk. This will give you a short overview, as shown in Figure 3-8.

```
                     Display Partition Information

     Current fixed disk drive: 1

     Partition  Status  Type    Volume Label  Mbytes  System  Usage
       C: 1       A     PRI DOS  BOOTDISK       1914    FAT16   100%


     Total disk space is 1914 Mbytes (1 Mbyte = 1048576 bytes)




     Press Esc to continue
```

Figure 3-8   *fdisk partition information screen*

In the leftmost column, you see the partition number and, if applicable, the drive letter associated with the partition. In the Status column, you see that one partition is marked A, which stands for active. When the computer is started, the BIOS looks at the partition record, finds the **active partition** (the partition currently used to store data, and from which the computer boots), and looks at the file system inside that partition to start the operating system. Only one partition on each disk should be marked active. Next is the Type, a textual representation of the Partition Type ID in the partition record.

The MS-DOS version of *fdisk* recognizes only a very limited number of partition types, namely those used by Microsoft operating systems in existence prior to the creation of the version of *fdisk* used. For example, the *fdisk* in MS-DOS 4.0 does not recognize partitions made with the Windows 98 *fdisk*. Most versions of *fdisk* show both FAT12 and FAT16 partition types as FAT. The **Volume Label** column shows the name of the file system in the partition. The Mbytes column represents the size of the partition in megabytes. System indicates what type of file system is inside the partition (in this example it is FAT). Finally, the Usage column indicates how much of the total available disk space is consumed by the file system.

You can use the other functions of the *fdisk* program to delete or add partitions to the drives in your system. Once again, remove a partition only when you are absolutely sure that is what you want to do. When you remove a partition, all data contained in the file system inside the partition is lost. You may want to remove an existing partition to replace it with another file system, for example, or add a file system to a disk previously configured with a single partition.

To remove a partition, select option 3 from the *fdisk* menu, which presents you with another menu for selecting which partition you wish to remove. You are then led through a series of confirmations before the partition is finally removed. You can change the active partition using option 2. Option 1 gives you the chance to create additional partitions on the disk by answering some questions.

 Using *fdisk* option 2 (changing the active partition) can sometimes be handy to enable booting from a different partition on the disk, but take great care. Setting the active partition incorrectly may make it impossible to boot your computer from the hard disk.

With a new system called **large block allocation (LBA)**, it is now possible to make file systems much larger than 512 MB under MS-DOS. LBA translates larger logical blocks to smaller ones for support of larger physical disks. However, the disk controller and disk must support LBA, and they must be configured for LBA. The trick to LBA is that MS-DOS is told that the sector size of the hard disk is greater than 512 bytes per sector, which results in the ability to have much larger file systems. Try Hands-on Project 3-4 to practice using *fdisk*.

Formatting

After you partition a disk, it is time to place the file system on the partition in a process called formatting. In MS-DOS (and in many Windows versions), the file system is placed on the partition using the *format* command. This command writes all of the file system structure to the disk. In the case of a floppy disk, it uses the first sector of the disk as the boot block. This block contains some information about the disk, such as the number of tracks and the number of sectors per track, in coded form. It can also contain a very small program that enables the computer to start the operating system from a floppy or hard disk, if *format* is used with the /S (system) switch: *format /s*. As with many system-level commands, *format* includes several additional switches that modify precise program

3

operation. You can view a list of these switches by typing *format /?* at the MS-DOS prompt. See Table 3-1 for a list of *format* switches.

Table 3-1   *format* Command Switches

Switch	Function
/V[:label]	Specifies the volume label
/Q	Performs a quick format
/F:size	Specifies the size of the floppy disk to format (such as 160, 180, 320, 360, 720, 1.2, 1.44, 2.88—where the file sizes are in MB or GB)
/B	Allocates space on the formatted disk for system files
/S	Copies system files to the formatted disk
/T:tracks	Specifies the number of tracks per disk side
/N:sectors	Specifies the number of sectors per track
/1	Formats a single side of a floppy disk
/4	Formats a 5.25-inch 360K floppy disk in a high-density drive
/8	Formats eight sectors per track
/C	Tests clusters that are currently marked "bad"

Command lines frequently use **switches** (extra codes) to change the way a particular command operates. In many operating systems, these extra commands follow a forward slash and take the form of a letter, or combination of letters, such as the *dir* command in MS-DOS, which can take several switches or arguments, including */p* (pause when the screen is full) and */s* (include subdirectories).

The boot block is placed in the first sector on the disk. Next comes the root directory, where the system stores file information, such as name, start cluster, file size, file modification date and time, and **file attributes** (file characteristics such as Hidden, Read-only, Archive, and so on). The root directory on every partition is a fixed size that can contain a maximum of 512 entries in FAT16 (and unlimited entries in FAT32). Behind this root directory are two copies of the file allocation table (FAT). The FAT on a floppy disk consists of several 12-bit entries. Each entry corresponds with a cluster address on the disk. When the file system performs its format operation, it divides the disk into clusters that are sequentially numbered. In the case of a floppy disk, each cluster corresponds to a sector on the disk. Each of the two copies of the FAT has exactly one entry for each cluster.

When a file is stored to disk, its data is written in the clusters on the disk. The filename is stored in the directory, along with the number of the first cluster in which the data is stored. When the operating system fills the first cluster, data is written to the next free cluster on the disk. The FAT entry corresponding with the first cluster is filled with the number of the second cluster in the file. When the second cluster is full, the operating system continues to write in the next free cluster. The FAT entry for the second cluster is set to point to the cluster number for the third cluster, and so on. When a file is completely written to the disk, the FAT entry for the final cluster is filled with all 1s, which means end of file. At this time, the directory entry for the file is updated with the total file size. This is commonly referred to as the "**linked-list**" method.

Clusters are of a fixed length, and if a file does not exactly match the space available in the clusters it uses, you can end up with some unused space at the end of a cluster. This is a little wasteful, and it also explains why a file's directory entry must include the exact file size. The operating system sets all FAT entries to 0s when it formats the disk, indicating that none of the clusters is being used. When you write a file to disk, the operating system finds free space on the disk by simply looking for the next FAT entry that contains all 0s. In most cases, the *format* command reads every address on the disk to make sure they are usable. Unusable spots are marked in the FAT as **bad clusters**, and these areas are never used for file storage. It then writes a new root directory and file allocation table, and the disk is ready for use.

Formatting a disk removes all data that was on the disk because you lost the directory and FAT data needed to get to the data. On disks that have never been formatted, the *format* command writes new sector and track markers on the disk. On disks used previously, you can use the */q* (Quick Format) option. This tells *format* to dispense with the disk check, and simply write a new root directory and FAT table. This makes the format operation a lot faster, obviously, but it also skips the detailed checking of the disk, which can cause trouble later if an application tries to write information to a bad disk location.

The format process on a hard disk is the same as on a floppy disk, with two exceptions. The first is related to the size of each entry in the FAT table, which is 16 bits long on any disk larger than 16 MB. The second difference is in the cluster size. On a floppy disk, there are very few sectors, and there are enough FAT entries to use a cluster size of one sector per cluster. On a hard disk, several sectors are combined into a cluster. Exactly how many sectors per cluster depends on the size of the hard disk, as shown in Table 3-2.

Table 3-2   Hard Disk Cluster Reference

Partition Size	Sectors per Cluster	Cluster Size
0–32 MB	1	512 bytes
32–64 MB	2	1 KB
63–128 MB	4	2 KB
128–256 MB	8	4 KB
256–512 MB	16	8 KB
512 MB–1 GB	32	16 KB
1 GB–2 GB	64	32 KB
2 GB–4 GB	128	64 KB

The largest possible partition in a FAT file system is 4 GB. Keep in mind that the smallest allocation unit is one cluster. If you store a file that is 300 bytes long on a file system that has clusters of 64 KB, you will waste a lot of space. It is for this reason that smaller cluster sizes are generally considered desirable. As a result, Windows or MS-DOS systems using FAT with large hard disks frequently have many hard disk partitions.

Each partition stores two copies of the FAT table as a backup in case one of the copies gets damaged. However, there is only one copy of the root directory on each partition. This concept is shown in Figure 3-9.

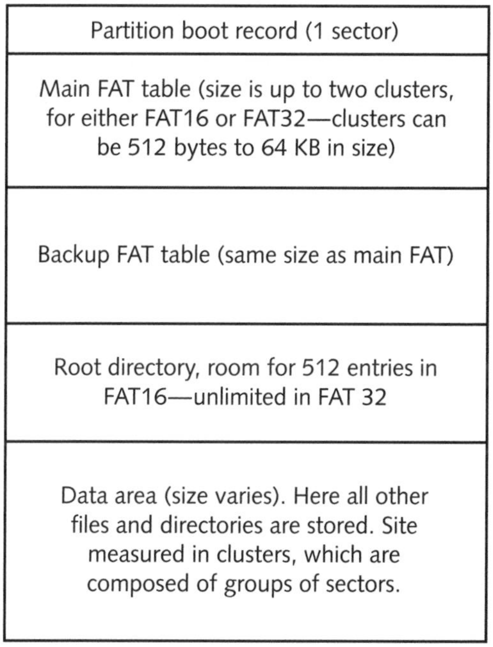

```
┌──────────────────────────────────────────┐
│     Partition boot record (1 sector)      │
├──────────────────────────────────────────┤
│  Main FAT table (size is up to two clusters,│
│  for either FAT16 or FAT32—clusters can    │
│       be 512 bytes to 64 KB in size)       │
│                                            │
├──────────────────────────────────────────┤
│                                            │
│  Backup FAT table (same size as main FAT)  │
│                                            │
├──────────────────────────────────────────┤
│                                            │
│  Root directory, room for 512 entries in   │
│         FAT16—unlimited in FAT 32          │
│                                            │
├──────────────────────────────────────────┤
│                                            │
│  Data area (size varies). Here all other   │
│  files and directories are stored. Site    │
│     measured in clusters, which are        │
│   composed of groups of sectors.           │
│                                            │
└──────────────────────────────────────────┘
```

Figure 3-9 Typical FAT directory structure

The FAT tables and root directory are found at the beginning of each partition, and they are always at the same location. This makes it possible for the boot program in MS-DOS to easily find the files needed to start the operating system. Other directories in the file system are specialized files. They are identical to any other file in the operating system, with the exception of having the directory attribute set in their own directory entry. There can be a virtually unlimited number of directories, with a virtually unlimited number of files in each.

The FAT directory structure is simple. Each item in a directory consists of 32 bytes. In each entry, information about the file is stored, including the filename, the file change date and time, the file size and the file attributes. As mentioned earlier, the filename consists of two parts: the name, which can be up to eight characters long; and the extension, which contains up to three characters. All letters in filenames are stored in uppercase, and the operating system treats all uppercase and lowercase letters as if they were all uppercase. In other words, the file named FILE.TXT is identical to the file named file.txt. Extensions can have a special meaning. Files with a .sys extension are generally device drivers; files with .com or .exe extensions are program files the operating system can execute; and files with the .bat extension are batch files of commands that can be executed as if they were typed on the keyboard. The filename and extension cannot contain spaces, and they are separated by a period.

Apart from the filename, each directory entry also contains some **status bits** that identify the type of filename contained in each entry. The status bits in use are Volume, Directory, System, Hidden, Read-only, and Archive. The Volume bit indicates a file system volume label, or a nickname for the file system. The volume name can be set with the */v* option of the *format* command, or by using the *volume* command. The volume name appears at the top of MS-DOS directory listings (using the *dir* command), in the Windows 3.1 File Manager, and in *fdisk* listings. The Directory bit is used to signify that a file contains directory data, and should as such be treated as a directory by the file system. Directories may in turn contain directories, as long as the names of all directories in a path do not exceed 80 characters. You will see a directory clearly marked with a <DIR> label when you look at a directory listing in MS-DOS, or with a file folder icon in Windows. The four remaining attributes indicate additional information about a file. Files that are part of the operating system and should not be touched by programs or users are marked with a System or *S* flag. Files that should not be visible to the user are known as Hidden files and marked with the *H* bit. Files that should not be written to are known as Read-only files and marked with the *R* flag. Lastly, files that should be backed up the next time a backup is made are said to have the Archive, or *A* flag, set.

All in all, there are four optional flags—*H, S, R,* and *A*. The *attrib* command can be used to look at or set these attributes. Typing *attrib* in a directory shows all of the attribute settings for all the files, whereas typing *attrib* followed by a filename shows only attributes specific to that file. The *attrib* command can also be used to set file attributes. To do this, the *attrib* command is followed by the attribute letter, the + sign to set, or the − sign to unset an attribute, and the filename in question. To make a file named test.txt hidden, for example, you would type *attrib h*+ test.txt. If you then typed *dir*, you would not see the test.txt file, but if you typed *attrib* test.txt, you would once again see test.txt, with the letter *H* in front of it, letting you know it is a Hidden file. A file with the *S* attribute set also does not show in directory listings, but you can view it with the *attrib* command, and you can remove the System attribute with *attrib* as well. Table 3-3 shows the various arguments and switches you can use with the *attrib* command.

Table 3-3   Attribute Command (*attrib*) Arguments and Switches

Argument/Switch	Description
R	Read-only file attribute
A	Archive file attribute
S	System file attribute
H	Hidden file attribute
/S	Processes files in all directories in the specified path

The Windows 95/98/Me FAT File Systems

The Windows 95, Windows 98, and Windows Me file systems are in many ways the same as the MS-DOS and Windows 3.x FAT file system. There are two versions of FAT that can be used with Windows 95, 98, and Me, depending on the version of Windows you are running, and the size of the disk you are using:

- FAT16, similar to the system used in MS-DOS/Win 3.x

- FAT32, a new system introduced in Windows 95, release 2 (OSR2)

Both FAT16 for Windows 95/98/Me and FAT32 have features in common with the MS-DOS version of the FAT16 file system, and some new features.

Windows 95/98/Me FAT16

The way the disk is organized is identical in both the Windows 95 and MS-DOS file systems. In Windows 95, as in MS-DOS and Windows 3.1, there is a Master Boot Record, followed by two FAT tables and a root directory. The function of the FAT tables and the root directory is the same as it is in the MS-DOS file system. However, in Windows 95, there is support for **long filenames (LFNs)**. A filename in the Windows 95 file system:

- Can contain as many as 255 characters

- Is not case sensitive

- Cannot include spaces and characters such as " / \ [ ] : ; = , (this applies to both 8.3 filenames and LFNs)

However, compatibility with the 8.3 naming convention of the MS-DOS file system is maintained. This is done through a clever trick with directory entries, which allows them to be converted into 8.3 equivalents. The first of the directory entries looks just like an MS-DOS directory entry, except in place of the filename, there is an abbreviated filename. This filename is obtained by taking the first six characters of the old filename, adding a tilde (~), and a number or letter behind it, such as the 8.3 name CIRC09~.TXT for the LFN circ09Copyright.txt. This process is performed automatically by the Windows 95 operating system when a file is written to the disk.

Since LFN characters are stored in **Unicode**, a coding system that allows for representation of any character in any language, it is possible to use any character known to Windows in a filename. The advantage of LFNs and Unicode is that LFNs can be read by Mac OS and UNIX systems (such as on a Windows 2000 server that has file services installed for Mac OS and UNIX clients).

Normally, letters and digits are represented by ASCII (American Standard Code for Information Interchange, pronounced "as-key") values. The problem with this standard is that it uses an entire byte to represent each character, which limits the number of characters that can be represented to 255. This is not enough to handle all the characters needed to represent world languages, including several different alphabets (Greek,

Russian, Japanese, and Hindi, for example). ASCII deals with this problem by employing many different character sets, depending on the characters you're trying to represent. The Unicode Consortium, a not-for-profit organization, represents an alternative in which there is a single, unique code for each possible character in any language. Unicode is a 16-bit code that allots two bytes for each character, which allows 65,536 characters to be defined. It includes distinct character codes for all modern languages. To the user who communicates primarily in English, Unicode will not make a big difference, but in this age of worldwide communication, it is becoming a necessity.

The filename directory entries are visible to older operating systems, such as MS-DOS and Windows 3.x, when they look at a Windows 95 directory, since the attribute bits for Volume, Read-only, System, and Hidden are set, a combination normally ignored by other operating systems. This is a pretty neat trick because it allows for the use of LFNs, while still maintaining compatibility with older versions of the operating system.

 Long filenames should be used and manipulated only with utilities that support LFN. MS-DOS and Windows 3.x utilities that support only 8.3 filenames can destroy LFN information, leaving only the 8.3 equivalents. This also happens if you move files with an older MS-DOS utility, such as an archiving utility. Only the short filenames will appear in the archive. This is one of the common problems with files on disks that are swapped between machines that run Windows 95/98/Me and Windows 3.x.

Two advantages of FAT16 are that, like FAT12, it is a simple file system supported by many small computer operating systems, and it has a low operating system overhead. The disadvantages are that FAT16 becomes corrupted over time as files are spread among disjointed allocation units (clusters) and pointers to each unit are lost, and FAT16 does not offer many file or directory security or auditing options.

FAT32

To accommodate the increasing capacities of hard disks, and avoid the problem of cluster size (the minimum increment of disk space that can be allocated), the second release of Windows 95 (OSR2) introduced an improved FAT file system called FAT32. FAT32 shares characteristics of FAT16 for Windows 95 (the way the disk is organized with the double FAT structure at the beginning of the disk, followed by a fixed main directory; use of LFNs; and Unicode). FAT32, however, allows partitions of up to 2 TB (theoretically); blocks can be allocated with clusters as small as 8 KB, and the maximum file size is raised to 4 GB.

 To determine which version of Windows 95 you are running, go to the Start menu, select Settings, click Control Panel, then select the System icon. On the General tab, you will see a System heading. The second line tells you what version you have. Earlier releases have a version number of 4.xxxx, which does not end in a B. If the version number ends in OEM-B, B, OSR-2, or –2, you have the newer OSR2, released on or after August 24, 1998. The latter version supports FAT32, whereas earlier releases do not.

FAT32 works by using many bits per FAT allocation unit, and is therefore incompatible with other operating systems such as MS-DOS and Windows NT. However, it is compatible with Windows 2000 and XP.

You can choose the FAT32 file system when the Windows 95/98 *fdisk* utility is run, but unfortunately, the utility does not simply ask if you wish to use FAT32. Instead, you are told that the computer contains a disk larger than 512 MB, and you are asked if you would like to use the large disk support (see Figure 3-10). In Windows 98, you can convert a drive to FAT32 from the Start menu by selecting Start, pointing to Programs, pointing to Accessories, pointing to System Tools, and then clicking Drive Converter (FAT32).

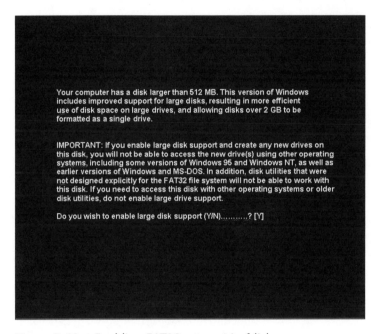

Figure 3-10   Enabling FAT32 support in *fdisk*

 DO NOT use FAT32 if you plan to access your hard disk from MS-DOS or Windows NT because it is not compatible with these systems. Use FAT16 instead. Also, do not convert to FAT32 if your drive is compressed, or you plan to compress the drive. If you do convert to FAT32, make a good backup first.

Windows 95/98/Me File System Utilities

The *fdisk* and *format* utilities in Windows 95, 98, and Me work identically to those in MS-DOS. There are now also graphical equivalents of these tools that you can launch from the Windows user environment, such as the Windows 95 *format* tool shown in Figure 3-11.

Although these graphical tools can be used in most cases, during initial installation and sometimes after a system crash, you must use the command-line or non-graphical versions.

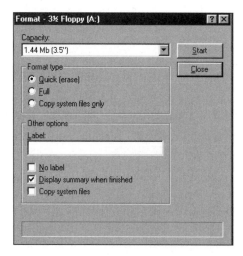

Figure 3-11 Windows 95 *format* utility

 The *format* and other MS-DOS-compliant utilities are accessed in Windows using the MS-DOS prompt (click Start, point to Programs, and click MS-DOS Prompt), and entering the filename of the utility, such as *format*.

Sometimes disk performance is affected by corrupted files, or when the file allocation table loses pointers to certain files. You can correct these problems in Windows 95 and maintain the integrity of the data by periodically running the "Checkdisk" utility, called *chkdsk*, by clicking Start, clicking Run, entering *chkdsk*, and clicking OK (or enter *chkdsk* in the MS-DOS Prompt window). In Windows 95, *chkdsk* checks the file allocation table, folders, files, disk sectors, disk allocation units, user files, and hidden files. If *chkdsk* finds any problems, it displays an error message. You then have the option of letting it fix such problems by using the */f*, or Fix option. Table 3-4 lists the switches associated with this command. The most common problems are files with 0 sizes, caused when a file is not properly closed; or chains of clusters (file allocation units) that have no directory entries attached. When *chkdsk* finds lost allocation units or chains, it prompts you with a yes or no question: Convert lost chains to files? Answer "yes" to the question so that you can save the lost information to files. The files that *chkdsk* creates for each lost chain are labeled Filexxx.chk, and can be edited with a text editor, such as Microsoft Word, to determine their contents. The presence of some bad sectors is normal.

 Many disks have a few bad sectors that are marked by the manufacturer during the low-level format, on which data cannot be written.

Table 3-4   Chkdsk Switch Options

Switch/Parameter	Purpose
[volume] (such as C:)	Specifies that *chkdsk* only checks the designated volume
[filename] (such as *.dll)	Enables a check of the specified file or files only
/F	Instructs *chkdsk* to fix errors that it finds, and locks the disk while checking
/V	Shows the entire path name of files

When you run *chkdsk* in Windows 98 and Windows Me, the utility does not perform a true disk check, but instead reports information about the volume serial number, total disk space, free disk space, distribution of allocation units, and lower memory allocation (under 640 KB). Instead of checking the disk, it recommends that you run the ScanDisk utility. Hands-on Project 3-5 lets you try the *chkdsk* utility.

ScanDisk is another disk checking utility, but it is a little more advanced. It has a nicer, menu-driven user interface, and it can do a surface scan to determine whether you have media problems on a disk. ScanDisk can also copy to another disk the files it is about to manipulate, a useful precautionary step to avoid inadvertently losing files or data. To launch ScanDisk, click Start, point to Programs, point to System Tools, and click ScanDisk. Select the drive to scan, and click Start (see Figure 3-12). Try Hands-on Project 3-5 to practice using ScanDisk.

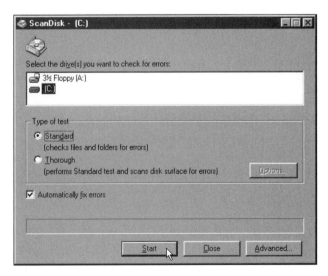

Figure 3-12   Starting ScanDisk

If you find that you frequently see errors when you run either *chkdsk* or ScanDisk, you should look for a bigger problem. Many times the operator is to blame. Systems that are not used properly—for example, because software is not closed correctly—can cause problems in the file system. Often, disks that are about to fail will show small glitches (such as ScanDisk or *chkdsk* errors) a long time before they finally fail, so be alert for possible future system failure if you see frequent errors.

Windows 95/98/Me includes the capability to create compressed disk volumes. When this option is used, a special device driver is loaded to compress data as it is written to the disk, and uncompress it as it is read. Disk compression was originally introduced in MS-DOS, during a time when hard disks were much more expensive and smaller than today.

The use of disk compression is not recommended. If something goes wrong, tools such as ScanDisk cannot be used effectively on compressed volumes, and there have been many problems with compressed volumes that resulted in loss of data.

Windows 95, 98, and Me also have a built-in disk defragmenting tool. When one of these operating systems writes a file to disk, it looks for the first place in the first empty FAT location and uses the cluster (allocation unit) indicated there. It continues to use the next empty cluster until there are no more clusters free immediately following the last cluster. At that point, it skips ahead to find the next open cluster. As a result, files written to disk may be scattered all over the disk. Imagine a scenario where four small files are written—we'll call them A, B, C, and D. On an empty disk, these files will occupy sequential clusters on the disk. If files A and C are removed, there will be some open clusters on the disk. If file E, which is larger than A and C combined, is written to the disk, it will start using the clusters formerly occupied by A, then use those formerly used by C, and then continue beyond the clusters occupied by D.

To start the disk defragmenter, click Start, point to Programs, point to Accessories, point to System Tools, and click Disk Defragmenter. The Disk Defragmenter can also be automatically started using the Scheduled Tasks tool. Figure 3-13 shows the Disk Defragmenter at work in Windows 98. In general, it is wise to defragment disks once a month for medium-use systems, and once a week for high-use systems. Defragmenting the disks yields better operating system response and extends the life of the disks.

It is VERY IMPORTANT that no other programs are running while the Disk Defragmenter program is running. Windows 95/98/Me is a multitasking operating system, and if any other program (including your screen saver or Solitaire) tries to access the disk while the Disk Defragmenter is running, the defrag process will restart from the beginning.

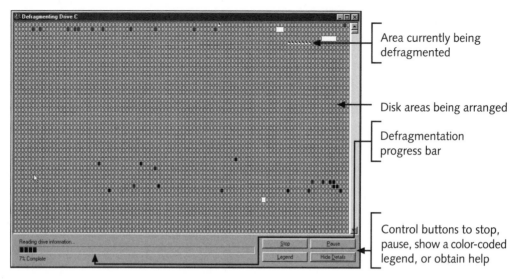

Area currently being defragmented

Disk areas being arranged

Defragmentation progress bar

Control buttons to stop, pause, show a color-coded legend, or obtain help

Figure 3-13   Windows 98 Disk Defragmenter

THE WINDOWS NT/2000/XP/.NET FILE SYSTEMS

Windows NT supports two types of file systems: the extended FAT16 system used by Windows 95, and the NTFS up through version 4 (for Windows NT 4.0). Windows 2000, XP, and .NET Server support extended FAT16, FAT32, and NTFS version 5. Also, Windows NT, 2000, XP, and .NET Server support file systems that enable use of CD-ROM drives.

Extended FAT16

The extended FAT16 file system under Windows NT/2000/XP/.NET has the same functionality as the FAT16 system under Windows 95, and it is possible to have multiple operating systems on one disk (called dual-boot or multiboot systems) with the FAT16 file system. For example, both Windows 2000 and Windows 98 can be on the same computer with options to select either operating system at boot time. In addition to all the features of FAT16 mentioned when we discussed the MS-DOS and Windows 95 file systems, FAT16 under Windows NT uses a few more bytes in the directory entry to store additional information. Besides the last modified date of a file, Windows NT/2000/XP/.NET tracks the file creation date and the last time a file was accessed. This data is simply ignored by MS-DOS and other operating systems using the directory entries, but Windows NT/2000/XP/.NET programs that are POSIX-compliant can access this data. **POSIX** stands for **Portable Operating System Interface**, a set of standards designed to guarantee portability of applications among different operating systems.

FAT32

Windows 2000, XP, and .NET Server all support FAT32, which is the same file system that is used in Windows 95 OSR2, Windows 98, and Windows Me. Sometimes users choose to employ FAT16 or FAT32 because they are familiar with these file systems, or they have dual-boot systems, such as a system with Windows XP and Windows 98. Another reason for using FAT16 or FAT32 is that these systems offer fast response on small 1 or 2 GB partitions.

 Sometimes Windows NT/2000/XP users create two partitions, one for FAT and one for NTFS. The FAT partition is relatively small, between 1 and 2 GB, and contains the system directory, \Winnt. Program and data files are kept on the larger NTFS partition. In this way, the FAT partition enables fast response for the system files, and the NTFS partition affords reliability and security for the application and data files.

Any Windows NT, 2000, XP, or .NET Server system can be converted from FAT16 or FAT32 to NTFS, either during installation or at a later date. If you convert at a later date, use the *convert* command at the command prompt. However, you cannot convert from NTFS to FAT16 or FAT32, except by reformatting to use FAT16 or FAT32 and then performing a full file restore.

 Converting from FAT16 or FAT32 to NTFS can take many hours on a volume that is over 1 GB, and the conversion process may appear hung, even though it is not. Thus, give any conversion a day or more to complete, and do not interrupt it by powering off the computer in the middle of the process.

 If a partition is set up for FAT, and is 2 GB or smaller, Windows 2000, XP, and .NET Server will format it as FAT16 during installation (if the option to use FAT is selected). Partitions that are over 2 GB are formatted as FAT32.

NTFS

New Technology File System (NTFS) is the native Windows NT/2000/XP/.NET file system, a modern system designed for the needs of a networked environment. Three important advantages of NTFS compared to FAT16 and FAT32 are:

- Ability to compress file and directory contents on the fly

- Better recoverability and stability

- Less disk fragmentation

- Local file and folder-level security

Windows NT 4.0 uses NTFS version 4 (NTFS 4), and Windows 2000, XP, and .NET Server use NTFS 5. The Windows NT Service Pack 4 update for Windows NT 4.0

provides an add-on that enables the operating system to read partitions that are formatted for NTFS 5. The basic features initially incorporated into NTFS 4 include:

- Long filenames
- Built-in security features
- Better file compression than FAT
- Ability to use larger disks and files
- File activity tracking for better recovery and stability than FAT
- POSIX support
- Volume striping and volume extensions
- Less disk fragmentation than FAT

NTFS enables the use of LFNs that are compatible with LFN FAT filenames. If an LFN is used in NTFS, that file can be copied to a FAT16 or FAT32 volume, and the filename remains intact (although the NTFS security permissions not supported in FAT16 or FAT32 are not carried over).

As a full-featured network file system, NTFS is equipped with security features that meet the U.S. government's C2 security specifications. C2 security refers to high-level, "top-secret" standards for data protection, system auditing, and system access, which are required by some government agencies. One security feature is the ability to establish the type of access allowed for users of folders and files within folders. The file and folder access can be tailored to the particular requirements of an organization. For example, the system files on a server can be protected so only the server administrator has access. A folder of databases can be protected with read access, but no access to change data; and a public folder can give users in a designated group access to read and update files, but not to delete files.

File compression is a process that significantly reduces the size of a file by removing unused space within a file, or using compression algorithms. Some files can be compressed by more than 40%, saving important disk space for other storage needs. This is particularly useful for files that are accessed infrequently. NTFS provides the ability to compress files as needed. Try Hands-on Project 3-6 to compress files in Windows 2000.

NTFS can be scaled to accommodate very large files, particularly for database applications. A Microsoft SQL Server database file might be 20 GB or larger, for example. This means an organization can store pictures, scanned images, and sound clips in a single database. The NTFS system can support files up to 2^{64} bytes (in theory).

Another NTFS feature is its ability to keep a log or journal of file system activity. This is a critical process should there be a power outage or hard disk failure. Important information can be retrieved and restored in these situations. FAT does not offer this capability.

NTFS supports POSIX standards to enable portability of applications from one computer system to another. Windows 2000 follows the POSIX 1 standard, which includes case-sensitive filenames and use of multiple filenames (called hard links, a concept discussed later in this chapter). For example, the files Myfile.doc and MYFile.doc are considered different files (except when using Windows Explorer or the Command Prompt window).

An important volume-handling feature of NTFS is the ability to create extensions on an existing volume, such as when new disk storage is added. Another feature is the ability to stripe volumes, which is a process that equally divides the contents of each file across two or more volumes to extend disk life, enable fault tolerance features, and balance the disk load for better performance.

Last, NTFS is less prone to file corruption than FAT, in part because it has a "hot fix" capability, which means that if a bad disk area is detected, NTFS automatically copies the information from the bad area to another disk area that is not damaged.

In addition to the NTFS 4 features already described, NTFS 5 adds several new features:

- Ability to encrypt files
- No system reboot required after creating an extended volume
- Ability to reduce drive designations
- Indexing for fast access
- Ability to retain shortcuts and other file information when files and folders are placed on other volumes
- Ability to establish disk quotas

With NTFS 5, files can be encrypted so that their contents are available only to those granted access. Also, volume extensions can be set up without the need to reboot the system (in NTFS 4 you must reboot after adding an extension onto an existing volume). Volume mount points can be created as a way to reduce the number of drive designations for multiple volumes, instead of designating a new drive for each new volume. NTFS 5 incorporates fast indexing in conjunction with Active Directory to make file searching and retrieval faster than in NTFS 4. A new technique called **Distributed Link Tracking** is available in NTFS 5 so that shortcuts you have created are not lost when you move files to another volume. Finally, NTFS 5 enables you to set up disk quotas to control how much disk space users can occupy. Disk quotas are a vital tool for disk capacity planning, to ensure that there is enough disk space for all server operations and critical files.

NTFS 4 does not have built-in disk quota capabilities, but third-party software is available to set up disk quotas.

3

The way NTFS keeps track of files and clusters is a little different from the FAT file systems. Rather than using a structure of FAT tables and directories, NTFS uses a **Master File Table (MFT)**. Like the FAT tables and directories, this table is located at the beginning of the partition. The boot sector is located ahead of the MFT, just as it is in the FAT system. Following the MFT, there are several system files that the file system uses to make all the features of NTFS work. Note that the MFT in itself is nothing more than a file on the file system, as are all other system files. The second file on the disk is a copy of the first three records of the MFT. This ensures that if the MFT is damaged, it can be re-created. File number five, known as $, contains the entries in the root directory, whereas file number six, known as $Bitmap, contains data about what clusters on the disk are in use. Normally, the MFT and related files take up about 1 MB of disk space when the disk is initially formatted. As you can see, this would make it impractical to use NTFS on floppy disks. It is therefore not possible to format floppy disks in NTFS format.

When a file is made in NTFS, a record for that file is added to the MFT. This record contains all standard information, such as filename, size, dates, and timestamps. It also contains additional attributes, such as security settings, ownership, and permissions. If there is not enough room in an MFT record to store security settings, the settings that don't fit are put on another cluster somewhere on the disk, and the MFT record points to this information. If a file is very small, there is sometimes enough room in the MFT record to store the file data. If there is not enough room, the system allocates clusters elsewhere on the disk. The MFT record reflects the sequence of clusters that a file uses. The attributes can generally be repeated; it is possible to have a whole series of different security attributes for different users. It also is possible to have multiple filenames that refer to the same file, a technique known as **hard linking**. This is a feature, also available in UNIX file systems, sometimes used to make the same file appear in multiple directories without having to allocate disk space for the file more than once. Table 3-5 provides a comparison of the most frequently used Microsoft file systems—FAT16, FAT32, and NTFS.

Table 3-5   FAT16, FAT32, and NTFS Compared

Feature	FAT16	FAT32	NTFS
Total volume size	4 GB	2 GB to 2 TB	2 TB
Maximum file size	2 GB	4 GB	Theoretical limit of 2^{64} bytes
Compatible with floppy disks	Yes	Yes	No
Security	Limited security based on attributes and shares	Limited security based on attributes and shares	C2-rated extensive security and auditing options
File compression	Supported with extra utilities	Supported with extra utilities	Supported as part of NTFS

Table 3-5   FAT16, FAT32, and NTFS Compared (continued)

Feature	FAT16	FAT32	NTFS
File activity tracking	None	None	Tracking via a log
POSIX support	None	Limited	POSIX.1 support
Hot fix	Limited	Limited	Supports hot fix
Large database support	Limited	Yes	Yes
Multiple disk drives in one volume	No	No	Yes

NTFS Utilities

Windows NT, 2000, XP, and .NET Server all come with the *chkdsk* utility, which is much more robust than in other Windows operating systems. Because *chkdsk* is more robust, these operating systems do not come with ScanDisk. *Chkdsk*, which starts the same way as in Windows 95/98/Me, can detect and fix an extensive set of file system problems in either FAT or NTFS systems. Table 3-6 presents a list of the switches that are available for this utility.

Table 3-6   Chkdsk Switch Options

Switch/Parameter	Purpose
[volume] (such as C:)	Specifies that *chkdsk* only check the designated volume
[filename] (such as *.dll)	Enables a check of the specified file or files only
/c	For NTFS only, *chkdsk* uses an abbreviated check of the folder structure
/f	Instructs *chkdsk* to fix errors that it finds, and locks the disk while checking
/i	For NTFS only, *chkdsk* uses an abbreviated check of indexes
/L:size	For NTFS only, enables you to specify the size of the log file created by the disk check
/r	Searches for bad sectors, fixes problems, and recovers information (if possible, or use the *recover* command afterwards)
/v	On FAT, shows the entire path name of files; on NTFS, shows clean-up messages associated with errors
/x	Dismounts or locks a volume before starting (/f also dismounts or locks a volume)

In Windows NT/2000/XP/.NET, *chkdsk* runs automatically at boot up if it detects that the operating system was previously shut down with a file system problem, or shut down before the operating system had the opportunity to clean up temporary files on the disk. Try Hands-on Project 3-8 to practice running *chkdsk* automatically.

3

Windows NT does not come with a disk defragmenter tool, so this must be purchased from a third-party vendor. Windows 2000, XP, and .NET Server all have Disk Defragmenter, which is initiated by clicking Start, pointing to Programs, pointing to Accessories, and clicking Disk Defragmenter. The Disk Defragmenter in Windows 2000, XP, and .NET can be used on volumes formatted for FAT16, FAT32, and NTFS.

Windows XP and Windows .NET Server both come with a Disk Cleanup utility that deletes temporary Internet files, temporary program files, program files that are not used, and files in the Recycle Bin. To start this utility, click Start, point to All Programs, point to Accessories, point to System Tools, and click Disk Cleanup.

 Care should be taken to use only utilities designed to work with NTFS; serious damage can occur if other utilities are used. If utilities designed for Windows 95/98/Me are used on NTFS file systems, they may reach incorrect conclusions regarding file system layout. As a result, they may actually destroy data by managing the file system as if it were a FAT system. This can result in loss of data, damaged files, or even destruction of the complete file system and all of its contents.

 When you copy a file from an NTFS system to a FAT16 or FAT32 system, the security permissions of the file that are not supported in FAT16 or FAT32 are lost. This may not sound like a big deal, but if you consider that all security settings to a confidential payroll spreadsheet can be lost by copying it to a temporary file on another partition, and then back to the NTFS partition, you may change your mind.

When you upgrade Windows NT Server 4.0 to Windows 2000 or Windows .NET, the current NTFS disk partitions are automatically converted to *basic* disks, which use traditional NTFS disk management techniques, with a limited number of volumes on one disk. Windows 2000 Server introduces the use of *dynamic* disks, a partitioning design that means there is no restriction on the number of volumes that can be set up on one physical disk. You can convert basic disks to dynamic disks by using the Disk Management tool. To access this tool in Windows 2000 Server, for example, click Start, point to Programs, point to Administrative Tools, and click Computer Management.

CDFS And UDF

Windows NT, 2000, XP, and .NET Server recognize two additional file systems used by peripheral storage technologies. The compact disc file system (CDFS) is supported so that these operating systems can read and write files to CD-ROM disk drives. CD-ROM capability is important for loading the operating systems, and sharing CD-ROM drives on a network. The **Universal Disk Format (UDF)** file system is also used on CD-ROM and large capacity **Digital Video Disc – Read Only Memory (DVD-ROM)** media, which are used for huge file storage to accommodate movies and games.

THE UNIX FILE SYSTEM

The UNIX file system works a little differently from anything discussed up to this point. "UNIX file system" is really a misnomer. There are, in reality, many different file systems that can be used, but some file systems are more "native" to specific UNIX operating systems than others. In Linux, for instance, the **extended file system (ext or ext fs)** is native and installed by default. Ext provides an advantage over all other file systems that can be used with Linux because it enables the use of the full range of built-in Linux commands, file manipulation, and security. If you are not sure what file systems are incorporated in UNIX, you can determine them by viewing the contents of the /proc/filesystems file, for example. Table 3-7 lists file systems that are compatible with UNIX systems. Also, try Hands-on Project 3-7 to determine what file systems are loaded in a Linux installation.

Newer Linux versions use the updated version of the extended file system, called the second extended file system (ext2). Also, Red Hat Linux 7.2 introduces ext3, which offers journaling. Journaling means that certain file changes are automatically backed up in a journal file.

The main difference between native UNIX file systems, such as ext3 and ufs, and those covered earlier in the chapter, lies in the way information is physically stored on the disk. The most popular file system across UNIX platforms is ufs, which we will detail here.

Table 3-7   File Systems Supported by UNIX

File system	Description
Extended file system (ext or ext fs) and the newer versions, second extended file system (ext2 or ext2 fs), and third extended file system (ext 3)	File system that comes with Linux by default (compatible with Linux and FreeBSD)
High-performance file system (hpfs)	File system developed for use with the OS/2 operating system
msdos	File system that offers compatibility with FAT12 and FAT16 (does not support long filenames); typically installed to enable UNIX to read floppy disks made in MS-DOS or Windows
International Standard Operating system (iso9660 in Linux, hsfs in Solaris, cd9660 in FreeBSD)	File system developed for CD-ROM use; does not support long filenames
Proc file system	File system that presents information about the kernel status and the use of memory (not truly a physical file system, but a logical file system)

Table 3-7   File Systems Supported by UNIX (continued)

File system	Description
Network file system (NFS)	File system developed by Sun Microsystems for UNIX systems to support network access and sharing of files (such as uploading and downloading files)
Swap file system	File system for the swap space; swap space is disk space used exclusively to store spillover information from memory, when memory is full (called virtual memory)
UNIX file system (ufs; also called the Berkeley Fast File System)	File system that is compatible with all UNIX systems
UmsMS/DOS	File system that is compatible with extended FAT16 as used by Windows NT, 2000, and XP, but it also supports security permissions, file ownership, and long filenames
Vfat	File system that is compatible with FAT32, and supports long filenames

The **ufs** UNIX file system (and also ext/ext2/ext3) uses the concept of **information nodes**, or **inodes**. This concept is shown in Figure 3-14.

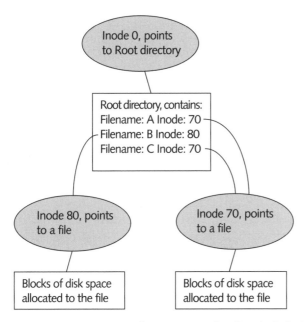

Figure 3-14   UNIX information nodes (inodes) design

Each inode can store some information about a file on the file system. The information stored on an inode identifies: the inode number, the owner of the file, the group in which the file is placed, the size of the file, the date the file was created, the date the file was last modified and read, the number of links to this inode, and information regarding the location of the blocks in the file system in which the file is stored. Blocks are typically 4096 or 8192 bytes in size, but the file system is capable of dividing these blocks, if required. Groups of blocks for cylinder groups and large files are allocated cylinder groups at the same time. The end of files, or small files, are stored in fragmented blocks. A block can be divided by two repeatedly until the smallest fractional block size is reached, which is typically equal to the size of a single sector on the disk.

When the file system is created, a fixed number of inodes is created. Since every unique file uses an inode on the file system, the number of inodes needs to be set high enough so that the system can hold enough files. It is not possible to increase or decrease the number of inodes, so, by default, a very conservative scheme is used, which allocates an inode for each 4 KB of disk space. Note that everything in the UNIX file system is tied to inodes. Inode 0 contains the root of the file system, the jump-off point that serves as the reference for everything else. Inode 1 contains the allocation of all bad sectors on the disk, and inode 2 contains the link to the root directory of the disk. Space is allocated one block, or fraction of a block, at a time. The directories in this file system are simple files that have been marked with a directory flag in their inodes. The file system itself is identified by the superblock. The **superblock** contains information about the layout of blocks, sectors, and cylinder groups on the file system. This information is the key to finding anything on the file system, and it should never change. Without the superblock, the file system cannot be accessed. For this reason, many copies of the superblock are written into the file system at the time of file system creation. If the superblock is destroyed, you can copy one of the superblock copies over the original, damaged superblock to restore access to the file system.

Note that the inode does not contain a filename; the filename is stored in a directory, which in itself is no more than a file. In it is stored the names of the files and the inode to which they are connected. Several directory entries can point to the same inode. This implements a *hard link*, which makes it possible to have one file appear in several directories, or in the same directory under several names, without using a lot of disk space. You can see how this works in Figure 3-15.

The inode keeps a counter that tells how many directory entries point to a file. Deleting a file is achieved by deleting the last directory entry, which brings the inode link count down to 0, meaning the file has effectively been removed.

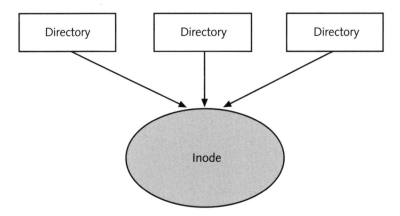

Figure 3-15   Multiple directory entries pointing to the same inode

A UNIX system can have many file systems. Unlike the MS-DOS/Windows environment, where each file system must have a letter of the alphabet assigned to it to enable access, UNIX mounts file systems as a sub-file system of the root file system. In UNIX, all file systems are referred to by a path (see Figure 3-16).

The path starts out with /, which indicates the root directory (inode 1) of the root file system. If other file systems are to be used, a directory is created on the root file system—for example, we will call it "usr." Then, using the *mount* command, the UNIX operating system is told to map the root inode of another file system onto the empty directory. This process can be repeated many times, and there is no hard limit to the number of file systems that can be mounted this way, short of the number of inodes in the root file system. Every file in every file system on a computer is thus referred to by a long directory path, and jumping from one file system to another is seamless. The *mount* command has several options; typing it without parameters results in a display of the disks that are currently mounted. For each disk, you will see the name of the partition and the path on which it was mounted. A typical *mount* listing for Red Hat Linux is shown in Figure 3-17.

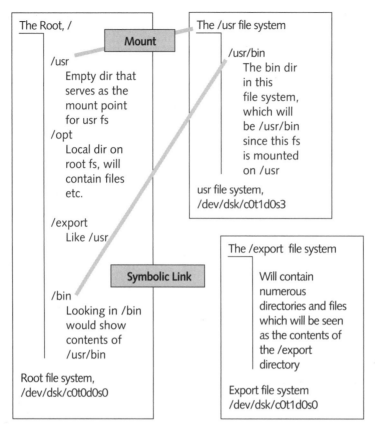

Figure 3-16   UNIX file system path entries

Figure 3-17   UNIX drive mount path

Directories in the file system contain a series of filenames, and directory names themselves are no more than filenames. UNIX allows you to use extremely long filenames, which may include any character that can be represented by the ASCII character set, including spaces.

 The UNIX operating system and file system treat uppercase and lowercase characters as different characters; a file named HELLO is a different file from one named hello, which is in turn different from one named Hello. It is, therefore, extremely important to type UNIX filenames exactly as they appear.

As we already mentioned, a directory is nothing more than a special file. There are several other special files in the UNIX file system. Disks themselves are, for example, referenced by a special inode called a device. There are two types of devices, **raw devices** and **block devices**. A raw device has no logical division in blocks, whereas a block device does. Every device the UNIX computer uses must be represented by a device inode, whether it is a disk, a serial port, or an Ethernet card. These devices have special parameters in the inode that enable the OS to figure out how to get to them. All partitions of all disks appear as devices. For example, an ext3 partition on a hard disk may be represented as /dev/hda1 (see Figure 3-17). Devices are normally kept in the /dev or /devices directory. When you look at the output of the *mount* command, you will see your disks referenced this way.

There is another special feature of the UNIX file system we should mention here, the symbolic link. As we previously indicated, it is possible to link multiple directory entries to one inode. For this to work, the inode and the directory entry must be on the same partition. If you want to link a directory entry to a file that is on a different partition, you must use a feature known as a **symbolic link**. This is a special file, which has a flag set in the inode to identify it as a symbolic link. The content of the file is a path that, when followed, leads to another file. Whenever one of these symbolic links is accessed, the operating system reads the contents of the symbolic link file, and interprets that as if it were the filename typed, referencing the directory entry, and then in turn the inode to which the symbolic link refers. Note that a hard link, when created, must point to a valid inode, and will therefore always be valid. A symbolic link is merely a pointer to a file. It is possible to create symbolic links that point to files that do not exist, or to remove the file to which a symbolic link points without removing the link. Doing this can result in having a symbolic link that, when looked at in a directory, appears to be a valid file, but when opened returns a "no such file" error. Another interesting effect of using links, both hard links and symbolic links, is that it is possible to create loops. You can make a directory A, which contains a directory B, which contains a link back to directory A. This is a feature that is nice, but can end up being extremely confusing. Links are made with the *ln* command, and the *−s* option is used to make a symbolic link. The first option is the name of the existing file, followed by the name of the link you wish to create.

One way to save time in typing is to create a link to a directory that has a long path. For example, assume that you store many files in the /user/bus/inventory directory. Each time you want to perform a listing of that directory, you must type *ls /user/bus/inventory*. If you enter *ln /user/bus/inventory* to create a link to that directory, in the future you only have to type *ls inventory* to see its contents.

As with all other operating systems discussed so far, you first have to partition a disk to use the UNIX file system. The command used to partition the disk differs slightly from one version of UNIX to another. In most UNIX systems, either *fdisk* or *format* does the job. The utility is generally text based, and it requires you to type commands. Typing *help* at the command prompt gives you an overview of available commands. In the *format* utility, you can type *partition* to set to the partition screen. The *print sub* command shows you current partition information, while the other menu commands can be used to adjust individual partitions on the disk.

Great care should be taken when changing partitions. UNIX lets you make any changes you want, without the extensive warnings found in operating systems like Microsoft Windows. This is because you make these changes using the root account for the system administrator, which gives you full access to the operating system.

After making your changes, the *write* command saves the label to the disk. Most versions of UNIX allow you to write a backup label in addition to the main disk label; this is a good idea, as it can be used to restore the original label if something goes wrong with the disk. The *fdisk* utility is similar to the partition section of the *format* utility. It usually has a print command that shows you the contents of the partition table, and other commands to edit partition information and write the disk label and backup label. The same caution applies here that applies to the partition editing tools in *format*. Linux uses an *fdisk* utility, but Solaris uses *format*, for example.

Once a partition is made, it is time to create the file system. To do this, you must know the device name of the partition on which you wish to create a file system. This name can be obtained from the *print partition table* command in *fdisk* or *format*. The most convenient way to create a new file system is the *newfs* command. Simply type *newfs*, followed by the name of the device. After you confirm that you wish to create a new file system, you will see a progress report showing you where copies of the superblocks are written, as well as some information about the cylinder group and the number of inodes. When *newfs* is completed, you can make a mount point for the new file system (remember that a mount point is nothing more than an empty directory) using the *mkdir* command. If, for example, you want to mount the new file system you just created on /dev/rdsk/c0t0d0s1 on the /test mount point, you type *mkdir /test*. Next, you mount the file system by typing *mount /dev/rdsk/c0t0d0s1 /test*, and now you are ready to use the new file system. In both Solaris and Linux, *newfs* is available. The *newfs* command in turn uses the *mkfs* program to actually create the file system. In UNIX varieties where *newfs* is not available, *mkfs* should be used instead. Use of *mkfs* is less desirable, since it requires the user to specify many parameters, such as the size of the file system, the block size, number of inodes, number of superblock copies and their locations, and a few others, depending on the version of UNIX. The *newfs* utility takes care of all these details automatically.

UNIX is very picky when it comes to file system consistency. If it finds problems on the file system in the inodes, superblock, or directory structures, it will shut down. When you save a file to disk, the system first stores part of the data in memory, until it has time to write it to disk. If for some reason your computer stops working before the data is written to disk, you can end up with a damaged file system. This is why UNIX machines should always be shut down using the proper shutdown commands, which ensure that all data is stored on disk before the machine is brought down. In normal operation, all data waiting to be saved to disk in memory is written to disk every 30 seconds. You can manually force a write of all data in memory by using the *sync* command. When the system is properly shut down, the file systems are unmounted. A flag is set in the superblock of each file system to indicate that the file system was properly closed, and does not need to be checked at startup. Whenever the machine starts up, UNIX checks the file systems to make sure they are all working properly. To do this, it verifies the integrity of the superblock, the inodes, all cluster groups, and all directory entries. The program that performs this operation is the file system checker, also known as *fsck*.

You can manually run *fsck* at any time to perform file system checks after the system is up, but take great care when doing this. If data on the disk is changed while an *fsck* is in progress, the results may be disastrous. The most common problems found when *fsck* is run are unlinked inodes, directory entries with no associated inodes, and wrong free block counts. All of these can be a result of a system that was not properly shut down. If these errors occur frequently, hardware failure may be imminent.

Typically, ufs file systems can be up to 4 GB in size, but by using larger block sizes, the systems can be made much larger. Depending on the implementation of UNIX being used, and the exact ufs version in use, it is possible to create file systems in excess of 32 exabytes. Typically, the maximum file size is 2 GB, but in some versions of UNIX it is possible to use special libraries that allow for the creation of larger files. Check your UNIX manuals to find out more about the particular file systems your implementation supports. Most of these systems use the standard commands discussed here. Table 3-8 presents a summary of useful commands for managing UNIX file systems.

Table 3-8   UNIX File System Commands

Command	Description
cat	Displays the contents of a file to the screen
cd	Changes to another directory
cp	Copies a file to another directory (and you can rename the file at the same time)
fdisk	Formats and partitions a disk in some UNIX systems, such as Linux
format	Formats and partitions a disk in some UNIX systems, such as Solaris
ls	Lists contents of a directory
mkdir	Creates a directory
mkfs	Creates a file system (but requires more parameters than newfs)
mount	Lists the disk currently mounted; also mounts file systems and devices (such as a CD-ROM)
mv	Moves a file to a different directory
newfs	Creates a new file system
rm	Removes a file or directory
sync	Forces information in memory to be written to disk
touch	Creates an empty file
umount	Un-mounts a file system

THE MACINTOSH FILE SYSTEM

The original **Macintosh Filing System (MFS)** of 1984 was limited to keeping track of 128 documents, applications, or folders. This was a reasonable limit when the only storage device was a 400 KB floppy disk drive. As larger disks became available, the need for directories and subdirectories became obvious, and Apple responded with the **Hierarchical Filing System (HFS)** in 1986.

Like FAT16, HFS divides a volume (the Mac term for a disk or disk partition) into, at most, 2^{16} (65,536) units. On PC systems, these units are called clusters or allocation units. On the Mac, they are called **allocation blocks**, but the principle is the same. Interestingly, while UNIX, MS-DOS, and Windows report file sizes in terms of their actual physical size, the Macintosh operating system typically reports file sizes in terms of logical size, based on the number of allocation blocks occupied by the file. The only way to find out the physical size is to use a third-party utility, or the Mac's Get Info command (see Figure 3-18). The Info screen shows logical file size, with physical file size in parentheses.

In 1998, Apple released Mac OS 8.1, which introduced a new disk format, Mac OS Extended Format, commonly referred to as HFS+. Like NTFS for Windows NT, 2000,

3

and XP, the new format increases the number of allocation blocks per volume to 2^{32}. This creates smaller allocation blocks (clusters) and more efficient disk utilization. Systems using Mac OS 8.1 or later can format disks in either Mac OS Standard (HFS) or Mac OS Extended (HFS+) formats. However, Macintoshes with pre-8.1 versions of the OS can't read disks in Extended format. Floppy disks and other volumes smaller than 32 MB must continue to use Standard format.

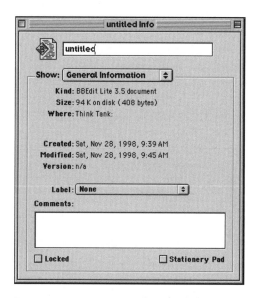

Figure 3-18   Macintosh Info dialog box

The first two sectors of a Mac-formatted disk are the boot sectors, or boot blocks in Macintosh terminology. The boot blocks identify the filing system, the names of important system files, and other important information. The boot blocks are followed by the **volume information block**, which points to other important areas of information, such as the location of the system files, and the catalog and extents trees.

The **catalog b-tree** is the list of all files on the volume. It keeps track of a file's name, its logical location in the folder structure, its physical location on the disk surface, and the locations and sizes of the file's data fork and resource forks (to be discussed later). The **extents b-tree** keeps track of the location of the file fragments, or extents.

Macintoshes can read and write to disks from other operating systems. For instance, Macs can read iso9660 CD-ROMs using the iso9660 CD-ROM driver. Macs can read all manner of MS-DOS- and Windows-formatted disks, from floppy and Zip disks, to almost any kind of SCSI device, thanks to Apple's PC Exchange control panel. Prior to Mac OS 8.5, PC Exchange assumed that PCs used short filenames, and truncated Mac filenames to 8.3 format when writing to PC-formatted media. Beginning with Mac OS 8.5, the Mac will write files with long names to PC disks without truncation.

In terms of filename length, the Mac OS has always supported what might be called **"medium" filenames** of up to 31 characters in length. Apple is gradually incorporating Unicode support into their operating system. HFS+ (Extended format) volumes can support Unicode characters in filenames. The use of the period as the first character in a filename is discouraged because older versions of the operating system used the period as the first character of invisible driver files (notably ".sony" for the Sony 3½" floppy disk drives). Any character may be used in a filename except the colon, which is used internally by the Mac OS as a directory separator, equivalent to slashes in other OSs. It's for this reason that Macintosh paths are written as colon-separated entities like this:

Hard Drive:System Folder:Preferences:Finder Prefs

UNIX and Windows operating systems use filename extensions such as .txt and .gif to identify file types. The Mac uses invisible **type codes** and **creator codes**. As an example, files created with Apple's SimpleText text editor have a type code of TEXT, and a creator code of ttxt. When a user double-clicks such a file, the Mac knows it must open the file with an application (type code APPL) with a creator code of ttxt. SimpleText, not surprisingly, has a type code of APPL and a creator code of ttxt. Type and creator codes are normally invisible to the user, but they can be viewed and modified using Apple's ResEdit program, or a variety of shareware programs (try Hands-on Project 3-9).

The type and creator codes facilitate the Mac's use of icons. Documents do not store their own icons, but rather, the Mac gets the icon from the creating application. Instead of accessing the application each time the icon must be displayed, the Mac stores the icons and file associations in invisible files called the desktop databases. Each disk or volume has its own desktop databases. "Rebuilding the desktop" on a Macintosh rebuilds these database files, and is a common troubleshooting step when icons appear incorrectly. You can rebuild the desktop on a disk at startup by holding the command and option keys. For removable media, hold down the command and option keys before inserting the disk.

One way in which Macintosh files are unique is that Mac files can contain two parts, or forks: the data fork and the resource fork. The **data fork** contains frequently changing information (such as word processing data), while the **resource fork** contains information that is fixed (such as a program's icons, menu resources, and splash screens). One advantage of resource forks for programmers is that they modularize the program. For instance, it becomes very easy to change the text of a warning dialog, or the name of a menu item, without having to change the underlying code, so customization and internationalization are easier. Most Mac documents contain only a data fork. Traditionally, Mac applications contained only a resource fork, but programs written for PowerPC-equipped Macintoshes store PowerPC code in the data fork.

One clever use of the data and resource forks is to store style information in a plain text file. The text is stored in the data fork, while the style information (font face, color, font size, italics, etc.) is stored in the resource fork. The advantage of this system is that the text file can still be read by any Mac text editing program, even if it doesn't understand the style information, and by any text editor on another operating system. This system is used by Apple's SimpleText program, America Online's text editor, and some other Mac programs.

Apple's free ResEdit utility can edit file resources. Using ResEdit, a programmer can modify a program's version number, splash screens, default memory allocation, icons, menu items, window resources, dialog text, and many other properties (see Figure 3-19). Users can also use ResEdit to modify the way programs operate.

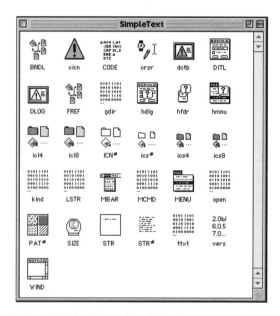

Figure 3-19   Mac SimpleText resources, as seen through ResEdit

The fact that Mac files have invisible type and creator codes and two forks can create problems when storing files on non-Macintosh servers (such as on a Windows 2000 server), or transferring files over the Internet. The need to store Mac files on non-Mac computers has led to several Mac file formats for bulletin board services, online services, and the Internet. One of these formats is **MacBinary**, which joins the two forks into one, and safely stores the type and creator codes and finder flags. For files that must be transferred through seven-bit gateways (such as Usenet news), the preferred format is BinHex. Like uuencode (a format used frequently in e-mail applications to convert binary files into text files transferable in e-mail systems), **BinHex** transforms all files into seven-bit files using the ASCII character set. Like MacBinary, BinHex preserves the two forks, the type and creator codes, and the finder flags. BinHex files can be identified by the .hqx filename extension.

Folders can be created using the New Folder command in the Finder's File menu (or the File menu's New Folder option in Mac OS X), and in the Save and Save As dialogs in most applications. All volumes have two special, invisible folders: Trash and Desktop. If you move a file's icon from a floppy disk to the desktop, the file still resides on the floppy disk's Desktop folder. Likewise, you can move the file's icon to the Trash can without deleting it, and it will still reside on the floppy disk's Trash folder. You can prove this to yourself by ejecting the floppy disk and inserting it in another Macintosh. The files will appear on the desktop, and the Trash can will bulge.

Apple's equivalent of the UNIX link and Windows shortcut is the **alias**, introduced in System 7.0 in 1991. Files, folders, applications, and disks can be aliased. Aliased disks can be placed in the Apple menu (for versions of Mac OS up to 9.x) for access to all files on the disk through the Apple menu. The system-level Alias Manager keeps track of the original, even if it is moved or renamed. The word "alias" is tacked onto the filename when the alias is created, and the filename is presented in italicized text. Beginning in OS 8.5, aliases also have small arrows on their icons, similar to shortcuts in Windows 95 and above. (Try Hands-on Project 3-10.)

The Mac OS ships with two basic disk utilities: Disk First Aid and Drive Setup. Drive Setup, a replacement for the older Apple HD Setup, formats and partitions Apple IDE and SCSI hard drives. Drive Setup checks the hard drive for a ROM that is present in drives shipped with Apple computers. If the ROM is not present, Drive Setup will not recognize the drive. Third-party hard drives must be formatted with third-party utilities, such as FWB Hard Disk Toolkit or La Cie Silverlining. Disk First Aid repairs minor hard drive problems, and can be used on any type of disk, whether or not it has an Apple ROM.

Most versions of the Mac OS include a basic find file utility. Mac OS 8.5 takes this one step further with the Sherlock program. **Sherlock** can search disks for filenames and text within files (see Figure 3-20). These operations are extremely fast because Sherlock pre-indexes local disks, just as search engines index Web pages. Because indexing takes significant processor time, indexing can be scheduled for times when the computer is not in use. Sherlock also functions as a program for querying multiple Internet search engines, or the site search engines available on many Web sites.

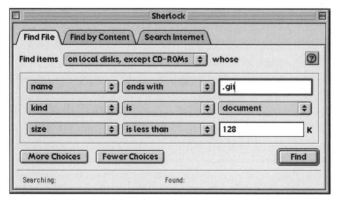

Figure 3-20   Mac OS 8.5's Sherlock search utility in file search mode

When the Mac is shut down normally using the Finder's Shut Down command (or the Shut Down option on the Apple menu in Mac OS X), a flag is set on the hard drive. In the event of a crash or forced reboot, this flag is not set. If the flag is not set, at the next startup, the Mac will see that the computer was not shut down properly and will run a disk integrity check.

The Mac is extremely versatile at booting from different devices. Like other operating systems, the Mac will boot from a floppy disk inserted during the boot sequence. If the floppy disk does not contain a valid System Folder, the Mac spits it out and continues searching for a bootable device. The Mac will also boot from various SCSI devices (Zip drives, Syquest drives, etc.) selected in the Startup Disk control panel. Since the early nineties, Macs have been able to boot from a CD-ROM drive. To boot from a CD-ROM, either press the "C" key while booting up, or insert the CD-ROM, select it in the Startup Disk control panel, and reboot. Pressing the Shift-Option-Delete-Apple (SODA) keys during the boot sequence will bypass the internal hard drive and boot from the next drive in the SCSI chain.

Chapter Summary

- ❏ For the user, files are the "bread and butter" of an operating system. Besides containing the operating system kernel, files hold documents and programs on which users rely. Files are made possible by a file system that enables them to be created, written, managed, and stored on disk media. All operating systems must have a file system that provides a file-naming convention, a way to store files, and a means to partition and format disks. Besides creating and modifying files, the file system also should offer the ability to defragment files, compress file contents, ensure file and data integrity, and control removable storage media, such as floppy and Zip disks.

- ❏ The file systems used by early Microsoft operating systems include FAT12 and FAT16. In these file systems, the file allocation table (FAT) file system creates a file allocation table to store information about files. The *fdisk* and *format* utilities are used with all versions of FAT file systems to partition and format disks, while the *chkdsk* and ScanDisk utilities give information about files and disks, and check for disk and file integrity. Some early versions of Windows, such as Windows 3.x, also support the *defrag* utility to defragment files, while most later Windows versions, beginning with Windows 95, have a GUI-based defragmenting utility.

- ❏ The FAT32 file system was introduced in the second release of Windows 95, and is also used in Windows 98 and Windows Me. FAT32 provides the capability to use long filenames, as opposed to the earlier "8.3" (eight characters and a three-character extension) convention. Windows 95, 98, and Me also include *fdisk*, *format*, ScanDisk, and disk defragmenter utilities.

- ❏ The native file system for Windows NT, 2000, XP, and .NET is called NTFS, but FAT32 is also supported by Windows 2000 and XP, while FAT16 is supported by Windows NT, 2000, and XP. NTFS is a more stable and secure file system than FAT, and in general, can handle larger disk and file sizes.

❑ UNIX file systems use information nodes (inodes) to organize information about files. A UNIX system can have many file systems mounted as subdirectories of the root. UNIX systems support multiple file systems, depending on the use of the system, such as UNIX file system (ufs), extended file system (ext), and network file system (NFS). Different varieties of UNIX use different file system utilities, such as *fdisk* (Linux) and *format* (Solaris), to partition and format disks. The *fsck* (file system checker) utility is used to verify the integrity of UNIX file systems.

❑ The Macintosh OS uses the Hierarchical Filing System (HFS). Like FAT, HFS divides a disk or disk partition (called a volume) into allocation units called allocation blocks. Unlike FAT, HFS has always allowed the use of relatively long filenames. The HFS+ (OS Extended Format) file system was introduced in 1998 with Mac OS 8.1. Like NTFS, HFS+ makes more efficient utilization of disk space and supports larger disk sizes. The Mac ResEdit utility is used to edit file resources. Two basic disk utilities are Disk First Aid and Drive Setup.

KEY TERMS

active partition — The logical portion of a hard disk drive that is currently being used to store data. In a PC system, usually the partition that contains the bootable operating system.

alias — In the Macintosh file system, a feature that presents an icon that represents an executable file. Equivalent to the UNIX link and the Windows shortcut.

allocation blocks — In the Macintosh file system, a division of hard disk data. Equivalent to the Windows disk cluster. Each Macintosh volume is divided into 2^{16} (65,535) individual units.

bad clusters — On a hard disk drive, areas of the surface that cannot be used to safely store data. Bad clusters are usually identified by the *format* command, or one of the hard drive utilities, such as *chkdsk* or ScanDisk.

BinHex — In the Macintosh file system, a seven-bit file format used to transmit data across network links that do not support native Macintosh file formats.

block allocation — A hard disk configuration scheme in which the disk is divided into logical blocks, which in turn are mapped to sectors, heads, and tracks. Whenever the operating system needs to allocate some disk space, it allocates it based on a block address.

block devices — In the UNIX file system, devices that are divided or configured into logical blocks. See also *raw devices*.

boot block — On a Mac-formatted disk, the first of two important system sections on the disk. The boot blocks identify the filing system, the names of important system files, and other important information. (See also *volume information block*, the second system section.)

catalog b-tree — In the Macintosh file system, a list of all files on a given volume. Similar to a directory in the Windows file system.

cluster — In MS-DOS and Windows-based file systems, a logical block of information on a disk, containing one or more sectors. Also called an allocation unit.

compact disc file system (CDFS) — A 32-bit file system used on standard-capacity CD-ROMs.

creator codes — Hidden file characteristics in the Macintosh file system that indicate the program (software application) that created the file. See *type code.*

data fork — That portion of a file in the Macintosh file system that stores the variable data associated with the file. Data fork information might include word processing data, spreadsheet information, and so on.

Digital Video Disc-Read Only Memory (DVD-ROM) — Also called Digital Versatile Disk, a ROM medium that can hold from 4.7 to 17 GB of information.

directory — Also called a folder in some file systems, an organizational structure that contains files and may additionally contain subdirectories (or folders) under it. In UNIX, a directory is simply a special file on a disk drive that is used to house information about other data stored on the disk. In other systems, a directory or folder is a "container object" that houses files and subdirectories or subfolders. A directory or folder contains information about files, such as filenames, file sizes, date of creation, and file type (for UNIX).

disk label — Used on UNIX systems, and is the same as a partition table in MS-DOS or Windows-based systems. The disk label is a table containing information about each partition on a disk, such as the type of partition, size, and location. Also, the partition table provides information to the computer about how to access the disk.

Distributed Link Tracking — A technique new to NTFS 5, so that shortcuts, such as those on the desktop, are not lost when files are moved to another volume.

extended file system (ext or ext fs) — The file system designed for Linux that is installed, by default, in Linux operating systems. Ext enables the use of the full range of built-in Linux commands, file manipulation, and security. Released in 1992, ext had some bugs and supported only files up to 2 GB. In 1993, the second extended file system (ext2 or ext2 fs) was designed to fix the bugs in ext, and support files of up to 4 TB in size. In 2001, ext3 (or ext fs) was introduced to enable journaling for file and data recovery. Ext, ext2, and ext3 support filenames of up to 255 characters.

extension — In MS-DOS, that part of a filename that typically identifies the type of file associated with the name. File extensions traditionally are three characters long, and include standard notations such as .sys, .exe, .bat, and so on.

extents b-tree — In the Mac OS HFS file system, keeps track of the location of the file fragments, or extents.

file allocation table (FAT) — A file management system that defines the way data is stored on a disk drive. The FAT stores information about file size and physical location on the disk.

file attributes — File characteristics stored with the filename in the disk directory, which specify certain storage and operational parameters associated with the file. Attributes are noted by the value of specific data bits associated with the filename. File attributes include Hidden, Read-only, Archive, and so on.

file system — A design for storing and managing files on a disk drive. File systems are associated with operating systems such as UNIX, Mac OS, and Windows.

folder — See *directory*.

hard link — In Windows NT/2000/XP and UNIX, a file management technique that permits multiple directory entries to point to the same physical file.

Hierarchical Filing System (HFS) — An early Apple Macintosh file system storage method that uses a hierarchical directory structure. Developed in 1986 to improve file support for large storage devices.

high-level formatting — A process that prepares a disk partition (or removable media) for a specific file system.

information node (inode) — In UNIX, a system for storing key information about files. Inode information includes: the inode number, the owner of the file, the file group, the file size, the file creation date, the date the file was last modified and read, the number of links to this inode, and information regarding the location of the blocks in the file system in which the file is stored.

large block allocation (LBA) — In MS-DOS, a technique to allow the creation of files larger than 512 MB. With LBA, MS-DOS is told that the sector size of the hard disk is greater than 512 bytes per sector, which results in the ability to have much larger file systems.

linked list — Used in FAT file systems so that when a file is written to disk, each cluster containing that file's data has a pointer to the location of the next cluster of data. For example, the first cluster has a pointer to the second cluster's location, the second cluster contains a pointer to the third cluster, and so on.

long filename (LFN) — A name for a file, folder, or directory in a file system in which the name can be up to 255 characters in length. Long filenames in Windows-based, UNIX, and Mac OS systems are also POSIX compliant in that they honor uppercase and lowercase characters.

low-level format — A software process that marks tracks and sectors on a disk. A low-level format is necessary before a disk can be partitioned and formatted.

MacBinary — A format for Mac OS files that joins type and creator codes, so that Mac files can be transferred over the Internet, or used via online services.

Macintosh Filing System (MFS) — The original Macintosh filing system, introduced in 1984. MFS was limited to keeping track of 128 documents, applications, or folders.

Master Boot Record (MBR) — An area of a hard disk that stores partition information about that disk. MBRs are not found on disks that do not support multiple partitions.

Master File Table (MFT) — In Windows NT, 2000, XP, and .NET Server, a file management system similar to the FAT and directories used in MS-DOS and Windows. This table is located at the beginning of the partition. The boot sector is located ahead of the MFT, just as it is in the FAT system.

medium filenames — In the Macintosh file system, the 31-character filename length that Macintosh OS has supported from the beginning.

New Technology File System (NTFS) — The 32-bit file storage system that is the native system in Windows NT, 2000, XP, and .NET Server.

partition table — Table containing information about each partition on a disk, such as the type of partition, size, and location. Also, the partition table provides information to the computer about how to access the disk.

partitioning — Blocking a group of tracks and sectors to be used by a particular file system, such as FAT or NTFS. Partitioning is a hard disk management technique that permits the installation of multiple file systems on a single disk. Or, the configuration of multiple logical hard drives that use the same file system on a single physical hard drive.

Portable Operating System Interface (POSIX) — A UNIX standard designed to ensure portability of applications among various versions of UNIX.

raw devices — In the UNIX file system, devices that have not been divided into logical blocks.

resource fork — In the Macintosh file system, that portion of a file that contains fixed information, such as a program's icons, menu resources, and splash screens.

root directory — The highest-level directory (or folder), with no directories above it in the structure of files and directories in a file system.

sector — A portion of a disk track. Disk tracks are divided into equal segments or sectors.

Sherlock — In the Macintosh file system, a file search utility that can find filenames or text within files.

status bits — Bits used as part of a directory entry to identify the type of filename contained in each entry. The status bits in use are Volume, Directory, System, Hidden, Read-only, and Archive.

superblock — In the UNIX file system, a special data block that contains information about the layout of blocks, sectors, and cylinder groups on the file system. This information is the key to finding anything on the file system, and it should never change.

switch — An operating system command option that changes the way certain commands function. Command options, or switches, are usually entered as one or more letters, separated from the main command by a forward slash (/).

symbolic link — A special file in the UNIX file system that permits a directory link to a file that is on a different partition. This is a special file, which has a flag set in the inode to identify it as a symbolic link. The content of the file is a path that, when followed, leads to another file.

track — Concentric rings that cover an entire disk like grooves on a phonograph record. Each ring is divided into sectors in which to store data.

type code — In the Macintosh file system, embedded file information that denotes what applications were used to create the files. Mac OS type codes are used in much the same way as Windows file extensions that identify file types with .txt, .doc and other extensions. See *creator code*.

ufs (UNIX file system) — A file system developed for UNIX operating systems that uses information nodes or inodes.

Unicode — A 16-bit character code that allows for the definition of up to 65,536 characters.

Universal Disk Format (UDF) — A removable disk formatting standard used for large-capacity CD-ROMs and DVD-ROMs.

volume information block — On a Mac-formatted disk, the second of two system sectors (see also *boot block*, the first sector). The volume information block points to other important areas of information, such as the location of the system files, and the catalog and extents trees.

volume label — A series of characters that identify a disk drive, or the file system it is using.

REVIEW QUESTIONS

1. When a disk drive is sent out by a manufacturer, it is _____ formatted.

2. What file system is native to Linux?

3. Which of the following must occur before you can write files on a hard disk using FAT32?

   a. It must be partitioned.

   b. It must be formatted.

   c. It must be spanned or extended.

   d. It must be primed.

   e. all of the above

   f. only a and b

   g. only a, c, and d

4. Which of the following information would you expect to be stored by a file system about a file?

   a. date and time it was created

   b. size

   c. attributes

   d. all of the above

   e. none of the above

   f. only a and b

   g. only a and c

5. Disk allocation tables are used to:

   a. allocate certain portions of a disk drive for the use of specific software applications.

   b. allocate certain portions of a disk drive for the use of specific users.

   c. track the location of data stored on the disk, and facilitate storing and retrieving data from the disk.

   d. allocate different disk drives in a hardware system to different file systems.

6. In the Macintosh file system, file type codes are used to _____.

7. Windows 95 only supports FAT16. True or false?

8. A technique for managing hard disks that enables the installation of multiple file systems on a single physical drive, or lets you configure multiple logical drives is called:

   a. disk partitioning.

   b. disk allocation.

   c. disk formatting.

   d. none of the above

9. You inadvertently turned off your Mac OS X system without using the Shut Down option. What will happen when you turn it back on, and why does this happen?

10. A newer text standard called Unicode is now used by many operating systems. What is the main difference between ASCII and Unicode?

11. You must make sure that only you can read the files in a folder on a Windows server. What version(s) of NTFS has (have) the ability to encrypt files?

12. Your Windows XP system has three files that report an error when you try to open them. What utility can you run to try to fix the errors?

13. Which of the following operating systems employs the ufs file system?

   a. Windows 98

   b. Windows XP

   c. UNIX

   d. Mac OS X

   e. all of the above

   f. only b and c

   g. only b, c, and d

14. A special link in UNIX permits directory pointers across partitions. This link is called a _____ link.

15. The NTFS entity that tracks directory entries is known as:

   a. Master Boot Record (MBR).

   b. Master File Record (MFR).

   c. Master File Table (MFT).

   d. File Table Master (FTM).

   e. none of the above

16. The UNIX file system uses a file system concept called:

   a. information node (inode).

   b. UNIX node (unode).

    c. Directory List Notation (DLN).

    d. UNIX File Allocation Table (UFAT).

    e. sector tracking number.

17. _____ is a tool that you can use to find a file in the Mac OS file system.

18. DOS and Windows file systems use disk clusters or file allocation units. In the Macintosh file system, this type of disk subdivision is called a (an) _____.

19. Macintosh files contain two structures, or forks. These are the data fork, which contains variable information, and the _____ fork, which contains fixed data about individual files.

20. You believe that your UNIX file system might be corrupted. What utility should you run to verify the file system?

    a. fdisk

    b. fsck

    c. newfs

    d. dskchk

    e. all of the above

    f. run a and then c

    g. run a and then d

HANDS-ON PROJECTS

Project 3-1

File systems store a wide range of information about files. In this project, you'll view the information that can be displayed about a file in Windows XP.

To view the information about the file in Windows XP:

1. Click **Start**, point to **All Programs**, point to **Accessories**, and click **Windows Explorer**.

2. Click **My Computer** in the left pane.

3. Double-click one of the disk drives in the right pane, such as **Local Disk (C:)**. (You may need to click *Show the contents of this folder.*)

4. Double-click a folder, such as **Program Files**.

5. Click **Show the contents of this folder**, if the files do not appear.

6. What information do you see in the right pane?

7. Click the **View** menu, and then click **Details**, if it is not already selected.

8. Click **Show the contents of this folder**, if necessary, to view the files and folders.

9. What information about files and folders now appears in the right pane?

10. Click the **View** menu again, and then click **Choose Details**.

11. What information about a file can you select to display? (Note that in the NTFS file system, under Windows XP, there is information associated with multimedia files that can be displayed—which is not typical of other file systems.)

12. Close the Choose Details box, and then close Windows Explorer.

Project 3-2

In this project, you'll learn how to create a directory or folder in different operating systems.

To create a new folder in Windows 95, Windows 98, Windows Me, Windows NT, Windows 2000, or Windows XP:

1. Click **Start** on the taskbar, and point to **Programs** (or **All Programs** in Windows XP).

2. In Windows 95, 98, or NT, click **Windows Explorer** (or **Windows NT Explorer** for Windows NT). In Windows Me, 2000, or Windows XP, click **Accessories**, and then click **Windows Explorer**.

3. In the left pane, double-click a drive, such as **(C:)**, to display all of the folders and files under it. (On some systems, such as Windows 2000 and XP, you may need to double-click My Computer and then double-click the drive.)

4. What are some of the existing folders on the drive that you displayed?

5. Click the drive to select it, click the **File** menu, point to **New**, and then click **Folder**.

6. What appears?

7. For the new folder's name, type in your initials, plus the word Folder, such as "JPFolder". Press **Enter**.

8. Close Explorer.

To create a new directory from the command line in Red Hat Linux (or in virtually any UNIX system):

1. Access the command line, such as via a GNOME terminal window.

2. If you are not already in your home directory, change to that directory by typing **cd /home/***homedirectoryname*, and press **Enter**.

3. Type **ls**. Are there any existing subdirectories in your home directory?

4. Type **mkdir** plus a space, then your initials and the word Directory, such as "JPDirectory", and then press **Enter**.

5. Type **ls** to verify that you successfully created the directory.

To create a new folder using the GNOME interface in Red Hat Linux 7.2:

1. Log onto your account.
2. Click the **Main Menu** (the foot icon), point to **Programs**, point to **Applications**, and click **Nautilus**. (Another way to start Nautilus is to double-click the Start Here icon on the desktop.)
3. Click the **Tree** tab (in the lower left portion of the window).
4. What folders do you see under the tree in the left side of the window? (If no folders are displayed, click the arrow in front of the top folder.)
5. If Nautilus has not automatically opened your home folder, click the **arrow** in front of the **home** folder, so that the folder's contents are displayed in the tree. Next, click your home folder, such as **mwalters**, so that you see its contents in the right pane (if the right pane is empty, this means thre are no subfolders or files under your home folder).
6. Click the **File** menu and click the **New Folder**.
7. Enter the name of the folder, combining your initials with Folder2, such as "JPFolder2". Press **Enter**.
8. Click the **x** in the upper right to portion of the screen to close the window.

To create a folder in the Mac OS (9.x and X):

1. First, open the Macintosh HD icon on the desktop to view folders already created. What folders do you see?
2. Click **File** on the menu bar.
3. Select **New Folder**.
4. Enter the name of the new folder, such as your initials plus "Folder".
5. Press **Enter**.

Project 3-3

A sudden power failure or a bad spot on a disk can cause the Master Boot Record to become corrupted, preventing a computer from booting. In Windows NT and Windows 2000, you can make an emergency repair disk from which to fix the Master Boot Record. This project gives you the opportunity to see how to fix the Master Boot Record in Windows NT or Windows 2000. You will need a blank formatted disk.

To fix the Master Boot Record:

1. Make an emergency repair disk (ERD) before there is a problem and store it in a safe place. To make an ERD in Windows NT, click **Start**, click **Run**, enter **RDISK** in the Open box, and click **OK**. Insert the blank disk, click **Create Repair Disk**, and click **OK**. To make an ERD in Windows 2000, click **Start**, point to **Programs**, point to **Accessories**, point to **System Tools**, and click **Backup**. Insert the floppy disk, click **Emergency Repair Disk**, click **OK**, and click **OK** again. Close the Backup utility.

2. Remove the ERD from the floppy disk drive.

3. Power off the computer.

4. If your computer supports booting from the Windows NT or 2000 Server CD-ROM, boot from it. If not, insert the Windows NT or 2000 floppy disk labeled Setup Disk 1 and boot from it.

5. Power on the computer, enabling it to boot from the CD-ROM or floppy disk. If you boot from floppy disk, follow the instructions to insert Setup Disk 2.

6. On the Welcome to Setup screen, press **R** for repair. What options are now available to you?

7. On the next screen, press **R** again to use the emergency repair disk to perform the recovery.

8. Insert the emergency repair disk.

9. There are two options that you can follow; one is to press M so that you can choose from a manual list of repair options, and the other is to press F to perform all repair options. If you select the manual option, you can select any or all of the following: inspect startup environment, verify Windows system files, and inspect boot sector. If you select F, all of these functions are performed.

10. Select **M**. Notice the options from which you can choose, but do not select any of the options unless you have your instructor's permission. If you have permission from your instructor, select to inspect the boot sector (which will fix any detected problems). If you do not have permission, exit by pressing **F3** to quit.

11. Reboot the computer.

 In Windows NT and 2000, it is wise to update the ERD any time that you make a change to the system, such as adding new software or device drivers. The ERD can be invaluable for fixing system file and boot sector problems when a system will not boot.

Project 3-4

The MS-DOS utility, *fdisk* is used to partition one or more hard drives in MS-DOS, Windows 95, and Windows 98. *fdisk* sets the file system type, and sets the size of each system by type. However, *fdisk* also can be used to help you understand the existing structure of your hard drive or drives. This project enables you to practice using *fdisk*.

 To view existing partition information in MS-DOS, Windows 95, or Windows 98:

1. Start up MS-DOS, or if you are using Windows 95, or Windows 98, click **Start**, point to **Programs**, and click **MS-DOS Prompt**.

2. At the MS-DOS prompt, type **fdisk**, and press **Enter**. If you have a hard drive larger than 512 MB, you may see the screen that asks if you wish to enable large disk support. Choose **Y** from this screen if you have a large disk drive to display the main FDISK screen, otherwise press **N**. What FDISK options do you see?

3. Choose menu item **4** to display current partition information. You may see only a single partition if you have only one disk drive and it is configured as one large partition. However, if you have a hard drive larger than 4 GB, you probably will see at least two partitions. Can you think why? What would you have to do to increase the partition size beyond 4 GB?

4. Press **Esc** twice to exit FDISK without making any changes.

 DO NOT CHANGE YOUR HARD DISK'S PARTITION INFORMATION. If you do, you may have to re-install your operating system and all applications. Be sure to press Esc to exit the *fdisk* program.

Project 3-5

In this project, you'll practice using *chkdsk* and ScanDisk in Windows 95, Windows 98, and Windows Me.

To use *chkdsk*:

1. Click **Start**, click **Run**, enter **chkdsk**, and click **OK**.

2. What information do you see?

3. Close the MS-DOS Prompt window.

To use ScanDisk to look for hard disk problems:

1. Exit all other running programs before starting ScanDisk.

2. Click **Start**, point to **Programs**, point to **Accessories**, point to **System Tools**, and click **ScanDisk**.

3. What drives can you scan? Choose the hard drive you want to scan. In most cases, you can accept the program's suggested drive. Also, what types of tests can be run?

4. Check **Automatically fix errors** if you want the program to automatically correct errors it finds.

5. Click the **Start** button to begin the disk scanning.

6. Watch the progress reporting screens as the program runs through its fairly extensive checklist. What information is reported in the Results dialog box?

7. Click **Close**, and then close the ScanDisk utility.

Project 3-6

In this project, you'll practice compressing all files in an NTFS 5 folder in Windows 2000. Before you start, ask your instructor about which folder to use for this project.

To compress the files in the folder:

1. Log on to Windows 2000.

3

2. Click **Start,** point to **Programs**, point to **Accessories**, and click **Windows Explorer**.

3. Scroll or browse to find the folder that your instructor designated for this assignment and right-click it.

4. Click **Properties**.

5. Click the **Advanced** button. What options do you see in the dialog box?

6. Click the check box **Compress contents to save disk space**. Click **OK**.

7. Click **OK** to close the folder Properties dialog box. (You may need to click OK again to confirm the attribute changes.)

8. Close Windows Explorer.

 You cannot compress a folder that is encrypted.

 ## Project 3-7

In this project, you'll determine what file systems are incorporated in a system running Red Hat Linux 7.x.

 To view the file systems:

1. Access the command prompt or a GNOME terminal window showing the command prompt.

2. At the command prompt, type **man mount** and press **Enter**. Continue pressing **Enter**, as necessary, to view the documentation for the -t parameter for the mount command. (If you are using a terminal window you may need to press Q to exit the text display mode, when you are finished.)

3. What file systems can be mounted?

4. Next, type **mount** and press **Enter** to determine what file systems are actually mounted. What file systems do you see?

5. If you are in a terminal window, type **exit** and press **Enter**.

 ## Project 3-8

Windows 95 and 98, Me, NT, 2000, XP, and UNIX systems include automatic checking routines to help avoid data loss or file damage. These utilities run automatically any time you fail to shut down your computer properly. You may already have seen how these programs work, but you can force them to run so you can see how these operating systems automatically handle potential problems.

 To force your operating system to launch some automatic diagnostics:

1. Close all running programs.

2. Make sure no other users are connected to the computer you are about to test. If so, ask them to log off temporarily.

3. Push the system hardware reset button, or simply turn off the power.

4. If you turned off the power, wait about 15 seconds, and turn the power back on. If you pushed the reset button, the system will automatically restart.

5. Monitor the boot process. At a certain point, you will see a screen informing you that the computer was not shut down properly. A disk scanning utility will be launched, and the drive and programs will be tested before the computer reboots.

This is basically a safe test. Even though it is not recommended that you shut down a computer in this way, it is doubtful that you will damage any data. However, don't do this test with a UNIX computer unless you are very familiar with UNIX in general, and the configuration of the test machine in particular. Further, note that Windows 2000, Windows XP, and Red Hat Linux 7.2 (if ext3 is installed), have new or improved journaling capabilities, and an improper shutdown of the system may not force an automatic file check.

Project 3-9

Unlike MS-DOS, Windows, and UNIX file systems, the Macintosh file system uses two separate file units to define file type and contents. These units are the data fork and the resource fork. Normally only applications interpret this information. It is transparent to the user. A free Macintosh utility called ResEdit lets you view and change this information. You can view file information with ResEdit, and learn a lot about the way the Macintosh tracks file data.

To open ResEdit and study file information:

1. Locate the ResEdit application icon on your Macintosh desktop, hard drive, or system folder.

If you don't find a copy of ResEdit in your operating system utilities, you can download a copy from the Internet by searching on "ResEdit download." You will be referred to several download sites where you can secure your own copy of this interesting utility.

2. Double-click the **ResEdit** icon to launch the application. You will see a jack-in-the-box opening screen with the program version number and other data. Click the ResEdit title screen to make the folder tree visible.

3. Navigate to a folder that contains the application program or file you want to view in ResEdit.

4. Click the program name to select it, and click **Open**. You should see a screen of resource icons.

5. Double-click one or more of these icons to view their contents. You will see different items depending on the type of file you are viewing. Among the items you might see are program startup icons, menu screens, sound icons, and so on.

We don't recommend that you make changes to information you see in ResEdit, unless you have a fair amount of experience, and make sure you made a backup copy of any file you do change.

3

Project 3-10

Aliases are among the useful Macintosh file system features. Like shortcuts in Windows, aliases let you create custom icons and names to place on your desktop, menus, or elsewhere to point to other applications. Aliases give you multiple ways to access the same application, and let you easily place these access points at various locations to help you get to them when you need them.

To create a program alias in the Macintosh file system:

1. Click once on an application icon to select it.

2. Click **File**, and then click **Make Alias** from the menu.

3. Type an alias name and other information you want on the Make Alias dialog box. For Mac OS X, the alias icon will be named with the old name plus "alias." Click within the name box for the new icon and type whatever name you wish for this new alias icon.

4. Drag the alias icon to the location where you want it to reside.

To find the original file or application associated with an alias:

1. Select the icon for the alias.

2. Click **File**, and then click **Show Original**.

3. What file or application is associated with the alias that you created?

4. Close the Applications window, if necessary.

Although an alias only points to the actual application, you can treat an alias like an application. For example, you can drag a file onto an alias icon to open the file with the application to which the alias points. You can also create an alias for a folder instead of an application. This lets you save files into a folder by choosing its alias. You can also create an alias from a network connection so you can open the server it represents by simply double-clicking the alias icon wherever it resides.

CASE PROJECT

Flatirons Metals is a large metal manufacturing company that makes steel and aluminum parts for aircraft, automobiles, and diesel trucks. They currently have 18 Microsoft Windows 2000 servers and want to implement five new Red Hat Linux 7.2 servers. The users who connect to these servers through the network use either Windows 98, Windows XP, or Mac OS 9.1 desktop computers. Flatirons Metals hires you to serve as a consultant for several questions they want to address about file systems in this environment.

1. The Flatirons Metal Information Technology Department does not have much experience with Red Hat Linux and asks you about compatible file systems. Explain what file systems can work with Red Hat Linux, and what file systems you recommend that the company use on the new Red Hat Linux servers.

2. The information technology director commented that the company wants to be able to take a floppy disk from a Windows 98 or XP computer and use it with Red Hat Linux to transfer files occasionally. Is this possible?

3. In your discussions with Flatirons Metals, you learn that they are using FAT32 on all of the Windows 2000 servers. The company is also complaining that there are some major security problems on these servers. What do you recommend to help solve these problems (explain why you make these recommendations)?

4. The Information Technology Department is curious about upgrading all of the Windows 98 systems to Windows XP. In terms of file system capabilities only, are there any advantages to upgrading, and if so, what are they?

5. The company's Macintosh computers are all formatted using Mac OS Standard (HFS). What advantage is there in formatting these computers to use Mac OS Extended (HFS+) instead? Are there any disadvantages?

OPTIONAL CASE PROJECTS FOR TEAMS

Team Case One

Your company put you on a team-based task force to determine the merits of implementing UNIX versus Windows XP desktop systems. You are specifically interested in the capabilities of the file systems available to these operating systems. Compare the file systems capabilities in terms of:

❑ Which file systems can be used in UNIX versus Windows XP

❑ The security features of the file systems in UNIX and Windows XP

❑ The reliability of the different file systems

❑ The types of problem-solving and troubleshooting tools available for the different file systems

❑ The ways in which the different file systems use hard disk storage

Consider developing tables or charts to illustrate the comparisons.

Team Case Two

Your company now wants to include a comparison of Mac OS file systems to Windows XP and UNIX. Expand the information that you developed in Team Case One to include the Mac OS. Also, now that you have developed a comparison of the file systems. Explain one or two work contexts for which the Mac OS file system is best suited. Next do the same for Windows XP and UNIX.

4

INITIAL INSTALLATION

After reading this chapter and completing the exercises you will be able to:

♦ Understand the overall process of operating system installation

♦ Prepare for operating system installation

♦ Install the following operating systems and understand the various options presented during the installations:

- Windows 95, 98, and Me

- Windows NT Server and Workstation

- Windows 2000 Server and Professional

- Windows XP Home and Professional

♦ Install Linux-variety UNIX and understand the basic differences between this installation and those of other operating systems covered in this chapter

♦ Install Mac OS version 9.x and understand the options presented during installation

For many, the installation of an operating system seems like a complex and worrisome task. This chapter takes the mystery out of operating system installation by showing you, step by step, how to install each operating system described in the book. An overview of the installations is given in the text portion of the chapter, and you can step through actual installations in the Hands-on Projects at the end of the chapter. By the end of the chapter, you will know what to expect, what to watch for, and what to avoid when you sit down at a computer to perform an operating system installation. It is beyond the scope of this book to cover all possible options and settings, so only usual installations are presented.

INSTALLING AN OPERATING SYSTEM

The process of installing operating systems varies from one operating system to another, but there are certain features common to all installations. Operating system installation can be divided into three general stages: preparation for installation, the installation itself, and any required or optional steps following installation.

Preparing for installation involves the following:

- Checking the computer on which you will install the operating system to make sure it meets or exceeds the hardware and/or software requirements for the operating system

- Ensuring that all equipment (computer and peripheral devices) is powered on and operating correctly

- Having the appropriate floppy disks or CDs on hand, including those for the operating system installation, and any floppy disks needed during the installation to create startup disks

- Understanding the general features of the operating system you are installing so you can decide which modules to install and which to omit

- Having the most up-to-date device drivers for your CD-ROM, SCSI devices, printers, modems, and so on, usually from the manufacturer's disk that came with the device, or downloaded from the manufacturer's Web site

- Having pertinent information available about your computer and peripheral devices

During the installation, you may need to provide some or all of the following information:

- Where (in which directory/folder or path) to install the operating system and what to name the directory/folder

- What type of installation you wish to perform (Typical/Default, Portable, Compact, or Custom, for example)

- Information about you, your company, and your computer (your name, company name, computer or workgroup name)

- Licensing information (usually a license key or ID number), verifying your right to install the operating system

- Which components of the operating system you want to install

After you complete an installation, keep the license key, ID number, or activation number in a safe place so you can reinstall the operating system in the event that your computer or hard drive fails. Some operating systems (Windows 95, 98, Me, 2000, and XP; Mac OS; and some versions of UNIX) can automatically detect and configure devices, such as monitors, keyboards, printers, mice, network cards, video cards, and sound cards. However, these operating systems also let you specify a device type or model that is different from the one they detect, in case the automatic detection made a mistake.

Installation programs can be primarily text based (some versions of UNIX, for example), use a combination of text-based and GUI (most Windows-based systems when booted from floppy disks or CD-ROMs), or use an automated "wizard" to step you through the process (all Windows-based systems when upgraded from a previous version of Windows, and Mac OS). Operating systems can be installed from floppy disks or CD-ROMs, and, in many cases, can be installed over a network. (Network installations are not covered in this book.)

The installation itself consists of some or all of the following general functions:

- Loading/running the installation program

- Gathering system information

- Determining which elements of the operating system are to be installed

- Configuring devices and drivers

- Creating a floppy disk used to boot the operating system in an emergency

- Copying operating system files onto your computer

- Restarting the system and finalizing configuration of devices

Not all of these functions are performed in every operating system installation. For some operating systems, devices and drivers are installed after the operating system installation (MS-DOS). For others, device/driver configuration is part of the OS installation. Operating systems from Windows 95 on have a feature called **Plug and Play (PnP)** that automatically configures internal and external devices as part of the installation, and at startup whenever a new device is added.

 Even with a Plug- and Play-capable operating system, you may have to configure memory for optimum performance, or configure devices to work with the operating system.

For example, in some operating systems, if your machine contains a CD-ROM drive, you must install a CD-ROM driver, or appropriate file system, before you can use the CD-ROM. In the following section, you will learn how to prepare for installation. After that, each operating system installation will be covered in more detail.

PREPARING FOR INSTALLATION

Before you can install any OS, you must make a few advance preparations. First, and most important, the machine must be working correctly. If you have defective hardware, such as a disk drive, CD-ROM drive, or bad section of memory, the operating system installation can be extremely difficult. Most operating systems interface with the hardware on many levels. Many of the operating systems covered in this book try to automatically detect the hardware connected to your computer. The result of nonworking hardware can be a failed installation.

Checking the Hardware

Before you begin an installation, you should be sure that all hardware is actually turned on and ready for use, including the computer and any external peripheral devices such as SCSI devices, tape drives, disk drives, modems, and scanners.

It is recommended that you remove any tapes or removable media that contain important data from tape and other drives. In general, an operating system installation will not destroy data on tapes or removable media, unless it is specifically instructed to do so. However, if important data is backed up, and removable media are out of the drives, there is no chance of losing anything.

You should also have available information about your hardware. This means that you should know how many hard disks you have, what size they are, and how they are connected to the machine. You should also know how much memory you have in your machine. For any expansion cards, such as your video card, network card, sound card, and SCSI cards, you should know the make and model. If you have a printer, modem, scanner, plotter, or other device, you should keep the device driver disks handy, and know their types. For some SMP (symmetric multiprocessor) systems, make sure that you have the multiprocessor driver, such as the HAL.dll (hardware abstraction layer driver). Table 4-1 is an example of how you might organize this information to have it available during installation.

Table 4-1   Hardware Component Information

Component	Description/Setting
CPU (type)	The system BIOS knows this information, and the operating system should automatically adjust anything required (unless you are using an SMP computer, in which case you should have the multiprocessor driver provided by the manufacturer).
Amount of RAM	Your operating system should automatically detect the amount of RAM in your system. However, guidelines supplied with your OS tell you how much RAM is recommended. You should know how much you have to ensure that the OS installs and operates properly.
Type of buses	You'll need this information if you install new expansion cards.
Hard disk(s)	Type, size, connection. Most new hardware includes BIOS routines to automatically detect the type of hard drive installed, as well as critical drive settings. It's also a good idea to write down hard drive statistics, such as number of cylinders, capacity, and number of heads. This information may be available in your owner's manual, on the case of the hard drive, or on the BIOS Setup screen. Try Hands-on Project 4-1 to learn more about the BIOS setup.

Table 4-1   Hardware Component Information (continued)

Component	Description/Setting
Keyboard	Unless your keyboard has special features that require custom drivers, the type of keyboard you have should not be a factor during OS installation.
Mouse	Standard, three-button, wheel mouse? Is a custom driver required? Does the mouse use a serial, parallel, or USB port?
Video card	Most modern operating systems will detect your video card and automatically include required drivers. However, special features of your video card may become available only with the use of a special driver provided by the manufacturer.
Floppy drive type	Your OS automatically detects this information.
Sound card	Some operating systems include drivers for common sound card hardware. If your card isn't one of the really popular models, make sure you have the required drivers supplied by the card's manufacturer.
NIC	Windows 95 and later Windows OSs, Red Hat Linux, and Mac OS probably will automatically detect your NIC. However, it may still be a good idea to use the manufacturer's custom drivers for best performance.
Printer	You should have custom drivers from your printer manufacturer.
Modem	Use manufacturer drivers, or those supplied with your operating system. You should know at least the manufacturer of your modem's basic chip set in case you must choose it during installation. If you have custom driver software that came with your modem, use it.
Other input/output devices	If your OS doesn't detect other hardware during the installation, you must understand hardware basics, and have access to any custom drivers required to make it function properly with your OS.

Chapter 6, "Output, Input, and Storage Devices," gives more detailed information on devices and device drivers.

Many cards installed in the machine include settings on the card. In the Intel PC architecture, these cards often must be configured to interface with the computer in a certain way. Windows 95 and later Windows products use the Plug and- Play system to do this. If you install a Plug and Play operating system, card configuration is automatic. If you do not use a Plug and Play operating system, or if your machine does not support the Plug and Play system, you may be in for a few surprises. Many Plug and Play cards come with a utility (usually included on the manufacturer's disk with the drivers) that lets you configure them to work in non-Plug and -Play mode. Currently, Windows 95 and later Windows products, other than Windows NT, support true Plug and Play mode. There is support in Windows NT 4.0 for something that looks like Plug and Play, but it is not truly Plug and Play! Windows NT 4.0 can detect some hardware features, but not as reliably as Windows 95 and later Windows products. Interface cards in the Macintosh architecture usually don't need any special configuration for the hardware to work properly because the Macintosh operating system is specifically designed for the Macintosh hardware.

With newer hardware, there may be BIOS settings that can turn Plug and Play compatibility on or off. Plug and Play should be enabled by default. If it isn't, check your computer's BIOS documentation to find out how to turn it on before installing a new operating system.

Checking Drivers

Many devices such as CD-ROM drives, SCSI drives, software-driven modems, and scanners, require special drivers to work correctly. In general, drivers are on the disks that come with the devices, but often these disks do not include drivers for all possible operating systems, or the most up-to-date drivers. Also, your device may not be on the list of drivers that come with the operating system, which can result in some installation problems.

If you install drivers that came with your hardware, the hardware should operate properly. However, in some cases (particularly with modems), you may experience significantly better performance by installing later drivers that you secure from the manufacturer. There are a few strategies to obtain the latest drivers for your particular device and operating system. If you have access to the Internet, simply go to your hardware manufacturer's Web site for drivers and support information. Or, contact the manufacturer and ask for the latest driver disks for your device. You don't want to have to abort an installation because of a lack of driver files.

Even though you may have driver disks in hand, it is best to get the most recent drivers because updates often fix bugs in older driver versions.

You should also check the documentation that came with any hardware you want to use with your new OS. In many cases, the manufacturer includes a disclaimer indicating which operating systems are certified for use with particular hardware.

Ensuring Hardware Compatibility

Because of the wide range of hardware available today, you will find that many operating systems have certain minimum hardware requirements. These are usually listed on the box, or in a section of the manual. More advanced operating systems often include a **hardware compatibility list (HCL)**. This is usually a list or book that contains brand names and models for all hardware supported by the operating system. Nearly all advanced Microsoft Windows, and some UNIX systems, for example, include an HCL. For Microsoft Windows-based operating systems, look on the installation CD-ROM for the HCL, or go to the Microsoft Web site at *www.microsoft.com*. Red Hat Linux lists hardware partners on its Web site at *www.redhat.com.* Unless you request it separately, you probably won't have an HCL with lower-level operating systems such as Windows 95 and Mac OS. Separate technical documentation may provide this information.

If you have hardware that is not on the HCL, all is not lost. If the hardware comes with appropriate drivers for the operating system you are about to install, your installation should be successful. However, if you do not have drivers, and your hardware is not on the HCL, you may be asking for trouble.

 If the hardware you plan to use is a clone, or an OEM (original equipment man-ufacturer) version of hardware that is on the list, proceed as if it is the hardware in question. If your hardware is not on the list of compatible hardware, or you do not have drivers, beware. The installation of the OS could fail, or the OS could become unstable after installation. Stick with compatible devices and drivers.

Regardless of the detail offered with your hardware, the OS manufacturer usually makes only minimal hardware recommendations. Many "minimal" recommendations are so small that you might be able to install the OS, but you probably won't be able to use it.

 If you need to partition and format the hard disk before you start, run *fdisk* from MS-DOS, as discussed in Chapter 3 (see Hands-on Project 3-4). When *fdisk* is finished, format the partition by running the MS-DOS command *format c: /s/u* (where c: is the drive letter) to unconditionally format the partition, and place the system files on it so that you can boot from that partition.

Making Time to Do the Job

Last of all, make sure you have enough time to complete the operating system installa-tion. Nothing is more frustrating than not being able to finish an install because you have some other obligation at an inconvenient moment. Coming back to the process later often turns out to be extremely confusing.

INSTALLING WINDOWS 95

Windows 95 comes in various versions or releases. You may see these referred to as ser-vice releases, identified by number. Updates to the basic operating system may be referred to as service packs. The differences in installation are minor from version to ver-sion. Newer releases have increased device support, and fewer bugs. Also, newer versions have more 32-bit code, and they include copies of Internet Explorer (the Microsoft Web browser) and the Active Desktop. You can get Windows 95 on floppy disks or on a CD-ROM. The version on floppy disk spans 26 disks, so it certainly pays to have a version you can install from a CD-ROM. Included with the CD-ROM is a Windows boot disk; it starts the Windows 95 command-line-only version from floppy, loads the CD-ROM drivers, and then runs the Setup program. You can practice installing Windows 95 in Hands-on Project 4-2 at the end of this chapter.

If you lost the Windows 95 boot disk, and you have a machine that runs MS-DOS, you can use the following steps to create a boot disk that will recognize a CD-ROM drive:

1. Obtain the necessary driver file from your CD-ROM manufacturer.

2. Obtain an MS-DOS disk that can be used to boot the computer (one that can boot into MS-DOS, and has at least the Command.com, Format.exe, Fdisk.exe, Autoexec.bat, and Config.sys files already on it). Using another computer, put the CD-ROM driver on the MS-DOS disk, and make sure that the disk has an Autoexec.bat file and a Config.sys file.

3. Use the MS-DOS Editor or Edlin line editor to edit the Config.sys file on the MS-DOS disk to include a line that points to the CD-ROM driver file, such as DEVICE=ACERCDH.SYS /D:IDECD000 (which starts the CD-ROM as drive D: in this example).

4. Boot the computer on which you want to install Windows 95 from the MS-DOS disk.

5. Insert the Windows 95 CD-ROM and run the Setup program.

You can make a boot disk from inside Windows 95, of course. Open the Control Panel (point to Start, then Settings, and choose Control Panel), choose Add/Remove Programs, click the Startup Disk tab, then click Create Disk (see Figure 4-1) and follow the instructions.

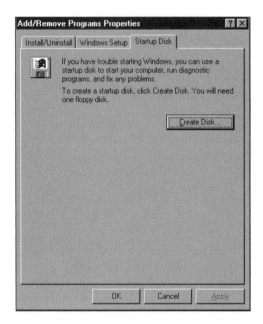

Figure 4-1   Creating a Windows 95 Startup disk

Hardware Requirements

To run Windows 95, you will need at least the hardware suggested in Table 4-2.

Table 4-2   Windows 95 Hardware Requirements

Hardware	Minimum	Recommended
CPU	386 DX	Pentium
RAM	4 MB	8 MB or more
Storage	45 MB	150 MB

The installation should take between 30 and 120 minutes, depending on whether you install from floppy disk or CD, and the speed of your machine. On a machine with a CD-ROM drive, 30–50 minutes for installation is about average.

The hard disk on your machine must already be formatted and have a partition.

 Review Chapter 3 on file systems before you decide to install a FAT32 file system on your machine!

 The FAT32 system is available only with the OSR2 release of Windows 95.

Windows 95 Installation Options

Windows 95 can be installed from either a CD-ROM or floppies. The setup program begins with a graphical user interface welcoming you to Windows 95. Clicking Continue and accepting the Software License Agreement initializes the Setup Wizard, an interactive utility, shown in Figure 4-2, which guides you through the setup process.

There are four Setup options for Windows 95. The Typical (default) installation installs the most popular Windows components for desktop computers. It performs most of the installation steps without much input from you; you only need to confirm the installation directory, and whether to create a startup disk. The Portable option provides support for options on portable computers such as **PCMCIA** (Personal Computer Memory Card International Association) cards (expansion cards used in laptops and desktop machines), and support for **LCD** (liquid crystal display) screens. This option is useful for mobile users with portable computers, and installs the Briefcase and support for direct cable connections. The Compact option performs an absolute minimum installation of Windows 95. This is for users with a limited amount of hard disk space. The Custom option allows you to choose the installation options you want.

Figure 4-2 Windows 95 Setup Wizard

 If you want to install mail and fax support, you must use the Custom option.

As with other Microsoft operating systems, we recommend that you use the Custom option so you can exercise control over what gets installed. You should install all of the Disk tools; by default, Backup is not selected! If you have plenty of disk space, it does not hurt to install all operating system components. Make sure each box is checked, as shown in Figure 4–3.

You can also choose whether to use the Windows 95 interface, which is the default selection, or the Program Manager (Windows 3.1) interface, if, for some reason, it is important to retain the look and feel of Program Manager.

Windows 95 asks if you want to create a **startup disk** (a bootable disk that can start the operating system if there is a problem with the hard disk). You should always create this disk; it will help you fix problems if you are unable to boot from the hard disk. This disk will be formatted, so any existing data on it will be lost.

During installation, you can choose to configure networking, printers, and modems, or you can bypass these options and set them up later from the Windows 95 Control Panel. The full steps for installing Windows 95 are provided in Hands-on Project 4-2.

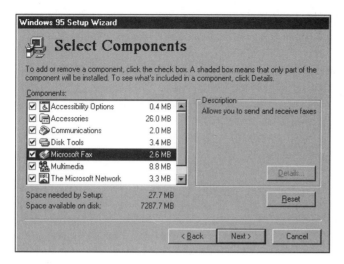

Figure 4-3   Windows 95 Select Components screen

Installing Windows 98

The Windows 98 installation is quite similar to the Windows 95 installation. This section addresses some of the elements that are different in Windows 98. It comes on either a CD-ROM or a large set of disks. Use the CD-ROM for speed and ease of installation.

Hardware Requirements

To run Windows 98, you will need at least the minimum hardware listed in Table 4-3.

Table 4-3   Windows 95 Hardware Requirements

Hardware	Minimum	Recommended
CPU	386 DX	Pentium
RAM	4 MB	8 MB or more
Storage	45 MB	150 MB

You will need one blank disk to make the system recovery disk, and the installation will take between 40 and 180 minutes.

As with Windows 95, you will need a startup disk with CD-ROM support. This disk comes with your Windows 98 bundle, but if you do not have it, you can make one yourself, as described in the Installing Windows 95 section of this chapter. You will also need a partitioned and formatted hard disk, a process detailed in Chapter 3.

You will need a Windows 95 OSR2 or a Windows 98 boot disk to format your hard disk with the FAT32 file system.

If there is no operating system currently installed on your computer, you may have to use the Windows 98 startup disk. Insert the startup disk, turn on your computer, and then insert the Windows 98 installation CD-ROM. By 1998, many computers could boot from a CD-ROM; you should make sure that the BIOS includes the CD-ROM drive as a bootable device (try Hands-on Project 4-1). If you already have an operating system installed, simply insert the Windows 98 installation CD-ROM. At this point, the Windows 98 Setup Wizard appears to step you through the installation. You can practice installing Windows 98 in Hands-on Project 4-3.

It's a good idea to choose the option to save your existing operating system files, which enables you to later uninstall Windows 98, and return to the prior operating system configuration.

If you try to use an Upgrade version of Windows 98 to do a full installation, you may see the Upgrade Compliance window, which appears because the setup routine could not find a previous version of Windows to verify that a license exists. If so, simply insert disk one, or the CD-ROM, of an older Windows version, and you should get past this point with no problems. If you do not have access to a previous version of Windows, you must obtain the Full version of Windows 98, rather than the Upgrade version.

You can choose from the same four types of installation as in Windows 95: Typical, Portable, Compact, or Custom, as shown in Figure 4-4. As usual, choosing Custom is the best option.

Figure 4-4   Windows 98 Setup Wizard

When you are able to select the components you wish to install, there are some options not included in Windows 95: Internet tools, Microsoft Outlook Express, Multilanguage Support, Online Services, and WebTV support. It is highly recommended that you add the Backup program to System Tools.

During the installation of Windows 98, the left side of the screen contains an outline of the portions of the installation process yet to be completed, and the estimated remaining install time. Don't make appointments based on the time estimate; it can be inaccurate.

In Windows 95, there is quite a bit of interaction required to configure devices after the basic operating system files are copied; in Windows 98 nearly everything is automatic up to the point of final configuration. Several restarts will occur automatically, whereas in Windows 95, you must be there to perform them. After the first restart, Windows 98 performs hardware detection, a process that may take several minutes. Your machine will start once again, and the drivers will be installed. Remember, no human interaction is needed for any of this to happen, so you can be doing something else. This is one of the biggest advantages of the Windows 98 installation.

 There are no questions about drivers or network cards, printers, or monitors during the Windows 98 installation; if these are not detected during installation, you must set them up after installation.

When you perform a Windows 98 installation, it will help a great deal if you have Internet access. This OS has a facility to access the Internet and download fixes and updated software, which is installed automatically. Additional information on Windows 98 upgrades is available in Chapter 5.

WINDOWS UPDATE

Beginning with the Windows 98 release, Microsoft includes an icon on the Start menu called Windows Update. **Windows Update** is a Web-based function that allows you to download and install fixes, updates, and enhancements to your Windows operating system. Product Updates and Support Information are the two main components in Windows Update.

Product Updates

Windows Update automatically scans your computer to determine your operating system and check on the installed updates. It then provides you with a list of components that you can choose to download and install on your computer. This list is divided into sections for Critical Updates, Picks of the Month, Recommended Updates, Additional Windows Features, and Device Drivers. You have the choice of which components, if any, you want to download and install.

Critical Updates listed for your system should be downloaded and installed. They will fix known bugs, security issues, and other problems that should be addressed as soon as possible.

Support Information

If you have never used Windows Update before, or have questions about it, the Support Information section provides several resources. These include Frequently Asked Questions; Known Issues; and Support options for your Operating System, Device Drivers, and Software Updates.

 Click the Installation History button to view a listing of all product updates previously performed on your computer.

INSTALLING WINDOWS ME

The installation for Windows Me is almost identical to the Windows 98 installation. The only real differences are the screens displayed during installation. They all mention Windows Me rather than Windows 98, and the information about the enhancements is, of course, new.

Hardware Requirements

To run Windows Me, you will need at least the minimum hardware listed in Table 4-4.

Table 4-4   Windows Me Hardware Requirements

Hardware	Minimum	Recommended
CPU	Pentium 150	Pentium 300 or faster
RAM	32 MB	64 MB or more
Storage	480-645 MB	2 GB

You will need one blank disk to make the system recovery disk, and the installation will take between 30 and 60 minutes, depending on the speed of your computer. Additional time will be required if you need to *fdisk* and *format* your hard drive. Check out Hands-on Project 4-4 for a complete Windows Me installation.

INSTALLING WINDOWS NT

Windows NT comes in two different configurations, Server and Workstation. The division of Windows NT into Workstation and Server occurred in 1994 with the release of version 3.5. Both Windows NT Server and Windows NT Workstation are designed as network operating systems, and either can be used for servers or workstations. The primary difference between them is the number of supported users that can be connected while the operating system is in server mode (NT Workstation is designed for no more than 10 simultaneous users, while Windows NT Server supports several thousand), and the features for network management (Windows NT Server has more extensive features). Windows NT 4.0, released in 1996, offered a new desktop interface, enhanced networking, Internet, directory services, and a more automated installation. This section will focus on installing Windows NT 4.0.

There are several ways to install Windows NT: directly from CD-ROM, from a combination of floppy disks and a CD-ROM, over the network, or using an answer file, which is a batch file that provides responses to questions that come up in the installation (sometimes called "unattended" installation). This chapter covers only installation directly from CD-ROM and from the combination of floppy disks and a CD-ROM (see Hands-on Project 4-5).

Hardware Requirements

Although Windows NT runs on many platforms, this chapter covers installation on the Intel platform. The installation on all platforms is nearly identical; just some specifics regarding hardware are different. You will need at least the hardware recommended in Table 4-5.

Table 4-5   Windows NT 4.0 Hardware Requirements for Intel-compatible Installations

Hardware	Minimum	Recommended
CPU	486 DX 33	Pentium 100 or faster
RAM	16 MB	32 MB
Storage (Server)	200 MB	500 MB
Storage (Workstation)	125 MB	400 MB

Your install time will be between 45 and 120 minutes.

Windows NT comes with an HCL (hardware compatibility list). Of the operating systems discussed so far, early releases of Windows NT (3.5 and 3.51) are the most selective about what hardware they support—later releases of Windows NT (4.0), starting in 1999, offer more built-in hardware driver support (equivalent to Windows 98).

To save yourself a headache, make sure that your hardware is on the HCL, or that you have Windows NT 4.0 drivers for the hardware you want to install. You cannot use any drivers with Windows NT 4.0 other than drivers made specifically for Windows NT 4.0. Using unsupported hardware and drivers can cause disastrous results! However, given the past popularity of Windows NT 4.0 among vendors and users alike, you should be able to find any drivers you require.

Although the HCL on your distribution CD-ROM may be out of date, you can update this list on the Internet. Point your browser to *www.microsoft.com* and search for "HCL" or "TechNet." TechNet is an online community sponsored by Microsoft that offers resources for IT professionals. When you register for TechNet, you can download the Windows NT 4.0 HCL, and find other recent information about Windows NT.

Starting the Installation

Windows NT 4.0 Server and Workstation come with an installation CD-ROM and three installation floppy disks. The disks can be used to start the installation on an Intel platform. If you lost the disks, you can make a set using another computer as follows:

1. Load the Windows NT CD-ROM in a working machine running MS-DOS, Windows 3.1x, 95, 98, or NT. Have three blank formatted floppy disks on hand.

2. From the MS-DOS prompt, navigate to the \i386 directory on the CD-ROM. (This directory contains installation files for 80486 and Pentium computers using Intel, Cyrix, or AMD processors.)

3. Run WINNT /OX.

4. Follow the prompts and you will end up with the startup disks for Windows NT.

Other platforms, such as the PowerPC, DEC Alpha, and RISC-4000, do not need the floppy installation disks; they will boot from the CD-ROM. Today, most Intel machines also include an option to boot from the CD-ROM.

Note that Windows NT 4.0 does not require a previously created and formatted hard disk partition. The Windows NT Setup program partitions and formats the drive(s) for you. Unless you need to retain a FAT partition (if you want to leave a portion of the disk for MS-DOS or Windows 95), you can install Windows NT on an NTFS file system (see Chapter 3). This is the default file system created by the Windows NT installer. You should make the Windows NT partition at least 500 MB, and preferably 1 GB. The maximum FAT partition space is 4 GB; you can create much larger partitions with NTFS.

Windows NT 4.0 only supports FAT16, not FAT32. Note that you cannot upgrade a volume that is already formatted for FAT32, such as a system already running Windows 98 and FAT32. You must use *fdisk* to reformat the volume to FAT16, and then proceed with the installation.

Windows NT installation is divided into two parts. The first part is character based, and focuses on detecting hardware and loading installation files. See Figure 4-5 for an example. The second part uses a graphical display (see Figure 4-6) with Windows-based dialog boxes, focusing on configuring the server or workstation.

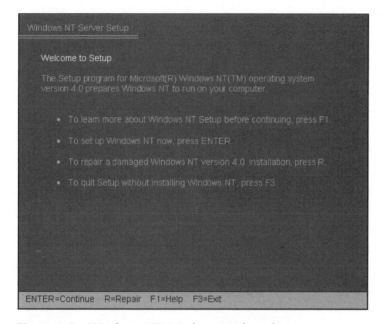

Figure 4-5   Windows NT 4.0 character-based screen

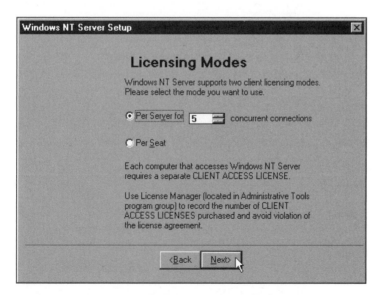

Figure 4-6   Windows NT 4.0 graphical display screen

If you install the Server version, you have two licensing options, depending on what you purchased. **Per-seat licensing** (a license for each workstation) makes sense in larger settings where you have more than one Windows NT server since one client can be connected to multiple servers with only a single per-seat license. In smaller settings with only one server, however, **per-server licensing** with a single server and a set number of workstations may make more sense.

If you install Windows NT Server, you must specify how this machine fits in the domain structure. A **domain** is a group of computers that share a common security database. If you install a single Windows NT server and do not plan to have other servers, or if you want it to participate only in a workgroup, or exist as a stand-alone server in an existing domain, you should choose the stand-alone server option during installation. If you want multiple Windows NT servers, and want to keep user and permission information consistent among all of them, put them all in a domain. There is only one **primary domain controller (PDC)** per domain, which is the main source for information about users and security rights for all the servers in the domain. Each domain has one PDC, and there can then be multiple **backup domain controllers (BDC)** per domain. More about domains can be found in Chapter 8 on Networking.

Windows NT also gives you the option to create a startup disk, called the Emergency Repair Disk (ERD). It is strongly recommended you make one. You will need one blank floppy during installation to make your ERD. This disk is unique to the machine on which you are installing, and you should make an Emergency Repair Disk for every Windows NT computer you have. Also, plan to update the ERD each time that you make a change, such as after adding a new device (and driver), installing new software, or adding many user accounts.

 Never use the Emergency Repair Disk from another computer! Doing so is likely to result in loss of data, and in many cases, require a new installation of Windows NT.

If your computer is connected to a network, you must answer questions about network connections and protocols. You can also install Remote Access Services (RAS) either during or after the Windows NT installation. RAS setup is covered in greater detail in later chapters.

You can also confirm or change **network bindings**, part of the Windows NT Server system, which are used to coordinate software communications among the NIC, network protocols, and network services. Setup automatically configures network bindings for protocols and services you selected.

Installing the Service Packs

With the basic installation of Windows NT completed, you can fix several bugs and problems in the operating system. Microsoft releases Windows service packs, known as SPs, to fix problems in the OS. In general, you should always apply the latest service pack right after you install any Windows operating system.

Before installing a service pack, always make a backup of your machine!

You can either download service packs from the Internet, or you can order a CD from Microsoft. If you have Internet access, go to *www.microsoft.com/windows/downloads/default.asp*, and select Windows NT Server 4.0. You will see a list of the service packs and upgrades available. Pick the service pack you want (see Figure 4-7), and find the download option on the bottom of the page. Choose this option to download the service pack, and then follow the instructions for installation.

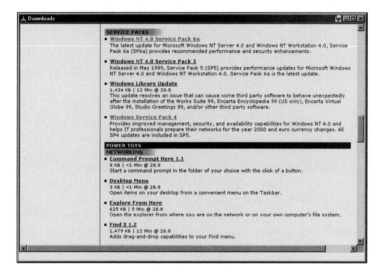

Figure 4-7   Download Windows NT service packs

When you are done with the service pack installation, you should make a new Emergency Repair Disk.

The latest service pack can be quite large, so downloading with a conventional modem connection may take a significant amount of time. Unless you have a high-speed connection, you probably should consider ordering the service pack on a CD.

When installing service packs, a folder is created that usually starts with "$uninstall." You can uninstall the service pack with the files found in this folder.

Installing Windows 2000

Windows 2000 is available in Server and Professional options, and is built on Windows NT technology. There are several ways to install Windows 2000, including floppy disks, CD-ROMs, over the network, and in unattended mode.

Hardware Requirements

You will need at least the hardware recommended in Table 4-6. It is important that your hardware is listed on the hardware compatibility list (HCL) for Windows 2000.

Table 4-6   Windows 2000 Hardware Requirements

Hardware	Minimum	Recommended
CPU (Server or Professional)	Pentium 133	Pentium 200 or faster
RAM (Server)	128 MB	256 MB
RAM (Professional)	64 MB	64 MB or more
Storage (Server)	1 GB	2 GB
Storage (Professional)	650 MB	1 GB

Your installation time will be between 45 and 120 minutes.

Starting the Installation

Two common ways to install Windows 2000 are by booting from the Windows 2000 CD-ROM, or by booting from the Setup disks. Both methods first go into a character-based screen that is actually started by the Winnt program.

 If you upgrade from an existing Windows NT installation, another way is to boot Windows NT, insert the CD-ROM, and run Winnt32—which is an all-GUI install, but does not follow all of the steps here.

The two common ways discussed in Project 4-6 will work every time, no matter what operating system is on the PC.

Project 4-6 addresses how Windows 2000 Setup provides a way to install a special mass storage driver, or special HAL, for SMP computers. **HAL** is the **hardware abstraction layer** consisting of the code that talks directly to the computer's hardware. This allows an application to use multiple processors if the need arises for additional processing power.

Windows 2000 also has the Windows Update feature. Please refer to the Windows Update section, which follows the Windows 98 discussion in this chapter. You will want to download and install any critical updates along with any optional updates you might want to use. Try Hands-on Project 4-6 to practice installing Windows 2000.

When you are done with the Windows Update installation, you should make a new Emergency Repair Disk.

INSTALLING WINDOWS XP

Windows XP, which stands for "experience," is designed for both Home and Professional use. The two versions are very similar, but the Professional version has more features, such as the ability to host up to 10 clients. Recreational users will probably use the Home version. Intended for office and networked environments, the Professional version adds support for multiple processors, software administration for the whole organization, and advanced security, to name just a few of the features provided.

Hardware Requirements

You will need at least the hardware recommended in Table 4-7. It is important that your hardware is listed on the hardware compatibility list (HCL) for Windows XP.

Table 4-7   Windows XP Hardware Requirements

Hardware	Minimum	Recommended
CPU (Home and Professional)	Pentium 233	Pentium 300 or faster
RAM (Home and Professional)	64 MB	128 MB or more
Storage (Home and Professional)	1.5 GB	5 GB or more

See Project 4-7 for practice installing Windows XP. Your installation time will be about 60 to 120 minutes.

The foundation for Windows XP, both Home and Professional, is a combination of Windows NT, Windows 2000, and Windows Me. You will notice several underlying similarities in Windows XP that remind you of features in these operating systems.

One new feature implemented in Windows XP is the concept of activation. Once you finish the setup and reboot your computer, you have 30 days to activate your copy of Windows XP. This can be done either by phone or online. Almost all new PCs with Windows XP installed have their activation linked solely to the BIOS. As long as the BIOS is not replaced, there should be no need for a reactivation.

Included with Windows XP is a new utility called the Files and Settings Transfer Wizard (see Figure 4-8). This allows you to transfer your files from your old computer to your new one via a direct cable or a network connection, if you are connected. You can transfer your display settings, browser favorites, desktop icons, and many other items to your new computer. This wizard is activated by clicking Start, then clicking Files and Settings Transfer Wizard.

Figure 4-8 Files and Settings Transfer Wizard

Windows XP also has the Windows Update feature. Refer to the Windows Update section, which follows the Windows 98 discussion in this chapter. You will want to download and install any critical updates along with any optional updates you want to use. Hands-on Project 4-7 enables you to practice a Windows XP installation.

INSTALLING UNIX: LINUX

And now for something completely different: UNIX. This section discusses installing one UNIX version—Linux—on the Intel PC platform. There are numerous other versions of UNIX designed for different hardware platforms. If you understand how Linux installs on the Intel platform, you should have no problem installing other versions of UNIX. Some UNIX flavors, such as **Solaris**, a version of UNIX developed by Sun Microsystems, are available for a variety of hardware platforms. Solaris was initially designed to run on many other platforms, including one based on Motorola 68000 CPUs and SPARC processors. A version for the Intel 80386 was introduced many years ago, but it was not a success. Now, functionally similar versions are released on both SPARC and Intel platforms.

Installing Linux

Linux is available in many shapes and forms. This section focuses on installing a commercial version of Linux, although there are shareware versions around. In the business environment, most companies choose to use operating systems for which they can get support. Using a commercial version of Linux guarantees support. Red Hat Linux 7.2 is the most recent commercial version at this writing.

Linux Hardware Requirements

The Red Hat Linux 7.2 operating system requires at least the hardware shown in Table 4-8.

Table 4-8   Red Hat Linux 7.2 Hardware Requirements

Hardware	Minimum	Recommended
CPU	386 DX 40	Pentium II series or faster
RAM	8 MB	64 MB or more
Storage (Server)	1 GB (minimal install)	4 GB (full install)

4

You will get a set of CD-ROMs in the package if you buy Red Hat Linux, or you can download the files from the Internet. For information on Red Hat Linux, point your browser to *www.redhat.com.* You can also search for "linux download" (use any Web search engine) to find many sites where you can download versions of Linux.

Install Red Hat from a CD-ROM. If your machine can boot from the CD-ROM drive, you will be able to boot Red Hat from the CD-ROM. You will need between 15 minutes to over one hour to install Red Hat Linux. You do not need to make partitions or format your disk ahead of time. Step-by-step instructions for installing Linux are included in Hands-on Project 4-8 at the end of this chapter.

The Linux operating system comes with the complete source code for the kernel, all the drivers, and most of the utilities. This is helpful if you are a computer programmer who wants to change code and make it do exactly what you want. This is probably the strongest advantage of Linux; because thousands of people worldwide are doing this kind of development, you will find a wide variety of programming tools and toys on the Internet. How well they work, and how well they are supported, is a different story. Linux is not for everyone!

INSTALLING MAC OS

The installations of Mac OS 9.x and OS X use a graphical interface and a Setup Assistant that functions similarly to the Microsoft Setup Wizards. Mac OS 9.x and OS X require a Macintosh with a PowerPC processor chip. They also require at least 32 MB of RAM, with virtual memory set to at least 64 MB.

The Mac OS installer does not require booting from a floppy disk, and can be installed from a CD-ROM, or over an AppleTalk network. The easiest way to install Mac OS is directly from the CD-ROM. The installation process has three parts: booting the CD-ROM, running the installer, and restarting from the hard drive. Complete, step-by-step instructions for installing Mac OS 9.x are given in the Hands-on Project 4-9 at the end of this chapter (if you are familiar with installing Mac OS 9.x, then you can install Mac OS X, which uses a similar installer).

Booting from the CD-ROM

A Macintosh will boot from the CD-ROM drive only if instructed to do so. This may be done either by selecting the CD-ROM icon in the Startup Disk Control Panel, or by holding down the C key on the keyboard at the very beginning of the startup process (put the CD-ROM into the machine, restart, and immediately hold down the C key). You will know you started from the CD-ROM when you see the desktop pattern, which will be tiled pictures of CD-ROMs.

At the end of the boot process, the CD-ROM icon appears in the upper-right corner of the screen, just below the menu bar, and the Mac OS 9.x window opens, showing you the contents of the CD-ROM, as shown in Figure 4-9.

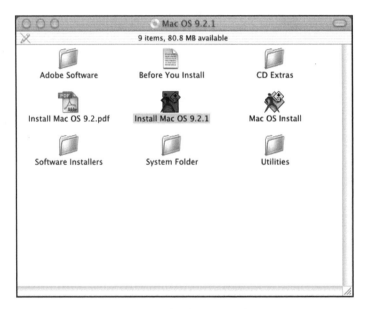

Figure 4-9   Mac OS 9.2.1 CD boot initial screen

 You may want to read the Mac OS Read Me files before starting the installation.

Running the Installer

To proceed with the installation, just double-click the Mac OS Install icon. The installer launches, and you are presented with the opening screen, which lists the steps for installation.

During this phase, you select a destination drive, read important information, agree to the software license, and then the installer copies operating system files to your hard drive. Copying files takes from about six minutes on a fast G4, to about 45 minutes on a 6100/60.

Restarting from the Hard Drive

When the installer finishes copying files, you are prompted to restart the computer. If you did a clean install, the operating system software that's appropriate for your Macintosh will appear on your hard drive, along with AppleTalk and TCP/IP networking software, and drivers for almost all Apple-brand printers. If you chose to install over existing system software, the installer may leave out printer drivers that do not match ones already on your system.

When you restart, the first thing you are presented with is the Mac OS Setup Assistant, shown in Figure 4-10.

Figure 4-10   Mac OS Setup Assistant

If you cancel this, you can use your computer right away, but it's a good idea to go through this final section of the installation to set up:

- The language you use
- Your name and organization
- The current time and date
- Your geographic location
- Your Finder preferences
- Local Network Introduction
- Computer name and password
- Whether or not you want to share a folder

Once you finish this and give the Assistant the go-ahead to set up everything, you can finish the installation, or continue with the Internet Setup Assistant.

Mac OS Installation Options

Up to this point, we have covered a basic installation. You can access additional installation options by clicking the Options or Customize buttons before starting the Mac OS Setup Assistant during the installation.

The Options button gives you the choice to not update your hard disk drivers, which should be updated unless you know with absolute certainty that the existing drivers are more recent than the version included with the operating system installer. You are also given the option not to create an installation log.

The Customize button allows you to control which components you want to install, down to the specific drivers. Use it if you know you don't want to install pieces, such as Personal Web Sharing, or know that you don't need to connect to the Internet. Unchecking components here is safe enough, unless you uncheck the Mac OS installer itself. Selecting the customized installation option of any of these components generally brings up many choices within the individual sections, and is not recommended unless you know exactly what you are doing.

CHAPTER SUMMARY

- ☐ This chapter provides an overview of the installation process for the operating systems covered in this book. You know how to prepare for operating system installation by checking hardware and gathering information about your system, and you surveyed basic installations of Windows 95, Windows 98, Windows Me, Windows NT (Server and Workstation), Windows 2000 (Server and Professional), Windows XP (Home and Professional), the Red Hat Linux 7.2 variety of UNIX, Mac OS 9.x., and Mac OS X.

- ☐ In addition, you learned how to configure networking and other hardware with each of these operating systems, and what hardware and software issues to watch for during operating system installation. And, you learned how to use the Windows Update option for Windows 98, Windows Me, Windows 2000, and Windows XP.

- ☐ The keys to making the most out of the information in this chapter are to try the hands-on exercises that follow, and practice installing various operating system functions. Nothing can replace experience in performing these installations. It takes several hours to install all of the operating systems, depending on the speed of your hardware. However, it will be time well spent, as you develop a broad understanding of general operating system theory, as well as the specifics of installing and configuring some of the most popular ones.

KEY TERMS

backup domain controller (BDC) — A server in the domain that has a copy of the domain's directory database, which is updated periodically by the primary domain controller (PDC). The BDC also can authenticate logons to the domain.

domain — A logical grouping of computers and computer resources that helps manage these resources and user access to them. A domain enables a group of computers to share a common security database.

HAL (hadware abstraction layer) — The hardware abstraction layer consisting of the code that talks directly to the computer's hardware.

hardware compatibility list (HCL) — A list of brand names and models for all hardware supported by an operating system. Adherence to the HCL ensures a more successful operating system install. HCLs can often be found on OS vendors' Web sites.

LCD (Liquid Crystal Display) — The display technology in some laptops and other electronic equipment.

network bindings — Part of the Windows NT Server and later operating systems, used to coordinate software communications among the NIC, network protocols, and network services.

PCMCIA (Personal Computer Memory Card International Association) — A standard for expansion cards used in laptops and desktop machines. Now usually shortened to PC Card.

per-seat licensing — A software licensing scheme that prices software according to the number of individual users who install and use the software.

per-server licensing — A software licensing scheme that prices software according to a server configuration that permits multiple users to access the software from a central server.

Plug and Play system (PnP) — In Windows 95 and later Windows products (except Windows NT), a protocol and hardware standard that permits the operating system to automatically recognize and configure compatible hardware.

primary domain controller (PDC) — A server in the domain that authenticates logons, and keeps track of all changes made to accounts in the domain.

Solaris — A Sun Microsystems operating system based on UNIX.

startup disk — A bootable floppy disk that includes the basic operating system, key disk utilities, and drivers (such as for the CD-ROM drive). This disk can be used to start the system in the event that the hard drive or its operating system is damaged.

Windows Update — A Web-based function that allows you to download and install product updates for your Windows operating system.

REVIEW QUESTIONS

1. What is the name of the program that sets up everything on your Mac after the installer is finished?

   a. Mac Installation Wizard

   b. Apple Post Installation Assistant

   c. Mac OS Setup Assistant

   d. Mac OS Setup Wizard

2. In Windows 95, you can format the hard drive with the FAT32 file system. True or False?

3. A Plug and Play operating system eliminates the need to understand operating system hardware requirements and limitations before installing the system. True or False?

4. Software driver requirements change as you add new hardware or install new software. Perhaps the best resource for updated drivers for any manufacturer's hardware is _____.

5. Windows 2000 ships in four configurations. Two of these configurations are Advanced Server and Datacenter Server. What are the other two?

   a. Home and Professional

   b. Server and Professional

   c. Home and Workstation

   d. Server and Workstation

6. Before installing the Red Hat Linux 7.2 operating system, you must partition and format the hard drive. True or False?

7. You are trying to install an operating system from the CD-ROM, but your computer won't boot from CD-ROM. Which of the following might be the problem?

   a. The computer is older and does not support booting from CD-ROM.

   b. Most operating system installations require that you use an installation boot disk.

   c. The computer's BIOS is not set up to boot from CD-ROM.

   d. all of the above

   e. only a and c

8. Windows 98 was the last operating system after Windows 95 to run on the Intel 386 platform. True or False?

9. The *fdisk* utility is used for what purpose?

10. If you use the Emergency Repair Disk from a Windows 2000 system on your Windows NT 4.0 system, the following will occur:

    a. New features in Windows 2000 will be added to the Windows NT 4.0 system.

    b. Nothing, Windows NT 4.0 will detect that it does not have the proper Emergency Repair Disk and notify you.

    c. There may be a loss of data, and a new installation of Windows NT 4.0 may be required.

    d. Windows 2000 does not support Emergency Repair Disks, so this could never happen.

11. Windows 98 and other operating systems frequently issue update files to fix bugs and add enhancements. In today's computing environment, there is a single source that is the best resource for obtaining operating system updates. What is it?

12. Windows XP is supplied in two configurations. What are they?

13. Sun Microsystems offers a popular UNIX version known as _____.

14. Why would you choose a commercial version of Linux over a shareware version?

    a. You have the money and don't want to take the time to download the shareware version.

    b. The source code for Linux comes with the commercial version.

    c. The commercial version comes with support for your company.

    d. The commercial version comes with a GUI interface, but no shareware versions have a GUI.

15. The HCL helps ensure that you have the proper hardware available during some Windows and UNIX installs. HCL stands for what?

16. To boot a Mac from the CD-ROM, you hold down what key during the bootup process? How do you know that it actually booted from the CD-ROM?

17. Choosing the Customize button during a Mac OS install allows you to:

    a. select which operating system to install.

    b. choose the install location.

    c. choose various OS components you want to install.

    d. None of the above

18. Windows Update is available in Windows 95 and later operating system releases. True or False?

19. What utility can you use in Windows XP to transfer Internet Explorer settings, Outlook Express settings, desktop settings, the My Documents folder, dial-up connections, and display settings to your new computer?

20. What three operating systems form the foundation for Windows XP?

HANDS-ON PROJECTS

Be sure to read the text sections on installing these operating systems before attempting the Hands-on Projects. The text contains important background information, such as hardware requirements, which you need to know before attempting the installations.

Project 4-1

Your hardware system BIOS controls many basic functions of your computer. This chapter discusses the need for being able to boot from a CD-ROM disk. You can find out how your system BIOS handles CD-ROM booting by displaying the Setup or Configuration screen on your computer.

To display your current booting options by looking at your BIOS:

1. Display your computer's BIOS Setup screen. How you do this varies with the machine, but common techniques are to press **Del** during the system bootup process, press **Ctrl+Alt+Esc** simultaneously, or press **F1**. If none of these works, study your computer's documentation, or carefully read all screens during system boot.

2. Look for settings for boot order. This usually involves using the cursor keys to position the cursor over a field, then pressing the space bar or Page Up/Page Down to step through the settings.

3. Step through the choices available on your machine.

4. If available, choose a CD-ROM boot, and save and exit the Configuration screen.

5. Insert your operating system CD-ROM disk and reboot the computer. Did the CD boot your computer? What error messages did you see, if any?

6. Can you reconfigure your system to boot from your hard disk drive?

Project 4-2

Most of us will probably never install an operating system from scratch. Usually when you buy a computer, an operating system is already installed. If you want to change the operating system, you'll probably purchase an upgrade version of the software that won't work by itself; it requires the presence of an earlier version of the operating system to function properly. (Chapter 5 covers upgrade installations.) However, if you build a computer yourself, or if you install a new boot hard drive, then you must install a Full version of an operating system. With modern operating systems, the process is very similar to installing an upgrade; however, there are some differences. For example, you must install a printer for the first time, install and configure communications components, and so on.

In this project, you'll install a Full version of Windows 95 from a CD-ROM distribution medium. We assume that: the new hard drive is already installed, you used *fdisk* to create an MS-DOS partition, and you used *format* to prepare it to receive the new operating system.

95

To install a Full version of Windows 95:

1. Obtain or create a bootable floppy disk. You'll need a bootable MS-DOS disk, a Windows 95 boot floppy, etc. Also make sure this bootable floppy includes support for your CD-ROM drive. Your installation will be easier if you installed MS-DOS-level support for a mouse. However, the setup routine itself also looks for a mouse, and probably will install the drivers needed for it if your mouse is a standard device that Setup can recognize.

2. Insert the floppy disk into the A: drive and boot the system.

3. Insert the Windows 95 CD-ROM into the CD-ROM drive. Type **d:setup**, where d: is the drive letter of your CD-ROM drive. You will see an information message that says "Setup is now going to perform a routine check on your system. To continue, press Enter. To quit Setup, press ESC."

4. Press **Enter**. Setup runs the Scandisk utility to verify the integrity of your hard drive. When Scandisk is finished, you will see a message that says "Copying files needed for setup." Next you will see a dialog box titled Windows 95 Setup with the message "Welcome to Windows 95 Setup."

5. Click **Continue**, or press **Alt+C**. You will see a message that says "Now preparing the Windows 95 Setup Wizard," and you'll see a progress bar in the Setup window while Setup copies files to your hard drive.

6. When the Software License Agreement dialog box appears, read the agreement, and click **Yes** to continue the Installation Wizard. The next dialog box summarizes the next steps the wizard will complete in the installation process: Collecting information, Copying Windows 95 Files, and Restarting the system. The first choice appears in bold face, indicating this is the next step. You will see this dialog box twice more during the installation process, as each section of steps is completed.

7. Click **Next** to continue.

8. Choose the directory where you want Windows installed. The default directory is C:\Windows. This is the best choice.

9. Click **Next**. You will see a Preparing Directory dialog box, then the Setup Options dialog box will appear. The choices in this dialog box are:

   ❑ Typical — Recommended for most computers

   ❑ Portable — Files required for portable computers

   ❑ Compact — A minimal install that includes no optional components

   ❑ Custom — Allows you to customize all installed components

   Although the onscreen prompt indicates that the Custom option is recommended only for advanced users, programmers, or system administrators, it is recommended that all users choose this option. If you choose Typical, the Setup Wizard determines which components to install. Later, as you install other software, you may be required to locate your Windows 95 CD and add more components. It is usually easier to install everything the first time. The rest of this project assumes you chose the Custom installation option.

10. Click the **Custom** option button to select it, and click **Next**. You will see a Certificate of Authenticity dialog box. Enter the CD key number, which may be printed on the cover of your Windows 95 manual, on a separate piece of paper supplied with the software, or on the back of the case in which the CD was shipped. If you are installing a version of the software that was shipped with your computer, this number takes the form:

    xxxxx-OEM-xxxxxxx-xxxxx

    If you purchased the operating system outright from another outlet, you won't see the OEM designation as part of the CD key.

11. Enter whatever key was provided with your version of the operating system, and click **Next**. A User Information dialog box appears.

12. Enter your name and company name, if applicable, in the fields provided, and click **Next**. The Analyzing Your Computer dialog box opens. It asks whether you want Setup to scan for available hardware, or if you want to manually install everything. You should choose the default, to scan the system.

13. Click **Next** to view a hardware list. This is a list of hardware Setup already knows about, such as a sound card, network interface card, and so on.

14. Click the check boxes beside the hardware you want to install. In general, this should be all of the hardware that appears in this dialog box.

15. Click **Next** to continue scanning the system for additional hardware. A progress bar in the middle of the dialog box shows how far along you are in the process. This part of the installation takes several minutes, until finally the Select Components dialog box appears. You should choose all possible options in this dialog box. Notice that in the list of components, there are check marks beside some, not others. In addition, some of the boxes with check marks are gray and some are white. Setup selected a subset of available components as a starting point.

16. Click any empty check boxes to select them. If a check box is gray, click **Details** to display a list of available components under that main heading. Check all of the options in this list, and click **OK** to return to the main Select Components dialog box. Repeat this process until all available components are chosen.

17. Click **Next** to select the options you chose, and continue the installation.

18. If you have a network adapter installed, you should see a Network Configuration dialog box. The default choices are:

    ❑ Client for Microsoft Networks

    ❑ Client for NetWare Networks

    ❑ Dial-Up Adapter

    ❑ IPX/SPX-compatible Protocol

    ❑ NetBEUI

    If you aren't using a network with this computer right now, or if you want to configure networking later, simply click **Next**.

19. If you aren't using a Novell network, you don't need the Novell networking components, so click **IPX/SPX-compatible protocol**, and click **Remove**. Setup removes this entry, as well as the Client for NetWare entry. This leaves everything you need to network in a Microsoft Windows environment, as well as sets the stage for dial-up networking, such as connecting to the Internet.

20. If you will be using the Internet, or if you are networking in a UNIX environment, you must install the TCP/IP protocol. We will assume you want to install the TCP/IP protocol.

21. Click **Add**, and choose **Protocol** from the list of available options. Click **Add**.

22. At the Select Network Protocol prompt, click **Microsoft** in the manufacturer list (left side of the dialog box), and then click **TCP/IP** from the Network Protocols list on the right side of the dialog box.

23. Click **OK**. TCP/IP appears in the Network Configuration dialog box.

24. Click **File & Print sharing** to display the File and Print Sharing dialog box.

25. Click in the boxes that turn on Share printers and/or Share files, and click **OK**.

26. Click **Next** to display the Identification dialog box.

27. Type a name for this computer.

28. Type a workgroup name. It is best if this is a relatively short, easy-to-use name. But remember that all computers on the network that you want to communicate with should be in the same workgroup.

29. Type a description in the Description field. This can be anything that describes this particular computer.

30. Click **Next** to display the Computer Settings dialog box. This is a recap of the configuration settings you just specified.

31. Review the settings, and click **Next** if everything is okay. To change an item displayed in this screen, click **Back** instead of Next.

32. The next window asks if you want to create a startup disk. You should click **Yes**, and then click **Next**.

33. The Start Copying Files dialog box appears. Click **Next**.

34. The next screen asks for a disk on which to copy the startup files. Insert a blank formatted disk, and click **OK**. A progress bar shows the file copy progress.

35. When you see "Setup has finished creating startup disk," remove the disk from the drive, and click **OK**. Setup continues by copying more files to your hard disk. Promotional and tip dialog boxes appear to introduce you to the Windows 95 environment.

36. When all files are copied, you should see the Finishing Setup dialog box. Click **Finish**. Setup will restart your computer. After the reboot, you will see "Getting Ready to Run Windows 95 for the First time." Setup is finishing the final Windows configuration, which may take several minutes.

37. Finally, you will see a user name and password dialog box. Type the name you want to use to log into Windows and your network, then click in the **Password** field and enter a password (if you are using a password, otherwise leave the Password field blank).

38. Press **Enter**, or click **OK**, and you will see the Set Windows Password dialog box. This is a crosscheck to make sure you haven't mistyped the password. Enter the password again, and press **Enter**, or click **OK**. You will see the Setting up Hardware and Plug and Play dialog box.

39. Set the system clock when you see the Date/Time Properties dialog box, then click **Close**.

40. If you included Windows messaging in your component choices at the beginning of this process, you will see a dialog box asking whether you have used Windows messaging before. Since this is a fresh install, the correct answer is **No**. Click **Next** to display the Inbox Setup Wizard opening dialog box.

41. Click the check boxes beside the services you want to use, and click **Next**. You may be asked for your area code and other information as part of dial-up networking configuration. Enter the requested data, and click **OK**.

42. Continue with the Inbox Setup Wizard, answering questions specific to your particular installation, and clicking **Next** on each wizard screen to move on to the next step.

43. You will be prompted to let Windows find and configure your modem, or you can manually set up the modem yourself. You should let the computer scan the system to find your modem and set it up for you.

44. If you included fax services as part of your original configuration specification, you will next see a dialog box asking whether you want the Fax server to answer every incoming call. Unless you have a dedicated telephone line for fax services, choose **No** here.

45. Click **Next** to display the Microsoft FAX dialog box. Enter your full name, country, and fax number with area code at the prompts.

46. Click **Next** to move to the next wizard screen, where you can enter the path to your post office. This information is required only if you will be using LAN-based e-mail. If you are using only Internet e-mail, you can bypass this option by entering a bogus directory (C:\ is a good choice), and accepting the entry when Windows warns that it can't find the post office. Otherwise, check with your LAN administrator for the correct location of the post office files.

47. Type a mailbox name and password. (Consult your LAN administrator, or enter bogus data. You can correct it later if necessary.)

48. Click **Next**, then click **Finish** to complete the Inbox configuration process. The Add Printer Wizard launches.

49. Click **Next**, and choose Local or Network printer from the next dialog box, depending upon which type of printer you are installing.

50. Click **Next**, and choose a printer from the list, or select the network host printer you want to use.

51. Click **Next**, and click **OK** when Setup says it wants to restart your computer.

52. After the reboot, enter your user name and password (the same combination you chose the first time the system rebooted). The startup process continues, and final setup is complete.

 If Setup didn't install or configure all of your hardware (your NIC, CD-ROM drive, or sound card, for example), click on Start, point to Settings, choose Control Panel, and select Add New Hardware. Let Windows scan your system for new hardware, or manually configure the missing pieces.

Project 4-3

In this project, you'll install a Full version of Windows 98 from a CD-ROM distribution medium. We assume that: the new hard drive is already installed, you used *fdisk* to create an MS-DOS partition, and you used *format* to prepare it to receive the new operating system.

The installation of Windows 98 is very similar to that of Windows 95. However, you will quickly notice that Windows 98 is more sophisticated. The setup program does more of the work for you, and there is less necessity for user intervention; for example, you don't have to keep clicking Next to continue the process. Once you chose the basic components you want, and specify the directory where you want Windows 98 to reside, the rest of the installation process is mostly automatic. Please read the section on Installing Windows 98 in this chapter before completing this exercise.

To install a Full version of Windows 98:

1. Obtain or create a bootable floppy disk. You'll need a bootable MS-DOS disk, or a Windows 98 boot floppy disk. Also make sure this bootable floppy includes support for your CD-ROM drive. Your installation will be easier if you installed MS-DOS-level support for a mouse. However, the setup routine itself also looks for a mouse, and probably will install the drivers needed for it if your mouse is a standard device Setup can recognize.

2. Insert the floppy disk into the A: drive and boot the system.

 If your computer can boot from the CD-ROM, you can skip Steps 1 and 2.

3. Insert the Windows 98 CD-ROM into the CD-ROM drive. Type **d:setup**, where d: is the drive letter of your CD-ROM drive. You will see an information message that says "Setup is now going to perform a routine check on your system. To continue, press Enter. To quit Setup, press ESC."

4. Press **Enter**. Setup runs the ScanDisk utility to verify the integrity of your hard drive. When ScanDisk is finished, you will see a message that says "Copying files needed for setup." Next you will see a dialog box titled Windows 98 Setup with the message "Welcome to Windows 98 Setup."

5. Click **Continue**, or press **Alt+C**. You will see a message that says "Setup is preparing the Windows 98 Setup Wizard" and you'll see the progress bar in the Setup window while Setup copies files to your hard drive. On the left of your screen is a menu that shows the steps to be completed, with the current step highlighted. You'll also see an estimate of the time remaining. At this stage, with a medium-speed CD-ROM and reasonably capable computer, you will see a time remaining of 35-40 minutes.

6. Click **Next**, and choose the directory where you want Windows installed. The default directory is C:\Windows. This is the best choice. However, if you want to change the directory, click the Option button beside the Other Directory prompt.

7. Click **Next**. You will see a Preparing Directory dialog box, and messages that say "Checking for installed components" and "Checking for available disk space." In a few moments, you will see the Setup Options dialog box. The choices in this dialog box are:

   ❏ Typical — Recommended for most computers

   ❏ Portable — Files required for portable computers

   ❏ Compact — A minimal install that includes no optional components

   ❏ Custom — Allows you to customize all installed components

   Although the on-screen prompt indicates that the Custom option is recommended only for advanced users, programmers, or system administrators, all users should choose this option. If you choose Typical, the Setup Wizard determines which components to install. Later, as you install other software, you may be required to locate your Windows 98 CD and add more components. It is usually easier to install everything the first time. The rest of this project assumes you chose the Custom installation option.

8. Click the **Custom** option button to select it, and click **Next** to select available components. As with Windows 95, you should select every available option during this initial installation to avoid having to repeat any of the installation process later.

9. Click **Next** to display an Identification screen. Enter a computer name, the workgroup, and a computer description.

10. Click **Next** to display the Computer Settings dialog box. This shows you a brief list of basic computer hardware, such as the keyboard layout and regional settings. You should accept the defaults on this screen (however, you can click **Change** to make any modifications you want to this list).

11. Click **Next** to view the Establishing Your Location dialog box. Accept the default, or choose from the list (United States, United Kingdom, Turkey, etc.).

12. Click **Next** to display the Startup Disk dialog box. When prompted, insert a blank floppy disk into the drive.

13. Click **OK**, and Setup begins copying files to the floppy disk. A progress bar shows how much is left to do. Eventually, you will see a message that says "Setup has finished creating your startup disk."

14. Remove the disk, and click **OK** to continue. You will see a dialog box that reports "Start Copying Files." This is an informational dialog box and Setup waits on this screen for you to click Next to continue the installation.

15. Click **Next**. The Welcome to Microsoft Windows 98 dialog box appears. You are invited to "Sit back and relax while Windows 98 installs on your computer." Note the time remaining at the lower left of the screen. At this point, it should be about 30 minutes. As more files are copied, you will see informational messages in the middle of the screen: promotional material, tips, and progress reports.

16. In the User Information dialog box, fill in your name and the company name, if applicable. Click **Next** to continue.

17. When the Software License Agreement appears, read the agreement, click the button beside the **I accept** prompt, and then click **Next**.

18. Setup then asks for the CD product key. It is located on documentation that came with your software, or on the back of the case in which the CD itself was delivered. The Windows 98 CD key takes the form:

    XXXXX–XXXXX–XXXXX–XXXXX–XXXXX

    You will enter a combination of letters and numbers to fill in all of the blanks. The key is not case sensitive, so enter the letters in either uppercase or lowercase. Click **Next**.

    Eventually, you will see a message that indicates that Windows is setting up hardware and Plug and Play devices. One or two more dialog boxes tell you that hardware is detected. Windows 98 does a pretty good job of detecting and configuring the hardware you installed. However, you must make sure all printers, scanners, and other devices are installed on the system and turned on before reaching this stage of the installation to ensure proper detection and configuration. You are 13 to 15 minutes away from finishing the installation at this point.

19. Set the system clock when you see the Date & Time Properties dialog box, then click **Close**. You will also see a dialog box that says "Windows is now setting up the following items:" followed by a list of remaining tasks, including Time Zone, Control Panel, Programs on the Start menu, and more. Additional dialog boxes show progress with each of these steps as they are completed.

20. Finally, you will see a dialog box that asks for your user name and password. Type the name and password you want to use to log into Windows, and click **OK**. The password in Windows 98 is not case sensitive. A Building Driver Information Database dialog box appears, then you will see various dialog boxes as Windows 98 finds your hardware components and installs the drivers they require.

21. Then you will see a large Welcome to Windows 98 dialog box with the following options:

   ❒ Register Now

   ❒ Connect to the Internet

   ❒ Discover Windows 98

   ❒ Maintain Your Computer

22. Click the **X** in the upper-right corner of this dialog box to close it.

23. If you want to install dial-up networking, double-click **My Computer**.

24. Choose **Dial-up Networking** and then choose **Make New Connection** to start the Make New Connection Wizard. Follow the on-screen instructions, clicking **Next** at each stage to move on to the next step. (For more information on setting up dial-up networking, see Chapter 7.) You have successfully completed the installation of Windows 98!

Project 4-4

In this project, you'll install a Full version of Windows Me from a CD-ROM distribution medium. We assume that: the new hard drive is already installed, you used *fdisk* to create an MS-DOS partition, and you used *format* to prepare it to receive the new operating system.

The installation of Windows Me is very similar to that of Windows 98. Once you choose the basic components you want, and specify the directory where you want Windows Me to reside, the rest of the installation process is mostly automatic. Please read the section on Installing Windows Me in this chapter before completing this exercise.

The installation of Windows Me should take between 30 and 60 minutes, depending on the speed of your computer.

To install a Full version of Windows Me:

1. Obtain or create a bootable floppy disk. You'll need a bootable MS-DOS disk, or a Windows 95 or 98 boot floppy disk. Also make sure this bootable floppy includes support for your CD-ROM drive. Your installation will be easier if you installed MS-DOS-level support for a mouse. However, the setup routine itself also looks for a mouse, and probably will install the drivers needed for it if your mouse is a standard device Setup can recognize.

2. Insert the floppy disk into the A: drive and boot the system.

 If your computer can boot from the CD-ROM, you can skip Steps 1 and 2.

3. Insert the Windows Me CD-ROM into the CD-ROM drive. Type **d:setup**, where d: is the drive letter of your CD-ROM drive. You will see an information message that says "Please wait while Setup initializes. Setup is now going to perform a routine check on your system. To continue, press Enter. To quit Setup, press ESC." Press **Enter**.

4. Setup then runs the ScanDisk utility to verify the integrity of your hard drive. When ScanDisk is finished, type an **X** to exit. You will then see a message that says "Copying files needed for setup." Next you will see a dialog box titled Windows Millennium Edition Setup Wizard with the message "Welcome to Windows Me Setup." See Figure 4-11. Click **Next**.

5. Next you are presented with the License Agreement screen. You should read this agreement using the Page Down key to move through the agreement. If you accept the agreement, click **I accept this Agreement**, then click **Next**.

6. Then you are asked to enter the unique product key for Windows Me. This 25-character product key is usually found on the back of the CD case. Type in the key, and click **Next**.

7. Now you are given the opportunity to choose the directory where you want Windows installed. The default directory is C:\Windows. This is the best choice. However, if you want to change the directory, click the Option button beside the Other directory prompt. Click **Next**.

Figure 4-11   Welcome to Windows Me Setup

8. You will see a Preparing Directory dialog box, and messages that say "Checking for installed components" and "Checking for available disk space." In a few moments, you will see the Setup Options dialog box. The choices on this dialog box are:

   ◘ Typical — Recommended for most computers

   ◘ Portable — Files required for portable computers

   ◘ Compact — A minimal install that includes no optional components

   ◘ Custom — Allows you to customize all installed components

   Although the onscreen prompt indicates that the Custom option is recommended only for advanced users, programmers, or system administrators, all users should choose this option. If you choose Typical, the Setup Wizard determines which components to install. Later, as you install other software, you may be required to locate your Windows Me CD and add more components. It is usually easier to install everything the first time. The rest of this project assumes you chose the Custom installation option. Click the **Custom** option button to select it, and click **Next**

9. On the User Information screen, enter your name and the name of your company. Click **Next**.

10. Next you will see the Select Components screen. As with Windows 98, you should select every available option during this initial installation to avoid having to repeat any of the installation process later. Click **Next**.

11. The Network Identification screen now appears. Enter a computer name, the workgroup, and a computer description. Click **Next**.

12. The next screen allows you to select your language. The default is English. Once you selecte the language, click **Next** to continue.

13. The next screen is Country/Region. Accept the default, or choose from the list (United States, United Kingdom, Turkey, etc.). Click **Next**.

14. The Keyboard Layout screen appears next. The default is United States 101, or you can select any of the other keyboards. Click **Next**.

15. Now you will see the Establishing Your Time Zone screen. Click on your zone, and then click **Next**.

16. The Startup Disk screen appears. You are asked to insert a floppy disk labeled "Windows Millennium Edition Startup Disk" in the floppy drive. Once you have done this, click **OK**. All existing files on the floppy will be lost. A progress bar shows how much is left to do. Eventually, you will see a message that says "Setup has finished creating your startup disk. Remove the disk, and then click OK to continue Setup." Remove the disk, and click **OK** to continue.

17. You will see a dialog box that reports "Ready to Begin Copying Files." This is an informational dialog box, and Setup waits on this screen for you to click Finish to continue the installation. Click **Finish**.

18. The Welcome to Microsoft Windows Millennium Edition dialog box appears. You are invited to "Sit back and relax while Windows Me installs on your computer." Note the time remaining at the lower left of the screen. At this point, it should be about 25 minutes, depending on the speed of your computer. As more files are copied, you will see informational messages in the middle of the screen: promotional material, tips, and progress reports. You will also see a progress bar on the lower left, showing a percentage of the file copy completed.

19. Setup now restarts your computer.

20. Next, the installation process inventories the driver database, and then sets up your computer hardware and any Plug and Play devices.

21. Setup restarts your computer.

22. The process continues, setting up the hardware and any Plug and Play devices.

23. The next screen you see shows Windows setting up the following items:

    ❐ Control Panel

    ❐ Programs on Start menu

    ❐ Windows Help

    ❐ Tuning up Application Start

    ❐ System Configuration

24. Setup now restarts your computer.

25. Finally, you will see a dialog box that asks for your user name and password. Type the name and password you want to use to log into Windows, and click **OK**. You are asked to retype the password to confirm it. Retype the password, and click **OK**.

26. You now see a dialog box showing "Updating System Settings". Once this is completed, you are logged on and ready to begin exploring Windows Me. Your installation was successfully completed.

Project 4-5

Please read the section on Installing Windows NT in this chapter before completing this exercise. You will need one blank floppy disk during installation to make your Emergency Repair Disk. This installation should be performed on a "clean" machine, one with no prior operating system installed.

    You do not need to partition nor format the hard disk. Windows NT will perform these tasks.

To install Windows NT Server 4.0:

1. Power off the computer.

2. If your machine can boot from a CD-ROM, insert the Windows NT CD-ROM, and turn on your computer. If not, insert Setup disk 1 into drive A: and turn on the machine, then insert the CD-ROM into the CD-ROM drive. This method automatically starts Winnt.exe, and the first screen of the installer appears.

3. Setup checks the system configuration. If you are installing from the setup disks, the installer requests you to insert Setup disk 2, and press **Enter**.

4. The Windows NT Server Setup options appear. Press **Enter** to continue the installation.

5. Setup attempts to automatically detect mass storage device controllers, such as ESDI, IDE, and SCSI. This process requires Setup to load device drivers from many hardware vendors, contained on Setup disk 3. Press **Enter**, and then you are prompted to insert disk 3. As requested, insert disk 3, and press **Enter**.

6. If Setup has problems detecting SCSI adapters for hard drives or CD-ROM drives, you might need a supplementary driver disk from the manufacturer to install these drivers. Press **S** if you need to manually select a driver from those suggested by Setup, or to install a driver from a manufacturer's disk.

 If Setup does not detect a SCSI adapter that is non-critical for the installation, such as a tape drive, you can install it later using the Windows NT Server Control Panel.

7. Press **Enter** to continue.

 If you receive a message that your hard disk may actually be larger than the size for which it is currently configured, press Enter to continue.

8. You now see the License Agreement. When finished reading, press **F8** to agree to the terms of the license.

9. If there is already a version of Windows NT loaded, you will see an upgrade choice. If there is an earlier version of Windows NT installed, press **Enter** to upgrade.

10. Setup lists information about your computer, such as type of PC, display, keyboard, and so on. If a change needs to be made, use the arrow keys to highlight the selection, and press **Enter** to view the alternatives. If the information is correct, highlight **No Changes: The above list matches my computer**, and press **Enter**.

11. The detected disk drives and partitions appear, and Setup asks you where you want to install Windows NT. If you already created a partition that you want to use, select it from this list, and press **Enter**. Figure 4-12 shows two partitioned disks, drives C: and D:. Choose the partition on which you want to install Windows NT, and press **Enter**.

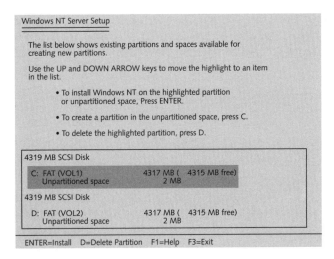

Figure 4-12   Selecting a partition for NT Server files

 You can also choose to press D to delete the FAT partition, and later repartition the drive for NTFS. You don't need to do this because Setup gives you an opportunity to convert the partition to NTFS in the next screen. Also note that deleting a partition permanently erases all data on the partition!

12. Setup confirms the drive location for the Windows NT Server partition and lists these choices: Format the partition using the FAT file system, Format the partition using the NTFS file system, Convert the partition to NTFS, or Leave the current file system intact (no changes).

 If you decide to use NTFS instead of FAT, you can either format the partition for NTFS, or convert the partition to NTFS. Either choice works. However, if you want to leave a partition for MS-DOS or Windows 95, choose to leave the current file system intact.

13. Highlight a selection (such as **Convert the partition to NTFS**). Then select **C** to confirm your choice. Press **Enter** to continue.

14. A screen may appear that shows the minimum and maximum partition size. Select the size for the partition; we recommend at least 500 MB, preferably 1 GB for Windows NT Server. Press **Enter** to continue.

15. If you choose to format the drive, a confirmation screen appears so you can confirm that the correct drive is selected. Press **F** to continue.

16. Setup shows the default path and name for the Windows NT Server files. As before, use the default values by pressing **Enter**. However, you can enter another directory path and name if you need to change it.

17. After selecting the path, Setup asks to check your hard disks. Press **Enter** to proceed with the check, which may take a few minutes. Upon completion of the test, a message appears indicating that the Windows NT files are being copied to the hard disk.

18. When the copy process is completed, remove all disks from the floppy and CD-ROM drives. Press **Enter** to restart the machine. This is the end of the text-based portion of the installation. Your computer may restart one or more times.

19. As prompted, insert the Windows NT CD-ROM, and the GUI part of the installation—the Windows NT Setup Wizard shown in Figure 4-13—will load. It shows the next three steps in Setup: Gathering information about your computer, Installing Windows NT Networking, and Finishing Setup. Click **Next**.

20. Follow the prompts on-screen to enter your name and your organization's name, click **Next**, then enter the CD key code from the sticker on the back of the Windows NT Server CD-ROM case, and click **Next**.

21. Next you see the license screen. Select the appropriate licensing option (Per-seat or Per-server) and click **Next**.

22. Enter the name of the server. This name must be unique on the network. Click **Next**.

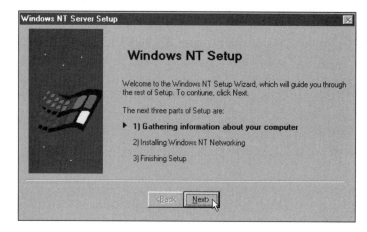

Figure 4-13 Windows NT Setup Wizard

23. Specify the server type, such as Stand-alone server or primary domain controller (PDC), and click **Next**. If you are installing a single Windows NT server, and do not plan to have other servers, choose Stand-alone server. If you want multiple Windows NT servers, and wish to keep user and permission information consistent among all of them, you might assign the first one as the primary domain controller (PDC), and other servers as member servers.

24. Enter the Administrator account password. Enter the password again in the confirmation box, then click **Next**.

This password is extremely important; without it, you will not be able to manage your Windows NT server. If you forget this password, the only way to get access to your server is to reinstall it!

25. Select the option to create the Emergency Repair Disk (ERD), if desired. If you choose this option, the ERD will be created near the end of the installation.

26. Specify the software components to add at the time of installation. Setup automatically marks the most commonly used components, as shown in Figure 4-14. To accept the components listed, click **Next**. (You can install other components after installation if you need them.)

27. The Windows NT Setup screen appears, showing you are entering Setup Step 2. Click **Next** to continue.

28. Now, specify network connection options. Indicate whether the server is directly connected to the network, used for dial-up access, or both. If you have a network interface card, click **Wired to the network**. If a modem is installed, you might also click the **Remote access to the network** option, which enables you to later set up Remote Access Service (RAS). RAS is covered in greater detail in Chapter 8.

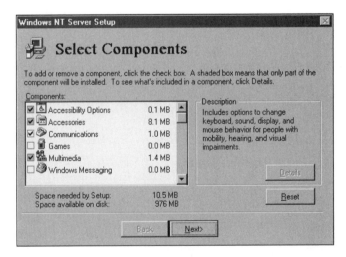

Figure 4-14   Selecting NT Server components to install

29. Select the option to install the Microsoft Internet Information Server (IIS), if desired, and click **Next**.

30. If you chose the Wired to the network option, click **Start Search** to have Setup automatically detect the network card. If the card is not detected, you can click **Select from List** to manually choose the card, or click **Have Disk** to use a driver from the NIC manufacturer's disk. Once the NIC is identified, click **Next**.

31. Select the protocol or protocols to be installed, and click **Next**. You may select all protocols, or only one, such as NetBEUI. Select only the protocols that you need—TCP/IP, IPX/SPX, and NetBEUI. If you select TCP/IP, you must enter the IP address information (get this from your instructor or network administrator) in another dialog box.

32. The networking services to be installed are listed, as shown in Figure 4-15. The list will vary according to which protocols and network options you selected. The checked services are required; you cannot unselect them. You can select other services by clicking **Select** from the list, but adding services after installation is better. Click **Next** to confirm the default selections.

33. Click **Next** to start the installation of network components by automatically detecting system settings for the NIC. Confirm the settings, or change any as needed.

34. Setup is ready to install selected components. If you installed a network card and the TCP/IP protocol, you may be asked whether there is a DHCP server on your network. Consult your instructor or network administrator for the answer. Once you click **Yes** or **No** to the DHCP question, the networking files are copied.

35. Confirm or change the network bindings, as desired. It is best to go with the defaults and make any necessary changes later. Click **Next** to accept the selections made by Setup.

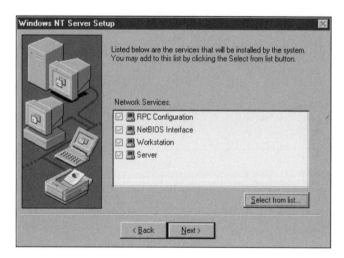

Figure 4-15   Selecting network services in Windows NT

36. If you elected to install TCP/IP, you will see the TCP/IP Properties window. You must provide the IP address and subnet mask, at a minimum. (Consult your instructor or network administrator on how to fill in this dialog box.) Make sure your server is connected to the network, and click **Next**. (Note: If you chose Yes for the DHCP option in Step 34, you may not see the TCP/IP Properties window. Proceed to Step 37.)

37. Click **Next** to start the network. The next windows you see depend on whether you chose to install a stand-alone server or a Workstation; you can choose to be part of a domain or a workgroup at this time. Enter the name of the domain or workgroup, and click **Next**. Setup checks for any identical domain or workgroup names on the network. Click **Finish** if instructed to do so. A short message tells you that the software is configuring the server.

38. If the Microsoft Internet Information Server (IIS) 2.0 Setup screen appears, choose any IIS components you wish to install, and click **OK**.

39. The Install Drivers screen appears. Choose an appropriate driver, and click **OK**.

40. Adjust the date, time, and time zone in the Date/Time Properties dialog box, if necessary. Click **Close**. (The time, date, and video settings can also be reset from the Control Panel after Windows NT is installed.)

41. Click **OK** to verify the display settings for the video card and monitor. (It's best to accept the defaults here. You can install new drivers after setup.) Click **Test**, and then click **OK** to check that the color and resolution are accurate. Click **Yes** to continue.

42. Click **OK** in the Display Settings dialog box, and click **OK** in the Display Properties dialog box.

43. Setup informs you that it is installing program shortcuts, security, and messaging services. When these tasks are done, it prompts you to insert a blank disk for the Emergency Repair Disk in Drive A:. Insert the disk, and click **OK**.

44. The last screen tells you the installation is complete. Remove any floppy disks, and click the **Restart Computer** button. The server is rebooted into Windows NT Server.

45. When the new server restarts, a logon screen appears with a message to press the Ctrl+Alt+Del keys at the same time. This combination is used to start the logon screen, and does not reboot the server. Press **Ctrl+Alt+Del**, enter **Administrator** as the account, and enter the Administrator password you supplied during installation. The Windows NT Server desktop appears.

Project 4-6

Please read the section on installing Windows 2000 earlier in this chapter for important hardware requirements.

To install the Windows 2000 Server operating system:

If you start from the floppy disk method:

1. Make sure the computer's BIOS is set to boot first from floppy drive A:.

2. Power off the computer.

3. Insert Setup Disk #1 into drive A: and the CD-ROM into the CD-ROM drive.

4. Turn on the computer, allowing it to boot from Setup Disk #1.

5. This method automatically starts Winnt.exe, and you follow the instructions on the screen, such as inserting Setup Disk #2 next.

If you start by booting from the CD-ROM (if your computer supports this):

1. Make sure the computer's BIOS is set to boot first from the CD-ROM drive.

2. Insert the Windows 2000 CD-ROM in the CD-ROM drive.

3. Power off the computer.

4. Turn on the computer, allowing it to boot from the CD-ROM. On some computers, you may be prompted to press Enter to boot from the CD-ROM.

5. This method automatically starts Winnt.exe and you follow the instructions on the screen.

When Winnt starts, the first screens are character based and you use the following steps:

1. Setup inspects the hardware configuration and loads the drivers and other files to get started. Next, Windows 2000 Server Setup provides a screen with three options: set up Windows 2000, repair an existing Windows 2000 installation, and quit Setup (Figure 4-16). Press **Enter** to begin the installation, but also make a note that you can later access the repair option at any time. The repair option enables you to access diagnostic and repair functions on the Emergency Repair Disk.

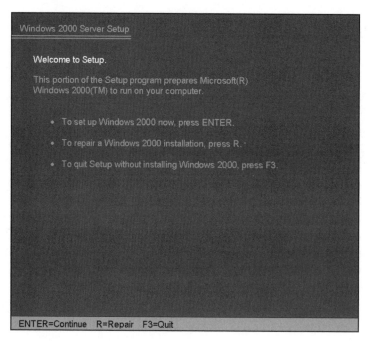

Figure 4-16   Beginning Setup options

4

 Setup provides a way to install a special mass storage driver, or special HAL, for SMP computers, in case the Windows 2000 Server CD-ROM does not contain the driver, or in case Setup cannot find storage devices when it inspects the computer. For special mass storage, press **F6** as soon as possible when Setup begins inspecting the hardware. Setup provides a special screen that enables you to install new drivers. Press **S**, insert the driver disk, and press **Enter**. Also, if Setup does not recognize the type of computer because it is an SMP computer, obtain a HAL driver from the vendor, press **F5** as soon as possible when Setup starts, select **Other** on the menu, and install the HAL driver from a floppy disk or CD-ROM.

2. Setup presents the license agreement for Windows 2000 Server. Use the Page Down key to read the agreement and when you are finished reading, press **F8** to indicate that you agree.

3. Setup scans the hard drive(s) to determine if there are any previous versions of Windows 2000 Server. If it finds one, you have the choice to repair it if it is damaged, or to install a new copy of Windows 2000 over the current version. If you see this screen, press **Esc** to install a new copy.

4. The hard drive scan also determines if any FAT16, FAT32, or NTFS partitions are already in place. Use the up and down arrow keys to select the unpartitioned space, or an existing partition, on which to install Windows 2000, and press **Enter**. If you use an unpartitioned space, Setup displays another screen to confirm the selection, and enables you to specify the size of the partition. If you select to write over an existing partition, Setup displays a warning screen on which you can enter **C** to continue.

5. Use the up and down arrow keys to select a file system, NTFS or FAT (a third option is to leave the existing file system, if the drive is already formatted). On the next screen, Setup warns that files will be deleted if you are formatting over an existing partition. Press **F** to format the partition. Or, if you change your mind at this point, press **Esc** to go back and select a different partition. After you start the format, a screen appears to show the progress of the format.

6. After the disk is formatted, there is a file copy stage and then Setup automatically reboots into the Windows 2000 graphical mode. If your computer is set up to boot first from a CD-ROM, depending on the computer, you may need to remove the Windows 2000 Server CD-ROM before it reboots, and then put the CD-ROM back in after it reboots.

After the system reboots, it goes into the Windows GUI mode. In this mode you make selections with a mouse or pointing device by clicking buttons at the bottom of dialog boxes, such as Back and Next.

The steps from the GUI mode are as follows:

1. The first dialog box is used to gather information about the computer, which includes the keyboard and pointing device. Click **Next**. An action bar in the next dialog box shows you the progress of the detection process, and automatically goes to the following dialog box when it finishes.

2. In the next dialog box, you have options to change regional and keyboard settings, such as to customize the server to use a specific language, or to customize a language for your locale. For example, you may set up to use English, but want to use the United Kingdom locale English. Complementing the language, you can customize number, currency, time, and date formats. Use the Customize buttons to make adjustments, and click **Next**.

3. Enter your name and the name of your organization in the Personalize Your Software dialog box. Click **Next**.

4. Enter the Product Key and click **Next**. You can find the key on a sticker attached to the reverse side of the Windows 2000 Server CD-ROM jewel case.

5. If you are installing a server, you will see a Licensing Modes dialog box. In the Licensing Modes dialog box, select the licensing mode (per-server or per-seat), and enter the number of licenses. You can add licenses later as needed, so only add the number of licenses you have now. Click **Next**.

6. Enter the name of the computer and provide a password for the Administrator account. Confirm the password, and click **Next**.

 Like Windows NT, Windows 2000 passwords are case sensitive.

7. Enter checks in the boxes of the components that you want to install. Windows 2000 Server offers more choices than Windows 2000 Professional. For example, you might install Message Queuing Services or Other Network File and Print Services (for UNIX and Macintosh communications). When you first install Windows 2000, it is recommended that you select only the services you need immediately and install others later, to minimize configuration difficulties. To view information about a particular component, click the component name, and click **Details**. Click **Next** after you make the selections.

8. If there is a modem installed in your computer, you must provide your region and country information, telephone area code, number you dial for an outside line (optional), and telephone line type (tone or pulse) in the Modem Dialing Information dialog box. This information is used to establish dial-up networking. Click **Next**.

9. Verify the accuracy of the date and time in the Date and Time Settings dialog box and make any needed changes. Also, make sure the time zone is correctly set, such as for Mountain Time. Click **Next**.

10. Setup next displays a dialog box to show it is configuring your network settings, and then enables you to select the Typical or Custom settings. Click **Typical settings** if you want to use Client for Microsoft Networks, TCP/IP, and Print Sharing for Microsoft Networks. Otherwise click **Custom settings** to establish a different setup, such as to install for connectivity to an older NetWare server. To keep the installation simple, it is recommended that you use the Typical settings

and make adjustments later. If you are not using dynamic IP addressing, you should configure the TCP/IP protocol manually. Click **Next** after you make your selection.

11. If the computer is not currently on a network, or if you want to specify a work-group for the computer, click the **No** radio button, or click **Yes** if the computer will join a domain. Enter the workgroup or domain name in the text box. Click **Next**. If you join a domain, you must enter the domain account and the password of the account you already created to enable the server to join the domain.

12. Setup now installs the components you specified (see Figure 4-17), sets up Start menu items, and removes the temporary files created by the installation process.

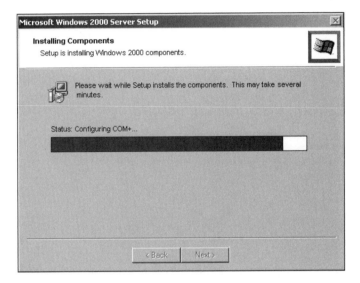

Figure 4-17   Installing components

13. Click **Finish**, remove the Windows 2000 Server CD-ROM, and wait for the computer to restart.

Project 4-7

In this project, you install Windows XP Professional using the CD-ROM installation method. Before you start, you will need the Windows XP Professional CD-ROM. Please read the section on Installing Windows XP in this chapter for important hardware requirements. The installation of Windows XP will take approximately 60 to 90 minutes. Similar to Windows 2000, the first part of the installation is in a text-based format and the second part is GUI-based. (Ask your instructor for the name of a workgroup or domain to join. If you join a domain, you will need to obtain an account name and password from your instructor.)

To start the first phase, the text-based installation:

1. Insert the Windows XP Professional CD-ROM and boot the computer from scratch so that it boots from the CD-ROM.

2. Windows XP Setup briefly inspects hardware components and then loads files onto the disk.

3. Press **Enter** if you see a Setup Notification screen (for evaluation copies).

4. Press **Enter** on the Welcome to Setup screen (see Figure 4-18).

5. Read the Windows XP Licensing Agreement and press **F8** to accept the agreement.

6. Use the up and down arrows to select the disk space on which to install Windows XP Professional and press **Enter**. Note that if there is already an operating system on the computer, such as Windows 98 or 2000, you can create a dual boot system by placing Windows XP Professional on another partition. Figure 4-19 shows the Setup screen on a computer that has two disk drives, one with Windows 98 (drive C:) and one with unpartitioned space (drive D:). In this situation, you can (1) select to install Windows XP Professional on drive C:, thus erasing Windows 98 or (2) install Windows XP on the unpartitioned space on drive D:, resulting in a dual boot system.

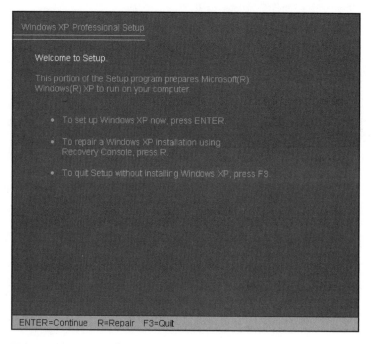

Figure 4-18   Windows XP Welcome to Setup screen

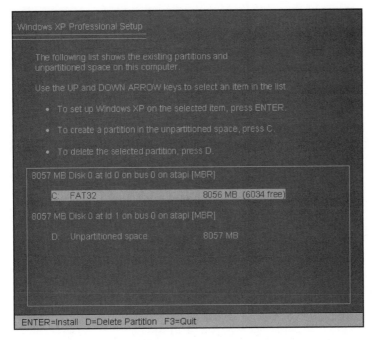

Figure 4-19   Selecting the partition for Windows XP

7. Use the up and down arrows to select **Format the partition using the NTFS file system** (which is selected by default). Press **Enter**. Setup takes a few minutes to format the partition and then it examines your disks.

 Avoid selecting the (Quick) format option, because this will not check the disk for errors and set aside bad spots on the disk so that they are not used.

8. Next, Setup copies files to the installation folders and then initializes the installation. Finally, Setup restarts the computer. If a floppy disk is loaded, remove it before the computer restarts.

To complete the GUI-based second phase of the installation:

1. Windows XP Professional restarts and immediately begins the installation. The first portion of the installation will take a few minutes. You will see an overview of Windows XP features in the right pane and the installation steps in the left pane. Also, the moving green square across the green dots in the bottom right side of the screen means that Setup is working.

2. Notice the bar that eventually appears in the bottom portion of the left pane that shows what is happening during the installation, such as installing devices.

3. When you see the Regional and Language Options dialog box, click **Customize** to review the regional options. Make sure that your format preferences are

selected, such as **English (United States)**. Also, select your present location, such as **United States**. Click **OK**.

4. Click **Next**.

5. Enter your name and the name of your organization. Click **Next**.

6. Enter the product key (look on the back of your Windows XP Professional CD-ROM's jewel case) and click **Next**.

7. Enter the name of your computer, such as XP plus your last name (XPPalmer). Also, enter the password for the Administrator account and then enter it again to confirm it. Click **Next**.

8. If there is a modem already installed in the computer, enter the country/region in which you reside, the area or city code, and a number to access an outside line (if necessary). Also, click the radio button for the type of phone system (tone or pulse dialing). Click **Next**.

9. Verify the date and time settings. For example, you may need to select the time zone (click the Time Zone list box down arrow). Click **Next**.

10. Setup continues the installation, starting with the installation of the network configuration.

11. On the Network Settings dialog box, for this project, select **Typical settings** (the default) to configure for a Microsoft-based network using the TCP/IP transport protocol. Click **Next**.

12. Select whether to make the computer a member of a workgroup or a domain (check with your instructor; or enter a workgroup name that consists of your initials plus "workgroup"). Click **Next**. (If you select to join a domain, another dialog box appears in which to provide the name of the account and password that you will use in the domain. Click OK after you enter the account and password.)

13. The installation proceeds, such as copying files to the newly formatted partition.

14. A display settings dialog box appears stating "To improve the appearance of visual elements, Windows will automatically adjust your screen resolution". Click **OK** to continue. Then a verification dialog box appears verifying that the new resolution is readable to the user. Click **OK** if you can read the information.

15. When the installation is finished, Setup restarts the computer so that you can access Windows XP Professional.

16. After the computer restarts, click **Next** on the Welcome to Microsoft Windows screen.

17. Windows XP checks your Internet connectivity. Click the appropriate radio button for how the computer will connect to the Internet. For this project, use the default option, **Yes, this computer will connect through a local area network or home network**. Click **Next** (or you can click Skip, if you do not wish to configure Internet access at this time).

18. The next dialog box that appears deals with IP and DNS information. Check with your instructor for the exact information you need to enter on these screens.

19. Select whether or not to activate Windows over the Internet or to wait until another time. For example, if you have Internet access, click **Yes, activate Windows over the Internet now**. Click **Next**.

20. Select whether or not to register online. For this project, click **No, remind me every few days**. Click **Next**.

21. Enter your name and click **Next**.

22. Click **Finish**.

Project 4-8

This project enables you to install Red Hat Linux 7.2 (workstation) using the text-based mode, which enables an installation to proceed even if there is not enough RAM. Please read the section on installing Linux earlier in this chapter for important hardware requirements.

To install the Red Hat Linux 7.2 operating system:

1. Boot the computer from the Red Hat Linux 7.2 Installation CD-ROM 1 of 2.

2. At the *boot*: prompt, type **text** and then press **Enter** to start the text-based installation. Instead of the mouse, the text-based installer enables you to use command keys, such as:
   - ◻ F1 for help
   - ◻ Tab to move between fields on the screen
   - ◻ Space to select options on the screen
   - ◻ F12 to go to the next screen
   - ◻ A Back option to return to the previous screen

3. Select the language that you use, such as **English** and tab to **OK**. Press **Enter**.

4. Select the model of keyboard that you wish to use, such as **us** for keyboards used by computers in the United States. Tab to **OK** after you make your selection, and press **Enter**.

5. Select the type of mouse, such as **Generic – 2 Button Mouse (serial)**. Tab to **OK,** and press **Enter**.

6. If you selected a serial or bus mouse in Step 5, another screen appears in which to select the device on which your mouse is located, such as **/dev/ttys (COM1 under DOS)**, tab to **OK**, and press **Enter**.

7. The Welcome to Red Hat Linux screen advises you to read the Linux manual and to register your version of Red Hat Linux. Select **OK**, and press **Enter**.

8. Select the type of system that you want to install, such as **Workstation**, for this hands-on project. Tab to **OK** after you make your selection, and press **Enter**.

> Notice that the other installation options include: Server, Laptop, Custom, and Upgrade Existing System.

9. The Disk Partitioning Setup screen enables you to use Autopartition, Disk Druid or *fdisk* to set up and partition the disk(s)—and to set up mount points. Follow the installation recommendation by selecting **Autopartition**, because it is easier to use. Press **Enter**, after you have tabbed to your selection.

10. Linux can recognize Linux and non-Linux partitions, such as FAT and NTFS. The options you'll see next are:

    ❏ Remove all Linux Partitions on this system

    ❏ Remove all partitions on this system

    ❏ Keep all partitions and use existing free space

    In this project, we assume that you will remove all partitions on the system, but check with your instructor about which selection to make. Select **Remove all partitions on this system**. Also select the drive on which to install Red Hat Linux, such as **hda**. Tab to **OK**, and press **Enter**. Tab to **Yes**, and press **Enter** to verify your selection.

11. Notice that on the Partitioning screen you can add a new partition, edit an existing partition, delete a partition, and configure RAID. Also, notice that a swap partition is created in addition to the main partition. Tab to **OK**, and press **Enter**. (If your computer does not have enough RAM for the installation, Red Hat Linux immediately turns on the swap space. If you see a Low Memory screen, select **OK** and press **Enter** to use the swap space.

12. Select **Use GRUB Boot Loader** (the default), tab to **OK**, and press **Enter**.

13. Use the default option for the boot loader configuration, such as **/dev/hda Master Boot Record (MBR)**. Tab to **OK**, and press **Enter**.

14. For this installation, do not select to pass special options to the kernel. Leave the option blank, tab to **OK**, and press **Enter**.

15. If you have more than one partition, on the next Boot Loader Configuration screen, leave the defaults as selected for other partitions from which to boot, tab to **OK**, and press **Enter**.

16. For this project, do not select to use a boot loader password. Tab to **OK**, and press **Enter**.

17. If you have an Ethernet card installed in your computer, you will see two screens from which to configure your network settings. On the first screen, provide the IP address information (see your instructor first about what to enter). Complete the IP address information, tab to **OK**, and press **Enter**. On the second screen, provide the host name for your computer (also ask your instructor about what hostname to use), tab to **OK**, and press **Enter**. (Note that even if you have an Ethernet card, you may not see these two screens. This is because there are DCHP and DNS servers on your network, which provide the information to the Red Hat Linux setup.)

18. Use the default **Medium** for the firewall configuration, tab to **OK**, and press **Enter**.

19. Select other languages that can be used, or simply leave **English (USA)** as the default. Tab to **OK**, and press **Enter**.

20. Select the time zone (use the arrow keys), such as **America/Detroit**. Tab to **OK**, and press **Enter**.

21. Enter a root password, and enter it again to confirm it. Tab to **OK**, and press **Enter**.

The password must be over six characters (Linux also treats upper- and lowercase letters differently).

22. Create a user account for yourself by entering:

   ❑ User ID

   ❑ Password

   ❑ Password (confirmation)

   ❑ Full Name

   Tab to **OK**, and press **Enter**.

23. Select the user account you want to use on the system, which is the account that you created in the last step. Notice that you can use the Add option to create more accounts, Delete to delete an account, and Edit to edit an account that you created. Tab to **OK**, and press **Enter**.

24. Select the packages that you want to install, such as GNOME (an X Windows interface similar to a Microsoft Windows interface). If there is an option to install KDE, select it as well (KDE adds more functionality to your GNOME interface). Tab to **OK**, and press **Enter**.

25. The installation process now checks for the dependencies of the packages that you selected in the last step.

26. Next, the installation process asks you to verify the video card type. Make sure that the default selections are correct (if not use the *Change* options for the video card and video RAM). Tab to **OK**, and press **Enter**.

27. Select **OK** to start the installation and press **Enter**. Notice that it will keep a log of the installation in /tmp/install.log so that you can go back to this log and examine it for possible errors.

28. Next, the installation process partitions and formats the disk(s).

29. After the partition and format process is done, it begins the installation of the packages and files.

This process can take from 15 minutes to over one hour, depending on the speed of your hardware.

4

30. As it is installing the files, the installation process shows the packages being installed. The screen includes two tables. One shows the name, size in K, and description of the file or package currently being installed. It also has a table that shows the progress of the installation, including what has been installed, and what remains to be installed.

31. When you are prompted (and the CD-ROM drive ejects the Installation CD-ROM 1 of 2), insert the Red Hat Linux 7.2 Installation CD-ROM 2 of 2. Press **Enter**.

32. Next, the system performs a post install configuration.

33. After the configuration screen, there is a Boot Disk screen from which to make a custom boot disk for booting into Linux, without depending on the normal boot-loader. Insert a blank floppy disk, and select **Yes** to create the boot disk. Press **Enter**.

34. Next, the system asks you to remove any disks that were previously inserted in the floppy drive and it warns that you will erase the disk currently in that drive. *Make sure your blank formatted floppy is the one in the drive.* Tab to **OK**, and press **Enter**.

35. Next, specify the monitor that you are using. If you are not sure, use the default that is already selected by the installation program (or use the Monitor and Hsync/Vsync Rate Change options to select a monitor other than the default). Tab to **OK**, and press **Enter**.

36. Use the X Customization screen to customize the color depth, resolution, and default login (graphical or text). For this project, use the defaults already selected, tab to **OK**, and press **Enter**.

37. The installation is now complete. Press **Enter** to reboot. Notice that the CD-ROM drive automatically opens to remind you to remove the Red Hat Linux Installation CD-ROM. Remove the CD-ROM, and make sure that the system reboots successfully. After it reboots, you can log on by entering the account and password that you created during the installation.

Project 4-9

Please read the section in this chapter on Installing Mac OS before completing this project.

To install Mac OS 9.x:

1. With the machine powered off, insert the Mac OS 9.x CD-ROM into the CD-ROM drive, restart the computer, and immediately hold down the **C** key to boot from the CD-ROM. You should see the CD icon in the upper-right corner of the screen, just below the menu bar, and the Mac OS 9.x window opens, showing you the contents of the CD.

2. If desired, double-click **Before You Install** and read the information.

3. To begin the installation, double-click the **Mac OS Install** icon. The installer launches, and the opening screen appears.

4. Click **Continue** to take you to the first step, selecting the drive for the installation. Select the drive you want to hold the operating system. This is usually your internal hard drive.

Clicking Options allows you to select a "clean" installation, which renames the System Folder currently on the drive to Previous System Folder. It then creates a new System Folder, and installs the operating system there. Creating a clean installation is a good idea if you aren't sure that all the extensions currently on the machine are compatible with the new OS, but it does require you to manually move the extensions and preferences from the old folder to the new one if you want to keep any of them.

5. Choose **Select**, which takes you to the Before You Install files. If you haven't already read this information, do so now. Otherwise, click **Continue**.

6. Next, you'll have to agree to the license agreement for the software: click **Continue**, and then click **Agree**.

7. Click **Start** to begin copying the installation files. This may take between 6 and 45 minutes.

8. A dialog box now appears prompting you to click continue to install additional software or quit to leave the program. Please click **quit** to leave this program.

9. When the installer finishes, restart the computer. The operating system loads from the hard drive, and you will see the Mac OS Setup Assistant, shown previously in Figure 4-10. Click the right arrow to continue.

10. Specify your preferred nationality/language, and click the right arrow

11. Enter your name, and then your organization. Click the right arrow.

12. Click **Yes**, if you are currently under Daylight Savings Time. Enter the correct time in the *What time is it?* Box, and enter the date in the *What is today's date?* box. (Select the time or date value that is wrong, such as the hour or year, and use the up or down arrows to reset the value.) Click the right arrow.

13. Select your geographic location, and then click the right arrow.

14. Review the information about Finder Preferences, and then click your preference, **Yes** (for fewer commands on the menu) or **No**. Click the right arrow.

15. Review the Local Network Introduction, and then click the right arrow.

16. Enter the computer name (or accept the default name), and then enter a password to protect access to your computer. Click the right arrow.

17. Review the information about shared folders. Click **Yes** if you want a shared folder, otherwise click **No**. If you click Yes, provide a name for the shared folder (or use the name already provided). Click the right arrow.

18. Click **Go Ahead**.

19. Click **Quit** on the Conclusion screen. (Clicking Continue instead of Quit starts the Internet Setup Assistant for creating Internet access. If you do this, you must provide information about your modem, the country and area code, and your Internet Service Provider.)

CASE PROJECTS

Your supervisor at Acme Insurance asks you to investigate the feasibility of installing several UNIX servers on your relatively large network. You are authorized to purchase one new computer as large as you need, within reason, but the remaining UNIX installs must be done on existing hardware. With this background, answer these questions:

1. What minimum hardware configuration would you recommend for the new UNIX network server?

2. How would you go about evaluating existing hardware to judge its feasibility for conversion to a UNIX box? Keep in mind such concepts as hard drive capacity, existing applications, memory size, and other storage devices.

3. What are the major software considerations in converting an existing machine with a different operating system to UNIX?

4. Cost is important; you can't go over the specified budget. What product might you consider in lieu of the standard commercial UNIX offerings? Why?

Now consider this project in light of the Windows and Macintosh operating systems. Replace the word "UNIX" with "Windows 2000 Server" or "Mac OS" and answer the four questions again.

OPTIONAL CASE PROJECTS FOR TEAMS

Team Case One

Your company has been short handed in the Information Technology Department for some time, and it has not been able to keep the desktop operating systems updated with the latest patches and service packs. You are asked to head up a team to implement this task.

❑ How will you determine what updates should be performed on each desktop?

❑ What other updates might you want to install at this time?

❑ Prepare a list of operating systems that have access to the Windows Update feature.

Team Case Two

Your company is so impressed with the proposal from your team on updating the desktop operating systems you prepared in Team Case One, that they wonder if the same type of update is available for the application software packages on the desktops. Explain the application software packages that your team can update with this same type of process.

5

UPGRADING TO A NEWER OPERATING SYSTEM VERSION

After reading this chapter and completing the exercises, you will be able to:

♦ Prepare for an operating system upgrade

♦ Understand the factors involved in making the decision to upgrade

♦ Test system upgrades before implementing them

♦ Understand how and why to make backups before upgrading your operating system

♦ Successfully upgrade the operating systems that are the focus of this text: Microsoft Windows-based, UNIX, and Mac operating systems

New computer hardware, software, and networking features are developed at a rapid pace, forcing operating system developers to feverishly keep their systems current. Most personal computer operating systems are enhanced every one to three years. When new capabilities are added, they typically signal a new version of an operating system, such as the new interface and multimedia features added to Windows XP, or the strikingly new Mac OS X interface. In between the release of new versions, operating system vendors offer minor enhancements and "bug" fixes. Whether it is a small upgrade to fix bugs, or a larger upgrade to introduce a new operating system, you may find it necessary to implement the upgrade. This is particularly true when an upgrade offers better security features, fixes a bug that causes you problems, or better enables you to run the software you need.

This chapter focuses on the steps involved in upgrading an operating system—from implementing minor updates, to installing a new operating system version. Many of the upgrade procedures are similar to those required for an initial installation, so it is valuable to complete Chapter 4 before reading this chapter. In this chapter, you'll learn about general upgrade considerations, backup and safety procedures, and finally, the specific steps (and possible pitfalls) involved in upgrading computer operating systems.

PREPARING FOR AN UPGRADE

Before you upgrade, the first thing to consider is whether an upgrade is truly necessary. If you are certain that an upgrade is necessary and desirable, then you must make sure that you have the necessary hardware and software (including device drivers) to perform the upgrade, as well as information about your system that may be needed during the upgrade. You should also make a complete backup of your current system and data before upgrading. If you are upgrading more than two or three computers at once, you may want to perform a test upgrade on one or two before doing a complete upgrade. These and other general upgrading considerations are discussed in the following sections.

Deciding to Upgrade

When new versions of operating systems are released that promise new features, bug fixes, enhanced capabilities, and more speed, it is tempting to jump immediately on the upgrade bandwagon. However, before taking such a step (especially in a large production environment), you should carefully consider (1) whether you need to upgrade, and (2) whether the time is right to upgrade. Although newer versions of operating systems promise great new features, you should ask yourself whether you actually need the new functionality. Objective analysis of the situation may show that an upgrade may not be cost effective. In other cases, such as upgrading a work environment from Windows NT to Windows 2000 or XP, the upgrade can be used to significantly lower the total cost of ownership (TCO) because Windows 2000 and XP enable you to manage users via group policies.

In some cases, upgrades to operating systems have little immediate effect on the functions performed by the computers and users for which you are responsible. You may also find that software or hardware that ran without difficulty on the older version of the operating system will not run on a newer version. Check with your software and hardware vendors before attempting an upgrade to ensure that the software and hardware will be compatible with the upgrade. Never assume that all of your current software and hardware will work flawlessly with the upgrade.

 Sometimes operating system vendors publish a list of the software tested on the upgraded operating system. These tests may not be comprehensive enough to ensure that all features of the software work properly, or that they work on all types of computers. Install the new operating system and the software your organization uses on a test computer so that you can personally verify the operating system and software before implementing it on a large scale.

Experience also has shown that it is best not to upgrade shortly after a new operating system is released. If you can put off an upgrade for several months, maybe even a year, you gain the benefit of the experiences of thousands of other users solving problems that might have been yours. If you wait, you will have access to many patches and bug fixes that are not available for early releases. If you feel you must upgrade soon after a new version is released, consider using the test upgrade strategy covered later in this chapter.

Some operating system vendors offer pre-release or **beta software** for you to try. Microsoft, for example, typically offers pre-releases in the form of **alpha**, beta, and **release candidate (RC)** versions. Never upgrade production computers to anything other than an official release of an operating system. Pre-release or beta operating system versions are in the preliminary to final test stages before release. They can have many bugs and may be unstable. A **production computer** is any computer used to perform real work, and which, if it were to become unusable for any reason, would cause an inconvenience, hinder workflow, or cause data to be lost.

5

 If you plan to implement an upgrade, consider obtaining a pre-release or beta version, and put it on a machine that is not a production computer. Use this computer for training and investigation to learn about the new features of the operating system and how they will affect your work environment, particularly your existing software.

Checking Hardware and Software

Before you decide to upgrade, you should carefully check the computers you wish to upgrade against the requirements of the new operating system. In many cases, newer operating systems require more hardware: increased memory, disk space, CPU speed, and sometimes even improved display properties. Some relatively new operating systems, such as Windows 2000 and Windows XP, offer a utility to examine the hardware for suitability before you upgrade (try Hands-on Project 5-1). Take special note of the hardware installed in the computer, such as network cards, scanners, sound cards, and other devices that require special drivers. If your organization supports many computers, consider obtaining network software that can automatically inventory the hardware components of the computers on your network. Or, you can develop a checklist so that you can inventory your hardware, as illustrated in Table 5-1.

Also, before you upgrade to a new operating system, make sure that the current drivers for input and output devices and storage media work with the new version, or that there are drivers available for these devices for the new operating system. It is a good idea to contact hardware vendors and get some assurance that their devices will continue to work properly after the upgrade. Do not leave this to chance; older or discontinued hardware may not be supported in newer operating system versions.

 The existence of drivers is another reason to delay your upgrade until an operating system has been on the market for several months. Sometimes operating system vendors release a system before hardware manufacturers have had time to develop and test new drivers. Waiting to upgrade usually means there will be more drivers—and hardware—available to use with an operating system.

Table 5-1   Hardware Checklist

Number of Computers	CPU/Clock Speed	RAM	Disk Capacity	CD-ROM	Video	Special Devices

Make sure that you have all the device drivers needed for the hardware available on floppy disk, Zip disk, or CD-ROM. If there are drivers that exist only on the hard disk of the computer, copy them to a floppy disk, or some other safe place. Otherwise, if the upgrade fails, you will not have the drivers you need to get the computer back to work. If there are new drivers for the new version of the OS, keep those handy, as well as copies of your current drivers. This will enable you to reinstall the old operating system if, for some reason, you are unable to complete the upgrade.

It is also a good idea to keep detailed records of custom software settings—changes in the defaults for the operating system and other software—so that these custom settings can be restored, if necessary, after any operating system or other software upgrade. For example, it is not uncommon for users to modify display or other settings after they run an operating system for a while; they may use an automated backup program, run special disk tools on a regular basis, or have customized network settings. Upgrade installations may reset some settings to their defaults, which may not be what you want.

Determine what software is used on systems prior to an upgrade so that you can check to see if there are any compatibility problems. For example, not all software written for Windows 95 can run in Windows XP, and the Windows 95 software that can run in Windows XP is run in Windows 95 compatibility mode (in Windows XP click Start, point to All Programs, point to Accessories, and click Program Compatibility Wizard). Further, some databases may not be accessible, or there might be access problems, such as with **Open Database Connectivity (ODBC)** drivers, when you upgrade. ODBC is a set of rules developed by Microsoft for accessing databases. Table 5-2 illustrates a checklist that you can make before upgrading software. Also, try Hands-on Project 5-2 to learn how to assess what software is loaded on an operating system.

Table 5-2   Software Checklist

Software	Vendor/Version	Operating System	Location	Future Software Upgrade Plans
Accounting				
Publishing				
Word Processing				
Spreadsheet				
Database				
E-mail				
Inventory				
Manufacturing				
Human Resources				
Custom-built				

CONDUCTING A TEST UPGRADE

You should plan to test an upgrade before you apply it to a production computer. If you have only one or two computers to upgrade, this may not be an option. But when you have five or more computers to upgrade, it can be beneficial to perform an upgrade test on a sample computer, or on several computers.

The purpose of an upgrade test is to simulate what would happen in a real upgrade. You can discover any problems that might occur, either with the upgrade itself, or with running hardware and software after the upgrade. To do this, you need a working computer that closely resembles the computers you will be upgrading. Choose a computer that resembles the "lowest common denominator" of the computers you are upgrading, in terms of the amount of memory, speed of the CPU, size of the hard disk, and any devices connected to the computer. You should also install all software that is typically found on a production computer in your situation. If you are in a network environment, connect the computer to the network and make sure everything is fully functional. You should be able to use this machine as if it were a production computer. At the beginning of the test, this computer will run the old version of the operating system, the version you currently run on your production computers. Part of the test is to practice upgrading this operating system.

If the test computer is also a production computer (because that is the only option available to you), it is important to back up all files—data, system, and software—before you start. Operating system upgrades can destroy application configuration files and data during the upgrade. See the backup section in this chapter for more information about backing up a computer.

When the test computer is fully functional, you can perform the upgrade. During this first upgrade, it is very helpful to take specific notes describing the steps of the installation and any problems that arose, and what you did about them. Also note any questions you had about the installation, and any information you had to look up to complete the installation. Write down drivers that you needed. These notes will serve as a guide in later installations.

When there are many computers to upgrade, it is common to upgrade them over a period of several weeks or months, so having notes on the exact steps of the upgrade process will help you remember the information you need, and the problems you found. Another approach is to create a written "script" that documents the upgrade process step by step, including how to handle problems, or special driver and software installations and configurations. Figure 5-1 illustrates a sample upgrade script for upgrading from Windows 98 to Windows XP using the Windows XP CD-ROM.

Once you complete the upgrade on the test computer, and note and immediately deal with any software issues that arise, test the computer for a couple of days. Perform tasks that you would normally perform, and take note of anything that changed in the way the computer, and in particular the user interface, works.

If you find no apparent problems, the next step is to ask an informed computer user, whose computer is on the list to be upgraded, to use this computer for day-to-day work for a few days. Keep in close communication with this person, taking note of any problems experienced, and anything that does not work properly. After any operating system upgrade, one of the first things to check is whether all application software functions normally. Sometimes after upgrades, particular functions in software packages do not work, or work differently. If there are problems, chances are that the problems will not surface until a user tries to access a certain function that you never think to test.

During the testing phase, ensure that the upgrade did not change any settings, move, or remove files or programs. If you do encounter significant problems with hardware or software, consider delaying the upgrade until these problems are resolved. Just as a pre-release test will uncover major and minor problems with a new operating system design, an upgrade test can uncover conflicts between the new operating system and your particular system configuration.

Windows 98 to XP upgrade script:

1. Obtain a software license for each system to be upgraded.
2. Make sure that the hardware fulfills the Windows XP hardware requirements.
3. Make sure that the hardware is on the Windows XP hardware compatibility list.
4. Determine if the BIOS needs to be upgraded, and obtain any BIOS upgrades on floppy or CD-ROM (particularly for portable computers that are part of the upgrade).
5. Determine if there are new drivers for XP, such as for SCSI devices, modems, etc., and obtain them.
6. Make sure that there is a key code available for each installation (associated with the individual license).
7. Be sure that a password is already selected for the Administrator account.
8. Before upgrading, get a fresh startup by rebooting, and then closing any open windows.
9. Insert the Windows XP CD-ROM and use the Autorun option to start the installation.
10. Use the option to check for system compatibility.
11. Use the option to upgrade rather than to install a new system (so existing settings are retained).
12. Prior testing shows there is no need to download updated setup files – thus choose No when this option appears.
13. Use the option to save existing operating system files so it is possible to uninstall if there are problems.
14. Click Next and OK, as appropriate, to the Setup dialog boxes.
15. Log in after you finish to make sure that the installation worked.
16. Obtain a product activation code via the Internet.

Figure 5-1   Sample upgrade script

After resolving any problems, repeat the test installation process starting with a **clean computer** (a computer from which all unnecessary software and hardware have been removed). Install the old OS, then all software, then upgrade the OS (using your initial set of notes), and make the changes you think will resolve the issues you encountered earlier. Test the computer yourself for a couple of days, and then let a user test the upgraded computer. In this way, you have another chance to test the upgrade and your installation notes.

These pre-upgrade tests can be time consuming; you may need a week or longer to get through them. In some cases, you may perform many test installs before you get every detail worked out. Or, you may decide after repeated tries that the upgrade will not work, and decide not to upgrade. Either way, the test results, when carefully documented, will tell you what to expect from your upgrade. Obviously it is better to find out in a test situation that an operating system upgrade won't work for you. Your test results also can be used as a tool to explain to employees and management why an upgrade should or should not be carried out. If you decide the upgrade should proceed, you will know the steps, you will know what to expect, and you will be efficient in performing the upgrade. A test upgrade is well worth your time.

MAKING BACKUPS BEFORE UPGRADES

A **backup** involves copying files from a computer system to another medium, such as tape, Zip disk, another hard drive, or a removable drive. It is essential to have a complete backup of your old operating system, software, and data before beginning an actual upgrade. Some operating systems, in particular the Windows series, can change many configuration files, even those not used exclusively by the operating system. As a result, some applications may not be able to locate data. There are cases in which operating system installers have altogether destroyed parts of application programs. As you learned earlier in the book, the operating system is responsible for, among other things, the management of files and disks, and at the same time it provides many services to application software. With this level of complexity, a change in even one file during an upgrade can drastically change the way the new operating system works.

Making backups of software and data also is a very important part of day-to-day computer operation because unexpected things happen, such as hard disk crashes or unintentional file deletions. As operating systems and computers get more complicated, failures can even happen for unexplainable reasons during normal computer operation. If you use computers long enough, eventually you will lose critical information. Backups are essential to recovering from such a loss.

Most operating systems have a backup utility. Figure 5-2 shows the Backup tool in Windows NT 4.0, which you would use to back up a computer before upgrading to Windows 2000 or Windows XP, for example.

 If a program is lost, you may be able to simply reinstall it. But when data files are lost, the damage may take hours to repair. For this reason, regular backup of your system during normal operations and absolute backup prior to an upgrade are necessities.

Here are some points to consider when backing up your information:

- Close all open windows, programs, and files before starting a backup because most backup tools do not back up open files (on systems that use swap files—most systems—the swap file is always open, but it is acceptable to omit the swap file contents in the backup).

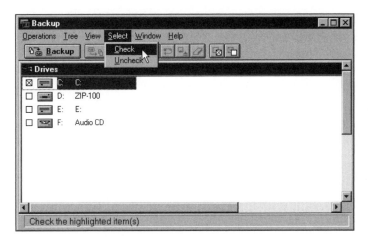

Figure 5-2   Windows NT 4.0 Backup tool

■ Make sure that you have the software needed to restore the backups under both the old and new operating systems. There is nothing more frustrating than having a backup, but not being able to restore it. Even though you tested the backup and restored software with the old operating system, there is no guarantee that it will work properly with the new one. Before you perform an upgrade, you should test the restore software, preferably by making a backup and restoring it to the computer you set up to test the new operating system.

■ Make sure that you actually make a full backup. Sometimes important files are not included in the backup process because of program error or human oversight. In addition, you should make a backup of all the contents of all fixed disks connected to the computer, not just the boot drive. If a disaster happens, it can save you a lot of time. You would then only need to restore backup tapes, instead of having to hunt all over the place to find installation disks for software programs.

 When you perform a backup, make sure that you back up critical system files, such as the system state data in Windows 2000/XP, which includes the Registry. In the backup utility that comes with these systems (and for some third-party utilities), you must manually select to back up these files. Another way to make sure that you have a backup of all files, including system files, is to perform an image (binary) backup by using tools in your backup or third-party software, such as Symantic/Norton's Ghost, or PowerQuest's Drive Image.

■ If you upgrade to a new version of backup software on your new operating system, make 100% sure, preferably by a test you perform yourself, that the new system will be able to read your backup without problems. For example, a Windows 95 backup is not compatible with a Windows XP backup.

Some computers that you upgrade will not have a built-in drive, such as a tape drive, that is suitable to make a full backup. If the computer is connected to a network, you may be able to use another computer on the network, which is equipped with an appropriate backup device, to make your backup. Alternatively, backup devices, such as tape drives or large removable disk drives, are now relatively inexpensive; almost all operating systems support easily removable external drives that connect to the parallel printer, USB, or SCSI port on a computer. It is worth the money to have one of these devices handy to make full backups of computers before an upgrade installation.

Upgrading an operating system can be very simple; it may take only 20 minutes, and you may never need those backup tapes that took two hours to create, or that test upgrade that took two weeks. However, if that 20-minute job turns into a three-week project, or if you must give up the upgrade and start from scratch, you will be very happy to have the backups. The time spent doing a test upgrade, including testing the backup, can prevent many headaches and problems with your larger system upgrade.

UPGRADING SPECIFIC OPERATING SYSTEMS

In the sections that follow, you'll learn how to upgrade the primary computer operating systems discussed in the book:

- Windows 95/98
- Windows Me
- Windows NT
- Windows 2000
- Windows XP
- UNIX
- Mac OS

Typically, the upgrade process is easier than a new installation, but this is not always the case. When it is relevant, the differences between the upgrade installation and the full installation of these operating systems are also described.

Upgrading to Windows 95

The authors realize that Windows 95 is a legacy operating system, and you won't have many occasions to upgrade to it. But there are still some situations in which this is possible. For example, your organization might have mission-critical legacy software or hardware that only runs on Windows 95 or earlier Microsoft operating systems. Upgrading to Windows 95 from an earlier operating system, such as MS-DOS or Windows 3.11, makes sense because Windows 95 offers more network functionality and speed. It may also make sense because support for early 16-bit MS-DOS, Windows 3.x, and Windows 95 applications is limited in newer operating systems, such as Windows 2000, and especially Windows XP.

You cannot directly upgrade from MS-DOS, Windows 3.x, or Windows 95 to Windows XP. However, you can upgrade from (1) MS-DOS or Windows 3.x to Windows 95, (2) from Windows 95 to Windows 98, and (3) from Windows 98 to Windows XP. If you need to use some or all of this upgrade path, then it is valuable to know how to upgrade to Windows 95, and then to Windows 98, from earlier systems.

5

Before upgrading to Windows 95 from either MS-DOS or Windows 3.x, for example, you must make a backup of your current operating system and data files. However, the backup programs provided with MS-DOS make backups that cannot be read with Windows 95. The Windows 3.x backup program writes backups that cannot be read with the Windows 95 Restore program. In addition, the Windows 3.x Restore utility cannot be used after an upgrade to Windows 95. For these reasons, use either of the following two strategies for making backups when upgrading from MS-DOS or Windows 3.x to Windows 95:

- The least expensive solution is to use the *backup* utility provided by the MS-DOS version on your computer; after the upgrade, you can boot into MS-DOS instead of Windows 95, and use the restore command for your MS-DOS version to restore files, if needed. Remember to copy that restore utility onto a floppy disk since it is removed by some Windows 95 installers during the upgrade.

- The second option is to find a third-party backup program that will write files from Windows 3.x or MS-DOS, which can be read in Windows 95. If you are in a networked environment, you can use a networked backup solution such as ARCServe from Cheyenne Software (now owned by Computer Associates).

An upgrade from MS-DOS to Windows 95 is almost identical to a fresh install of Windows 95. The Windows 95 installer runs as described in Chapter 4.

Microsoft does not consider the shift from MS-DOS to Windows 95 an "upgrade" so you either need to use the full version of Windows 95 (see Chapter 4), or you must provide the first disk of an older Windows version, such as Windows 3.11, as proof of ownership during the install of an upgrade-only version of Windows 95.

In an upgrade from MS-DOS to Windows 95, make sure that your CD-ROM drivers work correctly prior to starting installation (if you are installing Windows 95 from a CD-ROM). These drivers must load without your intervention when your computer starts because the installer will rely on them during installation. When the installation is complete, you will find that Windows 95 works exactly as it would if you had done a clean install. However, if you press the F8 key when the "Starting Windows 95" text message appears during initial boot, you will find that the boot selection menu has one additional option. This option enables you to boot the previous version of MS-DOS, which can be a useful feature because you may have older software that doesn't run correctly under the Windows 95 version of MS-DOS. By booting from the older MS-DOS version, you may be able to use utilities and other software that are totally unavailable in a Windows-only environment.

An upgrade from Windows 3.0, 3.1, or 3.11 to Windows 95 is almost the same as a clean install, but here again, some versions of Windows 95 can cause problems. For example, if you attempt to upgrade from Windows 3.1 or 3.11 to Windows 95 with a full version, you may not be able to do so. The installer may refuse to run, telling you this is not an upgrade product. You may face the same problem in upgrading from one version of Windows 95 to another. This is part of the Microsoft copyright protection scheme. The company wants to make sure you aren't indiscriminately installing versions of Windows on multiple computers. Presumably an upgrade is okay, but placing a full install on a computer with an operating system licensed only for new computers, for example, may not be allowed. You can solve this problem by renaming the Win.com file in your old Windows directory to something else, for example, Win.3. The installer tries to adopt as many of your old Windows settings as possible, and as a result, you will see that some questions in the installer have preselected answers that are a little different from those you may expect.

You may see some questions during installation that ask you whether you want to overwrite a file with a newer version. This happens when a file Windows 95 tries to install is already on the hard disk, and the version on the disk is newer than the version Windows is trying to install. Make a note of all files where this happens; be sure to write down the exact name, including the extension, and the version number and date information of the old and new files. Be aware that these may be shared files that are used by applications. These files may install with Windows, but later, when you install an application, the application installer may replace the original with one of its own. Now when you upgrade Windows, the Windows installer "knows" that the file placed there by the application isn't the same one being installed with the Windows upgrade. You can see that if you replace the application-specific file, there is a possibility that the program won't run properly.

Nevertheless, it is best to let Windows install the file it wants to install; note that in most cases, this is not the default option. If, after the installation is complete, you find that some software does not work, you can locate the file on your hard disk, and replace it with the original file from your backup. Note that when you do this, you should always keep a copy of the file you replace because Windows 95 may not let you restore the older file over the newer one.

There is one group of files that you should never replace with an older version: files that contain the **Microsoft Foundation Classes (MFC)**. MFC is a series of core routines used by almost all applications on your Windows 95 computer; the files are named

MFCxx.DLL, where xx is a numeric expression such as 32, 30, or 42. You can learn more about MFCs in Hands-on Project 5-3 at the end of this chapter.

Make sure you never replace any of the MFCs with an older version; doing so will seriously corrupt your operating system. In many cases, you may be unable to reboot the computer.

When the installation of Windows 95 is complete, you should see that all of your old Windows 3.x programs were moved into the Start menu, or the Program Manager if you chose to use that interface.

You may find that some of your programs do not work quite as you expected. Some Windows 3.x programs simply do not work under Windows 95 due to system incompatibilities. This is why performing a test installation is a good idea.

One reason that some Windows 3.x programs may not work under Windows 95 is that they rely on entries that are no longer in the Win.ini or System.ini files; the information in them was moved to the Registry. In some cases, you can edit the Win.ini and System.ini files to make these programs respond properly. Another problem with some upgrades to Windows 95 is caused by the use of older device drivers. If Windows 3.x device drivers are used in Windows 95, they can cause problems with power management and performance. Although the drivers may work, they generally do not support 32-bit operation, which can result in poor performance. With network or hard disk drivers, this can be quite a drain on system performance.

Because Windows 3.x did not provide for standardized power management, none of the Windows 3.x drivers supports Suspend mode, and computers using these drivers are unable to use all of the Windows 95 power management functions. The common solution for this problem is to obtain new, Windows 95-compliant drivers for the devices that don't work properly after the upgrade. These drivers can be installed, according to instructions provided with the drivers, after the initial Windows 95 upgrade is complete.

When you upgrade from Windows 3.x to Windows 95, file systems are not converted to the Windows 95 FAT32 system. Also, if you have a problem with an upgrade to Windows 95, the easiest solution is to perform a clean installation from scratch, making sure that you have all the device drivers you need prior to installation, and all your hardware is compatible with Windows 95.

Upgrading to Windows 98

The only upgrade path to Windows 98 is from Windows 95, and, fortunately, the Windows 98 Backup program can read Windows 95 backups. The step from Windows 95 to Windows 98 is in many ways not as big as the step from Windows 3.x to Windows 95, so this upgrade generally works well. Still, make a backup, and make sure your backup works before starting this upgrade (see Hands-on Projects 5-4 and 5-5 at the end of the chapter). Also, make sure that you back up the Windows 95 Registry. Most backup software offers an option to back up the Registry, which you should use. If your backup software does not allow you to back up the Registry, you can back it up yourself by copying the System.dat and User.dat files, both of which are hidden files in the Windows folder. You can copy these files from the MS-DOS command line, even though you won't see them if you display a directory list of the Windows folder. You can also use Windows Explorer to back up these files if you first turn on hidden files view, as shown in Hands-on Project 5-6.

To upgrade to Windows 98, start Windows 95, and make sure to close all other running programs. (The installer may crash if other software runs concurrently.) Then insert your Windows 98 Upgrade CD-ROM into the CD-ROM drive. When Autorun starts the CD-ROM, you are notified that the CD-ROM contains a newer version of the Windows operating system, and you are asked if you wish to upgrade. Click Yes, and you are on your way (see Figure 5-3). The complete steps for the upgrade are in Hands-on Project 5-7.

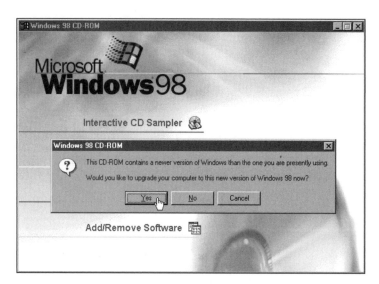

Figure 5-3   Upgrading Windows 95 to Windows 98

During the installation, you may be asked about certain files already installed on your computer because there is a version of a file on your computer that is newer than the version on the CD-ROM. As with Windows 95, keep notes on these filenames, and let Windows 98 install the versions provided with the upgrade CD-ROM for all files. If applications do not work after the upgrade, simply install the original versions from your backup. Also, if applications don't run after an upgrade, you'll probably see an error message that tells you which file is missing or incompatible. This is the file you want to restore. If you don't get a message that includes a filename, you may be able to determine which files need to be replaced from the name of the program executable file. Study the filenames in the directory in which the application is installed. Do any match names you noted during the upgrade?

 Under no circumstances should you replace any MFC file in Windows 98 with an MFC file from Windows 95. Doing so will result in a non-functional operating system installation.

Towards the end of the installation, if your computer is connected to the Internet, Windows 98 may use the Internet connection to look for newer drivers and components. As long as you have a reasonably fast Internet connection, there should be no problem. Also, near the end of the setup process, the Windows 98 installer attempts to set up drivers for all possible devices. When this is done, the installer looks at all the devices installed on your computer for which you have not yet removed the drivers. For example, if you once had a certain network card, and you removed the card without removing the drivers for it, the Windows 98 installer tries to determine whether or not those drivers should be installed in Windows 98. Although this is a good thing, it may take a while. You may have to wait for as much as half an hour or more, even though the installation "clock" shows only a minute or two to go.

 It is important that you do not interrupt this driver detection process. However, if nothing happens for more than one hour, something probably went wrong, and you should restart the installation.

If you previously upgraded the same computer from Windows 3.x to Windows 95, you may still have some older 16-bit drivers. You may end up with some devices that will not work properly with power management features, and system performance may not be optimal. The best solution is to obtain Windows 98 drivers from each device's manufacturer, or the manufacturer's Web site.

When the upgrade is complete, provided that you have Internet connectivity, use the Windows Update feature, as follows, to get the latest patches and upgrades:

1. After you complete the installation, click Start, and click Windows Update (see Figure 5-4); or click Start, choose Settings, then select Windows Update. You will be connected to the Internet if you are not already connected. Your Web browser starts, and you see the Microsoft Windows Update Web page.

 If you are using an older version of Internet Explorer, you may be asked whether or not you want to update it when you access the Microsoft Windows Update page.

Figure 5-4   Starting the Windows 98 Update feature

2. From the Windows Update page, select Product Updates. If you are asked to download a component, click Yes. You are asked for permission to scan your computer. If you click Yes, your computer is scanned for installed software, and you are presented with a list of all the patches you should install, as well as a list of available new software. It's helpful to at least pick every item on the list tagged as Critical Updates.

3. Click Download, located at the top or bottom of the page. Figure 5-5 shows how the page looks.

4. After you click Download, you will see that the next screen contains the patches you selected, how long it will take to download them, and a link to some instructions. Click Start Download. You receive one more warning (click Yes to continue), and the download begins.

5. After a while, you may be asked to restart your computer. Restart the computer as specified. Your Windows 98 is now up to date.

If you have permanent Internet access, you can set up Windows 98 so that it performs these updates periodically, and installs all software automatically. Some people see this last option as a security risk; you can periodically use the Windows Update feature to look at what is offered for installation, rather than setting up automatic updates.

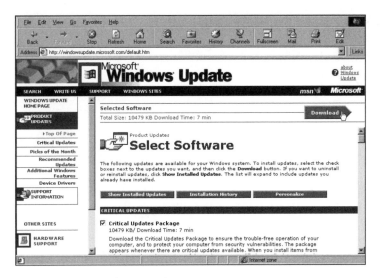

Figure 5-5   Windows Update page

Upgrading to Windows NT 4.0

Typically, you'll upgrade to Windows NT 4.0 from Windows NT 3.51. Windows NT 3.51 Workstation can be upgraded to Windows NT 4.0 Workstation, for example. An upgrade to Windows NT Server 4.0 is usually done by upgrading from Windows NT Server 3.51. Even though there are more advanced Windows server versions—Windows 2000 and Windows .NET Server—sometimes users choose to upgrade to Windows NT 4.0 Server because they currently have a Windows NT domain and are not yet ready to employ Active Directory.

Before starting the upgrade, making a backup of the system is critical. The Windows NT 4.0 Restore program is not capable of reading Windows NT 3.51 backups. Try using a third-party backup program that will work on both platforms, such as Cheyenne Software/CA's ARCServe. Make sure the backup software can back up the Registry, and supports NTFS.

 There is no uninstall feature in the Windows NT 4.0 installer. If you decide this upgrade does not work, you must rely on your backups to restore the NT 3.51 system.

The software driver model used in Windows NT 4.0 is quite different from that used in Windows NT 3.51. The other versions of Windows can use older drivers already installed; in a Windows NT 4.0 installation, this is not the case. You need drivers specifically designed for Windows NT 4.0 for the hardware installed in your computer.

One concern about Windows NT 4.0 when it was first released was the lack of a complete range of drivers for devices. Microsoft corrected this situation by eventually implementing nearly the same array of drivers as for Windows 98.

The Windows NT 4.0 upgrade is started from the 3.51 version of Windows NT, and proceeds as follows:

1. Make sure that no users are accessing the resources made available from this computer (Windows NT 3.51 Workstation supports up to 10 connected users over a network, while Windows NT 3.51 Server supports several hundred or more).

2. Insert the Windows NT 4.0 Upgrade CD-ROM, and double-click the Setup32.exe (or Setup.exe, depending on your version of the CD-ROM) program from the i386 directory on the CD-ROM. The Setup program copies all files to the hard disk, and after the computer restarts, the setup process continues, as described in Chapter 4.

The Windows NT 4.0 upgrade installer is identical to the non-upgrade (Full) version installer. However, you should be aware that some questions have already been completed according to your preferences from the previous installation of the earlier operating system version.

 During the installation, you can choose to convert some or all of your FAT file systems to NTFS. This process, if interrupted, will leave disks beyond repair, thereby making your reliance on a backup much greater. You should not use this option unless you are certain your backups are perfect. You can choose to update to NTFS at a later time, if you wish.

The networking setup changed significantly from Windows NT 3.51 to Windows NT 4.0, and you should pay special attention to the section of the installer that deals with the setup of your network hardware, addressing, and protocols. In many cases, the installer will configure the devices and fill in the information about them correctly, but for computers that have multiple network cards with a mix of protocols on each card, care should be taken to ensure that the information entered for all devices is correct. If there is a problem setting up networking during installation, you can reconfigure networking after the upgrade is completed (by using the Control Panel's Network icon).

When Setup is complete, follow the instructions given in Chapter 4 on the post-install setup of Windows NT. As part of this process, make sure that you install the most recent service pack and all the security updates, particularly for Windows NT Server 4.0.

At this writing, there are six service packs (up to Service Pack 6a) and additional security updates. You do not need to load all six service packs because the last service pack always contains the fixes and enhancements included in the previous service packs. Keep in mind that if you install new software or drivers, you typically must reinstall the service pack because the software or driver installation may write over one or more service pack files. Also, remember that a service pack can be removed, if there is a problem, by using the files in the $Uninstall folder. Always back up your system before installing a service pack.

Upgrading to Windows 2000

There are several upgrade paths to Windows 2000, such as from Windows 95, Windows 98, and Windows NT. The most common paths are to upgrade from Windows 95/98 or from Windows NT 4.0. Less common is to upgrade from Windows Me because Windows Me came out after Windows 2000 and was targeted primarily for home users.

Actually, there is no upgrade path from Windows Me to Windows 2000 because in order to upgrade, you must purchase a Full non-upgrade copy of Windows 2000 and install it from scratch.

When you upgrade from Windows 95/98, you will upgrade to Windows 2000 Professional. If you upgrade Windows NT Workstation 4.0 (or earlier), you will upgrade to Windows 2000 Professional. Windows NT Server 4.0 is upgraded to Windows 2000 Server or higher (Advanced Server or Datacenter Server).

For users who upgrade from Windows 95/98, there are several issues to consider:

- Determine if your computer meets the minimum system requirements for Windows 2000 (see Chapter 4).

- Determine if you need to obtain new drivers for the devices in your computer, such as for a modem or network interface card. Visit the Windows Compatibility Web site at *www.microsoft.com/windows2000/default.asp* (click or search for the link for compatibility) to check on compatible devices.

- Decide if you want to upgrade to NTFS from FAT16 or FAT32. It is recommended that you wait to upgrade to NTFS until after the installation is completed, and you have an opportunity to make sure your computer is working properly. Keep in mind that once you convert from FAT16 or FAT32 to NTFS, you cannot convert back without reformatting the hard disk and performing a restore.

- You will need a password for the Administrator account. Decide on a password before you start the installation.

When you are ready to upgrade from Windows 95/98 to Windows 2000 Professional, start Windows 95/98, close any open windows, and then insert the Windows 2000 Professional CD-ROM. The first box you see queries whether you want to upgrade to Windows 2000. Click Yes to view the Welcome to the Windows 2000 Setup Wizard dialog box. In this box, select the option to Upgrade to Windows 2000 (Recommended), as shown in Figure 5-6.

Figure 5-6   Windows 2000 Setup Wizard

After you select the upgrade option, you are on your way to upgrading to Windows 2000 Professional. The installation takes from 45 minutes to about an hour and a half. One way to save time during the installation is to go to the Windows 2000 Compatibility Web site in advance and make sure that your system and peripherals are compatible with Windows 2000 Professional. Also, obtain any new drivers or BIOS updates for Widows 2000 before you start. You may also need to obtain Windows 2000 updates for some of your software. Consult your software vendors' Web sites for Windows 2000 update information. You can install these software updates after you install Windows 2000 and determine that you need them. Try Hands-on Project 5-8 to upgrade from Windows 98 to Windows 2000 Professional.

The preparations for upgrading from Windows NT 4.0 to Windows 2000 are the same as those for upgrading from Windows 95/98, with a few exceptions. First, Windows NT 4.0 only uses FAT16 or NTFS, and not FAT32. If you are using FAT16 and want to continue using the FAT file system, the Windows 2000 Setup program upgrades your disk to FAT16 if it is 2 GB or smaller; it upgrades to FAT32 if your disk is over 2 GB. If your disk is already formatted for NTFS version 4, Windows 2000 Setup converts it to NTFS version 5. Second, make sure that you obtain Windows 2000 drivers for your Windows NT-supported devices. Third, the protocol of preference for Windows 2000 is TCP/IP. If you are using the legacy NetBEUI protocol, convert your Windows NT system to use TCP/IP before you upgrade (for a smoother upgrade path).

The actual upgrade steps from Windows NT Workstation to Windows 2000 are similar to those for Windows 98, which means that you can apply what you learn in Hands-on Project 5-8 to a Windows NT Workstation upgrade.

If you upgrade a Windows NT Server 4.0 domain to a Windows 2000 Server domain, the upgrade steps are more complicated than upgrading from Windows NT Workstation to Windows 2000 Professional. Use the following general steps to upgrade a Windows NT Server domain:

1. Coordinate a time when you can upgrade the servers and domain while no one is accessing these but you.

2. Back up each Windows NT 4.0 server that will be upgraded, including its Registry, before you start an upgrade. Also, make an Emergency Repair Disk before you start, and again just after you finish.

3. If TCP/IP is not already implemented, upgrade the servers to TCP/IP before you start; or, consider setting up the first upgraded server as a **Dynamic Host Configuration Protocol (DHCP)** server, and use the default TCP/IP configuration for each upgraded server (generally, however, it is better to give all servers a static IP address that is not assigned by DHCP, and use DHCP only for clients). A DHCP server automatically assigns IP addresses to network clients. Also, set up the first upgraded server to work as a **Domain Name Service (DNS)** server if one does not already exist on the network, such as via a UNIX server. A DNS server resolves domain and computer names to IP addresses (and vice versa).

4. If you are upgrading more than one server in a domain, start by upgrading the Windows NT 4.0 primary domain controller (PDC, the server that contains the master copy of the domain information) to the first Windows 2000 domain controller. Next, and one at a time, upgrade each Windows NT 4.0 backup domain controller (BDC, the servers that contain backup copies of the domain data) to be a Windows 2000 domain controller.

5. To begin the upgrade, use the Winnt32 program on the Windows 2000 Server CD-ROM by clicking Start, clicking Run, entering the path to the CD-ROM plus Winnt32, such as *D:\i386\Winnt32* (or use the browse option on the CD-ROM window that is displayed by the Autorun program when you insert the CD-ROM).

To view the command switches for Winnt32, click Start, click Run, enter the CD-ROM path plus \i386\Winnt32 /?.

6. Select Upgrade to Windows 2000 (Recommended) on the first screen when the Setup program starts so that you can retain existing settings, including the Windows NT Security Account Manager (SAM) database information about accounts and groups, and software.

7. Follow the directions in the Windows 2000 Setup.

8. During the upgrade, the Active Directory Wizard starts and provides the opportunity for you to specify if you want to join an existing domain tree or forest, or start a new one. Specify that you want to start a new one if you are upgrading the PDC. Specify that you wish to join an existing one if you are upgrading a BDC, and provide the name of the domain.

9. The Active Directory Installation Wizard upgrades the PDC or BDC to have Windows 2000 Server directory services and Kerberos authentication services. Also, it converts the SAM in the Windows NT Registry to the database used by Active Directory so that accounts, groups, and security information are retained.

10. After you upgrade a PDC, it is still recognized by any Windows NT BDC as the domain master, and can synchronize with live BDCs until they are upgraded. Leave a BDC running until all servers are upgraded (except for the last server to be upgraded, of course) because this gives you a backup alternative if there is a problem. (If you are concerned about upgrade problems, create an extra BDC to match the last BDC before it is converted. Remove the backup BDC from the network, and store it in a safe place until you feel assured the upgrade process is fully successful.)

11. Establish security policies for the domain via Active Directory, including logon restrictions.

12. After all servers are upgraded and there are no Windows NT servers connected to the domain, convert the domain (or all domains) to native mode, which reflects that there are no longer any Windows NT PDCs or BDCs on the network. You can do this by clicking the Start button, pointing to Programs, pointing to Administrative Tools, and clicking Active Directory Domains and Trusts. Right-click the domain you want to convert and click Properties. Click the Change Mode button.

After you finish upgrading any system to Windows 2000, connect your computer to the Internet (if you have access), and use the Windows Update option to obtain the latest patches and upgrades. The Windows 2000 Update option works in a way that is similar to the Windows 98 Update option described earlier because it connects to the Microsoft Windows Update Web page for Windows 2000. To access the Windows 2000 Update option, click Start, and click Windows Update at the top of the Start menu (or click Start, point to Settings, click Control Panel, double-click Add/Remove Programs, click Add New Programs in the left pane, and click the Windows Update button).

Also, obtain the latest service pack version from the Microsoft Web site (or order the CD-ROM from Microsoft), and apply the service pack to Windows 2000. This is particularly important for server and Web security. For example, there is a patch for the Code Red virus that affected many people connected to the Internet.

Upgrading to Windows XP

You can upgrade to Windows XP from any of the following Microsoft operating systems:

- Windows 98
- Windows Me
- Windows NT
- Windows 2000

5

Before you start an upgrade, keep in mind that you cannot upgrade Windows 95 or earlier operating systems to Windows XP. Also, as is true for any upgrade: (1) back up your system before you start, including the Registry, (2) make sure that your hardware matches the recommended hardware requirements for Windows XP (see Chapters 3 and 4), (3) check the hardware compatibility information on Microsoft's Web site, and (4) obtain any drivers that you may need before you start.

 If you have older hardware, such as a Pentium I or Pentium II computer, the manufacturer may offer a BIOS upgrade that makes the computer more compatible with Windows 2000 and Windows XP. Contact the computer manufacturer or visit its Web site to check on a possible BIOS enhancement that you can download or obtain on CD-ROM.

There is not room to explain how to upgrade from all possible operating systems to Windows XP, but it is not necessary because the upgrade process is virtually identical for Windows 98, Me, NT, and 2000. In this section, we provide the general upgrade steps for all of these systems.

 Microsoft considers Windows XP to be a "minor" upgrade from Windows 2000 because Windows 2000 and XP are built on nearly the same kernel. The primary differences are in the introduction of a relatively new GUI in Windows XP, and Windows XP has more functionality for multimedia applications, including photos, music, and video clips. Because Windows XP is a minor upgrade, some organizations that already use Windows 2000 are waiting for the version after Windows XP before upgrading.

To upgrade to Windows XP (Home or Professional) from Windows 98, Me, NT, or 2000, begin by closing all open windows, or reboot the computer and then close any windows that you don't need. Insert the Windows XP CD-ROM and wait for the Autorun program to automatically start the Setup program. Use the option to check system compatibility (see Figure 5-7) before you start the actual installation, and then select the option to check your system automatically. If you see the message "Windows XP upgrade check found no incompatibilities or problems" (see Figure 5-8), your system is ready for the upgrade. Click Finish and then Back so you can continue with the upgrade. If there is an incompatibility, stop the upgrade and check with your computer manufacturer for Windows XP updates.

Figure 5-7   Option to check compatibility with Windows XP

Figure 5-8   Viewing the compatibility test results

Next, begin the Windows XP installation, and specify that you want to use the upgrade option so that the settings you already have in Windows 98, Me, NT, or 2000 are carried into Windows XP. Read the license agreement, enter your product key, and complete the remaining steps in the Windows XP Setup program. The upgrade takes from 30 to 90 minutes to complete. Try Hands-on Project 5-9 to practice upgrading to Windows XP.

For all systems that you upgrade to Windows XP, you must obtain a product activation code by going to Microsoft's Web site. Also, keep in mind that if your computer stops working and you need to port Windows XP to another system, such as through a tape restore, you must obtain another product activation code for the new computer.

Finally, after you upgrade to Windows XP, use the Upgrade option to link to Microsoft's Web site for additional features and special upgrade options. To access the Upgrade option, click Start, select All Programs, and click Windows Update. Also, obtain the latest service pack for Windows XP.

Upgrading UNIX System V

There are many backup programs that can be used with UNIX. These programs are standardized; it is possible to make backups in one version and read them in many other versions, whether older or newer, from the same vendor or a different vendor. The standard UNIX backup utility is called a *dump* (*dump* in Linux and *ufsdump* in Solaris). Backups can be made to local devices or across a network. In Solaris, there is a backup program called tapetool with a graphical user interface. Since tapetool uses dump to make a backup, it too will be compatible with almost any UNIX version.

It is especially important to make backups of all the system configuration files on UNIX computers; if for some reason the upgrade does not work, you must do a full, fresh operating system installation. Having configuration files to fall back on can save a lot of time and trouble. You should make a backup of the contents of the entire /etc directory so that you have copies of all system configuration files. This can be done using the *tar* command. For example, to copy the contents of /etc to a file called myetc.tar in the root directory, you go to the root directory by entering *cd /*, and then enter *tar –cvf /myetc.tar etc*. You may also want to back up your /usr/local/etc directory, as illustrated in Hands-on Project 5-10.

The configuration files found in the /etc directory include the various *rc* startup scripts, the inittab file that helps your system start, and the disktab or vfstab files, which help you mount your file systems. They also include various service configuration files, such as the hosts file, which contains information needed to set up networking; the host.* files, which help configure the computer at startup; and the syslog.conf file, which tells *syslog* what to do and how. *Syslog* is a command-line utility that enables you to track system information, such as successful and failed events, hardware events, and security events. Depending on what services your computer runs, there may be additional configuration files; you should also back up your password (/etc/passwd and /etc/shadow in Linux and Solaris) and groups files (/etc/group in both Linux and Solaris).

If you installed any special kernel or device driver files, make backups of these as well. You may also want to back up your Web and other configuration files; these are generally found in /usr/local/etc. Exactly which files you should back up depends on your installation. Backing up both /etc and /usr/local/etc ensures that you have copies of any configuration files you may need. As with other upgrades, backing up these files and directories can make recovering from problems easier if things go wrong after the upgrade. The /etc/services and /etc/inetd.conf files are also likely to change; often you will find new services added, or some of your custom services removed, so a careful check of these files should be made. Also, the inittab and startup files should be checked to ensure that they function properly.

In the other operating system installations discussed in this chapter, if the upgrade installation fails, you simply restart it, and it either starts from the beginning, or detects that an error occurred, and tries to resume the upgrade from the point where it left off. In the world of UNIX, however, if an install or upgrade fails in the middle, you must reinstall the operating system as if nothing was on the disk. This is a weakness in UNIX that various vendors are trying to address. Meanwhile, you should be very certain your backups are in tip-top shape before starting an upgrade.

Once again, if you attempt a UNIX upgrade that fails, you cannot just restart the upgrade; you must do a new install.

The upgrade process described here is based on the Red Hat Linux 7.2 installer. Although the installers have changed significantly in appearance over the years, the functionality has not changed much. Upgrades from any version of Linux to this version should work, but in many cases the installer cannot determine the exact features installed on the previous version of Linux. It's recommended that you upgrade to Red Hat Linux 7.2 only from Red Hat version 3.0 or up. If you used a different Linux version, back up your data and perform a clean install, then restore your data.

Under Linux, the upgrade process works similarly to the installation process. You start the installation, as described in the previous chapter, then choose to perform an upgrade. The installer asks for some basic system information, such as which language and keyboard to use. Also, it checks to determine what hard disks to use for the installation. It then gets most system information previously stored on the hard disk by the old operating system. The appropriate system files are replaced, and the installer asks if you want to customize the package installation. If you select Yes, you can choose specific elements to install or update for each previously installed package. Note that many libraries and programs will be replaced, and if you add software to the computer, you should check carefully to ensure that everything still works as expected after installation. Try Hands-on Project 5-11 to practice updating a Red Hat Linux operating system.

An important caveat in UNIX upgrades is that many configuration files are overwritten during the upgrade. The mail system, printing system, window system, and other network services such as FTP and the World Wide Web server may be reconfigured. You should double-check configuration files on these services to make sure they did not change.

Solaris, like Red Hat Linux, comes in many versions. If you are comfortable with upgrading Red Hat Linux as described here, you should have no problems conducting a Solaris upgrade.

Upgrading Mac OS

Before attempting to upgrade the Mac operating system, you should always perform three basic steps:

1. As with other operating systems, you must perform a backup of all data and configuration files on the hard drive. This includes the entire System Folder, which may contain the user's browser bookmarks and Eudora address book and mail files.

2. Check the disk for errors using a utility like Norton Disk Doctor (part of Symantec's Norton Utilities for Macintosh) or Apple Disk First Aid. Otherwise, the installation could aggravate existing directory damage and cause new problems, including data loss. Newer versions of Apple installers perform a basic check automatically.

3. Always upgrade the hard disk drivers. Skipping this step can result in a loss of data if the old disk drivers are incompatible with the new OS. If you are using an Apple drive formatted with an Apple driver, newer versions of the installer handle this automatically. For third-party drives, contact the publisher of your disk-formatting utility for new disk drivers. If new disk drivers have not shipped, postpone the upgrade until the necessary software is available.

Clean versus Dirty Installs

There are two ways to install or reinstall the Mac OS: "dirty" and "clean." In a dirty install, the OS is installed on top of the previous System Folder. Files with the same name are overwritten, but older, obsolete components that don't have a modern equivalent are retained. Likewise, the dirty System Folder contains all the third-party software that was present in the old System Folder, including software that may not be compatible with the current OS. Any time you upgrade or reinstall the Mac OS on a volume that contains an existing OS install, you are performing a dirty install.

In a clean install, a fresh new System Folder is created. Clean installs are always the safest option. The technique for performing a clean install depends on the operating system version, as follows:

- Systems prior to 7.5: rename the old System Folder ("System Folder Old," for instance). Move the Finder from the old System Folder to another location.

- System 7.5: in the main installer window, press Command+Shift+K. A dialog box appears, giving you the option to install a new System Folder.

- OS 7.6: in the Software Installation window, click Options, and choose the "Create new System Folder (clean installation)" check box.

- OS 8.0/8.1: choose the Perform Clean Installation check box in the Select Destination window.

- OS 8.5 through OS X (including 9.x): in the Select Destination window, click Options and put a check next to Perform Clean Installation, as shown in Figure 5-9. Note that the old System Folder is renamed "Previous System Folder," and should be deleted after you verify the installation and set up panels and other elements.

Figure 5-9   Choosing a "clean" install of Mac OS

Sample Mac OS X Upgrade

The general steps to perform a Mac OS X upgrade from Mac OS 9.x are as follows:

1. From a computer already booted and running Mac OS 9.x, insert the Mac OS X CD-ROM.

2. Select Special, select Restart, and press and hold the C key.

3. Select the appropriate language for users of the computer and then click Continue.

4. Read the introductory information that appears on the screen and click Continue.

5. Review the "Important Information" that is displayed and select Continue.

6. Review the license agreement and click Continue.

7. Click the Agree button.

8. Click the icon for the disk that will hold the operating system and click Continue. (Do not select the Mac OS X CD-ROM.)

9. Click Install.

10. When the installation is completed, the computer reboots so that you can configure Mac OS X.

11. The configuration process enables you to configure your country, keyboard layout, registration information, and user account. You can also configure your Internet connection and local area network connection.

Merging the Old and New System Folders

Once you test the system to make sure it is functioning correctly, you must recover certain files from the old System Folder. For instance, you need certain extensions and control panels that are necessary for the operation of printers, disk drives, and other peripherals, as well as third-party fonts and application preferences files. If the preferences files are lost, you must reenter the serial numbers for some commercial programs. The serial numbers may be printed on manuals or installation disks now scattered to the four winds. Likewise, the Control Panels, Extensions, and Fonts folders may contain critical files whose installer disks can no longer be located.

When transferring these files, especially extensions and control panels, exercise caution. Some of the files may not be compatible with the new operating system. For instance, RamDoubler and SpeedDoubler are very likely to require maintenance upgrades to be compatible with a new version of the operating system because of the intimate way those programs interact with the operating system. If you are reinstalling the operating system because the computer was crashing, be especially wary. The crashes may be caused by a buggy extension or control panel, or by a corrupted font or preferences file. Keep that in mind when moving files into the new operating system. It's a good idea to transfer a few files at a time, and restart to make sure everything works.

When merging the old and new System Folders, you should concentrate on five folders and two subfolders: the Apple Menu, Control Panels, Extensions, Fonts, and Preferences folders; and the Modem Scripts and Printer Description subfolders inside the Extensions folder. Modem Scripts are modem configuration files used with Apple Remote Access and PPP. Printer Descriptions are PostScript Printer Description (PPD) files.

Files can be moved manually from the old System Folder to the new a few at a time. Files that exist in the new operating system (such as the Date & Time Control Panel) don't have to be moved. You'll mainly be moving third-party files. Again, it's a good idea to move a handful of files at a time, restart, and verify that the files are not causing problems. (There is third-party software, such as Cassady & Greene's Conflict Catcher, that can merge the old and new software at the touch of a button. Conflict Catcher can also diagnose extension and control panel conflicts, and is a useful addition to the system administrator's toolbox.)

When you upgrade from Mac OS 9.x to Mac OS X, the old Mac OS 9.x applications are treated as "classic applications" because they are not written to use the new interface, and they do not run as fast as the applications written for Mac OS X. When you open a Mac OS 9.x application, it automatically starts the classic applications environment for that application. Also, try Hands-on Project 5-12 to manually start and stop the classic applications environment.

CHAPTER SUMMARY

❑ No matter how comfortable you are with an operating system, there comes a time when you must upgrade to the next version. For instance, you may find that your current operating system version does not support new software or certain devices. Also, older versions of operating systems don't have the security features required for network and Internet access—or to protect e-mail systems.

❑ Upgrading an operating system is very similar to installing a new operating system, which you learned about in the last chapter. However, you should take certain steps in preparing for an upgrade. Before upgrading, make sure that an upgrade is necessary. For example, some organizations have decided not to upgrade from Windows 2000 to Windows XP because the software and network features they use are nearly identical in both systems. Also, when you decide to upgrade, check that your hardware meets the requirements for upgrading, and make sure you have the correct, most up-to-date drivers for the various devices on your system.

❑ Before you insert the upgrade CD-ROM, make sure that you have a working backup of the current operating system and data. Check your backup after it is made to make sure that you can perform a restore from it if the upgrade is unsuccessful, or if you need to retrieve data that was overwritten by the upgrade.

❑ There are specific issues associated with an upgrade of any operating system. Some issues are small, such as deciding on a password for the Administrator account when you upgrade from Windows 98 to Windows 2000 or XP. Other issues are more involved—deciding to convert from FAT16 to NTFS, for example.

❑ It's important to realize that when upgrading various UNIX versions, there are critical differences between a UNIX upgrade and a conventional Windows upgrade. Similarly, when upgrading your Mac OS to a later version, you must choose between a "clean" and "dirty" install.

❑ The information in this chapter, coupled with the original operating system installation information in the previous chapter, should give you a strong foundation for installing and upgrading your operating system on virtually any platform.

KEY TERMS

alpha software — An early development version of software in which there are likely to be bugs, and not all of the anticipated software functionality is present. Alpha software is usually tested only by a select few users to identify major problems and the need for new or different features before the software is tested by a broader audience in the beta stage.

backup — A process of copying files from a computer system to another medium, such as a tape, Zip disk, another hard drive, or a removable drive.

beta software — During software development, software that has successfully passed the alpha test stage. Beta testing may involve dozens, hundreds, or even thousands of people, and may be conducted in multiple stages: beta 1, beta 2, beta 3, and so on.

clean computer — A computer from which all unnecessary software and hardware have been removed. A clean computer is useful during software upgrade testing since a minimum number of other software and hardware elements are in place, making it easier to track down problems with new software.

Domain Name Service or System (DNS) — A TCP/IP application protocol that resolves domain and computer names to IP addresses, or IP addresses to domain and computer names.

Dynamic Host Configuration Protocol (DHCP) — A network protocol that provides a way for a host to automatically assign an IP address to a workstation on its network.

Microsoft Foundation Classes (MFC) — A series of core routines used by almost all applications on a computer running a Windows-based operating system.

Open Database Connectivity (ODBC) — A set of rules developed by Microsoft for accessing databases and providing a standard doorway to database data.

production computer — Any computer used to perform real work, which should be protected from problems that might cause an interruption in workflow or loss of data.

release candidate (RC) — The final stage of software testing by vendors before cutting an official release that is sold commercially. A release candidate is usually tested by a very large audience of customers. Some vendors may issue more than one release candidate if problems are discovered in the first RC.

REVIEW QUESTIONS

1. You are trying to upgrade Windows 98 with a FAT32-formatted drive to Windows NT Workstation 4.0, but the upgrade refuses to go from the beginning. What is the problem?

2. Each operating system upgrade is somewhat unique, but there are some general steps you should conduct with every upgrade. Which of the following apply? (Choose all that apply.)

   a. Test the upgrade on a non-production computer.

   b. Physically disconnect from the network, in case you have to change protocols during the upgrade.

   c. Back up all data and applications before starting the upgrade.

   d. Test backup and restore software before committing to the new software version.

   e. Completely remove the old operating system before starting the upgrade.

3. You only need to back up application files since an operating system upgrade won't touch your data files. True or False?

4. Which of the following operating systems requires that you obtain a product activation code after you upgrade to it?

   a. Windows XP

   b. Mac OS X

   c. Windows 2000

   d. Red Hat Linux 7.2

   e. all of the above

   f. only a and b

   g. only a and c

   h. only b, c, and d

5. In a Mac OS clean installation, a _____ is installed.

6. When you upgrade a Windows NT Server 4.0 domain to a Windows 2000 Server domain, which should you upgrade first?

   a. You must first upgrade all Windows NT clients to Windows 2000.

   b. You should first upgrade the Windows NT PDC.

   c. You must first upgrade all Windows NT BDCs, and then the Windows NT PDC.

   d. You should first upgrade all clients that are running Windows 95 and 98 to Windows XP.

   e. Both a and b should be done at the same time.

   f. All of a, b, and d should be done at the same time.

7. What backup utility are you likely to use when making a pre-upgrade backup in Linux?

   a. *ls*

   b. *vms*

   c. *dump*

   d. *grep*

   e. *mount*

8. You have Windows 95 and are trying to upgrade to Windows XP, but the upgrade won't work. What is the problem?

   a. You must first make a change to the Windows 95 Registry to allow upgrades.

   b. You cannot upgrade to Windows XP from Windows 95.

   c. Your Windows 95 system is using NetBEUI, and you must first convert to TCP/IP before starting the upgrade.

   d. Windows 95 is not compatible with the Windows XP Active Directory.

9. You just completed your upgrade to Windows 2000. What can you do now to obtain the latest patches and upgrades that are not included on your Windows 2000 CD-ROM?

10. Why is it ill advised to implement a beta version of an operating system on a computer that is in production use?

11. A user that you are helping upgraded from Windows 95 to Windows 98. After the upgrade, he copied some Windows 95 application files that he thought would be important over some Windows 98 files. Now Windows 98 does not work properly. Which of the following might be the problem?

    a. Windows 98 does not recognize the same printers as Windows 95, so the printers must be reinstalled.

    b. The user did not upgrade to the OSR2 version of Windows 98.

    c. The user inadvertently copied one or more Windows 95 MFCs over the Windows 98 MFCs.

    d. The user upgraded to use FAT16, but the security that he set in Windows 98 requires FAT32.

    e. The files that the user copied back into Windows 98 are formatted for FAT16, but the upgrade was to FAT32.

12. After you upgrade a Mac OS, you will likely need to recover some files from the _____.

13. Why should you back up the /etc directory in UNIX?

14. The only upgrade path to Windows 98 is from _____.

15. During installation of some versions of Windows, the installer may access the Internet. What is the purpose of this access? Is it desirable, or should you stop this process in the interests of local system security?

16. You upgraded from Mac OS 9.1 to Mac OS X, but some of your applications do not run using the new Mac OS X interface. What can be done?

    a. Stop using those old applications because they may damage your new system.

    b. Purchase the Mac application converter program that converts these applications to run in Mac OS X.

    c. Contact the old application vendors to obtain special .dll files.

    d. Use the classic environment to run these applications.

17. After installing Red Hat Linux 7.2, where can you look to view information about the status of the installation?

18. When you upgrade the Mac OS, make sure that you also upgrade the _____ to prevent _____.

19. One advantage to upgrading the Mac OS compared to other operating systems is that you do not need to make a backup. True or False?

20. When you upgrade from Windows 98 to Windows 2000, you:

    a. can use either the FAT or NTFS file systems.

    b. should run the Registry upgrade after the installation for compatibility with Active Directory.

    c. can select to use the Windows 98 desktop, the Windows Me desktop, or the Windows 2000 desktop.

    d. should delete the Administrator account because it is a security risk.

    e. all of the above

    f. only a and c

    g. only b, c, and d

HANDS-ON PROJECTS

Project 5-1

In this project, you'll learn how to determine if a computer has the proper hardware configuration for an upgrade to Windows 2000 or Windows XP. You will need the Windows 2000 or Windows XP (any version of these operating systems) CD-ROM.

To check the computer's hardware prior to an upgrade:

1. Start any of the following computer operating systems: Windows 95, Windows 98, Windows NT, Windows 2000 (for an upgrade to Windows XP), or Windows XP (if you do not have an earlier operating system).

2. Insert the Windows 2000 or Windows XP CD-ROM in the CD-ROM drive.

3. Click **Start**, and then click **Run**.

4. Enter the drive letter and path of the winnt32.exe file (on the CD-ROM) in the Open box, and enter **/checkupgradeonly**. Enter the command as in: **D:\i386\winnt32.exe /checkupgradeonly** (winnt32 is located on the CD-ROM in the \i386 folder for Intel-based computers). Click **OK**.

5. If you are connected to the Internet, you can use the Microsoft Windows Upgrade Advisor (which starts automatically) to obtain upgrade updates from Microsoft's Web site. To use the advisor, after it starts, click *Yes, download the updated Setup files (Recommended)* and then click *Next* View the information about incompatibilities and problems, and then click *Finish*. If you are not connected to the Internet, click *No, skip this step and continue installing Windows* and then click *Next*. Examine the report and click *Finish*. (In some versions of Windows 2000 you may not see the Microsoft Windows Upgrade Advisor. In these cases the Microsoft Windows 2000 Readiness Analyzer creates the report and you click *Finish* after you review it.)

Project 5-2

Before upgrading an operating system, it is important to know what software will be affected. In this project, you'll learn one place in which to look for the software installed on different operating systems.

To determine the software installed on Windows-based systems:

1. Begin by observing the application icons that are on the desktop. What software application icons or shortcuts do you see?

2. Click **Start** on the taskbar, and point to **Programs** (or select **All Programs** in Windows XP).

3. What programs are listed?

4. In Windows 95, 98, or NT, click **Windows Explorer** (or **Windows NT Explorer** for Windows NT). In Windows Me, 2000, or Windows XP, point to **Accessories**, and then click **Windows Explorer**.

5. Locate the main drive on the computer (most desktop computers have only one drive—also in some versions of Windows, you may need to open My Computer to see the drive). Double-click that drive, such as drive **(C:)**, if its contents do not appear under the drive.

6. Double-click the **Program Files** folder. (In some Windows versions the subfolders and files are not displayed until you elect to display them.)

7. What subfolders or programs do you see (such as MSOffice)?

8. Close Windows Explorer.

9. Next, in Windows 95/98/NT/2000, click **Start**, point to **Settings**, click **Control Panel**, and click **Add/Remove Programs**. Or, in Windows XP, click **Start**, click **Control Panel**, and click **Add or Remove Programs**.

10. What programs are listed as already installed?

11. Close the Add/Remove (or Add or Remove) Programs dialog box. Also, close the Control Panel if it still appears.

To determine the software installed in Mac OS 9.x:

1. Open Macintosh HD.

2. Select **Applications**.

3. What applications do you see?

4. Close the Applications window.

To determine the software installed in Mac OS X:

1. Select **Macintosh HD**.

2. Notice that there are two selections for Applications—*Applications (Mac OS 9)*, which is for Mac OS 9.x-compatible applications, and *Applications*, which is for Mac OS X-compatible applications.

3. Select **Applications (Mac OS 9)** and determine what applications are available.

4. Click the button on the right side of the top bar to display the options at the top of the window (Back, View, Computer, Home, Favorites, and Applications), if they are not currently displayed.

5. Click **Back**.

6. Next, select **Applications** and determine what applications can be accessed.

7. Close the Applications window.

 To determine the software installed in Red Hat Linux 7.2 (with the GNOME interface):

1. Click the **Main Menu** (foot) icon in the Panel.

2. Point to **Programs**, and then point to **Applications**.

3. What programs do you see?

4. If there is another Applications selection, point to it and determine the applications.

5. Move the pointer to a blank area of the screen and click it to close the menu, if necessary.

 To see a list of all of the software packages installed in UNIX:

1. At the Red Hat Linux 7.2 command line (or in the terminal window in the GNOME interface), type **rpm –qa**. Press **Enter**.

2. What are some examples listed of software (the list will be quite long)?

3. If you opened a terminal window to access the command line, type **exit** and press **Enter** to close the window.

 The command to view installed software packages is different in various UNIX systems. For example, you enter *pkginfo* in Solaris, *swlist* in HP UNIX, *pkg_info -a* in FreeBSD, and *lslpp -L all* in IBM's AIX.

 ## Project 5-3

MFC (Microsoft Foundation Classes) files are important files that may be used by many applications. These files are installed with your operating system, and also by some applications software.

 To view MFC files currently installed on your computer:

1. In Windows 95/98, click **Start**, point to **Programs**, and choose **MS-DOS Prompt**. In Windows NT, click **Start**, point to **Programs**, and click **Command Prompt**. In Windows Me, click **Start**, point to **Programs**, point to **Accessories**, and click **MS-DOS Prompt**. Or, in Windows 2000/XP, click **Start**, point to **Programs**, (in Windows 2000) or **All programs** (in Windows XP), point to **Accessories**, and click **Command Prompt**.

2. Type **CD ** and press **Enter** to make the root directory the current directory.

3. Type **dir mfc*.dll /s** and press **Enter**. You will see a list of directories and MFC files. What are some of these files and in what directories are they stored?

4. Close the MS-DOS Prompt window.

Project 5-4

Plan to back up system and application files prior to conducting an operating system upgrade. In this project, you'll back up files in Windows 98, such as in preparation to upgrade to Windows 2000 or Windows XP. You will need a medium on which to write the backup, such as a tape, Zip disk, network drive, or floppy disk—consult your instructor about which to use. Also, the Windows 98 Backup utility should already be installed. If it is not (see Step 1), obtain the Windows 98 CD-ROM and insert it in the CD-ROM drive. Click Start, point to Settings, and click Control Panel. Double-click Add/Remove Programs, and open the Windows Setup tab. Double-click System Tools, and click the box in front of Backup. Click OK and click OK again.

To back up specific directories or files in Windows 98:

1. Click **Start**, point to **Programs**, point to **Accessories**, point to **System Tools**, and click **Backup**.

2. If the Backup program does not detect any backup hardware installed on your computer, it will ask if you want AutoDetect to try to find it. If this occurs, click **No**.

3. On the opening Backup screen, choose **Create a new backup job**, and click **OK**.

4. Choose **Back up selected files, folders and drives**. You can use this choice to back up to floppy disks, or a removable high-density disk such as a Zip or Jazz drive. If you have a tape backup system, choose **Backup My Computer** to back up everything on your hard drive. Click **Next**.

5. Navigate to the folder(s) or file(s) you want to back up, and click the check boxes beside the entries you want to back up.

6. Click **Next**, and choose **All selected files** from the following dialog box.

7. Click **Next** and specify the backup location. This is where you choose the destination drive for the backup files. Note that you can back up to a network hard drive, or even to a file on a local hard drive, if you wish.

8. Click **Next** to continue the Backup Wizard, and choose whether you want to use file compression.

9. Click **Next** and name the backup job. This lets you repeat this process later, or modify the job for later backups.

10. Click **Start** to complete the backup process. A dialog box informs you when the operation is complete. Click **OK**.

11. Click **OK** in the Backup Progress window, and then close the Microsoft Backup window.

The backup process is very similar for Windows Me, Windows 2000, and Windows XP. With the guidance from these steps, you can find your way through nearly any Windows-based backup—begin by clicking Start, pointing to Programs, pointing to Accessories, pointing to System Tools, and clicking Backup. To start a backup in Windows NT, click Start, point to Administrative Tools (Common), and click Backup. (Windows 2000 and XP offer wizards to help you complete a backup.)

Project 5-5

No data backup is useful if the restore software or the backup media fail. Many critical failures occur during data restoration because of bad media and incompatibilities between the restore software and new system software. That's why backup and restore testing is critical during operating system upgrades. In this project, you'll practice a restore from the backup that you made in Hands-on Project 5-4. Make sure that you obtain permission from your instructor for the restore. If you do not have permission, only complete Steps 1 through 8.

To test the backup created in Hands-on Project 5-4:

1. Click **Start**, point to **Programs**, point to **Accessories**, point to **System Tools**, and click **Backup**.

2. From the opening Backup screen, choose **Restore backed up files**, and click **OK**.

3. Choose the source for the restored data from the next wizard screen. Click **Next**.

4. Choose from the list of backup sets displayed in the next dialog box. Click **OK**.

5. Click the check boxes beside the items within the backup set to select individual items to restore, and click **Next**.

6. Choose a restore location from the next dialog box. During testing, you should choose a destination other than the original, in case you encounter problems. Click **Next** to continue the wizard.

7. Choose the type of restore operation if the program finds existing files at the destination location. You can tell the program not to replace existing files, to replace files only if the ones on your computer are older, or to always replace existing files. (Close the Backup tool after this step if you do not have permission to complete the restore.)

8. Click **Start** to begin the restore. You will be prompted for the backup media originally used. Insert the requested media, and click **OK**.

9. Click **OK** in the *Operation Completed* dialog box, then click **OK** in the Restore Progress dialog box. Close the MSBackup window.

10. Test the restored data to make sure everything was restored properly.

As in Hands-on Project 5-4, you can use similar steps for Windows Me, Windows 2000, and Windows XP. To start a restore in Windows NT, click Start, point to Administrative Tools (Common), and click Backup.

Project 5-6

You can manually back up the Windows 95/98 Registry data by copying the System.dat and User.dat files, which are hidden files in the Windows folder. This project shows how to view the hidden files, and copy them to a Zip disk or network drive (ask your instructor which to use).

To manually copy Windows 98 Registry files to a Zip disk or network drive:

1. Click **Start**, point to **Programs**, and click **Windows Explorer**.

2. Click **View** on the menu, and choose **Folder Options** (for Windows 95, choose **Options**). You will see a display similar to the one in Figure 5-10 for Windows 98 (in Windows 95, you will see the Options dialog box).

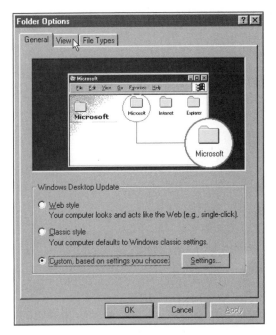

Figure 5-10   Windows 98 Folder Options dialog box

3. If necessary, click the **View** tab.

4. Make sure the **Show all files** option button is selected, as shown for Windows 98 in Figure 5-11.

5. Click **OK** to close the Folder Options (or Options) dialog box.

5

6. If you are using a Zip disk, label the Zip disk "Registry Backup" with today's date, and insert it into the Zip drive. Use Windows Explorer to determine the drive letter of the Zip drive. Or, if you are using a network drive, use Network Neighborhood to browse to that drive and map it—such as by finding another computer in Network Neighborhood, double-clicking it, finding the shared drive or folder on the computer, right-clicking the drive or folder, and clicking Map Network Drive (ask your instructor about which computer and drive/folder to use on the network). Choose a drive letter to use for the network drive and click **OK**.

7. In Windows Explorer, browse to and click the **Windows** folder, and click **Show Files**, if necessary, to display its contents.

8. In the right pane, browse to and click the **System.dat** file. Browse to and **Ctrl+click** the **User.dat** file so that the two files are highlighted.

9. Click the **Copy** icon, or press **Ctrl+C**, to copy the two files to the Clipboard.

10. In the left pane of Windows Explorer, browse to the Zip disk or network drive, and click to select it.

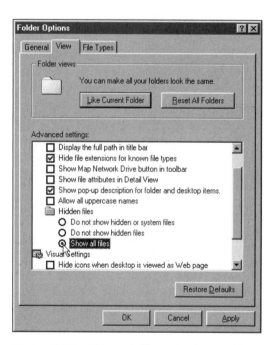

Figure 5-11 Show all files selection on View tab

11. Click the **Paste** icon, or press **Ctrl+V** to copy the two files to the Zip disk or network drive.

12. Click **View**, click **Refresh**, on the Windows Explorer menu, and check that the two files were successfully copied.

13. If you used a Zip disk, remove it now.

14. Close Windows Explorer.

Project 5-7

This project enables you to upgrade a computer running Windows 95 to Windows 98.

To upgrade to Windows 98 from Windows 95:

1. Start Windows 95 and make certain that all windows are closed. Insert the Windows 98 installation CD-ROM. A dialog box appears, indicating that the CD-ROM contains a newer version of Windows.

> If you don't see a message within a few seconds of inserting the CD-ROM disk, your CD-ROM drive doesn't support Autorun. You can launch the Windows 98 setup routine by pointing to the Start menu, choosing Run, and typing d:\setup in the Open field of this dialog box, where d: is the drive letter of your CD-ROM drive. Also, without Autorun, you will not see Step 2.

2. Click **Yes** to upgrade your computer to Windows 98. The Windows 98 Setup screen appears.

3. Click **Continue** to start the installation. The license agreement appears. Read and accept the agreement by clicking **I accept the Agreement**, and click **Next** to continue.

4. When prompted, enter the Product Key from your installation CD or documentation. Click **Next**. Windows creates a directory for system files.

5. Click an option to specify if you want to save your existing operating system files (recommended). Click **Next** to continue.

6. If you see a dialog box in which to specify the location for the uninstall files, accept the default location and click **OK**.

7. If you are installing using Windows 98 OSR2, you will see three additional dialog boxes. In the Setup Options dialog box, select **Typical** and click **Next**. Click **Next** on the User Info dialog box. Last, in the Windows Components dialog box, select to use the most common components and click **Next.**

8. Select your country from the list. The wizard uses this information to provide Web channels (specially designed Web sites that Windows can deliver automatically to your computer) it considers to be of interest to people in your country. Click **Next** to continue.

9. Setup now creates a startup disk to use if you have trouble starting Windows 98. Click **Next** to continue.

10. You are prompted to insert a floppy disk for the startup disk. Label the disk "Windows 98 Startup Disk," insert it in drive A: (or your floppy drive), and click

OK to continue. You will see a message when Setup finishes creating the startup disk. Remove the floppy disk from the drive, and click **OK** to continue.

11. Now Setup displays the Start Copying Files screen. If you want to go back to a previous step to change your answers, you can click Back. Otherwise, click **Next** to continue. It may take several minutes to copy all the files to your computer.

12. When all files are copied to your computer, you are prompted to restart the computer. Restart your computer. After it restarts, the wizard restarts your computer a second time and begins the final phase of installation. It sets up any hardware devices and Plug and Play devices it finds on your computer. If your computer has a network card, you may be asked to enter a password. If this happens, type your password and then press **Enter**. (If you used a password with the previous version of Windows, you can use the same password with Windows 98.) After the computer updates its settings, it may restart a third time.

13. Windows 98 starts and the Welcome to Windows 98 dialog box appears.

Project 5-8

In this project, you'll upgrade Windows 98 to Windows 2000 Professional. Make sure that your computer is compatible with Windows 2000 Professional before you start.

To upgrade from Windows 98 to Windows 2000:

1. Start Windows 98 and close any windows that are opened automatically at startup.

2. Insert the Windows 2000 Professional CD-ROM.

3. You will see an opening box that says: "This CD-ROM contains a newer version of Windows than the one you are presently using. Would you like to upgrade to Windows 2000?" Click **Yes**.

4. In the Welcome to Windows 2000 Setup Wizard dialog box, make sure that **Upgrade to Windows 2000 (Recommended)** is selected, and then click **Next**. (Refer back to Figure 5-6.)

5. Read the license agreement by using the scroll bar. Click the radio button for **I accept this agreement**, and then click **Next**.

6. Enter your product key (see Figure 5-12), which is usually found on the back of the jewel case or paper envelope for the CD-ROM (you can use the Tab key to advance from field to field). Click **Next**.

7. In the Preparing to Update to Windows 2000 dialog box, you can select *Click here* to go to the Windows Compatibility Web site to check for the latest hardware and software compatibility information. For the sake of this hands-on practice, and because your computer may not be connected to the Internet, click **Next**. (If you do select *Click here*, the Internet Connection Wizard is used to set up your Internet connection before you can connect to the Windows Compatibility Web site. Also, when you use the Internet Connection Wizard, if you have TCP/IP file and printer sharing enabled, you will see a warning box to disable it. Click **OK** if you see this warning box.)

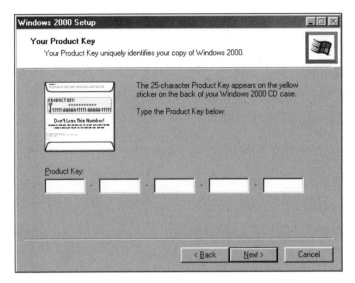

Figure 5-12   Windows 2000 Product Key dialog box

8. The next dialog box queries whether or not you have upgrade packs for your programs. These are upgrades so that the programs will work with Windows 2000. Since you can apply upgrade packs later, click the radio button **No, I don't have any upgrade packs** (which is the default), and then click **Next**.

9. You are given the option to upgrade from FAT16 or FAT32 (whichever is currently on your system) to NTFS (see Chapter 3). Although you will likely want to use NTFS in the future (there is a Convert program included with Windows 2000), for now, select **No, do not upgrade my drive** (the default)—the prudent selection. It is best to keep the upgrade process simple so that it is easier to troubleshoot problems. After you are certain that your system is working properly, then consider upgrading to NTFS for better file and workstation security. Click **Next**.

10. Windows 2000 Setup begins to prepare the Upgrade Report, and prepares to install the operating system.

11. If the Setup program detects hardware drivers that may need to be updated, particularly for Plug and Play, it provides a list of the hardware that may need new drivers in order to work with Windows 2000. Make a note of the hardware on the list, and then click **Next**. (After the upgrade, if you determine that this hardware is not working properly, contact the hardware manufacturers for new drivers. Or, if you have the drivers now, click Provide Files to install them.)

12. Depending on your version of Windows 2000 (you may not see this screen), the next screen enables you to access the Upgrade Report about possible installation issues concerning your hardware and software. You can click **Save As** to save the report as a file, or click **Print** to print it now (if your computer is connected to a printer). Determine which option you want, and complete the parameters for that option (provide a filename if you save it to a file, or select a printer if you print

it). Examine the report, if you printed it, or plan to examine the report file after the installation. Click **Next**.

13. In the Ready to Install Windows 2000 box, Setup informs you that it is ready to begin the upgrade, which will take 30 to 45 minutes (see Figure 5-13). Click **Next**. (Setup will reboot three times. Also, the first part of the process is in character mode, while the remaining setup process is in a GUI Windows mode.) *Make sure that you let Setup work automatically; you do not need to click any buttons, including the Next button, because Setup handles all of the work.*

If you did not have a workgroup or domain previously specified before upgrading Windows 98 to Windows 2000, you will see an additional dialog box after Step 13 that enables you to select whether or not to join a workgroup or domain. If the computer is not currently on a network or if you want to specify a workgroup for the computer, click the **No** radio button; or click **Yes** if the computer will join a domain. Enter the workgroup or domain name in the text box. Click **Next**. If you join a domain, you will need to enter the domain account and the password of the account you already created to enable the server to join the domain.

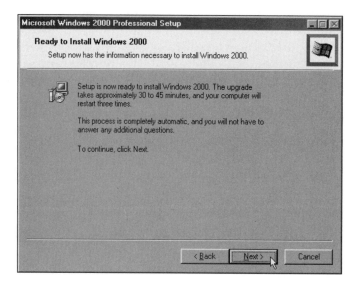

Figure 5-13 Beginning the Windows 2000 upgrade

14. Enter a password for the Administrator account, and then enter it again to confirm it. Click **Next**.

15. Log on to Windows 2000 using the Administrator account and your new password. After you enter the account and password, click **OK** in the Log On to Windows box.

16. Note that after you log on, the Getting Started with Windows 2000 window appears. From this window you can:

❑ Register your copy of Windows 2000

❑ Discover more about Windows 2000

❑ Connect to the Internet

Project 5-9

5

In this project, you'll upgrade Windows Me to Windows XP Professional.

To upgrade from Windows Me to XP:

1. Reboot your computer so you have a fresh system running. After it reboots, close all programs and windows.

2. Insert the Windows XP CD-ROM in the CD-ROM drive.

3. Wait for the Autorun feature to start up the Welcome to Microsoft Windows XP screen. Click the arrow in front of **Check system compatibility** (refer back to Figure 5-7).

4. Click the arrow in front of **Check my system automatically** (see Figure 5-14). This checks your system to make sure that the hardware is compatible with Windows XP. If you see a screen to enable you to connect to the Internet to download more setup files, click **No, skip this step and continue installing Windows** (or if you have Internet connectivity, click Yes and be prepared to supply information about how to configure for an Internet connection). Check for any incompatibilities, and if there are none, click **Finish** (refer back to Figure 5-8).

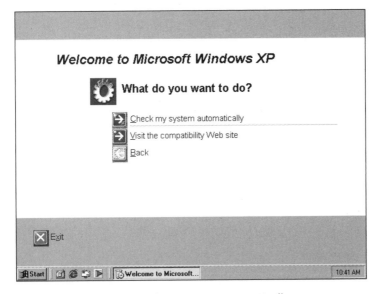

Figure 5-14   Checking the system automatically

5. Click the **Back** arrow to return to the first screen. Now you are ready to begin installing Windows XP.

6. Click **Install Windows XP**.

7. You will see the Welcome to Windows Setup screen. Click the down arrow in the Installation Type list box and you will see two choices for the setup: Upgrade (Recommended) and New Installation (Advanced). For this project, choose **Upgrade (Recommended)** as in Figure 5-15 and then click **Next**.

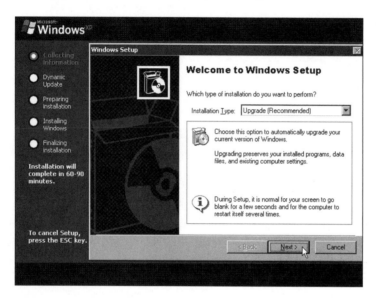

Figure 5-15   Selecting to upgrade to Windows XP

8. Next is the License Agreement screen. Read the agreement using the **Page Down** key to move through the agreement. If you accept the agreement, click **I accept this agreement**. Click **Next**.

9. Enter the unique product key for Windows XP. This 25-character product key usually is found on the back of the CD-ROM jewel case. Type in the key and click **Next**.

10. The Get Updated Setup Files screen enables you to obtain new setup files. If you have Internet connectivity and already downloaded the setup files in Step 4 or if you do not have Internet connectivity, click **No, skip this step and continue installing Windows**. If you have Internet connectivity, but did not download the new setup files – and want to now—click **Yes, download the updated Setup files (recommended)**. Click **Next** to continue. You may need to configure your Internet connection if you select to download the files. Ask your instructor for the configuration information.

11. Setup now analyzes your computer to collect information. This may take several minutes. During this time, information about new features and enhancements in Windows XP appears. After Setup analyzes the computer, it goes through additional steps. The green bar in the lower-left corner shows the progress for this section of the installation.

12. While it is preparing for the installation, Setup copies files from the CD-ROM to your computer. Once this is completed there will be an automatic reboot.

13. Next the Preparing installation step is highlighted along with additional information on Windows XP. You can watch the progress of this step in the green progress bar. There is an automatic reboot after this step has completed.

14. After the Installing Windows step starts, the screen may flicker, which is normal because Setup is installing and testing your screen type. What steps do you see being executed in the Installing Windows stage?

15. When you see the Finalizing installation screen, there is still more information for you to read along with the progress bar. Also, what steps do you see executed in this stage of the process?

16. Setup now reboots your computer.

17. After the computer reboots, you'll see a Display Settings dialog box. This informs you that Windows will automatically adjust your screen to improve the appearance of visual elements. Click **OK** to continue. (Depending on the display parameters set up before you started the upgrade, you may not see this step or step 18.)

18. The Monitor Settings dialog box appears, and you should click **OK** if you can read it.

19. Next, you will see the Welcome to Microsoft Windows screen. Click the **Next** arrow in the bottom right-hand corner of the screen to continue.

20. The *Ready to register with Microsoft?* screen is displayed. Click **Yes** if you have permissions from your instructor or register now or click or **No** to register later. Click the **Next** arrow in the bottom right-hand corner.

21. Now you will see the *Who will use this computer?* screen. Enter the name of each person that will use this computer in the appropriate box and click the **Next** arrow.

22. The *Thank you!* screen now appears. Click the **Finish** arrow in the bottom right-hand corner of the screen to continue.

23. The *Password Creation* screen enables you to enter a password for your account and the administrator's account. The password is the same for both accounts. You are asked to retype the password to make sure it is entered correctly the first time. Click **OK**. After the upgrade, you can change the password for either account by opening the Control Panel (click Start and click Control Panel) and selecting the User Accounts option.

When upgrading from Windows NT or Windows 2000, Setup uses the Administrator password that you set up prior to the upgrade, so you do not go through Step 23. For these systems, enter the Administrator password in Step 24.

24. Next you will see the Login screen. Enter your password (the one that you just configured), and then click the **arrow**.

25. Windows XP now welcomes you and applies your personal settings. After this is completed, you are ready to begin using Windows XP.

Windows XP will notify you about how many days you have left to complete the product activation.

Project 5-10

Before you upgrade to a new version of UNIX, it is crucial to make a backup of important UNIX configuration files so that it will be easy to restore your old system, if necessary. Many systems have important files in the /etc directory, and also in the /usr/local directory. In this project, you'll back up the UNIX configuration files.

To complete this exercise, you must have root privileges on the system.

To back up UNIX configuration files:

1. To make a backup to a disk:

   a. Use the *df* command to find a partition that has enough space to hold your backup. Type **df**, and locate a directory on your file system that has enough space. DO NOT use the TEMP or root (/) directory!

   b. Use the *tar* command to create a compressed format backup file. The syntax for *tar* is *tar -[command][options][parameters]*. For example, to back up the /etc and /usr/local directories and all their subdirectories to a file called *archive.tar* in the /home directory, you enter:

   tar −cvf /home/archive.tar /etc /usr/local

   The command *c* is used to create a new tar file; the *v* and *f* options are for verbose and file (to show you what is happening, and to indicate that what follows next is the path and filename of the file to be saved); and the parameters include the file or directory name(s) you are backing up.

2. To make a backup of /etc and /usr/local and all of their subdirectories to a tape drive using built-in compression:

   a. Load an empty tape in your tape drive.

   b. Enter the command **tar −cvf /dev/rmt/0c /etc /usr/local**.

   (If necessary, replace "rmt/0c" with the proper designation for your tape drive.)

Project 5-11

This project enables you to upgrade to Linux 7.2. Because your computer may have limited memory, we are using the text mode for this installation instead of the graphics mode (because the text mode will work on nearly all computers, even those that have limited RAM and video memory, such as under 64 MB of RAM).

To upgrade to Red Hat Linux 7.2:

1. Make sure that your system can boot from the floppy disk drive or the CD-ROM drive (you may need to change a parameter in the BIOS Setup regarding the disk boot order).

> If you have the Red Hat Linux CD-ROM (1 of 2), you can make a floppy disk with a boot image from a computer running MS-DOS (or the MS-DOS Prompt Window). To make the floppy disk, insert the Red Hat Linux CD-ROM and determine the drive it is in, such as D:. Insert a blank, MS-DOS formatted floppy disk. At the MS-DOS prompt, type *d:* and press Enter. Type *cd/dosutils* and press Enter. Last, type *rawrite* and press Enter.

2. Boot the system either from the Red Hat Linux CD-ROM or from a startup floppy disk containing the boot image (either way, make sure that you insert the Red Hat Linux CD-ROM before you start).

3. The boot screen provides you with several alternatives. At the *boot:* prompt, type **text** and press **Enter**.

4. Wait for a few minutes while the installer sets up files and runs the anaconda program.

5. Use the up and down arrow keys to select the language that you want to use, such as **English** (typically your language will be selected by default), and tab to select **OK**. Press **Enter**. (Note that on many screens you have the following key options: F1 provides help, Tab is used to move between fields, the spacebar is used to make a selection, and F12 is used to go to the next screen.)

6. Select the model of keyboard (or use the default), such as **us**, for computers in the United States. Tab to **OK,** and press **Enter**.

7. Select the type of mouse, such as **Generic – 2 Button Mouse (serial)**. Tab to the *Emulate 3 Buttons?* field and use the spacebar to select or de-select this option. Tab to **OK,** and press **Enter**.

8. If you selected a serial or bus mouse in Step 7, a screen appears from which to select the device on which your mouse is located, such as **/dev/ttyS0 (COM1 under DOS)**, tab to **OK,** and press **Enter**.

9. The Welcome to Red Hat Linux screen advises you to read the Linux manual and to register your version of Red Hat Linux. Select **OK,** and press **Enter**.

10. Use the arrow keys to select the option to **Upgrade Existing System**. Tab to **OK**, and press **Enter**.

11. The partition on which the upgrade will be made is automatically selected, such as **/dev/hda1**. Tab to **OK**, and press **Enter**.

12. The system enables you to customize the packages that are to be upgraded. Select **Yes**, and press **Enter**.

13. On the next screen there is an option to migrate to the ext3 file system, which enables journaling (keeping a running backup of data changes in case there is a disk failure or corrupted data). Select whether or not you want to migrate the existing partitions, such as **/dev/hda1 – ext2 - /boot**. It is recommended that you select to migrate all partitions currently formatted for ext2 or ext in earlier Red Hat Linux operating systems. Make your selections, tab to **OK,** and press **Enter**.

14. Select **Use GRUB Boot Loader** (which is the default), tab to **OK**, and press **Enter**.

15. Select the default option for the boot loader configuration, such as **/dev/hda Master Boot Record (MBR)**. Tab to **OK**, and press **Enter**.

16. For this installation, do not select to pass special options to the kernel. Leave the option blank, tab to **OK**, and press **Enter**.

17. If you have more than one partition, on the next Boot Loader Configuration screen, leave the defaults as selected for other partitions from which to boot, tab to **OK**, and press **Enter**.

18. For this project, do not select to use a boot loader password. Tab to **OK**, and press **Enter**.

19. The system will take several minutes to find the packages to upgrade.

20. On the Individual Package Selection screen, use the up and down arrows to select the packages that you want to upgrade. Notice what types of packages can be installed. Press the + key to add a package and press the – key to delete a package (or use the spacebar to toggle on and off selections). Tab to **OK**, and press **Enter**.

21. The installer now checks for dependencies of the packages and options that you selected.

22. If you earlier selected to install packages for which dependent packages are not installed, you will see a Package Dependencies screen from which to install the packages on which others are dependent. Select **Install packages to satisfy dependencies**, tab to **OK**, and press **Enter**.

23. Next, you'll see a screen that notes you can review a log of the installation when you are finished, located in /tmp/upgrade.log. Tab to **OK**, and press **Enter**.

24. The system takes a few minutes to transfer the install image to the hard drive and then to set up RPM transaction

25. As it is installing the files, the installation process shows the packages being installed. The screen includes two tables. One shows the name, size in K, and description of the file or package currently being installed/upgraded. It also has a table that shows the progress of the installation, including what has been installed, and what remains to be installed.

26. When you are prompted (and the CD-ROM drive ejects the Installation CD-ROM 1 of 2), insert the Red Hat Linux 7.2 Installation CD-ROM 2 of 2. Press **Enter**.

27. An information screen informs you that the installer is performing the post installation configuration and another screen shows the system is installing the bootloader.

28. Choose **Yes** to create a custom boot disk (to be able to boot from the floppy drive, in case there is a problem with booting from the hard drive). Press **Enter**.

29. Remove the installation floppy disk, if there is one, and then insert the blank floppy disk. Tab to **OK**, and press **Enter**.

30. The installation is now complete. Make sure **OK** is selected and press **Enter** to reboot. As the system is rebooting, the CD-ROM drive ejects the Linux CD-ROM so that you don't forget to remove it prior to rebooting.

Project 5-12

When you upgrade to Mac OS X, applications written for previous versions of the operating system must run in the classic environment. This project shows you how to start and stop that environment.

To start the classic applications environment:

1. Open the Apple menu and click **System Preferences**.

2. Click **Classic**.

3. Select the startup volume, or use the default.

4. How would you set up to use the classic environment each time you log into the computer?

5. Click **Start**.

6. What message appears now?

7. Close the Classic window.

To stop the classic environment:

1. Open the Apple menu and click **System Preferences**.

2. Click **Classic**.

3. Click **Stop**.

4. What happens to the Mac OS 9.x applications?

5. Close the Classic window.

CASE PROJECT

Merlinos Mills is a company that produces flours and grains for grocery stores. It owns mills and distribution centers in the northwestern and midwestern United States. The headquarters location in Bend, Oregon employs over 400 people, most of whom use computers. Also, the headquarters has 28 servers, all running either Microsoft Windows NT 4.0 or Red Hat Linux 4.0. The company employees use a full range of operating systems, including Windows 95, Windows 98, Windows 2000, Red Hat Linux 4.0 (Workstation), and Mac OS 8.1.

The management of Merlinos Mills wants each department to upgrade to the newer operating systems. Also, they are very concerned about network security, and they want to upgrade the servers to operating system versions that take better advantage of security features. Your role in the process is to work with each department to help ensure that the upgrades go smoothly.

1. The master distribution center in Bend, Oregon has 42 people, including nine Windows 95 diehards, 22 people using Windows 98, and 11 people using Windows 2000 Professional. The distribution center is slated to upgrade its computers to Windows XP Professional. What preliminary steps should be taken before starting the upgrades on these computers? In general, are there any problems involved in upgrading to Windows XP from each of these operating systems?

2. The 11 people in the distribution center who are running Windows 2000 Professional are currently able to use all software, such as office software, customized distribution software, and inventory software that is integrated with the distribution software. They are resisting the upgrade to Windows XP Professional, and the distribution manager asks for your opinion about whether or not to upgrade these computers. Should they upgrade from Windows 2000 Professional to Windows XP Professional?

3. The user support person for the distribution center has not performed an upgrade from Windows 98 to Windows XP. Tell her generally what to expect when performing this upgrade.

4. The IT Department already has been testing Windows 2000 Server, and some time ago purchased licenses to upgrade all of its Windows NT servers to Windows 2000. Explain the general process it must follow to upgrade to Windows 2000 Server, recognizing that there's already one Windows NT domain called merlinomills.

5. For the IT Department, review the general steps it must follow to upgrade Red Hat Linux servers to Red Hat Linux 7.2.

6. The Marketing Department strictly uses computers running Mac OS 8.1, and plans to upgrade to Mac OS X. What steps must it follow for the upgrade?

7. Before upgrading, the marketing director is concerned that some customized applications designed for Mac OS 8.1 might not run in Mac OS X. What is your answer to her?

OPTIONAL CASE PROJECTS FOR TEAMS

Team Case One

Merlinos Mills plans to upgrade its Windows NT servers and use Active Directory before upgrading any desktop operating systems. What problems might this cause in using older operating systems, such as Windows 95 and Windows 98, to connect to the upgraded servers? If there are problems, how might they be addressed? Form a team to research these issues.

Team Case Two

The IT Department at Merlinos Mills wants to know what new security and network features it will find in Red Hat Linux 7.x that are not in Red Hat Linux 4.0. Use your team to research the new security features, and define what general steps are required to configure them.

5

6

INPUT, OUTPUT, AND STORAGE DEVICES

After reading this chapter and completing the exercises you will be able to:

♦ Understand how operating systems interface with input, output, and storage devices

♦ Understand the need for software drivers for specific hardware output devices

♦ Discuss software driver installation within major operating systems

♦ Describe popular printer technologies, connections, and methods of installation

♦ Discuss general display adapter design, types of adapters, and hardware installation

♦ Understand basic disk drive interface technologies

Regardless of what you do with your computer, you must input commands and data in the form of text, sound, or visual input, and produce output—via the video display on your computer monitor, as printed hard copy, or as sound through your computer's speakers. In addition, you must be able to save information to disks or other storage devices so that all of your changes are not lost when your computer experiences a power failure, and so that you can make backup copies of important data. This chapter describes how major input, output, and storage components work, including installation and configuration considerations, and how various operating systems work with them.

OPERATING SYSTEMS AND DEVICES: AN OVERVIEW

As you learned in Chapter 1, one of the primary functions of any operating system is to provide basic input/output (I/O) support for application software—that is, to translate requests from application software into commands that the hardware can understand and carry out. For example, the operating system must:

- Handle input from the keyboard, mouse, and other input devices.

- Handle output to the screen, printer, and other output devices.

- Control information storage and retrieval using various types of disk drives.

- Support communications with remote computers.

There are two ways that an operating system accomplishes these tasks: through software (device driver code within the operating system itself, as well as accessing third-party device driver software) and through hardware (controllers and adapter boards for specific input or output devices) that is controlled by the operating system. Device drivers perform the actual communication between the physical device and the operating system. Adapters, which are circuit boards that plug into a slot on the motherboard of the computer, are the interface between hardware components (such as display adapters to produce video output, or sound cards to produce audio output). The particular configuration of device drivers and adapters varies from operating system to operating system, but they function in the same way in each operating system.

Likewise, setting up or installing input, output, or storage devices involves three general steps across operating systems:

1. Install any software drivers that are required

2. Install the input, output, or storage device

3. Set up the hardware

SOFTWARE CONSIDERATIONS

As necessary and common as printers, display adapters, and other devices are today, it may seem strange that you need a custom driver for each item you install—but it is true. The operating system provides the basic input/output support for the parallel, serial, bus, or other ports your printer and other hardware use, but it doesn't support specific features of individual devices you may connect to these ports. For that, you need a driver, which may be supplied by the hardware manufacturer or the producer of the operating system. (See the discussion of driver software in Chapter 1.)

Many hardware manufacturers supply a floppy disk or CD-ROM with drivers for current operating systems. In general, you should use the manufacturer's driver, if available, instead of the driver supplied with your operating system. Although many operating system drivers for specific hardware were developed by the hardware manufacturer in cooperation with the operating system producer, they may be generic—designed to support a range of hardware models—or they may be older than the specific hardware you are installing. Using the driver shipped with your particular printer or other device gives you a better chance of having the latest version designed for your specific hardware.

 Even if your hardware is brand new, it is good practice to check with the manufacturer for newer driver software. Drivers usually are designated by version number, and sometimes with a date. Drivers with later version numbers and dates may contain fixes for problems identified with earlier releases, and they sometimes enable or improve the performance of some hardware features. The best source of new driver software is the World Wide Web. Check the documentation that came with your hardware for a Web site for new drivers, or simply point your browser to the manufacturer's main Web site and look for downloads, product support, software updates, or pages with a similar title.

For example, to find drivers for a broad range of Epson printers, point your browser to *prographics.epson.com*, click Support Center, select a product, click Go, and choose Download. You'll find a range of printer drivers for Epson's high-end printer models and, typical of many hardware manufacturers, Epson also offers you a patch for third-party software, including PageMaker 6.5 to enable PageMaker to work better with Epson printers. Use *www.epson.com* to select a country, and then choose a specific Epson product line and browse for support software. Here are some other examples of Web support addresses, as this book is written:

- *www.hp.com/cposupport/eschome.html* Enter the product name or number for a specific Hewlett-Packard printer or plotter model, then click the arrow to obtain the latest drivers.

- *www.lexmark.com* Select the correct country, choose Drivers, and then select the product or model from the drivers page.

- *www.americas.creative.com/support* Navigate to the Creative Labs (SoundBlaster) pages to find drivers and review other support material.

- *www.matrox.com/mga/support/drivers/home.cfm* Choose a particular Matrox driver category to download the latest drivers.

 Remember that you can usually guess the home page for major companies. Simply type *www.companyname.com* in the address line of your browser, where *companyname* is the actual name of the manufacturer of your hardware product. If you don't find the page you want, try a variation of the company name. If this doesn't work, go to a Web search engine and search for information about a particular company or product.

The procedure for installing drivers varies slightly with the source of the driver and the operating system you are using. If you download a new driver from a manufacturer's Web site, you'll probably have to uncompress the file before you can use it.

For example, many PC users use the **PKZIP** or **WINZIP** compression/decompression utilities. Many software producers distribute software bundled and compressed with the PKZIP/WINZIP format. Compression software not only reduces the size of the supplied files by removing redundant information, it also groups multiple files into a single distribution file or archive. Distribution files may be supplied in self-extraction format, an executable file that decompresses the archive and expands individual files. PC-executable files normally use an .exe file extension. If you download a driver archive that includes this extension, it is a **self-extracting file**. If the file includes a .zip extension, on the other hand, you'll need a program such as PKZIP or WINZIP to expand the archive before you can install the driver software.

 If you don't have the PKZIP or WINZIP software, you can download it from the Internet at a variety of sites. There also are other programs that perform similar functions. One resource for a wide variety of shareware, freeware, and low-priced software is: *www.tucows.com*.

Macintosh users can use ZIP-format archives, but a more common format is **StuffIt**, a utility similar to PKZIP, which also bundles multiple files into a single distribution archive. StuffIt files can be self-extracting, or you can use StuffIt Expander or another utility to expand the archive into its individual components. If you don't have this utility, you can download the shareware StuffIt Expander from Aladdin Systems at *www.aladdinsys.com*. Even if you work primarily in Windows, you might want to retrieve this utility for your PC. It also supports ZIP format, and it lets you retrieve compressed or archived files from Macintosh users. For a small fee, you can purchase the full-blown StuffIt software so you can create archives for Mac and Windows environments. The ZIP utilities available for the Mac don't always produce files that are compatible with Windows systems. The StuffIt Expander software, on the other hand, works both ways quite well.

UNIX system users may retrieve drivers and other software in a *tar* format. **Tar** files also are archives that group multiple files into a single distribution file. *Tar* doesn't compress the files; it merely groups files to make it easier to copy and distribute multiple files together. You may find that a *tar* archive is also zipped. You can use a UNIX version of unzip to expand the compressed *tar* archive into an uncompressed file, then you issue a UNIX *tar* command to extract individual files from the archive. StuffIt is also available for Linux and Solaris systems.

Once you locate the driver you want to use, you generally have three choices for installation, depending on the source of the driver: you can use your operating system's install utility, the Plug and Play (PnP) feature of operating systems from Windows 95 and later, or the install utility provided by the hardware manufacturer. Procedures are slightly different among different operating systems, and precise steps differ with different equipment (a printer installs differently from a sound card, for example), but the general process is very similar. This section steps you through an operating system printer install, which is representative of how various operating systems handle hardware driver integration.

Manufacturer Driver Installation

When you use a hardware manufacturer's install utility, the process is usually fully automatic and well documented. In fact, newer printers, plotters, and other devices frequently come with extensive support material on CD-ROM. You might be presented with video or animated training material to teach you how to install or use the device. Certainly, you shouldn't have to know much about the way your operating system installs drivers or interfaces with the device you're installing because the manufacturer's install routine handles it all for you. Since each manufacturer has a different procedure with different devices and different operating systems, it is difficult to document each system and device type.

In general, however, the procedure is to insert a floppy disk or CD-ROM into a drive and either wait for a program to start automatically, or run a setup or install utility. Then, simply follow on-screen prompts. If you run into problems, look for a disk-based tutorial, or go to the manufacturer's Web site to search for more information. Some software suppliers also include .txt files on install disks to present new information or tips for the installer. You can use Notepad or any text program to look for these files and read them.

 Beginning with Windows 95, Plug and Play will, in most cases, automatically detect the new hardware and lead you through the process of loading the drivers.

Windows Driver Installation

Whereas installing a driver from a supplied floppy disk or CD-ROM usually involves interactive instructions from the install routine or Plug and Play system, when you install a driver with the operating system's routines, you may need to be a little more savvy. This section shows you the basics of installing drivers in the Windows environment, illustrated with sample printer installations. The following sections cover the procedures for other operating systems.

Windows 95/98/Me

The procedures for installing hardware in Windows 95, Windows 98, and Windows Me are very similar to one another. The Windows 98 perspective is shown here. If you're using Windows 95, some of the icons may look slightly different, but the process is essentially the same.

A nice thing about Windows 98 and Windows Me (and to a slightly lesser degree, Windows 95) is the Plug and Play feature. You can install a new printer in Windows 98 and Windows Me very quickly with these steps:

1. Shut down the system by choosing Shut Down from the Start menu.

2. Turn off the power.

3. Connect the printer to the computer's printer port.

4. Plug the printer into a power outlet and turn it on.

5. Turn on the computer.

When the operating system boots, it recognizes that a new piece of hardware is attached to the printer port and tries to locate the drivers for it. If Windows already has a built-in driver for this device, it finds the drivers on the Windows distribution disks or CD-ROM. Otherwise, you must insert the manufacturer's disk or CD-ROM into an appropriate drive when Windows asks for it.

If Windows doesn't recognize the new hardware, or if you simply want to conduct an install from scratch, you use the Printers dialog box, accessible through the Control Panel, or directly from the Start menu. To display the Printers dialog box in Windows 95, Windows 98, or Windows Me, click Start on the taskbar, point to Settings, and choose Printers from the supplemental list. You will see a window similar to the one in Figure 6-1.

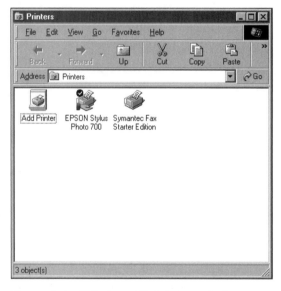

Figure 6-1   Windows 98 Printers window

Choose Add Printer from the Printers window to display a series of wizard screens that help you complete the installation. In the wizard screens, you answer questions about whether you want to set up a local or network printer, and specify the manufacturer and printer model, as shown in Figure 6-2. If you have a disk supplied by the manufacturer, you can click the Have Disk button and specify the path to the driver disk or CD-ROM.

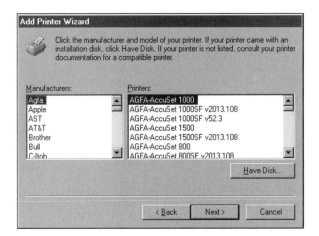

Figure 6-2   Choosing a printer manufacturer and model in Windows 98

You will also choose the port to which this printer is connected, and give a name that you want to use for the printer. You can probably accept the suggested printer name. However, if this is a networked printer, and you have more than one printer of the same model from the same manufacturer on this network, you must give the printer a unique name so everyone who uses it will know what printer to use. You also must specify whether you want Windows to use this new printer as the default printer.

Next you can choose to print a test page. This is a good idea when you first install a new printer to ensure that the physical connection to the printer is OK, and that the drivers were properly installed to create at least basic text and graphics images. After printing a test page, check to see if it printed correctly.

At the end of the installation, you will see the Printers screen with the new printer you just installed listed along with any others that were previously installed.

You can now use this new printer from any applications you have installed by selecting the printer from the Print dialog box of individual applications.

Windows NT/2000/XP

Many Windows NT/2000/XP screens look very similar to Windows 95/98/Me screens. In fact, with many screens, you must look closely to identify the operating system. The process of installing a new printer in Windows NT/2000/XP is also quite similar to installing a printer in Windows 95/98/Me.

You can install a new printer in Windows 2000 and Windows XP very quickly with these steps:

1. Shut down the system by choosing Shut Down from the Start menu.

2. Turn off the power.

3. Connect the printer to the computer's printer port.

4. Plug the printer into a power outlet and turn it on.

5. Turn on the computer.

When the operating system boots, it recognizes that a new piece of hardware is attached to the printer port and tries to locate the drivers for it. If Windows already has a built-in driver for this device it finds the drivers on the Windows distribution disks or CD-ROM. Otherwise, you must insert the manufacturer's disk or CD-ROM into an appropriate drive when Windows asks for it.

If you are using Windows NT 4.0, or Windows 2000/XP doesn't recognize the new hardware, or you simply want to conduct an install from scratch, click Start, choose Settings, and open the Control Panel. Double-click the Printers icon in the Control Panel to display the Printers dialog box, shown in Figure 6-3.

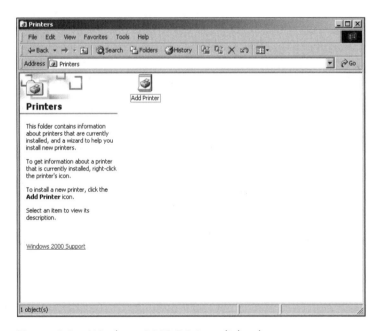

Figure 6-3   Windows 2000 Printers dialog box

Double-click the Add Printer icon in the Printers dialog box to start the Windows 2000 Add Printer Wizard. Click **Next** to display the screen shown in Figure 6-4.

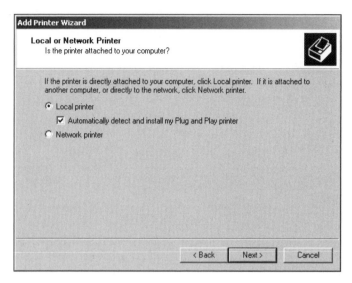

Figure 6-4   Windows 2000 Add Printer Wizard

As with Windows 98/Me, in the Add Printer Wizard, you choose whether the printer you are installing is connected directly to your computer, or already installed somewhere else on the network; select the port (for a local printer, or the previously installed network printer if the printer you are installing already exists somewhere on the network); choose the manufacturer and printer model; and enter the name you want to use for this new printer.

Then you specify whether you want to share this printer with other users on a network, as shown in Figure 6-5. If you choose Yes, you will need to enter a share name. This is the name other users on the network use to locate and connect to your printer. In this case, we chose to share the printer and use the name LJ4000.

On the next screen, you can choose to print a test page. Remember, it is always a good idea to print a test page when you install a new printer. This is especially true if you are installing a network printer.

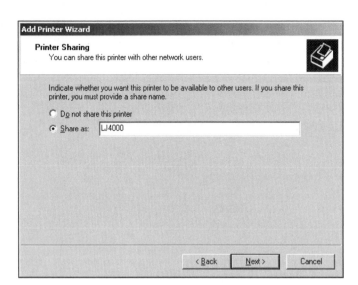

Figure 6-5   Windows 2000 Printer Sharing dialog box

Unless you installed this printer before, Windows NT/2000/XP also must retrieve the drivers required for this printer. You may be asked to insert the Windows NT/2000/XP disk or CD-ROM. You may also use your manufacturer's disk or CD-ROM. When you're done, you'll see a new printer icon that represents the just-installed printer in the Printers dialog box.

Mac OS Driver Installation

The Mac OS installation includes drivers for almost all Apple-brand printers. Unless you chose a customized installation of the operating system and intentionally removed the printer drivers, you already have the Apple drivers on your system.

If you do have an Apple printer, and the printer is not listed in the Chooser (Apple's tool for selecting the printer, found in the Apple menu for Mac OS up through version 9.x), you should first check to see if the currently installed drivers are compatible with your printer. In general, if your printer isn't listed, you should try the next higher numbered printer in the Chooser before installing software that is included on the disk with the printer. In Mac OS X, the Chooser is retired, and you must check the printers via the Print Center.

If you aren't sure that you have all of the Apple printer drivers installed, you may need to install them. For Mac OS versions up through 9.x, this requires rerunning part of the Mac OS installer.

To begin this process, launch the installer (there is no need to boot from a CD-ROM to do this, just insert the CD), and go through the install process, as described in Chapter 4, until you reach the last screen. Before you click Start, click the Customize button, as shown in Figure 6-6. Remove the checks from everything but Mac OS, then change the installation mode by clicking the Customized Installation selection, as shown in Figure 6-7.

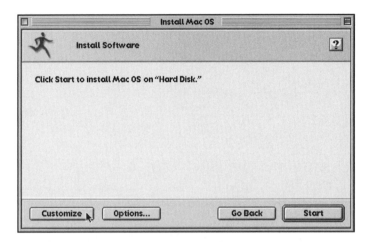

Figure 6-6   Customize button in Mac OS install

Figure 6-7   Customized Installation selection

A second window opens. Check Printing, and then click OK (see Figure 6-8).

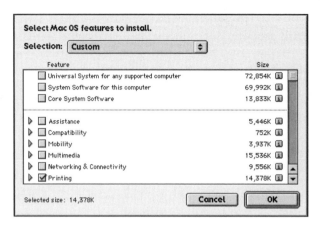

Figure 6-8   Choose Printing installation

On the next window (Figure 6-9), click the Start button. When the installer finishes, restart, and pick the correct driver and port using the Chooser.

Figure 6-9   Click Start to launch the printer driver installer

 If your printer is not manufactured by Apple, you must follow the instructions provided with that printer, and it might also be a good idea to check the printer manufacturer's Web site. Many printers include driver versions significantly older than the currently available downloadable versions, and these older versions can cause problems when used with the latest version of Mac OS.

In Mac OS X, most printer drivers are already installed when you install the operating system. If they are not installed through this means, make sure that the printer you buy has a CD-ROM to install the new printer driver. To set up a printer for use, open the

Mac OS X Print Center and display the Printer List window. Next, click the Add Printer button to install the printer.

UNIX Driver Installation

The concept of drivers in UNIX is slightly different from that in other operating systems. The central portion of the UNIX operating system, the kernel, is where most of the UNIX device drivers are loaded. Device drivers are either in the form of kernel modules, which are pieces of code that must be linked into the kernel, or loadable modules, similar pieces of code that are not linked into the kernel, but are loaded when the operating system is started. Device support in most UNIX versions is limited compared to other operating systems; manufacturers of devices often provide drivers for special hardware, which are then linked or loaded into the kernel.

Since UNIX is a multi-user, multitasking operating system, it uses a print queue. When a print job is sent from an application, a **print queue** or **spooler** temporarily stores the print job, from which it is sent to the printer. In order to configure a printer on a UNIX system, you first must define the printer parameters and the print queue. All definitions of printers and queues are kept in the file /etc/printcap. This file is maintained in plain ASCII text and can edited by hand. However, there are UNIX utilities to make this job easier; take advantage of these tools. Hands-on Project 6-5 steps you through the process of setting up printers in Red Hat Linux 7.2, using the printtool utility called *printconf*.

 You need root privileges to perform most UNIX printer maintenance.

The UNIX operating system provides a standard mechanism for network printing; a printer connected to one computer can be used to print jobs from another computer. Every computer that wants to use a printer, whether remotely or locally, must first create a print queue for that printer. If there is one computer with the printer connected, and three other UNIX computers that want to use the printer, a print queue for that printer must be created on all four computers. When a print job is submitted, it is queued in the local print queue. From there, it is submitted to the print queue of the computer to which the printer is connected, and then it spools to the printer.

Now that you're familiar with the basic process of installing device drivers in various operating systems, it's time to survey the various types of input, output, and storage devices you might want to install.

STANDARD INPUT DEVICES

There are two standard and universal computer input devices: the keyboard and the mouse. The keyboard is the single most important input device, and the second most important is the mouse (or one of the mouse alternatives such as a trackball, stylus, touch pad, or pointing stick). As universal as the mouse is today, it is a relatively new addition to the average user's computer hardware. Macintosh computers have used the mouse from the beginning, of course, but it was several years later before Microsoft-based computers routinely were supplied with a mouse. Today you wouldn't consider computing without a mouse—even if your preference is UNIX—assuming that you're in a networked environment where the X-Window graphical interface is pretty much the norm on these platforms. If you're using an older DOS computer, chances are there is no mouse support. However, some MS-DOS application software may offer a Windows-like user interface and install a mouse driver to support it.

Mouse and Keyboard Drivers

Because the input/output routines for the mouse and keyboard are highly standardized across operating systems, it is unlikely that you as an end user will need to interact with the operating system to set up these devices. Although mice and keyboards do use device drivers, unlike printers and other output devices, these drivers are standard and, in most cases, included as part of the operating system. The operating system provides only general support for output devices like printers (it includes routines to send data out a parallel port, for example, and to receive data sent to the computer from a device connected to this port, but has no intrinsic routines to support specific printer brands, models, or capabilities). For keyboards and mice, however, most operating systems contain intrinsic routines to handle these devices.

The mouse and keyboard use special ports—serial ports, basically—in a way similar to the way a printer uses a parallel port. Like a printer or other output device, the keyboard and mouse also need additional software to support specific functionality. However, the main difference between your mouse and keyboard and another device you may connect to your computer is virtually universal standardization. You can plug in a keyboard supplied with your computer, use a cheap replacement from a discount store, or pay the difference for a high-quality custom design, and, in most cases, you won't need any drivers beyond what is supplied with your operating system. For the most part, individual differences among keyboards are handled inside the keyboard itself. All the operating system cares about is the set of standard signals presented to the keyboard port when individual keys or key combinations are pressed. Different keyboards may include different hardware designs—switches or membranes for the keys, for example, and unique electronics for processing keystrokes. Some keyboards even include specialty keys that replace complex keystroke combinations or sequences. As long as these special keys send standard keystroke sequences to the keyboard port, the operating system doesn't really care how the codes are generated. These key closure codes or encoded sequences are captured at the port by intrinsic operating system routines and passed to higher level operating system applets and applications (word processing, spreadsheet, etc.) running under the operating system. No special drivers are required; the ones that install as part of your standard operating system will work just fine.

Newer operating systems include fairly sophisticated keyboard driver routines and custom configuration utilities, such as the one from Windows 2000, shown in Figure 6-10. Try Hands-on Project 6-8 to view basic keyboard configuration settings.

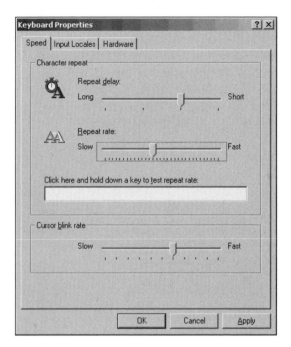

Figure 6-10   Windows 2000 Control Panel keyboard configuration utility

As you can see from this illustration, the degree of configuration is minimal. This simply points out the standard nature of the keyboard itself, and the drivers that support it. Earlier operating systems—particularly non-Windows systems—may have even more limited keyboard configuration options. You plug it in and it either works or it doesn't.

A mouse is a pointing device with a ball on the underside that rotates as you move the mouse across a desk or mouse pad, and one, two, or three buttons on top. As the ball rolls, it moves two **potentiometers** (variable resistors) positioned at 90-degree angles to each other. As this movement changes these resistor values, the operating system records the direction of movement, the distance moved, and even the speed of movement. The top-mounted buttons are connected inside the mouse housing to **micro-switches** that close when the buttons are pressed. Operating system drivers capture this switch closure and send the information to other operating system routines and application programs for interpretation. Try Hands-on Project 6-10 to view basic mouse hardware design and clean mechanical parts.

There are also mice that use optical sensors rather than a ball to determine movement. These mice are referred to as optical mice.

As with the keyboard, the intrinsic operating system mouse drivers may offer customization options to the user. Mouse options for Windows XP are shown in Figure 6-11. Try Hands-on Project 6-7 to view or change your basic mouse settings.

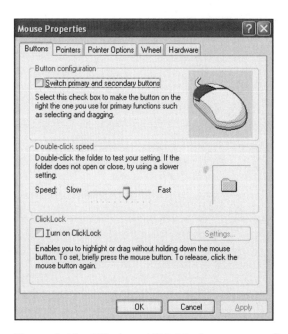

Figure 6-11   Windows XP intrinsic mouse configuration

Configuration routines such as this let you set the double-click speed, calibrate mouse movement and direction (based on how you hold the mouse as you roll it around the desk), and customize the pointer graphic and a variety of other features. The mouse, as the primary navigation tool, has expanded over the years in terms of the functions that can be customized. Consider the **wheel mice** popularized by the Microsoft IntelliMouse design. In addition to the standard ball and buttons, the IntelliMouse (and other wheel mice designs from companies such as Logitech) includes a wheel on top of the mouse that rotates front-to-back, parallel to the buttons. The wheel can be programmed for several application and operating system functions, but, by default, it replaces the vertical scroll bars used on many dialog boxes. In addition, a micro-switch mounted beneath the wheel is set, by default, to let you scroll horizontally by moving the mouse body itself after pressing the wheel downward to engage the switch. Other mice designs include trackballs and programmable keys.

In addition to adding special features to the function of the mouse itself, manufacturers' drivers also usually provide additional levels of user configuration, as you can see from the Microsoft IntelliMouse configuration interface, shown in Figure 6-12.

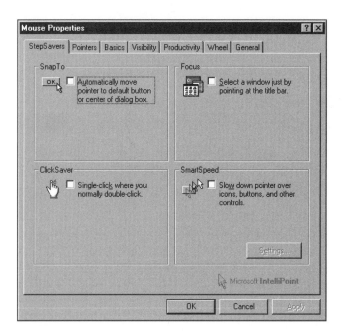

Figure 6-12   Microsoft IntelliMouse configuration dialog box for Windows XP

One thing most PC users notice about the Macintosh right away is the single mouse button. The Mac mouse has one button, whereas the PC mouse has at least two, and, in many cases, three. In Windows, you can right-click, which means you click with the rightmost button on your mouse. That's something a Mac user has never done; the right button doesn't exist. Mac users use keyboard shortcuts for most of the same functions that the right-click serves in the PC world. Additionally, Apple added contextual menus to Mac OS that are strikingly similar to the PC's properties menus. If you want second-button functionality on a Mac, you can add a third-party two-button mouse, or you can use a trackball or joystick with two or more buttons. Generally, these extra buttons are programmable with software that ships with the hardware.

Other Input Devices

The keyboard and mouse are ubiquitous and standard. If your computing needs stop with fairly common business applications such as word processing, spreadsheets, and databases, you probably won't need anything more. On the other hand, if you do graphics design, Web page development, digital photography, or movie or sound editing, then you will use one or more specialty input devices, such as digital tablets, scanners, joysticks and gamepads, digital sound input, or digital picture and video input. The following sections introduce these devices. Try Hands-on Project 6-9 to review installed devices on your computer, and Project 6-11 to view and configure multimedia devices.

Digital Tablets

A **digital pad** or **tablet** is really a different kind of mouse. A mouse is an excellent input tool for normal operations: choosing from a menu, selecting an icon or other graphic object, or dragging text or graphics to a new screen location. However, when you need to draw pictures, sign your name, color a detailed graphic image, or conduct other tasks that require a high degree of manual dexterity, then a digital pad or tablet is a useful addition to your computer hardware.

The same technology used in digital tablets is also used in **personal digital assistants (PDAs)**. PDAs are handheld devices, which, because of their size, are easily transported with you wherever you go. Features include a to-do list, calendar, appointments with reminder alarm, contact list, and the ability to synchronize this information with your desktop computer. PDAs and cellular phones are being combined into one unit for even more functionality.

A digital pad plugs into your computer via a standard or custom serial port, or through the USB or ADB (Macintosh) ports. After you install custom drivers (usually supplied by the pad manufacturer), then you can use the pad to conduct usual mouse operations, such as selecting menu items or moving objects. In addition, you can use the pad's electronic stylus for finer tasks, such as object drawing, capturing signatures, or manipulating specialty graphics programs, such as CorelDraw or Photoshop. If you've ever tried to use even a simple drawing program with a mouse as your only input device, you can appreciate the value of a digital pad that lets you write and draw in much the same way you would with a pen or pencil.

The digital pad, like the mouse, can range from fairly standard, simple hardware to specialty devices that include LCD display panels that mirror your computer's video display. Even the simplest pads require some custom software and a unique installation process. Refer to earlier sections in this chapter for general information on installing drivers (operating system support software) for specialty devices such as the digital pad.

Scanners

A **scanner** is like a printer in reverse, or maybe like an office photocopier that "prints" to your computer instead of onto plain paper. Instead of accepting digital data from the computer and converting it to hard copy like a printer, a scanner starts with hard copy—a photograph, negative or slide, newspaper article, book page, even a solid object—and creates a digital image, which is then transmitted to the computer. Once in the computer, this digital image can be saved in a variety of graphics image formats, edited, merged with other images or text, transmitted over the Internet or other network connection, or, of course, printed.

Scanners may also be used with **optical character recognition (OCR)** software. Instead of scanning the text into a digital graphic image, which does not allow for text manipulation, imaging software scans each character on the page as a distinct image. Then you can import the scanned results into a word processing document to work with the text.

Most scanners use some form of **Small Computer System Interface (SCSI)** hardware or the USB port. SCSIs are fast because they use wide data paths and rely less on the main system CPU than IDE controllers, freeing the CPU for other work. Some scanners are supplied with their own SCSI card, but you don't have to use this interface. If you have any standard SCSI already installed in your computer, chances are your scanner can use it. You will need drivers to enable the scanner to use any SCSI port. Interestingly enough, whereas the Mac OS has supported SCSI ports from the earliest days, Windows still doesn't support SCSI ports without custom drivers. One reason is the fact that different SCSI manufacturers implement the standard SCSI protocols in different ways, making it impossible for the operating system to support all versions. If you're using a USB scanner with a Windows 98 or later operating system, installation and configuration should be automatic. Figure 6-13 shows the Windows XP Scanner and Camera Installation Wizard screen, which is accessed by clicking Start; clicking Control Panel; clicking Sounds, Speech, and Audio Devices; clicking Printers and Other Hardware; and clicking Add an imaging device. You answer several questions about the scanner and the wizard does the complete installation.

Figure 6-13   Windows XP Scanner and Camera Installation Wizard

For the most part, you'll install custom drivers, and, in many cases, custom interface software supplied by the scanner manufacturer when you install the hardware. In most cases, the driver software—usually a driver with user interface and scanner control—links automatically with a variety of graphics software. If you're using PhotoShop, for example, the scanner may show up as an add-in; if you're using a Microsoft product such as Publisher or Photo Editor, you'll see a scanner icon on your toolbar. When you click the icon, the custom scanner software will load so you can use your scanner. These drivers and the user interface interact with the operating system to control the SCSI or USB port, and capture data supplied by the scanner.

Windows and other operating systems generally ship with several SCSI drivers—in much the same way as they ship with printer drivers—and you can probably find an intrinsic driver that will enable input and output through your SCSI port. However, to get the best and most reliable performance from any SCSI, you should install the drivers supplied by the manufacturer of the device itself. Again, you should check the vendor's online site to determine whether there are later versions of the required drivers for your hardware. This is true even if you just bought the hardware. Chances are the manufacturer posted the very latest driver versions on the Web page, which you can download over the Internet and install on your computer.

Joysticks and Game Pads

If your computer application is strictly business, you'll have no need for **joysticks** and **game pads**. On the other hand, if some part of your computer experience includes an occasional game, then one of these alternative input devices could be part of your hardware collection.

A joystick is more like a mouse than a digital pad. Like a mouse, the joystick uses a mechanical device to rotate one or more potentiometers. Changing resistance tells the joystick driver what value to feed to the operating system and any associated application software. You use the joystick for three-dimensional movement of an on-screen cursor or other object, such as a car, airplane, or cartoon character. Just as the digital pad makes it easier to input handwriting, picture retouching, and the like, the joystick offers a lot more control than a mouse when it comes to detailed movements of graphical screen objects. Although games are the primary application for joysticks, Mac users sometimes use them to supplement the mouse functionality. Joysticks can be used for virtually any application input task, given the proper driver.

In addition to the three-dimensional movements of the vertical joystick, this input device usually includes one or more push-button switches that can be associated with gun firings, boxing swings, menu selection, and so on. Like the digital pad, the joystick can use a conventional serial port, including the Mac's ADB or the PC and Mac's USB. Potentiometer settings or switch closures are sent through the I/O port as positive/negative pulses or as variable values on a scale. The operating system's basic port I/O routines grab this data, and then it is up to the associated application—a game, for example—to interpret this data in a meaningful way.

Game pads come in a wide variety of designs. As the name suggests, they are primarily designed for interaction with games, and include multiple buttons, wheels, or balls to effect movement of a variety of on-screen objects. As with the joystick, the game pad sends standard signals to a serial port where the operating system I/O routines take the data and pass it off to an application program or custom driver for interpretation.

Digital Sound Input

Almost every Mac, PC, and even workstation computer is supplied with some kind of analog sound card for sound input and output. For most of us, this sound capability is used pretty frivolously: software startup sounds, beeps when e-mail arrives, or playing music CDs. There are more serious applications for sound hardware, however. You can connect a microphone to an input port on your sound card and record voice mail that you can include with electronic mail, for example, or for narration of slide presentations. You can record custom sounds or music from a CD player or tape deck for use within software applications. Voice input to word processing and other programs is important for those unable to use a keyboard or mouse.

For more professional applications, such as editing music or voice for electronic journalism or training applications, you may want to add a digital I/O card. This lets you capture digital sound from a DAT recorder or digital camera directly into the computer, without having to convert to analog in the process. A digital card lets you copy digital audio directly from a recorder to your hard drive in much the same way as you would copy digital information from one hard drive to another. There is no loss of quality; you can edit the sound files in native digital format, and then copy the finished files back to tape, or burn them onto a CD for distribution or presentation.

There are multiple professional audio I/O standards, both optical and copper. Which one you use depends on the external hardware you will interface with your computer. Some DAT machines and digital cameras include more than one digital I/O port, so you can choose which format to use based on personal preference, your need to interface with other users, or which interface you can find. Most cards require custom driver software. And, like scanners, these cards usually can be controlled and accessed from inside application software, such as digital audio or video editing packages. Once the driver is installed, you can transfer audio information through the digital sound card from inside the application you are using to manipulate the audio files.

Most digital audio interfaces plug into the computer's internal bus—usually PCI—but there also are devices that use a USB port. If you need to transfer audio into multiple computers, the USB interface is a good choice since USB is self configuring for the most part, and most USB devices are external to the computer. By installing the required drivers on a second computer, you can easily add digital audio I/O capabilities by using the USB device.

Digital Picture and Video Input/Output

Digital picture and video I/O works similarly to digital audio I/O. You need a digital I/O interface and drivers to allow your operating system to recognize and use the card. And, as with digital audio, you import digital images into whatever application software you are using for picture or video editing. In some cases, you use a utility supplied by the interface manufacturer to import the digital image, then launch another application, such as Adobe Premier or PhotoShop, to conduct the actual editing. On the other hand, some card manufacturers include the ability to link their hardware drivers directly into editing software so you can import and export digital files from an external camera and edit the video or still images, all from the same application.

1394 Technology

IEEE 1394 is the specification for a digital interface that supports data communication at 100, 200, or 400 megabits per second. This technology is currently targeted at multimedia peripherals, which include digital camcorders and music systems. New extensions are being proposed to this standard that will allow gigabit speeds for data transfer. FireWire is the Apple Computer, Inc. implementation of this standard; Texas Instruments calls its Lynx, and Sony Corporation uses iLINK.

PRINTERS

A printer is an important part of nearly every computer installation. The following sections outline the most popular types of printers and printer connections.

 The installation of printers in various operating systems was covered earlier in the chapter, in the Software Considerations section.

Printer Types

The following types of printers are the most popular today:

- **Dot matrix printers**, which produce characters by slamming a group of wires (dots) from a rectangular grid onto a ribbon and then onto paper to produce characters (thus the designation "impact printer"). Dot matrix printers tend to be noisy, and the quality of the characters is not as good as laser and ink-jet printers. Although dot matrix printers are declining in popularity, you'll still find them behind sales counters to support point-of-sale (POS) computers, in hospitals, at airline counters, in insurance companies—anywhere a computer is used to fill out forms, or where multiple copies of the same document are needed simultaneously.

- **Ink-jet printers**, another printer that creates characters from dots by squirting tiny droplets of ink directly onto the page. Whereas impact dot matrix printers may be capable of printing a few hundred dots per inch, some ink-jet designs can lay down 2,880 dots in an inch. And, of course, full color—even near-photographic quality—printing with ink jets is quite common today. Ink-jet printers are popular personal printers in many offices, and dominate the bulk of the printer market for schools and homes. Small, quiet, and inexpensive, these printers are perfect for relatively low-volume letter-quality text and even graphics output. Models that deliver color and high resolution are used for proofing by graphics designers and printers, as well as home and office users. With the popularity of digital electronic cameras, high-resolution ink-jet printers are used increasingly to produce photograph-like output on heavy, slick paper, much like photographic paper stock.

- **Laser printers** use an imaging technology similar to copiers to produce computer output, and are probably the most popular printer design for business text and graphics. A typical laser printer contains its own CPU and memory since printed pages are first produced electronically within the printer. Laser printer prices have declined sharply over the past several years, so that even small businesses now can afford them. Color laser printers are popular in medium and large-scale companies. They are quickly gaining popularity in smaller offices as prices continue to drop.

In early dot matrix printers, the operating system, printer driver, and application software manage the printer at the character level; that is, directions are given for positioning the print head wires for every character. In later models, the printer itself may contain software that can receive basic character information from the computer, and adjust the quality level of the output by making multiple passes over the characters.

Early ink-jet printers also depended on character-by-character instructions from the operating system via the device driver, but later models include internal electronics and programs that can take more general formatting information from the operating system and device driver and translate it into output.

With laser printers, the printer's own CPU conducts most of the print processing in the memory of the printer itself. The operating system and application software send basic character and graphics information to the printer, and the printer handles the formatting, font and font attributes, and so on. The printer drivers interpret application output and convert it to a series of commands based on the printer programming language. These commands tell the printer how to format the output, but the actual formatting is conducted inside the printer.

The cost of printing is more than just the expense of the printer. Ink and laser cartridges add to printing costs. Depending on the cost for the cartridges, and the number of pages you are able to print with each one, many people are finding that a less expensive printer may cost more in the long run. Several computer magazines have published articles and comparisons on the Total Cost of Printing, and they can be found by searching the Internet using that phrase.

Aside from these three major printer types, there are some other printer designs that are used in specialized arenas:

- **Line printers**, one of the earliest impact printer designs, print an entire line at a time rather than a character at a time. Line printers are fast but extremely noisy, as the "line" is usually a metal chain. They use some form of tractor feed or pin feed. Line printers are rare these days; you may see them in government agencies, colleges or universities, or other venues that require large amounts of paper output, particularly paper output with multiple copies. Impact printers of this type are still the best way to produce multiple pages of the same document or form. You must repeatedly print the pages on a laser printer to achieve multiple copies.

 Vestiges of the line printer still remain: the main printer port on a PC is designated LPT1, which stands for Line Printer 1. It is doubtful that very many PCs ever were connected to a true line printer, but this big machine terminology stays with us.

- **Thermal-wax transfer** printers. Two basic thermal-wax transfer designs exist. One uses rolls of plastic film coated with colored wax, which is melted onto the page, one primary color at a time. A second type, known as phase change, melts wax stored in individual colored sticks and sprays the molten, colored wax onto the page. These printers generally produce very high-quality color output, but they also are relatively slow since they must pass the print head over each printed line once for each color. In addition, these printers frequently require special paper, which adds to the cost of the printed output.

- **Dye sublimation** (sometimes shortened to dye sub) printers. The dye sublimation design takes the concept of atomizing waxy colors onto the paper a step further. Dye sub printers don't just melt pigments and spray them onto the paper, they vaporize them. This colored gas penetrates the surface of the paper to create an image on the page. Dye sub printers produce high-quality output. Moreover, they can mix and blend colors to produce output at near-photographic quality. Thermal-wax transfer and dye sublimation printers are used in many graphics applications where very high-quality, color printed output is required. Graphics design shops, for example, use them to produce proofs for book covers, brochures, or other graphical materials that ultimately are produced on high-quality printing presses.

- **Imagesetter** printers, high-quality output devices frequently used in the printing industry to produce final output or to page masters for offset printing. Imagesetters frequently produce output directly to film rather than paper. The film is used in a printing press to produce the final output. In color printing, a separate piece of film is produced for each of the colors cyan, magenta, yellow, and black.

High-speed copiers, printers, and most other printing devices found in a printing shop are now connected to the network. This allows the device to receive materials electronically from any computer connected to the network. The operator of these printing devices schedules printing in accordance with the instructions submitted electronically with the materials.

 To find out what printers are installed on your system, try Hands-on Project 6-1 for Windows 95/98/Me, Hands-on Project 6-2 for Mac OS 9.x and Mac OS X, Hands-on Project 6-3 for most UNIX systems, and Hands-on Project 6-4 for Red Hat Linux 7.x.

In addition to traditional printers, another printer-like device called a **plotter** is popular in engineering, architecture, and other fields where hard copy output (such as blueprints) won't fit on standard paper sizes, or can't be produced by standard character or graphics printers. Plotter design is even more complex than printers, using pen and control mechanisms. As with printers, plotters require special drivers to enhance the operating system's intrinsic capabilities, but the process of installing plotter hardware and software is similar to that for printers. Likewise, plotters can be installed on a computer's parallel and serial ports in much the same way as printers (see the next section on Printer Connections).

Printer Connections

In the early days of computing, nearly all printers were connected to a **serial port**—the same port where you may connect your modem or mouse today. A serial port manages communications between the computer and devices in a one-bit-after-the-other (asynchronous) stream. Today, the most common PC printer connection is a **parallel port**, which manages communications between the computer and peripherals, in which data flows in parallel streams. Because more data can be sent at the same time (synchronously) in a parallel connection, it is generally a higher speed connection than a serial connection. The parallel port is sometimes called a **Centronics interface**, after the printer manufacturer that made it popular. The original Centronics interface used a 36-pin connector. Current PC platforms and most UNIX computers use a 25-pin **(DB-25)** connector since some of the original Centronics lines aren't necessary.

Some printers are designed with both parallel and serial interfaces so you can connect either way, depending on current needs.

 In general, a parallel printer connection is best since it provides a faster data path and better two-way communication between the computer and the printer. However, if you need to locate the printer more than 10 feet or so from the computer, a serial connection is the better choice. You can place a printer up to 50 feet from the computer if you use a serial connection.

Parallel printer communication is achieved in one of three ways. The first is compatibility or Centronics, which is one-way communication between the computer and printer. The second form of communication is referred to as nibble. This is a form of two-way communication, but it only allows communication one way at a time. The final way is usually referred to as **extended capability port (ECP)** communication, which allows for higher speed bidirectional communication between the computer and printer, as well as the printer and computer.

The printer cable must be bidirectional and the parallel port set to bidirectional in order for this type of communication to work properly. If the printer cable is not bidirectional, you must turn off this feature on the port.

Printer manufacturers are increasingly offering alternative connection methods. Printers designed for corporate environments, for example, frequently have a direct network connection option that lets you place the printer virtually anywhere on a LAN, where it can be shared among all of the computers attached to the LAN. If a particular printer doesn't include a networked option, you can purchase a network printer interface from a third party. These interfaces have one or more network ports plus one or more printer ports. You connect the network on one side and plug in the printer on the other. It is generally more efficient to use a direct network-attached printer rather than a printer attached to a computer on the network. Using a printer attached to a computer can be a drain on that computer's resources when others are using the printer, and a network interface is always on, making the printer always available to network users.

The **Universal Serial Bus (USB)** interface is very popular in today's printer market. Almost all printers now come with a USB port built into the printer. External disk drives, cameras, scanners, modems, and other devices also use this interface. Apple computers are also supplied with USB connectivity, but older Apple machines use a slower, similar technology, the **Apple Desktop Bus (ADB)**. The ADB is used for keyboard, mouse, printer, and other device connections in much the same way as the newer USB interface.

To experiment with the messaging that occurs between your operating system and printer, try Hands-on Project 6-6.

DISPLAY ADAPTERS

Once wildly diverse in design and features, display adapters today are reaching a common ground across operating systems and hardware platforms. The general industry acceptance of the **AGP (Accelerated Graphics Port)** bus standard has enabled adapter manufacturers to supply one hardware product, or a line of hardware products, to a variety of hardware platforms. The AGP bus enables high-performance graphics capabilities.

Basic Display Adapter Technology

If you are using a PC with a monitor, you have a display adapter card already installed in your computer. The display adapter is part of a standard computer package. No matter what computer platform you are using, the basic display (and the baseline standard in most cases) consists of 640 pixels horizontally and 480 pixels vertically. Depending on the display adapter in your computer and how the operating system detects the display adapter through PnP, your display may be at 800 × 600 or greater. There also is a minimum resolution associated with many operating systems. A **pixel**, remember, is a picture element, actually a small dot of light that represents one small portion of your overall screen display. Top-end display adapters today are easily capable of displaying 1280 × 1024 pixels, 1600 × 1280, or even 2048 × 1536 in some cases.

6

In general, as you display more pixels on the screen, you'll need a larger monitor to comfortably read the displayed data. For a given size of screen, higher resolution displays can present more data at a time on the screen, but this data will be presented in a smaller format. A 1024 × 768 display on a 15-inch monitor works okay, but is better on a 17-inch monitor. And if you need 1280 ÷ 1024 or higher resolution, you should consider at least a 19-inch monitor (a 21-inch monitor is a better choice).

Current operating systems support devices with the full range of resolution, so the major considerations in choosing an adapter are the adapter's resolution capabilities, the amount of memory included onboard the adapter (more memory on the adapter generally means faster performance when rendering screen images), type of video processor (display adapters may have their own CPU or accelerator to speed things up), and cost. As noted previously, you should also consider what kind of monitor you need as you decide on the screen resolution.

There's another aspect of screen resolution that isn't often discussed: the density of the displayed image, or bit depth. A resolution of 640 × 480 (the default resolution on PCs, Macs, and most other computers) simply means that images are displayed with 640 dots of light from left to right and 480 dots of light top to bottom. However, there is a third dimension to this display, the bit depth—how many of these dots of light can be crammed into an inch of display. All computer displays have a bit depth of 72 dots per inch (dpi), and this is probably why so many books and articles about computer graphics ignore this important aspect of image display. When you consider graphics programs (such as PhotoShop or CorelDraw), or choose a digital camera or other image source, this aspect of resolution becomes important. A high-quality photograph, for example, may contain 4,000 dots per inch. Books are printed at 133 lines, but to ensure good quality, files are usually produced at 200 dpi or greater; brochures may be printed at 1,200 dpi.

When you view graphics on your computer monitor, you see only 72 dots per inch because that's all your monitor is capable of showing. However, your printer may be able to reproduce 600 dpi, 1,200 dpi, 1,440 dpi, or even 2,880 dpi for some applications. It is important to know this third dimension when you spec printers, plotters, scanners, digital cameras, video editing software, and graphics programs. Print resolution, for example, may be more precise than the resolution of the monitor. The printer may show imperfections that the monitor does not display.

Although 640 × 480 is the basic **Video Graphics Array (VGA)** resolution, the majority of new computers ship with 800 × 600 set as the default. Larger monitors also are the norm. Whereas 15-inch monitors were the norm just a few years ago, 17-inch displays ship with most lower-end computers today. With the 17-inch monitor, you can routinely set a resolution of 1024 × 768 and still see everything you need to see.

Standard VGA adapters also have standard color rendition capabilities that range from 16 colors, at the very low end, to millions of colors at the top. At the mid range is a 256-color setting that lets you reproduce color material with reasonably good quality; that setting is compatible with the broadest range of display adapters. World Wide Web page designers frequently design their images for 256 colors to ensure the broadest possible compatibility with computer hardware in use by Web browsers. A 256-color setting is pleasing to the eye, but still very low quality compared to higher settings.

Installing Display Adapters

Unless you're building a computer from scratch, or you want to upgrade your existing video capabilities, there should be no reason for you to install a display adapter yourself. The computer should come from the manufacturer with a pre-installed adapter. If you designed your computer when you purchased it for the type of work you will do, the original adapter should last for the life of the computer.

However, there can also be good reasons for upgrading display hardware. Technology changes, software changes, and our personal needs change, all leading to potential upgrade situations.

By far, the majority of display adapters are supplied as AGP cards. The AGP bus has become a popular standard among computer hardware manufacturers, including Intel-based computers, Macintosh computers, and workstations designed for UNIX, Sun Solaris, and other systems. As with printers and other hardware, display adapters are installed in two phases, hardware and software.

Installing any display adapter bus card is similar to the next section on installing circuit boards. And, thanks to the industry's adoption of the AGP bus standard and similarities among computer case designs, you shouldn't have problems adapting any hardware install procedure you learn for one platform to any other platform.

INSTALLING CIRCUIT BOARDS

Today's computer hardware is pretty rugged. You can drop it, twist it, or mash it, and it will probably survive. Still, perhaps the biggest enemy of the devices supplied on circuit boards is static (high-voltage, low-current charges that can exist between any two devices, including human bodies). Static discharges are obvious when the voltage is high enough to cause a spark to jump between objects, or from an object to your finger. However, you can damage delicate computer parts with voltage levels below this sparking level.

To avoid damage to circuit boards during installation, follow these simple guidelines:

- Leave the card inside its protective cover until you are ready to install it.

- Disconnect all power to the computer.

- Prepare the computer by removing the case and any slot covers for the slots you will use.

- Position the card inside its cover, near the computer.

- Touch a grounded part of the computer. The power supply case is a good choice. Now, without removing your hand from the computer, open the bag and remove the card you are about to install. If you must, swap hands as you move the card into position, just be sure you keep touching the computer case. This is easier than it sounds. You can use your elbow, wrist, the back of your hand, and so on, to maintain contact with the computer as you handle the card.

- Insert the card carefully into the chosen slot and press it firmly into place. It is helpful to wiggle the card into position, pressing first one end, then the other, until it is firmly seated. You'll quickly get the hang of it as you work with more cards. Just remember that the card itself is quite rugged. Except for static discharge, it isn't likely that you'll hurt a modern computer card during installation. (See Figure 6-14.)

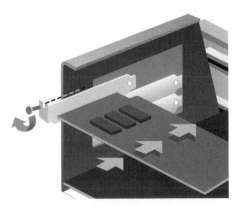

Figure 6-14 Typical card being placed in a computer

Electrostatic Discharge (ESD) straps can be used to prevent damage to your computer and cards. An ESD strap usually consists of a wrist strap with a grounding cord to clip to the computer's metal frame.

SOUND CARDS

In the past, computer support for sound and other multimedia devices was rare. Today there's hardly a computer that doesn't include high-end audio support. Multimedia, sound output, and even quality recording capabilities have become more important to a broader range of users. Businesses use sound as part of documentation or training, sales presentations, and even for music and motion video productions.

You'll find that support for a sound card is automatic with newer computers. The sound card comes pre-installed, and the operating system includes integral support for sound input and output. However, there are drivers for individual pieces of sound hardware that must be installed, as described in the earlier overview section. Also, if you format your hard drive (or replace it with a new one), you must install the proper drivers for your sound hardware for everything to work properly.

Sound devices are of two general types: bus cards and hardware integrated with the motherboard. Increasingly you will see sound cards built into the motherboard. This provides the easiest installation because the hardware is always there, and all you might need to do is install or configure drivers. The downside to motherboard sound hardware, as with built-in disk controllers, video adapters, and other devices, is that it may be harder to update or change the hardware.

OTHER OUTPUT DEVICES

In today's computer marketplace, there are so many output options that it would be impossible to cover them all here. Digital video, for example, is becoming a popular consumer and professional computer-based feature. Adapter cards that let you capture and output digital video to a camera or VCR are available, coupled with capable, low-cost video editing software to help you use them.

Enhanced sound output is also now reasonably priced. Instead of living with analog output, for a few dollars more, you can output (and input) a digital audio stream to minidisk or DAT (Digital Audio Tape) recorders. Multi-port sound cards are available today, which permit a computer to serve as a fully digital, multi-channel recorder for sound studio applications.

As you interact with a variety of computer systems and read specifications for products from a variety of industries, be aware of what hardware and software may be driving the features you are using or reading about. And, be aware that there's probably some specialty software required to make everything work properly.

COMPUTER STORAGE OPTIONS

Another kind of computer input/output device is disk storage. Storage devices are somewhat different from the other devices discussed so far in this chapter, but they also are an integral part of a functioning computer system and its associated operating system. This section briefly discusses various storage technologies and relates their functions to general operating system theory.

Today, most computer systems are supplied with a single 3.5-inch floppy drive, perhaps a high-density floppy or Zip disk, one or more internal, fixed hard drives, and a CD-ROM or DVD drive. These storage devices are mounted in the computer case and connect to the computer hardware through an electronic interface and cable system.

Floppy and hard disk drives include internal electronics and an external interface to connect the drive to the computer. In modern computers, the floppy drives and the hard drives may plug into the same bus interface card, which includes separate connectors and separate controllers that share some common components. The operating system acts as an interface between this controller and the rest of the computer. The operating system also provides services to application software that needs to read from and write to the drive. There are many controller designs. When they comply with the standards required by the operating system, what goes on inside the hard drive or the hard drive controller is not significant in terms of the user or the operating system.

The most popular hard drive interface in the Intel PC architecture is the **Integrated Drive Electronics (IDE)** interface. This interface is often built into the main board of the computer, or is otherwise present in the form of an interface card. A single IDE interface can support two devices, one so-called **master** (the first or main drive) and one **slave** (secondary storage device). The cable usually has three 40-pin header connectors. One connector plugs into the IDE card or into the appropriate connector on the main board. The other two can be used to connect to the IDE devices.

IDE has many subtypes that control the speed of data transfers between the devices and the computer. An advantage of IDE is that the controller and the devices are able to determine which of the various substandards they support, and as a rule of thumb, you, as the user, do not have to worry about the details. **Enhanced IDE (EIDE)** supports transfer speeds as high as 33 megabits per second. And, today's computer systems generally include dual EIDE controllers, usually built into the system motherboard. The primary controller interfaces the boot drive to the system. The secondary controller may be used for a CD-ROM drive, a second hard disk, and so on.

The last type of drive, which can be used on all PC platforms mentioned in this book, is the type that uses the Small Computer System Interface (SCSI). SCSI can be a confusing standard, partially because there are so many different SCSI designs, each with its own set of cables and rules. You might encounter a SCSI-1, SCSI-2 and Narrow SCSI-2, Wide SCSI-2, SCSI-3, Wide Ultra SCSI, Ultra2 SCSI, and Ultra3 SCSI, all of which use 50 pins in the cable. These can address eight or 16 devices per SCSI controller, depending on the type of SCSI. One of these devices is the controller. The disks are connected to each other and to the controller by a single cable. This cable, when it is run inside a computer, can be a ribbon cable with 50 wires and header connectors. SCSI cables can have as little as one, or as many as eight, of these connectors. There is a limitation in the length of the overall cable; it should not exceed 18 feet. Each end of the cable must be electrically terminated to prevent echoes and ghost signals on the cable. Termination is done with terminator resistors. Since one end of the cable is usually terminated in the SCSI controller, you will find that, in most cases, one of the terminators is built into the card. Either a disk drive or an external terminator typically terminates the other end of the chain. In the case of a drive, sometimes you will simply set a jumper on the drive to turn termination on or off. In other cases, you will actually plug **terminator resistor packs**, or **TRPs**, into the drive to set up termination. If SCSI drives are external to the computer, something you will find quite often, an external SCSI connection is used. This connection can take many forms.

SCSI-1 normally uses either a DB-25 connector (often used in the Apple Macintosh architecture, but now also popular in many Intel PC architecture designs), or a 50-pin Amphenol or Centronics connector, the format that is more standard.

 The DB-25 connector must be treated with care. On the Intel PC, it looks identical to the connector used for the printer port. Plugging the printer into the SCSI port or vice versa may lead to serious hardware damage.

SCSI-2 and above are typically brought out on either a DB-25 or a Mini DBC-50 connector. The Mini DBC-50 is the most popular connector format. It snaps in place and can be easily removed. The pins in this connector are spaced very closely, and connectors can be easily damaged by inserting them with too much force.

Terminators for SCSI-1 and SCSI-2 come in a few variations. For SCSI-1 and Narrow SCSI-2, you should use passive terminators. These terminators consist of simple resistors, and, in many cases, they will work fine. For Wide SCSI-2 and above, which use a higher clock speed and are therefore faster than Narrow SCSI-2, stricter requirements are imposed on the terminator. As a result, Active Terminators are often used for Wide SCSI-2 and above installations. These terminators contain electronics that can actively change the characteristics of the terminator.

The three most common problems you will see in SCSI installations are related to the terminators, total cable length, and SCSI device addressing. SCSI-1 is an 8-bit wide bus; SCSI-2 is 16 bits wide. SCSI-1 runs at a speed of 10 MHz, as does SCSI-2. Fast SCSI-2 runs at a speed of 20 MHz. Fast Wide SCSI-3 format is different in a few ways. It has a 32-bit data path, it supports 15 devices per cable, and runs at a speed of 20 MHz. The drives used for Wide SCSI are more expensive; the cables are slightly different. Internal cables are 68-pin Micro Header connectors; external cables are Mini-D 68-pin connectors. All terminators in this scheme are active. The most frequent problems with this type of SCSI are cable length, which may not exceed 15 feet, followed by termination problems. Interface speed of the various SCSI drives varies widely; SCSI-1 is typically able to transfer about 5 MB per second (MBps); Narrow SCSI-2 transfers about 10 MBps; Wide SCSI-2 transfers as much as 20 MBps; and Fast Wide SCSI-3 for RISC computers transfers as much as 100 MBps.

Advances in the SCSI industry have resulted in several enhancements. These include the Ultra SCSI, wide Ultra SCSI, Ultra2 SCSI, wide Ultra2 SCSI, Ultra3 SCSI (Ultra160), and now the Ultra320 SCSI, which is the seventh generation of SCSI technology. It transfers at a rate of 320 MBps, has a 16-bit bus, handles 16 devices, and is especially well positioned for servers and network storage. Information on current developments in the SCSI industry can be found at the SCSI Trade Associations Web page at *www.scsita.org.*

6

Several disk drives or other devices, such as a tape drive or CD-ROM drive, can be daisy-chained on the cable of a SCSI adapter. Wide Ultra SCSI and Ultra2 SCSI provide the best performance when devices are daisy-chained.

It is important to make sure each device connected to the SCSI has a unique address, with the first device addressed as 0. Problems occur if two devices have the same address. Also, when troubleshooting SCSI problems, make sure that the SCSI cable is properly terminated at both ends. Omitting the cable terminator at the last device in the daisy chain is a common problem when connecting several devices to one SCSI adapter. If your operating system experiences difficulty recognizing SCSI devices, check to make sure the terminator is connected to the last device on the SCSI cable.

The number of platters, heads, tracks, and sectors per track varies widely from hard disk to hard disk. This information is often stored in an area of nonvolatile memory in the computer. In addition, many operating systems keep a table somewhere on the disk that describes the disk in great detail. EIDE and SCSI provide ways for the controllers to communicate with the electronics on the disk, which enables the controllers to retrieve this information. However, this exchange of information does not always work correctly, and it is a good idea to have the information about a disk on hand. This data is known as the **disk geometry**.

Storage capacity of a single hard disk can be a few megabytes to several gigabytes. Hard disks are fast and allow the user to store large amounts of data and programs. In many computers, they are used to store the operating system, the application software, and all the data.

Because of the delicate mechanisms inside the disk, it is not uncommon for a hard disk to fail. When a floppy disk fails, only a small amount of data is lost. Because floppies fail often, users do not usually rely on floppies as their only data storage. Hard disks seem much more stable, and many users do not make copies of data stored on hard disks. As a result, hard disk failures are often catastrophic for a user. Backing up data on hard disks is an essential practice. Try Hands-on Project 6-12 to use the Windows 98 System Information utility to study your hard drive configuration.

RAID Arrays

Although hard disks can store large amounts of data and are relatively fast and fairly reliable, there is room for improvement on all three points. To address some of these issues, a group of researchers at the University of California in Berkeley introduced the concept of a **Redundant Array of Inexpensive Drives (RAID)**. They defined various levels of RAID technology; a brief discussion follows. (A more detailed discussion of RAID levels is found in Chapter 10.)

RAID arrays serve three purposes: increased reliability, increased storage capacity, and increased speed. Different levels of RAID focus on different purposes, and there is no RAID level that can be declared superior for all situations. Because RAID array implementation tends to be costly, they are used primarily on network servers, with network operating systems (NOSs).

RAID is implemented as a combination of hardware and software. The hardware can consist of simply a few hard disks connected to one controller, or something as complicated as a very large set of hard disks connected to several disk controllers equipped with processors to assist in running RAID software. The RAID software is typically a low-level device driver that works with any RAID hardware and provides an interface to the operating system to provide access to the special RAID features offered. Some systems are presented to the operating system as if they were simple drives; the RAID hardware interacts with the OS as if it were a hard disk.

CD-ROM and DVD

This section compares the **compact disc–read only memory (CD-ROM)** to its newer sibling, the **digital versatile disc (DVD)**.

Compact Disc (CD) Technology

CD-ROMs are very important in today's operating system environment because most software and documentation are distributed on these media. These disks are different from floppies and hard disks for many reasons, including the way data is stored. Instead of using a system of tracks and sectors like floppy and hard disks, CD-ROMs use a big "spiral" that starts at the inside of the disc and winds itself slowly toward the outside of the disc. Whenever data is needed from the disc, a laser pickup is pointed at a part of the disc surface.

The disc itself is rotated by a precision motor that keeps the disc speed constant. The optical pickup is typically moved by yet another motor under computer control. Extreme precision is required when moving the pickup, and there are a wide variety of mechanisms that connect to stepper motors and to the pickup. Most modern drives use a direct drive mechanism, where the motor moves a little rod that pulls the head to the correct position. Optical encoders are often used to make sure the head is positioned correctly. Older drives use worm wheel drives, which tend to develop mechanical problems after intense use.

When a disc is read, laser light is emitted by the CD-ROM head and reflected off the disc surface onto an optical pickup. The surface of the disc is covered with little indents, which shift the position of the reflected laser light as it is returned to the pickup. Depending on the size of the dents, ones or zeroes are returned. You are probably familiar with the CD-ROM disc itself, a silver disc about four inches in diameter. The surface of the CD-ROM reflects light during a data read operation. Although CD-ROM discs are extremely reliable, the large number of dents make this surface very sensitive to scratches and other kinds of damage that can hinder optical readout.

Because it is almost inevitable that the CD-ROM surface will become damaged through frequent use, the CD-ROM drive and disc are equipped with extensive mechanisms to protect the user from critical data errors. The data on the CD-ROM has **Cyclic Redundancy Check (CRC)** bits encoded in it as other disks do, and it also has error correction bits encoded on the disc. As long as there is not too much damage to the disc surface, the reading mechanism will recover from reading errors. Parity bits, which are interlaced in the data stream, are used to reconstruct any missing or damaged data before it is passed to the operating system. Although the CD-ROM is one of the more delicate media, its built-in error detection and correction make it one of the most reliable.

The storage capacity of a CD-ROM is fairly high. About 650 MB of data can be stored per disc. CD-ROMs are single-sided discs. The typical transfer speed of a single-speed CD-ROM drive is roughly 150 KB per second, with an average seek time of about 150 milliseconds (ms). CD-ROMs were originally invented for use as an audio storage mechanism to replace the old LP, and the single-speed nomenclature originates from this use. A single-speed CD-ROM player spins the disc and reads the data at the same speed as an audio CD-ROM player.

For many purposes, that speed is quite acceptable, but as always, faster is better. Not long after introduction of the single-speed CD-ROM came faster models. The main difference between the single-speed and multispeed CD-ROM drives is the speed at which they can spin the CD-ROM, and the speed at which they move the optical pickup heads from one place on the spiral to another. Rotational speeds can range from as little as twice the normal audio speed, or 2X, to as high as 72 times that speed (72X).

High-speed CD-ROM drives can reach data transfer rates of several megabytes per second, some as much as about 10 MB. The seek times vary widely. Many are in the 50 to 70 ms range; some of the fast ones are in the 20 to 30 ms range. This kind of performance is very close to what you would expect from some hard disks, but in most practical situations, CD-ROM drives appear to be a lot slower.

Digital Versatile Disc (DVD) Technology

The digital versatile disc, or DVD, works a lot like the CD-ROM. It is also an optical drive, and has the data written on the disc in the form of a spiral of blocks. All data is read from the disc with the use of a laser and an optical pickup. The storage capacity and data transfer rate of the DVD are much higher, but the size of the disc is the same. Almost all DVD drives can read CD-ROM as well as DVD discs. A computer equipped with a DVD drive must be able to read CD-ROMs for versatility. There is a physical similarity between the DVD and CD-ROM discs and drives.

The DVD disc can have two sides with up to two layers per side. All data on a hard disk, floppy disk, or CD-ROM is stored on one layer of material. On the CD-ROM, when laser light hits the layer, it is reflected. On a DVD, the same thing happens, but in addition to the first layer, which is a spiral that moves from the middle of the disc to the outside like a conventional CD-ROM, the DVD disk has a second layer. This layer is read by using light that hits the disk at a different angle. The second layer is also a spiral, this one written from the outside of the disk to the inside. Each side of a DVD disk may contain up to two layers, and each layer can hold 4.7 GB of data. The result: on each DVD, you can store roughly 17 GB of data. The trend toward more graphics and multimedia as part of operating systems and application programs is certain to make DVD a very popular format in the near future.

DVD drives are typically multispeed drives. The 1.0X (single-speed) benchmark for a DVD drive is the speed at which most DVD drives used for video applications retrieve video data. Typical computer DVD drives are in the 16X range, with faster drives to come in the future. When these drives read CD-ROM discs, they do so at about 48X speed. DVD has even better bit error correction than the CD-ROM format, but, like a CD-ROM, is very sensitive to damage to the disc surface.

The data transfer rate of DVD ranges from about 1.3 MB per second to about 21 MB per second. The average seek time is 85 milliseconds to about 200 milliseconds. Switching sides or layers tends to take a little longer, sometimes as much as about two-tenths of a second. For most applications, this performance is very acceptable.

 Look for much more DVD software in all forms in the future. DVD is fast enough to run applications directly from the DVD disc as you would from a hard disk. This could change the way application software is used, and may significantly increase the number of applications at your disposal at any given time.

CD-ROM and DVD-ROM Interfaces

CD-ROM and DVD-ROM drives are typically connected to the computer using a hard disk interface. Many PCs use the EIDE interface with SCSI as a close second. Because these discs have a distinctively different organization from hard disks, and because they cannot be written to, typically an operating system requires a special driver to read from them. The latest generations of PCs have drivers for CD-ROM and DVD-ROM drives built into the ROM BIOS, which allows them to use the drives without special drivers. This enables them to boot an operating system directly from a CD-ROM or DVD-ROM. Mac OS, Windows NT 4.0/2000/XP, and many flavors of UNIX can boot an operating system directly from the CD-ROM or DVD-ROM for initial installation.

Recordable and Rewritable CD and DVD

For some time it has been possible to record and rewrite CD-ROMs using CD-R and CD-RW devices. Only recently were devices introduced to record and rewrite DVD-ROMs using DVD-R, DVD-RW, and DVD+RW devices. CD-R and DVD-R can record data once on the media, and then it can be read many times. Thus, the R stands for recordable. CD-RW and DVD-RW can write on the media thousands of times. RW stands for rewritable. Currently, these devices can record up to 4.7 GB per side, depending on the manufacturer. A new standard called DVD+RW is backed by such vendors as Philips Electronics, Ricoh, Yamaha, Mitsubishi, Sony, Dell, Hewlett Packard, and Thomson Multimedia. It faces competition from vendors of the DVD-RW standard.

Network Storage

Many organizations are finding that with eBusiness, merger requirements, and other applications with lots of data, they need a method to manage this data. Backups, disaster recovery, and availability of data are just a few of the reasons organizations are beginning to implement **Storage Area Networks (SANs)**. SAN technology provides for interconnection between servers and storage systems without sending data over the corporate network. This is accomplished by tying the servers and storage systems together via a switched, full-duplex (data goes in both directions at the same time) **Fibre Channel** fabric. The servers are also tied to the network, but all data transfer between the servers and storage systems takes place on the Fibre Channel. The Fibre Channel runs between 1 gigabits per second (Gbps) and 2 Gbps, with 10 Gbps in the works.

Connecting Drives

All of the drives discussed in this chapter connect to the computer in much the same way as hard disks, typically through an EIDE or SCSI. The drivers needed for many of these drives are often quite specialized. It is very important to make sure you have the drivers required for the operating system with which you want the drives to function. Do not assume that any drive can be used with any operating system. When it comes to specialty drives like the ones discussed in this chapter, always make sure they are supported for your operating system.

Removable Disks

Removable disks, in most cases, are hard disks with a twist. These also come in many shapes, sizes, and formats, and we will briefly take a look at some of the more popular drives and disks available today. The first group of drives are those that use flexible magnetic disks, in particular the low-capacity **SuperDisk (LS-120)** and **Zip disks**, and the high-capacity **Jaz** drive. The second group consists of drives that use hard platters, much like a hard disk. Bernoulli, SyQuest, and Castlewood's ORB drives are examples of these technologies.

Removable Large-Capacity Floppy Drives

The SuperDisk, also known as the LS-120 floppy disk, uses a drive much like a 3.5" floppy. As a matter of fact, the drive is able to read from and write to 3.5" HD floppies. The SuperDisk looks a lot like a 3.5" floppy; however, the shutter mechanism is slightly different. The storage capacity of a SuperDisk is 120 MB. There are several types of SuperDisk drives: some connect to the computer's printer port, others replace an internal floppy drive, and others connect to the EIDE or SCSI of the computer. Software drivers for this format are currently available for the various versions of Microsoft Windows, the Mac OS, and UNIX.

The higher storage capacity (higher than floppy capacity) on the SuperDisk is achieved by using a higher density magnetic storage medium. The speed when using floppies is similar to that of a 3.5" disk drive. The medium is relatively cheap, so this seems to be a good alternative for exchanging moderate amounts of data. Note that there is physical contact between the heads and the disk, which makes this disk sensitive to wear, much like floppies.

A competitor to the LS-120 floppy is the Zip disk, designed by Iomega. The Zip drive is addressed by the system like a hard disk, and offers a storage capacity of 100 or 250 MB. Zip drives are available in both external and internal varieties with printer port, SCSI, EIDE, or USB connections. The newest generation of external Zip drives has a port that connects to a printer port, a SCSI port, or a USB port. It automatically adapts to the port to which it is connected. The Zip disk was initially plagued by mechanical problems, but newer models seem to be quite reliable. The disk consists of a cartridge that contains a magnetic disk. The medium is much like a floppy, and the size is similar to a 3.5" floppy. Unlike the LS-120, the Zip drive cannot read from or write to 3.5" floppy disks. The Zip drive was the first affordable, compact, medium storage capacity removable disk to hit the market, and it is a quite popular option. When connected to a native disk interface such as SCSI, USB, or EIDE, most operating systems do not need any special drivers to use a Zip drive. It is generally recognized as yet another hard disk connected to the system. There are, however, special drivers for the Zip drive, which enable some additional functions. As is generally the case with removable drives, some of the features the special drivers offer are related to change notification. This means that the operating system is notified when the disk is inserted or removed. Operating systems such as DOS and Windows 3.1 generally do not care about disk changes, but more advanced operating systems typically store some information about the disk in memory. It may be as little as the table of contents, or as much as some of the data stored on the disk.

If the operating system is not told when a disk is swapped, the results can be rather disastrous. For example, the operating system could blindly write data to an area on a disk that it assumes is empty, but if a disk was swapped without the operating system being notified, some of the data may be damaged beyond repair.

It is possible to use Zip drives with many operating systems without any special drivers, but *not recommended*, particularly with operating systems that cache part of the disk, such as Mac OS, UNIX, Windows 95, Windows 98, Windows Me, Windows NT, Windows 2000, and Windows XP.

Zip drives are available for many platforms. Some commercial computers, even some laptops, now have a built-in Zip drive. The media is slightly more expensive than that used in the LS-120 drive.

You can connect Zip and LS-120 drives to a computer's printer port, which is a great feature. In many cases, a Zip disk can hold enough information to install an entire operating system from one disk. This is convenient for fixing problems on computers that do not have a CD-ROM drive. In addition, disks that connect to the printer port can be easily connected and disconnected, and used on more than one computer.

The price you pay for this convenience is speed. When connected to the printer port, the speed at which the disk can be accessed is greatly reduced. Throughput may go down to as little as 140 KB per second. In addition, much of the CPU time may be used in making the drive work.

An alternative with much higher capacity is the Jaz drive, also made by Iomega. Jaz drives come in internal or external models, which are connected to the computer using either a SCSI or EIDE interface. The cartridge is slightly bigger than the Zip cartridge, but works much the same. Inside you will find a flexible plastic disk covered with a magnetic layer on which the data is stored. This disk also stores data much like a floppy disk. The heads are in continuous contact with the disk as data is read or written. There are two versions of the Jaz drive—a 1 GB and a 2 GB model. These drives are recognized by any operating system as a hard disk, but as with Zip disks, there are special drivers for many operating systems that enable them to work correctly when disks are swapped.

Removable Rigid Cartridges

The second class of removable disks have a disk made out of a solid material inside the cartridge, much like the platters found in a hard disk. The heads in these systems, much like the heads in a hard disk, are not in contact with the disk surface. Instead, they float above the surface at a very close distance. This has some advantages and some disadvantages. A very big advantage is that there is no mechanical contact between the heads and the disk, which means that both the heads and the disk last a lot longer. They suffer no wear and tear from the read/write head. A big disadvantage is that it is not easy to make a head float very close to a platter in a system where the platter is in a removable cartridge.

Bernoulli drives are semi-rigid, removable cartridge hard drives based on the Bernoulli aerodynamic principle. They can be used on desktop or laptop computers, and provide relatively high speed and high storage capacity. **SyQuest** makes a series of removable drives that are used with many operating systems. The drives work similarly to the Bernoulli drives in that they use a hard platter, much like the one in a hard disk, which is housed inside a hard plastic cartridge. The platter is also spun at high speed, and has heads floating above it to read and write data. However, the principle of an air cushion and positive air pressure is not used. The distance between the disk and the heads is slightly greater. A different technique is used in the heads, which makes it possible for them to be a little further away from the disk surface. Unfortunately, both Bernoulli and Syquest have experienced financial difficulties, and have either been purchased or are in the bankruptcy courts.

Castlewood Systems, Inc. makes the **ORB** 2.2 GB and the ORB 5.7 GB drives. The ORB 2.2 GB comes in EIDE, Ultra SCSI, Ultra Wide SCSI, Parallel Port, and USB models. The ORB 5.7 GB is only available in the EIDE model at this time.

Table 6-1 shows some of the major storage devices and their respective capacities.

Table 6-1 Storage Media with Respective Capacities

Storage Media	Capacity
Castlewood ORB	2.2 or 5.7 GB
CD-ROM	650 MB
CD-R	650 MB
CD-RW	650 MB
DVD-ROM	4.7, 8.5, 9.4, or 17 GB
DVD-R	4.7 GB
DVD-RW	4.7 GB
DVD+RW	4.7 GB
Iomega Zip disk	100 or 250 MB
Iomega Jaz	1 or 2 GB
SuperDisk (LS-120)	120 MB

Removable Storage

Microsoft introduced the Removable Storage system in Windows 2000. The Removable Storage system tracks removable storage media such as tapes, CD-ROMs, DVD-ROMs, optical disks, and even high-capacity disk drives, which might be contained in changers and jukeboxes. Applications such as backup software manage the actual data stored on these removable media. Removable Storage provides the mechanism for multiple applications to share the same media. All applications using the Removable Storage system must run on the same computer. Figure 6-15 shows the Removable Storage section under Computer Management in Windows 2000.

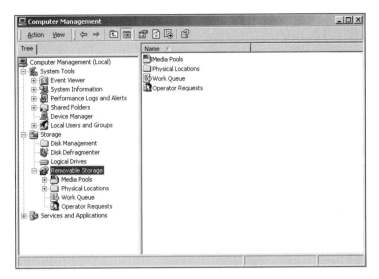

Figure 6-15   Removable Storage in Windows 2000

Chapter Summary

- This chapter provides a conceptual overview of how operating systems interface with input, output, and storage devices, and how such devices usually require both hardware and software setup. It is impossible to provide detail about every input, output, and storage device since each one is different and, moreover, works differently with different operating systems. You've learned the general steps to install required driver software, and special considerations of specific operating systems as they relate to some devices. This chapter covered various printer technologies, and discussed other output devices such as sound cards and display adapters.

- Basic keyboard and mouse technologies are available to users of all operating systems, and there are general considerations that are important when installing and using a variety of input devices, including digital pads (tablets), digital cameras, and digital scanners. You also learned about joysticks, game pads, digital sound input, digital video input, and 1394 technology.

- Popular computer storage technologies include hard disk drives, RAID arrays, CD-ROMs, and DVD drives. You saw how these storage devices interface to the computer hardware and learned basic operating system considerations in using them. Removable storage devices such as SuperDisk, Zip disk, Jaz disk, and ORB drivers provide several options for portable storage. You learned that, depending on the device, they can store between 120 MB and 5.7 GB. See Table 6-1 for a listing of storage media and their respective capacities. Network storage using Storage Area Networks (SANs) and Fibre Channel fabric was discussed for managing large amounts of data. You also learned that SANs transfer data without using the corporate network.

❏ Dot matrix, ink-jet, and laser printers in both color and black and white were discussed. In addition, you learned about specialty devices, such as line, thermal-wax, dye sublimation, and Imagesetter printers.

Key Terms

Accelerated Graphics Port (AGP) — A bus standard that has enabled adapter manufacturers to supply one hardware product to a variety of hardware platforms.

Apple Desktop Bus (ADB) — A serial bus common on the Apple Macintosh computer. ADB is used to connect the Macintosh keyboard, mouse, and other external I/O devices.

Bernoulli — A semi-rigid hard drive based on the Bernoulli principle. These high-capacity, removable cartridge drives provide reasonably high-speed, high-density add-on storage for desktop and laptop computers in data-intensive applications such as graphics.

Centronics interface — An industry standard printer interface popularized by printer manufacturer Centronics. The interface definition includes 36 wires that connect the printer with the computer I/O port, though all of these pins aren't always used, particularly in modern desktop computers.

compact disc-read only memory (CD-ROM) — A non-volatile, digital data storage medium used for operating system and other software distribution.

Cyclic Redundancy Check (CRC) — An error correction protocol that determines the validity of data written to and read from a floppy disk, hard disk, CD-ROM, or DVD.

DB-25 — A 25-pin D-shaped connector commonly used on desktop computers, terminals, modems, and other devices.

digital pad or digital tablet — An alternative input device frequently used by graphic artists and others who need accurate control over drawing and other data input.

digital versatile disc (DVD) — A high-capacity CD-ROM-like hardware device used for high-quality audio, motion video, and computer data storage.

disk geometry — Critical information about a hard drive's hardware configuration. This information is often stored in an area of non-volatile memory in the computer.

dot matrix printer — A character printer that produces characters by arranging a matrix of dots. Dot matrix printers can be impact, ink jet, or other technologies.

dye sublimation — A printer technology that produces high-quality, color output by creating "sublimated" color mists that penetrate paper to form characters or graphic output.

extended capability port (ECP) — A form of communication that allows for higher speed bidirectional communication between the computer and printer, and the printer and computer.

Enhanced IDE (EIDE) — A more modern, faster version of IDE.

Fibre Channel — A means of transferring data between servers, mass storage devices, workstations, and peripherals at very high speeds.

game pad — An input device primarily designed for interaction with games. Includes multiple buttons, wheels, or balls to effect movement of a variety of on-screen objects.

Imagesetter — A high-end printer frequently used for publishing. Capable of producing film output.

ink-jet printer — A character printer that forms characters by spraying droplets of ink from a nozzle print head onto the paper.

Integrated Drive Electronics (IDE) — A storage protocol popular in today's desktop computer systems. IDE is significant because it simplifies the hardware required inside the computer, placing more of the disk intelligence at the hard drive itself.

Jaz — An Iomega removable hard disk design capable of storing 1 or 2 GB of data, depending on the model.

joystick — An input device shaped like a stick that allows for three-dimensional movement of an on-screen cursor or other object, such as a car, airplane, or cartoon character.

laser printer — A high-quality page printer design popular in office and other professional applications.

line printer — A printer design that prints a full line of character output at a time. Used for high-speed output requirements.

LPT1 — The primary printer port designation on many desktop computers. Also designated Line Printer 1.

master — In an EIDE drive chain, the main or first drive. Most EIDE interfaces can support two drives. One is the master (Drive 0) and the second drive is the slave. See *slave*.

micro-switch — A small electronic switch used in a computer mouse, game pad, or joystick to connect and disconnect electronic circuits. These openings and closings can be monitored by driver software to enable certain software features or functions.

optical character recognition (OCR) — Imaging software that scans each character on the page as a distinct image and is able to recognize the character.

ORB – Drives manufactured by Castlewood Systems, Inc., in both 2.2 GB and 5.7 GB models.

parallel port — A computer input/output port used primarily for printer connections. A parallel port transmits data eight bits or more at a time, using at least eight parallel wires. A parallel port potentially can transmit data faster than a serial port.

personal digital assistant (PDA) — Handheld devices, which, because of their size, are easily transported wherever you go. They include features to assist you in organizing your time, such as a calendar, to-do lists, contacts, etc.

pixel — Short for picture element. The small dots that make up a computer screen display.

6

PKZIP — A utility program that archives files and compresses them so they require less disk storage and can be transmitted over a network faster.

plotter — Computer hardware that produces high-quality printed output, often in color, by moving ink pens over the surface of paper. Plotters are often used with computer-aided design (CAD) and other graphics applications.

potentiometer — A hardware device used to vary the amount of resistance in an electronic circuit. In computer I/O hardware, this variable resistance can be used to monitor mouse movement, joystick positioning, and so on.

print queue or print spooler — A section of computer memory and hard disk storage set aside to hold information sent by an application to a printer attached to the local computer or to another computer or print server on a network. Operating system or printer drivers and control software manage the information sent to the queue, responding to printer start/stop commands.

Redundant Array of Inexpensive Drives (RAID) — A relatively inexpensive, redundant storage design that uses multiple disks and logic to reduce the chance of information being lost in the event of hardware failure. RAID uses various designs, termed Level 0 through Level 5.

removable disks — A class of relatively high-capacity storage devices that use removable cartridges. These devices are used for data backup, long-term offline storage, and data portability among multiple computer systems.

Storage Area Network (SAN) — Technology that provides for interconnection between servers and storage systems without sending data over the corporate network.

scanner — Creates a digital image from a hard copy that is then transmitted to the computer.

self-extracting file — A compressed or archive file that includes an executable component, like an application program, which enables the file to separate into individual files and uncompress the files automatically. A self-extracting file does not require an external program to expand the file into its individual components.

serial port — A computer input/output port used for modem, printer, and other connections. A serial port transmits data one bit after another in serial fashion, as compared to a parallel port, which transmits data eight bits or more at a time.

slave — In an EIDE drive chain, the secondary storage device. See *master*.

Small Computer System Interface (SCSI) — A computer input/output bus standard and the hardware that uses this standard. There are many types of SCSI in use today, providing data transfer rates from 10 Mbps to 100 Mbps.

StuffIt — A Macintosh archive and compression utility.

SuperDisk (LS-120) — An increasingly popular high-capacity floppy disk design. SuperDisk / LS-120 drives can store as much as 120 MB of data on a single disk, but these drives also can read conventional 3.5" floppy disks.

SyQuest — The manufacturer of one of the earliest removable hard disk devices popular in Macintosh and PC systems. SyQuest drives use hard disk technology. Early drives stored only 40 MB, but later designs can hold upwards of 200 MB.

tar — A UNIX file archive utility.

terminator resistor packs (TRPs) — Sets of resistors used on a hard drive or other storage device. These resistors reduce the possibility of data echoes on the interface bus as information travels between the computer's controller and the storage device.

thermal-wax transfer — A printer technology that creates high-quality color printed output by melting colored wax elements and transferring them to the printed page.

Universal Serial Bus (USB) — A relatively high-speed I/O port found on most modern computers. It is used to interface digital sound cards, disk drives, and other external computer hardware.

Video Graphics Array (VGA) — A video graphics display system introduced by IBM in 1987.

wheel mouse — A relatively new mouse design, popularized by Microsoft's IntelliMouse, that includes a top-mounted wheel in addition to the standard mouse buttons. The wheel is programmable for a variety of operating systems and application functions. A switch integral to the wheel provides additional opportunity for programmable, custom functions.

WINZip — An archive and compression utility for Windows 95 and 98.

Zip disk — A removable high-capacity floppy disk design from Iomega. Zip disks store a nominal 100 or 250 MB of data.

6

REVIEW QUESTIONS

1. The main printer port on Windows computer systems is frequently designated as:
   a. Character Port.
   b. LPT1.
   c. Printer Port 1.
   d. Main Printer Port.

2. Describe how ink-jet designs differ from impact designs.

3. One type of popular computer printer could be described as a computerized copier. What printer technology is this? Is this analogy appropriate? Why or why not?

4. What are Imagesetter printers most often used for?
   a. low-resolution proofs
   b. high-resolution final output for publishing applications
   c. computer animation
   d. none of the above

5. A Centronics port can best be described as:

   a. a serial port sometimes used to connect a printer to a computer.

   b. a high-speed digital port frequently used for digital cameras.

   c. a parallel port that has become the standard printer interface for IBM-compatible PCs.

   d. an older printer interface that is rarely used today.

6. Two or three users can access a single printer by using a switch box that changes which computer is attached to the printer. When multiple users need access to the same printer, however, a better solution is a printer that includes:

   a. a network interface and support software.

   b. multiple parallel interfaces.

   c. multiple serial interfaces.

   d. More than two or three users can't use the same printer.

7. Although computer screens can display 640 × 480 pixels or more, the actual bit depth—the number of pixels per inch—is only _____ dots.

8. A bus that is common to PC, Macintosh, and UNIX computers, and that is most often used as the interface for modern display adapters is:

   a. PSI.

   b. AGP.

   c. IDE.

   d. none of the above

9. Describe why it is important to leave a new expansion card inside its shipping container until you are ready to install it into the computer. What additional precautions should you take in handling adapter cards during the installation process?

10. Even if your hardware is brand new, the driver software shipped with it may not be the latest and greatest. What is a good source of the most recent software drivers for a manufacturer's hardware?

11. What do the software utilities PKZIP, StuffIt, and tar have in common? For which operating system is each designed?

12. Describe the basic differences between the digital pad or tablet and a standard mouse. Under what circumstances would you most commonly use each of these input devices?

13. Some of the newer computer mice include a top-mounted wheel. What purpose does this wheel serve?

14. The most common hardware interface for a digital scanner is:

    a. USB.

    b. IDE.

    c. RS-232.

    d. SCSI.

15. For what applications might you expect to use a joystick for data input. (Choose all that apply.)

    a. playing games

    b. manipulating graphics objects

    c. text documents

    d. database applications

16. Hard disks are very different from floppy disks in the way they read and write data. The hard disk read/write heads don't _____.

17. RAID is a technology for:

    a. eliminating programming bugs during application development.

    b. using multiple hard drives in various configurations to provide data security through redundancy and error checking.

    c. storing data in a Redundant Access Integrated Drive arrangement.

    d. communicating configuration information between the computer and a remote user interface.

18. Describe the major design differences between DVD and CD-ROM that enable the much larger storage capacities of DVD.

19. The Removable Storage system manages the actual data stored on the removable media. True or False?

20. A Storage Area Network (SAN) interconnects servers and storage systems via:

    a. Ethernet.

    b. Token Ring.

    c. Fiber Channel fabric.

    d. Category 5e cable.

Hands-on Projects

Project 6-1

There are times when you must determine what printers are available on an operating system. In this project, you'll learn how to determine the printer setup in Windows 95/98/Me.

To find out what printers are installed on your Windows 95/98/Me system:

1. Move the mouse pointer to the bottom of the screen to display the taskbar, if it is not visible.

2. Click **Start**.

3. Point to **Settings**.

4. Click **Printers** to display the Printers window.

5. Now you can determine some of the settings for an individual printer by right-clicking one of the printer icons.

6. Choose **Properties** from the shortcut menu. You will see different properties displays for different printers. You probably will see a tabbed dialog box. Click on various tabs to view information such as paper trays available, quality setting, and so on.

7. Close the Properties dialog box by clicking **Cancel**, then close the Printers window.

Project 6-2

There are times when you must determine what printers are available on a Mac operating system. In this project, you'll learn how to determine the printer setup in Mac OS.

To find out what printers are installed in Mac OS 9.x:

1. Open the Apple menu (click the **Apple** icon at the upper left of your desktop).

2. Open the **Chooser**, which you should find near the top of the Apple menu.

3. If you have printers installed, you will see a separate icon for each one on the left side of the Chooser dialog box.

4. Click one of the icons to select it, and you will see information specific to that printer on the right side of the display.

5. Click the **Setup** button to display properties and options settings for this printer.

6. Click **Cancel** to close Setup, then close the Chooser to return to the Apple desktop.

In Mac OS X, the Chooser is replaced by the Print Center. To view the printers:

1. Click the **Go** menu, and then click **Applications**.

2. Double-click the **Utilities** folder.

3. Click the **Print Center** icon.

4. What printers appear in the Printer List window? (If the window does not open automatically, select the Printers menu and click View Printer List.)

5. How can you set up a new printer via the Printer List window?

Project 6-3

The UNIX operating environment can be very different from any of the Windows implementations or Mac OS, or it can be fairly similar, depending on whether you are running the X-Window shell or GNOME in Red Hat Linux.

To find out the status of printers in Red Hat Linux 7.x (and many other UNIX systems):

1. Log on as root.

2. At the command line or in a terminal window, type **lpc status all**.

3. The names of connected printers and whether or not they are enabled are displayed.

Project 6-4

Working on a UNIX computer, there will be times that you must determine what printers are available. In this project, you'll learn how to determine the printer setup in Red Hat Linux 7.x, using the GNOME interface.

To find out what printers are installed in Red Hat Linux 7.x, using the GNOME interface:

1. Type **printtool** from the GNOME terminal window, and press **Enter**. The list of printers appears in the printtool window. (You may need to enter the root account password.)

2. Click the **Close** box to close printtool.

Another way to run printtool in the GNOME interface is to click the Main Menu (foot) icon, point to Programs, point to System, and click Printer Configuration (see next project).

Project 6-5

In this project, you add a local printer to Red Hat Linux 7.2 by using the printtool utility, called *printconf*, via the GNOME Printer Configuration interface. You'll need root privileges before you start. Also, you should have a printer already connected to a parallel or USB port.

To add a printer to Red Hat Linux 7.2:

1. Log on as root.

2. Click the **Main** Menu (foot), point to **Programs**, point to **System**, and click **Printer Configuration**.

3. Click **New**.

4. Click **Next** on the Add a New Print Queue screen.

5. In the Queue Name box enter your initials plus "printer," such as **MWPrinter**.

6. Click the radio button for **Local Printer**. Notice that you can also use this screen to specify a remote printer (network printer) on another UNIX computer, a Windows computer, a Novell server, or a printer attached to a JetDirect network print server (see Figure 6-16).

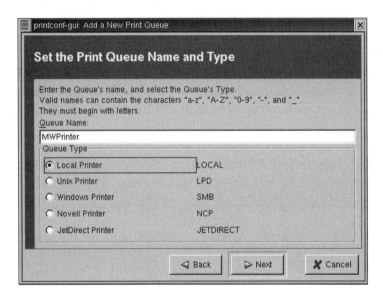

Figure 6-16   Selecting a queue name and queue type

7. Click **Next**.

8. The *printconf* program detects the printer that is attached to the computer. (If it does not detect the printer, click **Custom Device** and enter the device name. For example, specify /dev/lp0 if you are setting up a parallel printer or /dev/usblp0 for a USB printer. Click **OK**.)

9. Click **Next**.

10. On the Select a Printer Driver screen, you install the printer driver. If *printconf* automatically detected your printer in Step 8, it will highlight that printer and correct printer driver. If it did not automatically detect the printer, select the printer driver for your printer by clicking the arrow next to the printer in the list. Under the printer, you'll next see a list of drivers. Ask you instructor about which driver to use (or select the first one on the list, which is highlighted by default).

11. Click **Next**.

12. Click **Finish**.

13. In the printconf-gui screen, click **Apply** to save the changes you have made. Click **OK** in the information box.

14. Click **Test** to print a test page.

15. Select the type of test page that you want to print. For example, if you have a non-postscript printer, select **ASCII Text Testpage** or if you have a postscript printer select **A4 PostScript Testpage**.

16. Click **OK** in the information box.

17. Examine the test page to verify your printer setup.

18. Close the printconf-gui screen.

Project 6-6

One interesting facet of the operating system hardware interface is the way various devices communicate with the operating system. How detailed this communication is depends to some extent on the operating system, but mainly is a factor of the hardware and custom software driver designs.

To experiment with the messaging that occurs between your operating system and your printer:

1. Make sure your printer hardware is connected to your computer and that the printer is turned on.

2. Load a software application that can print to the connected printer. It doesn't matter much which application: word processor, spreadsheet, presentation package, etc.

3. Remove all paper from the printer and send a document to the printer. Note the error message you receive. Replace the paper. Does the printer begin printing without user interaction on the computer?

4. Send a large print job to the printer and quickly unplug the printer cable before the print buffer can be transferred to the printer. Does your application happily print to nothing, or does it recognize that no printer is physically attached to the system?

5. Open an MS-DOS window if you are working in Windows. Use the *copy* command to copy a text file to the printer (*copy filename lpt1*). Does the MS-DOS window communicate properly to the printer?

6. Open an application that will support a large graphics image such as a photograph. Send a photograph to the printer. Does it have enough memory to process the print job? If not, what error message do you see when the printer runs out of memory?

Project 6-7

Many of us never view or change the configuration settings for our computer's mouse. However, whether you are using a standard mouse or an extended version, such as a wheel mouse, configuration software is readily available to you.

To view or change your basic mouse settings:

1. Click **Start** on the taskbar.

2. Point to **Settings**.

3. Click **Control Panel**.

4. Double-click the **Mouse** icon to open the Mouse dialog box.

5. View or change available mouse settings, as desired.

6. Cancel the Mouse dialog box, and close all open windows.

Project 6-8

Many of us never view or change the configuration settings for our computer's keyboard. However, whether you are using a standard keyboard or an enhanced version, such as a Microsoft Natural Keyboard, configuration software is readily available to you.

To view basic keyboard configuration settings:

1. Click **Start** on the taskbar.

2. Point to **Settings**.

3. Click **Control Panel**.

4. Double-click the **Keyboard** icon to open the Keyboard dialog box.

5. View or change available keyboard settings, as desired.

6. Cancel the Keyboard dialog box, and close all open windows.

Project 6-9

Does your computer include any specialty input hardware? You can physically view the back of your computer to find special devices, or you can check the drivers installed on your system to get a line on what's in there.

To review installed devices:

1. Click **Start** on the taskbar.

2. Point to **Settings**.

3. Choose **Control Panel**.

4. Double-click the **System** icon to open the System dialog box.

5. Click the **Device Manager** tab to display installed devices (see Figure 6-17).

6. If necessary, click the plus sign to display additional information about any entry.

7. Select an entry and click **Properties** to display detailed information about any entry in this list.

8. Cancel the Device Manager dialog box, and close all open windows.

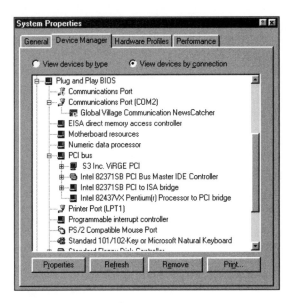

Figure 6-17   Windows 98 Device Manager

Project 6-10

Mouse hardware is fairly standard, even between very inexpensive models and high-end devices. For the most part the mouse just works. However, it does require periodic cleaning.

To view basic mouse hardware design and clean mechanical parts:

1. Turn over the mouse.

2. Notice the plastic cover over the mouse ball. In most cases, it is marked with clockwise and counterclockwise arrows.

3. Apply pressure on the cover in the direction the counterclockwise arrow points. The cover should slide a fraction of an inch to enable you to remove it.

4. Set the cover aside.

5. Place your hand over the bottom of the mouse and turn over the mouse. The mouse ball will fall into your hand. Set the ball aside.

6. Notice the internal components. You should see two horizontal rollers. In cheaper mice these are plastic. More expensive mice use stainless steel rollers. These connect to potentiometers that send mouse movement information to your operating system. A third roller is a tensioning device that helps keep the ball in place and rolling smoothly.

7. Is there any lint, hair, or other residue on any of these rollers? If so, that could explain why you have had difficulty positioning the mouse pointer accurately.

8. Use a soft rag or tissue and a little rubbing alcohol to clean the rollers.

9. Clean the ball by rubbing it with a soft cloth (rubbing the ball on your clothing works well as long as you don't use a sweater or other garment that might produce lint).

10. Turn over the mouse and drop the ball into the hole.

11. Set the cover in place, rotate it clockwise until it clicks, and reposition the mouse on its pad or your desktop.

Project 6-11

You can tell a lot about your system from the System Properties dialog box, as shown in Hands-on Project 6-9. There also are specialty utilities to let you view and configure other devices, such as multimedia.

To view and configure multimedia devices on your computer:

1. Click **Start** on the taskbar.

2. Point to **Settings**.

3. Click **Control Panel**.

4. Double-click the **Multimedia** icon to open the Multimedia Properties dialog box.

5. Click any of the tabs to view audio, video, and other settings.

6. To inspect available drivers and settings, click the **Devices** tab (see Figure 6-18).

7. Click **Cancel** or **OK** to close the dialog box. Close the Control Panel window.

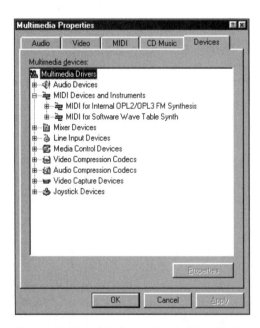

Figure 6-18   Windows 98 Multimedia Properties dialog box

Project 6-12

Windows 98 includes some useful system-level utilities that can help you find out more about your hard drive.

To use the Windows 98 System Information utility to study your hard drive configuration:

1. Click **Start**, point to **Programs**, point to **Accessories**, and point to **System Tools**.

2. Click **System Information**. The Microsoft System Information dialog box opens, as shown in Figure 6-19.

6

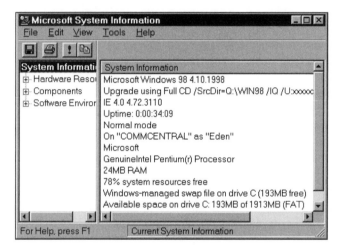

Figure 6-19   Microsoft System Information dialog box

3. Note the size of your hard drive and the amount of space used at the bottom of the first screen of System Information.

4. Use **File**, **Exit** from the menu to close this dialog box, and return to your desktop.

CASE PROJECTS

Case Project One

As MIS manager for a small business network, you are asked to research possible expansion of your network printer hardware. You currently support 10-15 users with a single, high-speed laser printer capable of 16 pages per minute. This printer works well for general business printing, but your firm is broadening its in-house technical capability to include advertising layout and Web page development. The Public Relations Department additionally wants to begin publishing a newsletter for your corporate clients, which will require some color printing capabilities.

From the information covered in this chapter, answer the following questions about your pending network printing upgrade:

1. Assuming you leave the existing laser printer in place, what additional shared printer might you install to expand general-purpose business printing capabilities?

2. Given that quality color printing is important—more important than speed for this application—what color printing solution might you suggest?

3. The Accounting Department needs a dedicated printer shared among three users to print private information such as financial reports and payroll checks. What type of printer might you suggest here?

4. That sounds like three additional printers at least. Can you estimate a budget for this network expansion?

Case Project Two

Your company's computer collection consists of a Macintosh for the Graphics Department, five PCs for Management and Accounting, and a UNIX-based Web and mail server to handle your e-mail and Internet presence needs.

All computers are equipped with standard input devices at this time. Based on the material covered in this chapter, answer the following questions:

1. What additional input device or devices might you suggest for the Macintosh?

2. Are there any advantages to changing or adding to the input devices already available on the PC platforms?

3. Would you consider installing a digital pad on the UNIX server computer? Why or why not?

OPTIONAL CASE PROJECTS FOR TEAMS

Team Case One

Your team has been assembled to discuss to which computer to add digital photography capabilities in your company. Which one would you recommend? Why?

Team Case Two

Your company asks you to lead a team to explore the Removable Storage system in Windows 2000. Explore how to use this tool and provide a scenario showing how your company might benefit from using this system. This might include archiving old data and files off a disk after End-Of-Year closing for Accounting, or use a scenario of your choice.

7

MODEMS AND OTHER COMMUNICATIONS DEVICES

After reading this chapter and completing the exercises you will be able to:

♦ Understand analog modem architecture

♦ Use the classic Hayes AT modem command set with computer communications applications

♦ Understand digital modem architecture and the telecommunications methods used with digital modems

♦ Describe the basics of telephone line data communications

♦ Understand modem communications in different operating systems

Long gone are the days when most computer users sat at isolated computers. Communications from your computer to another user's computer, and from your computer to many other computers on a wide area network, such as the Internet, are an important part of computer use today. We communicate among computers to share data and conduct research. If your computer is part of a local area network, you may communicate directly over the network connection. If you have a stand-alone computer, you probably communicate with other computers and networks using a modem attached directly to your computer— forming the most basic and most used type of wide area network (WAN).

This chapter gives you a foundation in how the different modem technologies work. You'll begin by learning about analog modems, which are now built into most computers purchased for home or office use. You'll also learn how digital modems work in the context of high-speed communications services, including ISDN, DSL, and cable modems. Finally, you'll learn how modems interact with operating systems, and how to configure an operating system to use a modem to connect to the Internet.

ANALOG MODEM ARCHITECTURE

Computers handle information in a digital format. Everything the computer understands is stored as a series of 1s and 0s, represented as the presence of voltage (a digital 1) or the absence of voltage (a digital 0). Information is sent over a telephone line in analog format—the rising and falling sounds produced when you speak into the telephone handset. The computer doesn't recognize the telephone system's analog data, and the telephone system—at its most commonly used level—can't use the computer's digital data format. A **modem** is a piece of hardware and associated software that connects these two incompatible systems in a way that lets them communicate with each other.

 The analog modems that you are most likely to use work over regular copper or fiber-optic telephone lines. Typically these are called **plain old telephone service (POTS)** lines, which is the old term, or **public switched telephone network (PSTN)** lines, which is the modern term.

Modem Hardware Basics

A modem consists of three basic electronic hardware or software components: the data pump, the controller, and the UART. The name modem comes from a description of what the modem does. A modem is a *MOdulator-DEModulator*. It modulates digital signals from the computer into analog signals that can be sent over the phone line, and demodulates incoming analog signals back into digital signals the computer can understand. The component that performs basic modulation/demodulation is sometimes called a **data pump**. Basic modem concepts are illustrated in Figure 7-1.

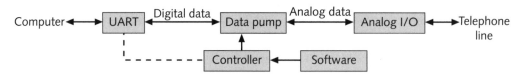

Figure 7-1   Basic modem concepts

The **controller** provides the modem's identity. This is where protocols for modulation (V.34, V.90, and V.92, for example), error correction (V.42), and data compression (V.42bis) are stored. A **protocol** is an established guideline that specifies how networked data, including data sent over a telephone network, is formatted into a transmission unit; how it is transmitted; and how it is interpreted at the receiving end. The controller also interprets **Attention (AT) commands**. After the modem receives AT, the modem interprets the next string of characters as a command instead of as data. The AT command set communicates configuration and operational instructions to the modem. More detailed information about communicating with modems using AT commands is provided later in this chapter.

Modem protocols define some of the basic operational parameters of your modem, and determine how compatible it is with other modems with which it communicates. Modem protocol standards are established by the **International Telecommunications Union (ITU)** and compose the ITU–T standards. The latest standards, V.90 and V.92, define a 56,000 bits per second (56 Kbps) communications protocol. These are by far the most popular choices for data communications requirements such as browsing the World Wide Web. (For more information about modem speed and testing your modem's performance, see Hands-on Projects 7-1, 7-2, and 7-3 at the end of this chapter.) Modem protocols are not presented in detail in this chapter, but it is important for you to understand the basics of modem protocols, and how their development has paralleled the development of modem technology. Historically, modem protocols have been a determining factor in modem speed and compatibility. Also, modems are the basis of the simplest and most commonly used wide area networks (WANs)—connecting a personal computer to the Internet, or to other computers through modems at both ends, joined by a telecommunications line. Table 7-1 presents the common standards and protocols that you may see as you read and learn about modems. The V.90 and V.92 standards popular today generally incorporate most of the earlier technologies and protocols listed in the table.

Even though modem technology currently seems stopped at the 56 kilobits per second (Kbps) standard used by the V.90 and V.92 standards, theoretically, PSTN can support up to 64 Kbps for standard analog modem communications.

Sometimes modems, particularly older modems, will not communicate because of how their settings are configured. For example, a 2400/4800 bps V.27ter modem cannot establish communications with a 36.6 Kbps V.42 modem if the 36.6 Kbps modem is not set to negotiate down to a slower speed. Also, when telephone lines are very noisy, some V.42bis modems attempt to step down to MNP-5, a proprietary version of data compression. If one of the communicating modems does not have MNP-5 compression capability (which is used concurrently with MNP-4 error detection), they may not be able to establish a link-up because V.42 error control does not work with MNP-5 data compression. Also, a modem using proprietary MNP-4 error control may not work with another modem using V.42 compression. Keep these precautions in mind when you set up network modems and work with users to solve modem communication problems—make sure that the modem standards used by a modem at one end are compatible with the modem standards used by a modem at the other end.

Table 7-1 Modem Standards and Protocols

ITU-T Modem Standard	Description
V.21	300 bps data transmission for dial-up lines
V.22	1200 bps data transmission for dial-up and leased lines
V.22bis	2400 bps data transmission for dial-up lines
V.23	600/1200 bps data transmission for dial-up and leased lines
V.26	2400 bps data transmission for leased lines
V.26bis	1200/2400 bps data transmission for dial-up lines
V.26ter	2400 bps data transmission for dial-up and leased lines
V.27	4800 bps data transmission on leased lines
V.27bis	2400/4800 bps data transmission on leased lines
V.27ter	2400/4800 bps data transmission on dial-up lines
V.29	9600 bps data transmission on leased lines
V.32	9600 bps data transmission on dial-up lines
V.32bis	14.4 Kbps data transmission on dial-up lines using synchronous communications
V.33	14.4 Kbps data transmission on leased lines
V.34	28.8 Kbps data transmission on dial-up lines with the ability to drop to slower speeds when there are line problems
V.34 (new)	Enhancement of the previous V.34 standard to reach 33.6 Kbps
V.35	48 Kbps data transmission on leased lines
V.42	Error detection and correction on noisy telephone lines
V.42bis	4:1 data compression for high-capacity transfer
V.90	56 Kbps data transmission on dial-up lines (actually is 33.6 Kbps upstream from the modem to the remote site and 56 Kbps downstream from the remote site to the modem)
V.92	56 Kbps data transmission (offering enhanced upstream transmissions at 48 Kbps)—also can temporarily stop data transmissions to take a voice communication

When a computer is connected to a modem, the data transfer speed is the **data terminal equipment (DTE)** communications rate. A desktop computer with a modem is an example of a DTE because it prepares data to be transmitted. The modem is called the **data communications equipment (DCE)** and its speed is the DCE communications rate. The computer's port setup for the modem (DTE rate) should be the same or higher than the DCE rate of the modem. For example, if you have a 56 Kbps modem, select a maximum port speed of 57.6 Kbps (the closest setting) in Windows 2000 or XP when you configure the computer for that modem. (Try Hands-on Project 7-1).

When two modems communicate over a telephone line, such as the modem on a remote workstation communicating with a modem on a network, they may not truly communicate at the maximum speed for both modems. For example, two V.90 modems may negotiate to transmit at 33.6 Kbps instead of 56 Kbps because of noise detected on the line. (Try Hands-on Projects 7-2, 7-3, and 7-6 to determine the actual transmission rate of a modem.)

Computer modems can be classified in several ways. One distinction is whether the modem is located inside the computer (an internal modem) or outside the computer (an external modem). Internal modems usually are built on expansion cards that plug into the computer's expansion bus, most commonly the PCI bus. They may also be part of the computer's main circuit board.

External modems are circuit boards that are placed inside a stand-alone case with its own power supply. External modems usually plug into the computer via a serial port or, with newer modems, the USB port. An external USB modem is an excellent choice for several reasons. For one thing, the USB port is a high-speed port that can supply power to peripheral devices, obviating the need for external power supplies or power "bricks." USB devices are self configuring. When you plug in a USB modem, the operating system recognizes the presence of the new device and automatically launches a configuration utility. In general, external modems are preferable to internal modems because they include status lights that tell you when the modem is connected, what state it is in, and whether data is being transferred. In addition, an external modem is a universal device that you can use with Windows, Mac OS, or UNIX.

The **UART** (pronounced "you art") is an electronic chip, the **Universal Asynchronous Receiver-Transmitter**. The UART converts data from the computer into data that can be sent to serial ports. The UART reads in one byte of data at the computer's bus speed, adds a start bit at the beginning, a stop bit at the end, generates an interrupt, and feeds the bits to the serial port at a slow speed that won't overwhelm the peripheral (a modem in this case, but the same system applies to other serial devices). External modems use whatever UART is attached to the serial port. Internal modems use their own UART, bypassing the computer's serial I/O port. (In Figure 7-1, you can see this internal UART concept. An external modem has serial port hardware and uses the computer's internal UART.)

Computers communicate with external serial devices in two basic modes: synchronous and asynchronous. These terms refer to the method used to keep the data streams on the local and remote devices aligned so proper data transfer can occur. Asynchronous communication is the most common method for today's desktop computers. Asynchronous communication uses fairly accurate clocks (timers) at both ends of the connection to synchronize data. The transmitting device sends a start bit, which is captured by the receiving device. The next eight bits are assumed to be data, and the final two bits are stop bits. The start and stop bits help the receiving device interpret data and stay in sync.

Synchronous communication, on the other hand, sends information in blocks (frames) of data that include embedded clock signals. Alternately, the clock data can be sent over a separate, dedicated clock line that is part of the connection. Synchronous data transfer usually is more efficient, but it requires more processing at both ends of the link. Synchronous communication is normally used to send data over very high quality, digital lines.

Software-Based Modems

All modems need the functions of the data pump, controller, and UART. However, some modems do not implement these functions in hardware. Software-based modems (often referred to as **Winmodems**, after the trademarked name of 3Com/U.S. Robotics popular models) replace one or more of these components with software.

The 3Com (formerly U.S. Robotics) Winmodem is a controllerless modem that retains a hardware data pump (a **Digital Signal Processor (DSP)** in the case of the 3Com Winmodem), but implements the controller functions in software. So-called **Host Signal Processor (HSP)** modems dispense with the controller and data pump hardware entirely. Instead of using their own signal processors, HSP modems use the host's central processing unit (such as the Pentium or PowerPC), along with special software, to handle the same jobs.

There is a third kind of modem unique to the Apple Centris and Quadra AV (Audio Visual) models. Apple's Geoport Telecom Adapter for these computers uses the AV computer's onboard DSP, rather than the computer's CPU, to perform modem functions. This DSP is also used for speech recognition, so you can conduct speech recognition and modem operations with these computers at the same time. The Geoport Telecom Adapter for the PowerPC models was a conventional HSP modem.

One disadvantage of implementing modem functions with software rather than hardware is that such software takes up memory and processor cycles, although these cycles are now quite inexpensive. The biggest disadvantage of software-based modems is their dependence on particular operating systems. A 3Com Winmodem won't work on a Mac, or even on a PC running Linux or OS/2, and a Geoport Telecom Adapter won't work on a PC operating system. In addition, many communications software packages simply aren't compatible with the Winmodem design because they expect to find a serial port and modem hardware at traditional locations, while many software modem designs use nonstandard address locations. Newer communications software can find such address locations, but older software won't always work properly with software-based modems.

In contrast, any external Hayes-compatible modem (hardware-based) can be used on virtually any computer made in the past 20 years. All that is required is a serial port on the computer that's compatible with the modem's serial port, and communications software that's capable of sending compatible commands through the computer's serial port to the modem, and receiving feedback and data from the modem.

The advantages of using a software modem are cost savings and upgradeability. By eliminating physical parts, the unit cost falls dramatically. In a completely software-based modem, drastic upgrades are possible by rewriting the software. In addition, many multimedia features, such as voice mail or speakerphones, are easier to implement in a software-based modem design.

Hayes AT Command Set

In the 1970s, modems were sold for specific purposes—such as connecting a particular remote dumb terminal (monitor and keyboard with no CPU) to a specific mainframe computer—and commanded high prices. Dennis Hayes devised a way to create a general-purpose modem that could be configured using a command language he invented, the **Hayes command** language, also called **Attention** (AT) **commands**. When a modem is said to be Hayes-compatible, it simply means that the modem supports all or part of the Hayes AT command set. Most chipset vendors support the standard Hayes command set and supplement it with additional commands.

Dennis Hayes commands begin with the letters AT, which tells the modem to interpret the next character string as a command. A Hayes-compatible modem is equipped with software that acts as a command interpreter. The command interpreter ignores spaces and dashes (which people are accustomed to using to separate area codes, exchanges, and extensions). Table 7-2 summarizes many commonly used AT commands. The commands are not case sensitive and can be issued in uppercase or lowercase. Although many modem manufacturers extend the basic AT command set or use proprietary commands, most modern modems still respond to the basic commands in the traditional ways. This command set is used extensively to set up and control modems so that they are compatible with a variety of host hardware.

Table 7-2   AT Command Set Summary

AT Command	Description
DT and DP	Dial the phone number that follows. DT is for touchtone phones. DP is for pulse dial phones. A complete touchtone dialing sequence would be: ATDT 555-5555 (the phone number you wish to dial).
, (comma)	Causes a delay before executing the next command. Often used to make sure the phone switch has recovered before dialing, as when dialing a 9 to get an outside line: ATDT 9,555-5555
W	Wait for the dial tone before dialing: ATDT 9W555-5555
+++	Escape from online mode into command mode. In command mode, AT commands can be sent to the modem.
H	Hang up. A typical hang-up sequence is +++ ATH.
O	Go from command mode back to online mode. This is the only occurrence of the letter "o" in the Hayes AT command set. All other occurrences of o-like shapes are zeroes.
S0=n	Answer incoming calls after n rings. Setting n to zero tells the modem not to answer incoming calls.
Mn	Turn modem speaker off (n=0) or on (n=1).
Ln	Set speaker volume for values of n equal to 0 (lowest volume), 1 or 2 (medium volume), or 3 (highest volume).
&Fn	Set modem to the default settings from the factory.
Z	Reset modem to defaults.

DIGITAL MODEMS

The name digital modem is a misnomer because there is no actual modulation or demodulation (of analog signals), but the usage persists. A digital modem performs the same basic function as an analog modem: it moves data out of a computer, across a telephone line, and into another computer at a remote location. The major difference is that the data is digital from start to finish. **Digital modems** are digital devices that use digital transmission media. Digital modems can be network devices (connected directly to the network) or serial devices (connected to the serial port). When connecting to TCP/IP networks, they connect via Point-to-Point Protocol (PPP), which is a popular communications protocol for Internet communications (see Chapter 8).

Today there are three popular telecommunications or cable networks, which each use different types of digital communications and digital modems:

- ISDN
- Cable networks
- DSL

ISDN

Integrated Services Digital Network (ISDN) uses a digital telephone line for high-speed computer communications, videoconferencing, Internet connections, and so on. This technology has been around for nearly 20 years, but only with the rise in Internet usage and videoconferencing has it gained much market penetration. ISDN uses standard copper telephone line pairs with digital equipment on either end of the connection to encode and transmit the information—an ISDN router (to route the transmission to the right place) and **terminal adapter (TA)**, a type of digital modem.

ISDN routers and TAs typically include analog telephone jacks so you can plug in a conventional telephone or modem for use over the digital line. With most ISDN hardware, you connect to a single telephone line copper pair (the same kind of wire that brings telephone service into your home or office consisting of two wires twisted together), but you get separate channels for computer data and analog telephone lines. You can use one analog line and one data line simultaneously, or two digital lines, or two analog lines.

Two interfaces are supported in ISDN: basic rate interface and primary rate interface. The **basic rate interface (BRI)** has an aggregate data rate of 144 Kbps. The BRI consists of three channels: two are 64 Kbps Bearer (B) channels for data, voice, and graphics transmissions; and the third is a 16 Kbps Delta (D, sometimes called Demand) channel used for communications signaling, packet switching, and credit card verification. The primary function of a D channel is for ISDN call setup and tear down for starting and stopping a communication session. BRI is used for videoconferencing, Internet connectivity, and high-speed connectivity for telecommuters and home offices. Multiple BRI channels can be "bonded" together for even faster communications. For example, one BRI line with two 64 Kbps channels can be bonded to achieve a 128 Kbps connection for actual data throughput. With the 16 Kbps D channel added, plus 48 Kbps for maintenance and synchronization, the total rate is 192 Kbps. Another example is the bonding of three BRI lines consisting of six 64 Kbps channels for an aggregate data throughput speed of 384 Kbps.

 Windows NT, 2000, XP, and many UNIX systems support bonding ISDN lines using Multilink PPP. Also, if you subscribe to BRI ISDN, look for telecommunications companies to soon implement download capabilities through the D channel, thus creating an additional 16 Kbps for downstream communications.

The **primary rate interface (PRI)** sports faster data rates, with an aggregate of switched bandwidth equal to 1.544 Mbps. In the United States and Japan, PRI consists of twenty-three 64 Kbps B channels and one 64 Kbps D channel for signaling communications and packet switching (plus 8 Kbps for maintenance). European PRI ISDN is thirty 64 Kbps channels and one 64 Kbps signaling or packet-switching channel. The PRI is used for LAN-to-LAN connectivity, ISP sites, videoconferencing, and corporate sites that support telecommuters who use ISDN.

7

 A third type of ISDN is broadband or B-ISDN, which currently supports 1.5 Mbps, but theoretically has a limit of 622 Mbps.

ISDN is generally more expensive than DSL and cable modems, which are discussed in the next sections. It is, however, a good alternative for those who need faster access than asynchronous modems can provide, particularly in areas that do not have DSL or cable modem access. Also, ISDN can be very economical for small businesses because it is possible to connect multiple digital devices (usually up to eight) to one incoming line, such as several digital telephones, computers, and faxes.

Cable Modems

In some areas, cable TV providers also offer data services to businesses and homes. A **cable modem** is used to attach to cable data services. This type of modem is usually an external device that plugs into a USB port or network interface card in your computer, and is connected to the coaxial cable used for the cable TV system. The cable modem communicates using upstream and downstream frequencies (channels) that are already allocated by the cable service. The upstream frequency is used to transmit the outgoing signal over a spectrum (contiguous range) of frequencies that carry data, sound, and TV signals. The downstream frequency is used to receive signals, and is also blended with other data, sound, and TV downstream signals. Depending on the modem, upstream and downstream data rates may or may not be the same. For example, one vendor's modem provides a 30 Mbps maximum upstream rate and a 15 Mbps maximum downstream rate. Another vendor offers a modem that has 10 Mbps for both the upstream and downstream rates. However, even though cable modems are built for high speeds, at this writing, a single modem user is likely to have access (bandwidth) in the range of 256 Kbps to about 3 Mbps. The actual speed is partially dependent on how many of your neighbors are using their cable modems at the same time because one cable run that connects a group of subscribers to the cable hub can handle a maximum of 27 Mbps of bandwidth. Also, a cable service provider may establish a limit on your bandwidth (how fast you can transmit and receive) so that the provider can give more users access to the cable network.

Cable modems are manufactured as either internal or external devices. When you purchase an internal device, it looks similar to a modem card that fits in a PCI expansion slot in your computer. External cable modems are more common, and typically connect to your computer in one of two ways. One way is to connect the cable modem directly to a conventional network interface card that is already in your computer, using twisted-pair wire (similar to telephone wire), an RJ45 connector, and Ethernet communications (see Chapter 8). The second type of cable modem connects directly to a USB port in your computer. Once the cable modem is installed in the computer, the other end is connected to broadband coaxial wire used for cable TV communications.

The advantage of cable modem communications is that currently unallocated bandwidth can be allocated to you, even for a millisecond or two, when you are downloading a large file, for example. This means that even when the cable is busy because you and your neighbors are all using TV, radio, or computer communications, the system is always dynamically allocating unused cable bandwidth. If your neighbor is connected via her cable modem, but is not sending or receiving, then you are allocated some of her bandwidth when you are downloading a file, for example.

 Because you share the same cable with your neighbors, it is possible for a knowledgeable user to view or access the files on your computer. For this reason, if you use a cable modem, it is vital that you protect your files and access to the computer through file security and personal firewalls. Windows XP, for example, enables you to set up a personal firewall, called the Internet Connection Firewall (ICF), via built-in software functionality. For even more security help, contact Microsoft to obtain its Security Tool Kit.

DSL Modems

Another high-speed digital data communications service that is challenging ISDN and cable modems is **Digital Subscriber Line (DSL)**. DSL is a digital technology that works over copper wire that already goes into most residences and businesses for telephone services (newer forms of DSL can be used over fiber-optic telephone lines). To use DSL, you must install an intelligent adapter in your computer, which is to be connected to the DSL network (see Figure 7-2). The adapter can be a card similar in appearance to a modem, but that is fully digital, which means it does not convert the DTE's (computer or network devices) digital signal to analog, but instead sends a digital signal over the telephone wire. Two pairs of wires are connected to the adapter and then out to the telephone pole.

Communication over the copper wire is simplex, which means that one pair is used for outgoing transmissions, and the other pair for incoming transmissions, thus creating an upstream channel to the telecommunications company (**telco**) and a downstream channel to the user. The maximum upstream transmission rate is 2.3 Mbps, while downstream communications can reach 60 Mbps. Also, the maximum distance from user to telco without a repeater (to amplify and extend the distance of the signal) is 5.5 kilometers (3.4 miles, which is similar to ISDN).

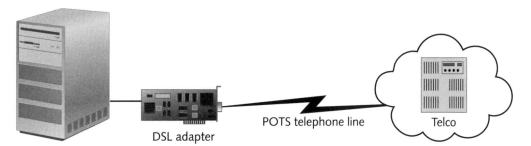

POTS telephone line

DSL adapter

Telco

Figure 7-2   Connecting to DSL

The actual transmission rate is determined by several factors, including the type of DSL service used, the condition of the cable, the distance to the telco, and the bus speed in the user's computer.

Like a cable modem, a DSL adapter offers high-speed data transmissions, but it also has some advantages over a cable modem. For example, a cable modem uses a line shared by other users, which means its signal can be trapped and read by another user. A DSL line is dedicated to a single user, which means that there is less likelihood that the signal can be tapped without the telco being alerted. Also, the DSL user employs the full bandwidth of his or her line, in contrast to the cable modem user who shares bandwidth with others.

On networks, DSL is connected by means of a combined DSL adapter and router. A **router** is a device that can be used to direct network traffic and create a firewall, so that only authorized users can access network services. This type of connection enables multiple users to access one DSL line, and it protects the network from intruders over the DSL line. Usually this type of connection comes with management software that enables you to monitor the link and perform diagnostics, such as Cisco's Commander software, as shown in Figure 7-3.

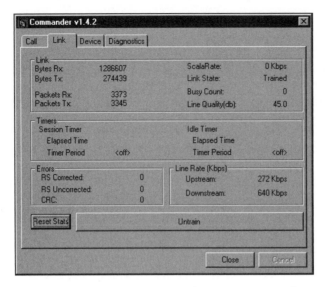

Figure 7-3   DSL monitoring and management software

There are five types of DSL services:

- Asymmetric Digital Subscriber Line (ADSL)
- Rate Adaptive Digital Subscriber Line (RADSL)
- High Bit-Rate Digital Subscriber Line (HDSL)
- Very High Bit-Rate Digital Subscriber Line (VDSL)
- Symmetric Digital Subscriber Line (SDSL)

ADSL is the most commonly used version of DSL. Aside from traditional data and multimedia applications, ADSL also is well suited for interactive multimedia and distance learning. Before transmitting data, ADSL checks the telephone line for noise and error conditions in a process called forward error correction. When it was first established, ADSL upstream transmissions were 64 Kbps, and downstream transmissions were 1.544 Mbps. At the time of this writing, those transmission rates are 576–640 Kbps for upstream, and up to 6 Mbps for downstream. ADSL also can use a third communications channel for 4 kHz voice transmissions that occur at the same time as data transmission—which means that the user can be on the Internet and the telephone at the same time.

 When you employ ADSL for simultaneous computer and telephone use, it is necessary to place an inexpensive filtering device between the ADSL line that comes in from the telco and the telephone. The filter is used to block line noise that can diminish telephone conversations. However, do not place the filter between the incoming line and the DSL digital modem.

Originally developed for on-demand movie transmissions, **RADSL** applies ADSL technology, but enables the transmission rate to vary depending on whether the communication is data, multimedia, or voice. There are two ways that the transmission rate can be established.

One is by the telco setting a specific rate per each customer line based on the anticipated use of the line. Another is for the telco to enable the rate to automatically adjust to the demand on the line. RADSL is an advantage to customers because they pay only for the amount of bandwidth they need, and it helps the telco by allowing it to allocate unused bandwidth for other customers. Another advantage of RADSL is that line length can be greater in situations where not all of the bandwidth is used, so it can accommodate customers who are more than 5.5 kilometers from the telco. The downstream transmission can be up to 7 Mbps, and the upstream transmission up to 1 Mbps.

Originally, **HDSL** was designed for full-duplex communications over two pairs of copper telephone wires at a sending and receiving rate of up to 1.544 Mbps for distances up to 3.6 kilometers (2.25 miles). Another HDSL implementation has been created to use one of the two pairs of telephone wires, but with a full-duplex transmission rate of 768 Kbps. One limitation is that HDSL does not support voice communications as well as ADSL and RADSL, in part because it requires the installation of specialized converters and adapters for voice transmission. The most significant advantage of HDSL is that it is particularly useful for businesses needing to join local area networks.

7

VDSL is intended as an alternative to networking technologies that use coaxial or fiber-optic cable. The VDSL downstream speed is 51–55 Mbps and upstream is 1.6–2.3 Mbps. Although it offers very high bandwidth, VDSL's range, or maximum distance from the telco, is relatively short at 300–1800 meters (980–5900 feet), which limits how it can be applied. VDSL works in a fashion similar to RADSL in that bandwidth can be automatically allocated to meet the existing demand, and it is similar to ADSL because it creates multiple channels over the twisted-pair wires, and enables voice transmission at the same time as data.

SDSL is similar to ADSL, but it allocates the same bandwidth for both upstream and downstream transmissions at 384 Kbps. SDSL is particularly useful for videoconferencing and interactive learning because of the symmetrical bandwidth transmissions. Table 7-3 provides a summary of the DSL technologies.

Table 7-3   DSL Technologies

DSL Technology	Upstream Data Transmission Rate	Downstream Data Transmission Rate
Asymmetric Digital Subscriber Line (ADSL)	576 – 640 Kbps	Up to 6 Mbps
Rate Adaptive Asymmetric Digital Subscriber Line (RADSL)	Up to 1 Mbps	Up to 7 Mbps
High Bit-Rate Digital Subscriber Line (HDSL)	Up to 1.544 Mbps	Up to 1.544 Mbps
Very High Bit-Rate Digital Subscriber Line (VDSL)	1.6 – 2.3 Mbps	51 – 55 Mbps
Symmetric Digital Subscriber Line (SDSL)	384 Kbps	384 Kbps

DATA COMMUNICATIONS OVER PHONE LINES

When two modems communicate, they must have a way to halt and resume the flow of data. Otherwise, data buffers would fill and then overflow, resulting in lost data. The buffers are prevented from getting too full through the use of **flow control**, which is accomplished using software or hardware.

Software Flow Control

A popular software flow control method from the early days of modems is called **Xon-Xoff.** Xon-Xoff uses the Ctrl+S character (ASCII 19) to stop the flow of data (Xoff), and Ctrl+Q (ASCII 17) to resume (Xon). When the receiving computer needs time to process the data in the buffers, perform disk I/O, and so on, it can send an Xoff request to the remote modem to stop the flow of data. Once it processes the data in its buffer, it can send an Xon to begin receiving data again. This receive, stop, resume process continues repeatedly throughout the data transfer or communications session.

In the days before online services had graphical user interfaces, you could manually type Ctrl+Q and Ctrl+S from the keyboard to issue the Xon-Xoff control signals to suspend and resume the flow of on-screen text. This was a common technique for users of dumb terminals connected to central computers as well. Some software in those days wasn't sophisticated enough to manage the dumb terminal screens automatically. Also, communications software running on early PCs or Macs simply emulated a dumb terminal to access text-based host computers.

One problem with Xon-Xoff flow control is that the data being transferred may contain Ctrl+S or Ctrl+Q characters, which can interrupt the data transfer. Another problem is that Xon-Xoff is a form of signaling that uses the bandwidth of the data stream to pass data about the condition of the data stream. This is inefficient because it reduces the amount of user data that can move over the phone line.

Hardware Flow Control

With the advent of faster modems, the industry moved to hardware flow control. Hardware flow control halts and resumes the movement of data by changing the voltage on specific pins in the serial interface. Controlling data flow with hardware eliminates the problem of the modem confusing data with control signals. If you are given a choice in configuring your modem for data communications, always use hardware flow control instead of Xon-Xoff. It is more reliable and permits faster modem performance. Figure 7-4 demonstrates the flow control options for a modem set up in Windows XP.

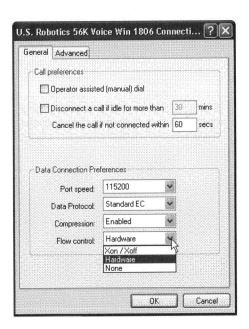

Figure 7-4   Flow control options

Error Correction

Sometimes errors are introduced into the data stream by the telephone lines or other equipment. Modems must check for these errors and resend bad blocks of data to ensure that the receiving modem gets the information exactly as it was transmitted.

Modems transfer bits (ones or zeroes) over the phone line. Three possible errors can occur: a bit can be lost, an extraneous bit can be introduced, or a bit can be flipped (changed from zero to one or from one to zero). The most basic form of error correction involves the start and stop bits. Each eight-bit byte is framed by a **start bit** at the beginning and a **stop bit** at the end (see Figure 7-5).

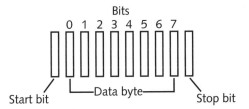

Figure 7-5   Data byte framing with start and stop bits

The start and stop bits always have the same value. If a bit is added or lost, the start and stop bits won't be in the right place. The receiving modem will notice this and request that the sending modem resend that block of data. The modem's UART adds start and stop bits to outgoing data, and strips them from incoming data.

There are always eight bits between the start and stop bit, even when communicating with systems that only require seven bits. That makes it possible to use the eighth bit for another form of error checking: parity checking. **Parity checking** is a data verification process that ensures data integrity through a system of data bit comparisons between the sending and receiving computer.

Parity can be either even or odd (or none, if parity checking is turned off). For example, assume that the seven bits are 0100101. Adding up the 1s yields 3. If parity is set to even, then an extra parity bit with a 1 value must be added to this byte: 01001011. The resulting byte + parity combination has an even number of 1s. A data byte that already has an even number of 1s gets a parity bit of 0 to maintain the even parity check. The receiving computer checks the number of 1s in each byte to make sure they sum to an even value (2, 4, 6, 8, etc.). If they are odd, the computer knows that a bit flipped, or that some other error occurred.

Most modems use the ITU's V.42 standard to provide error checking. V.42 employs an error-checking protocol called **Link Access Protocol for Modems (LAPM)**, which is used to construct data into discrete frame-like units for transmission over communications lines. Each frame is given a sequence number, and is stuffed with a fixed or variable amount of data (depending on the V.42 version used) and a checksum. When the frame is received by the remote modem, that modem verifies the sequence number and checksum. If the data is received out of sequence, or the received checksum is in error, then the data is retransmitted. V.42 comes in three versions: (1) Full V.42 uses a variable-length frame, (2) V.42-Lite uses a fixed-length frame and less error-detection coding in modems and smaller buffer sizes, and (3) V.42-Relay is used over digital TCP/IP networks and some high-speed networks. All versions of V.42 enable the communicating modems to detect the presence of noise on the communication line, which can lead to errors. When noise is detected through using V.42, the communicating modems can decide to transmit at a slower speed so that fewer retransmissions are required.

Data Compression

In addition to error correction, modems usually compress the data they send. The concept behind data compression is fairly simple. Consider a screen displayed on your computer, for example. There may be several icons, an application dialog box, and a solid blue background. A data compression routine can study this picture and see that there's a lot of repetitive blue in the picture. The "compressed" representation of the screen shows a blue dot and a number that represents the number of times the blue dot is repeated. This takes a lot less room than physically representing each blue dot.

Other file types are compressed using this same—very simplified—approach. Text usually contains repetitive data, as does program code. Virtually any computer file can be compressed to reduce the overall size of the file that must be transmitted. If you are familiar with compression utilities, such as PKZIP or WINZIP for the PC, or StuffIt for the Mac, then you have seen the results of data compression. Compression can reduce the size of a TIF (Tagged Image Format) file, for example, by more than 90 percent. In fact, many people compress large files before sending the files to their modems.

 Using file compression software prior to sending your file is one way to speed modem communications, so that the modem does not have to perform the compression.

Modem data compression uses a similar technique to reduce the total number of data bytes that must be transferred over the connection, but it does it "on the fly," compressing the data while you send it. Data compression is one way in which modem manufacturers are able to achieve some of the high-speed data transfers expected today.

Compression is typically accomplished by using the V.42bis standard, which employs the Lempel-Ziv-Welch (LZW) compression method. This method works "on the fly" in two important respects. One is that it compresses data as it is sent, rather than waiting for all of the data to be prepared in a buffer, compressing it, and then sending it. The second is that it can detect when the data is already compressed, such as a file that is compressed using PKZIP—and it does not attempt to compress this type of file. In ideal conditions, data can be compressed on a 4:1 basis, which means that optimal data transmissions are up to four times faster when data can be fully compressed (as long as there are no transmission errors because of line noise).

MODEMS AND THE OPERATING SYSTEM

All operating systems include a communications component, such as for communicating through modems. In fact, data communications is one of the most basic operating system duties. Data moves along the internal computer bus from the CPU to memory, and to peripheral devices that may be connected to the internal bus or external ports. Part of the data communications software that is vital to the operating system was already presented in Chapter 6. Keep in mind that monitors, keyboards, storage devices, and modems all have a cumulative affect on the software components of the operating system that manage the flow of data through the serial and parallel ports—and they work with the features of vendor-specific drivers.

In the case of modems, the serial communication protocols are used to manage data flow through the serial port, and communications programs external to the operating system handle the specifics of communicating with a remote host. Also, programs supplied with the operating system (but that are actually external applications) dial a remote computer and establish a communication link using PPP or another protocol. For example, Microsoft Dial-Up Networking is supplied with Windows 95/98/NT, and can be accessed from the My Computer icon on the desktop (try Hands-on Projects 7-4, 7-5, and 7-6). In Windows 2000, there is a Network and Dial-up Connections tool that can be opened by clicking Start and pointing to Settings (see Figure 7-6), or by opening the

Control Panel (try Hands-on Project 7-7). To set up a modem combined with Internet access in Windows XP, click Start, click Control Panel, and click Network and Internet Connections (try Hands-on Project 7-8). One advantage of the Windows XP setup is that you can configure an "Internet Connection Firewall" to help discourage intruders from accessing your computer, and to filter possible viruses from coming in over the Internet, or through FTP downloads. You should certainly configure this option if you are connecting through a cable modem.

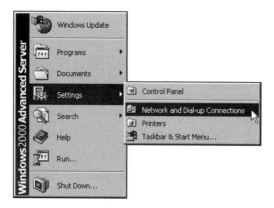

Figure 7-6   Opening the Windows 2000 Network and Dial-up Connections tool

In Windows 95/98 and Windows NT 4.0, you can set up modems individually by opening the Modems icon in the Control Panel—click Start, point to Settings, click Control Panel, and click Modems. In Windows 2000, open the Phone and Modem Options icon in the Control Panel by clicking Start, pointing to Settings, clicking Control Panel, and clicking Phone and Modem Options. And, in Windows XP, click Start, click Control Panel, open Printers and Other Hardware, and click Phone and Modem Options. Note that when you configure dial-up access in any of these systems, they will start the modem configuration process, if your modem has not already been configured by automatic PnP detection.

The Mac OS uses the PPP protocol and two major TCP/IP stacks—the MacTCP Control Panel and the TCP/IP Control Panel—to configure your computer for Internet or other TCP/IP remote host access. Older connection software and older Mac operating systems use MacTCP; newer versions of Mac OS, through version 9.x, use Open Transport or the TCP/IP Control Panel (try Hands-on Project 7-9). In Mac OS X, the Internet Connection software is introduced, which is accessed by opening the Apple menu, opening System Preferences, and clicking the Network icon (try Hands-on Project 7-10). You can use this tool to configure TCP/IP, PPP, and the modem.

Newer versions of Mac OS, through version 9.x, also have a built-in PPP Control Panel and Modems Control Panel. This is sometimes referred to as "PPP for Open Transport" because it requires Open Transport. Apple began including this software with Mac OS 7.6, and it is available as a separate download for System 7.5.3 and 7.5.5. Mac OS X includes TCP/IP and PPP tabs within the Network Control Panel as part of the System Preferences.

On systems that have Mac OS version 7.5.3 or 7.5.5, users can switch between Mac TCP and TCP/IP using Network Software Selector. Network Software Selector is easy to use. Double-click it, select either Classic Networking or Open Transport Networking, and restart the computer. Network Software Selector, if present, is located in Hard Drive:\Apple Extras\. If it is not present, you may need to reinstall the 7.5.3 or 7.5.5 update.

In UNIX, and in some configurations of Windows, a modem has two purposes. It can either be a dial-in device, or a dial-out device. When a modem is used as a dial-in device, it is treated like a terminal connected to the computer using a serial connection. Any such terminal is still referred to as a teletype, from the old paper-based terminals that were used many years ago. As such, the device port used for a modem is referred to as a TTY port, an abbreviation for teletype. To support dial-in connectivity on one of these TTYs, UNIX uses a **daemon** (an internal, automatically running program) called *getty*. There are numerous versions of *getty*; some simply answer a call and let a user use the TTY as if on a terminal. More advanced versions are capable of using fax modems, detecting when a fax is received on the modem line, and automatically invoking fax software.

Keep in mind that *getty* is very picky when it comes to what the modem will report, both in the form of control lines used and messages sent to the computer. In general, a modem should be used in factory settings with UNIX, with DCD signaling enabled, DTR set to drop the phone line, and DSR and DTS set to normal.

You should set the modem to Auto Answer mode for use with *getty*. This means the modem automatically answers the phone when there is an incoming call, and makes the connection to the other modem.

From the command line, many UNIX systems offer access to a modem through one of several possible programs, such as Minicom, which is included with Red Hat Linux. The first step in using Minicom is to create a modem configuration file using the options shown in Figure 7-7. You configure the file by entering *minicom -s* from the root account, selecting Modem and dialing (see Figure 7-7), and then selecting the options that you want to configure (you must use AT commands for some parameters). After the file is configured, connect via the modem by entering *minicom* at the command line. Once Minicom is started, you can use the AT commands shown in Table 7-2.

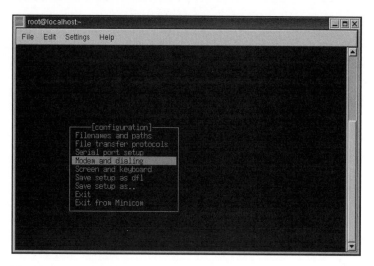

Figure 7-7   Using Minicom to configure a modem and dialing

Red Hat Linux 7.2 also simplifies modem setup and Internet setup by offering a *getty* called the Network Configuration tool (try Hands-on Project 7-11) and the Internet Configuration Wizard. The Network Configuration tool enables you to configure a modem. If you are connecting to an Internet service provider, you can use the Network Configuration tool to configure the modem and your Internet connection; or you can use the newer Internet Configuration Wizard. To start the Network Configuration tool from the GNOME interface, click the Main Menu (foot) on the panel, point to Programs, point to System, and click Network Configuration. Or, to start the Internet Configuration Wizard, click the Main Menu, point to Programs, point to System, and click Internet Configuration Wizard. You need access to the root account to use either tool; or if you start it from your own account, you will need to provide the password for the root account. Both the Network Configuration tool and the Internet Configuration Wizard enable you to configure access to an Internet provider through different types of access, such as ISDN, analog modem, and DSL. Some versions of Red Hat Linux (including version 7.2) also offer a Dial-up Configuration tool and a Red Hat Point-to-Point (RH PPP) Dialer for connecting to the Internet. For example, the Dial up Configuration tool presents an Internet Connections window (see Figure 7-8) from which you can configure your Internet connection to use PPP, install a modem, or reconfigure a modem. Click the Main menu (foot), point to Programs, point to Internet and click Dial-up Configuration to use the Dial-up Configuration tool. After you configure the connection, use the RH PPP Dialer to connect (click the Main Menu, point to Programs, point to Internet, and click RH PPP Dialer).

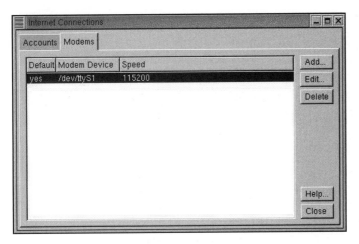

Figure 7-8 Red Hat Linux Internet Connections window

External communications programs can include simple terminal emulators (Microsoft Terminal), World Wide Web browsers (Microsoft Internet Explorer, Netscape Navigator or Communicator), e-mail programs (Outlook Express, Eudora), audio and video communications applications (Microsoft NetMeeting), or anything that uses a modem link to exchange data with a remote computer or remote computer network. UNIX supports many software packages that can use the modem to dial out. The earliest packages were for message exchange using the **UNIX to UNIX Copy Protocol**, or **UUCP**. These packages are found on almost all UNIX versions, including the very simple terminal program *tip* (Telephone Interface Program).

In addition, many UNIX platforms now run Netscape Communicator or Microsoft's Internet Explorer. For example, Red Hat Linux 7.2 typically comes with Netscape Communicator, when you install the GNOME interface. Also, there are now some advanced terminal emulation programs available as third-party add-ons to most UNIX operating systems. If you get your modem set up to work with *tip* or one of the PPP products, your modem will also work with any of these third-party programs.

Some *gettys* don't want to see any progress information from the modem (try Hands-on Project 7-12 to set up Solaris). To achieve this, use the following initialization string on most modems:

> AT&F&C1&D2E0V0Q1S0=2&W

This string has the following components and meanings:

- AT – Modem command prefix
- &F – Reset the modem to factory settings
- &C1– Turns on RTS/CTS control
- &D2 – Sets DCD control to follow carrier

- E0 – Enables the modem to forgo echoing commands sent to it back to the computer

- V0 – Instructs the modem to send numeric, as opposed to verbal, error and progress messages

- Q1 – Tells the modem not to return any error or progress messages

- S0=2 – Tells the modem to answer the phone after two rings

- &W – Writes these settings to the modem's NVRam (non-volatile RAM that stores configuration information), so the new settings are used the next time the modem is power cycled.

Dial out can be done with the same modem, but, in general, a different device name is used. This is done because UNIX does not normally operate with a modem that does not have the Data Carrier Detect (DCD) line raised. The initialization string for most dial-out applications is very similar to that for dial-in applications. The only change for most software is to use a Q0 instead of a Q1 setting, and for some software to use the V1 setting instead of V0. Some modems may differ, so consult your modem manual.

Once you install the modem hardware, you must configure your operating system dialer to communicate with your modem, dial a number, and log on to a remote host. This process is detailed in the step-by-step exercises in the Hands-on Projects section at the end of this chapter.

CHAPTER SUMMARY

- ❏ Understanding how operating systems govern modem communications provides an important background to understanding the powerful data sharing capabilities of modem-based WANs. For many people, their analog modems provide a window for communicating through the Internet, or telecommuting to work from a home office. Analog modems have a three-part architecture, consisting of a data pump, controller, and UART (Universal Asynchronous Receiver-Transmitter). These components may be implemented completely in hardware, or partially in software. The most common way to communicate through modems is by using the Hayes (AT) modem command set to control modem settings.

- ❏ Digital modems are not actually modems at all since they are entirely digital and do not perform the modulation/demodulation required for analog devices. They are called modems because they perform the same basic functions as analog modems, allowing communications between computers over a WAN connection, such as a telecommunication line. Digital modems work with digital telephone or cable systems, such as ISDN (Integrated Services Digital Network), cable TV networks, and Digital Subscriber Lines (DSLs).

- ❏ Both analog and digital modems communicate over telephone lines by using communications protocols, software flow control, hardware flow control, error correction, and data compression. Each of these techniques conforms to standards, such as the ITU-T standards, so that one type of modem can successfully communicate with a different modem or WAN communications device at the other end.

❑ All the operating systems discussed in this book include a communications component and methods for establishing dial-up networking through modems and other telecommunications devices. To configure a modem and dial-up networking, you must provide the operating system with information about your modem, such as networking protocol(s) and addresses, AT commands, and a dial-up access telephone number.

KEY TERMS

Asymmetric Digital Subscriber Line (ADSL) — A high-speed digital subscriber line technology that can use ordinary telephone lines for downstream data transmission of up to 6 Mbps, and 576-640 Kbps for upstream transmission.

Attention (AT) commands — A modem control command set designed by the Hayes company. This standard modem command set begins each command with AT (for Attention), and allows communications software or users to directly control many modem functions.

basic rate interface (BRI) for ISDN — An ISDN interface that consists of three channels. Two are 64 Kbps channels for data, voice, video, and graphics transmissions. The third is a 16 Kbps channel used for communications signaling.

cable modem — A digital modem device designed for use with the cable TV system, providing high-speed data transfer. It may include an analog modem component that is used with a conventional telephone line connection for information sent from the user to the ISP.

controller — A hardware or software component of a modem that defines an individual modem's personality. The controller interprets AT commands and handles communications protocols, for example.

daemon — An internal, automatically running program, usually in UNIX, that serves a particular function such as routing e-mail to recipients or supporting dial-up networking connectivity.

data communications equipment (DCE) — A device, such as a modem, that converts data from a DTE, such as a computer, for transmission over a telecommunications line. The DCE normally provides the clock rate/clocking mechanism necessary for communications.

data pump — The hardware or software portion of a modem that is responsible for converting digital data into analog signals for transmission over a telephone line, and for converting analog signals into digital data for transmission to the computer.

data terminal equipment (DTE) — A computer or computing device that prepares data to be transmitted over a telecommunications line, to which it attaches by using a DCE, such as a modem.

digital modem — A modem-like device that transfers data via digital lines instead of analog lines.

Digital Signal Processor (DSP) — A software data pump used in such software-driven modems as the 3Com Winmodem.

Digital Subscriber Line (DSL) — A technology that uses advanced modulation technologies on existing telecommunications networks for high-speed networking between a subscriber and a telco, and that offers communication speeds up to 60 Mbps.

flow control — A hardware or software feature in modems that lets a receiving modem communicate to the sending modem that it needs more time to process previously sent data. When the current data is processed successfully, the receiving modem notifies the sending modem that it can resume data transmission.

Hayes command — See *Attention (AT) commands.*

High Bit-Rate Digital Subscriber Line (HDSL) — A form of high-speed digital subscriber line technology that has upstream and downstream transmission rates of up to 1.544 Mbps.

Host Signal Processor (HSP) — A software approach to handling data pump duties in software-based modems such as the 3Com Winmodem.

Integrated Services Digital Network (ISDN) — A digital telephone line used for high-speed digital computer communications, videoconferencing, Internet connections, and telecommuting.

International Telecommunications Union (ITU) — An international organization that sets telecommunications standards—for modem and WAN communications, for example.

Link Access Protocol for Modems (LAPM) — An error-checking protocol used in the V.42 standard that constructs data into discrete frame-like units for transmission over communications lines. Error checking is made possible because each unit is given a sequence number and a checksum. If a received unit is out of sequence or has the wrong checksum, this signals an error in the transmission.

modem (MOdulator-DEModulator) — A hardware device that permits a computer to exchange digital data with another computer via an analog telephone line or dedicated connection.

parity checking — A data communications process that ensures data integrity through a system of data bit comparisons between the sending and receiving computer.

plain old telephone service (POTS) — Regular voice-grade telephone service (the old terminology).

primary rate interface (PRI) ISDN — An ISDN interface that consists of switched communications in multiples of 1,544 Mbps.

protocol — An established guideline that specifies how networked data, including data sent over a telephone network, is formatted into a transmission unit, how it is transmitted, and how it is interpreted at the receiving end.

public switched telephone network (PSTN) — Regular voice-grade telephone service (the modern terminology).

Rate Adaptive Digital Subscriber Line (RADSL) — A high-speed data transmission technology that offers upstream speeds of up to 1 Mbps and downstream speeds of up to 7 Mbps. RADSL uses ADSL technology (see *ADSL*), but enables the transmission rate to vary for different types of communications, such as data, multimedia, and voice.

routers — Network hardware that can intelligently route network frames and packets to different networks, and that can route multiple protocols.

Symmetric Digital Subscriber Line (SDSL) — A form of digital subscriber line technology that is often used for videoconferencing or online learning. It offers a transmission speed of 384 Kbps for upstream and downstream communications.

start bit — In data communication, an extra bit inserted by the sending modem at the beginning of a data byte to help ensure that the received data is correct.

stop bit — In data communication, an extra bit inserted by the sending modem at the end of a data byte to help ensure that the received data is correct.

telco — A telecommunications company.

terminal adapter (TA) — A digital modem that permits computer-to-computer data transfer over a digital line, such as ISDN.

Universal Asynchronous Receiver-Transmitter (UART) — An electronic chip that handles data flow through a serial port or modem.

UNIX to UNIX Copy Protocol (UUCP) — A protocol used by UNIX computers for communicating through modems. UUCP can also be used on networks, but for these applications, it is usually replaced by the faster TCP/IP technology.

Very High Bit-Rate Digital Subscriber Line (VDSL) — A digital subscriber line technology that works over coaxial and fiber-optic cables, yielding 51–55 Mbps downstream and 1.6–2.3 Mbps upstream communications.

Winmodem — A software-driven modem from 3Com Corporation that uses minimal hardware and the computer's CPU with software to conduct data communications.

Xon-Xoff — A software flow control protocol that permits a receiving modem to notify the sending modem that its data buffers are full, and it needs more time to process previously received data.

REVIEW QUESTIONS

1. The three basic modem components are _____, _____, and _____.

2. Which of the following are tools that enable you to configure dial-up access in Red Hat Linux?

   a. Dial Pro tool

   b. Network Configuration tool

   c. Dial Up Configuration tool

   d. all of the above

   e. only a and b

   f. only b and c

3. One problem with Mac OS X is that it does not support TCP/IP for Internet access; instead, you must go through AppleTalk's version of PPP. True or False?

4. Digital modems:

   a. are misnamed because they actually use analog signals, not digital signals.

   b. are used for DSL communications.

   c. can only be used when you have fiber-optic lines for access to the telecommunications company.

   d. all of the above

   e. only a and b

   f. only b and c

5. International modem standards define how modems communicate with each other and at what speed. Which of the following is a standard for 56 Kbps modem communications?

   a. V.34bis

   b. V.42

   c. V.190

   d. V.92

6. A UART is the electronic device that manages serial input/output data transfers for modems and other serial objects. UART stands for:

   a. United Access Reverse Transfer.

   b. Universal Area Remote Transmitter.

   c. Universal Asynchronous Receiver-Transmitter.

   d. Universal Accessible Reverse Transfer.

7. V.42bis is a:

   a. data compression standard.

   b. format for zipping graphics-only documents before they are sent to a modem.

   c. data error correction standard.

   d. data packing technique used exclusively by ISDN.

8. Flow control helps ensure accurate data transfer between modems. There are two general types of flow control in common use. They are _____ and _____.

9. In UNIX, a device port for a modem is treated as a:

   a. software modem.

   b. parallel interface port.

   c. teletype (TTY) port.

   d. display monitor port.

10. Adding an extra bit to each data byte for error correction is called _____ checking.

11. The Hayes command sequence that you would put in front of a telephone number for dial-up access over a touchtone line is:

    a. ATDP.

    b. ATDT.

    c. ATTOUCH.

    d. ATTH.

12. In Windows XP, the Phone and Modem Options configuration tool is found in the:

    a. Taskbar.

    b. System Tools menu.

    c. Control Panel.

    d. Internet options menu.

13. A TA is one example of a device that you can use to connect a computer to an ISDN network. True or False?

14. Software-based modems use electronic circuits called Digital Signal Processors, or DSPs, to emulate what major modem hardware component?

15. You have a Microsoft Word document that is about 1 MB in size. What should you do before sending it over a modem for faster transmission?

    a. disable error checking

    b. use two parity bits to signal use of the fast modem mode

    c. compress the file using a compression utility, such as PKZIP

    d. send the file early in the morning when there are fewer people on the Internet

16. An internal modem is most commonly attached to the computer through a _____ expansion slot.

17. Which is the most commonly used version of DSL?

    a. VDSL

    b. HDSL

    c. SDSL

    d. ADSL

18. The purpose of Xon-Xoff is:

    a. as an AT command to hang up the modem connection.

    b. as a special signal line for DSL.

    c. for flow control.

    d. to create a larger modem storage buffer for transmitting a large file.

19. You can configure an Internet connection in the Mac OS X by using _____.

20. Minicom is a modem connection software package that is typically included with the _____ operating system.

7

HANDS-ON PROJECTS

Project 7-1

This project enables you to check the modem port speed setup in Windows XP. In Windows-based systems, it is important to make sure that the port speed (the speed setup for the serial or parallel port to which the modem is connected) is the same as or higher than the speed capability of the modem. If it is not, then you will not be using the full-speed capability of the modem.

To check the modem port speed setup:

1. Click **Start**, click **Control Panel**, click **Printers and Other Hardware**, and click **Phone and Modem Options**.

2. Click the **Modems** tab in the Phone and Modem Options dialog box.

3. Click the **Properties** button, as shown in Figure 7-9.

Figure 7-9   Selecting to view modem properties in Windows XP

4. Click the **Modem** tab.

5. What is the value in the Maximum Port Speed box? Is it higher than the actual speed of the modem?

6. How can you change the port speed?

7. Click **Cancel** to close the modem Properties dialog box. Click **Cancel** to close the Phone and Modem Options dialog box. Close the Printers and Other Hardware window.

You can perform a similar check in Windows 95/98/NT/2000 by clicking Start, pointing to Settings, and clicking Control Panel. Open the icon for modems, select the modem, and select to view the properties of the modem.

Project 7-2

You can't always depend on achieving a data transfer rate equivalent to the speed of your modem. A 56 Kbps modem may only connect at 48 Kbps or less, for example, and even if you connect at a full 56K, you may not achieve an actual data throughput of 56K.

To test the performance of your modem:

1. Log onto an online service or remote computer with an FTP client. (For example, if you are using Internet Explorer, use a URL that starts with ftp:// and provide the name of the ftp site.)

To locate listings of ftp sites, go to a search engine, such as *www.lycos.com* or *www.yahoo.com*, and search for ftp sites or download sites.

2. Locate a compressed file of known size on the remote computer.

3. Start downloading the file.

4. Use a stopwatch or watch and time precisely how long it takes to download the file.

5. Conduct the following calculations, using your actual data, to determine the actual transfer rate in bits per second:

   For example, if your 56K modem downloaded a 100 kilobyte compressed file in 20 seconds, a simplistic calculation would be:

   100 kilobytes ★ 1024 bytes/kilobyte ★ 8 bits/byte = 819,200 bits

   819,200 bits/20 seconds = 40,960 bits per second

   This calculation assumes that the modem was transferring eight bits per byte. But what about start and stop bits? That would make the number 10 bits per byte, which makes the modem performance 51,200 bits per second. However, a 56Kbps modem is probably using V.42 hardware error correction, which strips out the start and stop bits, but adds other overhead. For quick calculations, call it nine bits per byte, or about 46,080 bits per second.

   Take note that the file was compressed. Otherwise, you would have to take into account the compressibility of the file and the efficiency of the modem's hardware compression! (Also, see Hands-on Projects 7-3 and 7-6 to gauge the actual transmission speed of a modem.)

7

Project 7-3

Testing modem performance with only a single type of file and a file of only one length won't give you a reliable test of modem performance over the phone lines with frequently used hosts. In this exercise, you'll conduct data transfer (upload and download) experiments using different file types, such as .zip, .gif, .jpg, and .txt. .zip files are efficiently compressed. .gif and .jpg files are somewhat compressed, and .txt files are not compressed at all.

When conducting data transfer tests, use sufficiently large files to ensure reproducible results. That minimizes the effect of latency and TCP/IP slow start. Files of about 200 KB in size are sufficient for analog modem testing.

To further test your individual modem performance by downloading various types of files:

1. Use any available FTP program or utility for the transfer, such as Internet Explorer for Windows-based systems, Fetch for the Macintosh, or FTP in UNIX.

2. Using the FTP program, log on to a remote site (an Internet site, public FTP site, or dial-in Remote Access Server). If you have an Internet Service Provider, you can probably upload files to a directory on the host, or use files already available in a public FTP site.

3. Identify the file or files you want to transfer (try to select a .gif file, a .zip or other compressed file, a .jpg file, and a .txt file). Download all files from the same location, and time the data transfer, as described in Hands-on Project 7-2. How much do the different file types affect modem efficiency?

Project 7-4

Dial-up networking is the way in which you configure modem communications in Windows 95/98. Although the Windows NT component operates slightly differently, the user interface and installation process are very similar, and are discussed in the next Hands-on Project. You'll need dial-up networking to enable modem communications to the Internet or another remote host if you're using Windows 95/98. Before you start, obtain IP configuration and gateway information from your instructor.

The figures in the following project are from Windows 98. Windows 95 screens are nearly identical.

To install and configure Windows Dial-Up Networking:

1. Verify that Dial-Up Networking is installed:

    a. Click **Start**, point to **Programs**, point to **Accessories**, point to **Communications**, and look for the Dial-Up Networking icon or entry.

If you don't see these items in your Start menu, double-click the My Computer icon, then verify that the Dial-Up Networking icon is present.

   b. If Dial-Up Networking is present, skip ahead to Step 2. If it is not present, continue with Steps c through j to install it.

   c. Click **Start**, point to **Settings**, click **Control Panel**, and double-click the **Add/Remove Programs** icon.

   d. Click the **Windows Setup** tab.

   e. Click **Communications**.

   f. Click **Details** and make sure Dial-Up Networking is selected. (The other components are not necessary for this project.)

   g. Click **OK**.

   h. Click the **Have Disk** button.

   i. Insert your Windows 95 or 98 CD-ROM, and click the **Browse** button. Select the CD-ROM drive in which the CD-ROM is loaded, such as drive D:. Windows 95 or 98 will install the Dial-Up Networking components.

   j. Restart your computer and continue with the next step.

2. Check your network settings:

   a. If the Control Panel is not still open, click **Start**, point to **Settings**, and click **Control Panel**. Double-click the **Network** icon.

   b. On the Configuration tab, the Primary Network Logon should be set to Windows Logon. If you are on a Novell network, Netware Login is appropriate. Client for Microsoft Network may cause problems and should not be selected as the Primary Network Logon.

   c. Check in the network components area for the following two components, which are necessary to use Dial-Up Networking: Dial-Up Adapter, and TCP/IP, or TCP/IP →Dial-Up Adapter. If you are missing one or both of these components, you must install them using the instructions in Steps 3 and 4. Otherwise, skip to Step 5.

3. Install the Dial-Up Adapter:

   a. Click the **Add** button.

   b. Double-click **Adapter**.

   c. Select **Microsoft**.

   d. Choose **Dial-Up Adapter**, and click **OK**.

4. Install TCP/IP:

   a. Click **Start**, point to **Settings**, and click **Control Panel**. Open the **Network** icon.

   b. Click the **Add** button.

c. Double-click **Protocol**.

d. Select **Microsoft**.

e. Choose **TCP/IP**, and click **OK**.

f. Click **TCP/IP** (or **TCP/IP→Dial-Up Adapter**), and click the **Properties** button. (In Windows 98, you may see a message box warning that changing settings could cause problems. Click **OK** to close this dialog box.)

g. Click the **IP Address** tab if it is not the default tab. For most computers, it should be set to "Obtain an IP address automatically."

h. Click the **WINS Configuration** tab. For most Internet services, this is set to "Disable WINS resolution." If you are running on a local area network, check with your LAN administrator for the proper setting here.

i. If you obtain an IP address automatically, the DHCP server will likely complete the gateway information. If not, click the **Gateways** tab. Type 0.0.0.0 in the New Gateway box, and click **Add**. If your Internet service provider or LAN administrator specifies a different setting here, use that instead.

j. Click the **DNS Configuration** tab.

k. Verify that **Enable DNS** is selected.

l. In the host text box, enter your username in all lowercase letters with no spaces.

m. The domain should be the domain to which you are connecting. If the connection is for an ISP, this is probably the ISP's domain, such as onemain.com. This should be entered in all lowercase characters with no spaces.

n. Under DNS Server Search Order, the Primary and Secondary DNS should be an IP address, such as 199.1.48.2. You'll need to check with your ISP or LAN administrator for the correct settings in these fields. Enter the IP Address, then click the Add button.

o. Under Domain Name Suffix Search Order, the domain should be your ISP's domain, or whatever domain is specified by your ISP or LAN administrator. Enter this data in all lowercase with no spaces. After entering the Domain, click the Add button. Figure 7-10 shows the DNS Configuration tab of the TCP/IP Properties dialog box.

p. Click **OK** to accept the configuration you entered.

q. Click the **Dial-Up Adapter**, and click the **Properties** button.

r. Click the **Bindings** tab. Only TCP/IP should be checked. Uncheck all other bindings. (Removing other protocols will help to make your transmissions faster.)

s. Click **OK**.

t. Click **OK** again to close the Network control panel.

u. You are prompted to restart Windows for changes to take effect. Restart Windows before attempting to log in.

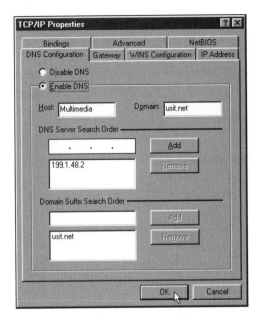

Figure 7-10   DNS Configuration tab of the TCP/IP Properties dialog box

5. Create a new connection icon:

   a. Choose **Start**, point to **Programs**, point to **Accessories** (for Windows 95); or click **Start**, point to **Programs**, point to **Accessories**, point to **Communications** (for Windows 98), and then click **Dial-Up Networking**. If you don't see these items in your Start menu, double-click the My Computer icon, then double-click the Dial-Up Networking icon. If you did not previously install dial-up networking, you will see a Connection Wizard that will step you through the process described here. If this happens, skip to Step 5c.

   b. Double-click **Make New Connection**.

   c. Type a title for the connection. Give the connection the same name as your Internet service provider, or use another name that will help you identify it later, such as your initials plus "connection." "U.S. Internet" is used in our examples.

   d. Your modem should be listed in the "Select a modem" area (in Windows 95), or "Select a device" area (in Windows 98). If it isn't, see the following Note.

If your modem is not listed in the Select a modem area, now is a good time to set up your modem to work with Windows 95 or Windows 98. Click Start, point to Settings, click Control Panel, click Add New Hardware, and follow the steps in the Add New Hardware Wizard. Click the Configure button. In the General tab, select your modem speed. For 14.4 Kbps modems, use 19200. For 28.8 Kbps modems, use 38400 or 57600, and use 57600 for 56 Kbps modems. DO NOT select "Only connect at this speed." You can ignore the settings in the Connection tab. Click the Options tab. Make sure "Bring up terminal window after dialing" is unchecked. Click OK.

e. Click the **Next** button. Enter the dial-up access phone number you want to use, and click **Next**. Click the **Finish** button. The icon for your new connection appears in the Dial-Up Networking dialog box.

6. Set the properties of your dial-up connection:

a. Click the new icon you just created for the dial-up connection to select it.

b. Right-click and choose **Properties** from the menu. You should now see a dialog box named after your icon.

c. Click the **Server Types** tab.

d. Under Type of Dial-Up Server, choose **PPP: Windows 95, Windows NT 3.5, Internet** (in Windows 95), or **PPP: Internet, Windows NT Server, Windows 98** (in Windows 98).

e. Verify that the advanced options are all OFF. Make sure Log on to network, Enable software compression, and Require encrypted password are not checked.

f. Verify that TCP/IP is the only allowed network protocol. Make sure that **TCP/IP** is checked. NetBEUI and IPX/SPX Compatible should not be checked, as shown in Figure 7-11.

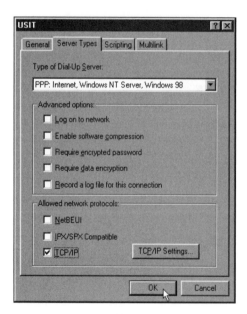

Figure 7-11   Windows 98 Server Types tab

g. Click the **TCP/IP Settings** button.

h. In the TCP/IP Settings dialog box, verify that **Server assigned IP address**, and **Specify name server addresses** are selected. Primary DNS and Secondary DNS should be set to the name server addresses specified by your ISP or network administrator. **Use IP header compression** should be checked, as should **Use default gateway on remote network**. Figure 7-12 shows the completed TCP/IP Settings dialog box, with Primary and Secondary DNS addresses for U.S. Internet.

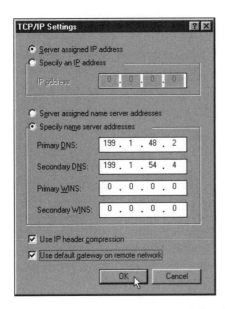

Figure 7-12   TCP/IP Settings dialog box

   i. Click **OK**. Click **OK** again to close the Properties dialog box.

   j. Set Dial-Up Networking to redial. From the Connection menu of the Dial-Up Networking window, choose **Settings**. Then put a checkmark in the **Redial** box, and click **OK**.

7. Use these settings to connect to an ISP or other remote host:

   a. Double-click your dial-up connection icon.

   b. Enter your username and password in the provided boxes. Please note: your username and password are case sensitive. Uppercase and lowercase are not the same.

   c. Click the **Connect** button; your modem should dial and connect. Windows 95/98 should now tell you it is connected, and a timer begins counting your time online. You can now launch your Internet software, such as a browser or e-mail software.

Project 7-5

Configuring dial-up networking for Windows NT is almost identical to Windows 95/98, although the dialog boxes you use are different. Before you start, obtain IP configuration and gateway information from your instructor.

To set up Windows NT 4.0 for Dial-Up Networking:

1. Double-click the **My Computer** icon on your desktop, then double-click **Dial-Up Networking**.

> **Note**
> If you did not previously install dial-up networking, you will see a dialog box to begin the installation. Click Install and insert the Windows NT CD-ROM if requested; then follow the directions on the screen. Choose Yes when you are asked if you want RAS setup to invoke the modem installer.

2. If you see a dialog box saying that the phone book is empty, click **OK**.

3. Launching RAS (Remote Access Service) for the first time starts the Phonebook Entry Wizard. If you have run RAS before, simply click the **New** button to start the Phonebook Entry Wizard.

4. Enter a name for this connection. You should give the connection the same name as your Internet service provider, or use another name, such as your initials plus the word "connection."

5. Click the **Next** button.

6. The Server dialog box tells your system what to expect from the server. Put a check mark next to all of the following three options (see Figure 7-13).

   ☐ **I am calling the Internet.**

   ☐ **Send my plain text password if that's the only way to connect.**

   ☐ **The non-Windows NT server I am calling expects me to type login information after connecting, or to know TCP/IP addresses before dialing.**

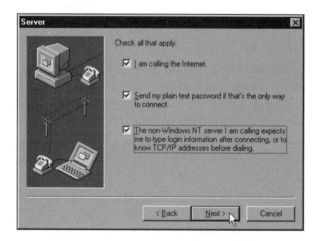

Figure 7-13   Windows NT Server dialog box

7. Click **Next**.

8. Supply a phone number for your dial-up connection. Do not select Use Telephony dialing properties. Click **Next**.

9. Set the serial line protocol to **Point-to-Point Protocol (PPP)**, and click **Next**.

10. Under Login Script, select **Use a terminal window**, and click **Next**.

11. If your ISP uses dynamic IP addressing, leave the IP address at 0.0.0.0. Otherwise, enter the IP address you were given for your workstation. Figure 7-14 shows the IP Address dialog box.

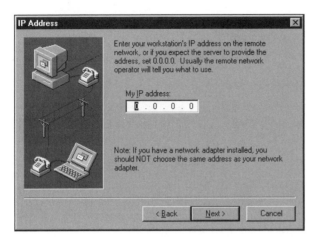

Figure 7-14   Windows NT IP Address dialog box

12. Click **Next**.

13. Set the Name Server Addresses. The DNS Server is the IP address supplied for this server (the example uses the IP address of the U.S. Internet DNS server); or if the DNS Server IP address is supplied automatically through DHCP, leave the entry as 0.0.0.0. WINS server will be left at 0.0.0.0 in most cases, as shown in Figure 7-15.

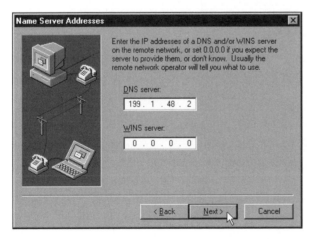

Figure 7-15   Windows NT Name Server Addresses dialog box

14. Click **Next**.

15. Click **Finish**.

16. At the main RAS connect screen, you must supply a secondary DNS. In the Dial-Up
Networking dialog box, click the **More** button, then select **Edit entry and
modem properties**, as shown in Figure 7-16. The Edit Phonebook Entry dialog
box appears, as shown in Figure 7-17.

Figure 7-16   Windows NT Dial-Up Networking dialog box

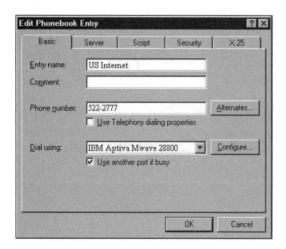

Figure 7-17   Edit Phonebook Entry dialog box

17. Click the **Server** tab. The settings on this tab should be:

  ❑ Dial-up server type: **PPP: Windows NT, Windows 95 Plus, Internet**

  ❑ Network protocols: **TCP/IP** only

  ❑ **Enable software compression**: checked

  ❑ **Enable PPP LCP extensions**: checked

If any of these items is not checked, click the empty box to select the item.

18. Click the **TCP/IP Settings** button to display the dialog box shown in Figure 7-18. These settings are typical, but you'll need the actual figures from your ISP or other host:

- ◻ **Server assigned IP address** (unless you have been assigned a static IP address, in which case you should select Specify an IP address and enter the address)

- ◻ **Specify name server addresses**

- ◻ Primary DNS: **199.1.48.2** (for U.S. Internet)

- ◻ Secondary DNS: **199.1.54.4** (for U.S. Internet)

- ◻ Primary WINS: **0.0.0.0** (not used)

- ◻ Secondary WINS: **0.0.0.0** (not used)

- ◻ **Use IP header compression**: checked

- ◻ **Use default gateway on remote network**: checked

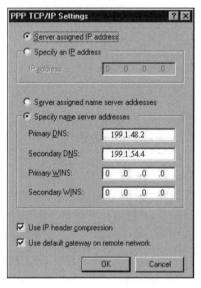

Figure 7-18   PPP TCP/IP Settings dialog box

19. Click **OK** to close the PPP TCP/IP settings dialog box and click **OK** to close the Edit Phonebook Entry dialog box.

20. Click **Close** or **OK** to close the Dial-Up Networking dialog box.

Project 7-6

Windows-based systems that use the Dial-Up Networking capability, such as Windows 95, 98, and NT, start the Dial-Up Network Monitor when a connection is made. You can use this tool to determine the speed of a dial-up connection.

To monitor the actual speed of a dial-up connection:

1. Open a connection by double-clicking **My Computer**, double-clicking **Dial-Up Networking**, double-clicking a previously defined modem, and clicking **Dial** (in Windows NT) or **Connect** (in Windows 95/98).

2. Click the **Dial-Up Networking** icon on the taskbar (usually near the clock).

3. Make sure that the **Status** tab appears (see Figure 7-19 for Windows NT 4.0), and if not, click it.

4. Check the line bps value and compare it with the speed capability advertised for your modem.

5. Click **Hang up**, and click **Cancel**.

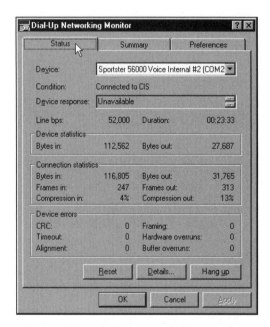

Figure 7-19   Dial-Up Networking Monitor

Project 7-7

In this project, you'll practice setting up a dial-up connection in Windows 2000 Professional.

To configure dial-up networking in Windows 2000:

1. Click **Start**, point to **Settings**, and click **Network and Dial-up Connections**.

2. Double-click **Make New Connection** (see Figure 7-20).

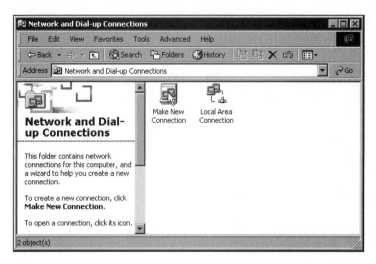

Figure 7-20   Creating a new connection for modem access

3. Enter your area code (required) and the number to dial an outside line (if necessary). Also, select whether to use tone dialing or pulse dialing (most telephone lines have tone dialing). (If you see the Network Connection Wizard in the background, ignore it for now.)

4. Click **OK**.

5. Click **OK** in the Phone and Modem Options dialog box.

6. Click **Next**, when you see the Network Connection Wizard.

7. What connection options appear?

8. Click **Dial-up to the Internet**, and click **Next**.

9. For this project, select **I want to set up my Internet connection manually, or I want to connect through a local area network (LAN)** (see Figure 7-21).

10. If your modem is not already installed, the wizard now installs it. Click **Next** if you see the Add/Remove Hardware Wizard. (If your modem is enabled for PnP, the wizard automatically configures it; otherwise, you must specify the type of modem and the port to which it is attached.) Click **Finished** when the Add/Remove Hardware Wizard is finished.

11. Click **I connect through a phone line and a modem**. Click **Next**.

12. Enter the telephone number for the connection, and click **Next**.

13. Enter the account or username and password used for the connection.

14. Provide a name for the connection, such as the name of your ISP, or your initials plus "connection."

15. Click **Next**.

Figure 7-21 Determining how to access the Internet

16. Click **No**, so that you do not set up an Internet mail account at this time. Click **Next**.

17. Click **Finish**.

18. If you are connected to a telephone line, you can click **Connect** now to test your connection. If you are not connected to a telephone line, close the Dial-up Connection box.

>
>
> When you use the Network Connection Wizard to set up an Internet connection, it automatically sets up to use TCP/IP and PPP. You can verify this by clicking Start, pointing to Settings, and clicking Network and Dial-up Connections. Right-click the connection that you just created and click Properties.

Project 7-8

This project enables you to configure dial-up networking in Windows XP Professional.

To configure dial-up networking:

1. Click **Start**, click **Control Panel**, and click **Network and Internet Connections**.

2. Click **Set up or change your Internet connection** (see Figure 7-22).

3. Click the **Setup** button in the Internet Properties dialog box.

4. The New Connection Wizard starts. Click **Next**.

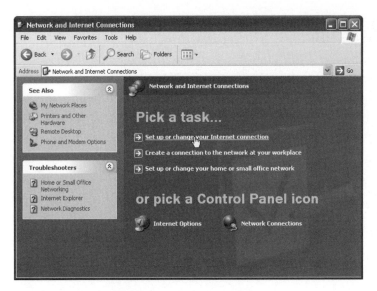

Figure 7-22   Configuring dial-up networking for Internet access

5. What network connection options do you see?

6. Select **Connect to the Internet**, and click **Next**.

7. What options are in the Getting Ready dialog box?

8. Click **Set up my connection manually**, and then click **Next**.

9. Click **Connect using a dial-up modem**. Notice that this option includes the ability to connect using an analog modem or an ISDN TA. There are also options in this dialog box to connect using DSL and cable modems. Click **Next**.

10. Enter the name of the ISP (or your initials plus "connection"), and then click **Next**.

11. Enter the phone number to use for accessing the ISP. Click **Next**.

12. Enter the user/account name for the ISP connection and the password. Enter the password again to confirm it. Also, make sure that the following are checked:

   ❑ **Use this account name and password when anyone connects to the Internet from this computer.**

   ❑ **Make this the default Internet connection.**

   ❑ **Turn on Internet Connection Firewall for this connection.**

13. Click **Next**.

14. Review the parameters that you entered, and click **Finish**.

15. On the Network and Internet Connections window, click **Network Connections**.

16. Right-click your new connection, and click **Properties**.

17. Click the **Networking** tab. Notice that TCP/IP and PPP are automatically configured for this connection. Also, what other option is configured by default?

18. Close the Properties dialog box and then close the Network Connections window.

Project 7-9

This project enables you to configure TCP/IP for network and Internet communications in the Mac OS through version 9.x.

To view or change your TCP/IP settings on the Mac:

1. Choose **Apple Menu** and then **Control Panels**. Open the **TCP/IP** Control Panel, shown in Figure 7-23.

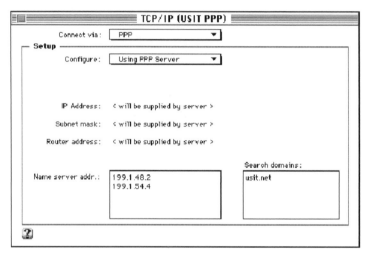

Figure 7-23   Mac TPC/IP Control Panel

2. There are several modes used in TCP/IP that affect the appearance of the Control Panel. The screenshot in Figure 7-23 shows the Basic mode. To change the user mode, select **User Mode** from the **Edit** menu (see Figure 7-24) to display the User Mode dialog box, shown in Figure 7-25.

Figure 7-24   Using the Edit menu to change the user mode

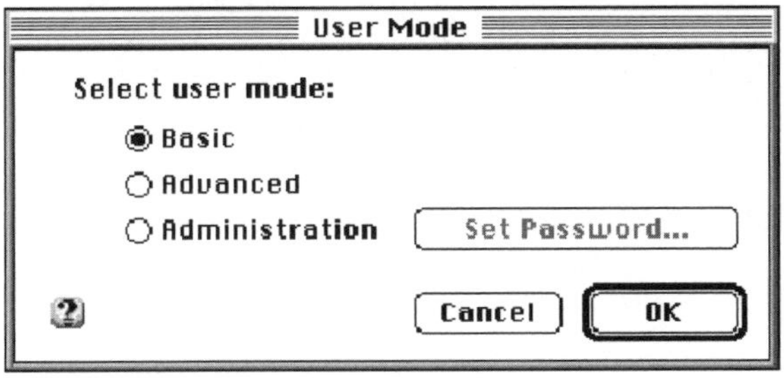

Figure 7-25   User Mode dialog box

3. Select the **Advanced** user mode, and click **OK**. The TCP/IP dialog box now shows an Options button.

4. If the Mac tries to dial in every time it's restarted, you probably have "Load Only When Needed" unchecked in the Options dialog box. Click **Options** in the TCP/IP dialog box to display the TCP/IP Options dialog box, shown in Figure 7-26. Put an "x" or checkmark next to **Load only when needed**, and the problem disappears.

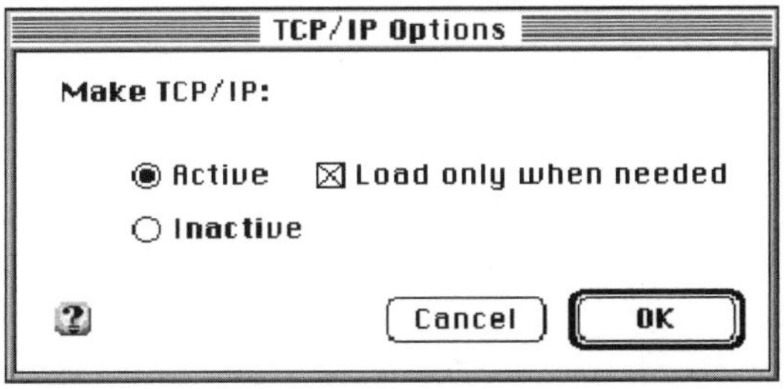

Figure 7-26   TCP/IP Options dialog box

5. The Connect via settings in the TCP/IP dialog box can be one of four things (though you may not see all options in all versions of Mac OS):

   ◻ Use "MacPPP" with FreePPP 1.05 or MacPPP 2.5

   ◻ Use "FreePPP" for use with FreePPP 2.5 and later

   ◻ Use "PPP" with Apple's PPP (part of 7.6 and later)

   ◻ Use "Ethernet" for computers attached to a router

All other settings should be as shown for server-assigned IP addresses. For static addresses used with an Ethernet-based ISDN router, change Configure to "Manually," and enter the correct numbers for IP, Subnet, and Router (ask your ISP or instructor).

Project 7-10

In this project, you'll configure TCP/IP and a modem connection for Internet connectivity in Mac OS X.

To set up TCP/IP and a modem connection in Mac OS X:

1. Open the **Apple** menu and select **System Preferences**.
2. Click the **Network** icon.
3. What tabs do you see?
4. Click the **TCP/IP** tab.
5. Select to configure **Manually**, and enter the TCP/IP, subnet mask, and router information provided by your ISP or instructor.
6. Click the **PPP** tab.
7. Enter the name of the ISP, the telephone number, the account name, and account password.
8. Click the **Modem** tab. Select the modem type, specify whether you want the sound on or off, and select whether your telephone line is tone or pulse (most are tone). Also, check the box to **Wait for dial tone before dialing**.
9. Click **Save**.

Project 7-11

Under Linux, normally the serial ports on the PC are automatically set up for modem use. All you must do is connect a configured modem. When done, you can dial into the desired computer with any terminal emulator; or use the RH PPP Dialer that was described earlier for Red Hat Linux. When you do, you will see the login prompt, and you will be in business. The *getty* provided with Linux self-detects the modem speed and parameters. This project enables you to configure Red Hat Linux 7.2 for a modem using TCP/IPP and PPP. There are two options illustrated here: one is to use the Network Configuration tool and the other is to use the Dial up Configuration tool.

In order to complete this exercise and effectively configure network interfaces, you must have root privileges.

To configure a dial-up modem interface via the Network Configuration tool in Red Hat Linux 7.2:

1. From the GNOME interface, click the **Main Menu** (foot) on the Panel, point to **Programs**, point to **System**, and click **Network Configuration**.
2. Make sure that the **Hardware** tab is displayed. Click the **Add** button and select **Modem** (see Figure 7-27).
3. Click **OK**.

4. The Network Configuration tool next automatically detects your modem. Verify each of the parameters: Modem Device (such as /dev/modem), Baud Rate (such as 115200), Flow Control (Hardware (CRTSCTS)), Modem Volume (Off, Low, Medium, High, or Very High). Also, if you have a touch tone line, check the box for **Use touch tone dialing**, if it is not already checked.

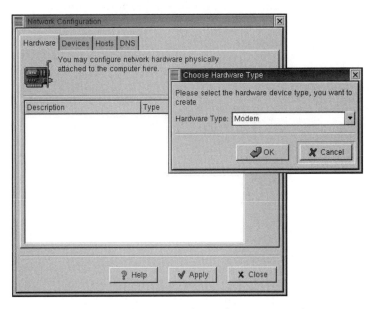

Figure 7-27   Using the Network Configuration tool

5. Click **OK**.

6. Click the **Devices** tab.

7. Click the **Add** button.

8. Select **Modem** as the device type, if it is not already selected.

9. Click **OK**.

10. On the General tab, provide a nickname for the modem, such as your initials plus the word "modem."

11. Click the **Protocol** tab. Make sure that **TCP/IP** already appears in the Protocol Type box. (If it does not, click the Add button to add it; or if it is already selected, the Add button may be deactivated.) The selection of TCP/IP also enables use of PPP.

12. Click the **Provider** tab and notice that you can use this tab to supply information about your Internet service provider or your dial-up connection provider, including the telephone access number, the provider name, your login name, and your password.

13. Click **OK**.

14. Click **Apply**.

15. Close the Network Configuration tool or click **Close**.

16. Click **Yes** to save your changes.

To configure a modem interface and PPP using the Dialup Configuration tool in Red Hat Linux 7.2:

1. Click the **Main Menu** (foot) icon in the Panel, point to **Programs**, point to **Internet**, and click **Dialup Configuration**.

2. Click the **Add** button.

3. Click **Next** when you see the Create a New Internet Connection screen.

4. Select the modem device, such as **/dev/modem** and click **Next**.

5. Enter the name you use for the Internet account, such as your user name (or enter a name to identify the Internet access). Enter the prefix (if you have one), the country or area code, and telephone number for your ISP. Note that you can move between fields by pressing the Tab key.

6. Click **Next**.

7. Enter the user name for the account and the password. Click **Next**.

8. Select your Internet provider or if it is not listed, select **Normal ISP**. Click **Next**.

9. Review the information that you have entered and click **Finish**.

10. Click **Close**.

11. Notice that the Internet connection you configured is now added to the Internet Connections window. (Also, a Choose window may be displayed, which is really the RH PPP Dialer. If it is, you can connect to the Internet by clicking the name of the Internet account and clicking **OK**.)

12. Click the **Modem** tab. Notice that you can add a new modem or modify an existing modem configuration from this tab.

13. Click **Close** to leave the Internet Connections window.

After you configure a connection (interface), you can access it at any time by starting the RH PPP Dialer. To start this tool, click the Main Menu, point to Programs, point to Internet, click RH PPP Dialer, select the interface, and click OK.

Project 7-12

In this project, you'll configure a modem in Solaris. To complete this exercise and effectively configure network interfaces, you must have root privileges.

To set up and configure a modem under Solaris:

1. Launch the Service Access Facility manager (SAF), which is part of the admintool, an X Window-based tool. From the command line, enter **admintool**. The Admintool window appears.

2. From the **Browse** menu, select **Serial** ports. The list of serial ports is shown.

3. Select one of the ports, then select **Edit**, **Modify** from the menu to change the settings for that port. The Modify serial window appears.

4. Click the **Expert** button to reveal all options.

5. From the Template list, choose **Modem**.

6. Check **Service Enable**.

7. In the options section, select **Initialize Only**, **Bi-Directional**, and **Software Carrier**.

8. For normal dial-in operation on this port, set the service setting to **/usr/bin/login**, and the streams modules setting to **idterm,ttcompat**.

9. Click **OK**, and you are ready to accept incoming calls on your modem.

The command string sent to a modem for it to work correctly under Solaris is AT&F&C1&D2E0V0Q0S0=2&W. Without this setting, the operating system will not work correctly with the modem. If no auto-answer is desired, the S0=2 portion may be left off.

CASE PROJECT

Trent and Williams, LLC is a tax accounting firm that provides modem access to 10 employees who telecommute from their home computers four days a week. The telecommuters dial into a bank of 10 modems at the firm that enable them to access the firm's small network and servers. The company hired you to consult about its modem communications needs.

1. Currently, the modem bank consists of analog V.90 modems, each connected to a separate telephone line (requiring the firm to pay for 10 telephone lines). The partners are curious about what other communications technologies might be appropriate for their communications needs. What technologies do you recommend?

2. One of the partners, Max Williams, is curious about modem standards. Generally explain the modem standards that are relevant to the firm's particular use of modems, and why the standards are important.

3. An accountant who telecommutes has Red Hat Linux 7.2 on her home computer. Prepare an explanation about how to set it up for dial-in use with your network.

4. One of the administrative assistants in the firm just received a computer running Windows XP Professional. Explain how to set up an Internet connection on this computer.

5. Alice Trent, the other managing partner, is running Mac OS X at home. Her ISP provided an IP address and network mask, but she is not certain what to do next. Explain what she must do.

6. One of the accountants has an older computer running Windows 95 that is equipped with a V.27ter modem. Frequently, there are times when he cannot access the firm's bank of modems. What might explain his access problems?

OPTIONAL CASE PROJECTS FOR TEAMS

Team Case One

Your boss is curious about the advantages of DSL compared to cable modems. Form a team and prepare a presentation that compares these two technologies.

Team Case Two

In addition to your comparison of DSL to cable modem technology, your boss is now interested in finding out what digital modem-based telecommunications services are available in your community. Use your team to research what services are available, the costs, the equipment needed for an individual user compared to a small business, and the communication speeds.

8

NETWORK CONNECTIVITY

After reading this chapter and completing the exercises, you will be able to:

♦ Explain basic networking theory, such as network topologies, packaging data to transport, and how devices connect to a network

♦ Describe network transport and communications protocols, and determine which protocols are used in specific computer operating systems

♦ Explain how bridging and routing are used on networks

♦ Explain LANs and WANs

♦ Describe how network and workstation operating systems are used for remote networking

Networking is an extension of the desire to share information instantly. This information may take the form of word-processed documents, graphs and charts, pictures, maps, x-rays, electronic mail, or full-motion video, for example. Using networks, a physician in New York City can help diagnose a patient who is with another physician in Los Angeles. Using networks, an engineer can coordinate the design of a new supersonic airplane by electronically sharing design diagrams with other engineers working on the same project in the same building. Students now use networks to obtain assignments from teachers, and to submit their completed work. Other students take entire classes or programs of study using the Internet.

As you learned in the last chapter, modems provide one of the first and most basic ways to build a network. Today, there are many new and evolving options to connect computers. Strong interest in setting up computers to communicate has spurred the development of an array of network technologies. In this chapter, you'll learn about basic networking theory and architectures, and how computers communicate through network protocols. You'll also learn how information is forwarded from one network to another. You'll discover the differences between local and wide area networks, and you'll learn how telecommuters remotely access their work from home. Most important, you'll learn about networking features that are included in operating systems. These features make it possible for even the most diverse combination of operating systems to be partners in shared network communications.

BASIC NETWORKING THEORY

A **network** is composed of communications media such as communications cable, used to link computers, printers, disk storage, CD-ROM arrays, and network communications equipment. The basic principle of networking is similar to connecting telephones for communications. In a telecommunications system, telephones are located in homes and businesses. Each telephone can communicate with other telephones by linking to the local main cable or trunk line that is on nearby telephone poles or that runs underground. For example, in a single neighborhood, 50 homes may connect to one trunk line. That trunk line goes to a local telephone switch that connects to other trunk lines throughout a city or town. The main components of a telephone system are telephones, telephone communications equipment like switches, and cable that links telephones and switches.

Most of us understand the basics of telephone communications because we have used them all of our lives. The basics of networking can be understood in a similar way because computer networks mimic the principles of telephone systems. To understand networking, think of the computer as similar to the telephone, in that each computer is linked to the network by cable, which is similar to telephone cable. The equipment between computers is similar to a switch, or central hub, that connects one telephone to another (see Figure 8-1).

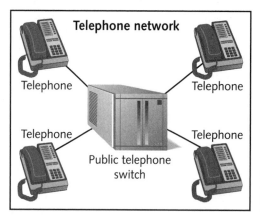
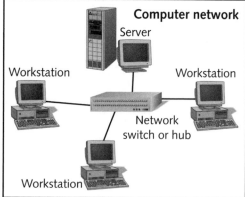

Figure 8-1   Telephone and computer networks compared

The hardware components of a computer network are computers, printers, communications cable, and internetworking devices such as bridges, switches, routers, and hubs (these devices are discussed later in this chapter). Computer networks also have software components consisting of client and server network operating systems. Windows 95, Windows 98, Windows NT 4.0 Workstation, Windows 2000 Professional, and Windows XP Professional are examples of client operating systems. A **client operating system** is one that enables a workstation to run applications, process information locally, and communicate with other computers and devices over the network. A **workstation** is a computer that has a CPU, and can run applications locally, or obtain applications and files from another computer on the network.

 Sometimes the term *workstation* is confused with the term *terminal*. The difference is that a **terminal** has no CPU or local storage for running programs independently. The main use of a terminal is to access a mainframe or minicomputer, and run programs on that computer.

A **network operating system (NOS)** is one that enables the coordination of network activities and the sharing of resources—network communications, shared printing, shared access to files, and shared access to software, for example. Windows 2000, Windows .NET Server, UNIX, and Novell NetWare are examples of NOSs. A **server** is a computer running a NOS, which provides resources, such as shared files and programs that are accessed by clients.

Reasons for a Network

Networks were invented for three interrelated reasons: to share resources, save money, and increase productivity. Most important, networks allow organizations to save money by sharing resources. For example, consider an accounting office in which there are 35 people, each with his or her own computer. Each person in the office uses word-processing software, spreadsheets, databases, and accounting software. Also, each needs to print documents and regularly back up files. Purchasing individual software packages and installing them on every office computer can be expensive and time consuming. Also, purchasing a printer for each computer is expensive, especially when each person does not require continuous use of a printer; and purchasing 35 tape drives to back up important information on each computer in the office is another expense. Buying a printer for each computer user was a particularly common practice when PCs were introduced, in the days before networks were common.

By installing a network, this office can save money by sharing resources (see Figure 8-2). For example, a server with one or two printers and a tape drive might be installed in a central location. One or two additional printers can be installed on the network in other locations, and those printer operations coordinated through the server. Software installations are made easier because a site license can be purchased so that an original copy of the software is placed on the server, and users can install the software on their workstations over the network. The advantage is that the software can be configured on the server so that it is installed in the same way on each workstation. Another advantage is that site licensing is often less expensive than purchasing individual software licenses for each user.

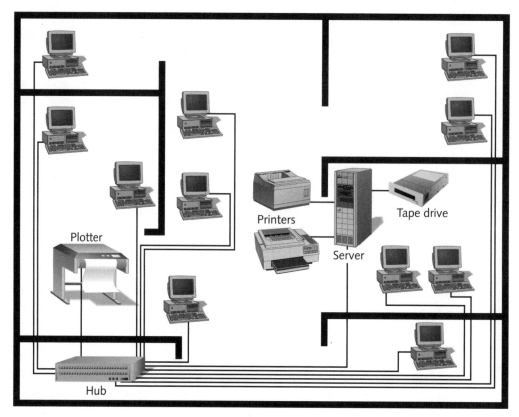

Figure 8-2   Sharing resources in an office

For instance, Windows NT Server 4.0, Windows 2000 Server, and Windows .NET Server offer several ways to save money and time by centralizing software and client operating system installation through a server. In Windows NT Server 4.0, the **Network Client Administrator** enables you to install the MS-DOS and Windows 95 operating systems on any client connected to a network. Windows 2000 Server and Windows .NET Server use **Remote Installation Services (RIS)** to install pre-configured client operating systems, such as Windows 2000 Professional, on a mass scale. When you use RIS to install a client operating system, you create an operating system image containing specific settings, and then the image is downloaded and installed on the client. For example, if all clients must have a particular desktop appearance, the image can be created to set up that desktop appearance on all computers.

Both Windows 2000 and Windows .NET Server also enable you to either assign or publish software applications through creating group policies. **Assigning applications** involves setting up an Active Directory group policy so that a particular version of software, such as Microsoft Word XP, is automatically started through a desktop shortcut or menu selection, or by clicking a file type. An example is starting Word XP when the user clicks a document with a .doc extension. A Windows 2000 or Windows .NET Server with Active Directory implemented can assign applications for a particular group, several groups, or all Windows 2000 or Windows XP Professional clients. If the user inadvertently deletes the shortcut or menu selection (or even the software), it is automatically re-installed the next time the user logs onto the network. **Publishing an application** means that the Windows 2000 Professional or Windows XP Professional client can open the Add/Remove Programs (Add or Remove Programs in Windows XP) icon in the Control Panel to install the pre-configured software from a central Windows 2000 or Windows .NET server.

Productivity is another reason for networks. Consider the accounting office example before the installation of a network. Each time an accountant needs to share a spreadsheet with another accountant, he or she makes a copy on a floppy disk and hand carries it to the other accountant. This is a process that we now call "sneakernet." Each act of sharing requires several time-consuming steps:

1. Finding and formatting the floppy disk

2. Copying the spreadsheet to the disk

3. Leaving your desk and walking to the other person's desk, which is perhaps on another floor, or in another building

4. Taking time for conversation with the other person as you deliver the disk

5. Walking back to your desk and possibly having more conversations with other employees along the way

Without a network, sharing one spreadsheet with one other person might take 10 minutes to one hour. If you need to share the file with several people, the process takes even longer. In the past, organizations sometimes hired an individual whose job it was to carry disks with shared files and printouts to other people within the organization. With a network, your productivity increases significantly without the need to hire an extra person. All you must do is copy the spreadsheet to a shared location on your workstation or on a server. If you need to share a printout as well, you just send it to a network printer in a location near the recipient.

Electronic mail (e-mail) is another example of how networking can increase productivity. With e-mail, you can reach someone on the first try. You also can attach a file, such as a word-processing document or spreadsheet, so that the recipient has it right away. If you need to contact several people, you can do so by sending one e-mail to a previously established address list, or to multiple recipients. Many organizations schedule meetings through e-mail and allow the e-mail program to send announcements automatically.

Electronic commerce is another network application that increases productivity. Computer companies such as Gateway and Dell can take thousands of orders a day through a Web site, as well as offer automated support or order information. The electronic capability to offer automated information saves time for customer service and support people, making them more productive.

Another growing area for networks is electronic conferencing. Advances in network technology coupled with advances in audio and video technologies enable organizations to hold conferences among sites in different parts of the country or around the world. For instance, a company that has manufacturing plants in three different sites can use a network so that members of project teams at each site can confer without leaving town. Electronic conferencing can save thousands of dollars in travel and employee time.

The Development of Network Operating Systems

Novell NetWare was one of the first network operating systems, initially demonstrated in 1982 at the National Computer Conference as a groundbreaking PC networking system. Windows 3.1, released in 1992, was one of the first Windows-based operating systems with network capabilities, enabling it to connect to NetWare, Microsoft, and other networks. (In 1992, Microsoft added basic workgroup capabilities to an updated version of Windows 3.1.) In 1993, Windows 3.11, also called Windows for Workgroups (WFW), constituted another significant step up in Windows network connectivity because it added peer-to-peer networking, expanded workgroup capabilities, and provided more support to connect to servers. Peer-to-peer networking enables basic PCs or workstations to share resources, such as files, with other computers. **Workgroups** (pre-defined groups of member computers) provide the ability to limit resource sharing on the basis of group membership.

Windows 95 represents yet another major step into networking because it expands peer-to-peer networking and has the ability to connect to more kinds of networks. Although Windows 98 looks similar to Windows 95 on the surface, it adds even more networking features, such as the ability to connect to very high-speed networks. Windows Millennium Edition (Me) is the last in the Windows 95/98 track of Windows operating systems. Windows Me was developed for home computer users to add multimedia capabilities, such as playing music, storing family photos, playing games, and accessing the Internet. It also makes it easier to connect all kinds of new devices to a computer, such as Internet cameras, digital cameras, scanners, read/write CD-ROM drives, TV converters, and specialized printers for color photo reproduction. Windows Me also comes with better networking capabilities for home use. Windows XP Home Edition, the latest addition, is meant as the next upgrade step from Windows Me. It is a scaled-down version of Windows XP Professional.

Representing a different Windows operating system track, Windows NT 3.1 was released just a little later than Windows 3.1, but Windows NT 3.1 was intended for industrial-strength networking from the beginning. The server version of Windows NT 3.1 was called Windows NT 3.1 Advanced Server, and was targeted to compete with NetWare. In 1994, Microsoft renamed the two versions of Windows NT to Windows NT Workstation and Windows NT Server, and considerably enhanced the networking capabilities of the Server version. The dawning of the millennium brought two new names for Windows NT: Windows 2000 Server and Windows 2000 Professional (Workstation). Today, Windows 2000 has evolved into two products, Windows XP and Windows .NET

Server, both containing the core elements of the Windows 2000 kernel. Windows XP (Home and Professional) is the desktop version of the new operating system, while Windows .NET Server is the server version. Besides having a new GUI, the Windows XP and .NET Server desktop stresses removing the clutter of icons by incorporating more functions into the Start menu. Windows XP and Windows .NET Server also offer better Internet security through a built-in firewall, and the ability to remotely control the computer over an Internet connection via a tool called Remote Desktop.

Both Windows 2000 and Windows XP have built-in options to configure home and small office networks, such as sharing a one modem-based Internet connection between multiple computers connected through a small network. Windows XP also has configuration options to enable novice users to quickly set up DSL or cable modem connections.

Besides the NetWare and Windows-based operating systems, there are several others designed for networking:

- UNIX
- Banyan Vines
- Pathworks
- LAN Manager

Three of these operating systems have not yet been mentioned in the text: Banyan Vines, Pathworks, and LAN Manager. All three are server operating systems that may be in use on networks, and that run on small to mid-sized computers. Banyan Vines, now known as ePresence, terminated all maintenance and support of Banyan products as of April 2001, and Pathworks is supported by Digital Equipment Corporation (now Compaq). LAN Manager was an early server operating system developed by Microsoft prior to Windows NT Server.

The Basics of Network Topologies

Networks are designed in three basic patterns, or architectures: bus, ring, and star. Each of these is called a network topology. A **topology** is the design of the network, as if you were looking at it from above in a helicopter, or following the path information takes when it goes from one computer to another. (You can practice identifying network topologies in Hands-on Project 8-1.)

A network that uses a bus topology is designed like a climbing rope with knots tied along the way for a foothold. There is a beginning and end to the rope, and junctures along the way for your feet. When you climb up the rope, you go from end-to-end, passing through each juncture. Like the climbing rope, a bus topology has two end points. Each end point has a terminator to keep the electronic data signal from reflecting back along the path it just traveled. Also like the knots in the rope, the bus topology network communications cable has junctures at which computers are attached. A data-carrying signal is transmitted onto the cable from the source computer, and it goes through all junctures on the bus. When the destination computer receives the signal, it picks it up from the cable and then codes it into data. Figure 8-3 shows a simple bus network.

8

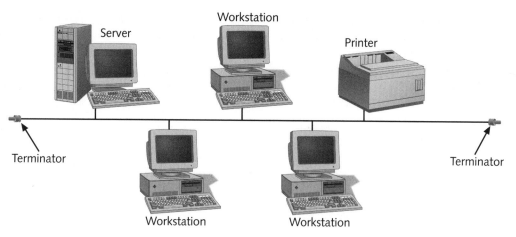

Figure 8-3   Bus topology

A ring topology is one in which the data-carrying signal goes from station to station around the ring, until it reaches the target destination. There is no beginning or end point, so there are no terminators (see Figure 8-4).

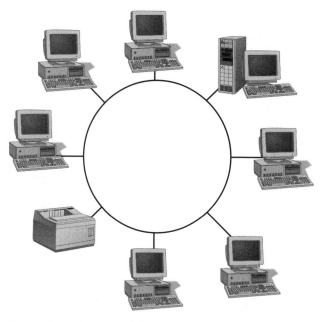

Figure 8-4   Ring topology

The star topology is one in which there is a hub in the middle, with cable segments coming out of the hub in all directions, as shown in Figure 8-5. The hub sends the signal onto each segment, which has a computer at the end. Every segment is terminated inside the hub at one end, and inside the computer at the other end (when it is used for Ethernet communications, discussed later in this chapter). The star topology was derived from the topology most frequently used in telephone networks. It is the oldest telecommunications topology, and has evolved into the most popular network topology because it has the most flexibility in terms of providing for future growth, and adding high-speed networking capability.

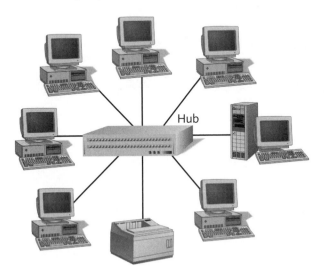

Figure 8-5 Star topology

Some hubs, called **passive hubs**, just pass the signal onto a segment without modifying the signal in any way. The disadvantage in using a passive hub is that the signal grows weaker each time it goes through the hub to the next segment. Networks that use passive hubs support fewer workstations because the signal eventually becomes too weak for reception. Networks that use **active hubs** support more computers because the signal is amplified to its original strength each time it goes through the hub.

Switched networks use switches in place of hubs. The switch learns what devices are located on each of the segments attached to it, and only transmits the information on the segment where the destination device resides. Traffic is not transmitted on all segments at once, as happens on hubs.

Packets, Frames, and Cells

Each computer or network device translates data into individual units, and then places the units onto the network cable. For example, if you obtain a file from a server and transport it to your workstation, the file is broken into hundreds of small data units, transmitted one unit at a time from the server to your workstation. Each data unit is called a **packet** or **frame**. These terms are sometimes used interchangeably, but they are not the same. Both consist of data and transmission control information contained in a header that is appended to the front of the data. The difference is that a packet contains routing information that can be read by specialized devices that are able to forward packets to specific networks. The actual data is placed after the header information, and followed by a footer or trailer that enables detection of a transmission error. Figure 8-6 shows a basic packet format. (Hands-on Projects 8-2, 8-3, and 8-4 show how to view the computers connected to a network, and the frame [packet] activity on a network.)

Figure 8-6   Basic packet format

Older networks transmit at speeds of 4 Mbps (megabits per second), 10 Mbps, and 16 Mbps. Newer networks transmit at 100 Mbps to 10 Gbps and faster, or consist of segments that transmit at 10 Mbps, 100 Mbps, 1 Gbps, or 10 Gbps. Network **backbones**, which are segments that join main networks, typically run at 100 Mbps or higher. A backbone might join networks on individual floors in a building, or link a LAN in one building to a network in another building.

Some networks require extra capacity for high-speed transmissions of over 100 Mbps, such as networks that have a high proportion of multimedia applications, or on which large files (1 MB and more) are regularly transmitted. On these networks, data may be transported in cells. A **cell** is a data unit designed for high-speed communications; it has a control header and a fixed-length payload (see Figure 8-7). The **payload** is that portion of a frame, packet, or cell that contains the actual data, which might be a portion of an e-mail message or word-processing file. One element of the cell header is path information that enables the cell to take the route through the network that is most appropriate to the type of data carried within the cell. For example, a large graphics file that holds a medical x-ray might take a different network path than a cell transmission containing streaming video for a movie clip.

Figure 8-7   Basic cell format

The exact format of a frame, packet, and cell is determined by the type of protocol used on a network. A **protocol** is a set of formatting guidelines for network communications, like a language, so that the information sent by one computer can be accurately decoded by another. Protocols also coordinate network communications so that data is transported in an orderly fashion, preventing chaos when two or more computers want to transmit at the same time. A network may use several different protocols, depending on the NOS and the types of devices that are connected (protocols are discussed later in this chapter).

Connecting to a Network

Computers and internetworking devices connect to a network through a **network interface card (NIC)**. A NIC is usually a card that goes into a computer's expansion slot, or that is built into a network device or a computer. The NIC is equipped with a connector that enables it to attach to the network communications cable. Each NIC has a unique hexadecimal address, called a device or physical address, which identifies it to the network. It is also called the **Media Access Control (MAC) address**. This address is used much like a postal address because it enables a computer (the source) to create a frame or packet and send it to a specific destination computer (see Figure 8-8).

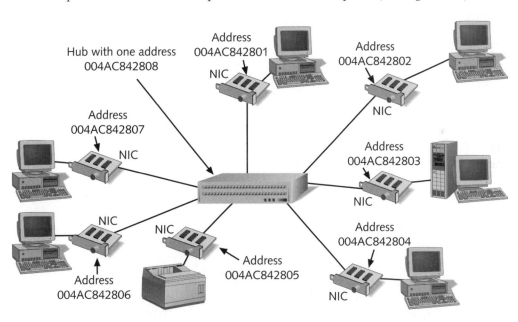

Figure 8-8 Devices on a network with unique physical addresses

A NIC is several devices built into one card. First, it is a transmitter and receiver (or transceiver) that can transmit a signal onto the cable and pick up a signal to decode. It also is a connection interface that matches the type of cable used on a network (twisted-pair, coaxial, or fiber-optic cable, for example). Finally, it contains computer circuits and chips that provide a home to software logic that translates data into packets and frames, and then sends the translated data onto the cable as an electrical or optical signal. Some NICs also transform data into radio frequency communications, called packet radio, for wireless networks. The software logic consists of one or more programs called **firmware** because it resides in a programmable chip on the card. Communication between the operating system and its NIC, like communication between the operating system and various input, output, and storage devices, is controlled by driver software written by the manufacturer of the device (in this case the NIC). Drivers are installed as part of the firmware on the NIC, and into the operating system on the computer when the NIC is installed. (Try Hands-on Project 8-12 to build a network cable for connecting to a NIC.)

One important step related to installing a NIC is to make sure you have the most recent software drivers for that NIC and for the operating system that is running on its host computer, such as NetWare, Windows NT/2000/XP, UNIX, Mac, or Windows 95/98/Me. Network communications are complex, and early versions of NIC drivers often contain errors that impede the NIC's performance. Most manufacturers offer the latest versions of drivers on their Web sites.

NETWORKING PROTOCOLS

Network communications are made possible through protocols. Protocols are used for many types of network communications, including the following:

- Coordinating transport of packets and frames among network devices
- Encapsulating data and communication control information
- Providing communications to accomplish a specific function, such as enabling the destination computer to tell the source computer to slow its transmission speed because it is too fast for the destination computer
- Enabling communications over a long-distance network, such as the Internet
- Enabling remote users to dial into networks

Two of the most important types of protocols are those that coordinate transport, and those that communicate and coordinate how data is encapsulated and addressed.

Transport Protocols

The commonly used transport protocols are Ethernet and token ring. Ethernet is in more installations than token ring because there are more network equipment options for it, and because modern Ethernet network designs are most easily expanded for high-speed networking. Token ring, an IBM-proprietary protocol, is used because it is reliable, and network problems were initially easier to troubleshoot on token ring networks than on early Ethernet networks.

Improved design options and equipment now make the complexity of troubleshooting Ethernet problems on a par with troubleshooting token ring problems.

Both Ethernet and token ring are defined as part of the networking standards established by the Institute of Electrical and Electronics Engineers (IEEE) through its 802 standards committee. The 802 standards are followed by network administrators and manufacturers to ensure consistent network communications, and the ability for one network to connect to another.

Ethernet

In **Ethernet** communications, only one station on the network should transmit at a given moment. If two or more stations transmit at the same time, frames collide. The transmission control method used by Ethernet is called **Carrier Sense Multiple Access with Collision Detection (CSMA/CD)**. In CSMA/CD, the NICs of computers and devices check the network communications cable for a carrier signal that contains an encoded frame. If the device's NIC detects a carrier signal, and if the NIC decodes its own device address within the frame, it forwards that packet to its firmware for further decoding. If the frame does not contain its device address, then the NIC does not process the signal any further.

When the detected carrier signal is twice (or more) the strength of a normal carrier signal, this indicates that at least two network stations transmitted at the same time. In this situation, a collision occurred, and a transmitting station sends a "jam" signal to warn all other stations. After the jam signal is sent, every station waits a different amount of time before attempting to transmit again. The amount of time that a particular station waits is determined by generating a random number for the wait period, on the assumption that each station will generate a different random number. If two stations generate the same random number and transmit simultaneously, then the collision recovery process starts again.

There are two mainstream varieties of Ethernet protocol communications: the IEEE 802.3 standard and Ethernet II. Both are nearly identical, but Ethernet II uses a slightly different frame format for modern network communications. In IEEE 802.3 and in Ethernet II, frames contain a header that has control information, along with source and destination addressing. The data portion of both frame types contains 576 to 12,208 bytes. Also, both frame formats contain a frame check sequence field as a trailer, which is used to alert the receiving station when a transmission error occurs, by showing that some portion of the received frame contents is not the same as when the frame was sent. If a transmission error is detected, the frame in error is retransmitted. Variations of the Ethernet protocol include Ethernet 802.2 and Ethernet 802.2 SNAP. Ethernet 802.2 is really combined with Ethernet 802.3 or Ethernet II so that there are newer service access points defined in the data-link LLC sublayer (OSI layer 2). **SNAP (SubNetwork**

Access Protocol) was added as a way to enable protocols that are not fully 802.2 compliant, such as AppleTalk, to operate on Ethernet networks. It creates open or unknown service access points that can be used by vendors. In essence, because vendors implement the standards differently, Ethernet is really not as pure under the hood as you might think. For example, Ethernet 802.3 or Ethernet II can incorporate Ethernet 802.2—or not, and both can incorporate Ethernet 802.2 SNAP—or not.

Networks that use Ethernet are designed in a bus topology, or a star topology, in which the internetworking devices simulate a logical bus. Ethernet hybrid star-bus networks are very common in modern network design because they are easier to troubleshoot and expand for high-speed networking than simple bus networks.

Originally, the speed of Ethernet was 10 Mbps. Newer Ethernet standards now include 100 Mbps and 1 Gbps versions that are called Fast Ethernet and Gigabit Ethernet, respectively. 10 Gbps is now delivered by several vendors. Fast Ethernet is becoming commonplace, and most NICs are currently designed to handle either 10 or 100 Mbps communications. Gigabit Ethernet is finding acceptance on busy network backbones, in which even Fast Ethernet does not provide enough capacity.

All versions of Ethernet are compatible with popular network operating systems such as:

- UNIX
- NetWare
- Windows NT, Windows 2000, Windows XP, and Windows .NET Server
- Windows 3.x
- Windows 95, Windows 98, and Windows Me
- Mac OS
- Banyan Vines
- Pathworks

Token Ring

In most versions of **token ring**, only one network station transmits at a time. The sequence of frame and packet transmissions is controlled by the use of a specialized frame, called a **token**. A token without data is transmitted around the network until it is captured by a station that wants to transmit. When the token is captured by a station, no other station can transmit until the station that has the token is finished (see Figure 8-9). The transmitting station packages data inside the token, so that part of the token is used as the frame header to indicate the beginning of a frame, and part is used as the frame trailer to indicate the last sequence of bytes in the frame.

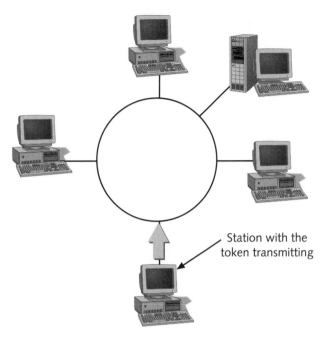

Figure 8-9   Station with the token in token ring

As the name suggests, token ring networks use the ring topology. Thus, the frame is transmitted from station to station around the ring, until it reaches the destination station. The destination station removes the frame from the network and decodes the frame's contents for local use. It also replicates the frame back onto the network to be forwarded around the ring to the sender, but changes two bits inside the frame indicating that the frame was successfully received and decoded at the destination.

On most token ring networks, the first station recognized as connected becomes the active monitor, and all other stations are standby monitors. The active monitor is charged with assessing transmissions to make sure that a token frame exists, the timing of packet transmissions is accurate, and standby monitors are responding. Each standby monitor periodically transmits a message to show that it is present and available to take over for the active monitor if it fails. If there is no token, the active monitor creates a new one and places it on the network. If the active monitor ceases to function, or if there is no response from a standby monitor, the token ring network goes into a beaconing condition, which is started when a station sends a beacon frame to warn that there is a problem. No tokens containing a data payload can be sent until the beaconing condition is solved, such as by assigning a new active monitor.

Older token ring networks transmit at 4 Mbps and newer networks transmit at 16 Mbps. IBM developed 100 Mbps fast token ring technology that is compatible with existing 4 Mbps and 16 Mbps networks. Fast token ring got off to a slow start in the market and, as a result, manufacturers discontinued production of internetworking devices that support it.

Token ring is compatible with the same mainstream network operating systems that are used with Ethernet, including:

- UNIX

- NetWare

- Windows NT, Windows 2000, Windows XP, and Windows .NET Server

- Windows 3.x

- Windows 95, Windows 98, and Windows Me

- Mac OS

- Banyan Vines

- Pathworks

Implementing a Transport Protocol in an Operating System

A transport protocol is interfaced with an operating system through three elements: a network driver specification built into the operating system, a NIC, and a NIC driver. Network operating systems are built to offer special elements, which programmers call "hooks," in the operating system kernel (program code), that enable the operating system to interface with a network. For example, Microsoft designed the **Network Device Interface Specification (NDIS)** and Windows-based NDIS drivers for this purpose. Similarly, NetWare uses the Open Datalink Interface (ODI) and ODI drivers.

 One way to think of networking "hooks" in an operating system, and how a NIC driver links into those hooks, is by using the analogy of a lock and key. The combined hooks are like a lock, and the NIC driver software is similar to a key that is specially cut to exactly match the unique configuration of the lock.

When you set up an operating system to work on an Ethernet or token ring network, the first step is to purchase an Ethernet or token ring NIC for the computer running the operating system. The NIC cable interface must also match the type of cable used on the network. After the NIC is installed in an open expansion slot in the computer, the next step is to boot the operating system and install the NIC driver software, which links the NIC into the network computing hooks in the kernel. For example, if you install an Ethernet NIC in a computer running Windows XP, then you must obtain an NDIS-compatible driver for that NIC, which is written for Windows XP Ethernet communications.

After the NIC setup is complete, and the computer is connected to the network, the operating system, NIC, and driver handle the work of converting data created at the computer to an Ethernet or token ring format for transport over the network. The same three elements also enable the computer to receive Ethernet or token ring packets or frames and convert them to data that the computer can interpret.

Communications Protocols

The development of communications protocols (the protocols that carry data between two communicating stations, and are encapsulated in Ethernet or token ring transport protocols) has been interrelated to the network operating systems in which they are used. For example, Novell NetWare, which grew out of experiments with network operating systems that began in the early eighties, became the first true network operating system. The **Internet Packet Exchange (IPX)** protocol was developed to enable a NetWare file server to communicate with its client workstations. Also, in 1982, researchers implemented and combined two protocols for use on the Advanced Research Projects Agency network, ARPANET, which was the long-distance network that set the foundation for the Internet. The ARPANET protocols now used worldwide over the Internet are **Transmission Control Protocol** (TCP) and **Internet Protocol** (IP). Since these are usually used together, the combination is called TCP/IP. Because many of the original ARPANET servers ran UNIX, this operating system was quickly adapted to employ TCP/IP. Two other important communication protocols are NetBIOS Extended User Interface (NetBEUI), a protocol developed for Microsoft networks, and AppleTalk, developed for Macintosh networks.

8

IPX

IPX is a protocol developed by Novell and modeled after the Xerox Network System (XNS) protocol. Xerox created XNS for Ethernet communications. Novell adopted XNS to use with NetWare and called the end product IPX. Although it was developed in the early eighties, IPX is still widely used because NetWare is one of the most commonly implemented network server operating systems. One reason IPX has survived is that it is tailored for NetWare environments, and it can be routed, which means that it can transport packets to specific networks, as designated in the packet addressing information.

IPX encapsulates data and transports it within a host transport protocol format— Ethernet or token ring, for example. IPX is a connectionless protocol, which means that it does minimal checking to ensure that a packet reaches its destination, leaving this task for the Ethernet or token ring communications layer within the packet. When there is a need for more reliable data transport, such as for data from a database, an application running via NetWare can use **Sequence Packet Exchange (SPX)**, a protocol that provides connection-oriented communications. In addition to Ethernet and token ring, IPX relies upon SPX at the transport layer to provide reliable, error-free communication. The limitation of IPX/SPX is that it is a "chatty" protocol. Servers and clients configured for IPX frequently broadcast their presence on the network, even when there are no requests to exchange actual data or information.

IPX works with other specialized service and NetWare protocols as follows:

- *Link Support Layer (LSL):* Enables one NIC to transmit and receive multiple protocols, such as IPX and TCP/IP
- *NetWare Core Protocol (NCP):* Used to access applications between a server and its client

- *NetWare Link Services Protocol (NLSP):* Enables routing information to be added to an IPX packet

- *Routing Information Protocol (RIP):* Enables a NetWare server to build tables of routing information about the location of particular network stations

- *Service Advertising Protocol (SAP):* Enables NetWare client computers to identify servers and the services offered by each server

IPX is the default communications protocol in all versions of NetWare up to version 5. The default protocol in NetWare 5 and Netware 6 is TCP/IP, although they still support IPX.

NetBEUI

NetBEUI (NetBIOS Extended User Interface) was introduced in the early nineties as the main protocol for LAN Manager, a network server operating system developed by Microsoft and IBM, and the forerunner of Windows NT Server. NetBEUI became a widely implemented communications protocol as the use of Windows NT Server on small networks grew through the mid nineties. This protocol continues to play an important role in all versions of Windows NT Server, up through version 4. The role of NetBEUI in Windows 2000 Server is diminished in favor of using the more versatile TCP/IP. Microsoft does not include support for NetBEUI in Windows XP and Windows .NET Server.

NetBEUI was developed from the **Network Basic Input/Output System (NetBIOS)**, which is a technique used to interface software with network services. NetBIOS also provides a naming service for computers on Microsoft networks. For example, if you view all of the computers on a Microsoft network that contains Windows NT servers and Windows 95 and Windows 98 workstations, you will notice that each has a unique name, such as a nickname of the user, an abbreviation of the computer user's title, or a name that is symbolic to the user, like Tophat or Sparrow. (You can view NetBIOS names in Hands-on Projects 8-2 and 8-3.)

 NetBIOS should not be confused with a protocol. It acts as a software interface only, providing a way for an application to export data to a network service, such as linking data in a word-processed document to a network mail service that attaches the document to an e-mail.

NetBEUI is designed for networks consisting of fewer than 200 stations, and is well suited for Microsoft networks. It is particularly compatible with applications that use NetBIOS and computers that run Microsoft operating systems, such as Windows NT, Windows 3.x, Windows 95, Windows 98, and Windows Me. Another advantage of NetBEUI is that later versions of this protocol can handle nearly limitless communication sessions (earlier versions were limited to 254). Thus, the limit on the number of clients that can be connected to a Windows NT server using NetBEUI depends on the server hardware and network resources, not the protocol. Other advantages of NetBEUI are:

- Low use of memory resources

- Quick transport of information on small networks

- Strong error detection and recovery

- Relatively easy configuration in the host operating system

An important limitation of NetBEUI is that it is not designed to carry routing information, which means it is not a good choice for medium and large networks. When it is used on these types of networks, it must be sent to every portion of the network, instead of limited to only specific smaller networks within the larger network scheme. This characteristic creates unnecessary traffic on a medium or large network that may already be bursting with high traffic. Figure 8-10 illustrates how NetBEUI is flooded to all networks within a large network setup when the goal is to reach only Station A.

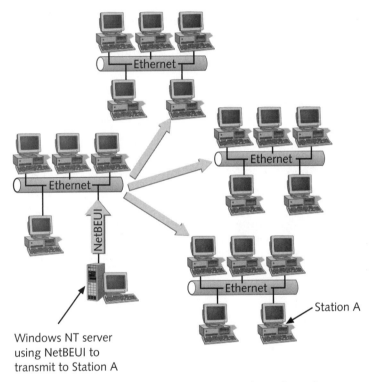

Figure 8-10   NetBEUI flooding all networks within a large network setup

TCP/IP

TCP/IP is one of the oldest protocols, initially developed for long-distance networking on ARPANET, and now used on most networks. One of the strongest influences on TCP/IP use has been the growth of the Internet. UNIX has always used TCP/IP as its main network communications protocol. NetWare versions 5 and 6, Windows 2000 Server, Windows 2000 Professional, Windows XP Home, Windows XP Professional, and Windows .NET Server also have adopted TCP/IP as the protocol of choice. Besides these server operating systems, TCP/IP is used to network IBM mainframe computers that run the Multiple Virtual Storage (MVS) operating system and Digital Equipment Corporation computers that run the Virtual Memory System (VMS). TCP/IP is also compatible with the following operating systems:

- Windows 3.1 and 3.11
- Windows 95/98/Me
- Windows NT 3.0, 3.5, 3.51, and 4.0
- Windows 2000/XP/.NET Server
- Mac OS
- Banyan Vines

TCP was developed for extremely reliable point-to-point communications between computers on the same network. This protocol establishes communication sessions among applications on two communicating computers, making sure there is a mutually agreeable "window" of transmission characteristics. Some of the communication functions performed by TCP are:

- Establishes the communication session between two computers
- Ensures that data transmissions are accurate
- Encapsulates, transmits, and receives the payload data
- Closes the communication session between two computers

The IP portion of TCP/IP is used to make sure that a frame or packet reaches the intended destination. IP performs the following complementary functions with TCP:

- Handles packet addressing
- Handles packet routing
- Fragments packets, as needed, for transport across different types of networks
- Provides simple packet error detection in conjunction with the more thorough error detection provided by TCP

IP addressing uses the dotted decimal notation that consists of four 8-bit binary numbers (octets) separated by periods. The format is as follows: 10000001.00000101.00001010.00000001, which converts to the decimal value 129.5.10.1. Part of the address designates a unique identifier for a network, called the network identifier (NET_ID). For example, a school or corporation has its own NET_ID, which distinguishes its network from all others. Another part of the address is the host identifier (HOST_ID) that distinguishes a computer or network device from any other computer or device on a network. There are five IP address classes, Class A through Class E, each used with a different type of network. The address classes reflect the size of the network, and whether the packet is unicast or multicast. In the **unicast** method of transmission, one copy of each packet is sent to each target destination. If there are eight workstations designated to receive a packet, such as a portion of a video clip, then it is transmitted eight times. In the **multicast** method, the recipients are placed in a group, such as a group of all eight workstations since they are on the same network. Only one packet is sent to the group, via a router or switch, which then sends the packet to each group member.

Classes A through C are intended as unicast addressing methods, but each class represents a different network size. Class A is used for the largest networks composed of up to 16,777,216 nodes. Class A networks are identified by a value between 1 and 126 in the first position of the dotted decimal address. The network ID is the first eight bits, and the host ID is the last 24 bits. Class B is a unicast addressing format for medium-sized networks composed of up to 65,536 nodes, and it is identified by the first octet of bits ranging from decimal 128 to 191. The first two octets are the network ID, and the last two are the host ID.   Class C addresses are used for unicast network communications on small networks of 256 nodes or less. The first octet translates to a decimal value in the range of 192 to 223, and the network ID is contained in the first 24 bits, while the host ID is contained in the last eight bits.

Class D addresses do not reflect the network size, only that the communication is a multicast. Unlike Classes A through C, the four octets are used to specify a group of nodes to receive the multicast, which consists of those nodes that are multicast subscription members. Class D addresses are in the range from 224.0.0.0 to 239.255.255.255. A fifth address type, Class E, is used for experimentation, and addresses range from 240 to 255 in the first octet.

Besides class addressing, there are some special-purpose IP addresses, such as 255.255.255.255, which is a broadcast packet sent to all network locations. Packets that begin with 127 in the first octet are used for network testing. An entire network is designated by providing only the network ID and zeroes in all other octets, such as 132.155.0.0 for a Class B network, or 220.127.110.0 for a Class C network.

A new way to ignore address class designation is by using **Classless Interdomain Routing (CIDR)** addressing that puts a slash (/) after the dotted decimal notation. CIDR provides more IP address options for medium-sized networks because there is shortage of Class B and Class C addresses. The shortage is due to the proliferation of networks, combined with the finite number of addresses numerically possible in the basic four-octet address scheme. For example, a CIDR network addressing scheme for a network that needs up to 16,384 (2^{14}) nodes might be 165.100.0.0/14.

Some network administrators also designate a **subnet mask** within the IP address which enables them to uniquely identify smaller networks or subnetworks within the larger network setup. For example, using a subnet mask enables the network administrator at a university to limit how much network traffic goes to certain networks on campus, as a way to reduce congestion and implement network security. In Figure 8-11, implementing a subnet mask enables a packet to be sent from one campus network to Station A on another network, without flooding all networks with traffic. The exact allocation of the IP address into NET_ID, HOST_ID, and subnet masks depends on factors unique to each network, such as its size, the number of computers connected to it, and the overall design of the network.

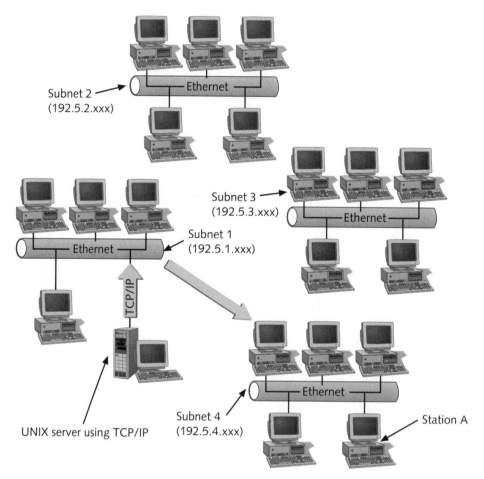

Figure 8-11   Using TCP/IP subnet masks

Consider a university's IP address of 129.72.22.124, in which the first half (first two octets) of the address is the NET_ID and the last octet is the HOST_ID. The first three octets are used to specify the subnet. In this address, the 129.72 identifies the university (NET_ID), 129.72.22 identifies the subnet on which the station is located within the university, such as the network in the English building, and 124 is the HOST_ID of a particular computer on that subnet. In this designation, the subnet is useful in several ways. One is that data, such as e-mail intended for English faculty, can be directed to the English building subnet so that it does not saturate other parts of a busy university network. Another advantage is that the English Department can set up its own private Web site containing salary, budget, and human resources information, and limit access to only those with the correct subnet as part of their IP addresses.

 By Internet convention, an IP address in which the first octet translates to a decimal number between 128 and 191 signifies a medium to large network consisting of 257 to 65,536 stations.

Computers and devices that use IP addressing actually have two addresses: a physical address and an IP address. The use of two addresses provides better insurance that a packet will reach the right destination, while expending the fewest network resources. For example, on a large network, a packet might be able to follow any of several paths to its destination, but some paths will be longer, or will involve using more expensive resources, such as high-speed backbone links. IP addressing makes it possible to send a packet along the best or fastest route for the type of information it contains.

Today IP version 4 is in use on nearly all networks, but its 32-bit (four-octet) addressing capacity is a problem. The explosive growth of networks and the Internet has created an address shortage. IP version 6 (there is no version 5), or IP Next Generation, is a new standard that is intended to solve the address shortage by using 128-bit addresses and providing more specialized networking implementations, including voice, video, and multimedia applications. Vendors are slowly releasing their implementations of IPv6, but it will be several years before IPv6 is broadly available. Microsoft released updates for Windows 2000, and Windows XP has IPv6 as part of the operating system. Also, Red Hat Linux 7.x supports IPv6.

TCP/IP works with a range of associated protocols that make this a powerful combination for networks of all sizes and types. Some of those protocols include the following:

- *Routing Information Protocol (RIP)*: Enables network routing devices to build tables of routing information about the location of particular networks and network stations

- *Simple Mail Transfer Protocol (SMTP)*: Used to transmit e-mail

- *File Transfer Protocol (FTP)*: Used to send and receive files over a network

- *Telnet*: Used to enable a PC workstation to emulate a terminal for connections to mainframes and minicomputers over a network

- *Hypertext Transfer Protocol (HTTP)*: Used for World Wide Web communications (for network browsers)

- *Point-to-Point Protocol (PPP)*: Enables a computer to remotely access a network, through a dial-up modem connection, for example

- *Simple Network Management Protocol (SNMP)*: Used to detect and track network activity, including network problems

- *Internet Control Message Protocol (ICMP)*: Enables reporting of network errors

8

- *Domain Name Service (DNS)*: For resolving domain and computer names to IP addresses, and IP addresses to domain and computer names (see Chapter 5)

- *Dynamic Host Configuration Protocol (DHCP)*: For automatically assigning IP addresses (see Chapter 5)

AppleTalk

AppleTalk is a network communications protocol used between Macintosh computers. It is designed primarily as a peer-to-peer protocol, rather than for combined peer-to-peer and client-to-server communications. As a peer-to-peer protocol, AppleTalk establishes equal communications between networked Macintosh computers, without the need for a server (see Figure 8-12). Most mainstream network operating systems, such as Windows NT/2000/.NET Server and NetWare, support AppleTalk as a means to communicate with Macintosh computers. For example, disk space can be specially configured on a Windows NT/2000/.NET server for access by Macintosh computers. Network communications are then configured by installing AppleTalk (and Services for Macintosh) in Windows NT/2000/.NET server.

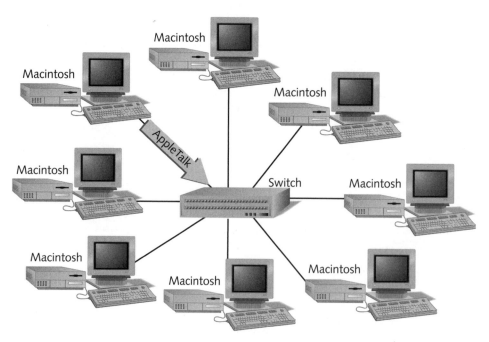

Figure 8-12   Peer-to-peer networking using AppleTalk and no server

AppleTalk performs three essential services: remote access to files over a network, network print services, and access to computers running MS-DOS or Windows operating systems. Examples of protocols designed for use with AppleTalk are as follows:

- *AppleTalk Address Resolution Protocol (AARP):* Converts computer names to IP addresses and vice versa for network and Internet communications

- *AppleTalk Data Stream Protocol (ADSP):* Ensures that streams of data are sent and received reliably

- *AppleTalk Session Protocol (ASP):* Used to ensure reliable network communications between two stations

- *Datagram Delivery Protocol (DDP):* Used for routing packets

- *Name-Binding Protocol (NBP):* Enables network services to be associated with specific computer names

- *Printer Access Protocol (PAP):* Used to communicate with network printers

- *Routing Table Maintenance Protocol (RTMP):* Enables routing table information to be built for routing packets

Early versions of AppleTalk are not very compatible with large networks that use multiple combinations of protocols, such as TCP/IP, IPX/SPX, and NetBEUI, over the same communication cable. AppleTalk Phase II is a newer version that is designed to work smoothly on large networks.

8

Implementing Communications Protocols in an Operating System

Most computer operating systems are designed to support one or more communications protocols. Those that support multiple communications protocols are able to do so through the same kernel interface hooks intended for transport protocols, such as NDIS for Windows-based operating systems and ODI for NetWare communications.

In general, there are two steps involved in setting up a communications protocol in an operating system. The first is to install the protocol software that is written for that operating system. For example, in Windows NT or 2000, you can install AppleTalk, IPX/SPX, NetBEUI, TCP/IP, or all four. The Windows-based software for each of these protocols is written to work in conjunction with NDIS so that these protocols can be carried over Ethernet or token ring networks. Step two is to bind the protocol with the NIC. Binding the protocol enables the NIC to format data for that protocol, and identify the most efficient methods for transporting it within Ethernet or token ring. When two or more protocols are used, binding also enables the NIC to set a priority for which protocol to process first. The protocol priority has a direct impact on how fast the computer and its NIC process network communications, and also affects network performance.

 In some operating systems, such as Windows 3.x, you manually bind the protocol, while in more advanced operating systems, such as Windows XP, the protocol binding occurs automatically (although you can still manually bind or unbind a protocol).

For example, consider a workstation that is configured for IPX/SPX, NetBEUI, and TCP/IP, and on which TCP/IP represents 80% of the communications. If its binding priority is set so that TCP/IP packets are processed after IPX/SPX and NetBEUI, then that workstation will take longer to process network communications than if TCP/IP is given the first priority. The end result is that the network must wait longer on that workstation, delaying communications to other workstations.

 Adjusting the priority of the network binding for workstations that support this, such as Windows NT/2000/XP, can make a significant difference in network performance. Figure 8-13 illustrates the screen used in Windows XP for setting the binding order.

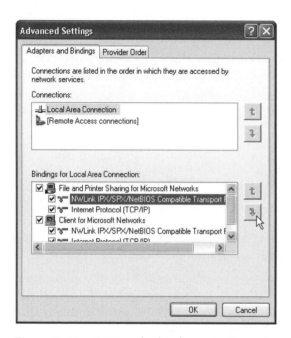

Figure 8-13   Setting the binding priority

The Mac OS up through version 9.x provides one of the easiest methods for setting up communications protocols. In the Mac OS, you use a Control Panel to designate a port for network communications associated with the NIC. After designating the port, you simply turn on AppleTalk from the Chooser window (try Hands-on Project 8-7). Binding takes place without user intervention.

In Mac OS X, setting up network communications is also simplified, but with more options than in Mac OS 9.x. You set up network connectivity through the Network panel that is accessed via System Preferences. This is the same panel that enabled you to configure network and Internet connectivity in Chapter 7. Through the Mac OS X Network panel, you can fully configure your Mac to use TCP/IP and TCP/IP network services, including the following:

- Manual configuration of IP address and subnet mask
- Automatic configuration of the IP address using DHCP
- Identification of the nearest router by IP address

- Identification of Domain Name Service (DNS) servers by IP address
- Identification of search domains by IP address

Most UNIX systems have TCP/IP networking support built in, and some of these automatically run a network configuration program when you first boot the computer with an installed NIC. NIC device drivers are loaded in the kernel. When the configuration program runs, you must supply information about the network connection, such as the IP address. If TCP/IP networking is not automatically configured when you first boot, it can be configured later by using the *ifconfig* command (for all versions of UNIX except HP-UX, which uses the *lanscan* command), when you log on as root. *Ifconfig* is a utility typically found in the /etc or /sbin directories (the /sbin directory in Red Hat Linux), which enables you to assign an IP address, turn on the network interface, and assign a subnet mask.

In most versions of UNIX, including Red Hat Linux and Solaris, type *ifconfig -a* to view the current IP and NIC settings (in HP-UX, type *lanscan -v*).

8

For some versions of UNIX, including Red Hat Linux, you must configure a loopback device, which is used to provide your computer with an internal IP address, even when it is not connected to the network. The IP address of the loopback device should be 127.0.0.1. Try Hands-on Project 8-8 to set up a loopback address and configure a network interface card.

In the Red Hat Linux GNOME interface, you can configure a network connection by clicking the Start icon on the panel, pointing to Programs, pointing to System, and clicking Network Configuration. The Network Configuration tool enables you to set up host and domain name, IP addressing, interface information, packet forwarding (for IPv4), and gateway information.

Communications protocols in NetWare, such as IPX and TCP/IP, can be set up in a window that appears when NetWare is installed. If TCP/IP is used, the setup process requires the IP address and subnet mask. Before version 5, NetWare uses IPX/SPX as the protocol of preference. In versions 5 and 6, TCP/IP is the preferred protocol, but NetWare can be configured to interoperate with TCP/IP and IPX/SPX (there is no support for NetBEUI).

In Windows 3.1 and 3.11, communications protocols are set up through the Main program group by opening the Windows Setup icon and the Options menu. For Windows 3.1, the network protocol configuration is modified by clicking Change System Settings and selecting the new setup. In Windows 3.11, the network protocol configuration is modified from the Options menu by clicking Drivers and modifying the protocol setup.

Communications protocols are set up in Windows 95, Windows 98, Windows Me, and Windows NT 4.0 through the Network icon in the Control Panel. In Windows 95, Windows 98, and Windows Me, you open the Network icon in the Control Panel and click the Configuration tab. Next, click the Add button and then double-click Protocol in the Select Network Component Type dialog box. (See Figure 8-14 and try Hands-on Project 8-9 to practice installing a protocol in Windows Me.) Windows NT 4.0 adds a slight variation in that you open the Network icon in the Control Panel, click the Protocols tab, and click Add to add a new protocol.

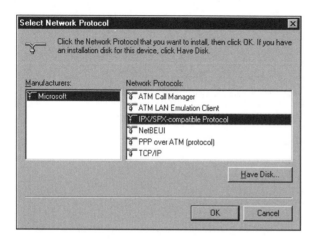

Figure 8-14   Installing IPX/SPX in Windows Me

Windows 2000 Server and Windows 2000 Professional use yet another method to set up a new protocol. In these versions of Windows, you open the Control Panel in the same way as in Windows 95, Windows 98, Windows Me, and Windows NT. Next, double-click the Network and Dial-up Connections folder. Use the Make New Connection Wizard to add a new setup for a NIC. Or, if there is already a connection, right-click it and select Properties (see Figure 8-15). Click Add and then click Protocols to add a new protocol.

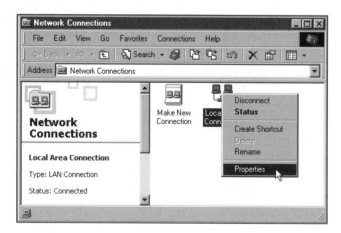

Figure 8-15   Installing a protocol in Windows 2000 Server

Finally, the network connection setup in Windows XP is performed through a wizard (see Figure 8-16), or manually via the Control Panel. To start the wizard, click Start, click Control Panel, click Network and Internet Connections, click Network Connections, and click Create a new connection. To configure the connection manually, open the Control Panel, click Network and Internet Connections, click Network Connections, right-click Local Area Connection, and click Properties. (Try Hands-on Projects 8-5 and 8-6 to practice installing a protocol in Windows 95, Windows 98, Windows NT, Windows 2000, and Windows XP.)

Figure 8-16 New Connection Wizard

Integrating Different Operating Systems on the Same Network

The key to implementing multiple operating systems on one network is to select a transport protocol and communications protocols that are supported in all of the operating systems that must be connected. Ethernet is particularly well suited to a network that has different operating systems. It is supported by Mac OS, UNIX, Windows-based operating systems, server operating systems, and mainframe operating systems. Also, the TCP/IP communications protocol is supported by most operating systems.

Ethernet is also a strong choice for mixed networks because there are more equipment, NIC, and driver options for it than for token ring. Also, there are more tools for troubleshooting problems. In general, Ethernet is also less expensive to implement than token ring. Most importantly, however, Ethernet has become the de facto standard for all modern networks.

In situations where TCP/IP is not supported by all operating systems, then multiple protocols can be configured, such as a combination of AppleTalk, TCP/IP, and IPX/SPX. For example, consider a network that has a combination of computers running Macintosh, Windows 95, Windows 98, Windows XP, Windows 2000 Server, and UNIX. This network might use AppleTalk and TCP/IP. AppleTalk might be used for communications between the Macintosh computers, and to enable them to access Windows 2000 Server resources. TCP/IP might be used for communications between the Windows-based computers, the server, and the UNIX computers. Another example is a small network of 120 computers in which the workstations run Windows 3.11, Windows 95, and Windows Me and access Windows NT 4.0 and NetWare 5 and 6 servers. This network might use both NetBEUI and IPX/SPX to enable communications among all of the workstations and servers.

BRIDGING AND ROUTING

One or more networks or segments can be linked by using internetworking devices such as bridges and routers. **Bridges** are used to link segments that are close together, such as on different floors in the same building. Another use for bridges is to extend segments, such as when more stations must be added, but the primary segment already contains the maximum length of cable or number of stations permitted by network standards. Bridges are also used to segment a network into smaller networks as a way to control traffic and reduce bottlenecks at busy network intersections. Finally, bridges can be used to link segments that use different cable types, such as linking a segment that uses twisted-pair cable to one that uses fiber-optic cable.

Bridges operate in what network administrators call promiscuous mode, which means that they examine the physical destination address of every frame that passes through them. Because they operate in promiscuous mode, bridge filters can be built to control which incoming frames are allowed to go out to specific bridge ports. For example, if a bridge has four ports connected to segments A, B, C, and D, it can build a table of known destinations. A frame sent from segment A that has a destination address on segment D can be prevented from reaching segments B and C (see Figure 8-17). The network administrator can build "filters" that use the bridge table information to control which segments receive traffic from other segments. This characteristic enables bridges to manage network traffic as a way to circumvent bottlenecks.

Bridges are protocol independent, a characteristic that permits them to forward all kinds of frame formats. Bridges can also accept frames from any computer operating system that can send frames. Bridges build tables of device or physical addresses to use in forwarding.

 Whenever two or more bridges are placed on a network, frames potentially can be forwarded in an endless loop. Network administrators prevent looping by implementing a programmed system of checks called the spanning tree algorithm.

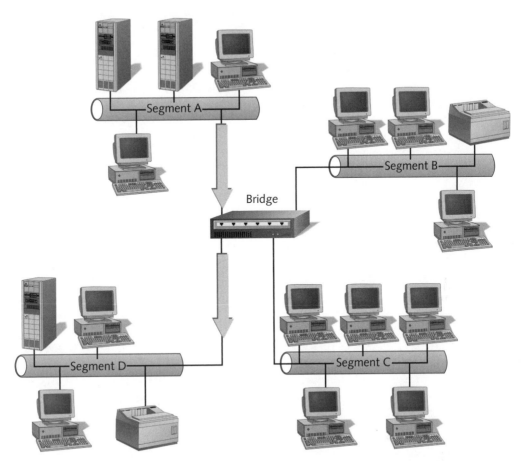

Figure 8-17   Using a bridge filter to direct Segment A frames to Segment D

Bridges are not designed to route packets from one network to another because they ignore routing information. Network designers use this characteristic in two positive ways. One is that because bridges do not look at or process routing information, they are able to forward frames faster than devices that process routing information (although this advantage is quickly disappearing because new routing devices use specialized computer chips to enhance their speed). Another advantage is that bridges can forward frames constructed by protocols that do not contain routing information, such as NetBEUI.

Most network administrators today use internetworking devices called switches instead of bridges. **Switches** operate in promiscuous mode like bridges, but they provide additional logic that enables them to move network traffic more efficiently than the old-style bridges. Also, some switches are starting to use mainstream network operating systems, such as Windows NT or Windows 2000, for managing the switch functions. Most manufacturers now use a Web interface to set up and maintain their switches. Statistics and reports are also generated through this same Web interface.

Routers are used to join networks, either locally or remotely. Unlike bridges, routers are designed to look at routing information in packets before forwarding those packets to another network. Routers also are sensitive to different network protocols and the resulting differences in packet formats. These characteristics of routers enable them to direct and control network traffic more effectively than bridges. Routers also make excellent firewalls because networks connected to a router can be divided into subnets as a way to control incoming and outgoing traffic to each subnet (see Figure 8-11). Because they truly route network traffic, routers are frequently used to prevent and cure network bottlenecks.

Routers that are equipped with multiple protocol interfaces can be used to translate traffic from one type of network to another, such as connecting a token ring network that uses TCP/IP, a token ring network that uses AppleTalk, and an Ethernet network that uses TCP/IP (see Figure 8-18). Like bridges, routers maintain tables, called routing tables, that store information about local networks and information obtained from routers connected to nearby and remote networks. Specialized routing protocols are used so that one router can transport part or all of its routing table information to another router.

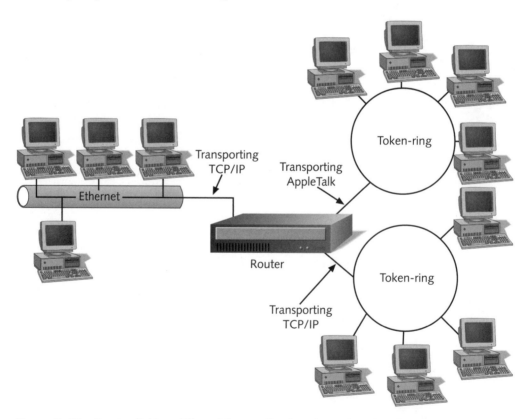

Figure 8-18   Router linking different types of networks and protocols

LOCAL AND WIDE AREA NETWORKS

Many networks are classified as local or wide area networks. A **local area network (LAN)** is one in which the service area is relatively small, such as a network in an office area, or one spread throughout a floor in a building. On a college campus, the Accounting Department computers might be connected to a LAN in the top floor of a classroom building, and the English Department computers might be on a different LAN within the main floor of the same building. Internetworking devices—a switch or a router, for example—might be used to connect these LANs.

A **wide area network (WAN)** is one that offers networking services over a long distance, such as between cities, states, or countries. For example, consider a documentary film company in Chicago that has a LAN that connects through a telecommunications line to the LAN of a film distribution company in St. Louis. The LANs and the telecommunications link compose a WAN. Further, the telecommunications link alone is also a WAN because it links two LANs over several hundred miles. An example of a simple WAN is using a modem and telephone line at your computer to dial into your Internet service provider.

 Metropolitan area network (MAN) is another term used to describe networks that cover more geographic area than LANs, but less than WANs. A MAN might consist of networks joined throughout a city, such as joining LANs among eight hospitals in one city. Another example might be linking the suburban branch campuses of a community college to the main campus in the inner city. The term MAN is used less and less, often replaced by WAN.

Because of the complexity of networking, it can be difficult to determine where a LAN ends and a WAN begins. There are several interrelated elements that can be used to determine the intersection of a LAN with a WAN. One element is that the network topology may change between the two, such as a LAN that uses a ring topology and a WAN that uses a star. Another factor is a change in cable type. In the previous example, the LAN might use twisted-pair cable and the WAN might use fiber optics. Protocols may change between a LAN and a WAN, which is another indication of where one ends and the other starts. Ownership is another factor because LANs often are private networks used by a restricted group, and WANs often are public, such as telecommunications lines operated by a telephone company.

USING OPERATING SYSTEMS FOR DIAL-UP ACCESS

As you learned in Chapter 7, users on remote computers can access host computers and networks through dial-up networking and modem connections. For example, a specialized Novell server can be configured, with the appropriate software, to be a NetWare Access Server (NAS) on a LAN. A user who wants to access the LAN from home or

8

while traveling simply dials up the NAS through software on the computer and a modem connection. Through the NAS, that user can gain access to files and software on one or more NetWare servers connected to the remote LAN.

Windows NT/2000/.NET Server offer a similar option for dialing into a LAN through a Remote Access Services (RAS) server. RAS is a set of network services that can be installed on any Windows NT/2000/.NET server connected to one or more modems. Once the services are installed and started, a remote user can dial into one or more Windows NT/2000/.NET servers, and also access NetWare servers on the same network through a single RAS connection.

Besides setting up a RAS server, there must be a way to set up remote access capability on client workstations. Windows 95/98/Me and Windows NT/2000/XP all have a dial-up networking service that can be configured to access a remote network, as shown in the Hands-on Projects in Chapter 7. The dial-up service is set up by specifying the telephone number used to access the remote network, the communication protocol (TCP/IP, IPX/SPX, or NetBEUI), and the remote communication protocol. Most users configure dial-up networking to use the Point-to-Point Protocol (PPP), which can encapsulate packets already formatted in TCP/IP, IPX/SPX, and NetBEUI for transmission over a telecommunications line (try Hands-on Projects 8-10 and 8-11). A close relative, Point-to-Point Tunneling Protocol (PPTP) can also be configured for making a remote connection to a LAN over the Internet. Another protocol, Serial Line Internet Protocol (SLIP) is sometimes used in UNIX for remote communications that transport TCP/IP.

Security for dial-up remote access is a very important topic because of potential threats from viruses or hackers. Two ways to enhance the security surrounding the use of remote access is with authentication and encryption. **Authentication** is the way you identify and validate who you are to the server. **Encryption** is the encoding of the data between you and the server so that only you and the server can decode the information.

CHAPTER SUMMARY

❑ A network is a system of information resources and productivity tools that facilitates our human need to communicate. Networks were invented because they enable us to share information and information resources over short and long distances. Today, networking is a vital part of society that enables us to communicate by e-mail, order products rapidly, and accomplish work without leaving our homes or offices.

❑ Networks are designed in standardized topologies (bus, star, and ring) and use standardized communication means, such as frames, packets, and protocols, with the end result that a network in Jackson, Wyoming can be connected to another in Denver, Colorado or Montreal, Canada. Protocols are particularly important to networking because they act as a common language for communication. Some protocols are used to provide orderly transport of data between computers. Other protocols package data so that it can be decoded and checked for errors when it arrives at its destination.

Protocols make communications reliable, enable the delivery of e-mail, and monitor networks for problems.

❐ Modern computer operating systems use a variety of network protocols for communication, such as TCP/IP, IPX/SPX, and NetBEUI. Even computers running very different operating systems, UNIX and Windows XP for example, are able to communicate and exchange information over networks. Network operating systems such as Windows NT, Windows 2000/.NET Server, NetWare, and UNIX offer a wide spectrum of services to client computers, including file sharing, printer services, backing up files, access to software applications, and access to databases.

❐ Tables 8-1, 8-2, and 8-3 provide a summary of the transport, communications, and remote protocols introduced in this chapter, and the operating systems that support those protocols.

8

Table 8-1   Summary of Transport Protocols

Transport Protocol	Communications Protocols Transported	Operating Systems that Support the Protocol
Ethernet	IPX/SPX, NetBEUI, TCP/IP, AppleTalk	Mac OS, NetWare, UNIX, Windows 3.1, 3.11, 95, 98, Me, NT, 2000, XP, .NET Server
Token ring	IPX/SPX, NetBEUI, TCP/IP, AppleTalk	Mac OS, NetWare, UNIX, Windows 3.1, 3.11, 95, 98, Me, NT, 2000, XP, .NET Server

Table 8-2   Summary of Communications Protocols

Communications Protocol	Operating Systems that Support the Protocol
AppleTalk (native to Mac OS)	Mac OS, NetWare, Windows NT, 2000, and Windows .NET Server
IPX/SPX (native to early versions of NetWare)	NetWare, Windows 3.1, 3.11, 95, 98, Me, NT, 2000, XP, and .NET Server
NetBEUI (native to early versions of Windows-based systems)	Windows 3.1, 3.11, 95, 98, Me, NT, and 2000
TCP/IP (designed for Internet and general networking and native to most current NOSs)	Mac OS, NetWare, UNIX, Windows 3.1, 3.11, 95, 98, Me, NT, 2000, XP, and .NET Server

Table 8-3   Summary of Remote Communications Protocols

Remote Comunications Protocol	Communications Protocols Transported over Remote Links	Operating Systems that Support the Protocol
SLIP	TCP/IP	NetWare, UNIX, Windows 95, 98, NT, 2000, XP, and .NET Server
PPP	IPX/SPX, NetBEUI, and TCP/IP	Mac OS, UNIX, Windows 95, 98, Me, NT, 2000, XP, and .NET Server

❑ Internetworking devices, bridges, switches, and routers, for example, enable network connectivity. Bridges, switches, and routers can be employed for network security and to control network traffic patterns. Each of these devices is used to achieve different connectivity goals, based on its capabilities.

❑ Networks are roughly categorized as LANs or WANs, depending on their areas of service. LANs are smaller networks that run throughout an office area or a floor in a building. WANs are long-distance networks that can span states and continents to join LANs and individual users. One of the simplest WANs consists of deploying a server on a LAN that is able to communicate with users by modem and telephone line connections. Also called dial-up access, modem communications with a LAN are made possible through remote communications protocols, such as SLIP and PPP. PPP is most commonly used because it can transport a combination of protocols, such as TCP/IP and IPX/SPX.

KEY TERMS

active hub — A central network device that connects multiple communications cable segments; it amplifies the data-carrying signal as it is transmitted to each segment.

assigning applications — An Intellimirror feature in Windows 2000, Windows XP, and Windows .NET Server that enables an Active Directory group policy to be set up so that a particular version of software is automatically started on a client (Windows 2000 or XP) through a desktop shortcut, via a menu selection, or by clicking a file with a specific file extension.

AppleTalk — Used for communications with Macintosh computers, this protocol is designed for peer-to-peer networking.

authentication — A scheme to identify and validate the client to the server.

backbone — A main connecting link or highway between networks, such as between floors in a building or between buildings. Main internetworking devices, such as routers and switches, are often connected via the network backbone.

bridge — A network device that connects two or more segments into one, or extends an existing segment.

Carrier Sense Multiple Access with Collision Detection (CSMA/CD) — A transmission control method used by Ethernet.

cell — Format for a unit of data that is transported over a high-speed network, usually at speeds of 155 Mbps to over 1 Gbps. Cells are mainly used for network communications that employ Asynchronous Transfer Mode (ATM).

Classless Interdomain Routing (CIDR) — A way to ignore address class designation by using addressing that puts a slash (/) after the dotted decimal notation.

client operating system — Operating system on a computer, such as a PC, that enables the computer to process information and run applications locally, as well as communicate with other computers on a network.

encryption — The encoding of data between the client and the server so that only the client or server can decode this information.

Ethernet — A network transport protocol that uses CSMA/CD communications to coordinate frame and packet transmissions on a network.

firewall — Hardware or software that can control which frames and packets access or leave designated networks, as a method to implement security.

firmware — Software logic that consists of one or more programs, which reside in a programmable chip on a card.

frame — A data unit sent over a network that contains source and destination, control, and error-detection information, as well as data (related to the data-link layer of network communications between two stations).

Internet Protocol (IP) — Used in combination with TCP, this protocol handles addressing and routing for transport of packets.

Internet Packet Exchange (IPX) — Developed by Novell, this protocol is used on networks that connect servers running NetWare.

local area network (LAN) — A series of interconnected computers, printing devices, and other computer equipment in a service area that is usually limited to a given office area, floor, or building.

Media Access Control (MAC) address — A unique hexadecimal address, called a device or physical address, which identifies a NIC to the network.

multicast — A transmission method in which a server divides recipients of an application, such as a multimedia application, into groups. Each data stream is a one-time transmission that goes to one group of multiple addresses, instead of sending a separate transmission to each address for every data stream. The result is less network traffic.

NetBIOS Extended User Interface (NetBEUI) — A protocol used on Microsoft networks that was developed from NetBIOS, and is designed for small networks.

network — A system of computing devices, computing resources, information resources, and communications devices that are linked together by communications cable or radio waves.

Network Basic Input/Output System (NetBIOS) — A technique to interface software with network services, and provide naming services for computers on a Microsoft network.

Network Client Administrator — A tool available in Windows NT Server 4.0 that enables clients to install any of the following operating systems: Windows 95, MS-DOS 3.x, and Microsoft LAN Manager for MS-DOS 2.x.

Network Device Interface Specification (NDIS) — Special elements, which programmers call "hooks," in the operating system kernel (program code) that enable the operating system to interface with a network. NDIS is from Microsoft.

network interface card (NIC) — A device used by computers and internetworking devices to connect to a network.

network operating system (NOS) — Computer operating system software that enables coordination of network activities, such as network communications, shared printing, and sharing files. Novell NetWare, UNIX, and Windows NT/2000/.NET Server are examples of network operating systems.

8

packet — A data unit sent over a network that contains source and destination, routing, control, and error-detection information, as well as data (related to the network layer of network data communications between two stations).

passive hub — A central network device that connects multiple communications cable segments, but does not alter the data-carrying signal as it is transmitted from segment to segment.

payload — That portion of a frame, packet, or cell that contains the actual data, which might be a portion of an e-mail message or word-processing file.

protocol — A set of formatting guidelines for network communications, like a language, so that the information sent by one computer can be accurately received and decoded by another.

publishing and application — Available in Windows 2000 Server and Windows .NET Server, setting an Active Directory group policy so that Windows 2000 and Windows XP Professional clients can install pre-configured software from a central server by using Add/Remove Programs (or Add or Remove in Windows XP) via the Control Panel.

Remote Installation Services (RIS) — Services in Windows 2000 Server and Windows .NET Server that enable clients to download an operating system over the network, such as downloading and installing Windows 2000 Professional on a client computer via RIS on a Windows 2000 Server.

router — A device that joins networks and can route packets to a specific network on the basis of a routing table it creates for this purpose.

Sequence Packet Exchange (SPX) — A protocol used on Novell networks that provides reliable transmission of application software data.

server — A computer running a network operating system that enables client workstations to access shared network resources such as printers, files, software applications, or CD-ROM drives.

subnet mask — A designated portion of an IP address that is used to divide a network into smaller subnetworks as a way to manage traffic patterns, enable security, and relieve congestion.

SubNetwork Access Protocol (SNAP) — A way to enable protocols that are not fully 802.2 compliant.

switch — A network device that connects LAN segments and forwards frames to the appropriate segment or segments. A switch works in promiscuous mode, similar to a bridge.

terminal — A device that has a keyboard but no CPU or storage, and is used to access and run programs on a mainframe or minicomputer.

token — A specialized frame that is transmitted without data around the network until it is captured by a station that wants to transmit.

token ring — A network that uses a ring topology and token passing as a way to coordinate network transport.

topology — The physical design of a network and the way in which a data-carrying signal travels from point to point along the network.

Transmission Control Protocol (TCP) — A communications protocol that is used with IP; it facilitates reliable communications between two stations by establishing a window tailored to the characteristics of the connection.

unicast — A transmission method in which one copy of each packet is sent to every target destination, which can generate considerable network traffic, compared to multicasting, when the transmission is a multimedia application.

wide area network (WAN) — A system of networks that can extend across cities, states, and continents.

workgroups — Pre-defined groups of member computers, which provide the ability to limit resource sharing on the basis of group membership.

workstation — A computer that has a CPU and usually storage to enable the user to run programs and access files locally.

REVIEW QUESTIONS

8

1. Which of the following computer operating systems are compatible with TCP/IP?
   a. NetWare 3
   b. Windows 95
   c. UNIX
   d. all of the above
   e. only a and b
   f. only b and c

2. Packet collisions are part of _____ networks, not _____ networks.

3. Which of the following resources can be shared through networks?
   a. files
   b. printers
   c. tape backup systems
   d. all of the above
   e. only a and b
   f. only a and c

4. The Internet Protocol (IP) handles _____ on networks.

5. Which of the following protocols is not designed to enable routing?
   a. NetBEUI
   b. IPX
   c. TCP/IP
   d. None of the above can be routed.
   e. All of the above can be routed.

6. List the possible protocols used by the Internet.

7. Which of the following operating systems cannot be used on an Ethernet network?

   a. Macintosh

   b. UNIX

   c. NetWare

   d. Windows 95

   e. None of the above can be used on Ethernet networks.

   f. All of the above can be used on Ethernet networks.

8. Dialing into a networked server at work from your home computer is a simple example of what type of network?

   a. Ethernet

   b. LAN

   c. WAN

   d. Token ring

9. A Remote Access Services (RAS) server for remote dial-in access runs on which of the following operating systems?

   a. NetWare

   b. Windows NT

   c. IBM MVS

   d. Dec VMS

   e. all of the above

   f. only c and d because they are mainframe and minicomputer operating systems

10. You are setting up a UNIX server for communications on a network. Which of the following protocols are you most likely to implement in the UNIX operating system for communications?

    a. NetBEUI

    b. IPX

    c. TCP/IP

    d. SNMP

11. Which of the following protocols would you set up on your Windows XP workstation to communicate with a UNIX server described in the previous question?

    a. NetBEUI

    b. IPX

    c. TCP/IP

    d. SNMP

12. You are configuring a Windows 95 portable computer that has an internal modem so that you can dial into Microsoft Windows NT servers that use TCP/IP on your network. Which of the following protocols would you configure on your portable for communications through the modem?

    a. TCP/IP

    b. PPP

    c. NetBEUI

    d. all of the above

    e. only a and b

13. List the possible Ethernet transmission speeds.

14. You are setting up a workstation running Windows NT so that it can access your network. To enable the computer to connect to the network cable, you must install a hardware card in the computer, called a(n) _____, and then you must install software into the operating system, called a(n) _____, which enables the hardware card to communicate with Windows NT.

15. Hypertext Transfer Protocol (HTTP) is used in association with which of the following protocols?

    a. TCP/IP

    b. XNS

    c. IPX

    d. NetBIOS

16. One problem with AppleTalk is that it cannot be used for network print services. True or False?

17. Which of the following topologies would you find on an Ethernet network?

    a. bus

    b. ring

    c. star

    d. all of the above

    e. only a and b

    f. only a and c

18. A firewall must be a hardware device because network security cannot be reliably set up through software. True or False?

19. A network that has a combination of NetWare and Windows NT servers can be either Ethernet or token ring. True or False?

20. 144.79.22.122 is an example of a(n) _____ address.

8

HANDS-ON PROJECTS

Project 8-1

In this hands-on activity, you'll examine a network to see if you can determine its topology.

To view a network topology:

1. Arrange to examine the network in a lab located in your school.

2. With the help of your instructor (or on your own), determine how each workstation is connected to the network. For example, are workstations connected directly to each other, to a wall outlet, or directly to a hub or switch?

3. If the workstations are connected to a wall outlet, ask if the connection eventually goes to a network device, such as a hub or switch.

4. Ask your instructor if the network employs Ethernet or token ring communications.

5. Determine if you can see any visible terminators.

6. Using the information that you gathered, and what you learned in this chapter, attempt to identify the network as a bus, ring, or star topology.

Project 8-2

In this assignment, you'll examine the computers connected to your school's network. You will need a workstation running Windows 95 or Windows 98 that has access to your school's network.

To observe the computers on your network:

1. Double-click **Network Neighborhood** on the desktop.

2. Observe the number of computers on the network and their computer names.

3. Notice if there is any apparent naming scheme for computers, or if users have a wide range of options in selecting their computer names.

4. Right-click one of the visible computers, and click **Properties**.

5. Look for the General tab in the dialog box and for Type, which shows the operating system running on the computer (see Figure 8-19). Close the Properties dialog box.

6. Repeat steps 4 and 5 to view other computers and their operating systems.

7. Back on the main Network Neighborhood screen, double-click **Entire Network**.

8. Notice if you see options, such as Microsoft Windows Network, and NetWare, or Compatible Network. If you do, first click one of the options to view its member computers. If you are using Windows 95, close the window; or if you are using Windows 98, click the **Up** button. Then click the other option to view its contents.

9. Close the Network Neighborhood windows that you opened.

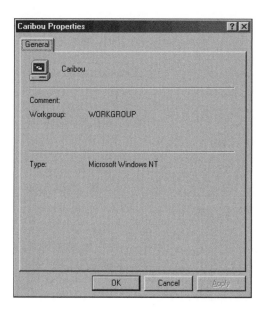

Figure 8-19   Viewing the connected computer's operating system

Project 8-3

In this project, you'll again examine the computers connected to your school's network. You will need a workstation running Windows Me or Windows XP that has access to your school's network.

To observe the computers on your network:

1. Double-click **My Network Places** on the desktop for Windows Me. For Windows XP, point to **Start**, click **My Computer**, click **My Network Places**, click **View workgroup computers**.

2. Observe the number of computers on the network and their computer names.

3. Notice if there is any apparent naming scheme for computers, or if users have a wide range of options in selecting their computer names.

4. Right-click one of the visible computers, and click **Properties**.

5. Look for the General tab in the dialog box and review the types of information displayed. Close the dialog box.

6. Repeat Steps 4 and 5 to view other computers and their information.

7. Back on the main My Network Places screen, double-click **Entire Network**. For Windows XP, click **View workgroup computers** and then press the **Up** button on the toolbar.

8. Notice if you see options, such as Microsoft Windows Network, NetWare, or Compatible Network. If you do, first click one of the options to view its member computers. Click the **Up** button. Then click the other option to view its contents. In Windows XP, you will need to double-click rather than single click.

9. Close the open windows.

Project 8-4

In this project, you'll view the number of packets transported across a network to your computer. You will need access to a computer running Windows 2000 Server that has the SNMP service installed. You also must ask your instructor for an account name and password to use in Windows 2000 Server.

To view the frame activity:

1. Click **Start**, point to **Programs**, and point to **Administrative Tools**.

2. Click **Performance**. Maximize the window, if necessary. Also, make sure that **System Monitor** is selected in the right pane (labeled the "Tree").

3. Click the **plus sign (+)** on the button bar.

4. In the Add Counters dialog box, make sure that **Select counters from computer** is selected, and that the name of your computer appears in the list box under this selection, or open the list box to find and select your computer.

5. Open the Performance object list box and select **Network Interface**.

6. Make sure that **Select counters from list** is selected, and then in the scroll box, select **Packets/sec**. This counter measures the total number of packets received by and sent from the NIC in your computer.

7. Make sure **Select instances from list** is chosen, and that your network interface card (NIC) is highlighted in the list, such as 3ComEtherlink PCI (do not select the loopback interface).

8. Click **Add**, and then click **Close** in the Add Counters dialog box.

9. View the graph for several minutes to see the frame activity.

10. Close the Performance windows when you are finished.

> **Note**
> Another way to view the network traffic is to use the Network Monitor in Windows 2000 Server. To open this tool, click **Start**, point to **Programs**, point to **Administrative Tools**, and click **Network Monitor**. Click the **Start Capture** button (the right arrow) on the button bar to view network traffic.

Project 8-5

In this project, you'll practice installing TCP/IP in Windows 95, Windows 98, or Windows NT 4.0 Server or Workstation.

To install TCP/IP in Windows 95 or Windows 98:

1. Click **Start**, point to **Settings**, and click **Control Panel**.

2. Double-click the **Network** icon (applet).

3. Click the **Configuration** tab (if not already selected), then click the **Add** button.

4. Double-click the **Protocol** selection in the Select Network Component Type dialog box.

5. Click **Microsoft** in the Manufacturers text box, and notice the protocols that can be installed under the Network Protocols text box (use the scroll bar if you are using Windows 98).

6. After you view the protocol selections, click **TCP/IP** in the Network Protocols text box.

7. Click **OK**.

8. If the setup program asks for a path from which to install the protocol software, insert the Windows 95 or Windows 98 CD-ROM. Then click **Continue** or **OK** (depending on the dialog box that appears).

9. In the Network dialog box, click TCP/IP –>*network adapter*, such as **TCP/IP –>3COM FastEtherLink XL 10/100**, then click **Properties** to open the TCP/IP Properties window. Make sure that the IP Address tab is displayed (see Figure 8-20). Notice that *Obtain an IP address automatically* is checked. This means that the default setting for TCP/IP is to use DCHP, which is fine for this project. Click **Cancel**.

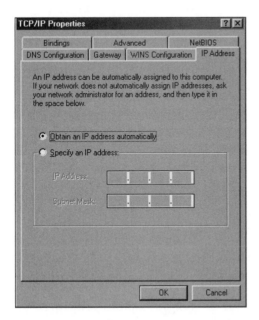

Figure 8-20   Selecting DHCP in TCP/IP Properties

10. Close the Network dialog box, and click **Yes** to reboot the computer (first save any other open work.)

To install TCP/IP in Windows NT 4.0:

1. Log on to the Administrator account, or to an account with Administrator privileges.

2. Click **Start**, point to **Settings**, and click **Control Panel**.

3. Double-click the **Network** icon.

4. Click the **Protocols** tab, and click **Add**.

5. Click **TCP/IP Protocol**, and click **OK**.

6. If the setup program asks for a path from which to install the protocol software, insert the Windows NT 4.0 CD-ROM and provide a path to the \i386 folder on the CD-ROM drive. Then click **Continue** or **OK** (depending on the dialog box that appears).

7. In the Network dialog box, click TCP/IP, then click **Properties** to open the Microsoft TCP/IP Properties window. Make sure the IP Address tab is selected. Notice that *Obtain an IP address from a DHCP server* is chosen by default, which is fine for this project.

8. Close the Network dialog box, and click **Yes** to reboot the computer (first save any other open work).

Project 8-6

In this project, you'll practice installing TCP/IP in Windows 2000 or Windows XP.

To install TCP/IP in Windows 2000 or Windows XP:

1. Click **Start**, point to **Settings** (Windows 2000 only), and click **Control Panel**.

2. Double-click the **Network and Dial-up Connections** icon (applet) in Windows 2000, or click **Network and Internet Connections**, then click **Network Connections** in Windows XP.

3. Double-click the **Local Area Connection** or your computer icon. Click the **Properties** button in the Local Area Connection Status dialog box.

4. Click the **Install** button in the dialog box.

5. Click **Protocol,** and then click **Add**.

6. After you view the protocol selections, click **TCP/IP**.

7. Click **OK**.

8. If the setup program asks for a path from which to install the protocol software, insert the Windows 2000 or Windows XP CD-ROM. Then click **Continue** or **OK** (depending on the dialog box that appears).

9. In the Local Area Connection properties window, double-click **Internet Protocol (TCP/IP)**, to open the TCP/IP Properties window. Make sure the General tab is displayed (particularly for Windows XP) and that *Obtain an IP address automatically* is checked as the default. Click **Cancel**.

10. Close the Local Area Connection Properties dialog box. Close the Local Area Connection Status dialog box and then close the Network and Dial-up Connections (for Windows 2000) or Network Connections (for Windows XP) window.

Project 8-7

In this project, you'll set up the Mac OS 9.x for AppleTalk communications. Next, you'll configure Mac OS X for TCP/IP network access using DHCP.

To set up AppleTalk in the Mac OS 9.x:

1. Make sure that the network cable is connected to the computer's NIC. If not, obtain a cable and connect it following directions from your instructor.

2. Open the **Apple** menu and **Control Panels**.

3. Select the **AppleTalk** Control Panel.

4. Select **Ethernet** as the port in the pop-up menu.

5. Close the AppleTalk Control Panel. (If the Save Changes warning box appears, click **Save**.)

6. Open **Chooser** in the Apple menu.

7. Click **Active** in the lower-right corner of the dialog box. Click **OK** for the warning to make sure you are connected to the network.

8. Exit Chooser.

To set up TCP/IP in Mac OS X:

1. Open the **Apple** menu, and select **System Preferences**.

2. Click the **Network** icon.

3. Click the **TCP/IP** tab.

4. View the options in the Configure pop-up menu.

5. Select **Using DHCP**.

6. Enter the IP address of any DNS servers, if your instructor provided this information.

7. Click **Save**.

Note that you learned how to manually configure TCP/IP in Chapter 7.

Project 8-8

In this project, you'll configure a loopback address, turn on TCP/IP networking, and assign an IP address in UNIX.

To configure a loopback address:

1. Log on as root.

2. At the command prompt or a terminal window, enter **ifconfig lo 127.0.0.1**, and then press **Enter**.

3. Type **ifconfig** or **ifconfig –a** to confirm that you created the IP information for the loopback address.

To set up and start TCP/IP communications in UNIX using the *ifconfig* command:

Do not execute this assignment if you are unable to obtain an IP address in advance because you run the risk of creating an address that may conflict with others, thereby causing network problems. If you do not have an IP address in advance, try only Step 5 to view the current configuration information.

1. Make sure that a NIC is installed in the computer, and ask your instructor for the NIC interface name, IP address, subnet mask, and broadcast address that you will use for this assignment.

2. Make sure that the network cable is connected to the computer's NIC. If not, obtain a cable and connect it following directions from your instructor.

3. Log in as root.

4. Access the command line, such as through the GNOME terminal window.

5. Run *ifconfig interface_name ip_address netmask subnetmask_value broadcasts broadcast_address,* such as **ifconfig eth0 129.72.10.188 netmask 255.255.0.0 broadcasts 129.72.1.1** (if you are using the SCO version of UNIX, use the format *ifconfig interface_name netmask subnetmask_value ip_address* and omit the broadcast address). Press **Enter**. You will see configuration information after you run the *ifconfig* utility. Note that when you designate an IP address, *ifconfig* also starts the interface. The actual parameters that you use should first be obtained from your instructor.

6. Check the configuration again by entering ifconfig interface_name, such as **ifconfig eth0**, or view all configuration information by entering **ifconfig –a**.

7. Close the GNOME terminal window, if you have opened it to access the command line.

8. Log off root when you are finished.

To configure an Ethernet NIC using the Red Hat Linux 7.2 GNOME interface:

1. Before you start, obtain information about your NIC from your instructor, such as the type of adapter, device type, and IRQ used in the computer.

2. Click **Main Menu** (the foot icon), point to **Programs**, point to **System**, and click **Network Configuration**.

3. Make sure that the Hardware tab is displayed. Click the **Add** button.

4. Select **Ethernet** in the Hardware Type box (see Figure 8-21) and click **OK**.

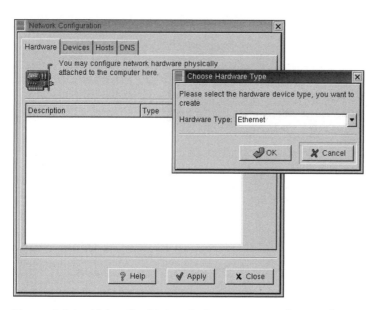

Figure 8-21 Using the Network Connection tool to configure a NIC

5. Enter the adapter type, such as **Intel EtherExpress Pro 100B** and the device type, such as **eth0**. Complete the remaining information using the parameters provided by your instructor. Click **OK**.

6. Click the Devices tab.

7. Select the device that you configured in Step 5, such as **eth0** and click **Edit**.

8. Click the Protocols tab and select the **TCP/IP**, if it is not already selected. Click **Edit**.

9. For this project, make sure **Automatically obtain IP address setting with** is checked and that **dhcp** is also selected in the box next to this selection. However, notice that you can manually enter an IP address, if necessary.

10. Click the **Hostname** tab and provide a name to identify your computer on the network, such as your last name.

11. Click **OK**.

12. On the Ethernet Device dialog box, click the **Hardware Device** tab.

13. Check Use Hardware Address.

14. Click the button to **Probe for Address**. Notice that the system automatically determines the device address of the NIC.

15. Click **OK**.

16. Click **Apply**.

17. Click **Close**.

18. Click **Yes** to save your changes.

Project 8-9

In this project, you'll set up Windows Me to use IPX/SPX communications with a NetWare server.

To set up IPX/SPX in Windows Me:

1. Point to **Start**, point to **Settings**, and click **Control Panel.**
2. Double-click the **Network** icon.
3. On the Configuration tab, click **Add** button.
4. Click the **Protocol** icon, and then click the **Add** button.
5. Click **IPX/SPX-compatible Protocol**, then click **OK**.
6. Click **OK**.
7. Save any previously opened work, if necessary, then click **Yes** to reboot.

Project 8-10

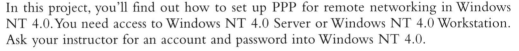

In this project, you'll find out how to set up PPP for remote networking in Windows NT 4.0. You need access to Windows NT 4.0 Server or Windows NT 4.0 Workstation. Ask your instructor for an account and password into Windows NT 4.0.

> If Dial-up Networking is not already installed on your computer, see Chapter 7 for information about how to install it.

1. Double-click **My Computer** on the desktop.
2. Double-click the **Dial-Up Networking** icon (applet).
3. In the Dial-Up Networking dialog box, click the **More** button.
4. Click the menu option to **Edit entry and modem properties**.
5. Click the **Server** tab in the Edit Phonebook Entry dialog box.
6. Notice the Dial-up server type box to see if **PPP: Windows NT, Windows 95, Internet** is the selected protocol.
7. Also on the Server tab, notice that you can specify which protocols will be carried via PPP.
8. Click **Cancel** in the Edit Phonebook Entry dialog box.
9. Click **Close** in the Dial-up Networking dialog box.

Project 8-11

As an alternative to Project 8-10, or in addition to that project, check the remote protocol setup in Windows 2000.

Note that Dial-up Networking should already be installed.

To check the remote protocol setup:

1. Double-click **My Computer**.
2. Double-click **Control Panel** and then double-click **Network and Dial-up Connections**.

If Dial-up Networking is not already installed on your computer, see Chapter 7 for information about how to install it.

3. Right-click an existing dial-up networking icon.
4. Click **Properties**.
5. Click the **Networking** tab.
6. Notice which protocol is set up in the Type of dial-up server I am calling list box.
7. Observe which network protocols are checked for transport over a remote connection.
8. Click **Cancel** in the Dial-up Connection Properties dialog box.
9. Click **Cancel** in the Network and Dial-up Connections dialog box.

Project 8-12

In this Hands-on Project, you'll attach a four-pair unshielded twisted pair (UTP) cable to an RJ-45 connector. You will need the cable, a crimper, a connector, and a wire stripper. (These instructions and Figure 8-22 follow the EIA/TIA-568 standard for constructing UTP network cable.)

To attach UTP cable to an RJ-45 connector:

1. Lay out the wires on a flat surface in the arrangement shown in Figure 8-22.
2. Trim the wires with a pair of wire cutters, all to the same length.
3. Use a wire stripper intended for twisted-pair cable.
4. Follow the directions from the stripper manufacturer to strip the cable.
5. Insert the wires into the RJ-45 connector, ensuring that the connector is oriented correctly, with the first pair of wires (blue and white/blue) to connectors 4 and 5 inside the RJ-45 connector, connecting the blue wire to connector 4 and the white/blue wire to connector 5 (see Figure 8-22).
6. Make sure the second pair of wires goes to connectors 1 and 2, connecting the white/orange wire to connector 1 and the orange wire to connector 2.

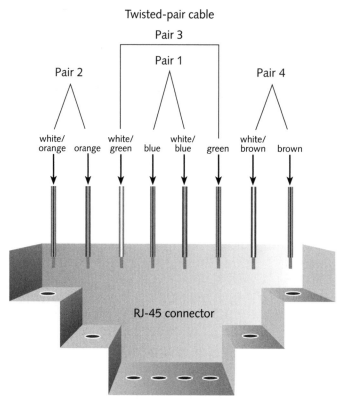

Figure 8-22 Attaching a connector to UTP cable

7. Make sure the third pair goes to connectors 3 and 6, connecting the white/green wire to connector 3 and the green wire to connector 6.

8. Make sure the fourth pair goes to connectors 7 and 8, connecting the white/brown wire to connector 7 and the brown wire to connector 8.

9. Make sure a portion of the cable jacket is inside the connector.

10. Insert the RJ-45 connector into the crimp tool and crimp the connector to the wires.

11. Test the installation by pulling the cable and connector in opposite directions to make sure your work does not come loose.

 If you have a cable tester available, put a second RJ-45 end on your cable and test it for continuity and correct wire layout.

 Now that you know how to build a cable, you are prepared for any emergency situation where you need a cable quickly. We recommend that you only build a cable in this type of situation. Otherwise, you should purchase pre-made, pre-tested cables that adhere to strict quality control standards.

CASE PROJECT

You are the network administrator for a group of 18 groundwater hydrologists who work in two adjacent buildings. Their company works with new housing construction all over the United States to determine if there is enough local ground water to support new housing developments. Each hydrologist has his or her own computer workstation. Two use computers running UNIX, three use Macintosh computers, and the rest use computers running Windows 98 or Windows 2000. These hydrologists work with a variety of software, including word processing, research databases, spreadsheets, mapping software, and mathematical calculation software. The buildings in which the hydrologists work are not networked, but the company plans to network each building and connect both networks. The company also decided to purchase a UNIX server and a NetWare server for all of the hydrologists to access. Both servers will be in a secure computer room in one of the buildings. Also, the company plans to connect to an Internet Service Provider so that each hydrologist can easily access the Internet. Explain how you would handle the following immediate concerns:

1. What type of network, Ethernet or token ring, do you believe should be implemented? Why?

2. What topology should be installed?

3. What equipment must be purchased in order for each hydrologist's computer to be connected to the network?

4. What protocols will you need to set up on each server and on all of the workstations? Why will you need these particular protocols?

5. Ten of the hydrologists travel frequently and need remote access to the network from portable computers that run Windows 98 or Windows 2000 Professional. What must be set up on the network for them to dial into it? What must be set up on each portable?

6. What internetworking device would you use to connect the networks in each building? Do you anticipate a need for routing capability on this network?

7. As you work to set up the network, two of the hydrologists are curious about the function of protocols. Briefly explain to them the function of network protocols.

8

OPTIONAL CASE PROJECTS FOR TEAMS

Team Case One

Tuesday morning you arrive at the office and your boss informs you that the CEO is concerned about hackers being able to break into the company's network. Your assignment is to form a team and prepare a report that discusses the use of firewalls to protect the company, including a discussion on both hardware and software firewalls.

Team Case Two

The CEO continues to be concerned about hackers, and asks your team to develop a presentation on security for the dial-up access the company provides to its employees. Your team should review the current authentication and encryption. Smart cards should be evaluated for possible use with remote access.

CHAPTER 9

RESOURCE SHARING OVER A NETWORK

After reading this chapter and completing the exercises, you will be able to:

♦ Explain the principles behind sharing disks and files on a network

♦ Set up accounts, groups, security, and disk and file sharing on network server operating systems

♦ Set up disk and file sharing on client operating systems

♦ Set up printer sharing on server and client operating systems

♦ Discuss how network and Internet servers are used for vast information-sharing networks

The power of networks and network-capable operating systems lies in their ability to share resources. The last chapter discussed resource sharing as the most fundamental rationale for a network. This chapter brings the concept to life by showing you how resources are shared in several network server and client operating systems. Most modern operating systems can share files, programs, printers, CD-ROM drives, tape drives, modems, fax machines, and other resources.

A cartoon showing two network experts attempting to connect an air conditioning unit to share its cooling capabilities over the network cable appeared several years ago in a popular computer magazine. The cartoon is a humorous illustration of the real trend toward sharing more types of resources over a network. In keeping with this trend, newer operating system releases offer more ways to accommodate resource sharing.

In this chapter, you'll learn how to share resources through operating systems such as Mac OS, NetWare, UNIX, and Windows-based systems. You'll learn about deploying user accounts, groups, and security to manage and protect shared resources. And finally, you'll learn how these capabilities enable network server operating systems to propagate information for businesses, schools, and government organizations.

SHARING DISKS, FILES AND PRINTERS

Most modern and many older computer operating systems can share files, directories, and entire disks on a network. The same operating systems also usually offer the ability to share printers. Sharing files was one of the first reasons for linking a workstation's operating system onto a network, and it remains one of the most important reasons for networking. In terms of network operating systems, NetWare was early on the scene at the start of the 1980s to enable file sharing through a server. This was possible through two methods: (1) by downloading a file from a file server to a workstation, and (2) by purchasing third-party software to create a special shared drive for other computers or workstations to access over a network. Downloading a file directly from a file server was one of the first methods for sharing files, and was incorporated in the first version of NetWare.

 Although NetWare is not one of the operating systems covered in this book, because of its importance in the development of network OSs, and the common use of computers running Windows, UNIX, and Mac OS as clients to NetWare servers, it is discussed in this chapter, and in Chapter 10.

When network operating systems such as NetWare, UNIX, and Windows NT became available, it was difficult for many users of mainframe computers to grasp the idea that entire applications could be loaded as files onto a networked workstation, instead of running on the mainframe. For instance, a word-processing package could be loaded onto the server and accessed by workstations. Each workstation would simply download the executable files, and perhaps a document file from a server, and run them in the local workstation's memory. Only one version of the word-processing software was needed at the server, which could be downloaded multiple times by authorized workstations, eliminating the need for the software on each workstation. In this arrangement, each workstation housed a specialized setup file for the word-processing software, but the executable files were always loaded from the server. Of course, it was still necessary, as it is today, to have the appropriate licenses, as mandated by the software vendor.

 Although it was common to download application software from a server and run it in memory on a workstation, it is less common today because many applications are too large to download every time a workstation needs them.

Another complexity is that as software applications have grown in size, downloading them each time you want to run them on a workstation creates excessive network traffic. For example, early versions of word processors might have had executable files in the range of a few thousand kilobytes, but today, executable files and associated components can be in the range of 1 MB and more because they contain many more functions. Consider a business where 100 employees arrive at work at 8 a.m., and all access the WordPerfect or Microsoft Word executable files from the server simultaneously. The resulting network traffic would be enough to bring the network to a standstill.

The concept of sharing resources quickly blossomed into other ways to access files, such as making shared drives available on a network, and making each shared drive look just like another local drive at the client. When a workstation accesses a shared drive, the process is called **mapping**. Mapping is a software process that enables a client workstation to attach to the shared drive of another workstation or server, and assign it a drive letter. The network drive that is attached is called a mapped drive in Windows-based operating systems. In the Mac OS, a mapped drive is called a **mounted volume**.

Sharing files also opened the way for printer sharing over a network. Organizations now save money on printer purchases because it is not necessary for each person in an office to have a printer. One printer connected to a network server operating system or network client operating system can be used by others in the same office area or location.

SECURING SHARED RESOURCES

Sharing disks, files, and printers is a potential security risk because it is then possible for non-authorized users to access a file or use a printer. This presents problems, for example, when a shared file contains sensitive employee or company information, or when a shared printer is overtaxed because more people are using it than was originally intended.

Fortunately, all of the operating systems discussed in this book offer security measures for protecting shared resources. For example, access to a file, directory, or disk can be denied to those who are not authorized. In some instances, you want people to be able to read a file (document), but not change it; or you want only specific people to be able to execute a file (program). For these situations, a file, directory, or disk can be assigned security privileges that limit users to only these capabilities, such as only read or only execute a file.

Similarly, access to a shared network printer can be given to only a specific group of people. Also, permission to manage print jobs, such as to delete or prioritize the jobs submitted by coworkers, can be granted only to one or two qualified people who have that responsibility.

In the sections that follow, you'll learn how to set up shared resources, and protect them so that they are used in the ways intended by your organization.

SHARING DISKS AND FILES THROUGH SERVER NETWORK OPERATING SYSTEMS

Windows NT Server, Windows 2000 Server, Windows .NET Server, UNIX, Mac OS X Server, and NetWare are prime examples of server network operating systems that can share disks and files over a network. Each of these operating systems offers a way for client workstations to access a combination of disk, file, and other shared resources.

Further, each operating system enables the network administrator to establish security through techniques such as assigning accounts, account passwords, groups, and access privileges. Windows NT Server, Windows 2000 Server, UNIX, Mac OS X Server, and NetWare are described in the next sections in terms of their capabilities to share disk and file resources, combined with the ability to secure those resources on a network. At this writing, Windows .NET Server is in the beta stage, and is discussed only briefly to describe new features.

Windows NT Server

Windows NT Server uses accounts, groups, and permissions; in this respect, it is similar to UNIX and NetWare. The steps involved in sharing Windows NT Server resources over a network include setting up the following:

- Groups
- Account policies
- User accounts
- Permissions
- Shared disks and folders

With Windows NT Server, you use groups to manage resources and permissions to resources in a way that is similar to NetWare and UNIX. Windows NT Server employs two kinds of groups: local and global. A local group is generally used to manage resources such as shared disks, folders, files, and printers. A global group typically consists of user accounts, and can be made a member of a local group that is in the same or a different domain. A **domain** is a grouping of servers in a particular geographic area, business unit, department, or other functional area. The process of controlling shared resources in Windows NT involves creating the resource, such as a shared folder, and then creating a local group that has specific permissions to that shared resource. Finally, a global group is created and user accounts are added to that global group, which is then designated as a member of an appropriate local group.

On the surface, this technique of managing shared resources sounds complex, but it ultimately reduces management effort. For example, consider a corporation that has business units and networks in five different geographical areas. Each network is designated as a separate domain, and has accounting and sales databases that are in shared folders. In this scenario, each domain would have a local group with permissions to the databases. The corporate headquarters domain would have a global group consisting of all members at each location who need access to the databases. Access could be controlled by making the headquarters global group a member of each local group (see Figure 9-1). If three employees leave the organization, the network administrator simply removes their accounts from the headquarters domain and global group. This is a simpler process than removing each account from each domain, and from a group in each domain, which would require more effort. Likewise, when three new people are hired, the network administrator creates an account for each person in the headquarters domain, and makes each a member of the global group in that domain.

 Directories are called folders in Windows 2000, Windows NT, Windows 95, Windows 98, Windows Me, and Windows XP.

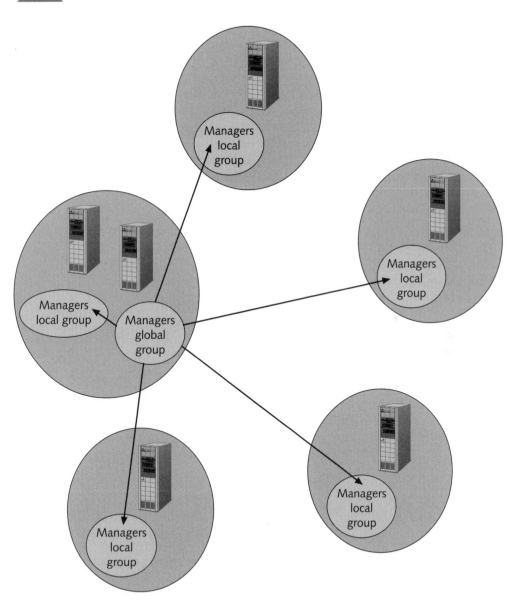

Figure 9-1   Managing shared resources using local and global groups

For the global and local group relationships to work between domains, as in Figure 9-1, trust relationships must be established among the domains. The headquarters domain that contains the global group for managers is designated as a **trusted domain**, which means that it is granted access to the resources in each of the other domains. Also, the four other domains are designated as **trusting domains**, which means that they grant permission to the headquarters domain to access their resources. Because they represent critical security relationships, trusts between domains are usually created and managed by a specially designated domain or security administrator.

Global and local groups are created by using the GUI tool, User Manager for Domains, in Windows NT Server. You access this tool in Windows NT Server 4.0 by clicking the Start button, pointing to Programs, pointing to Administrative Tools (Common), and clicking User Manager for Domains. Next, click the User menu, and select to create a new global or local group. Figure 9-2 illustrates the Windows NT dialog box that is used to create a new global group. (Try Hands-on Project 9-1 to view the global and local groups on a Windows NT server.)

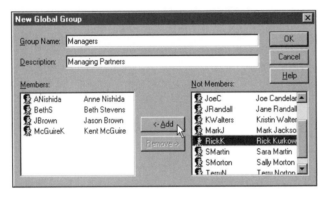

Figure 9-2 Creating a global group in Windows NT Server 4.0

 By now you understand that groups are a valuable tool for managing shared resources, but they can also introduce complexity in resource management when too many groups are used, and there is no documentation. As a rule, in NetWare, UNIX, and Windows NT/2000/.NET Server, keep resource management simple by planning groups in advance, and keeping their numbers to a minimum.

In Windows NT Server, access rights are controlled through setting rights policies in the User Manager for Domains, and by associating them with local groups. For example, the right to access a particular server over the network can be controlled this way, as well as the right to directly log onto a server from its console.

User accounts are also created through the User Manager for Domains. Windows NT Server uses account policies and restrictions, as does NetWare, which accomplish many of the same ends (but use different utilities) as follows:

- Require a password

- Set a minimum password length

- Require that a password is changed within a specified interval

- Require that a new password is used each time the old one is changed

- Limit the number of unsuccessful attempts to log onto an account

- Set time restrictions that specify when users can log on

- Set intruder detection capabilities

- Specify from which workstations an account can be accessed

- Control remote access to a server, such as over a dial-up line

Figure 9-3 shows the Account Policy dialog box in Windows NT Server 4.0, which is one place in which account restrictions can be set; another is through utilities provided at the time an account is created.

9

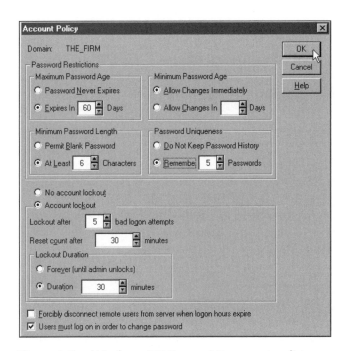

Figure 9-3   Windows NT Server 4.0 account policies

Some server operating systems, such as Windows NT Server and Windows 2000 Server, automatically create a Guest account. When an upgraded version of the operating system is released (or a service pack), the Guest account may not automatically have a password, but may have broad permissions to the server resources. Make sure these accounts get a password (or are disabled), and are given appropriate permissions.

As is true for UNIX and NetWare, access privileges (permissions) are associated with Windows NT Server disks, folders, and files. The ease with which you assign permissions is closely related to how the folder structure is set up. For example, it is easiest to share access for the installation of application programs by placing those programs in subfolders within a main folder intended for installing applications. The main folder might be called Program Files or Apps, and there might be subfolders such as MSOffice, Accounting, Drivers, CAD, and so on.

Windows NT Server recognizes two main file systems, FAT16 and the NT File System (NTFS). (See Chapter 3 for more information on file systems.) In virtually all cases, files that are shared on the network are set up in NTFS because this file system has better security. FAT16 can offer security through MS-DOS attributes, while NTFS can offer security by using a combination of MS-DOS attributes and NTFS permissions (see Table 9-1 for a comparison of security offered by FAT, NTFS, and other file systems).

Table 9-1   Attributes and File Permissions Compared

Description	MS-DOS Attributes (FAT)	NetWare Attributes and Trustee Rights	UNIX Permissions	Windows NT/2000/XP Attributes and Permissions (NTFS)
No access	N/A	N/A	Absence of X permission	No access or deny permission
Can read the contents of a file or directory	N/A	Read (R)	Read (R)	Handled through special NTFS permission (R)
Prevents directory or file from being changed or deleted	Read only (R)	Read only (Ro)	N/A	Handled through special NTFS permission (R)
Directory or file is new or changed and needs to be backed up	Archive (A)	Archive (A)	N/A	Archive (A)—file attribute
Compresses files to save disk space	N/A	Immediate Compress (Ic)	N/A	Compress (C)—file attribute

Table 9-1   Attributes and File Permissions Compared (continued)

Description	MS-DOS Attributes (FAT)	NetWare Attributes and Trustee Rights	UNIX Permissions	Windows NT/2000/XP Attributes and Permissions (NTFS)
In NetWare, Cc is automatically placed on files that should not be compressed, and Dc is placed on files by the administrator.	N/A	Cannot Compress (Cc) and Do not Compress (Dc)	N/A	N/A
File is used by the operating system and should not be viewed with ordinary list commands—used by NetWare directories but not NT/2000 directories	System (S)	System (Sy)	N/A	System (S)—file attribute
Directory or file cannot be viewed with ordinary list commands	Hidden (H)	Hidden (H)	N/A	Hidden (H)—file attribute (also can create a hidden share)
Directory or file can be viewed, changed, or deleted	No equivalent —file is not flagged with an R	Read Write (RW)	Read Write (RW)	Handled through special NTFS permissions (RW)
Can read and execute files, but not modify them	N/A	Read and Execute (RX)	Read and Execute (RX)	List or Read (RX) in NT; and Read & Execute in 2000
Can modify files and execute them	N/A	Write and Execute (WX)	Write and Execute (WX)	Add (WX) in NT; Modify in 2000

9

Table 9-1   Attributes and File Permissions Compared (continued)

Description	MS-DOS Attributes (FAT)	NetWare Attributes and Trustee Rights	UNIX Permissions	Windows NT/2000/XP Attributes and Permissions (NTFS)
Can read files, add new files, and execute programs, but cannot modify the file contents	N/A	N/A	N/A	Add & Read in NT (RWX); Modify plus Read in 2000
Can read, add, delete, modify, and execute files and directories	N/A	Read, Write, and Execute (RWX)	Read, Write, and Execute (RWX)	Change (RWXD) in NT; Modify in 2000
Cannot copy a file	N/A	Copy Inhibit (Ci)	N/A	Handled through special NTFS permissions
Cannot delete a directory or file	N/A	Delete Inhibit (Di)	N/A	Handled through special NTFS permissions
Can only execute a file (run the program)	N/A	Execute only (X)	Execute (X)	Handled through special NTFS permissions (X)
Flags large files for fast access	N/A	Indexed (I)	N/A	Handled by the NT operating system; set as an Indexed attribute in Windows 2000
Purge deleted directories and files so they cannot be salvaged	N/A	Purge (P)	N/A	Handled by the Recycle Bin
Cannot rename a directory or file	N/A	Rename inhibit (Ri)	N/A	Handled through special NTFS permissions
Read audit can be assigned, but has no function in NetWare 3.1 and later systems.	N/A	Read audit (Ra)	N/A	N/A

Table 9-1   Attributes and File Permissions Compared (continued)

Description	MS-DOS Attributes (FAT)	NetWare Attributes and Trustee Rights	UNIX Permissions	Windows NT/2000/XP Attributes and Permissions (NTFS)
Files can be accessed by more than one user at a time.	N/A	Shareable (Sh)	Execute (X)	Handled by creating a network share
For recovery of data files after a system interruption, such as a power failure	N/A	Transactional (T)	N/A	Handled by NTFS through directory and file recovery options
Can modify the contents of a file or folder	N/A	Write (W)	Write (W)	In NT, handled by creating a special NTFS permission (W); for Windows 2000, use Write (W) permission
Write audit can be assigned, but has no function in NetWare 3.1 and later systems.	N/A	Write audit (Wa)	N/A	N/A (however Windows NT/2000 NTFS enables many forms of file and folder auditing, including writing and read auditing)
Can read, add, delete, execute, and modify files and directories, plus change permissions and take ownership	N/A	N/A	N/A	Full control
Removes all attributes	N/A	Normal (N)	N/A	N/A

After groups, user accounts, and permissions are set up in Windows NT Server, disk volumes, folders, and files can be accessed through the network by creating shares. A **share** is an object—a disk or folder, for example—that is given a name and made visible to network users, such as through Network Neighborhood in Windows 95, Windows 98, and Windows NT, or My Network Places in Windows Me, Windows 2000, and Windows XP.

A disk or folder is shared through its properties. This is possible because Windows NT Server objects have associated properties that include sharing, setting permissions, and ownership. For example, to set up a shared folder, you locate that folder in My Computer or Windows NT Explorer, and then right-click the folder. Next, click the Sharing option and the Sharing tab in the folder's Properties dialog box. Sharing a folder entails clicking the Shared As radio button, and setting up the parameters for sharing, particularly the share permissions. Figure 9-4 illustrates the sharing properties for a folder called "Public". Share permissions (click the Permissions button in Figure 9-4) are another type of permissions, in addition to NTFS file and folder permissions.

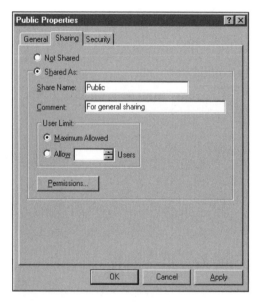

Figure 9-4   Setting up a shared folder in Windows NT 4.0

One of the problems associated with permissions is that there can be permission conflicts, such as between the NTFS permissions granted to a user account, and those granted to a group to which the user belongs. Or, there can be a conflict between the NTFS permission granted to a user or group and the share permissions granted to the same user or group. When you assign or troubleshoot permissions, remember that NTFS permissions are cumulative with one another (accept for No Access), but share permissions are not cumulative with NTFS permissions. An example of cumulative permissions in NTFS is: if a user account has Read permission for a folder, and belongs to a group that has Add permission, then that user has both Read and Add permissions. The exception is No Access, so that if the same user has Read permission on another folder, and belongs to a group with No Access, then that user does not have access to that folder.

NTFS and share permissions on the same folder are not cumulative, however. For example, if the Everyone group is granted NTFS Read access on a folder, but the share permissions for that folder are Full Control for the same group, the Everyone group still only has Read access to that folder. A summary of the permissions rules are:

- NTFS permissions are cumulative, with the exception that if an account or group is given No Access, this overrides other permissions.

- When a folder has both NTFS and share permissions, the most restrictive permissions apply.

You can practice setting up a shared folder in Windows NT Server in Hands-on Project 9-2.

There are only four share permissions, as follows:

- *No Access:* The specified groups and users have no access.

- *Read:* The specified groups and users can read and execute files.

- *Change:* The specified groups and users can read, add, modify, execute, and delete files.

- *Full Control:* The specified groups and users have full access to the files and folders, including the ability to take ownership or change permissions.

 Sharing resources through Windows NT Workstation involves nearly the same processes as sharing resources through Windows NT Server. The important differences are that Windows NT Workstation supports only local groups (not global groups), and Windows NT Workstation is designed to support 10 or fewer users logged on simultaneously.

Windows 2000 Server

Windows 2000 Server is similar to Windows NT Server in that it uses groups, account policies, user accounts, permissions, and shared disks and folders to offer resources over a network. The principles for how you use these elements are the same in Windows 2000, but new features are added because Windows 2000 can deploy Active Directory.

When Active Directory is not implemented in Windows 2000 Server, the scope of resources is limited to the standalone server, and only local groups are created. In contrast, the implementation of Active Directory increases the scope from a local server to all domains in a forest. The types of groups and their associated scopes are as follows:

- *Local*: Used on standalone servers that are not part of a domain. The scope of this type of group does not go beyond the local server on which it is defined.

- *Domain local*: Used when there is a single domain, or to manage resources in a particular domain so that global and universal groups can access those resources

- *Global*: Used to group accounts from the same domain so that those accounts can access resources in the same and other domains

- *Universal*: Used to provide access to resources in any domain within a forest

In Windows 2000, all of these groups are also defined as security or distribution groups. **Security groups** are used to enable access to resources on a standalone server or in Active Directory. **Distribution groups** are used for e-mail or telephone lists, to provide quick, mass distribution of information. In this chapter, the focus is on security groups.

When Active Directory is not installed, such as in a small office setting, only local groups can be created to manage access to an individual server. A local group usually contains both resources, such as the server or a printer, and user accounts that are given access to those resources.

When Active Directory is implemented, Windows 2000 Server adds the ability to have container objects that are larger than domains: **trees** and **forests**. A **container object** is an entity that is used to group together resources in a directory service, such as Microsoft's Active Directory. A tree consists of one or more domains, and a forest houses one or more trees. For example, in a large organization, domains that are in the same geographic location can be organized into trees. Further, trees that represent specific geographic regions, such as the eastern United States, can be organized into a forest. Although the concepts of domains, trees, and forests can be confusing, think of these organizational containers as a way to better manage multiple servers and computers in a very large organization, consisting of hundreds of servers and thousands of desktop computers.

Consider, for example, a large telecommunications company that has big offices in each state, regional offices in California and New Jersey, plus a headquarters office in Pennsylvania. In this case, each state office might be set up as a domain of computer resources—servers, desktop computers, and printers. The domains in the midwestern and western states might be organized into one tree in the California regional office, and the domains in the eastern states organized into another tree housed in the New Jersey regional office. Finally, a forest consisting of both trees would be set up at the headquarters, from which to set general security and group policies for all domains in both trees. For each region, more specific security and group policies could be set in each tree, while specific security and group policies that apply to each state office can be set in its domain. As you are probably thinking, managing security for this large organization of thousands of users and hundreds of servers can be complex. This is why Windows 2000 has three types of groups available when Active Directory is set up.

 Besides domains, trees, and forests, Windows 2000 Active Directory uses a container object, called an organizational object (OU), which is smaller than a domain. In the telecommunications company example, each department in each state office might be organized into a separate OU, such as an Accounting OU, a Research OU, a Sales OU, and so on.

As you think about the Windows 2000 groups, remember that the domain local and global groups work in about the same way as in Windows NT Server (refer back to Figure 9-1). Universal groups are added to the mix to take into account trees and forests—which are new to Windows 2000 Server. For example, the Active Directory administrators for the domains and trees of the telecommunications forest need broad powers. These administrators can be placed in a universal group that has forest-wide access. This access gives them the ability to add new domains and determine which domains are in which forest, for example.

When Active Directory is not installed, you create a local group or a user account by right-clicking My Computer on the desktop, clicking Manage, and clicking Local Users and Groups. When Active Directory is installed, you create domain local, global, and universal groups, and user accounts by clicking Start, pointing to Programs, pointing to Administrative Tools, and opening the Active Directory Users and Computers tool. Figure 9-5 illustrates how to use the Active Directory Users and Computers tool to create a new global security group. Hands-on Project 9-3 enables you to create a new account and group when Active Directory is installed.

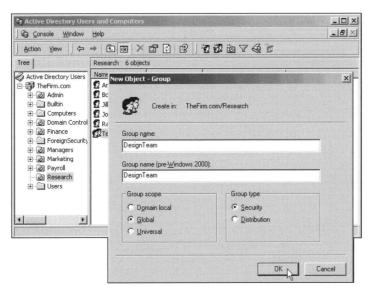

Figure 9-5   Creating a global security group

 When you upgrade from a Windows NT Server domain to Windows 2000 Server using Active Directory, the existing Windows NT local groups are automatically converted to domain local groups, and the Windows NT global groups are converted to Active Directory global groups. Windows 2000 Active Directory universal groups cannot be used until you convert a domain from a mixed mode of Windows NT and 2000 Servers to a native mode of only Windows 2000 Servers.

In Windows 2000 Server with Active Directory installed, access rights and account policies are set up through group policies that can apply to a local server, a domain, or an entire tree of domains. Before any accounts are created, it is wise to establish the account policies, such as for a domain. You can set account policies that are similar to Windows NT Server 4.0, but in Windows 2000 Server, there are more options, which are grouped in three categories:

- *Password Policy:* which includes setting a minimum password length, tracking old passwords so that they are not used over and over, setting password expiration, and encrypting passwords

- *Account Lockout Policy:* which is used to lockout accounts after failed login attempts

- *Kerberos Policy:* for configuring Kerberos security

To set up account policies for all users in a domain, click Start, point to Programs, point to Administrative Tools, and click Domain Security Policy. The account policies are found in the console tree under Windows Settings, Security Settings, and Account Policies, as shown in Figure 9-6.

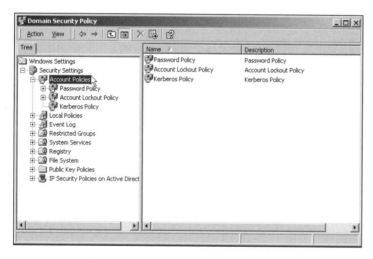

Figure 9-6   Windows 2000 account policies

Permissions on a file or folder in Windows 2000 are set by accessing the file or folder using My Computer or Windows Explorer. After you locate the file or folder, right-click it, click Properties, and click the Security tab (see Figure 9-7). In Windows 2000, permissions from a higher level folder can be automatically inherited by selecting *Allow inheritable permissions from parent to propagate to this object.* Table 9-2 shows the NTFS permissions available for files and folders in Windows 2000.

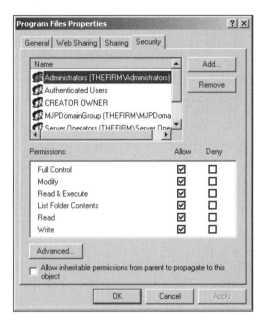

Figure 9-7   Setting NTFS permissions in Windows 2000

Table 9-2   Windows 2000 NTFS Folder and File Permissions

Permission	Description	Applies to
Full Control	Can read, add, delete, execute, and modify files, plus change permissions and attributes, and take ownership	Folders and files
List Folder Contents	Can list (traverse) files in the folder or switch to a subfolder, view folder attributes and permissions, and execute files, but cannot view file contents	Folders only
Modify	Can read, add, delete, execute, and modify files; but cannot delete subfolders and their file contents, change permissions, or take ownership	Folders and files
Read	Can view file contents, view folder attributes and permissions, but cannot traverse folders or execute files	Folders and files
Read & Execute	Implies the capabilities of both List Folder Contents and Read (traverse folders, view file contents, view attributes and permissions, and execute files)	Folders and files
Write	Can create files, write data to files, append data to files, create folders, delete files (but not subfolders and their files), and modify folder and file attributes	Folders and files

9

A Windows 2000 Server or Professional drive or folder can be shared across the network using a process that is similar to the one used in Windows NT. Again, this is accomplished by accessing the drive or folder in My Computer or in Windows Explorer. Right-click the drive or folder and click Sharing (see Figure 9-8). Click the radio button to *Share this folder*, provide a name for the share, and configure how many people can access the share at the same time. Click the Permissions button to set share permissions. The available share permissions are:

- *Read*: permits groups or users to read and execute files

- *Change*: enables users to read, add, modify, execute, and delete files

- *Full Control*: provides full access to the folder including the ability to take control or change share permissions

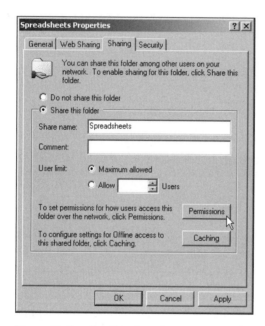

Figure 9-8   Configuring sharing in Windows 2000

Notice that the dialog box in Figure 9-8 has a button for caching. Caching enables you to set up a folder so that it can be accessed by a client, even when the client is not connected to the network. This option is particularly useful for laptop users who travel away from the network. The contents of the folder can be cached to the client's hard drive while he or she is not on the network.

Also, Windows 2000 enables you to set up Web sharing, which makes files available on a Web server for HTML or FTP access. By using Web sharing, you can make the file available to a Web server, but set your own permissions on that file. Tables 9-3 and 9-4 show the two sets of permissions used for Web sharing: access permissions and application permissions.

Table 9-3   Web Sharing Access Permissions

Access Permission	Description
Read	Enables clients to read and display the contents of folders and files via an Internet or intranet
Write	Enables clients to modify the contents of folders and files, including the ability to upload files through FTP
Script source access	Enables clients to view the contents of scripts containing commands to execute Web functions
Directory browsing	Enables clients to browse the folder and subfolders, such as for FTP access

Table 9-4   Web Sharing Application Permissions

Application Permission	Description
None	No access to execute a script or application
Scripts	Enables the client to run scripts to perform Web-based functions
Execute (includes scripts)	Enables clients to execute programs and scripts via an Internet or intranet connection

9

At this writing, Windows .NET Server is still under development. However, Windows .NET Server is built on Windows 2000, and so it offers many of the same features—but with the new Windows XP interface. Windows .NET Server also comes with utilities that support the Microsoft .NET initiative. These utilities include the Passport user authentication system, XML Web services, and .NET program language interpreters and compilers.

UNIX

Access to directories and files on a UNIX server is also governed through user accounts, groups, and access permissions. Each user account in UNIX is associated with a **user identification number (UID)**. Also, users who have common access needs can be assigned to a group via a **group identification number (GID)**, and then the permissions to access resources are assigned to the group, instead of to each user. When the user logs on to access resources, the password file is checked to permit logon authorization. The password file (/etc/passwd) contains the following kinds of information:

- The user name
- An encrypted password or a reference to the shadow file, a file associated with the password file that makes it difficult for intruders to determine the passwords of others
- The UID which can be a number as large as 60,000
- A GID with which the user name is associated

- Information about the user, such as a description or the user's job

- The location of the user's home directory

- A command that is executed as the user logs on, such as which shell to use

 Usually you will give users a unique UID; however, if there are more than one UNIX servers on a network, you might create accounts on each server with the same account name and UID, to simplify access and account administration.

 In many UNIX systems, including Red Hat Linux, any account that has a UID of 0 automatically has access to anything in the system. Occasionally audit the /etc/passwd file to make sure that only the root account has this UID. You can view the contents of the /etc/passwd file from the root account by entering *more /etc/passwd* at the command line, and then pressing *Enter* to view each page.

The shadow file (/etc/shadow) is normally available only to the system administrator. It contains password restriction information that includes the following:

- The minimum and the maximum number of days between password changes

- Information on when the password was last changed

- Warning information about when a password will expire

- Amount of time that the account can be inactive before access is prohibited

Information about groups is stored in the /etc/group file, which typically contains an entry for each group consisting of the name of the group, an encrypted group password, the GID, and a list of group members. In some versions of UNIX, including Red Hat Linux, every account is assigned to at least one group, and can be assigned to more. User accounts and groups can be created by editing the password, shadow, and group files, but a safer way to create them is by using UNIX commands created for this purpose. If you edit the files, you run the risk of an editing error that can create unanticipated problems. Also, it is important to make sure that each group has a unique GID because when two or more groups use the same GID, there is a serious security risk. For example, an obvious risk is that the permissions given to one group also inappropriately apply to the other.

The *useradd* command enables you to create a new user. The parameters that can be added to *useradd* include the following:

- *-c* gives an account description

- *-d* specifies the user's home directory location

- *-e* specifies an account expiration date

- *-f* specifies the number of days the account can be inactive before access is prohibited

- *-g* specifies initial group membership

- *-G* specifies additional groups to which the account belongs

- *-m* establishes the home directory if it has not previously been set up

- *-M* means do not create a home directory

- *-n* means do not set up, by default, a group that has the same name as the account (in Red Hat Linux)

- *-p* specifies the account password

- *-s* designates the default shell associated with the account

- *-u* specifies the UID

In Red Hat Linux 7.x, for example, the command *useradd -c "Lisa Ramirez, Accounting Department, ext 221" -p green$thumb -u 700 lramirez* creates an account called lramirez with a comment that contains the account holder's personal information, a password set to green$thumb, and a UID equal to 700 (see Figure 9-9). In Red Hat Linux, a UID under 500 is typically used for system-based accounts and user accounts have a UID of 500 or over. The parameters set by default, because they are not specified, are to create a group called lramirez, to create the home directory /home/lramirez (with lramirez as owner), and to set the shell as "bash" (Bourne Again Shell). **Home directories** are areas on the server in which users store data. If you do not want a group automatically created at the time you create an account, use the *-n* parameter with the *useradd* command. When you use the *-n* parameter, the account is automatically assigned to a general group called users (with GID 100), instead of to a newly created group with the same name as the account. Setting up a default group with a name that is the same as the account name is a characteristic of Red Hat Linux, but not generalized to other versions of UNIX. Hands-on Project 9-4 enables you to set up an account in Red Hat Linux (although the same steps apply to most UNIX versions).

In many versions of UNIX, such as Red Hat Linux, if no password is specified at the time the account is created, then the account is disabled by default.

The parameters associated with an account can be modified by using the *usermod* command. For instance, to change the password for the account lramirez, you would enter *usermod -p applebuTTer# lramirez*. Also, account setup can be automated by writing a shell script that contains prompts for the desired information. Accounts are deleted through the *userdel* command, which enables you to specify the username, and (optionally) delete the home directory and its contents. In Red Hat Linux and Solaris, to delete an account, the home directory, and all files in the home directory, use the *-r* parameter instead of specifying the home directory, such as entering *userdel -r lramirez*.

Figure 9-9 Creating an account in Red Hat Linux

Useradd, usermod, and *userdel* generally work in all versions of UNIX except IBM's AIX, which uses *mkuser, chuser,* and *rmuser.* Also, some installations of Red Hat Linux, such as those for servers, include a GNOME GUI option to configure user accounts. In the commercial version of Red Hat Linux 7.2, you can find this option by clicking the foot (Main Menu), pointing to Programs, pointing to System, and clicking User Manager.

Information about groups is typically stored in the /etc/group file (see Figure 9-10), and group security information is in the /etc/gshadow file (or the /etc/security/group file in AIX and the /etc/logingroup file in HP-UX). Groups are created using the *groupadd* command. There are typically two inputs associated with this command. The *–g* parameter is used to establish the GID, and the group string creates a group name. For example, to create the auditors group, you would enter *groupadd –g 2000 auditors.* Once a group is created, it is modified through the *groupmod* command. Groups are deleted through the *groupdel* command. (Try Hands-on Project 9-5.)

AIX UNIX uses the commands *mkgroup, chgroup,* and *rmgroup* to add, modify, or delete groups.

UNIX files are assigned any combination of three permissions: read, write, and execute. The permission to read a file enables the user to display its contents, and is signified by the letter *r.* Write permission entails the ability to modify, save, and delete a file, as signified by a *w.* The execute permission, indicated by an *x,* enables a user or group of users to run a program. When a directory is flagged with an *x,* that means a user or group can access and list its contents. Therefore, although a directory can be given read and write permissions for a user or group, these permissions have no meaning unless the directory is given the execute permission for that user or group.

Figure 9-10   Viewing the contents of /etc/group file

Executable programs can have a special set of permissions called Set User ID (SUID) and Set Group ID (SGID). When either of these is associated with an executable, the user or group member who runs it can do so with the same permissions as held by the owner. This provides more access permissions than when the file is executed simply by the user.

Permissions are granted on the basis of four criteria: ownership, group membership, other (or World), and all (all is not used in every version of UNIX, but is included in Red Hat Linux). The owner of the file or directory typically has all permissions, can assign permissions, and has the designation of *u*. Group members, designated by *g*, are users who may have a complete set of permissions, one permission, or a combination of two, such as read and execute. The designation other, or *o* (sometimes referred to as World), consists of non–owners or non-group members who represent generic users. Finally, the all or *a* designation represents the combination of *u+g+o*.

For example, the owner of a file has read, write, and execute permissions, by default. A particular group might have read and execute permissions, while others might only have read permissions, or perhaps no permissions. In another example, if there is a public file to which all permissions are needed for all users, then you would grant read, write, and execute permissions to all.

Permissions are set up by using the *chmod* command in UNIX. *Chmod* has two different formats, symbolic and octal. In the symbolic format, you specify three parameters: (1) who has the permission, (2) the actions to be taken on the permission, and (3) the permission. For example, consider the command *chmod go -r-w-x* * that is used on all files (signified by the *) in a directory. The *g* signifies groups and *o* signifies others. The – means to remove a permission, and *–r-w-x* signifies removing the read, write, and execute permissions (all three are removed; in some versions of UNIX, you might also enter *chmod go -rwx*). In this example, only the owner and members of the owner's group are left with read, write, and execute permissions on the files in this directory. In another example, to grant all permissions for all users to the data file in the /public directory, you would enter *chmod a+r+w+x /public/data*. (Try Hands-on Project 9-6 to practice setting permissions in UNIX.)

The octal permission format is more complex because it assigns a number on the basis of the type of permission, and on the basis of owner, group, and other (World)—all is omitted from this scheme. Execute permission is assigned 1, write is 2, and read is 4. These permission numbers are added together for a value between 0 and 7. For instance, a read and write permission is a 6 (4 + 2), while read and execute is a 5 (4 + 1). There are four numeric positions (xxxx) after the *chmod* command. The first position gives the permission number of the SUID/SGID, the second position gives the permission number of the owner, the third gives group permissions, and the last position gives the permission number of other. For example, the command *chmod 0755 ** assigns no permissions to SUID/SGID (0); read, write, and execute permissions to owner (7); and read and execute permissions to both group and other (5 in both positions) for all files (*).

Mac OS X Server

The Mac OS X Server is built on the Mac OS X foundation, but it is designed as a true server for file sharing, printer sharing, managing network users and groups, and providing Web services. A computer running Mac OS X Server can support up to several thousand users (depending on the network and computer hardware). You might deploy Mac OS X Server in a company that creates publications or advertising materials, for example. Or, Mac OS X Server might be deployed for a school laboratory consisting of Macintosh and other computers.

Mac OS X Server includes the Apache Web server software, which was originally designed for UNIX computers and has been adapted for Mac OS X Server. Through Apache, you can set up multiple Web sites and enable users to participate in Web authoring. Apache supports mainstream Web capabilities, including HTML documents, the HTTP Web protocol, and cgi-bin and scripts.

As is true of Mac OS X, Mac OS X Server supports TCP/IP and AppleTalk. These network protocols open the door for communications with Mac OS computers and other computers that use TCP/IP. This also means that Mac OS X Server is compatible with the Internet e-mail protocol Simple Mail Transfer Protocol (SMTP, see Chapter 2). Out of the box, Mac OS X Server includes a Sendmail interface and program for e-mail communications. Also, Mac OS X Server comes with an FTP Service that can be used to transfer documents to or from the server over the Internet.

Two important tools are included with Mac OS X Server that enable server management: Server Admin and Macintosh Manager. Accounts and groups can be created and managed through the Server Admin tool. Through this tool, users can be set up with a login shell (similar to a login script of actions that occur before the user logs on) and a home directory on the server. File and print sharing can also be managed through Server

Admin—for example, establishing sharing attributes (such as ownership of a share and group access to a share). Server Admin also establishes **share points**, which are simply shared resources on the server.

Through Server Admin, you can set up logging of events on a Mac OS X Server. The events log can include:

- Login and Logout events
- Opened files
- Newly created files
- Newly created folders
- Deleted files and folders

There is also a Printer Monitor in Server Admin, for monitoring print queues, holding print jobs, releasing print jobs, deleting jobs, setting printing priority, creating new printer queues, and so on.

The Macintosh Manger is a tool for managing users, groups, and computers that access the server. Through this tool, you can create users and groups by calling that part of the Server Admin tool that accomplishes these tasks. Also, a user account previously created through Server Admin can be imported into Macintosh Manager to fine tune management of that account, by establishing disk quotas to limit how much space that users can have to store files on the server, for example. Hands-on Project 9-7 enables you to import an account into Macintosh Manager.

NetWare

When a Novell NetWare server is installed, one of the first projects is to design a file structure that makes it easy to establish drive mappings. For example, important commands available to users are contained in a directory called Public. The System directory contains operating system files and utilities that the server administrator uses to manage the server. The Login directory has files that users can access before they log into a server, such as the executable file (Login.exe) used to log in, and other startup files needed by clients. Other information important to users is contained in home directories set up for each user. Users typically have control over whether to enable other users to access their data. Also, on NetWare servers, there may be directories from which to install applications, such as WordPerfect or Microsoft Word, (or perhaps to run other applications that do not have much network overhead).

Consider, for example, a NetWare server set up for use by accountants. The main disk volume composing the root directory is the system volume, called the SYS volume. The server would have default directories on the SYS volume created during installation, which are available to users, such as PUBLIC, LOGIN, HOME, APPS, and DATA (see Figure 9-11). The SYSTEM directory is also on the SYS volume, but full access is limited to the server administrator. If workstations access the server using a Windows-based client operating system, then the PUBLIC directory can have a subdirectory for utilities and programs related to a particular version of Windows, such as a subdirectory called WIN98 for Windows 98, or WIN2K for Windows 2000 Professional. The APPS directory might contain subdirectories for applications such as word processing, spreadsheets, and accounting software. The HOME directory would have one subdirectory for each user, and the DATA directory would contain database files for the accounting system.

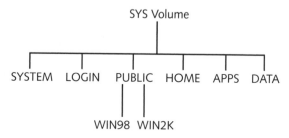

Figure 9-11   Sample NetWare directories available to users

Before users can access any shared directory, the network administrator performs several tasks to prepare the server before it is made available on the network. These tasks include the following:

- Set security on each directory, subdirectory, and on particular files
- Create an account and account password for each user who needs to access the server
- Set up groups as a way to provide shortcuts for managing security

After the server is prepared for network access, individual users log onto their accounts and map to particular drives. This can be done as a manual process, by mapping each drive at the beginning of every login session, or it can be done using a login script. Table 9-5 illustrates how drives might be mapped at the client workstation, which might be running Windows 95/98 or Windows 2000, for example.

With an account and the appropriate security, a client can access directories and files within NetWare directories over the network. The directories that are mapped using a letter of the alphabet are available as shared drives for users to view and access files, and copy files to their client workstations. The letters for these drives generally are those that follow letters allocated for local drives on the workstation, including local drive A: for a floppy drive, local drive C: for a hard drive, and local drive D: for the CD-ROM drive (depending on the number of hard drives installed).

Table 9-5   NetWare Network Drive Mappings

Mapped Drive Letter at the Workstation	Mapped Directory on the Server	Purpose of the Mapped Directory
F	SYS volume root	Access to the main volume and logon utilities
H	SYS volume HOME directory, and user's subdirectory (SYS:HOME\userdirectory)	Storing the user's files
P	SYS volume applications directory (SYS:APPS)	Accessing program files to download to the client
Q	SYS volume data directory (SYS:DATA)	Access to data files or a database
S1	SYS volume PUBLIC directory (SYS:PUBLIC)	Search access for NetWare utilities
S2	SYS volume, PUBLIC directory, and Windows 2000 subdirectory (SYS:PUBLIC\WIN2K)	Search access for clients using Windows 2000

9

Note

In MS-DOS, Windows 3.x, Windows 95, and Windows 98, the last drive letter allocated for a local drive can be specified in the Config.sys boot file using the *LASTDRIVE* command. Typically a computer that is not attached to a network is set up with the command *LASTDRIVE=E*; if it is connected to a network, *LASTDRIVE=Z* is used. Using this command occupies 40 KB of overhead in memory. When you do not use the command, these client operating systems default to using A: through E: for local drives, thus the first network drive is mapped as F:.

NetWare recognizes another type of network drive, called a **search drive**, which is given drive letters such as S1 for the first drive, S2 for the second drive, and so on. The difference between a mapped network drive and a mapped search drive is that NetWare can execute a file on a search drive, regardless of whether the file is in the main directory or in a subdirectory under the search drive. For example, if you want to execute a utility in a subdirectory under the S1 mapped directory for PUBLIC, you simply type the name of the program and NetWare searches all subdirectories under PUBLIC in order to execute it.

There are several ways to map a NetWare drive from a client workstation operating system. One way is to use the MAP command from the MS-DOS prompt, or MS-DOS command prompt window for Windows-based operating systems. The syntax of the MAP command is MAP *drive*:=volume:directory[\subdirectory] for regular network drives, and it is MAP S#: = volume:directory[\subdirectory] for search drives. For example, to map the PUBLIC directory as search drive S1, you would type MAP S1:=SYS:PUBLIC (try Hands-on Project 9-8). Another way to set up the same search drive (so that you map it each time you log onto your account) is to put the MAP command in a NetWare login script. A login script is a file of commands that is stored on the NetWare server and associated with an account or a group of accounts. The login script runs automatically each time a user logs onto the account. The network administrator can set up login scripts and enable users to customize their own login scripts. Figure 9-12 is an example of a NetWare login script (the arrows in the figure point to the description of each command).

```
MAP DISPLAY OFF ──▶ Turns off the display of map commands as they are executed
CLS ──▶ Clears the screen
WRITE "Welcome to the First National Bank network server" ──▶ Displays a message
PAUSE ──▶ Requires that a key be pressed to continue
MAP F:=SYS: ──▶ Maps drive F: to the SYS: volume
MAP H:=SYS:USERS\HERRERA ──▶ Maps drive H: to the home directory location
MAP INS S1:=SYS:PUBLIC ──▶ Maps search drive S1 to the PUBLIC directory
MAP INS S2:=SYS:PUBLIC\WIN98 ──▶ Maps search drive S2 to the WIN98 subdirectory in PUBLIC
#CAPTURE Q=HPLASER ──▶ Directs printer files from a local printer port to a network printer
```

Figure 9-12   Sample NetWare login script

 The MAP INS command is used to insert a search drive between two existing search drives. It is also used in login scripts to ensure that search drive mappings supercede those from another source.

Access to a NetWare shared drive is granted through creating an account for each user. A user account can be set up using several kinds of restrictions. The restrictions include:

- Requiring a password
- Setting a minimum password length
- Requiring that a password is changed within a specified interval of time
- Requiring that a new password is used each time the old one is changed
- Limiting the number of unsuccessful attempts to log on to an account
- Setting time restrictions that specify when users can log on
- Setting intruder detection capabilities

User accounts and restrictions are set up in NetWare by using the NetWare Administrator (see Figure 9-13). Also, multiple accounts can be set up by using the UIMPORT utility. UIMPORT is run in conjunction with an ASCII text file that contains information about the accounts to be set up, such as the login name, the user's actual name, information about the location of a home directory, password restrictions, and other information pertinent to each account.

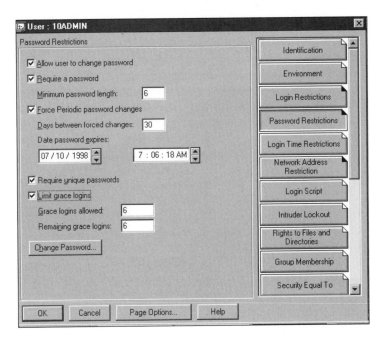

Figure 9-13   Password restrictions in NetWare Administrator

After accounts are set up, the network administrator can grant rights to access specific directories, subdirectories, and files. The rights control the ability to:

- Perform a directory listing
- Create a new directory, subdirectory, or file
- Read the contents of a directory, subdirectory, or file
- Write to the contents of a file
- Delete a directory, subdirectory, or file
- Change the security associated with a directory, subdirectory, or file
- Copy a directory, subdirectory, or file
- Rename a directory, subdirectory, or file

Rights are assigned by making a user or group a directory or file trustee. Rights also can be inherited on the basis of the rights already assigned to higher level directories, and they can be inherited based on container objects. In NetWare, a container object is an entity that is used to group together resources, such as an organizational unit, an organization, or a country, as specified in the directory services of NetWare.

An effective way to manage the rights granted to accounts is by creating groups that need the same kinds of access. After a group is created, the network administrator assigns rights to the group, and also assigns accounts to the group. Likewise, a group can be assigned to a specific login script containing mapped drives and other network parameters, such as network printer assignments, applicable to each group.

User accounts, groups, printers, directories, subdirectories, files, and other resources in NetWare are considered **objects** (and the same is true for Windows NT/2000/.NET Server). Information about objects, such as rights that are associated with them, is stored in the **Novell Directory Services (NDS)**. NDS is a comprehensive database of shared resources and information known to the NetWare operating system. A portion of the NDS is used to store information about clients, which is one example of NDS **leaf objects** in an organization container, given various levels of authorization to access NetWare servers. The information that is stored in the NDS includes the client login name, full name of the client, home directory location, and password information.

NDS and Windows 2000 Active Directory are examples of directory services. A **directory service** provides three important functions on a network: a central listing of resources, a way to quickly find resources, and the ability to access and manage resources.

ACCESSING AND SHARING DISKS AND FILES THROUGH CLIENT NETWORK OPERATING SYSTEMS

Many operating systems include the ability to act as clients, to map to disks and directories on servers, for example. Some client operating systems can share files and folders as well. In the sections that follow, you'll learn about the capabilities of major client operating systems including:

- Windows 95
- Windows 98
- Windows Me
- Windows NT
- Windows 2000
- Windows XP
- UNIX
- Macintosh

Accessing and Sharing Resources in Windows 95, Windows 98, and Windows Me

Windows 95, Windows 98, and Windows Me have nearly the same capabilities to access shared disks and folders. All three operating systems also can offer shared resources for other network workstations to access. These operating systems enable access to resources through two access control techniques. One, called share-level access control, creates a disk or directory share that is protected by share permissions, and on which the share owner can require a password for access. The second technique, called user-level access control, requires the share owner to create an access list of groups and users who are allowed to access the share. Both techniques are set up through the Control Panel and Network icon. After you open the Network dialog box, click the Access Control tab to select one of these methods (see Figure 9–14).

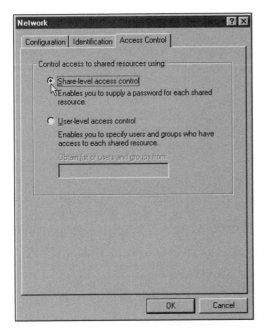

Figure 9-14   Windows 98 Access Control dialog box

In share-level access, you create a share that is similar to a share created on a Windows NT or 2000 server. The difference is that several hundred simultaneous users (depending on the server resources, such as CPU and memory) can access a Windows NT or 2000 Server share, whereas a share on a computer running Windows 95, 98, or Me is designed to host 10 or less (also depending on the workstation resources). Further, Windows NT and 2000 Servers provide a more comprehensive set of combined NTFS permissions and share permissions. There are three share-level access permissions in Windows 95, 98, and Me:

- *Read-Only:* Clients can read the contents of files and folders and copy them, but clients cannot modify files and folders

- *Full:* Clients can read, copy, add, remove, and modify files and folders

- *Depends On Password:* Clients are given access on the basis of a read-only or full-access password.

The Read-Only and Full permissions can be assigned with or without a password. The default is to use no password, which simply means that you leave the password box empty. The Depends On Password permission requires that you enter a password on the basis of whether the client is to have read-only or full access. There is no option to leave the password boxes empty.

User-level access enables you to specify access on the basis of user accounts and groups that are already defined through Windows NT or 2000 servers that authorize users to log on to a domain. A list of users and groups also can be obtained from Windows NT Workstation or Windows 2000 Professional. To obtain a list of valid users and groups, you specify either the domain name or the name of a computer that has a defined set of users and groups. Users and groups are given three kinds of access:

- *Read-Only:* Clients can read the contents of files and folders and copy them, but clients cannot modify files and folders

- *Full:* Clients can read, copy, add, remove, and modify files and folders

- *Custom:* Clients are given access using any combination of the permissions listed in Table 9-6

Try Hands-on Project 9-9 to practice setting up a shared folder in Windows 95/98 Me.

Before setting up share-level access or user-level access, it is necessary to install file and printer sharing services. These services can be installed for Microsoft networks, older NetWare networks, and newer NetWare networks that use NDS. File and printer sharing services are installed from the Control Panel and Network icon. Click the Add button, double-click Service, and double-click *File and printer sharing for Microsoft Networks* to install the services for a network running Microsoft operating systems. After you install the services, return to the Configuration tab and the Network dialog box, and check the options to enable others to have access to files and printers.

With file and printer sharing services installed and the access level selected, you are ready to create a shared disk, folder, or file (or printer). For example, to share a folder, right-click the folder in My Computer or in Windows Explorer, click the Sharing option on the menu, and click the Shared As radio button. The parameters that you complete will depend on which access level was designated previously.

Table 9-6   Windows 95, 98, and Me Custom Share Permissions for User-level Access

Permission	Description
Read-Only	Read the contents of files and folders and copy them, but cannot modify files and folders
Full	Read, copy, add, remove, and modify files and folders
Read (R)	Read the contents of files and copy them
Write (W)	Modify the contents of files
Create (C)	Create new files and folders
Delete (D)	Delete files
Change file attributes (T)	Change share permissions on files, such as adding or removing read, write, and delete to the customized access granted to a list of users and groups
List files (F)	View a listing of files in a folder
Change access control (A)	Change the type of access to files and folders, such as from read-only to full

9

To map a drive that is shared by another computer, Windows 95 and 98 use the Network Neighborhood utility on the desktop, while Windows Me uses the newer My Network Places. You map a drive by double-clicking Network Neighborhood or My Network Places to view the computers on the network. Both utilities are used to display a list of computers by name. To access the resources offered by a particular computer, double-click that computer to view the shared resources, which can be folders and printers. Next, map a folder by right-clicking it and selecting Map Network Drive on the menu (see Figure 9-15). In the Map Network Drive dialog box (see Figure 9-16), you specify a drive letter to which it is mapped, and you can check a box to make sure the drive is mapped each time you start the operating system. After the drive is mapped, it appears in My Computer and in Windows Explorer.

Figure 9-15   Windows 98 selection menu

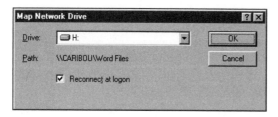

Figure 9-16   Mapping a drive in Windows 98

To disconnect a mapped drive, you right-click the drive in My Computer or Windows Explorer, and click Disconnect on the menu.

 Shared drives in Windows NT Server and Windows NT Workstation are mapped using the same utilities as in Windows 95 and Windows 98— Network Neighborhood and the Map Network Drive dialog box. Also, mapped drives appear in My Computer and Windows Explorer.

Accessing and Sharing Resources in Windows 2000 Professional

Mapping a drive in Windows 2000 Professional and Server is similar to the process used for Windows 95/98/Me, but Network Neighborhood is replaced by My Network Places. The steps for mapping a drive in Windows 2000 are:

1. Double-click My Network Places on the desktop.

2. Double-click Entire Network.

3. Click the hyperlink for entire contents.

4. Double-click the network in which you want to look, such as Microsoft Windows Network.

5. Double-click the workgroup or domain in which to look.

6. Find the computer that offers the shared resource, and double-click it to view the folders and printers it shares.

7. Right-click the folder or printer that you want to access, and click Map Network Drive.

8. Specify a drive letter to assign to the network drive, and click Finish.

The process for sharing a drive in Windows 2000 Professional was discussed earlier in the section about Windows 2000 Server. To disconnect a shared drive, find it in My Computer or Windows Explorer, highlight the drive, click Tools on the menu bar, and select Disconnect Network Drive.

Accessing and Sharing Resources in Windows XP

Windows XP uses My Network Places to locate and map network drives, but this tool offers more options in Windows XP than in Windows 2000. You can access My Network Places using several techniques, such as through the Control Panel or Windows Explorer, but among the fastest is to use the following steps:

1. Click the Start menu, right-click My Computer, and click Map Network Drive.

2. Click the Browse button.

3. Find the workgroup or domain in which the computer sharing the drive resides, and click it (see Figure 9-17).

4. Click the folder that you want to access, and click OK.

5. Set the drive letter to which you want to map the network drive.

6. Click Finish.

9

Figure 9-17   Mapping a drive in Windows XP

Disconnecting from a shared drive in Windows XP involves the same steps as in earlier versions of Windows: find the drive in My Computer or Windows Explorer, right-click the drive, and then click Disconnect.

Sharing a drive or folder using Windows XP can be accomplished from either My Computer or Windows Explorer. For example, to share a folder, open Windows Explorer, find the folder that you want to share, right-click it, and click Sharing and Security. Figure 9-18 shows the dialog box used to configure a shared folder called Spreadsheets (try Hands-on Project 9-10).

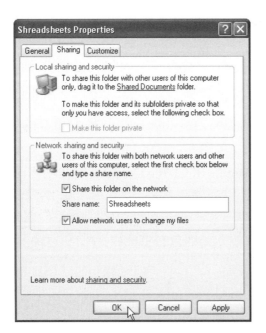

Figure 9-18   Configuring a shared folder in Windows XP

Accessing Shared Resources via UNIX and Specialized Utilities

UNIX computers can access resources on other computers that support the **Network File System (NFS)**, which provides file transfer capabilities. Accessing shared resources on a Windows NT Server provides one example of how UNIX can participate as a network client with the ability to access shared resources. One way to support a UNIX client in Windows NT Server is to implement third-party disk sharing software that employs NFS, such as Intergraph DiskShare (recommended by Microsoft as compatible).

With the third party's software installed, you can copy the UNIX password file, located in \etc\passwd, to a Windows NT server at the folder location, Winnt\System32\Drivers\Etc. This step enables the Windows NT logon authentication to work with the third-party software to match the authentication used at the UNIX workstation, so both employ the same username and password, for example. The authentication is performed by creating an account in Windows NT Server, and linking the same rights and privileges assigned to the UNIX user account with those of the corresponding Windows NT Server account. Intergraph DiskShare, for instance, is installed in Windows NT Server, and provides an NFS server and an administrator utility that is used to link and administer the rights and permissions granted to the NT Server account. The NFS server utility is used to set up shares that are available to UNIX, and assign share permissions. With this in place, the UNIX client accesses the shared disk or folder through its *mount* command, which is the same command used to mount local and remote resources, including non-UNIX file systems such as FAT and NTFS. Typically UNIX share permissions include:

- *Root:* Includes all permissions, and is similar to Full Control in Windows NT

- *Read-write:* Encompasses permissions to mount the shared disk or folder, read the contents of files and folders, and modify files and folders

- *Read-only:* Gives permission to mount the shared resource, but only read the contents of files and folders

- *No access:* Prevents mounting the shared disk or folder

The NFS server acts as a two-way utility because it also permits a Windows NT server or NT workstation to access a computer running UNIX. When Windows NT is a UNIX client, the UNIX computer authorizes the logon, and enables the Windows NT computer to mount the UNIX shared resources as a mapped drive that appears in Windows NT Explorer and My Computer. The drive is mapped in Windows NT using the same utility as for mapping any other network drive.

Windows 2000 Server comes with a software component called Services for UNIX that can be installed using the Add/Remove Programs icon on the Control Panel. This software component works with Sun Solaris, DEC/Compaq/HP UNIX, and Hewlett-Packard's HP-UX. Services for UNIX includes the following components:

- Server and client software to run NFS for file sharing between UNIX and Windows 2000 computers

- Server and client software for Telnet, so that a UNIX computer can log on remotely to a Windows 2000 server and vice versa

- Ability to synchronize passwords between Windows 2000 servers and UNIX computers for accounts used by the same account holders

- Various UNIX utilities that can be used from Windows 2000, such as the Korn shell

 Services for UNIX is now also available from Microsoft for Windows NT Server 4.0.

Accessing and Sharing Resources via Mac OS

The Mac OS offers two ways to connect to shared resources on a network: the Chooser and the Network Browser. The Chooser is the original way to access shared network volumes, which can be an entire disk drive or a directory, depending on the way in which the resource is set up. The Chooser is available up through Mac OS 9.x. The Network Browser is a utility that is new to Mac OS 8.5 and above. For example, you might use either utility to mount a shared drive set up for AppleTalk on a NetWare or

Windows 2000 server. Another way to use these utilities is to connect to shared files and volumes on another Macintosh workstation, or on Mac OS X Server.

The Mac OS uses the term *mount* instead of map when accessing a shared disk volume over the network.

To use the Chooser in Mac OS 9.x, for example, you select it from the Apple menu, and then click the AppleShare icon in the Chooser window. If your network consists of more than one zone, select the zone that is home to the computer you want to access. Next, choose the computer that contains the shared volume or files, and click OK (see Figure 9-19). A dialog box appears that enables you to mount the resource as a guest, or as a registered user. Typically, you access the shared resource as a registered user, providing your name and password. If you access the resource as a guest, you do not enter your name and password because guest access is intended for anonymous users who access resources available for anyone on the network. After you make your selection, click Connect. A list of resources, called volumes, appears in the next dialog box, enabling you to click the one you want to access. You can select multiple volumes by pressing the Shift key and clicking those you wish to mount. There is also an option to check volumes that you wish to open at system startup time, which means that these volumes are automatically connected each time you start up the operating system. Once your selection is made, click OK to have it appear as an icon on the desktop.

If the Mac OS is set up to use TCP/IP, then you can use the Chooser to connect to a server by entering its IP address. Also, you can set up the operating system for PPP communications over a remote network (see Chapter 8).

The Mac Network Browser presents an interface that is similar to a Windows drop-down or scroll box, or like the Open dialog box that is new to Mac OS 8.5 through Mac OS 9.x. The Open dialog box is a scroll box that lists items, and presents a small identifying icon in front of each item. Hands-on Project 9-11 demonstrates how to use the Network Browser. Unmounting a volume entails dragging its icon to the trash, which does not delete the volume contents, but only disconnects access to the volume at the computer that mounted it.

In Mac OS X, you connect to another computer that is sharing a disk or folder by using the Go menu. To mount a shared drive, open the Go menu, and select Connect To Server. Mac OS X regards both computers configured as servers and computers that share drives or folders as servers. The Connect to Server window provides a list of computers to which you can connect, and gives you three ways to connect to a computer:

- By selecting the computer in the pop-up menu

- By selecting the computer from the list in the right pane

- By entering the AFP (Apple File Protocol) or IP address of the computer in the Address box—by typing afp://200.92.10.8, for example

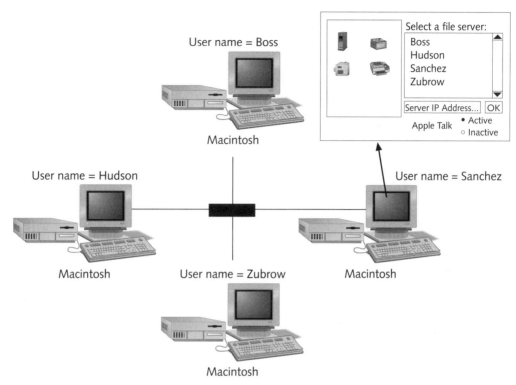

Figure 9-19   Using the Chooser

After you select the computer, click Connect, enter your account name and password, and click Connect again. Hands-on Project 9-11 enables you to mount a volume in Mac OS X.

Files are shared from a Macintosh workstation by first creating users and groups, and then defining which files to share. As in server operating systems, a Macintosh user is set up by assigning an account and a password. Also, groups can be established that consist of accounts with the same access. Up through Mac OS 9.x, users and groups are set up by opening the Apple menu, clicking Control Panels, and then Users & Groups. In Mac OS X, there are two ways to create users. One way is to open the Users icon in System Preferences. A more advanced way to manage users and groups in Mac OS X Server is through the Macintosh Manager. To start the Macintosh Manager, locate it in the Dock (or taskbar) at the bottom of the desktop (Macintosh Manager is set up in the Dock, by default). Click the Users tab, and click the Import button to start a Users & Groups window, from which you can create a new user account, a new group, or import a user. You can also create users and groups by using the Server Admin tool in Mac OS X Server. Computers running the Mac OS typically have two users already defined—Owner and Guest. After a user is created, it can be added to one or more groups.

The process of creating a new user in Mac OS 9.x involves these steps (which you can practice in Hands-on Project 9-7):

1. Provide the user's name.

2. Provide a password.

3. Enable the user to change his or her password (an optional check box).

4. Enable sharing and allow the user to link to programs on the computer.

Creating an account in Mac OS X involves parameters that are similar to Mac OS 9.x, but you create an account via the Users icon in System Preferences. However, if you set up an account to be managed in the Mac OS X Server Macintosh Manager, besides the username and password, you can configure the type of user, the type of access allowed to the user, e-mail preferences, and disk quotas. See Hands-on Project 9-7 to learn more about managing an account through the Mac OS X Server Macintosh Manager.

Creating a group is an equally straightforward process in which you define the name of a group, and then drag selected users into the group. Also, you can modify or delete users and groups from the Users & Groups control panel in Mac OS 9.x, from System Preferences in Mac OS X, and from the Users & Groups window in the Server Admin or Macintosh Manager tools in Mac OS X Server. As is true with network server operating systems, it is a good practice to keep the number of groups to a minimum for easier management.

After the users and groups are created, you are ready to share files. The first step in preparing to share files is to establish a network identity for the computer. You establish a network identity in the Mac OS 9.x File Sharing control panel by providing your name as the owner, the password to associate with the owner name, and a computer name. The computer name is the one that other computers on the network use to identify yours. After the network identity is established, it is necessary to turn on file sharing, which is accomplished through the File Sharing control panel in Mac OS 9.x. Also, it is possible for users to "link" to your computer so that you can share programs with them. If your computer has programs that can be linked, you can choose to turn on linking as part of the file sharing process. File sharing and linking can be turned off through the File Sharing control panel at any time.

In Mac OS X, you establish the network identity and turn on file sharing through System Preferences. Open the Apple menu, select System Preferences, and select Sharing. At the bottom of the pane, enter the computer name that you want to use for the network identity. Next, click the Start button at the top of the pane to turn on file sharing (but do not click it if the button says Stop because sharing is already turned on).

Privileges are set in order to enable users and groups to access the folders and files you wish to share. There are four kinds of privileges that can be set:

- *None:* No access to files

- *Read only:* Access to only read the contents of files only

- *Write only:* Access to write files, but not open them
- *Read & write:* Access to open and write files

The access privileges can be assigned to any of four types of users: owner, users, groups, and everyone. The owner is the one who holds all access privileges and can set them. Users and groups consist of the user accounts and groups currently set up on the computer. Last, everyone consists of those who do not belong to any of the following: users already assigned privileges, groups already assigned privileges, or the owner.

SHARING PRINTING DEVICES

All of the operating systems discussed in this book have the ability to share printers as well as disks, directories, and files. The sections that follow describe how printers are shared through these operating systems. (For more information on setting up printers in various operating systems, see Chapter 6.)

Windows-based Systems

Printing is configured in Windows-based systems by using the Add Printer Wizard to set up a printer (see Chapter 6). Once a printer is set up, it appears in the Printers folder. In Windows 95 through Windows XP, you share a printer by first opening the Printers (or Printers and Faxes) folder. In Windows 95/98/NT/Me/2000, click Start, point to Settings, and click Printers. In Windows XP, click Start, and click Printers and Faxes. Select the printer you want to share and right-click it to access menu options, such as those shown in Figure 9-20 (for a printer that is not the default printer) for Windows XP. Click Sharing and select the option to enable sharing of the printer—such as *Shared As* in Windows 95/98/Me/NT/2000, or *Share this printer* in Windows XP. Enter a name for the shared printer and a comment, if there is a Comment box in your version of Windows. In some versions of Windows, such as Windows 95 and 98, if share-level access is used, then you also have the option to require a password to access the printer, as shown in Figure 9-21. Also, in Windows 95/98, if user-level access is used, then you can specify a list of users and groups who have access to the printer.

Figure 9-20   Configuring a shared printer in Windows XP

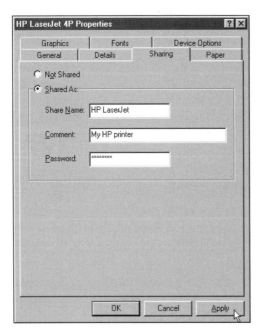

Figure 9-21   Setting up shared printer parameters in Windows 98

 To share a printer, file and printer sharing services must first be installed in Windows 95, 98, Me, 2000 Professional, and XP. For example, in Windows 98, open the Network icon in the Control Panel and click File and Print Sharing; or, in Windows XP, click Start, click Control Panel, click Network and Internet Connections, click Network Connections, right-click Local Area Connection, click Properties, click Install, and double-click Service. In Windows NT and Windows 2000 Server, the server, spooler, and workstation services should be running (you can check these through the Control Panel and Services icon in Windows NT, or in Windows 2000, right-click My Computer, click Management, and click Services and Applications in the console tree).

When you configure sharing in Windows NT and Windows 2000, particularly in the Server versions, make sure that you configure sharing permissions for the shared printer. In both of these operating systems, you configure the share permissions by right-clicking the printer in the Printers folder, and opening the Security tab. The printer share permissions for Windows NT are:

- *No Access:* Cannot access the shared printer

- *Print:* Can send print jobs and manage your own jobs

- *Manage Documents:* Can send print jobs and manage yours or those sent by any other user

- *Full Control:* Have complete control, including the ability to change share permissions, turn off sharing, and delete the share

For Windows 2000, the following share permissions are checked for *allow* or *deny*:

- *Print:* Can send print jobs and manage your own jobs

- *Manage Documents:* Can send print jobs and manage yours or those sent by any other user

- *Manage Printers:* Can access the share, change share permissions, turn off sharing, configure printer properties, and delete the share

 The Windows NT Server and Windows 2000 Server Add Printer Wizard enables you to designate a printer as shared at the same time you install it. It also enables you to set up and manage shared printers at other Windows-based workstations on the network. Because the wizard does not include setting share permissions, make sure that you set these after the wizard completes the printer installation.

Mapping to a shared printer is an easy process in Windows 95 through Windows XP. To map a printer, open Network Neighborhood (Windows 95/98/NT) or My Network Places (Windows Me/2000/XP), find the computer that offers the shared printer, and double-click it. In the list of shared resources, right-click the printer, and click Install or Connect (depending on your version of Windows). Hands-on Project 9-12 enables you to access a shared network printer from Windows XP.

UNIX

UNIX printing in a networked environment is essentially the process of logging on to the UNIX server and printing to one of its printers. Typically, when a UNIX server is accessed through network connectivity, it is set up to use the BSD or the SVR4 spooling systems, as described in Chapter 6. As a review, BSD uses three components for printing: the *lpr* print program, the *lpd* daemon, and the file /etc/printcap to specify printer properties. The file /etc/printcap is a text file that can be modified via a text editor. In SVR4, the spooling system consists of the *lp* print program and the *lpsched* daemon. SVR4 printer properties are stored in the file /etc/printcap, which is modified by using the *lpadmin* utility.

 If your version of UNIX can use either BSD or SVR4 spooling, note that administrators often consider BSD spooling to be more adaptable for network clients.

In Red Hat Linux 7.2, you can set up a printer and start *lpd* by using the GNOME Printer Configuration tool. To access the tool in some versions of GNOME, click the foot icon, point to Programs, point to System, and click Printer Configuration. You can set up printers and print queues with this tool. Also, you can start *lpd* in the Printer Configuration tool by opening the File menu and clicking *Start lpd*; or if *lpd* is already running, and you suspect it is hung, open the File menu and click *Restart lpd*.

Mac OS

The Mac OS can make a connected local printer available to other computers running the Mac OS on a network. Also, the Mac OS can attach to a shared printer offered by another workstation on the network. In Mac OS 9.x, you use the Chooser utility to set up a printer to share, and to attach to a shared printer through the network.

For many earlier versions of the Mac OS, to share a printer, first install the printer and set it up. Once a printer is installed, it appears in the Chooser window. Select the printer in the Chooser window, and click Setup. In the Sharing Setup dialog box, click the check box next to Share this Printer, and enter a name for the shared printer. There are also optional parameters that enable you to set a password required by others to access the shared printer, and a check box to enable the Mac OS to keep a log of its use.

Accessing a shared printer requires that you first install a printer driver for the printer, such as a driver for a LaserWriter 8 or a StyleWriter 1200. After the printer driver is installed, click it in the Chooser window, and select the appropriate zone, if applicable. A list of shared printers appears, enabling you to select the one to use over the network.

In Mac OS 9.x, there is the option to share a USB printer. You access this option by opening the Apple menu, selecting Control Panels, and selecting USB Printer Sharing. Select to view the Start/Stop tab, and click the Start button. Open the My Printers tab and click the Share box next to the printer that you want to share. Other users who want to use the shared printer can do so by opening the USB Printer Sharing control panel, selecting the Network Printers tab, and clicking the Use box next to the printer that they want to use.

For Mac OS X, printer sharing and accessing a shared printer are handled through the Print Center. You can access the Print Center by opening the Applications icon in a Finder window. In the Applications window, open Utilities, and then the Print Center icon. The Print Center shows a list of available printers and has an Add Printer button for adding a printer. When you add a printer, you can specify the type of printer, such as an AppleTalk printer, or a TCP/IP-based LPR printer with an IP address.

NetWare

Shared printing in NetWare is accomplished by using two different approaches. Both approaches are relatively complex and are only summarized in this chapter. The first approach is to employ queue-based printing, which is used for MS-DOS or Windows applications. The second is **Novell Distributed Print Services (NDPS)**, which is used for Windows applications, and printers that have options tailored to NDPS.

In queue-based printing, the network administrator performs several functions to set up a shared printer. The first is to install the printer and its driver in NetWare. The next step is to create a print queue for the printer. For versions of NetWare that use NDS, the next step is to set up an NDS printer object, which defines the printer to NDS. After the printer object is defined, a print server object is also defined, which links a printer to one or more print queues. The last step is to load the print server on the NetWare server so that the printer and its queue are shared through the NetWare server's operating system. After the printer is shared, clients access it by using the NetWare *capture* command, which captures the output from the client's designated printer port, such as LPT1, to the network printer associated with the queue.

NDPS is a print service capability added in NetWare 5.0 and above. It is designed to work with printers that have built-in NetWare printer agent software. These printers are simply attached to the network as a printing agents, and the NDPS on the NetWare server handles the details of directing client print requests to the correct printer. Because some printers do not come with printer agent software, NetWare provides a printer gateway that acts as printer agent, and runs on the NetWare server. When printers without built-in agent software are attached, NetWare provides the NDPS Manager utility to manage their connectivity for client access.

9

NETWORK AND INTERNET RESOURCE SERVERS

NetWare, UNIX, Windows NT/2000/.NET, and Mac OS X servers can be set up as resource servers to provide network and Internet resources. All of these operating systems can act as servers for many kinds of functions. One of the most common is to handle e-mail. There is a wide range of programs that can turn a NetWare, UNIX, or Windows NT/2000/.NET Server system into an e-mail server. Also, Mac OS X Server can process e-mail through its Sendmail program. A close relative of e-mail is e-commerce, which consists of thousands of servers connected to the Internet conducting business, such as taking and fulfilling product orders. These servers process billions of dollars in business transactions.

Another area in which these operating systems participate as resource servers is in videoconferencing and multimedia. Many companies are implementing videoconferencing capabilities on servers and workstations as a way to save money by reducing travel expenses. For example, meetings that once required people to fly to a location from different parts of the country are now conducted through networks and server operating systems. Multimedia servers are also growing in use for business applications, education, government, and entertainment purposes. In a short time, computer owners will access a variety of rental movies through multimedia servers connected to the Internet. Movies that are shown in movie theaters now, in some cases, are delivered through the Internet. Currently, you can go to virtually any news organization's site and play news clips from a multimedia server. Many of these servers run NetWare, UNIX, Windows NT/2000/.NET, and Mac OS X Server. Another growing use for multimedia is to provide academic courses that you can access from a home computer over the Internet.

Client/server applications are also a reality, and are made possible by networks and servers. A typical client/server application consists of three components: a workstation running a Windows-based operating system, a server from which to run applications, and one or more database servers. These applications are made possible because database software runs well on NetWare, UNIX, and Windows NT/2000/.NET Server. For instance, Oracle is a database system that can run on these operating systems. Informix is another database system designed for UNIX, and SQL Server is a database system designed for Windows NT/2000/.NET Server. All of these database systems are used frequently in client/server applications.

Web servers are another fast-growing implementation of NetWare, UNIX, Windows NT/2000/.NET, and Mac OS X servers. Web servers provide a huge range of services that include the ability to quickly access information and download it through FTP. This means that many Web servers also act as FTP servers. Before long, most software that you purchase will be downloaded from an Internet server instead of purchased in a box at a store.

Companies, schools, and government organizations are quickly implementing intranet and virtual private network (VPN) servers that enable information to be obtained through private networks. For example, some companies enable employees to change personnel information by accessing an intranet/VPN server and completing a form in a Web-based environment. You may already have services at a bank that enable you to access your account information from a home computer by dialing into an intranet server available over the Internet. Or, your school may post grade and degree completion information on a server that you access through your campus network or the Internet.

The uses for network servers are growing at an unimaginable rate. As networks are able to transport higher volumes of traffic at faster speeds, the implementation of servers grows reciprocally. Complementing the growth in the use of servers is equivalent growth in the capabilities of their operating systems, and in the number of server programs written for them. For example, only a few years ago, most database systems were written for mainframe computers. NetWare and Windows NT servers, in particular, were not considered robust enough to handle large databases. Today, major database systems run on NetWare and Windows NT/2000/.NET, and databases often grow to be multigigabyte-sized files.

CHAPTER SUMMARY

❏ Resource sharing is why networks exist and are thriving. At first, networks were particularly designed to share files. One of the first methods of doing this was by using protocols such as FTP to upload and download individual files. Network file servers quickly followed with the ability to share disks, directories, and files. Before long, they were also sharing other services, such as printing and program services. Today, these functions on servers are commonplace and compose the vital network infrastructure of information and services.

❏ One way to distinguish network-capable operating systems is by classifying them as server or client operating systems, although in some cases, the distinctions are slight. NetWare, UNIX, Windows 2000 Server, and Mac OS X Server are four current popular server network operating systems. Each of these enables you to create user accounts to access shared resources, and create groups to help manage user accounts, resources, and security. Security is becoming a critical capability as more servers are implemented on networks and more resources are shared. Some server network operating systems offer extensive security, such as Windows 2000 Server.

❏ Mac OS, UNIX, Windows 95/98/Me, Windows NT Workstation, Windows 2000 Professional, and Windows XP are examples of client network operating systems. All of these operating systems can share disks, directories, and files for other computers to access through a network. Each of these also can map to the shared resources made available on a network. Most of these operating systems enable you to control who accesses their shared resources. Table 9-1 presents a security summary by comparing FAT attributes (DOS and Windows-based systems configured for FAT), NetWare attributes and trustee rights, Windows NT, 2000, and XP (NTFS) attributes and permissions, and UNIX permissions.

❏ Network server operating systems will be particularly interesting to watch as they provide more and more shared network and Internet resources. Already, network server operating systems handle functions such as e-mail, e-commerce, network conferencing, multimedia distribution, database access, and education through the Internet.

9

KEY TERMS

client/server application — A software application that divides processing between a client operating system and one or more server operating systems (often a database and an application server). Dividing processing tasks is intended to achieve the best performance.

container object — An entity that is used to group together resources, such as an organizational unit, an organization, or a country, as specified in the directory services of NetWare; or an organizational unit, domain, tree, or forest in Microsoft Active Directory.

directory service — A large container of network data and resources, such as computers, printers, user accounts, and user groups, that (1) provides a central listing of resources and ways to quickly find specific resources, and (2) provides ways to access and manage network resources.

distribution group — A list of Windows 2000 Server users that enables one e-mail message to be sent to all users on the list. A distribution group is not used for security.

domain — A grouping of resources into a functional unit for management. The resources can be servers, workstations, shared disks and directories, and shared printers.

forest — An Active Directory container that holds one or more trees.

group identification number (GID) — A unique number assigned to a UNIX group that distinguishes that group from all other groups on the same system.

home directory — Also called a home folder, a user work area in which the user stores data on a server, and typically has control over whether to enable other server users to access his or her data.

leaf object — An object, such as an account, that is stored in an organization or organizational unit container in the NetWare NDS.

mapping — The process of attaching to a shared resource, such as a shared drive, and using it as though it is a local resource. For example, when a workstation operating system maps to the drive of another workstation, it can assign a drive letter to that drive, and access it as though it is a local drive instead of a remote one.

mounted volume — A shared drive in the Mac OS. See *mapping*.

Network File System (NFS) — Enables file transfer and other shared services that involve computers running UNIX.

Novell Directory Services (NDS) — A comprehensive database of shared resources and information known to the NetWare operating system.

Novell Distributed Print Services (NDPS) — Services used in NetWare version 5 and above that enable printers to attach to the network as agents, to be managed through a NetWare server, and to be accessed by NetWare and Windows-based clients.

object — An entity, such as a user account, group, directory, or printer, that is known to a network operating system's database, and that the operating system manages in terms of sharing or controlling access to that object.

search drive — A mapped NetWare drive that enables the operating system to search a specified directory and its subdirectories for an executable (program) file.

security group — A group of Windows 2000 Server users that is used to assign access privileges, such as permissions, to objects and services.

shadow file — With access limited to the root user, a file in UNIX that contains critical information about user accounts, including the encrypted password for each account.

share — An object, such as a folder, drive, or printer, that an operating system or a directory service, such as Active Directory, makes visible to other network users for access over a network.

share-level access control — Access to a shared folder in Windows 95 and Windows 98 by creating a disk or folder share that is protected by share permissions, and on which the share owner can require a password for access.

share points — Shared resources on a Mac OS X server.

tree — An Active Directory container that houses one or more domains.

trusted domain — A domain granted security access to resources in another domain.

trusting domain — A domain that allows another domain security access to its resources, such as servers.

user identification number (UID) — A number that is assigned to a UNIX user account as a way to distinguish that account from all others on the same system.

user-level access control — Access to a shared folder in Windows 95 and Windows 98 in which the share owner creates a list of groups and users who are allowed to access the share.

REVIEW QUESTIONS

1. Which of the following enables you to access a shared volume in Mac OS 9.x?

   a. Network Neighborhood

   b. Chooser

   c. My Computer

   d. all of the above

   e. only a and b

   f. only b and c

2. You can use the GNOME _____ tool to start *lpd* in Red Hat Linux 7.x.

3. Which of the following is an access method that can be used in Windows 95?

   a. user-level

   b. share-level

   c. privilege level

   d. all of the above

   e. only a and b

   f. only a and c

4. Which of the following is NOT a printer share permission in Windows NT 4.0?

   a. Full Control

   b. Print

   c. Manage Documents

   d. Manage Printers

5. Which operating system enables you to set up a search drive?

   a. Mac OS X

   b. NetWare

   c. Windows 2000

   d. UNIX

9

6. The utility that is used to set up accounts for Active Directory in Windows 2000 Server is called:

   a. Server Manager.

   b. Active Directory Account Manager.

   c. User Manager for Domains.

   d. Active Directory Users and Computers.

7. The x permission on a UNIX directory enables you to:

   a. write to a file in the directory.

   b. delete the directory contents.

   c. execute a file.

   d. keep date stamps on files in the directory.

8. Each account created in UNIX is identified by a number called the _____ number.

9. The Web service program included with Mac OS X Server is called _____.

10. Which of the following is a security measure that you can associate with a NetWare account?

   a. intruder detection

   b. requiring a minimum password length

   c. requiring the user to periodically change his or her password

   d. all of the above

   e. only a and b

   f. only b and c

11. Which of the following are configured in account policies in Windows 2000 Server?

   a. time and date stamp

   b. password policy

   c. Kerberos security

   d. all of the above

   e. only a and b

   f. only b and c

12. The share permissions used to share a folder in Windows 2000 Server are _____, _____, and _____.

13. Which of the following file systems recognized by Windows NT Server has the greatest security capabilities?

   a. FAT

   b. NFS

    c. NTFS

    d. OSPF

14. Both users and groups can be configured in Mac OS 9.x. True or false?

15. What command-line utility in UNIX is used to configure permissions?

    a. chmod

    b. addmod

    c. mkgroup

    d. permconfg

    e. none of the above

16. Before you share a folder in Mac OS 9.x or X, you must _____.

17. What tool can you use in Windows 2000 or XP to connect to a shared network printer?

    a. Network Neighborhood

    b. My Network Places

    c. Printer sharing icon in the Printers folder

    d. Printer sharing icon in the Control Panel

18. Which type of Windows NT or 2000 Server group is typically used for managing user accounts?

    a. resource

    b. global

    c. share

    d. local

19. In Mac OS 9.x, it is possible to access another network computer by using the name of the computer or its network address. True or false?

20. You are creating an account in Red Hat Linux 7.x using the *useradd* tool. What parameter can you enter to prevent the tool from automatically creating a group with the same name as the account you are creating?

    a. -p

    b. -gr

    c. -ng

    d. -n

    e. none of the above, because no groups are created when you use this utility

9

HANDS-ON PROJECTS

Project 9-1

In this project, you'll view the global and local groups on a Windows NT server. You will need access to a computer running Windows NT Server, and access to an account that has Administrator privileges (ask your instructor how to access the account).

To view the global and local groups:

1. Click **Start**, highlight **Programs**, and highlight **Administrative Tools (Common)**.

2. Click **User Manager for Domains**. Maximize the screen, if necessary.

3. View the groups listed in the bottom half of the screen, under the Groups column.

4. Notice which groups have the word Domain in front, such as Domain Admins and Domain Guests, and notice their descriptions. These are global groups.

5. Notice the groups that do not start with the word Domain. These groups are local.

6. Double-click a global group to view its members. Next, close that dialog box and double-click a local group to view its members. Close that dialog box when you are finished viewing the members.

7. Close the User Manager for Domains when you are finished.

Project 9-2

In this project, you'll practice setting up a shared folder in Windows NT Server 4.0. You'll also set up share permissions by deleting the Everyone group from access, and then by giving full access only to the Backup Operators local group. As in the previous Hands-on Project, you will need access to a computer running Windows NT Server (formatted for NTFS), and an account assigned Administrator privileges.

To set up the shared folder:

1. Open **My Computer** on the desktop and double-click drive C: (or another appropriate drive).

2. Select an existing folder to share, such as the **Temp** folder, and right-click it.

3. Click **Sharing** on the menu.

4. Click the **Shared As** radio button. Enter a name for the shared folder in the Share Name box, such as **TestShare**.

5. Enter **Share test** in the Comment box.

6. Click the **Maximum Allowed** radio button, so that there are no restrictions to the number of users who access the share simultaneously.

7. Click the **Permissions** button to open the Access Through Share Permissions dialog box.

8. Select the **Everyone** group from the Name list, and click **Remove**.

9. Click **Add**.

10. Select **Backup Operators** in the Names list box, and click **Add**.

11. Select **Full Control** in the Type of Access list box.

12. Click **OK**, and then click **OK** again. The Server Operators group now has Full Control access to that folder.

 Your instructor may ask that you remove the share when you finish. If so, repeat Steps 2 and 3. On the Sharing tab, click the Not Shared radio button, then click Apply and OK.

Project 9-3

In this project, you'll create an account and a global group in Windows 2000 Server. Active Directory must be installed in advance for this project, and you will need access to an account that has Administrator privileges.

To create a user account:

1. Click **Start**, point to **Programs**, point to **Administrative Tools**, and click **Active Directory Users and Computers**.

2. Open the **Users** container in the tree, if it is not already open. In the right pane, notice that existing accounts have a one-headed icon, and groups have a two-headed icon. What are some accounts and groups that have already been created?

3. Right-click the **Users** folder in the tree, point to **New**, and click **User**.

4. Enter your first name, initial, and last name.

5. In the User logon name box, enter your first initial plus your last name plus Test, such as **MWaltersTest**.

6. Click **Next**.

7. Enter a password and confirm the password.

8. Click the box for **User must change password at next logon**. Why is this parameter important?

9. Click **Next**, and then click **Finish**.

To create a global security group:

1. Right-click the **Users** folder, point to **New**, and click **Group**.

2. Enter a name for the new group consisting of your initials plus Global, such as **MWGlobal**.

3. What options do you see for the group scope? What do you see for the group type?

9

If the Universal option is deactivated, this means that you are working in a mixed mode of Windows NT and Windows 2000 servers. Universal groups cannot be used in the mixed mode.

4. Click **Global** for the Group scope, if it is not already selected, and click **Security** for the Group type, if it is not selected.

5. Click **OK**.

6. In the right pane, find the new group that you created and double-click it.

7. Click the **Members** tab, and then click the **Add** button.

8. In the top box, find the account you just created and double-click that account so that it appears in the bottom box. The new account you created is now a member of the global group.

9. Click **OK**, and click **OK** again.

Project 9-4

In this project, you'll create an account in Red Hat Linux 7.x by using the *useradd* command. (These steps also work in most versions of UNIX, other than AIX.)

To create an account:

1. Log onto the computer as root and access the command prompt (for example, by opening a terminal window in Red Hat Linux if you are using the GNOME interface).

2. When you set up the account, use your own name or initials, plus the word "test." For example, type *useradd -c "Mac Arthur, practice account" -p practice -n MArthurtest*, and press **Enter**. (Note that when you do not specify the UID, Red Hat Linux will use the next available number over 500.)

3. What is the purpose of typing *-n* in Step 2?

4. Type **more /etc/passwd** to view the contents of the password file. Do you see the account that you created? (You may need to press **Enter** one or more times to go to the end of the file—and in some terminal windows, you may need to press Q or q to exit the file contents display mode.)

5. Test your new account by logging off the root account and then logging onto the new account.

If your instructor wants you to delete the account after you finish, log onto root, type *userdel -r* plus the name of the account.

Project 9-5

In this project, you'll create a new group in Red Hat Linux 7.x (but these steps also work in nearly all versions of UNIX, except AIX), change the group's name, and finally delete that group. Before starting, ask your instructor for a GID. For the group name, use the first and last initials of your name appended to test, such as mptest.

To create, modify, and delete a group:

1. Log onto Red Hat Linux as root and access the command prompt.

2. At the command prompt, type *groupadd –g GID* (provided by instructor) *groupname* (your first and last initials + test), such as **groupadd –g 800 mptest**, and press **Enter**. Note that if the GID is already in use, the system reports this information and does not create the group. If you omit the *-g* parameter, the system will use the next available GID. (Also, in some versions of UNIX, you will see a return code of zero that indicates you successfully added the group. If a return code is displayed that is other than zero, make sure that you correctly typed the command, used a unique GID and group name, and that you have proper access to create groups; or, ask your instructor for help.)

3. Change the group name by using your first and middle initial appended to test, using the command *groupmod –n newname oldname*, such as **groupmod –n mjtest mptest**, and press **Enter**. (Again, in some versions of UNIX, you will see a zero return code to indicate that you have successfully changed the group name.)

4. Type **more /etc/group** and press **Enter** to view the groups and verify that you successfully changed the group name (you may need to press Enter several times to get to the end of the file, and press Q or q to exit the text display).

5. Delete the group by entering the *groupdel* command and the group name, such as **groupdel mjtest**, and press **Enter**.

6. Type **more /etc/group** and press **Enter** to verify that the group you created is truly deleted.

7. Log off root when you are finished.

Project 9-6

In this assignment, you give read permissions to a directory to all user accounts on a UNIX server. You will need access to a computer running Red Hat Linux or UNIX, a user account, and a practice directory containing files.

To set the permissions:

1. Log on to the UNIX computer and access the command-line prompt.

2. Switch to your practice directory, such as by typing **cd /home/mpalmer**, and press **Enter**.

3. At the command prompt, type **chmod a+r ***, and press **Enter**.

4. View the change by listing permissions via the command **ls –1**, and press **Enter**.

9

5. How would you remove the permissions that you just set?

6. Log off when you are finished.

Project 9-7

This project enables you to practice creating a new user in Mac OS 9.x. Also, in the second half of this project, you'll transfer a user that was created via Server Admin in Mac OS X Server into the Macintosh Manager (find out from your instructor which user to transfer).

To create a new user in Mac OS 9.x:

1. Open the Apple menu.

2. Select **Control Panels**.

3. Click **Multiple Users** and then click **New User**.

4. Enter the new user's name and password.

5. Select the type of user privileges: Normal, Limited, or Panels.

6. Click **Show Setup Details** and then click the **User Info tab**.

7. Select a picture to appear next to the user's name in the Login window.

8. Next, you can allow the user to change the password you initially set by checking **User can change password**.

9. Make sure that **Can log in** is checked so the user account is available.

10. You can also check **Can manage user accounts** which makes this user an account manager with create, delete, and modify privileges for other accounts. (The option, Can manage user accounts, is deactivated if you are creating a Limited user, but is activated if you are creating a Typical user.)

11. Close the window to save the settings and click **Multiple User Accounts On**.

To transfer a user in Mac OS X Server to the Macintosh Manager:

1. Open the **Macintosh Manager** from the Dock at the bottom of the desktop.

2. Open the **Users** tab, if it is not already open.

3. Click the **Import** button.

4. In the Users & Groups dialog box, find the user that you want to transfer into the Macintosh Manager. While you look for the user to import, notice how you can create a new user or group.

5. Drag the user from the Users & Groups dialog box into the Imported Users pane in the Macintosh Manager in the background.

6. While you are in the Macintosh Manager, determine what parameters can be set for a user account via the Basic tab. What parameters can you set from the Advanced tab?

7. Close the Macintosh Manager.

Project 9-8

In this hands-on activity, you'll practice mapping a search drive to a NetWare server, and then delete the drive. You will need network access from Windows 95, Windows 98, Windows Me, Windows NT, Windows 2000, or Windows XP, and an account on a NetWare server. Also, you'll need to obtain directions from your instructor about how to log onto the NetWare server for your particular network.

To map and then delete a search drive:

1. Log on to the NetWare server.

2. Open an MS-DOS Prompt window (in Windows 95/98/Me) or Command Prompt window (in Windows NT/2000/XP), type **MAP** at the prompt, and then press **Enter** to view the current drive mappings.

3. Determine the last search drive in use from the list of mapped drives, which is the S# drive that has the highest number.

4. Using the next S# number (use S1 if no search drives are defined), map a search drive to the PUBLIC directory, or to another directory specified by your instructor. Type **MAP S1:=SYS:PUBLIC**, and press **Enter**.

5. Type **MAP** again to see if your drive is in the list of mapped drives.

6. Finally, type **MAP DEL S1:** (or S and the number of the drive you used in Step 4), and press **Enter** to delete the drive mapping.

7. Type **exit** at the command prompt to close the MS-DOS or Command Prompt window.

> You may need to install Client Service for NetWare before you start. For example, to install Client Service for NetWare in Windows XP: click Start, click Control Panel, click Network and Internet Connections, click Network Connections, right-click Local Area Connection, click Properties, click Install, double-click Client, and double-click Client Service for NetWare.

Project 9-9

In this project, you'll create a shared folder in Windows 95, Windows 98, or Windows Me that employs user-level access. You need a computer running Windows 95, Windows 98, or Windows Me set up for user-level access, and on which file and printer sharing services are installed. The computer should also be set up in advance as a member of a Windows NT or Windows 2000 domain or workgroup. Also, a folder to share, such as Temp, should already be created.

To create the shared folder:

1. Open **My Computer** or **Windows Explorer**. Right-click a folder to share, such as **Temp**.

2. Click the **Sharing** option on the menu and then the **Sharing** tab, if necessary.

3. Click the **Shared As** radio button and enter a name for the share, such as **Test** or **Temp**, in the Share Name box. Also, document your share by entering a comment, such as **Temporary share**, in the Comment box.

4. Click **Add**.

5. In the Add Users dialog box, select a user, such as **Administrator**, and click the **Full Access** button. Notice that Administrator moves into the box at the right of the Full Access button.

6. Select another user on the list, such as **Guest**, and click the **Read Only** button. Also, notice that Guest moves into the box at the right of the Read Only button.

7. Click **OK**.

8. Click **Apply** and **OK**.

Project 9-10

In this project, you'll set up a shared folder in a domain or workgroup in Windows XP Professional.

To configure a shared drive:

1. Click **Start** and click **My Computer**.

2. Double-click a drive, such as **Local Disk (C:)**.

3. Create a new folder to share by clicking the **File** menu, pointing to **New**, and clicking **Folder**. Enter a name for the new folder by combining your initials with the word "folder," such as **MWFolder**.

4. Right-click the folder and click **Sharing and Security**.

5. If you are sharing a folder (or drive) via a workgroup for the first time, you may need to click **If you understand the risk but still want to share the root of a drive, click here.**

6. In the *Network sharing and security box*, click **Share this folder on the network**. What would you select to enable other network users to change your files in this folder?

 If you do not see *Share this folder on the network* as an option, click the option to start the Network Configuration Wizard, and configure your computer on the network. Then come back to the same file properties Sharing tab.

7. For this project, verify that the share name is the same name as the folder. How would you change the share name so that it appears on the network as a different name than the folder?

8. Click **OK**. Notice that the folder now has a hand under the icon to show that the folder is shared.

9. Close the volume window.

Project 9-11

In this project, you'll connect to a computer using the Network Browser in Mac OS 9.x, and the Go menu in Mac OS X. Besides Macintosh computers that run these operating systems, you will need shared resources set up on other network computers that these Macintosh computers can access.

To use the Network Browser in Mac OS 9.x:

1. Open the Apple menu and click the **Network Browser**. Click the **AppleTalk** option, if the Network window appears.

2. Double-click the appropriate zone containing the computer with the shared volume, if requested.

3. Double-click the computer containing the shared volume.

4. Enter your name and password (or a name and password provided by your instructor) in the text boxes. Click **OK**.

5. Double-click the volume you want to access.

6. Make sure that the icon for the volume is now on the desktop and that you can open it.

7. Close the Network Browser.

To connect to another computer via Mac OS X:

1. Open the **Go** menu and select **Connect To Server**.

2. Find and select the computer to which you want to connect in the right pane of the browser window, which is in the middle of the Connect to Server dialog box.

3. Click **Connect**.

4. Click the radio button for **Registered User**, if it is not already selected.

5. Enter your account name and password (or a name and password provided by your instructor).

6. Click **Connect**.

7. If there are two or more volumes shared by the computer you've selected, you'll see a dialog box from which to select the volume or volumes to which you want to connect. You can select two or more volumes at the same time by pressing the Command key and selecting the appropriate volumes. Click **OK**.

8. Open the **Finder** to locate the volumes that you mounted.

Project 9-12

In this project, you'll connect to network printers via Windows XP. Before you start, ask your instructor for the name of the computer that is offering the shared printer.

9

To connect to the shared printer:

1. Click **Start** and click **My Network Places**.

2. Click **Search** in the button bar at the top of the window.

3. In the Computer name box, enter the name of the computer that offers the shared printer and click **Search**.

4. Double-click the computer that offers the shared printer (you may need to provide an account and password if this is required by the computer).

5. Right-click the printer and click **Connect**.

6. Close the networked computer's window from which you selected the printer.

7. Click **Start** and click **Printers and Faxes**.

8. Do you see the shared printer?

9. Close the Printers and Faxes window.

Case Project

Your state's university has a large Engineering College consisting of 52 faculty members who use computers that run Windows 98, Windows 2000 Professional, Windows XP Professional, Red Hat Linux 7.2, Solaris, and Mac OS 9.1. The department also maintains four labs. One of those consists of computers running Mac OS 9.1, while the other three labs have computers that run a combination of Windows 98 and Windows 2000 Professional. Further, the dean's office maintains a NetWare server and a Windows 2000 server. You are employed by the department as the main support person for all of these computer operating systems.

1. Ten faculty members use Mac OS 9.1, and their students use the Macintosh lab. They want to enable students to submit assignments over the network from the lab. Also, they want to make new assignments available for students to pick up at any time of day through the network. Are these goals possible? If so, how can the Macintosh computers be set up to accomplish these goals? Must they first have a Mac OS X server in the labs?

2. The dean wants to set up the Windows 2000 server so that the five department heads in the Engineering College can access her spreadsheets reflecting the college's budget, and several department management programs written and installed by graduate student employees. You are charged with explaining to the department heads how the Windows 2000 server will be set up to share the spreadsheets and management programs. What explanation would you give in a presentation? Also, the dean asks you to show each department head how to access the shared information from computers that run Windows XP Professional. Develop a set of instructions for the deans, and explain how you would use the instructions to supplement a live demonstration.

3. The Electrical Engineering department head has two folders that he wants to share over the network. One folder contains professor evaluations that he wants to enable his faculty members to access and review, while restricting access so that each faculty member can only view his or her evaluation. A second folder consists of text files that are assigned readings for his class of 19 students. How would you advise him to set up these shared folders on his Windows 2000 Professional workstation? Keep in mind that the faculty members use Windows 2000 Professional and Windows XP Professional. His students use a lab that has a combination of Windows 2000 Professional and Windows XP Professional operating systems.

4. The dean's office associate wants you to make two expensive color laser printers in the front office available to any department member. One is attached to his Macintosh computer and the other is attached to the Windows 2000 server. Can you make the printers available throughout the department? If so, how?

5. The dean purchased an Oracle database of technical information for all members of the Engineering College to access. What department computer would you use as home for this database? Why?

6. Four faculty members have Solaris workstations. How can you set up the Windows 2000 server to be accessed by these workstations? Can they use their existing accounts and passwords for access?

7. A faculty member who uses Windows 98 wants to set up a shared folder so that others can only read the contents and access it via a password. How would you set up the computer to accomplish this?

OPTIONAL CASE PROJECTS FOR TEAMS

Team Case One

Your publishing company employs 150 users who have a combination of networked Mac OS 9.1 and Mac OS X computers. Form a team and research how installing a Mac OS X server can benefit this company.

Team Case Two

Your boss is curious about developing a comparison of Windows NT Server 4.0 and Windows 2000 Server. Establish a team to create a chart that shows a comparison of the features in these two operating systems. (If you have access to information about Windows .NET Standard Server, add its features to the comparison.)

10

STANDARD OPERATING AND MAINTENANCE PROCEDURES

After reading this chapter and completing the exercises, you will be able to:

♦ Explain file system maintenance techniques for different operating systems

♦ Perform regular file system maintenance by finding and deleting unused files and directories

♦ Perform disk maintenance that includes defragmenting, relocating files and folders, running disk and file repair utilities, and selecting RAID options

♦ Set up and perform disk, directory, and file backups

♦ Explain how to install software for best performance

♦ Tune operating systems for optimal performance

Computer operating systems are similar to cars in that they need regular maintenance to achieve the best performance. A new car, like a new computer, delivers fast responses, and every component usually functions perfectly. To keep the car at its best, you must perform regular maintenance, such as changing the oil and performing tuneups. If you neglect maintenance, the car's performance suffers and the wear shows quickly. Maintenance is as important for computers as it is for cars because it does not take long for an operating system, software, and hardware to degrade in performance. Computer operating system maintenance consists of deleting unnecessary files, tuning memory, regularly backing up files, defragmenting disks, and repairing damaged files. Maintenance is particularly important for computer systems connected to a network because a poorly responding computer has an impact on network operations.

In this chapter, you'll learn a variety of techniques for maintaining and tuning workstations and servers. One of the most important steps in making disk and file maintenance easy is to start with a well-designed directory structure, which makes finding unused files and folders a straightforward process. Two other important tasks are to perform regular backups and run disk maintenance utilities. How and where software is installed is also vital to how a computer performs. Finally, there are tuning options, such as adjusting virtual memory, that can immediately enhance performance.

FILE SYSTEM MAINTENANCE

Successful file system maintenance is closely linked to the file structure on a computer. On both workstation and server operating systems, a well-planned file structure makes it easy to locate files, update files, share folders and files, back up and archive files, and delete unwanted files. In addition, on server operating systems, well-designed file structures favorably impact network performance and security.

Some basic rules for creating a file structure include:

- Keep a manageable number of directories in the root directory.
- Keep operating system files in the default directories recommended by the vendor.
- Keep different versions of software in their own directories.
- Keep data files in directories on the basis of their functions.
- Design home directories to match the functions of users in an organization.
- Group files with similar security needs within the same directories.

It does not take long for the number of directories in the root directory (often called the "root") to proliferate. For example, many software vendors attempt to install software into the root, by default. If you have many software applications, this kind of file structure quickly becomes confusing and hard to manage. It makes more sense to create one or two directories within the root that are intended for software applications, and then create subdirectories within each main applications directory to contain particular applications. In Chapter 3, you learned that software applications can be placed in a directory called Apps, for example. Another technique is to create a general applications directory and separate directories for main software vendors. If you use Microsoft applications, consider using the Microsoft default directory, Program Files, or if you use other applications, such as the WordPerfect Office suite, use its default Corel directory. An example of a file structure in which you might use three directories for applications in the root of the main volume, Applications, Corel, and Program Files is illustrated in Figure 10-1. The figure also shows two other directories usually found in the root—for Windows system files and utility programs. Depending on the version of Windows, the Windows directory may be called \Winnt, or a name that the installer chose, such as

Win2000 or WinXP. Later versions of Windows do not create the Utilities directory, but instead create a directory called Documents and Settings, or My Documents.

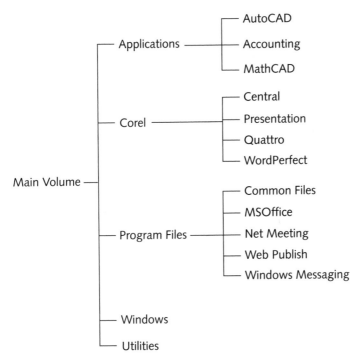

Figure 10-1   Example applications directories and subdirectories

Some users and system administrators prefer to limit the number of entries in the root directory to only the number that can be displayed in one or two screens when you are at the command level in an operating system, or in a utility such as Windows Explorer. On a typical system, this might translate to a maximum of 10 to 15 directories per hard disk volume.

Well-organized directories and subdirectories enable you to have a relatively small number of main directories in the root. Figure 10-2 illustrates a typical root directory structure in UNIX (also see Chapter 3). The directories in this example are as follows:

- *bin* for user programs and utilities (binary files)
- *lib* for libraries
- *usr* for users' files and user programs
- *var* for files in which the content often varies, or that are only used temporarily
- *tmp* for files used only temporarily
- *dev* for devices

- *mnt* for floppy drives, CD-ROM drives, and other removable media that can be mounted

- *etc* for system and configuration files

- *sbin* for user programs and utilities (system binary files)

- *home* for users' home directories

- *proc* for system resource tracking

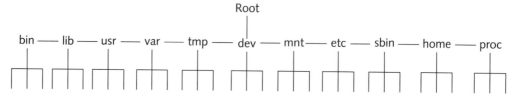

Figure 10-2   Typical UNIX root directory structure

Examples of important folders in the root of a Mac OS X system include:

- *Applications* for software applications (there is an Applications folder off the root, plus each user may have an Applications folder)

- *Documents* for storing documents (typically there is one off the root and one for each user)

- *Library* for library files that include fonts, preferences, and graphics, for instance

- *System* for system files

- *Users* for user accounts (containing a subfolder for each account)

In addition to folders off the root, each user account in Mac OS X contains folders such as:

- *Music* for music files

- *Movies* for movies that can be played on the computer

- *Pictures* to sort picture files

- *Public* for files to share with others over the network

- *Applications* for applications used by the account

- *Library* for support files, such as fonts used by the account

- *Documents* for storing documents

- *Desktop* for files that are on the user's desktop

Operating system directories are typically placed in the root directory and have appropriate subdirectories under a main directory. For example, Windows XP operating system files are contained in the Windows folder (see Figure 10-3), which has subdirectories such as System and System32. Macintosh system files are likewise kept in the System folder. Table 10-1 illustrates typical locations for system files.

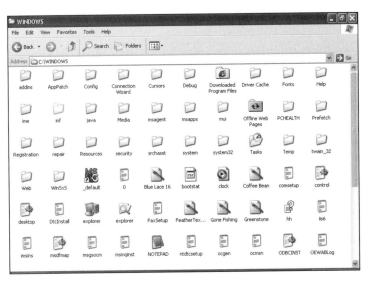

Figure 10-3   Windows XP operating system files in the Windows folder

Table 10-1   Operating System Directories

Operating System	System Directory or Directories from the Root
Mac OS	System (in Mac OS X the *System* folder contains the system files, and the *System Folder* contains Mac OS 9.x system files for running the classic environment)
NetWare	System
UNIX	Bin, etc, and sbin
Windows 3.x	Windows
Windows 95	Windows
Windows 98	Windows
Windows Me	Windows
Windows NT	Winnt
Windows 2000 Server and Professional	Winnt
Windows XP Home and Professional	Windows

There are several advantages to installing and leaving operating system files in the directories created by the operating system, instead of trying to hide these files, or use other directory locations (see the caution that follows). One reason is that it is easier for others to help with computer problems as they arise. For example, in organizations that have user support departments, it is easier for support professionals to assist in solving problems with drivers and network access when system files are easy to find. Another reason for leaving system files in the default directories is that many software installations expect operating system files to be in the default locations, and they work best when it is easy for them to find specific subdirectories and key files related to the operating system.

 When you install server operating systems, there may be a temptation to hide or rename default system directories as a way to protect them from intruders. However, most intruders will not be deterred by this attempt to hide files. A better approach is to understand and implement the security available in the operating system.

In most Windows-based systems, installed software is also tracked in the Registry, which contains configuration information, as well as information about individual components of a software installation. Thus, it is easier for the operating system to assist when it is necessary to uninstall or upgrade software because it is able to quickly identify and find the components to be deleted or upgraded. In Windows 95/98/Me and Windows NT/2000/XP, these vital files are kept in the operating system's folder and subfolders. For example, in Windows 95/98/Me and Windows XP, these files might be located in the \Windows, \Windows\System, or \Windows\System32 folders. In Windows NT/2000, they are found in the \Winnt and \Winnt\System32 folders. Table 10-2 lists examples of typical Windows-based application software components. Application software and operating system enhancements are easier to install when these components are in known locations.

Table 10-2 Examples of Windows-based Application Software Components

File Type	File Extension	File Type	File Extension
Application	.exe	Initialization	.ini
ActiveX Control	.ocx	Installation	.inf
Backup	.bak	MS-DOS application	.com
Bitmap image	.bmp	Microsoft Common Console Document	.mcs
Control Panel extension	.cpl	OLE common control	.ocx
Configuration	.cfg	Precompiled setup information	.pnf
Data	.dat	Screen Saver	.scr
Device driver	.drv	Text	.txt
Dynamic link library	.dll	TrueType font	.ttf
Help	.hlp	Virtual Device Driver	.vxd
Help context	.cnt	Visual Basic application	.vbx

Sometimes, particularly on network servers, it is necessary to keep several versions of a software application available for different uses. For example, an organization may have some users who still use earlier versions of WordPerfect or Microsoft Word. In a department or organization in which software applications are developed, it may be necessary to keep different versions of compilers or development tools available. Some users may have operating systems that only support 16-bit applications, whereas other users may have operating systems that support 32-bit applications. In these situations, one way to easily handle having more than one version of the same software is to put different versions in different subdirectories under a main applications directory. For example, in Windows 2000 Server, you can support different versions of Microsoft Word by having a Program Files directory, and subdirectories called Word2, Word95, Word97, Word2000, and WordXP. In this case, one version is installed to run locally, and the other versions are available to clients for network installations (given appropriate licensing considerations).

Some directory structures include special locations for data files. For example, if the computer contains files for word processing, spreadsheets, and databases, then those files might be stored as subdirectories under a root directory called Data. On a file server, the files might be stored on the basis of directories set up for departments. In a company that has a business department and a research department, the main directories might be Business and Research, with subdirectories under each for shared word-processing, spreadsheet, and database files.

Home directories on a server often reflect the organizational structure. In a college, the home directory might be called Home within the root directory. Under the Home directory, there might be subdirectories for each department in the college: Business, Registrar, Anthropology, Biology, Chemistry, English, Music, Psychology, and so on. Finally, under each department subdirectory, there would be subdirectories for that department's faculty and staff members.

10

FINDING AND DELETING FILES

A solid file structure on the computer makes it easier to find and delete unneeded files on a regular schedule. It does not take long on any computer system for such files to accumulate and occupy a large amount of disk space. One example is the temporary files created when you install new software and run many types of applications. Most installations create a temporary directory and a set of temporary files that are stored in the temporary directory. Some software applications do not completely delete temporary files when the application installation is finished. These files may be stored in a temporary directory in the root or operating system directory. Also, some software applications create temporary files that are not deleted when the application is improperly terminated. For example, many word-processing programs create temporary files that are used for backup purposes, or to save the most immediate changes. These files may not be completely deleted when the application is closed, or when the application is shut down improperly, such as because of a power failure. It is a good practice to implement a regular schedule for finding and deleting these unneeded files, using the methods available in different operating systems, detailed in the following sections.

Deleting files is vital as a means to make the best use of disk storage resources, and it can help extend the life of hard disks. One rule of thumb is that hard disk drives should be kept under 80% full. Those that grow over 80% full are subject to excessive wear, and are more likely to have problems or fail. This provides added incentive to make sure that files are regularly deleted as a means of keeping disk utilization under 80%.

Windows 95, Windows 98, and Windows Me

Temporary files are equally problematic in Windows 95/98/Me. The software in many office suites enables you to create a backup or temporary file (sometimes multiple files) of a document or spreadsheet, for example. If you improperly exit from the office software, or improperly shut down the computer, these temporary files are not deleted. Even when you do properly exit the software, the files sometimes remain. The temporary files often begin with a tilde (~) as a first character, or have a .tmp extension, and typically are found in the following places:

- A temporary directory in the root, such as C:\Temp

- A temporary directory in the Windows directory, such as C:\Windows\Temp

- A DOS directory in the root (Windows 95)

- A data directory in which word-processing, spreadsheets, or database files are stored

- The applications directory that contains the executable file, which created the temporary file

 If you are using an application, such as Microsoft Word, in which the file you are accessing is reported as corrupted, close the file and all applications. Next, delete all temporary files and try opening the file again to see if the error message is gone. Often this action alone can repair a corrupted file, and it is one of the first tasks that a Microsoft technician has you carry out to repair a corrupted file.

Web browsers also write an impressive number of temporary Internet files that are not deleted, unless you set an expiration date, or delete them using a Windows utility or utility that comes with the Web browser. In Windows 95/98/Me, these files are typically found in the temporary Internet files folder in the \Windows folder. For example, in Windows 95/98/Me, that folder is called \Windows\Temporary Internet Files. In most cases, the files can be deleted regularly, except for **cookies** that contain specialized information for accessing particular Web sites. Cookies are text files that have the preface *Cookie:*—for example, in many Windows operating systems, a cookie created after you access the Lycos Web site from your main (Windows 98) or Administrator (Windows 2000) account is Cookie:administrator@lycos.com. The temporary files that you delete often have extensions such as .html, .htm, .jpg, and .gif.

When you use a Windows-based utility or browser utility to delete files, the utility provides a warning dialog box for each cookie encountered, and you can choose whether or not to delete a cookie by selecting Yes or No.

There are three ways to search for and delete temporary files:

- Use the Disk Cleanup utility
- Use your browser tool (for Web-based temporary files only)
- Use Windows Explorer

Before you search for and delete temporary files, make sure you close all active applications so that there are no open temporary files.

Windows 98 and Windows Me both have a Disk Cleanup utility that enables you to delete unneeded files, such as temporary files created by applications and your Internet browser. To access this tool in both operating systems, click Start, point to Programs, point to Accessories, point to System tools, and click Disk Cleanup. Another way to access Disk Cleanup is to find the disk you want to clean in Windows Explorer, right-click it, click Properties, and click Disk Cleanup on the General tab. Figure 10-4 illustrates the types of files you can choose to delete. Hands-on Project 10-4 enables you to use the Disk Cleanup tool.

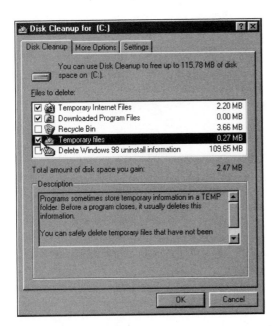

Figure 10-4   Windows 98 Disk Cleanup tool

If you want to clean up only temporary Internet files, you can do this periodically when you start your Web browser, such as Microsoft Internet Explorer or Netscape's browsers. For example, in Microsoft Internet Explorer, open the browser, click the View or Tools menu (depending on your version of Internet Explorer), click Internet Options, and click Delete Files.

Finally, you can search for temporary files by using Windows Explorer. Open Windows Explorer from the Start button and Programs menu in Windows 95 and 98; or click Start, point to Programs, point to Accessories, and click Windows Explorer in Windows Me. Click the Tools menu, move to Find, and click Files or Folders. To find temporary files created by applications, in the Find: All Files dialog box, enter *.tmp in the Named: text box; enter C:\ in the Look in: box; check the box to include subfolders; and click Find Now (see Figure 10-5). Select the files you wish to delete in the Find: Files named window (see Figure 10-6, or press Ctrl+A to select all files), press Delete, and click Yes to delete the files. Windows 95, Windows 98, and Windows Me show a warning box in case any files are still open, such as temporary files in current use by the operating system.

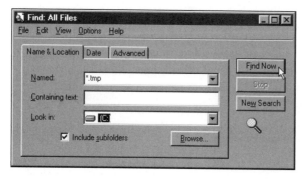

Figure 10-5   Windows 98 Find dialog box

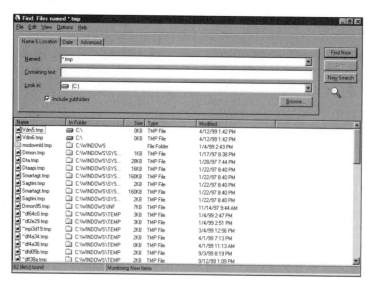

Figure 10-6   Temporary files found in Windows 98

Windows 95, Windows 98, and Windows Me retain deleted files in the Recycle Bin, by default. You can turn off retention of deleted files, or periodically empty the Recycle

Bin. To empty the Recycle Bin, double-click its icon on the desktop, in Windows Explorer, or in My Computer. Use the scroll bar to view the files before you delete them, and then select to delete all the files or only certain files. To delete selected files, highlight those files, click the File menu, and click Delete; to delete all files, click the File menu, and click Empty Recycle Bin (try Hands-on Project 10-5).

 By default, the Recycle Bin can grow to occupy 10% of the available hard disk storage. Computers that are configured for two or more volumes have a Recycle Bin on each volume. You can resize the maximum allocation for the Recycle Bin by right-clicking its desktop icon, selecting Properties, clicking the Global tab, and moving the slider bar to the desired maximum size.

Windows NT, Windows 2000, and Windows XP

Temporary files accumulate in Windows NT, Windows 2000, and Windows XP systems, and can be deleted using utilities that are similar to those in other Windows-based systems. In Windows NT and Windows 2000, temporary files from applications are typically written to the \Temp, \Winnt\System32, and \Winnt\Temp folders. Temporary Internet files in Windows NT are in the \Winnt\Temporary Internet Files and \Winnt\Profiles*account*\Temporary Internet Files (where account is the name of a particular account set up for a user) folders. In Windows 2000, the temporary Internet files are stored in the \Documents and Settings\Administrator\Local Settings\Temporary Internet Files and \Documents and Settings*account*\Local Settings\Temporary Internet Files folders.

In Windows XP, the temporary files are located in the \Temp, \Windows\Temp, and \Windows\System32 folders. Windows XP temporary Internet files are in the \Documents and Settings*account*\Local Settings\Temporary Internet Files folder.

There is no Disk Cleanup tool for Windows NT, which means that the easiest way to find and delete unwanted temporary files is by using Windows NT Explorer, following the same steps that you would use in Windows 98. Delete temporary Internet files in Windows NT by using the tools in Internet Explorer or Netscape's browsers, such as by opening Internet Explorer, clicking Tools, clicking Internet Options, and clicking Delete Files.

The best way to use the Disk Cleanup tool in Windows 2000 and Windows XP is to start it from Windows Explorer by opening Windows Explorer, right-clicking the disk you want to clean, clicking Properties, and clicking Disk Cleanup on the General tab (see Figure 10-7). When you start Disk Cleanup, it scans your disk to determine the amount of space that can be restored after cleaning specific types of files. The types of files that you can select to delete are:

- Downloaded program files
- Temporary Internet files
- Recycle Bin

10

- Temporary files

- Compress old files (not really an option to delete, but to save space by compressing files)

- Catalog files for the Content Indexer

- WebClient/publisher temporary files (only in Windows XP)

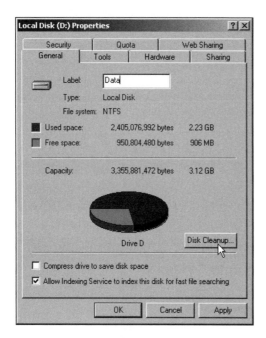

Figure 10-7 Windows 2000 Disk Cleanup tool

Windows NT/2000/XP all come with a Recycle Bin on the desktop, which contains files that have been deleted, but that you can still restore. Regularly open the Recycle Bin to delete its files, which purges them from the system. One way to delete files in the Recycle Bin is to use the Disk Cleanup tool in Windows 2000 or XP. The fastest way to delete these files, however, is to open the Recycle Bin and delete selected files or all files. To delete all files in Windows NT/2000/XP, double-click the Recycle Bin, click the File menu, and click Empty Recycle Bin.

UNIX

You can view UNIX files by using the *ls* command, along with one or more options for listing particular file qualities. Some of the options associated with this command in Red Hat Linux are as follows:

- *-a* lists all files

- *-C* formats the listing in columns for easier reading

- *-d* lists directories

- *-f* displays files in an unsorted list

- *-F* identifies the directory contents on the basis of directory, executable files, and symbolic links

- *-i* displays the inode number for each file

- *-l* presents a detailed information listing including permissions and file size

- *-n* displays UIDs and GIDs of those who have access to files

- *-r* sorts files in reverse alphabetical order

- *-s* displays the size of files (in kilobytes)

- *-t* displays files on the basis of the date they were last modified

- *-u* displays files on the basis of the time they were last modified

In the Red Hat Linux 7.2 GNOME interface, you can view files and directories in the GUI windows-like Nautilus tool by double-clicking the Home icon on the desktop, such as root's Home, when you are logged on as root, and then clicking the Tree tab. In the left pane, click the right arrow in front of a directory to display its subdirectories, or directly click a folder representing a specific directory to view the files it holds (displayed in the right pane). In Figure 10-8, the left pane shows the subdirectories under the /etc directory, and the right pane shows the files in the /bin directory.

10

Figure 10-8   Viewing files and folders in the GNOME interface

Files and folders are deleted in UNIX by using the remove (*rm*) command. The two options commonly added to the command are *-i* and *-r*. The *-i* or interactive option results in a query about if you really want to delete the file or directory; the -r or recursive command is used to delete the entire directory contents, including all subdirectories and files within a directory.

In the Red Hat GNOME Nautilus tool, you can delete a file by finding its folder in the tree, displaying the folder contents in the right pane, selecting the file in the right pane, and pressing Delete.

A file can be found by using the *find* command. This command enables files to be found on the basis of the filename, a wildcard character (*) associated with part of the name, the size of the file, and the last time it was accessed or modified. For example, to find and print a list of all temporary files modified in the last 30 days, you would enter *find -name temp* -mtime -30 -print*. (Try Hands-on Project 10-2 to practice finding and deleting temporary files in UNIX.)

Typical options used with *find* are as follows:

- *-atime* for last accessed time
- *-ctime* for last changed time
- *-mtime* for last modification time
- *-name* for the filename, including the use of wildcard searches
- *-print* to print the results of the find
- *-size* for file size (in blocks or bytes; with bytes specified by a "c" after the size value)
- *-user* to delete files by ownership

Similar to the Windows-based and Mac OS GUI interfaces, the Red Hat Linux 7.2 GNOME interface offers a trash can from which deleted files can be retrieved. The trash can appears on the desktop overflowing with papers when it contains files that can be retrieved or purged. Periodically view the contents of the trash can to purge files, which you can accomplish by double-clicking the trash can icon, and clicking the Empty Trash button in the left pane.

UNIX provides commands to help you assess the allocation of disk space. One command is *df*, which enables you to view information on the basis of the file system. It provides statistics on the total number of blocks, the number used, the number available, and the percent of capacity used. While *df* provides gross file system statistics, the *du* command is used to display statistics for a given directory and its subdirectories, or for a subdirectory alone. (Try Hands-on Project 10-3.)

On a UNIX computer that acts as a server, the administrator can set up disk quotas. For example, a disk quota can be established in blocks for each user as a way to make sure that users do not occupy all of the disk space (see Figure 10-9). A quota is set by using the *edquota* command that opens the quota file for editing. The quota file must first be created by the administrator, or in some versions of UNIX, it is created automatically when you first use *edquota*.

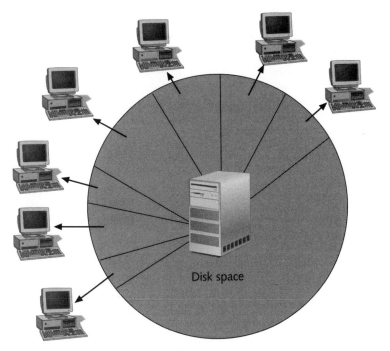

Figure 10-9 UNIX disk quotas for server users

 It is easier to start off by establishing an agreed-upon disk quota for each user, rather than start with no quotas and attempt to impose them later. Disk quotas are a good reminder to server users that they must periodically delete temporary and unused files. Providing training at the time accounts are created, or when a new server is installed, is one way to help users learn to monitor disk usage before they receive notification that their disk quotas have been exceeded.

Mac OS

One particularly important reason for deleting files in the Mac OS is to make sure that you do not run out of disk space. Regularly deleting files enables you to make sure there is enough disk space on hand for all needs. The Mac OS provides an easy way to assess available disk space by simply checking the header information (in Mac OS versions up through 9.x) when you open the Macintosh HD window, or a window to display the contents of any folder. The header provides information about the number of items and available disk space in MB.

 Mac OS X windows often have a list option that shows files and the size of each file. Click the List view button in the window to see file sizes.

The Mac OS (including Mac OS X) has a Find utility on the File menu that can be used to find files that are no longer needed. To use the Find utility, simply click the folder, and in the dialog box, enter the string you want to use to find an unneeded file, such as a Web-related graphics file called netnews.gif. Once an unneeded file is found, drag it into the trash. The Mac OS is forgiving because the deleted item can be brought back from the trash by opening the trash and moving the item back to the desktop. The Mac OS also has a Finder tool that can be used to display files and folders. For example, to access the Finder in Mac OS X, open the Finder icon (the icon at the far left) in the Dock (see Figure 10-10).

Figure 10-10   Mac OS X Finder

 Use the Sherlock utility, as described in Chapter 3, for complex search criteria including name, kind of file, creation date, modification date, size, version, and folder attribute. Sherlock also has the ability to index information for faster access.

 Files are not truly deleted until they are purged by emptying the trash. The trash should be emptied on a regular schedule so that disk space occupied by deleted files is returned for use by other files. (Try Hands-on Project 10-1 to practice emptying the trash.)

NetWare

There are several ways to manage files and folders in NetWare. NetWare Administrator is one tool that is available to view and manage directories and files on the server. Another option for Windows-based NetWare clients is to use Network Neighborhood or My Network Places to view folder and file information, including information about properties.

A third utility that can be very effective is called NDIR, and is run from a NetWare DOS window. NDIR includes several commands that enable you to find files on the basis of specific criteria, such as date or owner. NDIR can also provide important information about directory space that is in use. The commands include the following:

- /AC BEF to view files not accessed since the date specified
- /DATE to view information based on date
- /DO to view all information on directories
- /OW to view files by owner
- /REV SORT SI to sort files listing the largest first
- /SPA to view how directory space is used
- /SORT SI to sort files on the basis of size
- /SORT OW to sort files on the basis of ownership
- /VOL to view the information by volume

10

You can delete directories and files by using NetWare Administrator, or the delete (DEL) command in a DOS window. As is true for the Mac OS, NetWare files can be salvaged until they are purged. To salvage files from Network Neighborhood, for example, right-click the folder containing the files to be salvaged, and then click Salvage Files. Another option to salvage files is to use the Salvage command in the DOS window. Because file space is not returned until deleted files are purged, it is wise to establish a schedule for regularly purging them. For example, the deleted files in a directory called Data can be listed and purged by right-clicking the directory and clicking Purge Files. Next, click Purge all and click Yes. Another way to purge files is to open the DOS window, switch to the Data directory, and enter the PURGE command at the DOS prompt, such as PURGE *.* to purge all files, or PURGE *.doc to purge word-processed files only.

 When you create a home directory for a user, you can restrict the size of the directory by using NetWare Administrator. This technique ensures that there is a limit to the amount of disk space available to a single user. In fact, in some instances, users produce so many undeleted temporary files that they occupy all available disk space on a server. When this happens, no space is left to perform even the simplest functions until the administrator deletes these files.

Novell provides a utility called the NetWare Remote Manager, starting with version 6 of NetWare. This utility allows you to manage servers, applications, hardware, etc. You can also access the server console. This is all accomplished through your Web browser. The following are some of the options of this utility found on the main screen:

- Diagnose Server
- Manage Server
- Manage Hardware
- Manage eDirectory
- Use Server Groups
- Access Other Servers

 NetWare Management Portal in NetWare 5.1 was renamed NetWare Remote Manager, starting in NetWare 6.

MAINTAINING LARGE AND SMALL SYSTEM DISKS

In addition to finding and deleting unneeded files, there are other disk maintenance techniques that are valuable in terms of maintaining the integrity of files and ensuring disk performance. These include the following:

- Defragmenting disks
- Moving files to spread the load between multiple disks
- Using disk utilities to repair damaged files
- Deploying RAID techniques that extend the life of disks and provide disk redundancy

Defragmenting Disks

Hard disks in any operating system are subject to becoming fragmented over time. **Fragmentation** means that unused space develops between files and other information written on a disk. When an operating system is first installed, disk files are positioned contiguously on a disk, which means there is little or no unused space between files. Figure 10-11 is a simple conceptual illustration of a hard disk without fragmentation. The shaded areas represent files that are arranged in contiguous fashion, and the white areas are unused disk space.

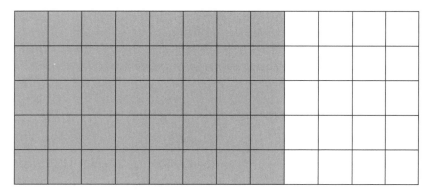

Figure 10-11   Files located contiguously on a disk

As the operating system deletes files, creates new files, and modifies files, the unused space between them grows and becomes scattered throughout the disk (see Figure 10-12). The greater the fragmentation, the more space that is wasted. Equally important, the disk read-write head begins to work harder to find individual files and data in files. When the disk read-write head must move over more disk area to find information, two problems result. One problem is that disk performance suffers because it takes the read-write head longer to find information, and it takes longer to find an appropriately sized unused location on which to write information. The second problem is that the read-write head works harder when there is more disk fragmentation, resulting in a possible hardware failure.

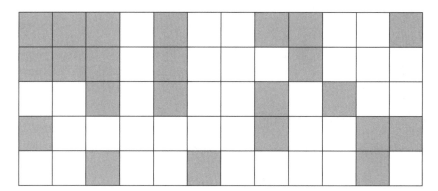

Figure 10-12   A fragmented disk

In older mainframes and minicomputers that have large hard disks, fragmentation is sometimes obvious because the constant activity of the read-write head causes the disk drive cabinet to literally move across the floor. In small disk drives, the problem is apparent through excessive noise and hard disk activity.

Defragmentation is the process of removing the empty pockets between files and other information on a hard disk drive. There are two ways to do this. The oldest method is to take a complete backup of a disk's contents and perform a full restore. Some administrators also run a **surface analysis** of a disk before performing the full restore, as a means of finding damaged disk sectors and tracks. Some surface analysis tools are destructive to data and attempt to reformat the damaged area to determine if it can be recovered. Others are not destructive to data because they relocate information from a damaged disk area to an undamaged location, and then mark the damaged area as off limits so that no files can be written there.

 As a precaution, back up a hard disk before running a disk surface analysis or defragmenting it. Also, consult the documentation to make sure you know if a disk analysis tool is destructive to data before you run it. For example, sometimes disk analysis tools provided on the system troubleshooting disk made available by computer manufacturers perform a format along with the surface analysis of hard drives. Also, some disk troubleshooting tools that accompany hardware RAID are destructive to data because they initialize and format individual or all disks within the RAID.

A second option that is usually easier than backing up and restoring a hard disk is to run a disk defragmentation tool. Many operating systems come with a built-in tool to defragment disks. In some cases, it is necessary to purchase the tool from a third-party vendor, which is true for Windows NT 4.0 owners. Some defragmentation tools can run in the background as you continue to use the operating system. Many also provide a quick analysis of the hard disk, and advise whether or not it is necessary to defragment it. For example, if disk fragmentation is 20% or less, the disk does not need to be defragmented immediately. Server operating systems often experience more rapid fragmentation than workstation operating systems. Server administrators should develop a regular schedule to defragment the hard disks. Some administrators defragment once a week to once a month, during times when no one is on the server other than the administrator. In some situations where a server is under constant and heavy use, such as one used for a client/server application, it can be necessary to defragment disks every few days.

As introduced in Chapter 3, MS-DOS, Windows 3.x, Windows 95/98/Me, and Windows 2000/XP are examples of operating systems with built-in defragmentation utilities. In Windows 95/98/Me, defragmentation is accomplished through a Windows utility accessed from the Start button, Programs menu, and Accessories menu. On the Accessories menu, select System Tools and Disk Defragmenter. Choose the drive to defragment in the Select Drive dialog box and click OK. Click Show Details to view a complete cluster-by-cluster display of the defragmentation process.

In Windows 2000/XP, defragmentation is also accomplished through the Start button, Programs menu (All Programs in Windows XP), Accessories menu, and System Tools menu. On the System Tools menu, select Disk Defragmenter. Next, highlight the drive you wish to work on, and then click Analyze to check fragmentation of the drive, or Defragment to actually defragment the drive. Figure 10-13 shows the Windows XP Disk

Defragmenter dialog box. Also, try Hands-on Project 10-6 to run the Disk Defragmenter in Windows 95/98 and Windows 2000/XP.

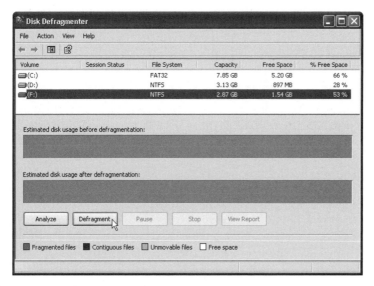

Figure 10-13   Disk Defragmenter in Windows XP

 If a disk contains an error, the Disk Defragmenter detects the error and requires that it is repaired prior to defragmenting that disk. Errors can be repaired using the ScanDisk or *chkdsk* utilities, discussed later in this chapter.

Windows NT 4.0 does not come with a defragmenting tool, but third-party software companies offer them. Executive Software, for example, developed a Windows NT version of Diskeeper that can defragment disk drives, including the page file (or files) on disk volumes (paging is discussed later in this chapter). SYMANTEC's Norton Utilities for Windows NT also includes the SpeedDisk defragmenting tool.

Defragmenting a Windows NT or Windows 2000 server can be an effective way to enhance performance, depending on how the server is used. For example, a Windows NT or Windows 2000 server that has frequent write and update activity may need to be defragmented every month. Also, active Internet and intranet servers may need regular page file defragmentation.

 When you defragment the drives on a server, make sure that you schedule a time when no users can access the server.

Some versions of UNIX come with defragmenting tools, such as *defragfs*. The tools are limited in that they defragment and return to use existing empty space, but they may not rearrange files. Compunix, DEC (Compaq/HP), Eagle Software, and other companies offer full-feature UNIX disk defragmentation tools.

 Recent versions of Red Hat Linux use the ext2 and ext3 (new with Red Hat Linux 7.2) file systems, which are designed to keep disk fragmentation to a minimum. When this operating system writes files to disk in ext2 or ext3, it works to write them in consecutive space, or if consecutive space is not available, it writes to free blocks that are as close as possible to one another. However, if you are using other file systems with Red Hat Linux, consider purchasing a disk defragmenting tool for these file systems.

 As for any system, an alternative to defragmenting disks on UNIX systems is to perform a full backup and restore.

The Mac OS is designed to minimize disk fragmentation, but third-party tools are available for systems that experience high use. For example, SYMANTEC's Norton Utilities for Macintosh includes a Mac OS version of SpeedDisk for defragmenting. One problem that is more likely to need attention in the Mac OS is memory fragmentation, in which pockets of empty unused space develop in memory. An indication of memory fragmentation is when you receive a message that there is not enough memory. There are four ways to handle memory fragmentation. The first and simplest is to implement virtual memory, as described later in this chapter. Two other approaches are to close all open applications, or shut down and restart the computer. The fourth technique is to open your least used applications first and the most used applications last; also, close the applications in the reverse order in which they were opened.

Moving Disk Files to Spread the Load

Another technique that can help extend the life of disk drives is to spread files evenly across disks when there is more than one disk. This technique is used mainly on computers with multiple-user access, such as servers, and on which there is frequent disk activity. Before files are moved, the server administrator examines disk and file activity to determine how to spread files across the disk drives to achieve even loading in terms of activity. Also, files must be moved on the basis of their functions so that files that contain related information are on the same drive. Disk activity is monitored in Windows NT and Windows 2000, for example, by using the Performance Monitor tool (in Windows NT) or the System Monitor (in Windows 2000), and monitoring the LogicalDisk and PhysicalDisk objects. Also, Windows NT resources in use are monitored by clicking the Server icon in the Control Panel. Windows 2000 and XP resources in use can be viewed by right-clicking My Computer, clicking Manage, and clicking

Shared Folders under System Tools in the tree. (See Figure 10-14 and try Hands-on Project 10-7 to study users and resource use across disks in Windows 2000 and XP.)

The *diskperf* utility must be started from the command prompt in Windows NT and Windows 2000 in order for Performance Monitor or System Monitor to gather statistics on disk use.

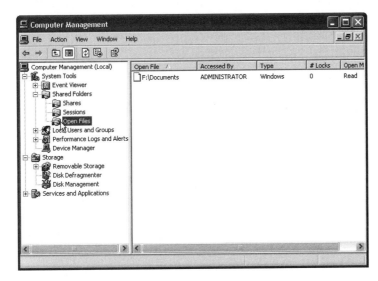

Figure 10-14   Studying resource use in Windows XP via the Computer Management tool

In Windows NT 4.0 Server (with Service Pack 4 or higher), Windows 2000, and Windows .NET Server, you can use the distributed file system (Dfs) to share files across many computers and achieve load balancing.

Using Disk Utilities to Repair Damaged Files

Some operating systems have utilities that enable you to repair damaged files and file links. Four examples of these utilities are:

- Disk First Aid in the Mac OS

- *fsck* and *p_fsck* in UNIX

- *chkdsk* in MS-DOS, Windows 3.1, Windows 3.11, Windows 95, Windows 98, Windows NT, Windows 2000, and Windows XP

- ScanDisk in MS-DOS, Windows 3.1, Windows 3.11, Windows 95, and Windows 98

Disk First Aid is a Mac OS utility that verifies files, folders, and mounted disks. Before you verify a disk, it is necessary to turn off file sharing. In Mac OS 9.x, you start Disk First Aid by opening the Disk First Aid icon—located in the Utilities folder, which is found in the Applications folder. Choose the disk that you want to verify, or press Shift and click several disks, and click the Verify button. Another option is to click the Repair button, if you know that a disk needs to be repaired.

In Mac OS X, Disk First Aid is combined with the Disk Utility. To access Disk First Aid, open the Applications folder, the Utilities subfolder, and select Disk Utility. After Disk Utility is opened, click the First Aid tab, select the disk or disks to verify, and click Verify; or to repair a disk, select it and click Repair.

The *fsck* utility in UNIX is used to check one or more file systems. For example, it looks for orphaned files without names, bad directory pointers, inode problems, directories that do not exist, bad links, bad blocks, duplicated blocks, and pathname problems. It also makes other file system checks. If it discovers a problem with one or more files, it gives you the opportunity to fix or disregard the problem. Unless you have a reason not to (such as a database file on which you want to try a database repair tool first), the best approach is to fix any problem found. To use *fsck*, enter the command along with a file list, which is provided in one of two formats. One format is to specify the device name of the file system, such as /dev/devicename. Another format is to specify the mount point of a particular file system so that the utility can determine it from the file /etc/fstab, which contains a list of file systems. If you do not specify a file system to check, *fsck* assumes that it should check all file systems, or you can instruct it to check all file systems by including the *-A* option. Also, some versions of UNIX have a *-y* (*-a* in Red Hat Linux) option that causes *fsck* to make its own decision about whether to fix a problem it finds, and a *-n* (*-N* in Red Hat Linux) command to have *fsck* check the file system and report problems, but not fix them. Hands-on Project 10-8 enables you to use *fsck*.

Besides *fsck*, there is the *p_fsck* utility in some UNIX versions. This utility checks two or more file systems simultaneously, instead of checking only one at a time, as is done by *fsck*. The drawback in using *p_fsck* is that it should not be applied to the root file system.

 In most UNIX systems, *fsck* starts automatically each time the operating system is booted. If *fsck* cannot run when you boot these systems, that means the root system is likely corrupted. To fix this problem, you must use the rescue disk or emergency boot disks for your version of UNIX to boot to a minimal system and restore the root system.

The *chkdsk* disk utility runs in the MS-DOS Prompt window in Windows 95/98/Me, or in the Command Prompt window in Windows NT/2000/XP. The Windows NT/2000/XP version of the utility is more powerful than the ones used in other versions of Microsoft Windows because it incorporates some of the features of ScanDisk (Windows NT/2000/XP do not have a ScanDisk utility). In Windows 95/98/Me, ScanDisk is usually recommended because it has a GUI-like interface, and contains more interactive utilities for checking the integrity of a disk. In Windows 98 and Windows Me, *chkdsk* does not check for errors, but only provides information about the volume serial number, disk space allocation, and lower memory allocation (under 640 KB). Also, switches for *chkdsk* that are available in other versions of Microsoft Windows are not implemented in Windows 98/Me (try Hands-on Project 10-9 to run *chkdsk* in Windows 98). Figure 10-15 shows *chkdsk* after it was run to check an NTFS volume on a Windows 2000 server.

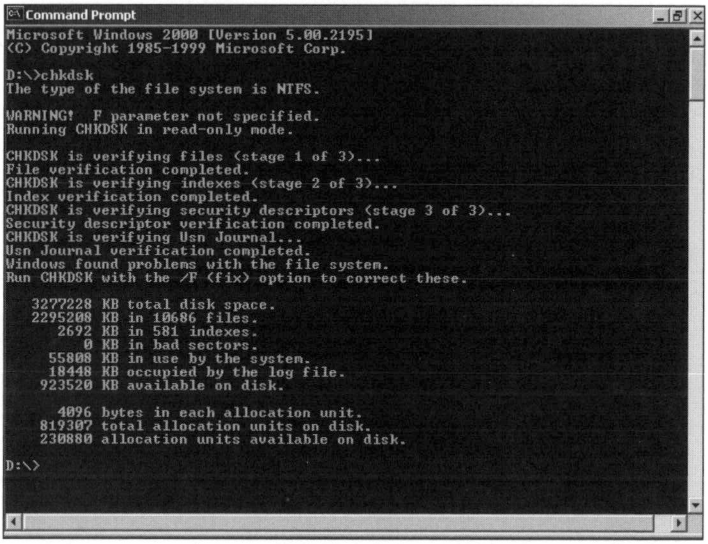

```
Command Prompt                                                    _|8|X|
Microsoft Windows 2000 [Version 5.00.2195]
(C) Copyright 1985-1999 Microsoft Corp.

D:\>chkdsk
The type of the file system is NTFS.

WARNING!  F parameter not specified.
Running CHKDSK in read-only mode.

CHKDSK is verifying files (stage 1 of 3)...
File verification completed.
CHKDSK is verifying indexes (stage 2 of 3)...
Index verification completed.
CHKDSK is verifying security descriptors (stage 3 of 3)...
Security descriptor verification completed.
CHKDSK is verifying Usn Journal...
Usn Journal verification completed.
Windows found problems with the file system.
Run CHKDSK with the /F (fix) option to correct these.

   3277228 KB total disk space.
   2295208 KB in 10686 files.
      2692 KB in 581 indexes.
         0 KB in bad sectors.
     55808 KB in use by the system.
     18448 KB occupied by the log file.
    923520 KB available on disk.

      4096 bytes in each allocation unit.
    819307 total allocation units on disk.
    230880 allocation units available on disk.

D:\>
```

Figure 10-15   *Chkdsk* in Windows 2000

For versions of Windows other than Windows 98 and Windows Me, *chkdsk* can find and fix the following (depending on the version of Windows):

- Damage to the root directory or another directory
- Problems with the directory structure that cause *chkdsk* to be unable to process the full tree
- Indexes created by indexing (such as when you use the Index attribute in Windows 2000)
- Security descriptors
- Unallocated disk space
- Files that share the same allocation units
- A file pointer to an allocation unit that does not exist
- Files assigned more allocation units than they need
- Directories without entries
- Damaged directories that cannot be repaired

- A full root directory (the limit is 512 files in some operating systems)

- Unreadable disk sectors

- Damaged subdirectory entries, such as damaged pointers to parent directories

- File Allocation Table entry problems, or a damaged File Allocation Table

- Allocation units that contain partial information, but have no links to files

- Bad file attributes

Chkdsk only checks the first 640 KB of RAM, and only for the purpose of determining how much of that is free for use by programs.

Users frequently employ the */f* switch with *chkdsk*, which instructs it to repair errors without a yes or no interactive query. On FAT volumes, the /v switch causes *chkdsk* to display all files as it checks them. The advantage to this is that you can see a particular file that is damaged, but the disadvantage is that you may have to watch it display hundreds of files. You can also instruct *chkdsk* to check a specific drive, directory, or file by using the drive letter or path after the *chkdsk* command. For example, *chkdsk D: /f* checks drive D and automatically fixes errors.

Use the */f* option with care: when *chkdsk* finds and fixes file errors, it may need to eliminate data that it cannot associate with a file; it fixes errors automatically and you may lose data. Also, in Windows NT, 2000, and XP, you should dismount a volume before you check it—use the */f* or */x* switches to dismount a volume, but first make sure that all windows are closed, programs stopped, and that there are no users accessing the volume. See Chapter 3 for more information about *chkdsk* switches.

If you do not specify the */f* option, *chkdsk* reports errors in terms of a query, such as: "xx lost allocation units found in *yy* chains. Convert lost chains to files (Y/N)?" If you automatically fix errors, or reply with yes to fix errors, *chkdsk* writes the lost data to one or more files in the root directory that have a .chk extension, as in Figure 10-16. Use an editor to examine the contents of the .chk files (some of the information consists of values you cannot read or interpret) in case there is information you want to retain. Once you extract the useful information, or determine that the information in the files is not needed, make sure that you delete the files to recover the space they occupy.

Two additional switches are available in the Windows NT/2000/XP *chkdsk* version: */r* and */l:size*. The */r* switch instructs *chkdsk* to look for bad sectors, and attempt to relocate information that it is able to read. The */l:size* switch is used to change the size of the log file in NTFS. Another difference between Windows NT/2000/XP and some other versions of Microsoft Windows is that *chkdsk* runs automatically when the operating system boots, and determines if there may be disk or file corruption.

```
IMAGE    BAK      137,728 05-19-96  10:23p
TREEINFO IDX          871 10-10-96   1:28p
FILE0001 CHK       32,768 11-10-98  10:14p
FILE0002 CHK       98,304 11-10-98  10:14p
FILE0003 CHK       32,768 11-10-98  10:14p
FILE0004 CHK       32,768 11-10-98  10:14p
FILE0005 CHK       65,536 11-10-98  10:14p
FILE0006 CHK       98,304 11-10-98  10:14p
FILE0007 CHK       65,536 11-10-98  10:14p
FILE0008 CHK       65,536 11-10-98  10:14p
FILE0009 CHK       98,304 11-10-98  10:14p
FILE0010 CHK       32,768 11-10-98  10:14p
FILE0011 CHK       32,768 11-10-98  10:14p
FILE0012 CHK       32,768 11-10-98  10:14p
COLLWIN      <DIR>          03-04-99   3:45p
SCANDISK LOG          520 03-31-99  11:10a
DOSBAK       <DIR>          04-05-99  11:22a
DOSMJP       <DIR>          04-16-99   3:45p
WIN31        <DIR>          04-16-99   3:48p
CONFIG   SYS          305 04-17-99  12:08p
AUTOEXEC BAT          178 04-16-99   5:39p
        51 file(s)       1,031,178 bytes
                       973,766,656 bytes free

C:\>
```

Figure 10-16   Examples of .chk files

ScanDisk is a disk verification utility available in Windows 95 and Windows 98. In these operating systems, ScanDisk is a Windows-based application run from the Start button, Programs menu, Accessories menu, and System Tools. The Windows-based version has more options than the earlier MS-DOS versions, and they can be set after ScanDisk starts. Another advantage of the Windows-based version is that it can be set up to start automatically each time you boot Windows 95 or Windows 98. The Windows-based version has two initial options—to perform a standard test or a thorough test. The standard test verifies files and folders, whereas the thorough test is a complete disk surface analysis that is not destructive to data. When you use the thorough option, you can specify whether to scan the system and data areas, only the system area, or only the data area. You can also specify whether or not to perform write testing, and whether or not to repair bad sectors in hidden and system files. This version of ScanDisk also offers the following advanced options:

- Selections for how to display the summary information
- Selections for handling cross-linked files
- Selections about how to handle lost file fragments
- Selections about how to verify files
- Selections on whether or not to report DOS name-length errors

Try Hands-on Project 10-10 to practice using ScanDisk and view its options.

Deploying RAID Techniques

As you learned in Chapter 6, deploying a redundant array of inexpensive drives (RAID) is a technique used by server operating systems, such as UNIX, NetWare, Windows NT, Windows 2000, and Windows .NET Server, for three purposes: increased reliability (providing data recovery when a disk drive fails and extending the useful life of disks), increased storage capacity, and increased speed. This section focuses on how RAID is used to extend the life of a set of disks. RAID does this by using **disk striping**, a technique for spreading data over multiple disk volumes. For example, when a file is written to a striped disk set, portions of that file are spread across the set. Striping ensures that the load resulting from reading and writing to disks is spread evenly across the set of disks. This means that the disks experience equal wear, rather than placing extra load on one or two disks that are then likely to wear out sooner.

There are six basic RAID levels:

- RAID level 0: Provides disk striping only, and requires the use of two or more disks

- RAID level 1: Uses two disks that are mirror images of one another so that if one fails, the other one takes over; however, it does not use disk striping to extend the life of disks

- RAID level 2: Provides disk striping, and all disks contain information to help recover data in case one fails

- RAID level 3: The same as RAID level 2, but error recovery information is on one disk only

- RAID level 4: Provides disk striping, as in RAID level 2, and adds checksum verification information that is stored on one disk in the array

- RAID level 5: The same as RAID level 4, except that checksum verification information is stored on all disks in the array, and level 5 includes the ability to replace a failed drive and rebuild it without shutting down the drive array or server

There are two general ways to deploy RAID: hardware RAID and software RAID. Hardware RAID is controlled through a specialized RAID adapter that has its own RAID software on a chip, which usually provides extra redundancy, such as a battery backup for the RAID logic in the adapter. Software RAID is set up and managed by the server operating system, and does not have as many redundancy features as hardware RAID. Generally speaking, software RAID is slower than hardware RAID.

 When given the choice, most server administrators use hardware RAID because it enables them to bypass some restrictions that the operating system places on software RAID. For example, Windows 2000 Server does not permit boot and system files to reside on software RAID, but the restriction does not apply to hardware RAID. Also, most hardware and software RAID is deployed as RAID level 1, RAID level 5, or a combination of these, in order to achieve the best performance combined with optimal data protection.

MAKING BACKUPS

In Chapter 5, you learned that it is vital to back up your operating system and data files before an operating system upgrade. It is also essential to back up these files as a regular maintenance practice. Disk drives fail, files can be lost or corrupted, and database files can get out of synchronization on any workstation or server. The best line of defense is to develop a strong backup plan. Most computer operating systems have built-in backup software, or backup software can be purchased separately. Typically, backups are written to tape, but other backup options include floppy disks, Zip drives, Jaz drives, and CD-ROMs.

In general, there are several types of backup techniques. One type of backup is called a **binary backup** because it backs up the disk contents in binary format to create an exact image of the disk contents. The advantages of this backup is that it is simple to perform, and includes everything on the disk. The disadvantages are that in many versions, you cannot restore individual files or directories, and when you perform a restore, the target disk drive must be the same size or larger than the disk drive from which the backup was made.

Another backup technique is called a **full file-by-file backup**, in which all of the disk contents are backed up, but as individual directories and files. This type of backup is commonly used on workstations because it enables you to restore a single directory or a given set of files without restoring the entire disk contents. Full file-by-file backups also are performed on servers, depending on the backup scheme that is in place. Some backup schemes call for a full file-by-file backup to be performed at the end of each workday, as long as the total amount of information on the disks is not too prohibitive. If the disks hold lots of information, then it is common to perform a full file-by-file backup once a week, and partial backups on the other days of the week. There are typically two kinds of partial backups—differential and incremental. A **differential backup** backs up all files that have an archive attribute (file attribute that indicates that the file needs to be backed up), but does not remove the archive attribute. An **incremental backup** backs up all files that have the archive attribute, and removes the attribute from each file after backup. The differences between using differential or incremental backups between full backups are in the number of tapes required for these backups, and the number of days that must be restored when a complete restore is necessary. For example, assume that a business needs to restore all files because of a catastrophic disk failure during the day on Thursday. Also, assume that the business performs a full file-by-file backup each Saturday evening, and differential backups Monday through Friday evenings. To recover after the disk drives are replaced, it first restores the full file-by-file backups from the previous Saturday, and then restores the differential backup from Wednesday night. If the same business had been performing incremental backups, it would restore the full file-by-file backup from Saturday, and then restore the incremental backups from Monday, Tuesday, and Wednesday.

10

Windows 95, Windows 98, and Windows Me

Windows 95, Windows 98, and Windows Me have a Backup utility that you access from the Start button, Programs menu, Accessories menu, and System Tools menu. Backups are created as jobs that are given titles. The Backup utility displays all drives recognized by Windows 95/98/Me, including mapped drives. You can back up an entire drive, a directory, a file, or any combination of these by placing a check in the box in front of the entity (see Figure 10-17). Also, there are options to back up all files (full file-by-file), or only files that are new or have changed since the last backup (incremental). After you choose what you want to back up, you must provide a job name, specify parameters for the backup, and start the backup. The parameters include the ability to compress files on the backup medium, and perform a read verification after each file is backed up.

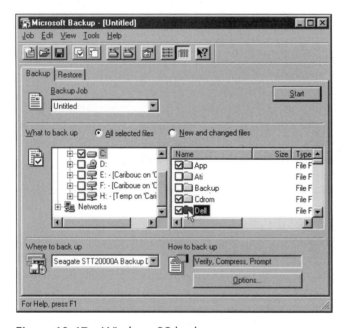

Figure 10-17   Windows 98 backup

 A read verification is advantageous because it provides initial assurance that a file can be read from the backup medium; it is disadvantageous in that it makes the backup take twice the time.

Windows NT, Windows 2000, and Windows XP

Windows NT 4.0, Windows 2000, and Windows XP all have a Backup utility that allows different combinations of full and partial backups, along with the ability to restore backed up information. The options in the Backup utility are as follows:

- Normal backup (full file-by-file backup)

- Incremental backup

- Differential backup

- Daily backup for files that changed on the same day as the backup

- Copy backup that is performed only on specified files

Prior to backup, the backup media and the driver that integrates the backup media with the operating system must be installed. For example, if you back up to tape, it is necessary to have the tape adapter and tape device driver installed, and the tape drives detected by the operating system. With these installed, you are ready to start a backup by starting the Backup utility. In Windows NT 4.0, click the Start button, point to Programs, click Administrative Tools (Common), and click Backup. When you start the Backup utility, it automatically detects the tape system. To back up a particular disk volume, click its check box (see Figure 10-18), or check all volumes to back up the entire server. Click the Backup button to specify the backup parameters, which include whether to back up the Registry, a description of the backup, and the type of backup, such as normal or incremental.

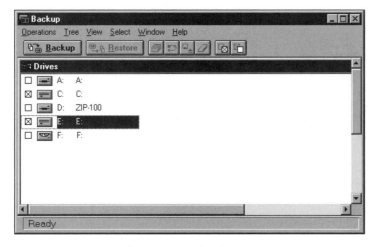

Figure 10-18   Windows NT 4.0 backup

To perform a backup in Windows 2000 or XP, click Start, point to Programs (in Windows 2000) or All Programs (in Windows XP), point to Accessories, point to System Tools, and click Backup. In Windows 2000, select the button to use the Backup Wizard (see Figure 10-19). In Windows XP, the Backup and Restore Wizard starts automatically to guide you through a backup or restore (see Figure 10-20).

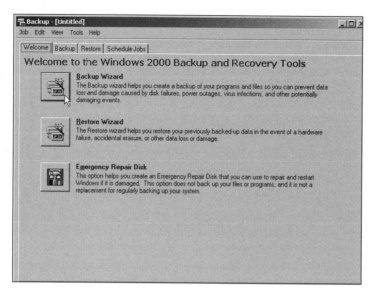

Figure 10-19   Starting with Windows 2000 Backup Wizard

Figure 10-20   Windows XP Backup or Restore Wizard

UNIX

Two main utilities in UNIX for backing up files are *volcopy* and *dump*. *Volcopy* (not available in Red Hat Linux) is a binary backup that creates a mirror image of a disk onto the backup medium, such as a tape or Zip drive. *Volcopy* requires that you provide specifics about the length and density of the information to be backed up. *Volcopy* can write to one or multiple tapes, calling for additional tapes if the information does not fit on the first one. The utility also can back up to multiple tape drives. *Volcopy* is sometimes used with the *labelit* utility, which can label file systems or unmounted volumes to provide unique identification for each one copied in the backup.

The *dump* utility (used in Red Hat Linux) is used for full or partial file-by-file backups. (These backups are often called "dumps.") The *dump* utility backs up all files, files that have changed by date, or files that have changed after the previous backup. Files can be backed up using a dump level that correlates a dump to a given point in time. For example, a Monday dump might be assigned level 1, Tuesday's dump level 2, and so on. Up to nine dump levels can be assigned. A dump is restored via one of three commands, depending on the flavor of UNIX: *restore* (in Red Hat Linux), *ufsrestore*, and *restor*.

A third backup utility called *tar*—available in most versions of UNIX, including Red Hat Linux—is sometimes used in addition to *volcopy* and *dump*. *Tar* is designed for archiving tapes, and includes file information, as well as the archived files, such as security information and dates when files were modified. (You used *tar* in a Hands-on Project in Chapter 5 to back up configuration files before upgrading UNIX.) Also, there are several third-party utilities that employ *tar*-based backups and restores, which offer many added features. Two examples of these utilities are CTAR from UniTrends Software and BRU from the TOLIS Group. A comprehensive backup and restore solution for networked systems is available in Cheyenne's ARCserve/Open.

NetWare

NetWare uses its Storage Management System (SMS) to create backups. Typically, three NetWare Loadable Modules (NLMs) are loaded at the server console by using the LOAD command. They include the target server software (TSA410), the target NDS agent (TSANDS, to back up the NDS database), and backup device drivers (SBACKUP).

After these NLMs are loaded, you highlight the Backup From or Restore To option on the SBACKUP menu at the console, and select the server to back up. Next, access the Backup menu, and provide a name and location for the backup log file. Specify the directories and files to back up using the Backup Selected Target selection, and provide a name for the backups. Use the Start backup now option to run the backups.

OPTIMIZING SOFTWARE INSTALLATION

One aspect of software installation already discussed in this chapter is to plan and set up a well-organized directory structure. The directory structure influences the ease of the installation, provides the ability to keep different versions in separate places, and enables you to smoothly uninstall software. The following is a checklist of additional guidelines for software installation:

- Make sure that the software is compatible with your operating system.

- Check the CPU, RAM, disk storage, audio, and other requirements to make sure your computer is a match for the software.

- Find out if there are different installation options, such as one with or without tutoring applications to help you to learn the software.

- For Microsoft operating systems, determine if the software is DOS-based or Windows-based, and if any special drivers are required. Keep in mind that Windows NT/2000/XP may not run some DOS-based software, games, and 16-bit Windows-based software.

- Check to determine if there are programs that attempt to directly manage hardware and peripherals because these may not be allowed to function in Windows NT and Windows 2000 since these functions must go through the system kernel.

- Use any utilities provided by the operating system for installing software. For example, Windows 95/98 and Windows NT/2000/XP use an Add/Remove Programs (or Add and Remove Programs in Windows XP) utility in the Control Panel.

- Look in the documentation, or ask your vendor, for software that is written to take advantage of the Registry for Windows 95/98 and Windows NT/2000/XP/.NET applications.

- Check the vendor's "bug" list for the software to make sure there are no bugs that will impact the way you will use it. Bug lists are often posted on the vendor's Internet site in the software support area.

- Make sure that the software is well documented and supported by the vendor, and that the vendor can provide the required drivers, if applicable.

- Determine, in advance, how to back up important files associated with the software, and find out the locations and purposes of all hidden files.

- Determine if running the program requires adjustments to page or swap files used by the operating system.

- Find out what temporary files are created by the program, and where they are created.

- For Windows-based software, always install the latest versions of components, including .dll, .ocx, .ini, .inf, and .drv files. (These are generally available directly from the software vendor or on the vendor's Web site.)

- Do not mix .inf and driver files between different versions of Windows because some other software on the computer may no longer work.

- Always keep service patches up to date for all software. **Service packs** are issued by the vendor to fix software problems, address compatibility issues, and add enhancements.

Installing software on a network server requires some additional considerations, which include:

- Make sure there are enough licenses to match the number of users, or that you have metering software that limits simultaneous use to the number of valid licenses.

- Determine the network load created by software, such as client/server, database, and multimedia applications.

- Consider purchasing management software, such as Microsoft System Management Server, that can automatically update system-wide software when there is a new release. This ensures that all users are on the same version of word-processing or database software, for example.

- Determine if the software will be loaded from the server each time it is used, or if it will be installed permanently at workstations from the server. (Windows 2000 Server Terminal Services, for example, enables users to run software on the server.)

- Publish or assign software offered from Windows 2000 or Windows .NET Server.

- Determine if the server or client workstations must be tuned for the software in a particular way, such as by modifying page files or Registry entries.

- For operating systems that support two or more file systems, make sure that the software is compatible with the file system used by the operating system.

TUNING THE OPERATING SYSTEM

After an operating system is installed, you may notice that its performance is not what you expected, or that performance seems to decrease with time. Just as a car needs periodic tuning, so do workstation and server operating systems. One critical reason for tuning operating systems is that slow workstations and servers have a cumulative impact on a network. Sometimes poor network performance is not the result of network problems or too little bandwidth, but instead, a preponderance of workstations and servers that cannot keep up with the network. This is an often overlooked area that can result in huge dollar savings for an organization. It is much less expensive to tune servers and workstations (often at no cost) than invest in faster and very expensive network devices such as routers and switches. There are many ways to tune operating systems to achieve better performance, including tuning virtual memory, installing operating system updates and patches, and tuning for optimal network communications.

Tuning Virtual Memory

Some operating systems supplement RAM by employing virtual memory techniques. **Virtual memory** is disk storage that is used when there is not enough RAM for a particular operation, or for all processes currently in use. The computer's CPU, in conjunction with the operating system, can swap to disk processes and data in RAM that temporarily have a low priority, or that are not in immediate use. When the operating system and CPU need to access the information on disk, they swap something else to disk, and read the information they need back into RAM, using a process called paging. The information that is swapped back and forth from RAM to disk and from disk to RAM is stored in a specially allocated disk area called the **paging** or **swap file** (or swap file system in UNIX).

Some operating systems that use virtual memory and paging enable you to tune the paging file by adjusting its size. Tuning the paging file can result in better operating system performance. For example, you can adjust the virtual memory allocation, disk cache, and RAM disk settings in the Mac OS (through Mac OS 9.x) by opening the Apple menu, Control Panels, and the Memory option. To adjust the allocation, click the radio button to turn on virtual memory, and make sure that it is set to equal the amount of RAM in the computer, plus 1 MB or more (try Hands-on Project 10-11).

In Mac OS X, there is no option for turning on virtual memory because it is always enabled. The use of virtual memory is built into the operating system, and is not subject to user intervention.

In UNIX, you can use the *vmstat* utility, recognized in all UNIX versions, to monitor paging (see Figure 10-21). Another tool that you can use to track disk activity is *iostat* (recognized in all UNIX versions except Linux). Paging in UNIX is accomplished by creating a swap file system using the make file system command appropriate to the flavor of UNIX (see Chapter 3), such as the *nsfs* or *mkfs* commands in Solaris and Linux. The swap file system is mounted like any other file system. If the swap file system is often over 80% full, increase its size. Also, if there frequently is a high rate of swapping, consider spreading the swap space over multiple disks on different controllers. Try Hands-on Project 10-12 to monitor swap space.

Virtual memory in Windows NT/2000/XP is adjusted to set an initial starting size, and a maximum size to which it can grow. Generally, the rule for sizing the page file is to set the initial size to equal the amount of RAM (in megabytes), plus 12 MB. The maximum pagefile size should allow for adequate growth in order to handle the most active times. You can monitor RAM and page file activity through the Task Manager's Performance tab (see Figure 10-22 and try Hands-on Project 10-12), the Performance Monitor in Windows NT, or System Monitor in Windows 2000.

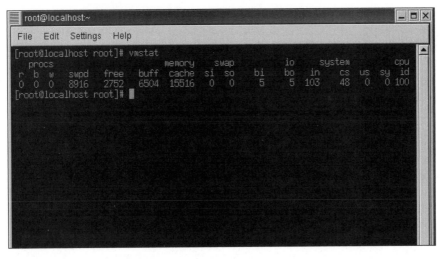

Figure 10-21   Monitoring virtual memory information in Red Hat Linux

 The default page file size in Windows NT/2000/XP is determined by multiplying the amount of RAM by 1.5, with the maximum pagefile size being 4,095 MB per volume.

10

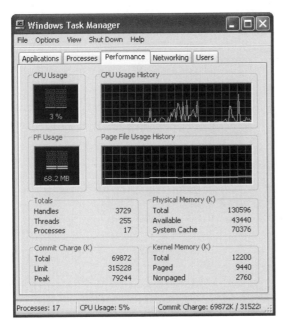

Figure 10-22   Monitoring memory and page file activity in Windows XP

To adjust the page file size in Windows NT, open the Control Panel, double-click the System icon, click the Performance tab, and the Change button. The page file size is specified in the Initial Size (MB) and Maximum Size (MB) boxes. Also, you can create a page file on each physical hard disk. As a general rule, it is a good idea to create multiple page files (one for each disk), with the following exceptions:

- Avoid creating a page file on the disk that contains the system files (if possible).

- Do not create a page file on a RAID set of disks when using software RAID levels 0 or 5 (not a problem in hardware RAID).

- Do not create a page file on the backup volume in a mirrored set.

These restrictions are another reason to use hardware RAID instead of software RAID.

For Windows 2000, you can configure the page file by opening the Control Panel, clicking the System icon, clicking the Advanced tab, clicking Performance Options, and clicking the Change button. To set the page file size in Windows XP, click Start, and click Control Panel. Click the System icon, click the Advanced tab, click the Settings button for Performance, click the Advanced tab, and click the Change button to view the screen in Figure 10-23.

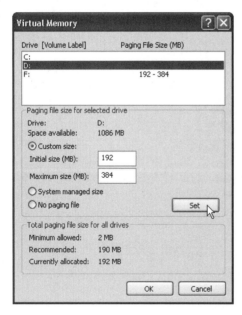

Figure 10-23   Creating page files in Windows XP

Windows 95/98 also make use of paging. In these operating systems, you can adjust the paging file size by opening the Control Panel, double-clicking the System icon, and clicking the

Performance tab. Click the Virtual Memory button, and click "Let me specify my own virtual memory settings" to enter the minimum and maximum sizes for the paging file.

 Unless it is specifically required by a software application, or you frequently see messages that you are out of memory, it is recommended that you let Windows 95/98 automatically adjust the paging file size.

Installing Operating System Updates and Patches

One of the most important ways to keep your operating system tuned is by installing operating system updates and patches issued by the vendor. Often problems with an operating system are not fully discovered until it has been released and used by thousands, or even millions, of users. Once enough problems are discovered and reported, vendors create updates or patches. For example, Microsoft issues service packs for operating systems and software, which contain a wide range of updates and patches. If problems are discovered between service packs, you can obtain individual program fixes or updates by using the Windows Update capability in Windows 98/Me, and Windows 2000/XP (see Chapter 5). System updates and patches can be downloaded from the vendor's Web site, or ordered on the appropriate medium, such as on CD-ROM.

Red Hat Linux 7.2 includes Netscape Communicator, which you can use to access *www.redhat.com* and obtain operating system updates via the Network Software Manager on the Internet.

 Often when you call a vendor to get help for an operating system problem, the representative will ask what service releases, upgrades, or patches you have installed, and may request that you install them as the first step in problem resolution.

Tuning for Network Communications

Any computer connected to a network should be checked periodically to make sure that the connectivity is optimized. An obvious, but often ignored, step is to periodically inspect the cable and connector into the computer for damage. A crushed or severely bent cable, or one in which wires are exposed at the connector, should be replaced immediately. Also, make sure that the NIC connector is in good condition. When the NIC is purchased, it should be high quality, and designed for use in the fastest expansion slot in the computer, such as a PCI slot in an Intel-based computer.

Just as operating systems need periodic patches, so do NIC drivers. Periodically check the NIC vendor's Web site for updated drivers that you can download and use immediately. Another problem with NICs is that they occasionally experience problems that cause them to saturate the network with repeated packet broadcasts, called a broadcast storm. Network administrators can regularly monitor the network and individual nodes to make sure none are creating excessive traffic.

Sometimes an operating system is configured for protocols that are not in use on a network. An easy way to tune the operating system is to periodically check which protocols are configured, and eliminate those that are no longer used. On many networks, only TCP/IP is in use, but workstations and servers are still configured for IPX, NetBEUI, or both.

A workstation running Windows NT, Windows 2000, or Windows XP (see Chapter 8) enables you to specify the order in which the workstation handles protocols on a multi-protocol network—called the protocol binding order. One very effective way to tune the response time of the workstation and improve the network response is to set the protocol binding order so that the most frequently used protocol is handled first. For example, consider a network that uses peer-to-peer communications and server communications that involve TCP/IP, NetBEUI, and IPX, plus printer communications that use IPX. In this example, most of the peer-to-peer and server communications involve TCP/IP, then NetBEUI, and last IPX. The workstation owner in this situation should set the order of Network Providers in Windows 2000, for example, as TCP/IP, NetBEUI, and IPX. Also, he or she should set the order of Printer Providers so that IPX is first. You can tune the access order in Windows NT 4.0 by opening the Control Panel, double-clicking the Network icon, clicking the Services tab, and then Network Access Order (see Figure 10-24). In Windows 2000, you set the protocol binding order by right-clicking My Network Places, clicking Properties, selecting Local Area Connection, clicking the Advanced menu, clicking Advanced Settings, and selecting the Provider Order tab (see Figure 10-25). Finally, in Windows XP, the screen to set the network binding order is nearly identical to that in Windows 2000, but you initially follow somewhat different steps to access it. In Windows XP, click Start, click Control Panel, click Network and Internet Connections, click Network Connections, select Local Area Connection, click the Advanced menu, click Advanced Settings, and select the Provider Order tab (try Hands-on Project 10-13).

Figure 10-24 Windows NT network binding order

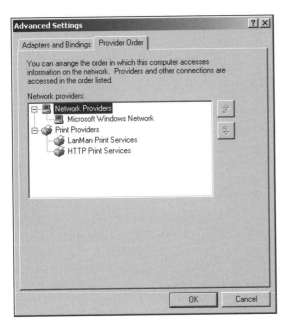

Figure 10-25   Windows 2000 network binding order

10

Testing Network Connectivity

Often questions arise about whether or not the network is working, or whether a particular workstation's network connection is working. TCP/IP-based networks have a protocol, called **Internet Control Message Protocol (ICMP)**, that is used for network error reporting, and to determine if there are network problems. Through ICMP, anyone can poll another network device, using the *ping* utility. *Ping* offers a simple and quick way to determine if a workstation or server's network connection is working. It also offers a fast means to determine if one network is communicating with another network because *ping* can be transported through network devices, such as routers.

Windows 95, 98, Me, NT, 2000, and XP all support *ping*. *Ping* is also available in UNIX and the Mac OS. Many of these operating systems support *ping* as a command-line command. Others, such as Mac OS X, include a GUI interface from which to use the utility. In all of these operating systems, you can use *ping* by entering the command plus the IP address of another computer or network device that you want to poll. Many versions of *ping*, such as in Windows-based operating systems, also let you poll by using the computer name or computer and domain name of the device you want to poll—such as *ping antelope*, where *antelope* is the NetBIOS name of a computer on a Windows NT or 2000 network.

If you poll a computer and receive a reply showing its address along with other information, that means your computer's connection is working. Also, if the computer that you poll is on another network or across the Internet, that means all of the network connections between your computer and the other computer are communicating. Try

Hands-on Project 10-14 to use the *ping* utility in Mac OS X, Red Hat Linux 7.2, and Windows XP.

CHAPTER SUMMARY

❒ Maintaining an operating system is as important as setting it up. There are many procedures you can follow on a regular schedule to ensure that your operating system is at its best. One important technique for maintaining an operating system is to regularly find and delete unused files. Disk space is often at a premium, and there is no reason to leave unused files on a system, particularly because they are easy to delete. Designing a well-organized file structure is a vital part of this maintenance technique.

❒ Other ways to maintain disks include defragmenting disks, moving files to relatively unused disks, finding and repairing disk problems, and setting up RAID. Many operating systems have built-in utilities that can determine if disks are fragmented, and then defragment them. Regularly defragmenting disks is an inexpensive way to extend disk life and improve performance. Disk scan and repair tools are another inexpensive way to work on disk problems and prevent them from growing more serious. Equalizing the disk load by periodically moving files is another way to extend the life of disks. Also, RAID techniques are frequently used to extend longer disk life, as well as protect data when a disk fails.

❒ An important part of maintaining a system is to make regular backups. Backups are vital at times when a hard disk fails, or after you delete and purge files that you later wish you had retained. Backups can also be used to restore drivers or other operating system files that were damaged or overwritten.

❒ There are many considerations when installing software. Two of the most important are to make sure that the software is compatible with the computer hardware and operating system. Another is to use the software installation tools and features built into the operating system.

❒ Finally, all operating systems should be tuned periodically. Adjusting paging is one way to tune for better performance. Another way is to make sure that you keep current with operating system patches and updates. Networked systems should be tuned so that only the necessary protocols are in use, NIC drivers are current, and the network cable is in good condition. Also, TCP/IP-based network systems include the *ping* utility for testing a network connection.

KEY TERMS

binary backup — A technique that backs up the entire contents of one or more disk drives in a binary or image format.

cookie — A text-based file used by Web sites to obtain customized information about a user, such as the user's name, the user's password to access the site, and information about how to customize Web page display.

defragmentation — The process of removing empty pockets between files and other information on a hard disk drive.

differential backup — Backs up all files with an archive attribute, but does not remove that attribute after backup.

disk striping — A disk storage technique that divides portions of each file over all volumes in a set as a way to minimize wear on individual disks.

full file-by-file backup — A technique that backs up the entire contents of one or more disk drives on the basis of directories, subdirectories, and files so that it is possible to restore a combination of any of these.

fragmentation — Developing more and more empty pockets of space between files on the disk due to frequent writing, deleting, and modifying files and file contents.

incremental backup — A technique that backs up all files with an archive attribute, and then removes the attribute after backup.

Internet Control Message Protocol (ICMP) — A TCP/IP-based protocol used for network error reporting, particularly through routing devices.

paging file — Also called the page or swap file, an allocated portion of disk storage reserved for use to supplement RAM when the available RAM is exceeded.

service packs — Software "fixes" issued by the vendor to repair software problems, address compatibility issues, and add enhancements.

surface analysis — A disk diagnostic technique that locates damaged disk areas and marks them as bad. Some surface analysis tools are destructive to data because they also format a disk. Others can run without altering data, except to move data from a damaged location to one that is not.

swap file — Also called the page or paging file, an allocated portion of disk storage reserved for use to supplement RAM when the available RAM is exceeded.

virtual memory — Disk storage that is used when there is not enough RAM for a particular operation, or for all processes currently in use.

REVIEW QUESTIONS

1. The *ping* utility is used for _____.

2. In disk striping:

   a. a disk array is specially coated to reduce wear.

   b. portions of files are spread over several disks in a set.

   c. redundancy is not needed because mirrored data is stored on a chip in the disk adapter.

   d. all of the above

   e. only a and b

   f. only b and c

3. In which of the following operating systems can you adjust virtual memory?

   a. Mac OS 9.x

   b. Windows XP

   c. Red Hat Linux 7.2

   d. all of the above

   e. only a and b

   f. only a and c

4. How can you purge a file in Mac OS X?

   a. Right-click the file and click purge.

   b. Send the file to the trash can and then delete it from the trash can.

   c. Copy the file to another hard drive and then delete it.

   d. Unlike Mac OS 9.x, Mac OS X files are always purged as soon as they are deleted.

5. Performing a complete backup and then fully restoring a disk is one way to eliminate heavy fragmentation. True or False?

6. The swap or page file is used for _____ memory.

7. Which of the following utilities in Windows 98 or Windows Me can be used to find and delete temporary files created by programs?

   a. Disk Tracker

   b. Recovery Console

   c. Disk Cleanup

   d. Control Panel System icon

8. _____ and _____ are examples of partial backups.

9. Which of the following backup utilities are available in Red Hat Linux 7.2?

   a. NLMs

   b. *volcopy*

   c. *dump*

   d. all of the above

   e. only a and b

   f. only b and c

10. Which of the following utilities would help you acquire information about paging in Windows 2000 or XP?

    a. PageScan

    b. Task Manager

    c. ScanDisk

    d. all of the above

    e. only a and b

    f. only a and c

11. UNIX has no built-in tools to fix file and directory problems, which means that you must always perform a complete system installation in these situations. True or False?

12. Which of the following are characteristics of RAID level 0?

    a. It involves disk striping.

    b. Four or more disks are required.

    c. It involves disk mirroring.

    d. all of the above

    e. only a and b

    f. only a and c

13. ScanDisk can repair file and directory problems in which of the following?

    a. Windows NT 4.0

    b. Windows 2000

    c. Windows 98

    d. all of the above

    e. only a and b

    f. only b and c

14. Which of the following is not a backup option in Windows 2000?

    a. normal

    b. incremental

    c. daily

    d. binary image

15. In most directory structures, the directory that contains the operating system is:

    a. in the root.

    b. hidden in a remote subdirectory for security.

    c. in server operating systems, located as a subdirectory under the /usr directory, a technique used to enhance performance.

    d. placed as a subdirectory in the main directory for all software applications.

10

16. In Windows XP, you can optimize the network binding order as a way to improve network performance. True or False?

17. You are at the Red Hat Linux 7.2 command prompt and have changed to a large directory in which you want to delete a file that you recall begins with the letter "w," but you're unsure of the exact name. Which of the following *ls* command switches might help you find the file faster?

   a. *-F*

   b. *-l*

   c. *-r*

   d. *-n*

18. Your Windows 2000 Professional workstation's hard drive seems to be laboring to find files, possibly because you added and deleted hundreds of files without performing any special disk maintenance. To improve the hard drive's performance you should _____.

19. You use the Internet frequently. What simple step should you perform on a regular basis to maintain your computer?

   a. Tune your Internet browser to automatically delete all cookies.

   b. Reset the protocol binding order in the Internet browser to give priority to IPX/SPX communications because accessing multiple sites can change the binding order.

   c. Check to make sure that your Internet browser's speed is always maintained between 128 Kbps and 20 Mbps.

   d. Use your Internet browser to delete temporary Internet files.

20. You need to restore two files from a backup. Fortunately, an image backup enables you to quickly restore only those two files. True or False?

HANDS-ON PROJECTS

Project 10-1

In this hands-on activity, you'll empty the trash in the Mac OS.

To empty the trash in Mac OS 9.x:

1. Double-click the **Trash** icon to view its contents.

2. Make sure that there are no files you want to salvage from the trash.

3. Close the Trash window.

4. Open the **Special** menu on the menu bar.

5. Click **Empty Trash**.

6. The warning dialog box provides a summary of the contents that will be deleted and the disk space occupied by the contents. Click **OK** to finish emptying the trash.

To empty the trash in Mac OS X:

1. Click the **Trash** icon on the Dock to view its contents.

2. Make sure that there are no files you want to salvage from the trash.

3. Close the Trash window.

4. Open the **Finder** menu.

5. Select **Empty Trash**.

6. Click **OK** in the warning dialog box.

In Mac OS 9.x, if the trash can has a closed lid, it is empty, but if the lip is opened with overflowing papers, it contains files to be deleted. In Mac OS X, if there are no files in the trash can, it appears as an empty wire basket on the Dock; if it contains files to delete, the wire trash can shows papers inside.

Project 10-2

In this assignment, you'll search for and delete all temporary files in the temp directory on a UNIX computer. (*Note:* Use the /temp directory created by your instructor for this assignment, or use the /tmp directory if your instructor specifies it; or, as another alternative, create a /temp directory in your home directory and populate it with one or more files.)

To find and delete the files using the command line:

1. Change to the temporary directory. Enter **cd /temp** or **cd /user/temp**, for example.

2. Type **ls –l temp.***.

3. Type **rm temp.***. In Red Hat Linux, the interactive option is used, by default. Thus, each file selected for deletion is displayed, and you must type **y** and press **Enter** to delete it.

4. Type **ls –l temp.*** again to make sure the files are deleted.

5. Log off when you are finished.

Project 10-3

In this project, you'll use the *df* and *du* commands in Red Hat Linux 7.2 to examine disk space use.

To examine disk space use:

1. Log on as root.

2. Enter **df –a** to view information on all mounted file systems.

3. Enter a **df** *directory*, such as **df /var**, to view information about the file system in which that directory resides.

10

4. Switch to a directory of your choice, and enter **du** to view how large each directory is within the main directory.

5. To view the total size of a directory and the directories under it, enter **du -s** *directoryname*.

Project 10-4

This project enables you to use the Disk Cleanup tool in Windows 98 or Windows Me to delete temporary Internet files and temporary files created by applications.

To use the Disk Cleanup tool:

1. Close all active windows and programs.

2. Click **Start**, point to **Programs**, point to **Accessories**, point to **System Tools**, and click **Disk Cleanup**.

3. Select the drive to clean up, such as drive **C:**, and click **OK**.

4. What types of files can be deleted?

5. Make sure the **Disk Cleanup** tab appears. Check the boxes for **Temporary Internet Files** and **Temporary files**.

6. Click the **More Options** tab. What can you do on this tab?

7. Return to the **Disk Cleanup** tab and click **OK**.

8. Click **Yes** to verify that you want to delete the files.

Project 10-5

In this project, you'll find and delete temporary files in Windows 95, Windows 98, or Windows NT. Then you'll purge the files from the Recycle Bin.

To find, delete, and purge the temporary files:

1. Close all active windows and programs.

2. Click **Start**, point to **Programs**, and click **Windows Explorer** (or in Windows NT, click Windows NT Explorer).

3. Click the **Tools** menu, move to **Find**, and click **Files or Folders**.

4. Enter ***.tmp** in the Named box and enter **C:** in the Look in list box (or click the list arrow and select (C:) from the list).

5. Check **Include subfolders**, if necessary, and click **Find Now**.

6. Press **Ctrl+A** and press **Del**. Click **Yes** to confirm the deletion.

7. Close the Find dialog box.

8. Scroll to the bottom of the left pane in Explorer and double-click **Recycle Bin**.

9. Scroll through the right pane in Explorer to view the Recycle Bin contents.

10. Click the **File** menu, click **Empty Recycle Bin**, and click **Yes**.

11. Close Explorer.

Project 10-6

In this project, you'll practice using Disk Defragmenter in Windows 95, Windows 98, Windows 2000, or Windows XP.

To start the Disk Defragmenter in Windows 95/98:

1. Click **Start**, point to **Programs**, point to **Accessories**, point to **System Tools**, and click **Disk Defragmenter**.

2. Select drive **C:** in the Select Drive dialog box, and click **OK**.

3. Click **Start**, if necessary, in the Disk Defragmenter dialog box.

4. Click **Show Details** to see the complete step-by-step sequence of the defragmentation process.

5. Click the **Legend** button to see an interpretation of the color-coded activities.

6. Click **Yes** to exit the Disk Defragmenter when the process is complete.

To run the Disk Defragmenter in Windows 2000/XP:

1. Click **Start**, point to **Programs** (in Windows 2000) or **All Programs** (in Windows XP), point to **Accessories**, point to **System Tools**, and click **Disk Defragmenter**.

2. Click **Defragment**.

3. Click **View Report** after the disk is defragemented. What type of information is in the report?

4. Click **Close** to close the report window.

5. Close the Disk Defragmenter tool.

Project 10-7

In this project, you'll use the Computer Management tool to view the resources available for sharing on a computer running Windows 2000 or Windows XP. This project works best if you have one or more shared drives already set up, and one or more clients accessing those drives.

To view the resources in use:

1. Log on as Administrator, or access an account that has Administrator privileges.

2. In Windows 2000, right-click **My Computer** and click **Manage** (or in Windows 2000 Server, click Start, point to Programs, point to Administrative Tools, and click Computer Management). In Windows XP, click **Start**, right-click **My Computer**, and click **Manage**.

3. Notice the options in the left pane. What kinds of tasks can be accomplished through the Computer Management tool?

4. Double-click **Shared Folders** in the tree (under System Tools).

10

5. Double-click **Shares** in the tree. Notice that the right pane displays the drives and folders that are shared from your computer.

6. In the tree, click **Sessions** to view the users connected to a share on your computer.

7. Click **Open Files** in the tree to view the files that have been opened by a client.

8. Close the Computer Management window.

Project 10-8

In this project, you'll perform a file system check that works in most versions of UNIX, including Red Hat Linux 7.2. Before you start, ask your instructor for a device name, such as /dev/hda1, and ask whether or not to use the –N or –n option.

To check the file system:

1. Log on as root.

2. Enter the command **fsck /dev/*devicename***. In Red Linux 7.2, if you are using the ext2 or ext3 file system, you can type **fsck.ext2** or **fsck.ext3** instead. Press **Enter**. Or, if your instructor is concerned about fsck causing a file problem in Red Hat Linux 7.2, just run **fsck.ext2 –n /dev/*devicename*** or **fsck.ext3 –n /dev/*devicename***, press **Enter**, and skip to Step 5.

3. Notice the phases of *fsck* operations as it runs.

4. Select **Yes** to correct any problems the utility finds as it works.

5. Notice the statistics produced by the utility.

6. If you see a message to reboot the system, use the **halt –n** command and reboot.

When you run *fsck* (without the -N option) or fsck.ext2/fsck/ext2 (without the -n option) in Red Hat Linux, an error code is printed. The ideal is to have an error code of 0. To view what the error codes mean, type *man fsck*.

Project 10-9

In this project, you'll run *chkdsk* in any or all of Windows 95, Windows 98, Windows NT, Windows 2000, and Windows XP. On these systems, close all windows and programs before you run *chkdsk*. Also, make sure that no one is accessing a shared resource. (See Hands-on Project 10-7, for example.)

To run *chkdsk* in Windows 95:

1. Click **Start**, highlight **Programs**, and click **MS-DOS Prompt**.

2. At the MS-DOS prompt, type **chkdsk**, and press **Enter**.

3. Notice the information about the disk volume presented on the screen.

4. Type **exit**, and press **Enter** to close the MS-DOS Prompt window in Windows 95.

98

To run *chkdsk* in Windows 98 and Windows Me:

1. Click **Start**, highlight **Programs**, and click **MS-DOS Prompt** for Windows 98; or click **Start**, highlight **Programs**, highlight **Accessories**, and click **MS-DOS Prompt** in Windows Me.

2. At the DOS prompt, type **chkdsk**, and press **Enter**.

3. Notice the information that appears on the screen. At the beginning, you should see a comment that says *chkdsk* has not checked the drive for errors, and you must use ScanDisk to detect and fix errors.

4. Close the MS-DOS Prompt window.

NT

To run *chkdsk* in Windows NT:

1. Click **Start**, point to **Programs**, and click **Command Prompt**.

2. Type **chkdsk /f** at the command prompt, and press **Enter**.

3. Notice the information on the screen and any errors that are fixed. You can run chkdsk on a FAT or NTFS volume.

4. Close the Command Prompt window when you are finished.

2000/XP

To run *chkdsk* in Windows 2000 or XP:

1. In Windows 2000, click **Start**, point to **Programs**, point to **Accessories**, and click **Command Prompt**. Or, in Windows XP, click **Start**, point to **All Programs**, point to **Accessories**, and click **Command Prompt**.

2. Type **chkdsk /f** at the command prompt, and press **Enter**.

3. Notice the information that appears, and whether or not any errors are fixed (refer back to Figure 10-15 for Windows 2000 Server, as an example).

4. Close the Command Prompt window.

10

Project 10-10

In this project, you'll run ScanDisk in Windows 95 or Windows 98.

95/98

To run ScanDisk:

1. Click **Start**, point to **Programs**, point to **Accessories**, point to **System Tools**, and click **ScanDisk**.

2. Select or click drive **(C:)**.

3. Click **Standard** as the type of test.

4. Check **Automatically fix errors**.

5. Click the **Advanced** button.

6. Check all three boxes under Check files for, which includes **Invalid file names**, **Invalid dates and times**, and **Duplicate names** (if you get a message asking if you are sure you want to check for duplicate names, click **Yes**). Click **OK**.

7. Click **Start** and notice the action bar as the utility checks files and folders.
8. Notice the ScanDisk Results dialog box, and click **Close**.
9. Click **Close** to exit ScanDisk.

Project 10-11

In this project, you'll tune memory settings in Mac OS 9.x.

To tune the memory settings in Mac OS 9.x:

1. Open the Apple menu.
2. Select **Control Panels** and click **Memory**.
3. For Disk Cache, click the **Custom setting** radio button, and set the disk cache using the following formula: **(32 KB) * (Amount of RAM in megabytes)**. If you see a message that says you may decrease performance by changing this setting, click **Custom** to continue.
4. For Virtual Memory, click the **On** radio button, and set the amount according to the formula: **(1 MB) + (Amount of RAM in megabytes)**.
5. Close the Memory Control Panel.

Project 10-12

This project enables you to view the virtual memory information in Red Hat Linux 7.x, Windows NT, Windows 2000, and Windows XP.

To monitor the use of swap space in Red Hat Linux:

1. At the command line, type **vmstat**, and press **Enter**.
2. How much swap space is in use?

The value under "swpd" is the amount of swap space used. Type *man vmstat* to learn more about how to interpret the other information that appears.

To monitor page file and memory use in Windows NT, 2000, and XP:

1. Right-click the **taskbar**.
2. Click **Task Manager**.
3. Click the **Performance** tab.
4. Notice the memory usage statistics and graphing information.
5. Notice the amount of memory that is paged compared to the amount that is not paged (see the Kernel Memory (K) section).
6. Close the Task Manager.

Project 10-13

In this hands-on activity, you'll view where to set the binding order in Windows NT 4.0, Windows 2000, and Windows XP. For all three operating systems, you will need access to an account with Administrator privileges. (This project works best if all of the operating systems are configured for at least two network providers [protocols such as TCP/IP and IPX/SPX] and two print providers.)

To view where to set the binding order in Windows NT 4.0:

1. Click **Start**, point to **Settings**, and click **Control Panel**.
2. Double-click the **Network** icon, and then click the **Services** tab.
3. Click the **Network Access Order** button.
4. What network and print providers are configured (refer back to Figure 10-24)? What buttons can you use to change the order of the network and print providers?
5. Click **Cancel**.
6. Click **Cancel** again, and then close the Network dialog box.

To view where to set the binding order in Windows 2000:

1. Right-click **My Network Places** on the desktop, and click **Properties** on the menu.
2. Click the network connection that you want to change – ask your instructor which connection to use, or click **Local Area Connection**.
3. Click **Advanced** on the menu bar in the Network and Dial-up Connections dialog box.
4. Click **Advanced Settings** on the Advanced menu.
5. Make sure the **Adapters and Bindings** tab is selected so that you can view the current bindings. What bindings exist on your computer?
6. Click the **Provider Order** tab (refer back to Figure 10-25). What is the network binding order for the providers?
7. Click **Cancel**. Close the Network and Dial-up Connections window.

To view where to set the binding order in Windows XP Professional:

1. Click **Start** and click **Control Panel**.
2. Choose **Network and Internet Connections**.
3. Click **Network Connections**.
4. Double-click the network connection that you want to change – ask your instructor which connection to use, or click **Local Area Connection**.
5. Click **Advanced** on the menu bar.
6. Click **Advanced Settings** on the Advanced menu.

10

7. Make sure the **Adapters and Bindings** tab is selected so that you can view the current bindings. What bindings exist on your computer?

8. Click the **Provider Order** tab. What is the network binding order for the providers?

9. Click **Cancel**. Close the Network Connections window.

Project 10-14

In this project, you'll use *ping* in Windows XP, Red Hat 7.2, and Mac OS X. Before you start, obtain an IP address from your instructor that you can poll across a network. If you don't have an address to *ping*, use the IP address of your workstation.

 For example, in Windows XP, you can determine your own IP address by opening the Command Prompt window and typing *ipconfig* and then Enter. Or, in any operating system, you can determine your IP address by using the network configuration tools (but do not change the IP address).

 To use *ping* in Mac OS X:

1. Open **Macintosh HD**.

2. Select **Applications**.

3. Click **Utilities**.

4. Select **Network Utility**.

5. Open the **Ping** tab.

6. Enter the IP address that you want to poll, such as **17.254.3.183** (the Apple Web site).

7. Select **Send only ___ pings** and enter **5**.

8. Click the **Ping** button. You should notice that the address you specified is returned with other information. (If the *ping* failed, that means there is a problem with your connection to the network.)

9. Close the Network Utility window.

 To use *ping* in Red Hat Linux 7.2:

1. At the command line, type **ping –c 5** (–c 5 limits the number of polls to five) plus the IP address you are polling, such as **ping –c 5 216.148.218.195** (the Red Hat Web site).

2. Press **Enter**.

3. What information do you see on the screen?

 To use *ping* in Windows XP:

1. Click **Start**, point to **All Programs**, point to **Accessories**, and click **Command Prompt**.

2. Type **ping** plus the IP address to poll, such as **ping 207.46.197.101** (for the Microsoft Web site).

3. What information is returned?

CASE PROJECT

The National Center for Weather Research (NCWR) is funded by 22 state universities and eight foundations to study all areas relating to weather patterns, forecasting, cloud seeding, and other weather phenomena. In NCWR's building, there is a network consisting of 295 workstations, supercomputers, and Red Hat Linux, Windows NT 4.0, Windows 2000, and NetWare servers. The workstations run Red Hat Linux 7.2, Windows 98, Windows NT Workstation 4.0, Windows 2000 Professional, Windows XP Professional, and Mac OS X. The network protocols are TCP/IP, AppleTalk, NetBEUI, and IPX/SPX. You are one of 10 computer professionals who provide support to users on this network.

1. Over 50 users who run Windows 98, Windows NT Workstation 4.0, and Windows 2000 Professional are certain they need to purchase additional disks because they are nearly out of space. What options can you show them before their department heads order new disks?

2. The executive director of NCWR is experiencing slow network response at her Windows XP Professional workstation, but the network administrator can find no apparent network problems after monitoring the network with a protocol analyzer. What alternatives might you examine to solve this problem?

3. Your boss hired a new computer professional who formerly worked as a database support specialist in the business office, but who is relatively inexperienced in operating systems. The boss assigned you to train your new colleague. One area that you are covering now is how to find and repair disk and file problems. Explain the tools available for the following operating systems:

   ❑ Red Hat Linux 7.2

   ❑ Mac OS X

   ❑ Windows 95/98

   ❑ Windows NT

   ❑ Windows 2000/XP

4. As you discuss the progress of the new employee, your boss mentions that he has an important word-processing file that opens with a message that it is corrupted. Is there anything he might do to keep this from happening again in Windows 2000 Professional?

5. The chief financial officer of NCWR keeps a huge number of reports, spreadsheets, and other critical financial information on his computer, which runs Windows 2000 Professional. As you walk by the CFO's office, you notice that the disk drive on his

10

computer sounds like it might have some mechanical problems. The CFO does not have a tape drive, and has not backed up his computer in over a year. However, you have a tape drive on your computer that runs Windows 2000 Professional, and there is a tape drive on one of the Windows 2000 servers in the computer room. Can you back up his computer on either of these computers? How?

6. The director of publications uses Mac OS X and has been working on so many projects for the past six months that she has had no time to perform maintenance tasks. She wants to spend some time tomorrow morning on these tasks. What maintenance tasks do you recommend?

7. Your new associate has not yet learned how to adjust the page file size in Windows 98 and Windows XP Professional. Explain how this is done.

OPTIONAL CASE PROJECTS FOR TEAMS

Team Case One

Your department manager at NCWR wants you to form a small team of computer professionals and give a presentation on the hard disk troubleshooting tools available through the System Monitor in Windows 2000 Server. Prepare a presentation that discusses the tools and how to use them to identify specific hard disk problems.

Team Case Two

Your manager now wants you to develop a network troubleshooting guide for Red Hat Linux 7.2 workstations and servers. Create a small troubleshooting guide that discusses tools you can use to identify network problems.

APPENDIX

A

AN OVERVIEW OF
COMMAND-LINE COMMANDS

The sections in this appendix present an overview of general commands that you can execute at the command line in Windows-based, UNIX, and Mac OS operating systems.

WINDOWS 95/98/ME MS-DOS PROMPT COMMANDS

The commands presented in Table A-1 are general MS-DOS Prompt window commands for viewing or controlling different aspects of Windows 95, Windows 98, or Windows Me. In Table A-2, the MS-DOS Prompt network-related commands are listed. To open the MS-DOS Prompt window in Windows 95 or Windows 98, click Start, point to Programs, and click MS-DOS Prompt; or to open it in Windows Me, click Start, point to Programs, point to Accessories, and click MS-DOS Prompt. To find out more about a command, open the MS-DOS Prompt window, type the command plus /?— such as *attrib /?* — and press Enter.

Table A-1   Commonly Used Windows 95/98/Me MS-DOS Prompt Command-Line Commands

Command	Description
attrib	For viewing the attributes set for a file, and to change one or more attributes
break	Causes MS-DOS to check for a break key only during standard MS-DOS operations, such as making input or output (*break off*), or during all program execution options (*break on*)
call	Used to call a batch file from within another batch file
cd or chdir	Enables you to change to a different folder, or view the name of the current folder
chkdsk	Used to report the disk file system statistics (Windows 95/98/Me), and correct file system errors such as lost clusters (Windows 95)
cls	Clears the information currently displayed on the screen
copy	Copies files from one disk location to another
date	Enables you to view the date and reset it
del or erase	Deletes specified files on a volume
dir	Lists files and subfolders within a folder

Table A-1 Commonly Used Windows 95/98/Me MS-DOS Prompt Command-Line Commands (continued)

Command	Description
diskcopy	Copies information on a floppy disk to another floppy disk
doskey	Starts the recall of previously used MS-DOS commands, and is used to create command macros
echo	Shows an associated message, or turns screen messages off or on
exit	Used to close the MS-DOS Prompt window session
fc	Enables you to compare the information in two files or two sets of files to determine the differences in content
find	Used to find a designated set of characters contained in one or more files
format	Formats a floppy or hard disk for FAT
keyb	Enables you to set the keyboard language or layout (not available in Windows Me)
label	Modifies the label on a disk volume
md or mkdir	Used to set up a new folder
mem	Displays memory usage statistics on your computer
mode	Sets up parameters for a device or communications port
more	Used to limit the display to one screen at a time so that information does not rush by faster than it can be read
move	Enables you to move files from one disk location to another on the same volume
path	Used to establish the path or list of folders to search in order to run a program or command
prompt	Modifies the format of the command prompt shown in the Command Prompt window
rd or rmdir	Deletes a folder or subfolder
ren or rename	Renames a file or group of files
share	Enables two programs to share use of the same file on one computer, while ensuring that both programs do not write to that file at the same time (Windows 95 only)
sort	Sorts lines input into a file, written to the screen, or sent to a printer from a file
start	Starts a new Command Prompt window in which to run a program or a command
subst	Used to link a path or volume with a designated drive letter
time	Used to view the time of day and reset it
type	Shows a file's contents on the screen, or sends the contents to a file
ver	Shows the current version of the operating system
verify	Instructs the operating system to verify that each file is accurately written to disk at the time it is created, copied, moved, or updated
vol	Used to view the volume label, if there is one, and the volume serial number
xcopy	Designed as a fast copy program for files, folders, and subfolders

Table A-2   Commonly Used Windows 95/98/Me MS-DOS Prompt Command-Line Commands for Network Functions

Command	Description
ipconfig	Displays information about the TCP/IP setup
net config	Shows the services that are currently started and that can be configured from this command, such as the Server and Workstation services
net diag	Displays network diagnostic information
net help	Shows help information for *net* commands
net init	Loads protocol and NIC drivers (but does not bind them)
net logon	Logs on this computer to enable access to network resources
net password	Changes your network access password
net print	Used to view and manage queued print jobs by computer, share name, and job number
net time	Used to synchronize the server's clock with that of another computer in the same or different domain; or to view the time as set on another computer in the same or different domain
net use	Shows information about shared resources, or is used to configure, connect, and disconnect shared resources
net ver	Shows the version of the network redirector
net view	Presents a list of domains and workgroups, plus the computers and servers in the domains and workgroups
ping	Used to poll another TCP/IP node to verify you can communicate with it (for help about this command, simply type *ping* and press Enter)
tracert	Used to view the number of hops and other routing information on the path to the specified server or host (for help about this command, type *tracert* and press Enter)

WINDOWS NT/2000/XP COMMAND PROMPT COMMANDS

The commands presented in Table A-3 are general Command Prompt window commands for Windows NT, Windows 2000, or Windows XP. Table A-4 lists the Command Prompt window commands that address network functions for these operating systems. To open the Command Prompt window in Windows NT, click Start, point to Programs, and click Command Prompt. In Windows 2000, click Start, point to Programs, point to Accessories, and click Command Prompt. And, in Windows XP, click Start, point to All Programs, point to Accessories, and click Command Prompt. To find out more about a command, open the Command Prompt window, type *help* plus the command—such as *help attrib*—and press Enter. To learn more about a network command, such as the *net* command, type *net /?*, and press Enter; or type the full command set and */?*, such as *net accounts /?*, and press Enter.

Table A-3   Commonly Used Windows NT/2000/XP Command Prompt Commands

Command	Description
assoc	Used to view and change file associations in Windows
at	Enables you to schedule one or more programs to run at a designated date and time
attrib	For viewing the attributes set for a file, and to change one or more attributes
break	Causes the system to check for a break key only during standard operations, such as while making input or output (break off), or during all program execution options (break on)
cacls	Enables you to view the permissions (access control list or acl) set for a file and change one or more permissions
cd or chdir	Enables you to change to a different folder, or view the name of the current folder
chcp	Used to view the currently active code page number, or set a different code page number
chkdsk	Used to report the disk file system statistics, and correct file system errors such as lost clusters (for FAT and NTFS)
chkntfs	Used to report the disk file system statistics, and correct file system errors such as lost clusters (for NTFS)
cls	Clears the information currently displayed on the screen
cmd	Used to start a new NTDVM session
color	Sets up the foreground and background screen colors
comp or fc	Enables you to compare the information in two files or two sets of files to determine the differences in content
compact	Compresses files and subfolders within a folder, or removes the compression attribute
convert	Converts a FAT formatted volume to NTFS at the time a server is booted
copy	Copies files from one disk location to another
date	Enables you to view the date and reset it
del or erase	Deletes specified files on a volume
dir	Lists files and subfolders within a folder
diskcomp	Checks the contents of one floppy disk against the contents of another
diskcopy	Copies information on a floppy disk to another floppy disk
diskperf	Installs, starts, or stops the Performance/System Monitor disk counters
doskey	Starts the recall of previously used MS-DOS commands, and is used to create command macros
echo	Shows an associated message, or turns screen messages off or on
exit	Used to close the Command Prompt window session
find	Used to find a designated set of characters contained in one or more files
findstr	Used to find one or more sets of characters within a set of files

Table A-3   Commonly Used Windows NT/2000/XP Command Prompt Commands
(continued)

Command	Description
format	Formats a floppy disk
ftype	Provides detailed information about file associations, and is used to change associations so as to link them with a designated program
graftabl	Displays characters and code-page switching for a color display monitor
help	Provides a list of the Windows NT/2000/XP command-line commands, and is used to display help about a particular command
keyb	Enables you to set the keyboard language or layout (works only in Windows NT)
label	Modifies the label on a disk volume
md or mkdir	Used to set up a new folder
mode	Sets up parameters for a device or a communications port
more	Used to limit the display to one screen at a time so that information does not rush by faster than it can be read
move	Enables you to move files from one disk location to another on the same volume
path	Used to establish the path or list of folders to search in order to run a program or command
popd	Deletes a specified drive letter that was temporarily created by *pushd*
print	Prints a designated file
prompt	Modifies the format of the command prompt shown in the Command Prompt window
pushd	Creates a temporary drive letter to a network resource
rd or rmdir	Deletes a folder or subfolder
recover	Enables you to try recovering files and data from a damaged or unreadable disk
ren or rename	Renames a file or group of files
replace	Compares files in two disks or folders, and synchronizes the files in one to those on another (similar to My Briefcase)
set	Shows a list of currently set environment variables and is used to modify those variables
setlocal	Used to start command process extensions via a batch file, such as for detecting error level information
sort	Sorts lines input into a file, written to the screen, or sent to a printer from a file
start	Starts a new Command Prompt window in which to run a program or command
subst	Used to link a path or volume with a designated drive letter
time	Used to view the time of day and to reset it
title	Modifies the title in the titlebar of the Command Prompt window
tree	Used to show a graphic of the folder and subfolder tree structure

Table A-3 Commonly Used Windows NT/2000/XP Command Prompt Commands (continued)

Command	Description
type	Shows a file's contents on the screen, or sends the contents to a file
ver	Shows the current version of the operating system
verify	Instructs the operating system to verify that each file is accurately written to disk at the time it is created, copied, moved, or updated
vol	Used to view the volume label, if there is one, and the volume serial number
xcopy	Designed as a fast copy program for files, folders, and subfolders

Table A-4 Commonly Used Windows NT/2000/XP Network Command Prompt Commands for Network Functions

Command	Description
ipconfig	Displays information about the TCP/IP setup
net accounts	Used to change account policy settings and synchronize BDCs
net computer	Adds or removes a computer in a domain
net config	Shows the started services that can be configured from this command, such as the Server and Workstation services
net continue	Resumes a service that was paused
net file	Shows the currently open shared files and file locks, and is used to close designated files or remove file locks
net group	Shows the existing global groups, and is used to modify those groups
net help	Displays help information for the net command
net helpmsg	Used to determine the meaning of a numeric network error message
net localgroup	Shows the existing local groups and is used to modify those groups
net name	Used to display, add, or remove computer names that can participate in the Messenger service
net pause	Pauses a service
net print	Used to view and manage queued print jobs by computer, share name, and job number
net send	Sends a message to designated users or all users currently connected to the server
net session	Shows the users currently connected to the server and is used to disconnect designated user sessions or all user sessions
net share	Used to create, delete, or show information about a shared resource
net start	Shows the started services, or is used to start a designated service
net statistics	Shows the accumulated statistics about the Server or Workstation service
net stop	Stops a network service on a server
net time	Used to synchronize the server's clock with that of another computer in the same or different domain; or to view the time as set on another computer in the same or different domain

Table A-4   Commonly Used Windows NT/2000/XP Network Command Prompt Commands for Network Functions (continued)

Command	Description
net use	Shows information about shared resources, or is used to configure, connect, and disconnect shared resources
net user	Used to view, add, or modify a user account set up on the server or in a domain
net view	Presents a list of domains, the computers and servers in a domain, and all resources shared by a computer in a domain
nbstat	Shows the server and domain names registered to the network (used only on server versions)
netstat	Used to display information about the TCP/IP session at the server
ping	Used to poll another TCP/IP node to verify you can communicate with it
tracert	Used to view the number of hops and other routing information on the path to the specified server or host

Red Hat Linux Command-Line Commands

The commands presented in Table A-5 are general Red Hat Linux command-line commands, and the commands in Table A-6 are network-related commands. If you are using the GNOME interface, click the GNOME Terminal emulation program on the panel to access a command-line window. When you are ready to close the window, type *exit*, and then press Enter. To access documentation on any of these commands, type *man* and the command, such as *man at*, and press Enter. Press Enter to advance through lines in the documentation, and type *q* in the text window to leave it and return to the normal command prompt.

Table A-5   Commonly Used Red Hat Linux Command-Line Commands

Command	Description
at	Runs a command or script at a given time
atq	Shows the jobs that are scheduled to run
atrm	Used to remove a job that is scheduled to run
batch	Runs a command or script and is really a subset of the *at* command. If you type only *batch*, this takes you to the at> prompt. In Red Hat Linux, the *batch* command is used so that a command or script is only run when the system load is at an acceptable level that is determined by your instructions. In the absence of your instructions, this level is automatically determined by the system.)
cat	Displays the contents of a file to the screen
cd	Changes to another directory
chgrp	Changes group ownership of a file

Table A-5 Commonly Used Red Hat Linux Command-Line Commands (continued)

Command	Description
chmod	Controls file security
chown	Changes file ownership
chsh	Sets your login shell
cmp	Used to compare two files
cp	Copies a file to another directory (and you can rename the file at the same time)
df	Shows a report of how the disk space is used
dump	Backs up files
edquota	Used to edit disk quotas associated with user accounts
fdisk	Formats and partitions a disk
file	Displays the file type
find	Used to find specific files
fsck	Performs a verification of the file system
grep	Searchs for a particular string of characters in a file
groupadd	Creates a new group
groupdel	Deletes an exising group
groupmod	Modifies an existing group
kbconfig	For configuring a keyboard
kbdrate	Sets the repeat rate for the keyboard
kill	Stops a process
less	Shows the contents of a file, with the ability to go back or move ahead in the file
ln	Creates symbolic file links
lpd	Configures a printer
lpq	Used to check a print queue
lpr	Prints a file
lprm	Removes print jobs from the queue
ls	Lists the contents of a directory
man	Displays documentation in Linux
mkdir	Creates a directory
mkfs	Creates a file system (but requires more parameters than *newfs*)
more	Displays text in a file—one screen at a time
mount	Lists the disks currently mounted; also mounts file systems and devices (such as a CD-ROM)
mv	Moves a file to a different directory
newfs	Creates a new file system
passwd	Used to change a password

Table A-5 Commonly Used Red Hat Linux Command-Line Commands (continued)

Command	Description
pr	Used to format a file into pages or columns for printing
printenv	Prints environment variables that are already set up
ps	Shows currently running processes
pwck	Checks the /etc/passwd and /etc/shadow files to make sure password authentication entries are valid
pwd	Shows the directory you are in
quota	Displays the disk quota for users
quotacheck	Verifies the disk quota files, including a report of disk usage
quotaon/quotaoff	Enables or disables disk quotas
repquota	Makes a report of disk quotas
restore	Restores files (from a dump)
rm	Removes a file or directory
rmdir	Deletes a directory that is empty
sort	Sorts the contents of a text file
swapon/swapoff	Turns page file devices on or off
sync	Forces information in memory to be written to disk
tar	Used to archive files
top	Shows a report of the main, current processes engaging the CPU
touch	Creates an empty file
umount	Dismounts a file system
uname	Shows information about the operating system
useradd	Configures a new user account
userdel	Removes an existing user account
usermod	Modifies an existing user account
vmstat	Displays a report about virtual memory use
whereis	Used to locate information about a specific file, such as a program
who	Shows who is logged on

Table A-6 Commonly Used Red Hat Linux Network Command Prompt Commands

Command	Description
finger	Provides information about a user
ftp	Enables file transfers
ifconfig	Used to set up a network interface
ipchains	Used to manage a firewall
netstat	Shows network connection information
nfsstat	Shows statistics for NFS (file upload and download) activity
nslookup	Used to query information on Internet DNS servers

Table A-6   Commonly Used Red Hat Linux Network Command Prompt Commands
(continued)

Command	Description
ping	Used to poll another TCP/IP node to verify you can communicate with it
route	Displays routing table information, and can be used to configure routing
showmount	Shows clients that have mounted volumes on an NFS server
who	Shows who is logged on
wvdial	Controls a PPP-based modem dialer

MAC OS X COMMAND-LINE COMMANDS

The Mac OS X kernel (also called Darwin) is based on UNIX FreeBSD 3.2, which means that you can access a terminal window in which to execute UNIX commands. To open the Mac OS X Terminal window, open Macintosh HD, double-click Applications, double-click Utilities, and double-click Terminal. Tables A-7 and A-8 list commands that you can use in the Mac OS X terminal window. Notice that these commands are nearly identical to those available in Red Hat Linux, including the use of *man* to read manual pages.

Table A-7   Commonly Used Mac OS X Command-Line Commands

Command	Description
cat	Displays the contents of a file to the screen
cd	Changes to another directory
chgrp	Changes group ownership of a file
chmod	Controls file security
chown	Changes file ownership
chsh	Sets your login shell
cmp	Used to compare two files
cp	Copies a file to another directory (and you can rename the file at the same time)
df	Shows a report of how the disk space is used
dump	Backs up files
edquota	Used to edit disk quotas associated with user accounts
fdisk	Formats and partitions a disk
file	Displays the file type
find	Used to find specific files
fsck	Performs a verification of the file system
grep	Looks for a string of characters in a file

Table A-7   Commonly Used Mac OS X Command-Line Commands (continued)

Command	Description
kill	Stops a process
less	Shows the contents of a file, with the ability to go back or move ahead in the file
ln	Creates symbolic file links
lpq	Used to check a print queue
lpr	Prints a file
lprm	Removes print jobs from the queue
ls	Lists the contents of a directory
man	Displays documentation
mkdir	Creates a directory
more	Displays text in a file—one screen at a time
mount	Lists the disks currently mounted; also mounts file systems and devices (such as a CD-ROM)
mv	Moves a file to a different directory
newfs	Creates a new file system
passwd	Used to change a password
pr	Used to format a file into pages or columns for printing
printenv	Prints environment variables that are already set up
ps	Shows currently running processes
pwd	Displays the directory you are in
quota	Displays the disk quota for users
quotacheck	Verifies the disk quota files, including a report of disk usage
quotaon/quotaoff	Enables or disables disk quotas
rcp	Performs a remote copy
repquota	Makes a report of disk quotas
restore	Restores files (from a dump)
rm	Removes a file or directory
rmdir	Deletes a directory that is empty
scp	Secure version of ftp or rcp (remote copy procedure)
sort	Sorts the contents of a text file
ssh	A secure version of ftp
sync	Forces information in memory to be written to disk
tar	Used to archive files
telnet	Used to remotely connect to another computer
top	Shows a report of the main, current processes engaging the CPU
touch	Creates an empty file

Table A-7   Commonly Used Mac OS X Command-Line Commands (continued)

Command	Description
umount	Dismounts a file system
uname	Shows information about the operating system
vm_stat	Displays a report about virtual memory use
whereis	Locates a specific file
who	Shows who is logged on

Table A-8   Commonly Used Mac OS X Command Prompt Commands

Command	Description
finger	Provides information about a user
ftp	Enables file transfers
ifconfig	Used to set up a network interface
netstat	Shows network connection information
nfsstat	Shows statistics for NFS (file upload and download) activity
nslookup	Used to query information on Internet DNS servers
ping	Used to poll another TCP/IP node to verify you can communicate with it
route	Displays routing table information, and can be used to configure routing
showmount	Shows clients that have mounted volumes on an NFS server
who	Shows who is logged on

Glossary

Accelerated Graphics Port (AGP) — A bus standard that has enabled adapter manufacturers to supply one hardware product to a variety of hardware platforms.

Active Directory — A Windows 2000 database of computers, users, shared printers, shared folders, and other network resources and resource groupings that is used to manage a network and enable users to quickly find a particular resource.

active hub — A central network device that connects multiple communications cable segments; it amplifies the data-carrying signal as it is transmitted to each segment.

active partition — The logical portion of a hard disk drive that is currently being used to store data. In a PC system, usually the partition that contains the bootable operating system.

ActiveX — An internal programming standard that allows various software that runs under the Windows operating system to communicate with the operating system and other programs.

address bus — An internal communications pathway inside a computer that specifies the source and target address for memory reads and writes. The address bus is measured by the number of bits of information it can carry. The wider the address bus (the more bits it moves at a time), the more memory available to the computer that uses it.

alias — In the Macintosh file system, a feature that presents an icon that represents an executable file. Equivalent to the UNIX link and the Windows shortcut.

allocation blocks — In the Macintosh file system, a division of hard disk data. Equivalent to the Windows disk cluster. Each Macintosh volume is divided into 2^{16} (65,535) individual units.

alpha software — An early development version of software in which there are likely to be bugs, and not all of the anticipated software functionality is present. Alpha software is usually tested only by a select few users to identify major problems and the need for new or different features before the software is tested by a broader audience in the beta stage.

Apple Desktop Bus (ADB) — A serial bus common on the Apple Macintosh computer. ADB is used to connect the Macintosh keyboard, mouse, and other external I/O devices.

AppleTalk — Used for communications with Macintosh computers, this protocol is designed for peer-to-peer networking.

Application Program Interface (API) — Functions or programming features in an operating system that programmers can use for network links, links to messaging services, or interfaces to other systems.

application software — A word processor, spreadsheet, database, computer game, or other type of application that a user runs on a computer. Application software consists of computer code that is formatted so that the computer or its operating system can translate that code into a specific task, such as writing a document.

arithmetic logic unit (ALU) — A part of the CPU that handles all arithmetic computations.

assigning applications — An Intellimirror feature in Windows 2000, Windows XP, and Windows .NET Server that enables an Active Directory group policy to be set up so that a particular version of software is automatically started on a client (Windows 2000 or XP) through a desktop shortcut, via a menu selection, or by clicking a file with a specific file extension.

Asymmetric Digital Subscriber Line (ADSL) — A high-speed digital subscriber line technology that can use ordinary telephone lines for downstream data transmission of up to 6 Mbps, and 576-640 Kbps for upstream transmission.

Attention (AT) commands — A modem control command set designed by the Hayes company. This standard modem command set begins each command with AT (for Attention), and allows communications software or users to directly control many modem functions.

authentication — A scheme to identify and validate the client to the server.

backbone — A main connecting link or highway between networks, such as between floors in a building or between buildings. Main internetworking devices, such as routers and switches, are often connected via the network backbone.

backup — A process of copying files from a computer system to another medium, such as a tape, Zip disk, another hard drive, or a removable drive.

backup domain controller (BDC) — A server in the domain that has a copy of the domain's directory database, which is updated periodically by the primary domain controller (PDC). The BDC also can authenticate logons to the domain.

bad clusters — On a hard disk drive, areas of the surface that cannot be used to safely store data. Bad clusters are usually identified by the *format* command, or one of the hard drive utilities, such as *chkdsk* or ScanDisk.

Basic Input/Output System (BIOS) — Low-level computer program code that conducts basic hardware and software communications inside the computer. A computer's BIOS basically resides between computer hardware and the higher level operating system, such as UNIX or Windows.

basic rate interface (BRI) for ISDN — An ISDN interface that consists of three channels. Two are 64 Kbps channels for data, voice, video, and graphics transmissions. The third is a 16 Kbps channel used for communications signaling.

batch processing — A computing style frequently employed by large systems. A request for a series of processes is submitted to the computer; information is displayed or printed when the batch is complete. Batches might include processing all of the checks submitted to a bank for a day, or all of the purchases in a wholesale inventory system, for example. Compare to *sequential processing*.

Beginner's All-purpose Symbolic Instruction Code (BASIC) — An English-like computer programming language originally designed as a teaching tool, but which evolved into a useful and relatively powerful development language.

Berkeley Software Distribution (BSD) — A variant of the UNIX operating system upon which a large proportion of today's UNIX software is based.

Bernoulli — A semi-rigid hard drive based on the Bernoulli principle. These high-capacity, removable cartridge drives provide reasonably high-speed, high-density add-on storage for desktop and laptop computers in data-intensive applications such as graphics.

beta software — During software development, software that has successfully passed the alpha test stage. Beta testing may involve dozens, hundreds, or even thousands of people, and may be conducted in multiple stages: beta 1, beta 2, beta 3, and so on.

binary backup — A technique that backs up the entire contents of one or more disk drives in a binary or image format.

BinHex — In the Macintosh file system, a seven-bit file format used to transmit data across network links that do not support native Macintosh file formats.

block allocation — A hard disk configuration scheme in which the disk is divided into logical blocks, which in turn are mapped to sectors, heads, and tracks. Whenever the operating system needs to allocate some disk space, it allocates it based on a block address.

block devices — In the UNIX file system, devices that are divided or configured into logical blocks. See also *raw devices*.

boot block — On a Mac-formatted disk, the first of two important system sections on the disk. The boot blocks identify the filing system, the names of important system files, and other important information. (See also *volume information block*, the second system section.)

bridge — A network device that connects two or more segments into one, or extends existing segment.

bus — A path or channel between a computer's CPU and the devices it manages, such as memory and disk storage.

cable modem — A digital modem device designed for use with the cable TV system, providing high-speed data transfer. It may include an analog modem component that is used with a conventional telephone line connection for information sent from the user to the ISP.

cache controller — Internal computer hardware that manages the data going into and loaded from the computer's cache memory.

cache memory — Special computer memory that temporarily stores data used by the CPU. Cache memory is physically close to the CPU, and is faster than standard system memory, enabling faster retrieval and processing time.

Carrier Sense Multiple Access with Collision Detection (CSMA/CD) — A transmission control method used by Ethernet.

catalog b-tree — In the Macintosh file system, a list of all files on a given volume. Similar to a directory in the Windows file system.

cell — Format for a unit of data that is transported over a high-speed network, usually at speeds of 155 Mbps to over 1 Gbps. Cells are mainly used for network communications that employ Asynchronous Transfer Mode (ATM).

central processing unit (CPU) — In today's computer, typically a single chip (the microprocessor) with support devices that conducts the majority of the computer's calculations.

Centronics interface — An industry standard printer interface popularized by printer manufacturer Centronics. The interface definition includes 26 wires that connect the printer with the computer I/O port, though all of these pins aren't always used, particularly in modern desktop computers.

Classless Interdomain Routing (CIDR) — A way to ignore address class designation by using addressing that puts a slash (/) after the dotted decimal notation.

clean computer — A computer from which all unnecessary software and hardware have been removed. A clean computer is useful during software upgrade testing since a minimum number of other software and hardware elements are in place, making it easier to track down problems with new software.

client — In a networking environment, a computer that handles certain user-side software operations. For example, a network client may run software that captures user data input and presents output to the user from a network server.

client operating system — Operating system on a computer, such as a PC, that enables the computer to process information and run applications locally, as well as communicate with other computers on a network.

client/server application — A software application that divides processing between a client operating system and one or more server operating systems (often a database and an application server). Dividing processing tasks is intended to achieve the best performance.

client/server systems — A computer hardware and software design in which different portions of an application execute on different computers, or on different components of a single computer. Typically, client software supports user I/O, and server software conducts database searches, manages printer output, and the like.

cluster — In MS-DOS and Windows-based file systems, a logical block of information on a disk, containing one or more sectors. Also called an allocation unit.

clustering — The ability to share the computing load and resources by linking two or more discrete computer systems to function as though they are one.

code — Instructions written in a computer programming language.

compact disc file system (CDFS) — A 32-bit file system used on standard-capacity CD-ROMs.

compact disc-read only memory (CD-ROM) — A non-volatile, digital data storage medium used for operating system and other software distribution, and to play and record multimedia.

Complex Instruction Set Computer (CISC) — A computer CPU architecture in which processor components are reconfigured to conduct different operations as required. Such computer designs require many instructions and more complex instructions than other designs.

Component Object Model (COM) — Standards that enable a software object, such as a graphic, to be linked from one software component into another one. COM is the foundation that makes Object Linking and Embedding (OLE) possible.

container object — An entity that is used to group together resources, such as an organizational unit, an organization, or a country, as specified in the directory services of NetWare; or an organizational unit, domain, tree, or forest in Microsoft Active Directory.

control bus — An internal communications pathway that keeps the CPU informed of the status of particular computer resources and devices, such as memory and disk drives.

controller — A hardware or software component of a modem that defines an individual modem's personality. The controller interprets AT commands and handles communications protocols, for example.

cookie — A text-based file used by Web sites to obtain customized information about a user, such as the user's name, the user's password to access the site, and information about how to customize Web page display.

cooperative multitasking — A computer hardware and software design in which the operating system temporarily hands off control to an application and waits for the application to return control to the operating system. Compare to *preemptive multitasking*.

creator codes — Hidden file characteristics in the Macintosh file system that indicate the program (software application) that created the file. See *type code*.

Cyclic Redundancy Check (CRC) — An error correction protocol that determines the validity of data written to and read from a floppy disk, hard disk, CD-ROM, or DVD.

daemon — An internal, automatically running program, usually in UNIX, that serves a particular function such as routing e-mail to recipients or supporting dial-up networking connectivity.

data bus — An internal communications pathway that allows computer components, such as the CPU, display adapter, and main memory, to share information. Early personal computers used an 8-bit data bus. More modern computers use 32- or 64-bit data buses.

data communications equipment (DCE) — A device, such as a modem, that converts data from a DTE, such as a computer, for transmission over a telecommunications line. The DCE normally provides the clock rate/clocking mechanism necessary for communications.

data fork — That portion of a file in the Macintosh file system that stores the variable data associated with the file. Data fork information might include word processing data, spreadsheet information, and so on.

data pump — The hardware or software portion of a modem that is responsible for converting digital data into analog signals for transmission over a telephone line, and for converting analog signals into digital data for transmission to the computer.

data terminal equipment (DTE) — A computer or computing device that prepares data to be transmitted over a telecommunications line, to which it attaches by using a DCE, such as a modem.

DB-25 — A 25-pin D-shaped connector commonly used on desktop computers, terminals, modems, and other devices.

defragmentation — The process of removing empty pockets between files and other information on a hard disk drive.

desktop operating system — A computer operating system that typically is installed on a PC type of computer, used by one person at a time, and may or may not be connected to a network.

device driver — Computer software designed to provide the operating system and application software access to specific computer hardware.

Dial-Up Networking (DUN) — A utility built into Windows 95, Windows 98, and Windows NT to permit operation of a hardware modem to dial a telephone number for the purpose of logging into a remote computer system via standard telephone lines.

differential backup — Backs up all files with an archive attribute, but does not remove that attribute after backup.

digital modem — A modem-like device that transfers data via digital lines instead of analog lines.

digital pad or digital tablet — An alternative input device frequently used by graphic artists and others who need accurate control over drawing and other data input.

Digital Signal Processor (DSP) — A software data pump used in such software-driven modems as the 3Com Winmodem.

Digital Subscriber Line (DSL) — A technology that uses advanced modulation technologies on existing telecommunications networks for high-speed networking between a subscriber and a telco, and that offers communication speeds up to 60 Mbps.

Digital Video Disc-Read Only Memory (DVD-ROM) — Also called Digital Versatile Disk, a ROM medium that can hold from 4.7 to 17 GB of information. Used for high-quality audio, motion video, and data storage.

directory — Also called a folder in some file systems, an organizational structure that contains files and may additionally contain subdirectories (or folders) under it. In UNIX, a directory is simply a special file on a disk drive that is used to house information about other data stored on the disk. In other systems, a directory or folder is a "container object" that houses files and subdirectories or subfolders. A directory or folder contains information about files, such as filenames, file sizes, date of creation, and file type (for UNIX).

directory service — A large container of network data and resources, such as computers, printers, user accounts, and user groups, that (1) provides a central listing of resources and ways to quickly find specific resources, and (2) provides ways to access and manage network resources.

disk geometry — Critical information about a hard drive's hardware configuration. This information is often stored in an area of non-volatile memory in the computer.

disk label — Used on UNIX systems, and is the same as a partition table in MS-DOS or Windows-based systems. The disk label is a table containing information about each partition on a disk, such as the type of partition, size, and location. Also, the partition table provides information to the computer about how to access the disk.

Disk Operating System (DOS) — Computer software that manages the interface between the user and computer components, and among various components inside the computer. A Disk Operating System manages the low-level computer instructions for operation of and communication with such devices as storage hardware, a keyboard, a display adapter, and so on. Also the specific name for the operating system popular with IBM-compatible PC computers, also called MS-DOS and PC DOS.

disk striping — A disk storage technique that divides portions of each file over all volumes in a set as a way to minimize wear on individual disks.

Distributed Link Tracking — A technique new to NTFS 5, so that shortcuts, such as those on the desktop, are not lost when files are moved to another volume.

distribution group — A list of Windows 2000 Server users that enables one e-mail message to be sent to all users on the list. A distribution group is not used for security.

domain — A logical grouping of resources into a functional unit for management. The resources can be servers, workstations, shared disks and directories, and shared printers.

Domain Name Service or System (DNS) — A TCP/IP application protocol that resolves domain and computer names to IP addresses, or IP addresses to domain and computer names.

dot matrix printer — A character printer that produces characters by arranging a matrix of dots. Dot matrix printers can be impact, ink jet, or other technologies.

DUN server — In Windows 95, Windows 98, and Windows NT, a software utility that permits a desktop computer to answer incoming calls, log on a user, and, with other software, permits the user access to the computer's resources.

dye sublimation — A printer technology that produces high-quality, color output by creating "sublimated" color mists that penetrate paper to form characters or graphic output.

Dynamic Host Configuration Protocol (DHCP) — A network protocol that provides a way for a host to automatically assign an IP address to a workstation on its network.

encryption — The encoding of data between the client and the server so that only the client or server can decode this information.

Enhanced IDE (EIDE) — A more modern, faster version of IDE.

Ethernet — A network transport protocol that uses CSMA/CD communications to coordinate frame and packet transmissions on a network.

Explicitly Parallel Instruction Computing (EPIC) — A computer CPU architecture that grew out of the RISC-based architecture, and enables the processor to work faster by performing several operations at once, predicting and speculating about operations that will come next (so that they are even completed before requested). EPIC uses larger and more work area registers than CISC or traditional RISC-based CPU architectures.

extended capability port (ECP) — A form of communciation that allows for higher speed bidirectional communication between the computer and printer, and the printer and computer.

extended file system (ext or ext fs) — The file system designed for Linux that is installed, by default, in Linux operating systems. Ext enables the use of the full range of built-in Linux commands, file manipulation, and security. Released in 1992, ext had some bugs and supported only files up to 2 GB. In 1993, the second extended file system (ext2 or ext2 fs) was designed to fix the bugs in ext, and support files of up to 4 TB in size. In 2001, ext3 (or ext fs) was introduced to enable journaling for file and data recovery. Ext, ext2, and ext3 support filenames of up to 255 characters.

extension — In MS-DOS, that part of a filename that typically identifies the type of file associated with the name. File extensions traditionally are three characters long, and include standard notations such as .sys, .exe, .bat, and so on.

extents b-tree — In the Mac OS HFS file system, keeps track of the location of the file fragments, or extents.

external clock speed — The speed at which the processor communicates with the memory and other devices in the computer; usually one-fourth to one-half the internal clock speed.

external commands — Operating system commands that are stored in separate program files on disk. When these commands are required, they must be loaded from disk storage into memory before they are executed.

Fibre Channel — A means of transferring data between servers, mass storage devices, workstations, and peripherals at very high speeds.

file allocation table (FAT) — A file management system that defines the way data is stored on a disk drive. The FAT stores information about file size and physical location on the disk.

file attributes — File characteristics stored with the filename in the disk directory, which specify certain storage and operational parameters associated with the file. Attributes are noted by the value of specific data bits associated with the filename. File attributes include Hidden, Read-only, Archive, and so on.

file system — A design for storing and managing files on a disk drive. File systems are associated with operating systems such as UNIX, Mac OS, and Windows.

File Transfer Protocol (FTP) — In some networking environments, a software utility that facilitates the copying of computer files across the network connection from one computer to another.

firewall — Hardware or software that can control which frames and packets access or leave designated networks, as a method to implement security.

firmware — Software logic that consists of one or more programs, which reside in a programmable chip on a card.

flow control — A hardware or software feature in modems that lets a receiving modem communicate to the sending modem that it needs more time to process previously sent data. When the current data is processed successfully, the receiving modem notifies the sending modem that it can resume data transmission.

folder — See *directory*.

forest — An Active Directory container that holds one or more trees.

fragmentation — Developing more and more empty pockets of space between files on the disk due to frequent writing, deleting, and modifying files and file contents.

frame — A data unit sent over a network that contains source and destination, control, and error-detection information, as well as data (related to the data-link layer of network communications between two stations).

full file-by-file backup — A technique that backs up the entire contents of one or more disk drives on the basis of directories, subdirectories, and files so that it is possible to restore a combination of any of these.

game pad — An input device primarily designed for interaction with games. Includes multiple buttons, wheels, or balls to effect movement of a variety of on-screen objects.

graphical user interface (GUI) — An interface between the user and an operating system, which presents information in an intuitive graphical format that employs multiple colors, figures, icons, windows, toolbars, and other features. A GUI is usually deployed with a pointing device, such as a mouse, to make the user more productive.

group identification number (GID) — A unique number assigned to a UNIX group that distinguishes that group from all other groups on the same system.

HAL (hardware abstraction layer) — The hardware abstraction layer consisting of the code that talks directly to the computer's hardware.

hard link — In Windows NT/2000/XP and UNIX, a file management technique that permits multiple directory entries to point to the same physical file.

hardware — The physical devices in a computer that you can touch (if you have the cover off), such as the CPU, circuit boards (cards), disk drives, monitor, and modem.

hardware compatibility list (HCL) — A list of brand names and models for all hardware supported by an operating system. Adherence to the HCL ensures a more successful operating system install. HCLs can often be found on OS vendors' Web sites.

Hayes command — See *Attention (AT) commands*.

Hierarchical Filing System (HFS) — An early Apple Macintosh file system storage method that uses a hierarchical directory structure. Developed in 1986 to improve file support for large storage devices.

High Bit-Rate Digital Subscriber Line (HDSL) — A form of high-speed digital subscriber line technology that has upstream and downstream transmission rates of up to 1.544 Mbps.

high-level formatting — A process that prepares a disk partition (or removable media) for a specific file system.

home directory — Also called a home folder, a user work area in which the user stores data on a server, and typically has control over whether to enable other server users to access his or her data.

Host Signal Processor (HSP) — A software approach to handling data pump duties in software-based modems such as the 3Com Winmodem.

Imagesetter — A high-end printer capable of producing film output, frequently used for publishing.

incremental backup — A technique that backs up all files with an archive attribute, and then removes the attribute after backup.

information node (inode) — In UNIX, a system for storing key information about files. Inode information includes: the inode number, the owner of the file, the file group, the file size, the file creation date, the date the file was last modified and read, the number of links to this inode, and information regarding the location of the blocks in the file system in which the file is stored.

Infrared Data Association (IrDA) — A group of peripheral manufacturers that developed a set of standards for transmitting data using infrared light. Printers were one of the first devices to support the IrDA specifications.

ink-jet printer — A character printer that forms characters by spraying droplets of ink from a nozzle print head onto the paper.

input/output (I/O) — Input is information taken in by a computer device to handle or process, such as characters typed at a keyboard. Output is information sent out by a computer device after that information is handled or processed, such as displaying the characters typed at the keyboard on the monitor.

instruction set — In a computer CPU, the group of commands (instructions) the processor recognizes. These instructions are used to conduct the operations required of the CPU by the operating system and application software.

Integrated Drive Electronics (IDE) — A storage protocol popular in today's desktop computer systems. IDE is significant because it simplifies the hardware required inside the computer, placing more of the disk intelligence at the hard drive itself.

Integrated Services Digital Network (ISDN) — A digital telephone line used for high-speed digital computer communications, videoconferencing, Internet connections, and telecommuting.

internal clock speed — The speed at which the CPU executes internal commands, measured in megahertz (millions of clock ticks per second) or gigahertz (billions of clock ticks per second). Internal clock speeds can be as low as 1 MHz and as high as over 2 GHz.

internal commands — Operating system commands that load with the main operating system kernel or command module.

International Telecommunications Union (ITU) — An international organization that sets telecommunications standards—for modem and WAN communications, for example.

Internet Control Message Protocol (ICMP) — A TCP/IP-based protocol used for network error reporting, particularly through routing devices.

Internet Packet Exchange (IPX) — Developed by Novell, this protocol is used on networks that connect servers running NetWare.

Internet Protocol (IP) — Used in combination with TCP, this protocol handles addressing and routing for transport of packets.

Interrupt Request (IRQ) — A request to the processor so that a currently operating process, such as a read from a disk drive, can be interrupted by another process, such as a write into memory.

Jaz — An Iomega removable hard disk design capable of storing 1 or 2 GB of data, depending on the model.

joystick — An input device shaped like a stick that allows for three-dimensional movement of an on-screen cursor or other object, such as a car, airplane, or cartoon character.

Kerberos — A security system developed by the Massachusetts Institute of Technology to enable two parties on an open network to communicate without interception by an intruder, creating a unique encryption key per each communication session.

kernel — An essential set of programs and computer code built into a computer operating system to control processor, disk, memory, and other functions central to the basic operation of a computer. The kernel communicates with the BIOS, device drivers, and the API to perform these functions. It also interfaces with the resource managers.

large block allocation (LBA) — In MS-DOS, a technique to allow the creation of files larger than 512 MB. With LBA, MS-DOS is told that the sector size of the hard disk is greater than 512 bytes per sector, which results in the ability to have much larger file systems.

laser printer — A high-quality page printer design popular in office and other professional applications.

LCD (Liquid Crystal Display) — The display technology in some laptops and other electronic equipment.

leaf object — An object, such as an account, that is stored in an organization or organizational unit container in the NetWare NDS.

Level 1 (L1) cache — Cache memory that is part of the CPU hardware. *See* cache memory.

Level 2 (L2) cache — Cache memory that, in most computer CPU designs, is located on hardware separate from, but close to, the CPU.

Level 3 (L3) cache — Cache memory that is located on a chip or daughter board, which is separate from, but close to the CPU, when L1 and L2 cache are both already built into the CPU.

Light Emitting Diode (LED) — An electronic device frequently used to display information in electronic devices, such as watches, clocks, and stereos.

line printer — A printer design that prints a full line of character output at a time. Used for high-speed output requirements.

Link Access Protocol for Modems (LAPM) — An error-checking protocol used in the V.42 standard that constructs data into discrete frame-like units for transmission over communications lines. Error checking is made possible because each unit is given a sequence number and a checksum. If a received unit is out of sequence or has the wrong checksum, this signals an error in the transmission.

linked list — Used in FAT file systems so that when a file is written to disk, each cluster containing that file's data has a pointer to the location of the next cluster of data. For example, the first cluster has a pointer to the second cluster's location, the second cluster contains a pointer to the third cluster, and so on.

local area network (LAN) — A series of interconnected computers, printing devices, and other computer equipment in a service area that is usually limited to a given office area, floor, or building.

long filename (LFN) — A name for a file, folder, or directory in a file system in which the name can be up to 255 characters in length. Long filenames in Windows-based, UNIX, and Mac OS systems are also POSIX compliant in that they honor uppercase and lowercase characters.

low-level format — A software process that marks tracks and sectors on a disk. A low-level format is necessary before a disk can be partitioned and formatted.

LPT1 — The primary printer port designation on many desktop computers. Also designated Line Printer 1.

MacBinary — A format for Mac OS files that joins type and creator codes, so that Mac files can be transferred over the Internet, or used via online services.

Macintosh Filing System (MFS) — The original Macintosh filing system, introduced in 1984. MFS was limited to keeping track of 128 documents, applications, or folders.

mapping — The process of attaching to a shared resource, such as a shared drive, and using it as though it is a local resource. For example, when a workstation operating system maps to the drive of another workstation, it can assign a drive letter to that drive, and access it as though it is a local drive instead of a remote one.

master — In an EIDE drive chain, the main or first drive. Most EIDE interfaces can support two drives. One is the master (Drive 0) and the second drive is the slave. See *slave*.

Master Boot Record (MBR) — An area of a hard disk that stores partition information about that disk. MBRs are not found on disks that do not support multiple partitions.

Master File Table (MFT) — In Windows NT, 2000, XP, and .NET Server, a file management system similar to the FAT and directories used in MS-DOS and Windows. This table is located at the beginning of the partition. The boot sector is located ahead of the MFT, just as it is in the FAT system.

math coprocessor — A module optimized to perform complex math calculations. Early system architectures have a processor and an optional slot for a math coprocessor. Modern system architectures have a CPU with a built-in math coprocessor.

Media Access Control (MAC) address — A unique hexadecimal address, called a device or physical address, which identifies a NIC to the network.

medium filenames — In the Macintosh file system, the 31-character filename length that Macintosh OS has supported from the beginning.

micro-switch — A small electronic switch used in a computer mouse, game pad, or joystick to connect and disconnect electronic circuits. These openings and closings can be monitored by driver software to enable certain software features or functions.

microprocessor — A solid-state electronic device that controls the major computer functions and operations. See also *CPU*.

Microsoft Foundation Classes (MFC) — A series of core routines used by almost all applications on a computer running a Windows-based operating system.

modem (MOdulator-DEModulator) — A hardware device that permits a computer to exchange digital data with another computer via an analog telephone line or dedicated connection.

mounted volume — A shared drive in the Mac OS. See *mapping*.

multi-user environment — A computer environment that supports multi-user access to a computer's hardware and software facilities.

multicast — A transmission method in which a server divides recipients of an application, such as a multimedia application, into groups. Each data stream is a one-time transmission that goes to one group of multiple addresses, instead of sending a separate transmission to each address for every data stream. The result is less network traffic.

Multimedia Extension (MMX) — A CPU design that permits the processor to manage certain multimedia operations—graphics, for example—faster and more directly. MMX technology improves computer performance when running software that requires multimedia operations.

multiprocessor computers — A computer that uses more than one CPU.

multitasking — A technique that allows a computer to run two or more programs at the same time.

multithreading — Running several program processes or parts (threads) at the same time.

NetBIOS Extended User Interface (NetBEUI) — A protocol used on Microsoft networks that was developed from NetBIOS, and is designed for small networks.

network — A system of computing devices, computing resources, information resources, and communications devices that are linked together by communications cable or radio waves.

Network Basic Input/Output System (NetBIOS) — A technique to interface software with network services, and provide naming services for computers on a Microsoft network.

network bindings — Part of the Windows NT Server and later operating systems, used to coordinate software communications among the NIC, network protocols, and network services.

Network Client Administrator — A tool available in Windows NT Server 4.0 that enables clients to install any of the following operating systems: Windows 95, MS-DOS 3.x, and Microsoft LAN Manager for MS-DOS 2.x.

Network Device Interface Specification (NDIS) — Special elements, that programmers call "hooks," in the operating system kernel (program code) which enable the operating system to interface with a network. NDIS is from Microsoft.

Network File System (NFS) — In UNIX and other operating systems, a system-level facility that supports loading and saving files to remote disk drives across the network.

network interface card (NIC) — A device used by computers and internetworking devices to connect to a network.

network operating system (NOS) — Computer operating system software that enables coordination of network activities, such as network communications, shared printing, and sharing files. Novell NetWare, UNIX, and Windows NT/2000/.NET Server are examples of network operating systems.

New Technology File System (NTFS) — The 32-bit file storage system that is the native system in Windows NT, 2000, XP, and .NET Server.

Novell Directory Services (NDS) — A comprehensive database of shared resources and information known to the NetWare operating system.

Novell Distributed Print Services (NDPS) — Services used in NetWare version 5 and above that enable printers to attach to the network as agents, to be managed through a NetWare server, and to be accessed by NetWare and Windows-based clients.

object — An entity, such as a user account, group, directory, or printer, that is known to a network operating system's database, and that the operating system manages in terms of sharing or controlling access to that object.

Open Database Connectivity (ODBC) — A set of rules developed by Microsoft for accessing databases and providing a standard doorway to database data.

operating system (OS) — Computer software code that interfaces with user application software and the computer's BIOS to allow the applications to interact with the computer hardware.

optical character recognition (OCR) — Imaging software that scans each character on the page as a distinct image and is able to recognize the character.

ORB — Drives manufactured by Castlewood Systems, Inc., in both 2.2 GB and 5.7 GB models.

packet — A data unit sent over a network that contains source and destination, routing, control, and error-detection information, as well as data (related to the network layer of network data communications between two stations).

paging file — Also called the page or swap file, an allocated portion of disk storage reserved for use to supplement RAM when the available RAM is exceeded.

parallel port — A computer input/output port used primarily for printer connections. A parallel port transmits data eight bits or more at a time, using at least eight parallel wires. A parallel port potentially can transmit data faster than a serial port.

parity checking — A data communications process that ensures data integrity through a system of data bit comparisons between the sending and receiving computer.

partition table — Table containing information about each partition on a disk, such as the type of partition, size, and location. Also, the partition table provides information to the computer about how to access the disk.

partitioning — Blocking a group of tracks and sectors to be used by a particular file system, such as FAT or NTFS. Partitioning is a hard disk management technique that permits the installation of multiple file systems on a single disk. Or, the configuration of multiple logical hard drives that use the same file system on a single physical hard drive.

passive hub — A central network device that connects multiple communications cable segments, but does not alter the data-carrying signal as it is transmitted from segment to segment.

path — In a computer directory structure, both a command and a path designation that specifies the complete location of a specific file or directory. Computer files are stored in files, which in turn reside in directories (folders). Directories can be stored within other directories. To access a specific file, you must also specify the series of directories, the path that must be traversed to reach the desired file.

payload — That portion of a frame, packet, or cell that contains the actual data, which might be a portion of an e-mail message or word-processing file.

PCMCIA (Personal Computer Memory Card International Association) — A standard for expansion cards used in laptops and desktop machines. Now usually shortened to PC Card.

peer-to-peer network operating system — A network operating system through which any computer can communicate with other networked computers on an equal or peer-like basis without going through an intermediary, such as a server or network host computer.

per-seat licensing — A software licensing scheme that prices software according to the number of individual users who install and use the software.

per-server licensing — A software licensing scheme that prices software according to a server configuration that permits multiple users to access the software from a central server.

personal digital assistant (PDA) — Handheld devices, which, because of their size, are easily transported wherever you go. They include features to assist you in organizing your time, such as a calendar, to-do lists, contacts, etc.

pipelining — A CPU design that permits the processor to operate on one instruction at the same time it is fetching one or more subsequent instructions from the operating system or application.

pixel — Short for picture element. The small dots that make up a computer screen display.

PKZIP — A utility program that archives files and compresses them so they require less disk storage and can be transmitted over a network faster.

plain old telephone service (POTS) — Regular voice-grade telephone service (the old terminology).

plotter — Computer hardware that produces high-quality printed output, often in color, by moving ink pens over the surface of paper. Plotters are often used with computer-aided design (CAD) and other graphics applications.

Plug and Play (PnP) — Software utilities that operate with compatible hardware to facilitate automatic hardware configuration. Windows versions starting with 95 recognize PnP hardware when it is installed, and, in many cases, can configure the hardware and install required software without significant user intervention.

Portable Operating System Interface (POSIX) — A UNIX standard designed to ensure portability of applications among various versions of UNIX.

potentiometer — A hardware device used to vary the amount of resistance in an electronic circuit. In computer I/O hardware, this variable resistance can be used to monitor mouse movement, joystick positioning, and so on.

power management — A hardware facility in modern computers that permits certain hardware to shut down automatically after a specified period of inactivity. Proper use of power management facilities reduces hardware wear and tear, as well as energy usage.

preemptive multitasking — A computer hardware and software design for multitasking of applications in which the operating system retains control of the computer at all times. See *cooperative multitasking* for comparison.

primary domain controller (PDC) — A server in the domain that authenticates logons, and keeps track of all changes made to accounts in the domain.

primary rate interface (PRI) ISDN — An ISDN interface that consists of switched communications in multiples of 1,544 Mbps.

print queue or print spooler — A section of computer memory and hard disk storage set aside to hold information sent by an application to a printer attached to the local computer or to another computer or print server on a network. Operating system or printer drivers and control software manage the information sent to the queue, responding to printer start/stop commands.

production computer — Any computer used to perform real work, which should be protected from problems that might cause an interruption in workflow or loss of data.

protocol — A set of formatting guidelines for network communications, like a language, so that the information sent by one computer can be accurately received and decoded by another.

public switched telephone network (PSTN) — Regular voice-grade telephone service (the modern terminology).

publishing and application — Available in Windows 2000 Server and Windows .NET Server, setting an Active Directory group policy so that Windows 2000 and Windows XP Professional clients can install pre-configured software from a central server by using Add/Remove Programs (or Add or Remove in Windows XP) via the Control Panel.

Rate Adaptive Digital Subscriber Line (RADSL) — A high-speed data transmission technology that offers upstream speeds of up to 1 Mbps and downstream speeds of up to 7 Mbps. RADSL uses ADSL technology (see *ADSL*), but enables the transmission rate to vary for different types of communications, such as data, multimedia, and voice.

raw devices — In the UNIX file system, devices that have not been divided into logical blocks.

Read Only Memory (ROM) — Special memory that contains information that is not erased when the power is removed from the memory hardware. ROM is used to store computer instructions that must be available at all times, such as the BIOS code.

real mode — A limited, 16-bit operating mode in PCs running early versions of Windows.

real-time systems — An operating system that interacts directly with the user, and responds in real time with required information.

Reduced Instruction Set Computer (RISC) — A computer CPU design that dedicates processor hardware components to certain functions. This design reduces the number and complexity of required instructions and, in many cases, results in faster performance than CISC CPUs.

Redundant Array of Inexpensive Drives (RAID) — A relatively inexpensive, redundant storage design that uses multiple disks and logic to reduce the chance of information being lost in the event of hardware failure. RAID uses various designs, termed Level 0 through Level 5.

Registry — A Windows database that stores information about a computer's hardware and software configuration.

release candidate (RC) — The final stage of software testing by vendors before cutting an official release that is sold commercially. A release candidate is usually tested by a very large audience of customers. Some vendors may issue more than one release candidate if problems are discovered in the first RC.

Remote Access Service (RAS) — A computer operating system subsystem that manages user access to a computer from a remote location, including security access.

Remote Installation Services (RIS) — Services in Windows 2000 Server and Windows .NET Server that enable clients to download an operating system over the network, such as downloading and installing Windows 2000 Professional on a client computer via RIS on a Windows 2000 Server.

removable disks — A class of relatively high-capacity storage devices that use removable cartridges. These devices are used for data backup, long-term offline storage, and data portability among multiple computer systems.

resource fork — In the Macintosh file system, that portion of a file that contains fixed information, such as a program's icons, menu resources, and splash screens.

resource managers — Programs that manage computer memory and CPU use.

root directory — The highest-level directory (or folder), with no directories above it in the structure of files and directories in a file system.

routers — Network hardware that can intelligently route network frames and packets to different networks, and that can route multiple protocols.

scanner — Creates a digital image from a hard copy that is then transmitted to the computer.

search drive — A mapped NetWare drive that enables the operating system to search a specified directory and its subdirectories for an executable (program) file.

sector — A portion of a disk track. Disk tracks are divided into equal segments or sectors.

security group — A group of Windows 2000 Server users that is used to assign access privileges, such as permissions, to objects and services.

self-extracting file — A compressed or archive file that includes an executable component, like an application program, which enables the file to separate into individual files and uncompress the files automatically. A self-extracting file does not require an external program to expand the file into its individual components.

Sequence Packet Exchange (SPX) — A protocol used on Novell networks that provides reliable transmission of application software data.

sequential processing — A computer processing style in which each operation is submitted, acted upon, and the results displayed before the next process is started. Compare to *batch processing*.

serial port — A computer input/output port used for modem, printer, and other connections. A serial port transmits data one bit after another in serial fashion, as compared to a parallel port, which transmits data eight bits or more at a time.

server — A computer running a network operating system that enables client workstations to access shared network resources such as printers, files, software applications, or CD-ROM drives.

server operating system — A computer operating system usually found on more powerful PC-based computers than those used for desktop operating systems, which is connected to a network, and that can act in many roles to enable multiple users to access information, such as electronic mail, files, and software.

service packs — Software "fixes" issued by the vendor to repair software problems, address compatibility issues, and add enhancements.

shadow file — With access limited to the root user, a file in UNIX that contains critical information about user accounts, including the encrypted password for each account.

share — An object, such as a folder, drive, or printer, that an operating system or a directory service, such as Active Directory, makes visible to other network users for access over a network.

share points — Shared resources on a Mac OS X server.

share-level access control — Access to a shared folder in Windows 95 and Windows 98 by creating a disk or folder share that is protected by share permissions, and on which the share owner can require a password for access.

shell — The operating system user interface. In MS-DOS, UNIX, and some other systems, the shell interface is text based and command oriented.

Sherlock — In the Macintosh file system, a file search utility that can find filenames or text within files.

Simple Mail Transfer Protocol (SMTP) — In a networked computer environment, a software utility that manages the transfer of electronic messages among various users.

single-processor computers — Computers capable of supporting only a single CPU.

single-tasking — A computer hardware and software design that can manage only a single task at a time.

single-user — A computer hardware and software system that enables only one user to access its resources at a particular time.

slave — In an EIDE drive chain, the secondary storage device. See *master*.

Small Computer System Interface (SCSI) — A computer input/output bus standard and the hardware that uses this standard. There are many types of SCSI in use today, providing data transfer rates from 10 Mbps to 100 Mbps.

Solaris — A Sun Microsystems operating system based on UNIX.

start bit — In data communication, an extra bit inserted by the sending modem at the beginning of a data byte to help ensure that the received data is correct.

startup disk — A bootable floppy disk that includes the basic operating system, key disk utilities, and

drivers (such as for the CD-ROM drive). This disk can be used to start the system in the event that the hard drive or its operating system is damaged.

status bits — Bits used as part of a directory entry to identify the type of filename contained in each entry. The status bits in use are Volume, Directory, System, Hidden, Read-only, and Archive.

stop bit — In data communication, an extra bit inserted by the sending modem at the end of a data byte to help ensure that the received data is correct.

Storage Area Network (SAN) — Technology that provides for interconnection between servers and storage systems without sending data over the corporate network.

StuffIt — A Macintosh archive and compression utility.

subnet mask — A designated portion of an IP address that is used to divide a network into smaller subnetworks as a way to manage traffic patterns, enable security, and relieve congestion.

SubNetwork Access Protocol (SNAP) — A way to enable protocols that are not fully 802.2 compliant.

superblock — In the UNIX file system, a special data block that contains information about the layout of blocks, sectors, and cylinder groups on the file system. This information is the key to finding anything on the file system, and it should never change.

SuperDisk (LS-120) — An increasingly popular high-capacity floppy disk design. SuperDisk / LS-120 drives can store as much as 120 MB of data on a single disk, but these drives also can read conventional 3.5" floppy disks.

surface analysis — A disk diagnostic technique that locates damaged disk areas and marks them as bad. Some surface analysis tools are destructive to data because they also format a disk. Others can run without altering data, except to move data from a damaged location to one that is not.

swap file — Also called the page or paging file, an allocated portion of disk storage reserved for use to supplement RAM when the available RAM is exceeded.

switch — A network device that connects LAN segments and forwards frames to the appropriate segment or segments. A switch works in promiscuous mode, similar to a bridge.

switch — An operating system command option that changes the way certain commands function. Command options, or switches, are usually entered as one or more letters, separated from the main command by a forward slash (/).

symbolic link — A special file in the UNIX file system that permits a directory link to a file that is on a different partition. This is a special file, which has a flag set in the inode to identify it as a symbolic link. The content of the file is a path that, when followed, leads to another file.

Symmetric Digital Subscriber Line (SDSL) — A form of digital subscriber line technology that is often used for videoconferencing or online learning. It offers a transmission speed of 384 Kbps for upstream and downstream communications.

symmetric multiprocessing (SMP) — A computer design that supports multiple, internal CPUs that can be configured to work simultaneously on the same set of instructions.

SyQuest — The manufacturer of one of the earliest removable hard disk devices popular in Macintosh and PC systems. SyQuest drives use hard disk technology. Early drives stored only 40 MB, but later designs can hold upwards of 200 MB.

system architecture — The computer hardware design that includes the processor (CPU), and communication routes between the CPU and the hardware it manages, such as memory and disk storage.

tar — A UNIX file archive utility.

task supervisor — A process in the operating system that keeps track of the applications that are running on the computer and the resources they use.

task switching — A single-tasking computer hardware and software design that permits the user or application software to switch among multiple single-tasking operations.

telco — A telecommunications company.

terminal — A device that has a keyboard but no CPU or storage, and is used to access and run programs on a mainframe or minicomputer.

terminal adapter (TA) — A digital modem that permits computer-to-computer data transfer over a digital line, such as ISDN.

terminator resistor packs (TRPs) — Sets of resistors used on a hard drive or other storage device. These resistors reduce the possibility of data echoes on the interface bus as information travels between the computer's controller and the storage device.

thermal-wax transfer — A printer technology that creates high-quality color printed output by melting colored wax elements and transferring them to the printed page.

time-sharing system — A central computer system, such as a mainframe, that is used by multiple users and applications simultaneously.

token — A specialized frame that is transmitted without data around the network until it is captured by a station that wants to transmit.

token ring — A network that uses a ring topology and token passing as a way to coordinate network transport.

topology — The physical design of a network and the way in which a data-carrying signal travels from point to point along the network.

total cost of ownership (TCO) — The cost of installing and maintaining computers and equipment on a network, which includes hardware, software, maintenance, and support costs.

track — Concentric rings that cover an entire disk like grooves on a phonograph record. Each ring is divided into sectors in which to store data.

Transmission Control Protocol (TCP) — A communications protocol that is used with IP; it facilitates reliable communications between two stations by establishing a window tailored to the characteristics of the connection.

Transmission Control Protocol/Internet Protocol (TCP/IP) — A networking communications protocol. Used on the Internet and other UNIX networking environments.

tree — An Active Directory container that houses one or more domains.

trusted domain — A domain granted security access to resources in another domain.

trusting domain — A domain that allows another domain security access to its resources, such as servers.

type code — In the Macintosh file system, embedded file information that denotes what applications were used to create the files. Mac OS type codes are used in much the same way as Windows file extensions that identify file types with .txt, .doc and other extensions. See *creator code*.

ufs (UNIX file system) — A file system developed for UNIX operating systems that uses information nodes or inodes.

unicast — A transmission method in which one copy of each packet is sent to every target destination, which can generate considerable network traffic, compared to multicasting, when the transmission is a multimedia application.

Unicode — A 16-bit character code that allows for the definition of up to 65,536 characters.

Universal Asynchronous Receiver-Transmitter (UART) — An electronic chip that handles data flow through a serial port or modem.

Universal Disk Format (UDF) — A removable disk formatting standard used for large-capacity CD-ROMs and DVD-ROMs.

Universal Plug and Play (UPnP) — An initiative of over 80 companies to develop products that can be quickly added to a computer or network. These include intelligent appliances for the home. More information can be found at the Web site, www.upnp.org.

Universal Serial Bus (USB) — A relatively high-speed I/O port found on most modern computers. It is used to interface digital sound cards, disk drives, and other external computer hardware.

UNIX to UNIX Copy Protocol (UUCP) — A protocol used by UNIX computers for communicating through modems. UUCP can also be used on networks, but for these applications, it is usually replaced by the faster TCP/IP technology.

user identification number (UID) — A number that is assigned to a UNIX user account as a way to distinguish that account from all others on the same system.

user-level access control — Access to a shared folder in Windows 95 and Windows 98 in which the share owner creates a list of groups and users who are allowed to access the share.

Very High Bit-Rate Digital Subscriber Line (VDSL) — A digital subscriber line technology that works over coaxial and fiber-optic cables, yielding 51–55 Mbps downstream and 1.6–2.3 Mbps upstream communications.

Video Graphics Array (VGA) — A video graphics display system introduced by IBM in 1987.

virtual memory — Disk storage that is used when there is not enough RAM for a particular operation, or for all processes currently in use.

Virtual Private Network (VPN) — A private network that is like a tunnel through a larger network—such as the Internet, an enterprise network, or both—and restricted to designated member clients.

volume information block — On a Mac-formatted disk, the second of two system sectors (see also *boot block*, the first sector). The volume information block points to other important areas of information, such as the location of the system files, and the catalog and extents trees.

volume label — A series of characters that identify a disk drive, or the file system it is using.

Web browser — Software to facilitate individual computer access to graphical data presented over the Internet on the World Wide Web, or over a local area network in a compatible format.

Web server — In a networked environment, a computer that runs special software to host graphical data in a World Wide Web format. Data on a Web server is accessed with a computer running a Web browser.

wheel mouse — A relatively new mouse design, popularized by Microsoft's IntelliMouse, that includes a top-mounted wheel in addition to the standard mouse buttons. The wheel is programmable for a variety of operating systems and application functions. A switch integral to the wheel provides additional opportunity for programmable, custom functions.

wide area network (WAN) — A system of networks that can extend across cities, states, and continents.

Windows Update — A Web-based function that allows you to download and install product updates for your Windows operating system.

Winmodem — A software-driven modem from 3Com Corporation that uses minimal hardware and the computer's CPU with software to conduct data communications.

WINZip — An archive and compression utility for Windows 95 and 98.

workgroups — Pre-defined groups of member computers, which provide the ability to limit resource sharing on the basis of group membership.

workstation — A computer that has a CPU and usually storage to enable the user to run programs and access files locally.

X Window — A windowed user interface for UNIX and other operating systems.

Xon-Xoff — A software flow control protocol that permits a receiving modem to notify the sending modem that its data buffers are full, and it needs more time to process previously received data.

Zip disk — A removable high-capacity floppy disk design from Iomega. Zip disks store a nominal 100 or 250 MB of data.

Index